Winnipeg
L. of the Woods
L. Superior
L. Michigan
L. Huron
L. Erie
L. Ontario
St. Lawrence R.
Richelieu
Mohawk
Connecticut R.
Hudson R.
Delaware R.
Susquehanna R.
Allegheny R.
Monongahela R.
Potomac R.
James R.
Maumee R.
Mississippi R.
Illinois R.
Wabash R.
Ohio R.
Ohio R.
Tennessee R.
Alabama R.
Savannah R.
Santee R.
Mobile R.
Kansas R.
Arkansas R.
Red R.
CENTRAL
PLAINS
APPALACHIAN MOUNTAINS
PIEDMONT
COASTAL PLAIN
ATLANTIC OCEAN
GULF OF MEXICO
BAHAMA ISLANDS
CUBA

WILLIAM MORSE
302 E JOHN ST.
CHAMPAIGN ILLINOIS

FINAL
SAT - JAN 20

EXAM
SAT JAN 20
1:30 P.M - 112 GREG. HALL

BOARD OF GOVERNORS
OF THE FEDERAL RESERVE SYSTEM
WASHINGTON D.C.

THE FEDERAL RESERVE SYSTEM

American Economic History

American Economic History

DONALD L. KEMMERER

Professor of Economics
University of Illinois

C. CLYDE JONES

Associate Professor of Economics
University of Illinois

McGRAW-HILL BOOK COMPANY, INC.

New York Toronto London

1959

AMERICAN ECONOMIC HISTORY

 Library of Congress Catalog Card Number 58-14352

II

33930

THE MAPLE PRESS COMPANY, YORK, PA.

Preface

This book is intended primarily for use in a freshman-sophomore course in American economic history, although it is suitable for use at higher levels. It was written with a major and a minor goal in view. The major goal is to provide the students with an understanding of how the United States developed into the powerful industrial economy that it is today. The minor goal is to introduce some elementary economic institutions and principles and to show their application in history. Many of these same students will soon be taking a course in economics. This is not, however, merely an economist's economic history. Both of the authors are trained historians. They happen to have taught most of their careers in economics departments and have at various times taught several other economics subjects. Long ago they came to the conclusion that students must understand the nature and purpose of economic institutions before they can grasp the role of those institutions in the country's economic development. The authors also learned early to see illustrations of basic economic principles in sequences of historical events. They believe that using economic principles as teaching devices helps the students to a better understanding of economic history. Moreover they are convinced that historians teaching a similar course in a history department would find these methods easy to master and well worth the effort. The senior author has employed them successfully during the twenty-two years he has been in charge of this work at the University of Illinois. Enrollment has averaged about 500 students per year.

A more than customary integration of economics and history is, then, the special feature of this textbook. The following is an abbreviated example of that integration which illustrates the method used. Over a century ago the problem of overproduction began to plague one segment of the American economy after another. It was a result of many new technological advances. It appeared, for example, in oil refining and in agriculture during the 1870s. John D. Rockefeller sought to solve it by establishing a monopoly, reducing the supply of refined oil, and thereby raising the price. The farmers, unable to form a monopoly, found their best solution was to cut costs. The public resented private monopolies and so the government tried to break them up with antitrust laws. In the 1930s, the same problem rose again in agriculture and in various industries. This time the government itself set up a farmers' monopoly (the Agricultural Adjustment Administration) and temporarily encouraged industry to set up monopolies under government-approved codes (the National Industrial Recovery Administration). In short, Rockefeller's solution—establishing a monopoly—was now acceptable if carried out under government direction. Thus the students' attention is drawn not only to the details of historical events in the 1870s and 1930s but to the similarities of the basic problems and solutions employed.

The authors seek to introduce the students to still other economic concepts in economic history. They use national income figures as much as they think practical in this text. They also stress the tremendous importance of capital growth in making the American economy what it is today and they explain how directly and indirectly America has accumulated this capital. Indeed, they point out that the United States has moved from being an economy in which land and resources were plentiful, with capital and labor relatively scarce, to one in which labor was moderately plentiful (around 1900), to one in which capital is so plentiful that it no longer enjoys the respect that it once did. That last condition has probably never before occurred in the economic history of nations. Each of these basic changes has produced new attitudes on the part of the public and new economic legislation.

Yet there is also much that is familiar in the text. The economic historian who likes the traditional organization in an American economic history text will find that the authors have made but minor departures from it. They have done so only when they thought it would contribute to a better understanding by the student. They divide America's economic development into four fairly standard periods, the first ending about 1789, the second in 1860, the third in 1914, and the fourth at the present time. Treatment of the colonial period, however, is briefer than the other three. Each period has eight general topics, not seven as has been customary. The eighth is capital formation, for reasons already given. The others are physical expansion, transportation, manufacturing, money and banking, commerce, labor, and agriculture. Physical expansion includes not only the westward movement but population growth as well. It is in keeping with recent economic thinking to put population growth here rather than in the labor chapter. The topic of expansion for the period since 1914 includes, too, a discussion of the greater role recently played by this nation in world affairs. A frequently neglected area of economic history, domestic marketing, likewise receives more than usual attention.

Finally, taxation is stressed, for governments today spend a third of what their citizens earn.

Professor Kemmerer wrote twenty-three chapters and the introductions and summaries. With minor exceptions he has not drawn on the text that he wrote in collaboration with the late Professor Ernest L. Bogart. This is a new book. Professor Jones wrote eight chapters—those on agriculture, labor and slavery before the Civil War, agriculture and transportation after the Civil War, and agriculture, transportation, and labor in the recent period. Professor Kemmerer's areas of special interest are money, banking, and finance, whereas those of Professor Jones are agriculture and transportation. Professor Jones is editor of *Agricultural History*. Each of the authors has generously criticized the other's chapters.

The authors have experimented with a paperbound version of this text for two years at the University of Illinois, thanks to the cooperation of the Stipes Publishing Company of Champaign. Two colleagues at other institutions also used it in this trial form and gave much helpful advice drawn from their experience with it. They were Professor Jack Blicksilver of Georgia State College and Professor Fayette Shaw of the University of Illinois in Chicago. Three colleagues at the University of Illinois criticized the chapters in their particular fields: Robert W. Harbeson in transportation and antitrust policy, Fred M. Jones in domestic commerce, and John B. Parrish in labor. Margaret Scheldrup Jones constantly edited the work, and Mrs. Jean Masterson helped greatly in organizing the lists of charts, maps, illustrations, and tables.

Donald L. Kemmerer
C. Clyde Jones

Contents

PART FOUR. PROBLEMS OF PLENTY—GOVERNMENTAL SOLUTIONS 1914–1959

List of Maps

List of Charts

List of Illustrations

List of Tables

PART ONE

Dependence and Independence

INTRODUCTION

The first half of American history, from the founding of Jamestown in 1607 to the American Revolution, was devoted to establishing a European foothold in the New World. The "mother country," England, directed operations to a certain degree or, like many mothers, tried to. The term "mother country," used then and since, suggests a degree of dependence. Dependence was especially characteristic of the first century. The colonies were dependent on the mother country for many things: for capital and people to set up each of the sixteen new colonies up to 1733; for supplies and equipment to keep them going and to build them up; for military and naval protection against Spain, Holland, and France, for markets for their staples like tobacco and rice; for bounties; and finally for their very form of government and the democratic and capitalistic traditions that went with it. Even so, the American colonies enjoyed more freedom than neighboring colonies belonging to Spain, Holland, or France.

As time went on, a growing independence began to manifest itself. After all, a distance of some 3,000 miles, or six weeks by ship, of necessity made the colonies self-reliant. They had to learn how to defend themselves against barbarous Indians and yet how to make use of suitable methods of surviving in the wilderness. They learned how to eat corn, grow tobacco, paddle canoes, and live in log cabins. After about 1700, some of them became more out of touch with the mother country by moving farther inland where ocean ships could no longer penetrate. The settlers also altered their economic and social values: they economized on labor by making less careful use of land. To increase the labor supply, they acquired indentured servants and then Negro slaves, thus endangering a cherished principle of freedom. They experimented with paper money as a substitute for scarce capital. They preferred a wilderness brand of *laissez-faire* to the mother country's system of regulated economy, called *mercantilism.* Some of these choices were sensible ones and some were unwise, but in any event they demonstrated an independence of thinking and a willingness to experiment. Finally in 1776 these colonies, feeling that they could now stand on their own feet, took the most independent step of all by declaring their freedom from English rule. Subsequent events showed that they could survive independently only in a shaky fashion until they had adopted a constitution binding them more closely together and had fought a second war against England.

CHAPTER 1

Resources and Colonization

It is hard for Americans today to appreciate how much higher their standard of living is than that of most peoples in the world. Half the world is on the brink of starvation and tens of millions of families subsist on an annual income of under $300 a year. All this seems beyond belief to a nation whose average family enjoys an annual income of $5,500 a year and has its own automobile, radio, and television set. It is equally hard to appreciate how far the United States has advanced, from a material point of view, in the last 350 years. When Virginia was founded, the standard of living in Europe was little better than that in Asia today. America, not yet settled by white men, had an even lower standard of living. The one million American Indians were in Stone Age civilization. They had not yet discovered the wheel or how to smelt metals; the dog was their largest domesticated animal. Their writing, by hieroglyphics, and trading, by exchange of gifts, were likewise primitive. Rapid progress took place partly because England was one of the more advanced nations of Europe and also because America had tremendous potentialities. Although life on the edge of the frontier, in places like Jamestown and Plymouth at first, was crude, only rarely did people starve; very soon the people of the New World were enjoying a higher standard of living than the average man in the Old World. That has been true ever since. What was the nature of America that from the beginning made possible such strides?

PHYSICAL CHARACTERISTICS

Size. The United States today has close to 3.6 million square miles within the fifty states and is comparable in size to Australia, Brazil, Canada, or China. China and Canada are somewhat larger and Soviet Russia is twice as large as the United States. On the other hand, the United States is 36 times as large as Great Britain, which is the same size as New York and Pennsylvania combined, or approximately the size of any far western state. This country has a wide variety of climates and resources, extending as it does some 3,200 miles north and south, from the 71st parallel on the north to about the 25th at the southern tip of Florida, and some 5,000 miles east and west. It comes closer to being economically self-sufficient than any other political area in the world except perhaps Russia. The settled portion is the eastern half, that is, up to about one tier of states west of the Mississippi River. Attention thus should be centered on this half of the country plus the west coast and Texas, which have developed so fast in the last century. These have 50 per cent of the territory and 93 per cent of the population. The Rocky Mountain and Plains states and Alaska are valuable chiefly for their mineral resources, grazing lands, and some grain production.[1]

Climate. The outstanding characteristic of the northern two-thirds of the country is a temperate climate with prevailing westerly winds. Average temperatures vary 40 to 50 degrees between January and July, and the extremes vary over 100 degrees, especially in such northern areas as Maine and Minnesota. Equally important is the fact that temperatures may vary 20 to 40 degrees within a few hours' time. According to geographer Ellsworth Huntington, such changes stimulate a high degree of activity in human beings.[2] Virtually all the world's more advanced nations today are to be found in regions with this climatic characteristic.

South of about the 35th parallel, which runs through North Carolina, Tennessee, and Oklahoma, the climate is mild, the changes in temperature are less pronounced, snow is less frequent, and the summer heats are slightly more severe. Although there is much economic activity in the Deep South, especially in recent years, that area has been slower to develop, and the climate is usually blamed in part. Southern California, whose climate is essentially Mediterranean, does not have climate extremes in winter or summer, or sharp changes during the day.

As a general rule, at least 20 inches of rainfall per year, reasonably distributed, are needed to carry on satisfactory farming operations. When the rainfall is more than 60 inches, it becomes excessive; it raises the humidity, which is enervating, and it tends to erode the soil. The United States is fortunate as regards its rainfall. The common figure is between 25 and 40 inches, as can be seen in Table 1-1. Only in parts of the South and far Northwest does rainfall border on the excessive. In other regions too little rainfall, however, is a more serious problem; this explains to a large degree why settlement has been so light in the Plains

[1] The chief result of the admission of Alaska and Hawaii in 1959 was to enlarge the nation by one-fifth and extend its boundaries. In most respects Alaska and Hawaii are not representative states so that their coming does not materially alter the succeeding statements already written concerning the other 48 states.

[2] Ellsworth Huntington, *Principles of Human Geography* (New York: John Wiley & Sons, Inc., 1934), p. 291.

and Rocky Mountains area. In general, rainfall averages below 20 inches west of the 100th meridian, which runs through central Nebraska and the Dakotas. The population on the west coast is concentrated in river valleys like the San Joaquin in California or the Willamette in Oregon. In places irrigation is used generously to supplement the inadequate rainfall. In regions of light rainfall, sometimes it is only the lack of water that keeps the soil from being very productive. On the other hand, in certain regions of adequate rainfall periods of drought appear so frequently as to be a

Table 1-1
American Climates

Region	Representative cities	Average temperature, January, °F	Average temperature, July, °F	Annual rain, in.	Annual snow, in.
Northeast	Boston, Mass.	29	72	39	42
North Central	Minneapolis, Minn.	15	74	33	42
	Omaha, Nebr.	23	79	26	28
South	Charlotte, N.C.	42	77	43	6
	New Orleans, La.	56	83	64	0
Mountain	Boise, Idaho	27	74	13	21
	Albuquerque, N.M.	34	79	9	9
Pacific coast	Los Angeles, Calif.	55	73	15	0
	Spokane, Wash.	25	68	15	38

SOURCE: U.S. Bureau of the Census, *Statistical Abstract of the United States, 1956* (Washington, 1956), pp. 166–173.

serious menace to the farmer. This happens in central New England, northern Pennsylvania, Ohio, Indiana, and Illinois, and quite regularly in the Dakotas, Kansas, and Nebraska.

Mountains. Although a large portion of the United States is fairly flat country, there are three major north-south mountain ranges: the Appalachians in the East, the Rocky Mountains 2,000 miles inland, and the Sierra Nevada–Cascades in the far West. These mountains are significant for several reasons. For one, they affect the amount of rainfall, especially in the far Northwest where rainfall is heavy on the west side of the mountains but light on the east. Also, many rivers find their beginnings in the mountains. Most important, however, they have directed and deflected the flow of settlement. This was more noticeable to pioneers, who had to choose whether or not to drive creaking wagons over rough trails leading to mountain gaps, than it is to us today driving powerful automobiles on graded highways. The Appalachian Mountain range, stretching from Maine to northern Georgia, affected the nation's early economic destinies, as it kept the colonists from moving inland as fast as they otherwise would have done. Through the one north-south break in this mountain chain, out of which the Hudson River flows, Americans traded with or fought against the French in Canada. Through the one east-west break, out of which the Mohawk River empties into the Hudson at Albany, they built the only waterway connections to the West. The Appalachians were actually several ranges thick, ran in a southwesterly direction, and had their best southern exit into the West at the Cumberland Gap, in the far southwestern corner of Virginia. Accordingly, it was backwoodsmen from the North who settled the western areas of Virigina and North Carolina and who founded the first states west of the Appalachian Mountains—Kentucky (1792) and Tennessee (1796). Later in history, the more formidable Rocky Mountains, which reach from Canada to Mexico, made the long trek to California slower and more difficult. So also did the high Sierra Nevada and Cascade Mountains in the Pacific coast states. In fact, it was not until the 1840s that a wagon could make the trip to the Oregon territory, so steep were some of the trails.

Natural Waterways. If the Pacific and Atlantic coasts had been switched, North America would have been much harder to settle. All in all, the east coast offered many advantages to the sailing vessels and settlers of the seventeenth century. It has deep indentations such as Long Island Sound, Delaware Bay, Chesapeake Bay, and Pamlico Sound. Many rivers empty into it and offer access some distance into the interior, the best being the Hudson, up which vessels could sail 150 miles before encountering the first block to navigation. In general, they could penetrate farther inland in the South than in the North, for the mountains lay deeper in the interior. During the first century of settlement, the populace lived along these various rivers and as far up them as the first rapids or falls. Within this Tidewater area, supplies from overseas could be brought in or exports sent out without great difficulty. A line drawn to connect the first falls or rapids, as one ascends from the ocean, is known as the "fall line." At these navigation barriers, where transshipments of cargo had to be made, forts sprang up, power resources were later available, and cities appeared. Beyond the fall line lay the Piedmont, or foothills, scene of the second century of settlement.

Between the Appalachian Mountains in the East and the Rockies in the West lay the Mississippi Valley. The Mississippi River was navigable virtually without interruption from the Gulf of Mexico clear to Minneapolis. The two chief tributaries of the Mississippi are like two outstretched arms of the Father of Waters: they are the Ohio, rising in Pennsylvania and flowing in from the East, and the Missouri, rising in Montana and flowing in from the West. Both are navigable most of their length. Other important tributaries of the Mississippi, in its lower reaches, are the Arkansas and the Red, both entering from the West. Each of these tributaries has its own sizable tributaries feeding it, and some of them in turn have navigable tributaries. The whole Mississippi Valley on the east and south is a network of waterways that were very useful to early settlers. But in the arid northwestern quarter of the valley only the Missouri was of much use. Its chief tributary, the Platte, for example, was reputed to be a mile wide and a foot deep.

In the North are the five Great Lakes, among the largest fresh-water lakes in the world, all navigable and fairly well connected. These inland highways are an invaluable gift of nature to the economic development of the nation. They have only been used extensively, however, for about 135 years, since the opening of the Erie Canal in 1825 made them accessible to the East.

Still farther west were rivers like the Colorado and Rio Grande, which supplied water in a very arid region. In the far Northwest there was the Columbia, navigable at an early date as far as the Willamette River Valley, which was the scene of the early Oregon settlements. It was later made navigable still farther and provided water for irrigation and for making electric power. The west coast, unlike the east coast, has only three good harbors—Seattle, Portland, and San Francisco. California has no river of consequence extending into the interior.

Soils. The soils of this nation, on the whole, are good. The Indian farmer had rarely exhausted them, and the extensive cover of forest was adding to the topsoil all the time. The soils in the Northeast near the coast were thin but moderately good, and the sandy loams of the southern Tidewater area were better. Farther inland where the soil was more sandy and scrub pines abounded, the Southern soil was poor again. The best soils were to be found in the Mississippi Valley. The black prairie soils of Iowa, the northern half of Illinois, and southern Minnesota are especially fine for growing grain. Also rich are the alluvial soils of Mississippi, Arkansas, and Louisiana near the Mississippi. When there is adequate moisture, the brown soils of Kansas, the Dakotas, and Montana are likewise fine for grain production. The Western soils are not of especially high quality, although there are good soils in the San Joaquin Valley in California and the Willamette Valley in Oregon. Yet given some water, the results are sometimes surprising. It should be remembered that different crops thrive in different soils; sandy or clayey soils are less satisfactory than loam soils, for a sandy subsoil will lose moisture fast, and a clayey subsoil will hold too much moisture. Because this country is relatively flat and still young, America has better soils than are found in most parts of the world.

NATURAL RESOURCES

Among the chief natural resources are forests, wildlife, fisheries, coal, oil, metals, and important miscellany such as building materials, sulfur, salts, and fertilizers. The country is richly endowed with nearly all of these.

Forests. Originally, over 40 per cent of the nation was covered with forests (see Map 1-1). The entire East and most of the Middle West up

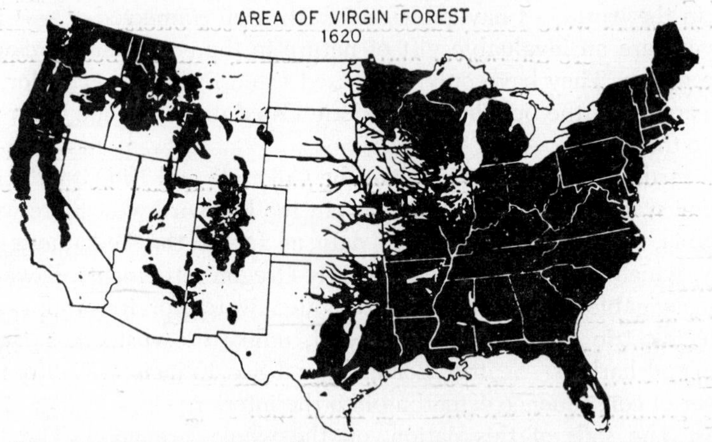

MAP 1-1. (*From C. O. Paullin, Atlas of Historical Geography of the United States, Carnegie Institution, Washington, 1932, plate 3A.*)

to the eastern borders of the Dakotas, Nebraska, and Kansas were forested. True, much of Iowa and central Illinois was prairie, with grass growing as high as a man's head. East of Illinois large stretches of open country were rare. Farther west were large wooded areas in eastern Texas, central Colorado, Idaho, western Washington and Oregon, and northern California. To the pioneer the forests had disadvantages as well as advantages. Although they provided timbers for buildings, crude furniture, and fuel, they also had to be removed before much cultivation could be undertaken, and they sometimes concealed marauding Indians.

Some 1,100 different tree forms have been counted in America, most of them useful. In the Northeast and in Michigan, Wisconsin, and Minnesota were vast evergreen forests, of which the white pine was the most sought after. Such forests were also found in Idaho, Colorado, and northern California. Another type of evergreen, the yellow pine, faster growing but of poorer quality, appeared all along the seacoast and several hundred miles inland from southern New Jersey around to eastern Texas. Between these two evergreen forests were vast leafy forests of oak, maple, hickory, chestnut, walnut, elm, birch, and others. In eastern Oregon and Washington were various fir trees, the Douglas fir being the most important. Since it takes water to grow a tree, the Great Plains and Rocky Mountain regions were largely unforested except near rivers.

Wildlife. The first settlers commented enthusiastically upon the abundance of wildlife such as deer, wild turkeys and other wildfowl, and bear (which were looked upon as great sport to hunt). Although these creatures provided much needed meat, another form of wildlife was just as seriously sought. These were the fur-bearing animals, namely, meat eaters, gnawers, and grazers, important in that order, as a rule. Among the meat eaters were foxes, raccoons, martens, sea otters, and seals. The chief gnawers were the beaver and the muskrat, with the beaver long the most prized catch. Deer and bison ranked high among the grazers. These last had many uses to both Indians and white men, who obtained food, clothing, and shelter from slaughtering them. The Plains Indians followed the enormous herds of bison, which drifted as far east as the western slopes of the Appalachians, obtaining food from the carcass, clothing and shelter from the hide, and fuel from "buffalo chips" (droppings).

Fisheries. It was ocean fisheries that lured western Europeans to America at an early date and that kept them coming all during the sixteenth century before there were any permanent settlements in British or French North America. Dozens of ships went out each year to the cod-feeding grounds off Newfoundland. Later they sought the cod nearer the New England coast, off Cape Cod. In addition to cod, other important fish that abounded off the Atlantic seacoast were haddock, flounder, mackerel, ocean perch, and herring. On the west coast the tuna fish and the sardine have been important, and of course the salmon in the far Northwest. The salmon was the "staff of life" of the Indians of that area and is still basic to an important canning industry. The chief other sea animal of importance is really a mammal, the whale, which was found off New England two centuries ago and later off the Pacific coast, but which was so hunted that by the early nineteenth century he had to be sought in the far corners of the world. He was killed for his oil, which was used in lamps to light homes, and for the "whalebone" in his mouth, which long served many of the purposes that light steel does today.

Coal. Coal may be broadly classified into four groups, namely, anthracite or hard coal, semibituminous, bituminous, and inferior grades, chief of which is lignite. Only two are to any degree scarce. These are anthracite, mostly used for heating homes, and semibituminous coking coal for making steel. Coal is important because for the past century it has been the leading source of home heat, industrial power, electricity, and railroad fuel. This nation is rich in coal and has enough to last for many centuries even at the present tremendous rates of use.

There are four major coal regions in the United States, plus a few other areas that have as yet not been greatly developed. In general, the farther west one goes, the poorer the quality of the coal becomes, primarily because it is less old. The Appalachian Mountains region, from Pennsylvania to northern Alabama, contains the major anthracite deposit (in eastern Pennsylvania), the best semibituminous or coking coal deposits (in western Pennsylvania, West Virginia, and Virginia), and the leading sources of bituminous coal today. The next major coal region to the west is the Illinois deposit, which actually extends into Indiana and Kentucky. Much of Illinois is underlain by coal. It is good bituminous coal but there is no anthracite and little coking coal in this region. The third coal region extends north and south from central Iowa, down the Kansas-Missouri border and into Oklahoma and Arkansas. This also is bituminous coal except for some coking coal deposits at the southern end. The fourth great deposit is in the Rocky Mountain states from the Canadian border down to Arizona and New Mexico. Most of it is inferior coal, that is, lignite or brown coal in South Dakota and subbituminous coal farther south. Four regions of the nation have virtually no coal at all, namely, New England, the Southeast, the far upper Middle West, and the Pacific coast. In the last century, this has at times handicapped their industrial development.

Oil. Today oil and natural gas are as important fuels as coal, but they came into prominence much later than coal. At first oil was primarily used as kerosene for lighting homes; only secondarily was it developed as a lubricant that could stand the heats and pressures of the new heavier industrial machines. Only in the present century has the chief use of oil become gasoline for our cars. Frequently large amounts of natural gas are found on top of the oil. It has been possible to use the natural gas to any great degree only in the last thirty years. Earlier much of it was thrown away or burnt at the well, because it was essential to draw off the gas to get to the oil and there was no way to store or transport the gas without installing very expensive pipelines and other equipment. Now this best of all fuels is being used. It is "the only fuel that mines, transports and feeds itself," that needs no processing, for it may be used as it comes from the earth. All one needs to do, once the piping facilities are installed, is turn a stopcock and light a match. It is twice as effective as gas produced from coal.

American oil and natural gas resources are found chiefly in six areas. The most easterly deposit and the one first developed, a century ago, lies in the Appalachian range from western New York south to northern Tennessee. A second deposit is in western Ohio, central Indiana, and southern Illinois. The third, and most important of all, the mid-continent, is found in Kansas, Oklahoma, and northern and central Texas. There is a fourth in Louisiana and along the east coast of Texas, a fifth in the upper Rocky Mountain area, especially in Wyoming and Montana, and a sixth in southern California, this last being less important than it once appeared to be. It may be noted that in a general way the chief oil and natural gas deposits coincide with the chief coal deposits, or at least are not too far removed from them. In World War II, the Germans actually got much of their oil from processing coal. Essentially the same four regions that lack coal also lack oil and natural gas, namely, New England, the Southeast, the far upper Middle West, and the northern part of the Pacific coast.

Metals. The metals may be classified under four heads: (1) iron; (2) nonferrous metals like copper, lead, zinc, aluminum; (3) alloying elements; and (4) others, chiefly precious metals. Ample supplies of most of these exist in the United States. Metals, unlike fuels, are not lost with one use; the scrap may be reused.

By far the most important metal is iron, from which steel is made. For nearly a century Americans have lived in an "Age of Steel." Iron constitutes 85 per cent by weight of all the metals mined. Early settlers found small but adequate iron deposits near Lynn, Massachusetts, and Salisbury, Connecticut, in Virginia and Pennsylvania, and in fact in all the colonies but Georgia. Later deposits were found in Ohio, Tennessee, Alabama, Wisconsin, and Utah. During the latter nineteenth century, when American industry needed iron in larger quantities, prospectors discovered huge deposits, first in Upper Michigan and then in eastern Minnesota. Six enormous iron ranges were eventually developed, the Marquette in 1848 being the first and the Mesabi, opened in 1892, the most famous. In recent years about 85 per cent of American iron ore has come from these two states. The location of the mines near the Great Lakes makes it easy to transport the ore. A smaller but sizable deposit in Alabama is significant chiefly because it exists alongside coal and limestone deposits.

Of the nonferrous metals the nation is best endowed with copper. Small deposits in New Jersey and other parts of the East served inadequately in early times. Later rich ores were found in southwestern Tennessee and especially on the Kewanee Peninsula in Upper Michigan. But the richest finds had to wait until later, and today half of the copper comes from southern Arizona and much of the rest from New Mexico, Utah, Nevada, and Montana. In early times copper was used as ship sheathing or for kettles; in recent times it is the chief conductor of electricity. Prospectors found the large Western mines in time to fill this modern need.

Lead was also in great demand in colonial times, mostly for shot for guns but also to mix with tin to make pewter plates and other tableware. In the eighteenth century lead mines were worked in Dutchess County, New York, near Southampton, Massachusetts, and in Virginia. Early in the nineteenth century the Galena deposit in northern Illinois was developed. In more recent times, Missouri has provided much of the lead, but now that these deposits seem to be running out, new ones are opening in Idaho.

Zinc, another dull metal, is associated with lead in many ways. It was not found to any extent in colonial times. Brass, made from copper and zinc, was imported. Zinc mines were opened in Pennsylvania and New Jersey in the mid-nineteenth century. Later in the century zinc mines were found near lead mines in the Middle West, and in recent times most zinc has come from Oklahoma and Idaho.

Aluminum, virtually unknown until a century ago, was first looked upon as a precious metal. The research of Charles Hall toward the end of the nineteenth century brought the price down and made it available for everyday use. It ought to be the most common metal of all, for aluminum ore exists in every claybank and in much of the earth underfoot. It takes terrific heats, however, to obtain aluminum from this source. Thus far aluminum has been obtained chiefly from bauxite, which will give up the metal somewhat more readily. Bauxite deposits are not large in this country, the chief ones being in Arkansas. If the atomic age can soon provide terrific heat at low cost, the aluminum all about us may be available. Aluminum is a good substitute for copper and to some extent for wood and iron.

Tin is about the only important nonferrous metal that the United States has lacked entirely at all times.

Alloying elements were not important until the appearance of specialized steels in the past century. The United States is moderately well equipped with these elements. The greatest asset is a mountain of molybdenum in Colorado. Molybdenum intensifies the effects of other alloys. The next most common one is tungsten, found in some quantity in Nevada. It imparts a fine cutting edge. The United States also has a little, but nowhere near enough, vanadium and manganese, and Canada has quantities of nickel. Chrome and other alloying elements have to be imported from afar.

As for the precious metals, the United States is the world's third largest producer of gold today. Some gold was found in North Carolina in the 1830s, and large amounts in California after 1848. Today gold and silver are found chiefly as joint products of copper, lead, and zinc mining.

Other Minerals. The nation has never lacked for building materials. Deposits of natural cement were worked in New York and Pennsylvania and elsewhere early in the nineteenth century. Vermont and later Georgia became famous for marble and New Hampshire for granite. Likewise, there are ample industrial chemicals, such as sulfur in Louisiana and Texas. Salt licks have not been unduly difficult to find, although their presence affected the location of settlements and trails in pioneering days. The areas that have most needed soil fertilizers have been the Southern states. When a soil becomes acid, it must be neutralized to regain its productivity. For that purpose there have been, fortunately, large quantities of marl, gypsum, and lime fairly handy. The other major soil fertilizers, such as potassium and phosphorus, are found chiefly in the Southwest and the Rocky Mountain states.

Altogether this country is richly endowed with the resources that a nation needs to be self-sufficient and great. Moreover, many of these have been found conveniently and in adequate amounts at about the time that they were needed.

EUROPEAN BACKGROUND

A number of remarkable changes, both intellectual and political, took place in Europe between about 1450 and 1550, and directly and indirectly they affected the settlement of America. A German named John Gutenberg invented the printing press around 1450; this made it cheaper and easier for people to buy and read books, which accentuated certain trends already under way. The Crusades had made western Europeans more aware of the ancient civilizations of eastern Europe. Reading stimulated people to think for themselves, to reinterpret the Bible for themselves, to do a little scientific experimentation, and to want to learn more about remote corners of the world. Henry VIII (1491–1547) in England, John Calvin (1509–1564) in France, Martin Luther (1483–1546) in Germany, and others led in throwing off the religious and political control of the Pope in Rome, and caused various Protestant groups to set up their own separate churches. These in time splintered into smaller sectarian groups. In science the teachings of Pythagoras began to gain in esteem. He had said that the sun was the center of our universe, in contrast to Ptolemy who said that the earth was the center. Both had agreed, however, that the earth was round, although the common man persisted in believing that it was flat.

DISCOVERY OF AMERICA

Meanwhile, there was an economic as well as an intellectual incentive for further exploring the face of the earth. The demand for silks and spices which came from India was growing, but the interference of the

Arabs with this trade was constantly raising the cost of these articles. There was also dissatisfaction with the exorbitant profits of Italian trading monopolies. The merchants of western Europe were beginning to wonder whether they could not find a way to avoid paying tribute to the Arabs and a profit to Italian merchants by themselves trading directly to India. During the fifteenth century, the Portuguese in particular sought to do this by exploring a way to India around the southern tip of Africa. Eventually, in 1498, Vasco da Gama succeeded, making a fabulous profit in the process. Meanwhile, another solution seemed possible in theory. If the earth was round, as educated men believed, why not sail west to reach India? In 1492, Christopher Columbus, an Italian from Genoa, sailing under the Spanish flag, tried to do just this. In some respects Columbus was a failure, for he did not reach India and he did not realize that he had found a new continent, or rather two of them. Actually, he never touched the mainland of North America. John Cabot, another Italian from Genoa, did this in 1497 for Henry VII, and was granted 10 pounds by that close-fisted monarch for discovering "a new continent." English claims to North America rested on his discovery. Nevertheless, Columbus's inadvertent discoveries set in motion a train of events that was henceforth to affect Europe profoundly. More and more, Europe turned its attention from the Mediterranean, the Near East, and Asia and looked west toward the New World. Spain, Portugal, France, England, and Holland, instead of being on a far corner of the stage, were increasingly in the center. Their trade grew and that of the Mediterranean states declined, relatively speaking. This is called the "commercial revolution."

Although Columbus discovered America for Spain in 1492 and Cabot did so for England in 1497, and the French sent out John Verrazano in 1524 and Jacques Cartier in 1534, no one but the Spanish did much settling in the sixteenth century. They concentrated on South and Central America and as far north as Mexico. One outpost did appear in North America, St. Augustine, Florida (1565). The English, French, and Dutch did not establish anything that lasted until the start of the seventeenth century. Their interest lay in seeking a water passage through or around America to India, and in doing a considerable amount of fishing off Newfoundland, Nova Scotia, and New England. Frequently the fishermen erected scaffoldings for drying their fish; they took on water, traded with Indians, frolicked with Indian maidens, and occasionally a few sailors would spend the winter here. They also explored the coast line and even carried back some Indians to Europe as souvenirs.

Colonization Begins. By the start of the seventeenth century England began to take a greater interest in the New World. A series of naval victories over Spain, the greatest being the defeat of the Spanish Armada in 1588, gave her merchants the courage to invade this part of the world. The success of the East India Company, which had reaped fabulous profits since its founding in 1600, led the serious and industrious merchants to think of developing other corners of the world being opened before them. The Virginia Company was chartered in 1606 with merchants of two ports, London and Plymouth, each enjoying a claim to a large segment of the coast. The King allotted the London merchants a region from latitude 34 to 41 (southern Virginia to New York City) and the Plymouth merchants a region from latitude 38 to 45 (southern Maryland to southern Nova Scotia). (All North America that England claimed was then called Virginia.) The two groups of merchants hoped that their colonists would search for gold, trade with the Indians, look for a water passage to the Pacific, and send back naval stores. Both sent out expeditions late in 1607, the Plymouth group settling at Sagadahoc (see Map 1-2, p. 18) on the Kennebec River in southern Maine, and the London group settling at Jamestown on the James River in southern Virginia. Both groups had an extremely hard time, but the Jamestown colony, in a milder climate and perhaps with somewhat better leadership, managed to survive, although it was not until about 1612 that Jamestown was on a fairly sound footing. Economically, the colonists there devoted their attention not to gold mining, Indian trade, or exploration, but chiefly to tobacco culture. Meanwhile, years went by and the Plymouth merchants were without a settlement. Finally, in December of 1620, a group of Pilgrims settled at Plymouth in southern Massachusetts.

The Plymouth Colony. The background and experience of this second successful English colony illustrate the attitudes, conditions, and problems of New World settlement in this period. The Pilgrims, sometimes called Separatists, were extreme Puritans who believed in local autonomy for their church. They wanted no interference from Church of England bishops and archbishops. This threatened to get some of them into serious trouble, and 125 fled to Leyden, Holland, where the Dutch treated them well. After about ten years, however, they felt they were losing their national identity, they feared the Spanish invasion then threatening Holland, and they wanted to establish their own separate community. Emigrating to America seemed a solution; the main barrier was lack of funds. Eventually they borrowed the money, on harsh terms, through a sharp promoter named Thomas Weston and were able to buy supplies and outfit two ships, the 180-ton *Mayflower* and the less seaworthy, smaller *Speedwell*. There were many delays; leaks caused the *Speedwell* to turn back; and some of the Pilgrims became discouraged and dropped out. Weston insisted on crowding in other passengers who wanted to go to America but who were not congenial to the Pilgrims. After a stormy two-month voyage, the *Mayflower* made a first landing at what is now

Provincetown on the end of Cape Cod. A good site was shortly chosen in southern Massachusetts at Plymouth. The group of ninety-nine set to work putting up frame dwellings. The winter was severe and the group had probably been weakened by close confinement during the voyage. Over half of them had died by spring; three families were entirely wiped out; and at one time only two men were well enough to tend to all the others. A group of people with less character and persistence would have

Fig. 1-1. The *Mayflower* II, a 92-foot replica of the original *Mayflower*. (*Courtesy of United Press.*)

given up or would never have come in the first place. The secret of success of this little colony was the determination and intelligent leadership of four or five leaders, such as William Bradford and Myles Standish.

A short time before, a plague had also struck the Indians living in the region and sharply reduced their numbers, even exterminating some villages. Had the Indians been more crowded, they might have been annoyed at the appearance of the Pilgrims and attacked the weakened group. Instead, the Indians feared their own Indian enemies more and looked upon the white men with their guns as desirable allies. Accordingly, the Indians were a great help to the Pilgrims. In March, 1621,

Samoset, a subchief who had dealt with English fishermen for twenty years and learned some English, walked into the village and greeted them, "Hello, Englishmen." He soon introduced them to Squanto, who had been kidnapped some years before and carried to England, where he had lived a while before finding his way back to America. Since his tribe, living about where Plymouth was, had been wiped out by the plague, he threw in his lot with the Pilgrims until he died two years later. Squanto showed them when and how to plant corn and pumpkins, where and how to fish, and taught them many of the tricks of living in the wilderness. Thanks also to Squanto, a treaty of friendship was drawn up with Massassoit, leading chieftain of the region, who protected them especially during their first decade of growth when they were so outnumbered. After the third year, the colonists always had plenty to eat. New groups of settlers kept being added to the colony. Livestock was imported. The Pilgrims never seemed able to master the art of fishing commercially, but they became expert fur traders and would have liquidated their debt to Weston and his associates at an early date were it not for pirates intercepting the furs and for crooked practices by Weston's associates and even by some of the Pilgrims' representatives in London. Morison estimates that the Pilgrims expended £20,000 at one period to reduce the debt by £1,800.[3]

Massachusetts Bay Colony. In 1628 the Council for New England, successors to the Plymouth Company, granted a charter to a large and moderately well-to-do group of Puritans to establish a self-governing colony in America. These founded Boston in 1630. The expedition numbered eleven ships and was under the leadership of John Winthrop. Within ten years, some 20,000 persons came over. The Massachusetts Bay settlement at Boston was so large that it made the "Old Colony" (Plymouth) less fearful of an Indian uprising. At first it also provided them an excellent market for their surplus farm crops. But the Bay community was so large that it dominated the other settlements around it. For this reason, two or three dissident groups split off from it, such as those going to Rhode Island under Roger Williams, those to New Haven under John Davenport and Theophilus Eaton, and those to Connecticut under Thomas Hooker and Governor Winthrop the Younger. There is not space here to examine the reasons leading to the founding of each colony. A few broad and fairly valid generalizations must suffice.

Other Colonies. The process of founding colonies went on for 126 years starting with Jamestown in 1607 and ending with Georgia in 1733. From the point of view of internal organization, several of the early ones were charter colonies, in particular, Massachusetts Bay, Connecticut, and

[3] Samuel E. Morison, *The Story of the "Old Colony" of New Plymouth* (New York: Alfred A. Knopf, Inc., 1956), p. 130.

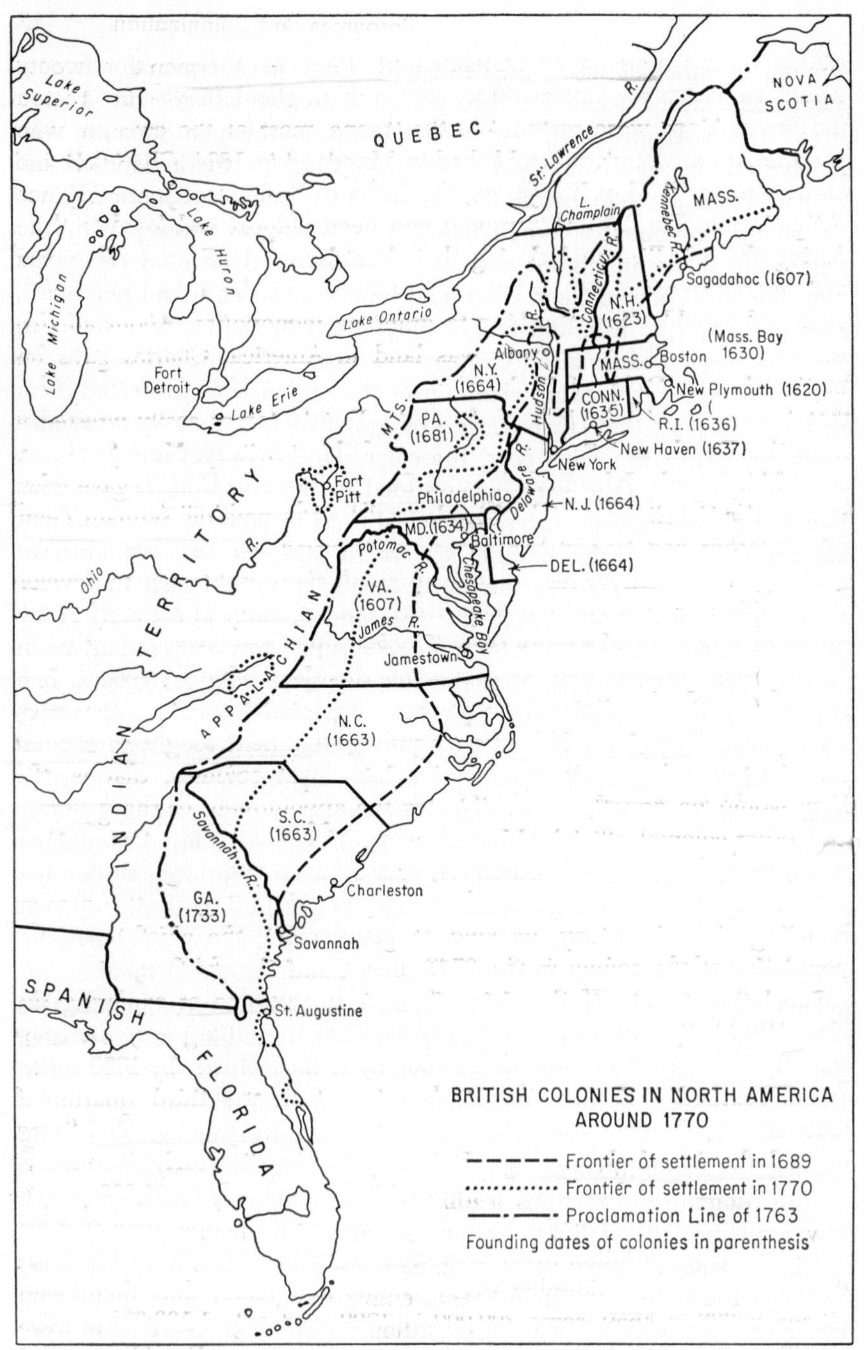

MAP 1-2. (*Adapted from Hammond's Atlas of American History, C. S. Hammond & Co., Inc., New York, 1953; frontier line of 1689 is from Dixon Ryan Fox, Harper's Atlas of American History, Harper & Brothers, New York, 1920.*)

Rhode Island. They were administered much as a business company would be. After the Cromwellian period in England (1642–1660) when the Stuart kings were restored to the throne, most of the colonies were proprietary, a precedent established in Maryland in 1634. Charles II and his successor (his brother James, the Duke of York, later James II) had obligations to English nobility who had been helpful and loyal to them during the rebellion and during their banishment to France afterward, and wanted to reward their friends. But Parliament kept the royal family poor and would allow the king to grant no monopolies. About all that the Stuarts had to give away was land in America. Charles gave his brother James, Duke of York, what soon became New York, provided that James would take it away from the Dutch. James easily wrested it from the Dutch and then gave a part of this territory, New Jersey, to two of his friends, John Berkeley and George Carteret. Charles gave what is now the Carolinas to eight friends, and he also paid off William Penn, whose father had loaned him money and served him in other ways, by granting him Pennsylvania. It was up to all these noblemen to develop their wilderness real estate if they could. Indeed, many of the early settlements of America make more sense if looked upon primarily as real estate development projects than as havens for dissident religious groups. It is rather that these religious groups were expected to make satisfactory customers. After about 1688 the English government sought to convert the charter and proprietary colonies into royal colonies; that is, the king would be directly responsible for the appointment of the governor and other colonial officials. Massachusetts, New York, New Jersey, New Hampshire, Virginia, the Carolinas, and eventually Georgia were royal colonies by the early eighteenth century. Table 1-2 gives the date of founding of each colony, its kind of government, the chief town, the population of the colony in the 1749 census, and the chief export.

Population Trends. If the sixteenth century was one of exploring the New World, the seventeenth century was one of settling only the coast line. By 1700 settlements extended roughly to the fall line. By 1750 settlements reached well into the Piedmont and in the third quarter of that century, Daniel Boone and a few other daring persons tried living beyond the Appalachian range. It is easy to visualize early America as far more populous than it actually was. There were only 2,500,000 people in the mainland colonies in 1775. At present, more people than that are added to the population every year. Starting about 1650, it is safe to say that the population doubled every twenty-five years; thus there were about 75,000 in 1650, some 300,000 in 1700, and only 1,100,000 in 1750. Families were large; it may be recalled that Benjamin Franklin was the tenth child of a family in which seventeen children were born.

Once the first colonists had arrived and a settlement had been planted,

Table 1-2

Data on the English Colonies on the American Mainland

Colony	Date of founding by English	Kind of government	Chief town, 1749	Chief export	Population, 1749* (000 omitted)	Other comments
Virginia	1607	charter	Williamsburg	tobacco	85	Became royal colony in 1624
New Plymouth	1620	charter	Plymouth	fish	220	Absorbed by Massachusetts, 1691
Massachusetts Bay	1630	charter	Boston	fish		Lost charter, became royal in 1684
New Hampshire	1623	proprietary	Portsmouth	fish	30	Became royal colony in 1679
Maryland	1634	proprietary	Baltimore	tobacco	85	Chief Catholic colony
Rhode Island	1636	charter	Newport	fish	35	Four towns: Providence, Portsmouth, Newport, Warwick
Connecticut	1635	charter	Middletown	fish	100	Charter obtained, 1662
New Haven	1637	....	New Haven	fish		Absorbed by Connecticut in 1664
North Carolina	1663	proprietary	New Bern	naval stores	45	Separated, 1712. Became royal, 1729
South Carolina	1663	proprietary	Charleston	rice	30	Separated, 1712. Became royal, 1719
New York	1664	proprietary	New York	grain	100	Settled by Dutch, 1624. Captured by English, 1664. Became royal, 1685
East New Jersey	1664	proprietary	Perth Amboy	grain	60	Settled by Dutch, 1624. Captured by English, 1664
West New Jersey	1664	proprietary	Burlington	grain		Two Jerseys united as royal colony, 1703
Delaware	1664	proprietary	Newcastle	grain	250	Settled first by Swedes, 1638. Dutch captured it in 1655, English took it in 1664; under Pennsylvania 1682–1704. Had own government from 1704 on
Pennsylvania	1681	proprietary	Philadelphia	grain		Settled by Swedes, 1647. Captured by Dutch, 1655; by English, 1664. United with Delaware 1682–1704
Georgia	1733	charter	Savannah	rice	6	Became royal colony, 1760
Total					1,046	

* From 1749 reports to British government, quoted in Timothy Pitkin, *Statistical View of the Commerce of the U.S.A.* (Hartford, 1816).

most of the growth in population was owing to natural increase rather than to migration from the Old World. Moreover, the population, by modern standards at least, was remarkably homogeneous. The majority were of English descent; the three great exceptions to this generality were the Negro slaves, the Germans (usually called Pennsylvania Dutch), and the Scotch-Irish. The Negroes, mostly slaves and in the South, numbered about 450,000 in 1775 and had come largely in the eighteenth century. The Germans who settled so heavily in Pennsylvania also came in the eighteenth century. The German word for German is Deutsch, which was easily confused with Dutch. The Scotch-Irish were descendants of lowland Scots who were transplanted to northern Ireland early in the seventeenth century. They left in large numbers a century later because, like the native Irish, they received poor treatment at the hands of the English. The English resented the competition first of their livestock in English markets, and then of their wool, and imposed harsh laws limiting the trade of these products. This in turn induced the Scotch-Irish to leave for a country where they would have more freedom. The Scotch-Irish hated to buy land and often settled on the frontier to avoid doing so. They were fine frontiersmen. On the whole the American population was white, Anglo-Saxon, and Protestant in character. Moreover it was a young people: there were many children and life expectancy at birth was under thirty-five. Since Americans were so busy opening a new continent, they had relatively little time for education. That made them less acquainted with the experiences of the past and forced them to solve problems with their own ingenuity. The fact that conditions were different in the New World contributed further to American resourcefulness.

Colonial Wars. In opening the new continent, the English and their colonists had more than the Indians to contend with, barbarous as these generally were. In the sixteenth century of exploration, the Spanish were England's great enemy. In the seventeenth century, England fought three important wars with the Dutch, whose trading genius exceeded that of the English at times. The Dutch merchant marine outshone the English, especially in the Cromwellian period, 1642–1660. The Dutch competed with the English in the Far East, for the African slave trade, and for territory around New York. The English drove them out of New York in 1664 and defeated them finally in 1674.

In the eighteenth century, France was the great enemy. The period from 1689 to 1815 has sometimes been called the Second Hundred Years' War because in that 126 years the two nations went to war six times and were in conflict half the time. Prussia, Austria, Spain, and others might side with England one time and with France another, but England and France were always opposed in the eighteenth century wars. Generally the wars were fought on several fronts, too, that is, in India and in

America as well as in Europe. Each nation had Indian tribes friendly to its cause. The French were trying to extend their control from Canada to the Gulf of Mexico; the English were reaching westward. To the colonies, asked to contribute men and money and to suffer Indian raids, these were wars of the kings: for example, King William's War, 1689–1697; Queen Anne's War, 1701–1713; and King George's War, 1739–1745. The same wars went by other names in Europe. The first really major conflict was the French and Indian War (1754–1763), as a result of which the French were driven out of Canada. After that, the Americans were less in need of English protection. Just when the Americans became less dependent on the English militarily, the English sought to increase their political control. The result was the American Revolution. But it had taken 168 years of economic growth before Americans felt able to undertake this war or even thought much of doing so. That was nearly half the history of the United States, for the halfway year from 1607 to 1959 is 1783.

CHAPTER 2

Colonial Agriculture and Labor

In colonial times, most people were farmers, but farming in the New World differed from farming in the Old World. Land was more abundant and the soil was usually more fertile. There were many new crops. Markets were fewer in number and farther away. These and other factors obliged the colonists to make numerous adjustments in their agricultural methods. European travelers rarely grasped the need for these adjustments and were usually critical of American farming methods.

WHAT THE EARLY SETTLERS FOUND

Indian Farmers. The common conception of the American Indian is that he was nomadic and made his living by hunting and fishing. This is partly incorrect. Along the east coast, in the South, and in the Southwest, most of the Indians lived in villages and farmed the land about them. The women and the younger people did most of the work in the fields, whereas the men supplemented the family income by hunting and fishing and, of course, were the tribal militia. On the Great Plains, the tribes were more nomadic and followed the great herds of buffalo whose flesh and hides provided them with food, clothing, and shelter. In the far Northwest, salmon was the staff of life; the backward Indians in California eked out a living from eating wild seeds. Of the million Indians in America in the seventeenth century, some 500,000, or half, should be classified as making their living from farming.

Indian farming was primitive and their methods of cultivation exhausted the soil within a few years. The Indians cleared land by girdling trees, and when the land was eventually worn out, the tribe would move on and find a new location. They lacked plows and horses or oxen and their chief grain was Indian corn. In New England "when the oak leaf was as big as a mouse's ear," the Indian women planted corn by scratching a hole with a sharp stick and dropping in four kernels and perhaps a dead fish or some other fertilizer. The hills were about three feet apart and laid out in rows. Weeding by hoeing was done with crude mattocks.

When harvested, the ears were husked and then stored in corn cribs standing off the ground, or sometimes in baskets in underground bins lined with straw matting. The good Indian farmer selected the best ears as his next year's seed corn; thus he practiced seed selection. The early settlers in Virginia got much of their food from these storage places, sometimes by gift, more often by trade, and occasionally by robbery. When deprived of their corn stores, one Virginian tribe came begging most piteously for its return. Other crops which the Indians raised were beans, squash, pumpkins, and watermelons. They also gathered various kinds of berries and preserved them by sun-drying. In the South, they cultivated tobacco for tribal rituals.

New Crops. The agriculture of America greatly enriched the diet of Europeans. It was estimated that new crops and plants carried to Europe augmented the variety of food crops by about one-third. By far the most important of the new crops was corn, called Indian corn by the settlers or maize by Europeans. The English word "corn" means essentially small grain such as wheat, oats, barley, and rye, and accordingly they christened this totally new small grain Indian corn. It was never too well received in the Old World, but its importance to the settlers in the New World can scarcely be exaggerted. All the major forms of corn such as field corn, sweet corn, and popcorn were already known to the Indians. The Indians taught the white man various ways of preparing corn as food, too, such as corn pone, hominy, mush, succotash, johnny cake, and roasting ears. For its weight, corn had more nutritive value than wheat, and so was ideal to carry on long journeys (johnny cake originally meant journey cake).

Next in importance was tobacco, because it soon became the chief export of Virginia and Maryland and of course made possible smoking, which had its beginnings in the late sixteenth century. So astounded was Sir Walter Raleigh's manservant on finding his master smoking that he threw a basin of water at him to save him from burning up. The pumpkins, squash, watermelon, and all kinds of delicious berries were also new crops. Although a variety of strawberry was known in Europe, it was scarcely edible, whereas the American strawberry was widely praised for its size and luscious flavor. Maple sugar was another Indian contribution. In addition, there were a number of plants brought in from the West Indies or from South and Central America. These regions had as much to offer in the way of new food plants as North America. There were the white potato from Peru, the sweet potato and pineapple from the West Indies, peanuts from Brazil, and tomatoes, cassavas, and peppers from Central America. The white potato went to Spain and also was taken to England and Ireland by Sir Francis Drake. For a while people did not regard the potato highly, because they did not know how to cook it. It finally gained popularity in Ireland and so came to be known as the Irish potato. Not until early in the eighteenth century did it gain wide acceptance in America. Altogether, the existence of many foods previously unknown in Europe meant that early colonists sometimes went hungry in the midst of plenty.

Fewer Animals. The North American continent added almost nothing of importance to the variety of livestock that is found on a farm. In fact, most of the Old World's farm animals did not exist here. There were no horses, oxen, cows, hogs, goats, sheep, or chickens in America. About the only domesticated animal that the Indian had was the dog, who served as a guard and a small-scale draft animal. In the latter capacity, he was hitched to a "travois." This consisted of two poles and a crosspiece, the whole shaped like a letter A, with the wide ends dragging on the ground and the closed ends pointed over the back of the dog and attached to him by a simple harness. Small loads were fastened to the crosspiece of the A. Lacking knowledge of the wheel, the Indians had no carts. Turkeys were North America's chief contribution to the farmyard. The Indian had not domesticated them, but the white man did. Although the first white men to reach the Great Plains found the Indians riding horses, this did not mean that the horse was native to America, although for a time such was thought to be the case. These Indian horses were the descendants of escaped or stolen horses from Mexico. The Spanish had introduced the horse there long before the first western explorers encountered Plains Indians on horseback. Two wild animals, the deer and buffalo, were of greater use to the Indian than any domestic animals they had before the white man came. The deer was already well known in Europe. The buffalo simply could not be domesticated and would not have been much use to an American farmer, anyway. Thus the settlers had to import virtually all their farm animals to America.

SOME FARM PROBLEMS

Acquiring Land. Land was a great deal more plentiful in America than in England, and this attracted many settlers. Yet land was by no means free in the New World. The farmer had to get it from the merchant company or proprietor owning the colony. He did this in one of two ways. He might pay his own transportation over the ocean to the colony at an early date and put up with all the inconveniences and hazards which first comers had to face, but he got his land free. For example, in 1664, the New Jersey proprietors promised 150 acres of land to every able-bodied person who arrived with half a year's supply of food before January 1, 1665. The amount of land granted declined each year for four years thereafter. Children and weaker persons got only half portions at all times. Later arrivals had to pay cash for their land. Moreover, for many settlers who came in the early years there was often, in actual practice, another landowner to pay, namely, the local Indians or Indian tribe. They had no legal rights according to English law, and individual Indians even had dubious rights under tribal law, but just the same the discreet thing to do, in order to avoid trouble, was to pay the Indians something. On top of these, there was a third payment to face, or at least the annoying possibility that it might be demanded. This was the annual quitrent of customarily half a penny an acre. The quitrent was a survival of the manorial dues owed by the serf to the lord in medieval times for protection. The early proprietors hoped originally to realize a substantial income from collecting a half-penny an acre from many thousands of acres, but they were largely disappointed in these hopes. The quitrent was least successful in New England, where it was early eliminated; it was only occasionally paid in the Middle Colonies, where it was a source of friction and worry; but it was an important form of taxation in Virginia.

Clearing Land. Most of the east coast was in forest. There were of course clearings, but frequently these were former farm lands of Indians which had been abandoned after the land had been worn out. Thus a farmer had to clear his own land. The Indians taught them that the best manner of doing this was to kill the trees by girdling them. The trees could later be felled at leisure, or they would fall themselves in a few years and could then be removed. Meanwhile, they put out no foliage, and the pioneer farmer could break the ground with a hoe and plant hills of Indian corn. Often he planted beans with the corn, letting the corn stalk serve as a bean pole, and frequently he grew pumpkins and squash as well. Thus he acquired a crop within a few months of his arrival. Only after the trees had been removed and the land broken by a heavy plow and by cross-plowing and harrowing could he produce such civilized crops as wheat. Corn was a frontier crop which required a minimum of preparation and attention. Using it solved many of the problems associated with frontier farming, especially the shortage of labor.

Erecting a House. The first dwellings of the colonists were often dugouts or shelters, the sort of thing with which a shepherd in the hills might content himself. That helps explain why so many of the early comers died. Since the colonists wanted homes that would be more livable, before the second winter they managed to put up simple frame houses, with a clapboard exterior, such as they had had back in England. As for the celebrated log cabin, that was unknown during most of the seventeenth century, except within the few Swedish and Finnish settlements along the Delaware River. Log cabins were unknown in England, Scotland, Ireland, Holland, and France, and it would have been very ingenious if people from these lands had thought immediately to erect such a dwelling, suitable as it might be to this country. Rather, in each colony the people first built the kind of house they were used to in their own country. It was the Swedes and Finns, coming from forested regions, who brought over the idea of the log cabin. Since the log cabin was ideally adapted to conditions in a forested New World, its use spread. By the start of the eighteenth century it was fairly common knowledge and typified the frontier thenceforth.

Farm Equipment. The equipment of the colonial farmer was simple and primitive. It was sometimes said that he could hoist all of it over his shoulder and carry it to the field in one load. This was almost true. The implements that he used most were his ax, a broad hoe, and a narrow one for cultivating, a mattock for breaking the ground and removing roots, a shovel, a pitchfork, a sickle, and a flail. Even the plow was lightweight, mostly of wood, with a metal point and a few pieces of metal fastened on the moldboard. It did not dig very deep into the soil. The four-sided harrow, with wooden teeth, was heavier but many a farmer just had his ox drag a heavy branch across the plowed field to break up the clods. Some farmers were fortunate enough to have a cart or even a wagon, and if so, this was the largest and most valuable piece of equipment of all. The chief draft animal was the strong, patient, almost indestructible ox.

Crop Rotation. Crop rotation appeared in medieval Europe when the population became sufficiently dense that it was inconvenient to move on when a piece of land wore out from planting the same crop year after year. So each field was allowed to lie fallow, or rest, every other year. Thus a two-field system supplanted a one-field system. The two-field system persisted in parts of England until the eighteenth century. In the more fertile valleys, however, a three-field system had been adopted. This consisted of wheat, barley or oats, and fallow. The American version later substituted corn for wheat. Regardless of the number of fields involved, letting a field lie fallow was wasteful, for weeds could exhaust the soil almost as much as crops. In time the English learned to substitute turnips or clover for fallow and thus get a forage crop for their animals at the same time that these crops also rebuilt the soil. It is clear that the scarcity of good land had prompted the English to make considerable progress in a thousand years or so. But land was not yet scarce in America. The Indians were still operating under a one-field system and most early colonists slipped back into that ancient regime too. It saved them from clearing more land until they were ready to do so and thus was a laborsaving device. But the whole line of thinking of the English agriculturalists who visited America was to promote ways to preserve the fertility of the land. They were shocked at the wasteful and primitive methods they found in use here and invariably lectured the colonists on this point. What they failed to realize was that Americans were conserving scarce labor at the expense of cheap land, whereas Europeans were conserving scarce land at the expense of cheap labor. The system was more sensible than it might appear, in view of the fact that American wheat could invade English markets more easily than the reverse.

REGIONAL CHARACTERISTICS

Farming in such widely separated regions as New Hampshire and South Carolina was bound to differ, for different climates and soils favor different crops. Colonial agriculture may be treated, geographically, in terms of three regions, namely, New England, the Middle Colonies, and the Southern Colonies.

New England. The New England community differed in appearance from that found in other regions; it looked strikingly like the medieval manorial community found in southern England. There was the village itself, usually surrounding a church, with a minister's house, a cemetery, a school, and a market place nearby. Every member of the community had a home lot in the village and lived there. Outside the village were the "upland and meadows" which were cut into strips and divided among the village families. Each family usually had several such strips, which they had acquired on the occasion of different "dividends" of the property that had been granted the town fathers or local proprietors. Some of this land would be kept as woodland, and some as pasture. Regular community members might also pasture their animals in the proprietors' commons, that is, in any land not yet divided up. The size of the family holdings depended on each family's investment in the original enterprise and on its ability to make use of the land. The average holding was relatively small in the seventeenth century, perhaps 50 to 60 acres, with about nine acres in tillage. Farmers sometimes cultivated their fields together, rather than each fencing in and tilling his own. Later, as people bought one another out and divided up all the proprietary lands, the holdings became larger. There were distinct reasons for the reappearance of this medieval type of village in the New World. A village was better protected against Indians than an isolated home. The church, which was very important in New England, wanted to keep close touch with its members. And with labor so scarce, close cooperation was a most helpful way of using the limited supply efficiently.

The New England soil was reasonably good, but it was thin and much of it was covered with granite rocks of all sizes. These had to be gathered up and stacked together into the fences so characteristic of the New England landscape to this day. It was not a soil likely to produce a surplus of crops. Farming in New England was more on a subsistence basis than it was in other sections. In fact, New England's chief cash "crops" came from the sea rather than from the land. Yet from nearly the beginning there were some agricultural exports from New England. From about 1640 to about 1675, wheat and flour were important exports, but then the wheat blast, a disease, stopped much of the wheat cultivation in that region. Other exports were peas, beef, pork, and butter. Nearly all of these went to the West Indies. New England horses were also in demand there.

The Middle Colonies. New York, New Jersey, and Pennsylvania were the "melting pot" in colonial times, for many Dutch and Swedes lived there when the English took over, and many Germans and Scotch-Irish came later. There was also some migration southward from New England, for the Middle Colonies were settled a generation later than New England. All these peoples, with their differing backgrounds, influenced the manner of disposing of land. The overriding fact, however, was that all three colonies, under the English, were proprietary colonies at first, and the proprietors were first of all interested in turning some of their land into cash. Compact settlements were thus the exception rather than the rule. People lived some distance apart with their land holdings spread about them, much as most farmers do today. Although some effort at first was made in East New Jersey to limit the sale of lands to those who were actually settlers, this good intention could not last long, and soon large sales of land were being made. But the intention of large landholders, too, was to find customers and sell them enough land for a farm, and so in time the large holdings were broken up. On the whole, the farmsteads were larger in the Middle Colonies than in New England, ranging between 100 and 200 acres and not infrequently reaching 500 acres.

The land in the Middle Colonies was better than in New England, except of course on the pine barrens of southern New Jersey or in some of the mountain regions. The other name for these three colonies, the "Bread Colonies," told rather well what the chief surplus farm product was. An early chronicler spoke of New York and East New Jersey as "the Granary or Storehouse of the West Indies, without which Barbadoes and the Leeward Islands could not subsist." Pennsylvania, the last but biggest of the three, also exported much grain, flour, and biscuit. Other exports were peas, pork, beef, and horses, the same sort of products that came from New England, except that the Middle Colonies were larger producers of them.

The Southern Colonies. Most of the people in these six colonies lived in Virginia and Maryland, with South Carolina in third place, North Carolina fourth, and Delaware and Georgia unimportant. There was more land in the South, too, since the mountains lay farther inland, and the soil was better than in the North. Also the climate was more favorable for the rough life which first settlers always had to endure.

Three methods of granting lands existed in the South. Efforts were made to introduce the medieval manorial system, involving a nobility, large land grants, and serfdom, into Maryland and Carolina, but these soon broke down, especially in Carolina. Town settlements later appeared in South Carolina and Georgia and enjoyed partial success. Both colonies were in their early days buffer colonies against further encroachments from the south by the Spanish. The land system most prevalent in the South resembled the individual holding found in the Middle Colonies except that these holdings may have been slightly larger. Any man might acquire a share in the London branch of the Virginia Company simply by coming to Virginia. He would shortly receive 50 acres of land as his "headright." For each other person, either of his family or a servant whom he brought over, he also received 50 acres. Supposedly these people were to be "seated" in compact areas, but this rule was poorly observed. After a few years a pioneer would locate his claim in any place he thought still open, so that settlement took place in a quite haphazard fashion. Such a pioneer might soon acquire more land by purchase, by importing more servants, or simply by fraud. Examples of fraud were two men buying a servant jointly and each claiming 50 acres, or alleging that an occupant of a grave was a servant. The secretary of Virginia eventually sold headrights for a few shillings. In this fashion, some individuals built up rather large land holdings. Nevertheless, the picture of Virginia as a land primarily of large planters has been a false one; most farmers had relatively small holdings of about 100 acres.

Virginia, Maryland, and northern North Carolina were the tobacco colonies. From a very early date in their history, tobacco was the chief surplus crop and chief export. The Indian princess, Pocahontas, is famous for saving the life of John Smith, which she probably never did. She ought to be famous for helping her husband, John Rolfe, find a way to cure tobacco so that its taste would be as acceptable to European pipe smokers as the taste of West Indian tobacco. As soon as this problem was solved, about 1616, Virginia could sell as much tobacco as she could produce. The profit was considerable, and as exports grew into millions of pounds, the price dropped from two shillings a pound to half a penny a pound in the 1660s. In Virginia, especially, this gave rise to a depression, to a revolution, to experiments in crop restriction, and to increased substitution of Negro slaves for white indentured servants to cut labor costs. Actually, tobacco is most successfully grown on relatively small farms, for its cultivation requires much careful labor, which must be closely supervised.

Farther to the south, other staple crops appeared during the colonial period. Rice began to be cultivated in the moist lowlands of South Carolina about 1695. Rice culture could be carried on only where there was an ample water supply to flood and drain the fields. Indigo was later associated with rice, because it thrived in the same kind of climate and its planting and cultivation schedule dovetailed very neatly with that of rice. A young girl, Eliza Lucas, left in charge of her father's plantation when she was only sixteen, is usually given credit for introducing indigo culture in South Carolina about 1741. Indigo, like tobacco, requires much careful attention. From it came the most popular vegetable dye for clothing of the period. Other staples were wheat in Virginia and North Carolina and cattle in North and South Carolina, which boasted a number of cowpens (ranches) in the eighteenth century. Cattle raising even then was a frontier industry.

Two staples normally associated with the South were conspicuous for their absence in the colonial period. These were cotton, which was known and home-grown but could not be cleaned fast enough to be sold commercially, and sugar cane, which cannot easily be grown north of Louisiana.

On the whole, farming was on a more commercial basis in the South than it was in the Middle and New England Colonies, because England wanted most of the southern staples. Yet at the same time, farming was much more on a subsistence basis in all regions than was to be the case in later centuries, when improved transportation made specialization more practical.

NEW ENGLAND'S FISHERIES

Because the New England soil was not particularly productive and the region had few agricultural staples to trade for the products of the outside world, the people of that region soon took to harvesting the sea instead of the land. In no sense did they plant and cultivate sea life; they simply took what was there. Off New England there was a great deal. In general, as one moved from north to south, the sea had fewer commercial products to offer and the land had more. It is understandable then that the staple of New England was codfish. Other fish such as haddock, flounder, hake, pollack, and perch existed in abundance, but the people of that era would not think of eating them.[1] Bartholomew Gosnold discovered and named the Cape Cod fishing grounds in 1602, and John Smith predicted a great future for the New England fisheries as early as 1616. New England fishermen of course ranged north to the fishing banks

[1] Samuel E. Morison, *The Story of the "Old Colony" of New Plymouth* (New York: Alfred A. Knopf, Inc., 1956), p. 122.

off Nova Scotia and Newfoundland. By 1700, Massachusetts was exporting a $400,000 crop of fish annually, mostly to the West Indies and southern Europe.

Hunting whales developed somewhat later than fishing. The first whales were drift whales, washed ashore dead and cut up for their oil, fat, and whalebone. During the later seventeenth century, whales were hunted in boats offshore. Indians appear to have been particularly skilled harpooners. After about 1700, whaling ships began to put out from places like Nantucket to make more distant voyages. Whale oil was used in lamps, the spermaceti made fine candles, and whalebone had many uses. Fish and whaling products were the leading staples of New England, exceeding, in terms of exports, anything produced on the land.

THE SCARCITY OF LABOR

Labor was scarce in colonial times. For example, in the 1690s New England wage earners got six times what those in Sweden earned, and wage earners in Pennsylvania did three times as well as those in Old England. That was because there was so much cheap land and so many natural resources available to be worked. The anonymous author of *American Husbandry* wrote in the 1760s, "I have more than once mentioned the high price of labor; this article depends on the circumstances I have now named; where families are so far from being burdensome, men marry very young, and where land is in such plenty, men very soon become farmers, however low they set out in life. Where this is the case, it must at once be evident that the price of labor must be very dear; nothing but a high price will induce men to labour at all, and at the same time it presently puts a conclusion to it by soon enabling them to take a piece of waste land. By [With] day laborers, which are not common in the colonies, one shilling will do as much in England as half a crown [2½ shillings] in New England. This makes it necessary to depend on [indentured] servants . . . ."[2]

The colonists sought to overcome this scarcity of labor in various ways. They had large families; they worked long hours; they made play out of their work by devising all kinds of cooperative undertakings; they let an apprentice climb the ladder to journeyman and master more rapidly than was the custom in Europe; they imported indentured servants, accepting even convicts in this capacity; and they encouraged Negro slavery, especially in the South.

Large Families. There was no economic incentive to keep families small, rather the contrary, and so families of ten or twelve children were

[2] Harry J. Carman (ed.), *American Husbandry* (New York: Columbia University Press, 1939), pp. 53–54.

frequent. From the age of about seven onward, a child could be assigned enough work to do on the farm to more than pay for his keep. For boys, there was weeding in the fields, shelling corn, combing wool, chopping wood, feeding the farm animals, gathering berries, and running errands, and for girls, helping mother in all kinds of household chores. Speaking of the Germans in 1789, one writer commented, "Upon the birth of a son, they exult in the gift of a plowman or waggoner; and upon the birth of a daughter they rejoice in the addition of another spinster or milkmaid to the family."[3] Since by the time the child was twenty he had probably married and set up housekeeping for himself, it was well to have younger ones growing up to assume the responsibilities that the older ones would shortly be leaving. Since all but wealthy families usually divided the property evenly on the death of the parents, there was incentive for each member to build up the family fortune.

Long Hours of Work. There were no clocks to watch in colonial times, there was no talk of an eight-hour day or of a forty-hour week. Instead there were tasks to be done and it was clear that if they were not, the worker, or a member of his family, would not be as well fed, clothed, shod or kept as warm as he should be. Much of the time the producer was working directly for the consumer—either for himself or for a member of his own family. The hours were from sunup to sundown, and usually a couple of good hours of work were put in before breakfast. Breakfast, accordingly, was a hearty meal, with meat, vegetables, and pie on the table. Thus ten to fourteen hours a day, depending on the season, was a fairly normal day's work for all the family and any servants or slaves. The compulsory quiet of church attendance and no work on Sunday actually supplied much-needed physical rest.

Cooperative Undertakings. It would be a mistake to assume that our forefathers drove themselves for all these ten to fourteen hours and never took time off for recreation. They made play out of part of their work, or, looked at in reverse, much of their play had a productive end in view. Games and sport for the pure sake of exercise were less common than in modern times. When our forefathers hunted deer, small game or even bear, or went fishing, it was to fill the family larder or to supply other family needs. The fact that hunting and fishing were fun as well made it easier to do this work. The men also made gay occasions out of putting up the framework of a house or barn, or putting on the roof. These were jobs in which "many hands made light work," they offered a chance to visit with the neighbors, and the womenfolk customarily provided sizable picnics for the ravenous workers. Husking bees in the autumn were fun because anyone who uncovered a red ear of corn was entitled to kiss

[3] Quoted in Curtis P. Nettels, *The Roots of American Civilization* (New York: Appleton-Century-Crofts, Inc., 1938), p. 448.

the partner of his choice. The husks flew as the search for the prized reds went on. Quilting bees were also gossip sessions, but far more productive than afternoon teas. There were joint undertakings, too, of community projects such as laying out roads, erecting bridges, or building schools or churches. Although cooperative activities were easier and more frequent in New England where people lived closer together, they were found everywhere to some extent. Anyone who lived too much alone, in fact, was suspect, as witness Poor Richard's saying, "He that drinks his cider alone, let him catch his horse alone."

Apprenticeship. The custom of apprenticing a lad to a master workman for training prevailed in America much as it did in England. The boy became an apprentice at from twelve to fifteen and usually remained until he was twenty-one, giving his labor and receiving in return schooling and training in a craft. Because labor was so scarce in the colonies, the term was often set below the seven years customary in England, and the quality of the training and workmanship of the journeyman was inferior.

Indentured Servitude. The bulk of servant labor was performed by persons who contracted to work a certain number of years, usually four, in exchange for being transported to America and for receiving certain "freedom dues" at the end of the term of service. These dues were food, clothing, a gun, some land, and farm equipment; they varied from colony to colony, and with the contract. From Pennsylvania southward they usually included 50 acres of land. The contract itself was the indenture. It was written in duplicate on a piece of paper, with a white strip between the two parts, and then was torn or cut in a saw-tooth fashion, with the servant keeping one half and the buyer of his services the other half. Since no two parts would fit unless they were originally together, the teeth or indenture guaranteed the genuineness of the document. Unfortunately, not all indentured servants obtained indentures or even written contracts, or, if they did, managed to keep them.

There were three types of indentured servants. Although the name was frequently used in a general sense to apply to all three types, it was also used in the narrow sense to apply to the earliest form of contract labor. This was the kind most generally used during the seventeenth century. An indentured servant in this narrow sense made a contract with someone in England to sell his services for four or five years, under specified conditions of servitude, in America. The servant either knew for whom he was going to work or at least had a say as to the conditions of work.

Occasionally a good bargainer or a desirable servant such as a skilled craftsman or schoolmaster might get written into the contract that he was not to be required to work in the fields. A servant was usually worth £10 to £20, of which about £5 represented his costs of transportation.

The difference was profit, or went to pay past debts of the servant. There were merchants who made a specialty of dealing in indentured servants. The people who placed themselves in servitude in this way might have friends or relatives in America, or be in debt, or simply want to start life anew in a world they hoped was better, or be persuaded by the glib talk of the merchant. Once over the ocean, the merchant, or his representative, would advertise and sell these servants, supposedly according to the terms of their contracts.

Toward the end of the seventeenth and in the eighteenth century a looser and less desirable type of contract servitude appeared. These people were called "free willers" or "redemptioners." Most of them came from the Continent, especially from Germany, and they often came in families. They were people who had sold their land and chattels and were on their way to America but found at the point of embarkation that they were short of funds. This happened so often that it indicates there were ways of causing it to happen. The family then paid the ship captain what they could toward the passage and agreed to supply the balance within, say, ten days or two weeks of their arrival in America, with the understanding that if they did not do so, they could be sold as indentured servants. Some of these emigrants hoped that friends or relatives would help them out, some hoped to strike a better bargain in America than the ship captain was likely to, and some expected to sell the services of their children as apprentices. Whatever the plan, they were all too often disappointed. They could not go far from the ship, communication was slow, anyone to whom they talked knew they were in a poor bargaining position, the ten days were soon gone, and the captain sold them for what he could get. The individuals largely responsible for encouraging so many naïve persons to decide to go to America when they lacked adequate funds were known as "newlanders" or "soul sellers." These were a class of people operating in Germany at this time who purported to be wealthy ex-Germans from America. They dressed well, sported gold watches as evidence of their success, and of course talked glibly about the fabulous opportunities and easy life in America. For every person whom a "newlander" directed to a ship, he received a commission from the captain.

Contract servants of a third type were not voluntary, but they were still better off than the Negro slaves. These were convicts, felons, and vagrants, or sometimes kidnapped persons. Jernegan reports that 10,000 were taken from Old Bailey prison in London and shipped to America between 1717 and 1775, and estimates that altogether 50,000 such persons were shipped over. Maryland is assumed to have received the largest share. As early as 1670 Virginia forbade the importation of convicts. For a time the English government desisted, but by the early eighteenth century the banishment to America of jailbirds had begun again. The situation was not good when a shipload of convicts was unloaded for sale in a colonial port, but even so its seriousness was probably exaggerated. In seventeenth and eighteenth century England there were literally hundreds of crimes punishable by death. Horse stealing was one, for example. Many a humanitarian judge ordered a prisoner sold into servitude in America to avoid having him executed. And if the guilty one were not a hardened criminal, he often mended his ways and did well in America. These people were familiarly known as "His Majesty's seven-year passengers," although the term of service was sometimes as much as fourteen years.[4]

Indentured servants were the most important form of labor, outside of the family, in colonial times, and also the most important type of emigrant. How important they were may be sensed from the fact that they were 40 per cent of the population in Virginia in 1625, that between 1635 and 1705 the tobacco colonies imported well over 100,000, and that two-thirds of the emigrants to Pennsylvania in the eighteenth century were white indentured servants. Moreover the system, taken as a whole, was advantageous to those who made use of this way to come to America. No matter how thrifty they had been with their Old World wages, many of them never could have saved enough to transport their families to America, and perhaps not even themselves. This method enabled them to pay for their passage by working it out while simultaneously gaining knowledge of the New World. True, for many individuals it was not a satisfactory arrangement. On the ships coming over, the servants were packed in almost like sardines for several weeks on end, and many died. Families were sometimes separated at the time of sale in America. Some servants were bought by cruel and thoughtless masters, although these were the exceptions. On the other hand, some masters got servants who shirked work and were not worth their keep. Many servants went on to become respected and even prosperous members of the community. In general, the system provided America with labor that was greatly needed at this period of development. At a later period when the standard of living was higher and labor was more plentiful, the government outlawed contract labor (1885). The institution of indentured servitude, however, must be judged against the background and needs of the seventeenth and eighteenth centuries.

Negro Slavery. In 1619 a Dutch privateer put in at Jamestown, Virginia, and disposed of several Negro slaves. This was the start of Negro slavery in the English mainland colonies. But Negro slavery was not adopted on any appreciable scale until later in the century. The activities of an

[4] Marcus W. Jernegan, *Laboring and Dependent Classes in Colonial America, 1607–1783* (Chicago: University of Chicago Press, 1931), p. 45.

English slave-trading company, founded about 1662 and later known as the Royal African Company, broke the Dutch slave-trading monopoly and brought increasing shipments of Negro slaves to the British colonies in America. Slaves were customarily acclimatized three years in the West Indies before being resold on the mainland. From the British point of view it was better that the colonists have slaves, for the British were beginning to be concerned over the depopulation of England. From the colonists' viewpoint, slaves were preferable to convicts and had advantages over other indentured servants. They lasted for life instead of for four or five years, they did not receive freedom dues, and they reproduced themselves. Slaves in Virginia in 1672 sold at £18 per head, about as much as indentured servants. Negro slaves became increasingly popular in the Southern Colonies. The Quakers of Pennsylvania opposed Negro slavery on religious grounds. The colonists of New England had no religious scruples but found the slave not versatile enough for their type of farming, and besides the Negroes were not accustomed to the Northern climate. Thus relatively few were found in the North, and then chiefly as house servants. In the tobacco fields of Virginia, Maryland, and northern North Carolina, however, and on the rice and indigo plantations of South Carolina and Georgia, they were used in ever-increasing numbers. An early prohibition of slavery in Georgia lasted only sixteen years. Virginia's slave population increased from 2,000 in 1671 to 4,000 in 1690; by 1700 there were over 20,000 in all the colonies. From then on, the slave population and the traffic in slaves grew more rapidly, the imports averaging 2,500 a year from 1715 to 1750, and 7,500 a year in the 1760s. At all time of the Revolution there were some 450,000 Negro slaves.

It may well be asked why a barbaric institution like slavery, closely akin to serfdom, should appear and be so readily accepted in America in a period when serfdom was dying out in the more enlightened areas of western Europe. The colonizer-statesman of the nineteenth century, E. G. Wakefield, gave this logical explanation of the institution in America. Although slave labor is more costly than free labor, it is adopted "because at the time and under the circumstances there is no other way of getting laborers to work with constancy and in combination. It happens whenever population is scanty in proportion to land." He cited as proof the presence of slavery in ancient Greece and Rome, the serfdom of the Middle Ages in Europe, and in Russia in the nineteenth century.[5]

The outstanding characteristic of colonial labor is that it was scarce and there was little of it for hire. Most of it was family labor or some kind of slave labor.

[5] Guy S. Callender, *Economic History of the United States* (Boston: Ginn & Company, 1909), pp. 743–744.

CHAPTER 3

Transportation, Manufacturing, and Capital

Most colonists were busy farming and remained fairly close to home. In the North where the mercantile activity was greater people traveled more than in the South. Traveling was confined mostly to businessmen and occurred chiefly by water. Some manufacturing was also found in the North, but the bulk of it was in the handicraft stage, to provide goods for local needs and to trade to the West Indies.

COLONIAL TRANSPORTATION

Ocean Shipping. In the seventeenth and eighteenth centuries a normal-sized ship was between 100 and 200 tons. The *Mayflower* weighed 180 tons, was about 100 feet long and 25 feet wide, was three-masted and square-rigged, had two decks, and traveled at 2½ miles an hour. It was characteristic of the *Mayflower* and other ships of this period to have high towering upper works at the bow and stern of the vessel. These had to be constructed of rather lightweight materials to keep the ships from capsizing, and consequently they often leaked in foul weather. But they did enable a ship to carry many people. The *Mayflower* carried 102 passengers and a crew of about 30 on the trip to New Plymouth. The outward voyage took place in October and November, with the weather so stormy that the trip took sixty-six days. Returning in the spring with "brave west winds" back of the ship, the passage took only thirty-one days. This was fast.

In the eighteenth century ships became larger and more streamlined—the high construction at bow and stern was removed—and the ships were heavier, better built, and faster. Greater use was made of the fore-and-aft sail and many combinations of square sails and fore-and-aft sails were devised. One of these, a distinctly American invention, was designed by Andrew Robinson of Gloucester, Massachusetts, in 1713; it was a sleek, low-lying vessel of two masts, with fore-and-aft sails set from gaff and boom and with a jib forward. Because she glided so gracefully over the water when launched, a spectator cried out, "See how she scoons," and Captain Robinson promptly named her a "schooner." Any vessel with less than three masts was not considered a ship but rather a schooner, bark, snow, or brig, depending on her design.

During most of the colonial period it was well to count on not less than six weeks to cross the Atlantic to America, although the time could easily exceed that. The eastward passage was usually faster, for it was more direct and the ship had the advantage of westerly winds and the Gulf Stream. Coming west from Europe, ships frequently sailed south to the latitudes of the trade winds, which blow from the east, and then came up the coast again. With crossings taking six or more weeks each way, few vessels made more than two round trips a year, for not many sailed at all during the winter. It can easily be seen how difficult it was for England to govern her colonies or for her merchants to take very quick advantage of business opportunities. Battles were even fought after wars were over. The whole tempo of that age was much slower than it is today. There is no place in the world today that is as far off, timewise, as the colonies then were from England or, in the case of most of them, from one another. Most people were discouraged from traveling by the dangers of ocean storms and pirates and the rigors of weeks aboard a small ship, often in cramped quarters with none too tasty food and water. These conditions were particularly bad for passengers, like indentured servants, who were often crowded below decks for days at a time, like so much baggage. When in 1710 some 3,000 Germans from the Palatinate came to New York, 500 died en route. This was not considered an abnormally heavy loss of life for the voyage at the time.

In general, ships followed no set schedule of departure. When enough freight and passengers were on board or available to ensure a profitable voyage, the ship departed. There was also no certainty that the ship would turn about shortly and make the return voyage, or that it would follow the same route. Captains and shipowners were opportunists and their ships went where there was profit to be made.

Intercolonial Transportation. Water transportation was also the chief form of transportation within the colonies. The ocean lay at the front door, so to speak, of every colony, and in most of them the settlements were near the coast. Thus the simplest way to travel from one colony to another was by sailing vessel. The fishing folk of New England turned early to commerce and provided most of the coastwise shipping. Ships drew such a shallow draft that many of them could sail up small rivers, such as the Schuylkill, Merrimac, Kennebec, or Raritan, tie up to a tree trunk, and unload on the river bank. Until the outset of the eighteenth century, most settlements lay east of the fall line.

Within the colonies, especially after settlements appeared west of the fall line in the eighteenth century, water was still the chief means of transportation. Nature had provided these highways and it required little or no effort on man's part to maintain them. The colonist was happy indeed to be spared that chore, for he had plenty of work to do making a living, opening up a new continent, and fighting Indians. Labor was always scarce. To transport heavier loads, there appeared at an early date the two basic types of boat later associated with western rivers, namely, the flatboat and the keelboat. The flatboat, often called an ark, was crudely built of heavy timbers, had a flat bottom and a square bow, and usually a cabin on deck. It was guided downstream and broken up for its timbers on reaching its destination. Only rarely did boatmen try to bring these cumbersome craft upstream again. The keelboat, barge, or poleboat, as its various forms were called, might be 30 feet long, 5 feet wide, and 3 feet deep; it had a flat bottom and a pointed prow. It could carry a sizable cargo of goods. Shallow of draft, even when fully loaded, it could navigate far upstream. It was propelled by poles: the crew stood near the bow of the boat, set their poles in the river bottom, and pushed against them as they walked toward the stern. They then carried the poles back to the bow and repeated the process. The work was extremely hard. A Durham boat was a larger version of the keelboat, wider and equipped with sails. Found chiefly on the Delaware, it was 60 feet long and 8 feet wide; it could carry 150 barrels of flour, and yet had only a 28-inch draft.

The Indian canoe was a favorite from early times on the smaller streams. In the North this was a light wooden frame covered with birch bark or sometimes elm bark and sealed with pitch. The means for repairing it were always at hand in the forest. The canoe was extremely light and had almost no draft at all—it was said to be able to float on damp ground. The colonists soon acquired the necessary skill to paddle it and keep it from capsizing. Trappers and pioneers could paddle a canoe almost to the source of a stream, if they wished, then portage their canoe and gear overland to the next nearest suitable stream, and thus travel long distances by water. A good pioneer knew the waterways in his region just as we know our numbered highways today. In the South the somewhat heavier wooden dugout—a carefully hollowed-out log fashioned in the shape of a canoe—took the place of the birchbark canoe. Long canoes of bark could carry quite sizable loads. George Washington and fourteen men and their supplies moved about in one for a week in the Ohio region in the 1750s.

In the North there was still another method of using the rivers—when they froze over in the winter. On such occasions they made excellent highways for sleighs, carioles, pungs, pods, or whatever the local citizenry called them. Since little farm work could be done in such weather, it was a good season for visiting.

On the whole, however, our colonial forefathers traveled rather little and this explains why their outlook was so provincial. It also caused the people of each colony to be suspicious of their neighbors and to find it difficult to cooperate with them. The greatest opportunities for mass traveling were the various colonial wars, most of which involved expeditions against the French in Canada. The route to Canada, whether with goods for trade in peacetime or with armies bent on destruction in wartime, was due north up the Hudson, then by small streams to Lake George, over to Lake Champlain, and down the Richelieu River to the St. Lawrence and Quebec. Forts lay all along this route, at every portage point or narrow strait on a lake. Crown Point, Fort Ticonderoga, Fort William Henry, and others are all famous in eighteenth century colonial military annals, for each changed hands several times in the frequent fighting.

Overland Travel. For a long time overland travel was the least frequent form of travel. When a boy named Lewis Morris, who later became governor of New Jersey, ran away from home in the 1680s and got as far as Virginia, people looked upon the escapade as remarkable because he went by land instead of by water. The earliest roads were Indian trails, which to some extent were based on game trails. Lumber roads also were forerunners of early highways. Explorers too laid out trails which by frequent use gradually became crude roads. Examples were the Old Mine Road along the upper Delaware, set out in the 1660s, and the Wilderness Road to Kentucky—attributed to Daniel Boone—just before the Revolution. During most of the colonial period there were few good roads. Those far from towns were nearly always crude and poorly kept, if indeed they deserved to be called roads at all. The colonial legislatures passed laws for the laying out of roads, but the system looked better on paper than it was in fact. There were few people to build and maintain them, and not a strong demand to keep them up. After all, as late as 1740 only a million people lived along a thousand-mile coast line; few traveled, and even when they did they preferred to go by water. On the outbreak of the Revolution there were but 2,400 miles of post roads, of which the best known were the Albany Post Road and the Boston Post Road, each starting from New York.

Bridges were rare and a stone bridge was rarest of all because it was so expensive to build. Travelers crossed rivers by ferries and expected to ford the smaller streams. Overnight accommodations were generally poor to mediocre. The blazing fire, tasty food, and genial hospitality of a good tavern were especially welcome to a weary traveler when he found them.

Within towns, travel was also limited. For a long time there were no private carriages on the cobbled streets of Boston. The simple Puritans frowned upon such ostentation, and the Quakers of Philadelphia were similarly minded. In 1685, carriages at last appeared in Boston, and by 1700 there were perhaps a dozen. About this same time, Philadelphia boasted thirty carts and wheeled carriages of all kinds. New Yorkers, although less opposed to riding, were about as well off.

Out-of-town travelers went chiefly by horseback. Fifty miles was a good day's ride, and it took a week to go from New York to Boston in relative comfort. As late as 1716 the tolls at the New Brunswick ferry, on the route between New York and Philadelphia, provided only for a "horse and man" and a "single person." New Jersey, which "enjoyed a greater amount of intercolonial travel than any other part of America," did not have stage coaches until just before the Revolution.[1]

Farther from the coast, the chief means of transportation along primitive roads was the pack horse. Pack trains of a score or more of loaded horses might be encountered on these trails. As the trails or roads improved, wagons replaced the pack horses. In the Conestoga Valley on the lower Susquehanna River, near Lancaster, Pennsylvania, the Conestoga wagon developed in the 1750s. It was later known as the covered wagon. Customarily hauled by six horses, the body was somewhat bowed like a boat. It was in effect a boat on wheels, constructed that way to make it easier to ford streams. This region was likewise famed for its sturdy Conestoga horses. There was considerable traffic between the rich farm country around Lancaster and the port city of Philadelphia. As the colonial period ended, overland transportation was starting to develop in the colonies, but it did not make rapid progress until the 1790s. Partly for this reason, manufacturing developed slowly in colonial times.

MANUFACTURING

The outstanding characteristics of manufacturing establishments in colonial times were that they were on a small scale and largely extractive in nature. They were small scale because the markets were limited. They were extractive because ample supplies of raw materials in the forests, fields, mines, and sea made simple processing of these the most obvious and easy thing to do. Also the shortage of capital and labor made more complex operations very expensive. Finally, the British government discouraged colonial manufacturing, for Britain wanted to reserve this more lucrative business for herself.

Forest Products. The tree was much less prized in the colonial period than it is today. Forests were everywhere and had to be cleared before

[1] Wheaton J. Lane, *Indian Trail to Iron Horse* (Princeton: Princeton University Press, 1939), pp. 47, 48, 55.

much farming could be done. One way of turning this clearing operation to some account was to burn the hardwood trees, then leach the ashes with water and boil the resulting lye with more water in large open kettles. The thick brownish residue was potash. Potash was sold in England for making soap, bleaching, and making glass, and it also served as a fertilizer. Pearlash, a more valuable refinement of potash, was made by baking potash in a hot oven until the carbon was removed. It was used chiefly as baking powder and for making soap. The proceeds from the sale of potash and pearlash would about meet the expenses of clearing a piece of land.

Naval stores, masts, and ship timbers were among the very earliest products to interest the English. In that day of wooden vessels they were as important to a major sea power such as England as steel and oil are to modern nations. White pines made magnificent masts, spars, and deck planking. Oaks were also in great demand for ship timbers of all kinds. Only one oak tree in many hundreds would yield the properly curved compass pieces needed to construct certain portions of a ship, and it took a century or more for such oaks to grow to maturity. Naval stores were pitch, tar, turpentine, and resin. Unless coated with resin and pitch, the planks of a vessel could not resist dry borers or marine rot, and the spaces between planks likewise had to be calked with oakum and pitch. The ship's rigging would also decay unless treated with tar. Britain's forests were becoming exhausted in the seventeenth century. Either Britain had to obtain her naval stores from the Scandinavian nations, especially Sweden, which would make her dependent on them in case of war or the threat of war, or else she had to develop a source of supplies of her own. The colonies seemed the obvious answer. A shipload of masts and naval stores was among the first commodities shipped home from the first Virginia settlement. Just before the Revolution, the colonies sent fifty shiploads of white pine timbers to England annually. A mast, 3 feet at the base, was worth $750 delivered in England. King's officers marked straight trees with the "broad arrow" to save them for the navy. First New England and later North Carolina became the leading suppliers of naval stores and masts.

The colonists soon became competent and industrious builders of ships themselves. The industry began with the launching of the *Blessing of the Bay*, a 30-ton sloop, at Medford, Massachusetts, in 1631. With fine timbers virtually at the water's edge, the American shipbuilders had a competitive advantage over the British. Governor Bellomont of New York said in 1700 that it cost only 60 per cent as much to build a ship here as in Britain. Although New England built three-quarters of all colonial-built ships, every colony turned out a few. Most of the ships were small, being under 75 tons in the West Indian trade and about 175 in the

European. Just before the Revolution the colonies were producing 20,000 to 25,000 tons of shipping a year. There were some 2,000 American-built ships afloat, comprising an estimated one-third of all ships flying the British flag.

This was an age of wood rather than of metals, and wood was the basic material for a wide variety of other industries. Nearly all houses were of wood, with stone or brick almost a rarity as a building material. Within the house the furniture was of wood; within the barn the equipment was chiefly of wood. People heated their homes with wood-burning fires and the annual demands of northern towns like Boston, New York, and Philadelphia caused the forests in their vicinity to recede rapidly. Ironmaking furnaces were likewise heavy consumers of firewood. The tanning industry made use of the bark of oak and hemlock trees. Maple-sugar making in the North was another forest industry, although less demanding on the trees. Even the bowls and dishes from which people ate were often made of wood.

Agricultural Industries. Historically the transition from farming to manufacturing is not as clear-cut as might be supposed. At first the raw materials for manufacturing came from the farm. Early manufacturing was but the further processing of grain, fibers, hides, or meat. At what point did simple processing of farm products cease and manufacturing begin? Probably, paradoxically enough, at about the point at which manufactured goods ceased to be "made by hand," which is the original meaning of manufacture. Colonial manufacturing took place largely in the home, or in a mill or shop close by the home, and the producer generally dealt directly with the customer.

In the grinding of grain the farmer customarily brought his grain to the mill, waited while it was ground, and paid for the service by letting the miller keep a fraction of the flour. He might also ask the miller to dispose of any surplus. From an early date nearly every community had a gristmill, usually run by water power although there were a few windmills. Towns would often give the mill site to a person who would erect a mill and would exempt it from taxes for a number of years. The miller was generally an important person in the community. Furthermore, the mill, which was the community's chief power plant, was frequently so constructed that it would also saw wood and full cloth. In the eighteenth century some mills near the coast, especially in the Middle Colonies, began to engage in the business of exporting flour. Since the overseas customers demanded products even more finished than flour, millers sometimes erected bake ovens and produced biscuits for export. This was virtually manufacturing in the modern sense of the term.

Alcoholic beverages have always been another destination for grain. Beer was made from wheat, barley, corn, or rice but had to be consumed almost immediately, for it would not keep. The Scotch-Irish introduced whisky distilling into the western settlements of Pennsylvania in the early eighteenth century, but whisky did not gain general popularity until later. Rum and cider were the preferred tipples of the colonial period. Rum was manufactured from molasses, which in turn is a by-product of the refining of sugar cane into sugar. The New England traders who carried sugar from the West Indies to England obtained the molasses from the West Indies at the same time for their own rum distillers.

There were three basic fibers that were made into cloth, namely, flax, from which linen is made, wool, and cotton. During much of the colonial period they were important in about that order. There were of course all possible combinations of these fibers; for example, wool and linen was known as linsey-woolsey; wool and cotton as homespun jeans or druggets; and linen and cotton as fustians. At first the whole process of clothmaking was likely to be found in the farmhouse, from spinning the yarn through weaving the cloth to making the clothes. All this was a tedious operation, as may be seen simply by listing the various steps that had to be performed, say, in the preparing of wool. The sheep had to be raised, his fleece sheared, the wool cleaned of the dirt and grease and then combed and carded. Next it had to be spun into yarn and the yarn woven into cloth, and the hard, rough product softened and smoothed, a process called fulling. After that, the piece of clothing had to be made according to pattern, and the result dyed and fitted to the person who would wear it. There were even more steps in the making of linen out of flax. With clothmaking so time-consuming, it is small wonder that people prized their linen napkins, tablecloths, shirts, and handkerchiefs. They patched clothes endlessly rather than throw them away, and they put leather on places that got the most wear, like the elbows and the seat of the pants. Furthermore, people, at least the common folk, did not wear as much clothing as would be the case in the nineteenth century.

The heavier operations of making cloth, such as fulling and weaving, were among the first to be taken out of the home. At an early date weaving was performed by men in shops set up for the weaving of cloth. Fulling was done at the local fulling mill. Dyeing was again a household operation; the smelly dye tub, its lid on tight because it contained uric acid to make the colors hold, occupied a warm spot near the fireplace. The coloring matter was found in the woods and fields—red oak provided brown, sassafras yellow, and madder root red. Blue, which was such a favorite color in the eighteenth century, came chiefly from indigo, bought from a peddler.

Paper was made largely from old linen in this era, rather than from wood pulp as it is today. Such paper was of better quality and lasted longer. The chief center of papermaking was in Pennsylvania because more raw material was available there. The people of colder New England wore more wool garments whereas those of Pennsylvania, where the climate was less severe, preferred linen. Benjamin Franklin, printer and statesman, promoted eighteen mills in the Philadelphia region. It required considerable power to grind the rags into pulp; then they had to be molded into sheets, pressed, dried, and glazed. Thus papermaking was not a household industry. The best known papermaker of Philadelphia was William Rittenhouse, who established the first paper mill there in 1690. Most of his early output was taken by one of the colonies' first printers, Thomas Bradford.

Hides of all kinds provided leather, which was used for articles of clothing much more in colonial times than now. It was more plentiful than today, easier to convert into wearable form, and it wore a longer time than cloth. Pioneers quite early learned from Indians how to make jackets and trousers from deerskin. The deer's own brains provided a good material for tanning the deerskin, making it quickly usable. The hides of cattle required a longer processing. Tanning pits had to be dug, bark of oak or hemlock gathered, and the hides sandwiched between layers of bark; the pits were then covered and watched until just the right time for removal. Later the hide had to be softened, cut, sewed, and fitted. The demand for leather was great. It not only went into shoes and clothing for both men and women (leather aprons and petticoats) but it was also used for hinges and straps of all kinds, and even as springs for wagons. The actual tanning of leather was a cumbersome and delicate operation requiring considerable skill, and so, like fulling and weaving, it left the home for the shop at an early date in many communities. One of the earliest tanneries in New England was at Lynn, Massachusetts. Lynn soon attracted cobblers and became the birthplace of making shoes for export in the eighteenth century.

Processing of meat consisted chiefly of salting it. Both beef and pork were brine-packed in barrels and shipped out, especially to the West Indies. The fertility of the Connecticut River Valley made it a cattle-raising area as early as the mid-seventeenth century. William Pynchon of Springfield was the best-known cattle raiser and the first packer of note. He bought quantities of hogs from other farms for packing and export. Boston and Worcester were the chief markets for meat in New England, whereas New York, Philadelphia, Chester, and Newcastle were in the Middle Colonies. Faneuil Hall in Boston became a supervised market in 1742 with regulations enforced on the quality of the meats sold. The hogs were chiefly razorbacks produced near the frontier and driven to markets along the coast. No effort was made to fatten them before marketing. The majority, however, of all animals were slaughtered and consumed in the same locality, if not on the same farm, where they were raised.

The products of the sea likewise provided some raw materials that had to be processed. Boston, the "home of the bean and the cod," salted codfish for preservation and exported it and other fish products. Although most candles were made in the home from surplus animal fats, the best candles in the eighteenth century were produced from spermaceti, or head matter, which was "a white waxy substance found in the cranial cavities of the sperm whale." The Brown brothers of Providence, Rhode Island, manufactured what were generally recognized as the best spermaceti candles in America in the early 1760s. They went so far as to put their trademark on every box, at a date when product differentiation was unusual. The candle manufacturers were ahead of their day in other respects, too. Since this was a profitable business, more manufacturers entered it; then because the amount of spermaceti coming on to the market was fairly constant, the price for the raw material started rising. If the candle manufacturers had raised their prices, they would have priced themselves out of the market, for they were in competition with tallow candles and whale-oil lamps. Accordingly, they agreed among themselves to put a ceiling on the price they would pay for spermaceti and a ceiling on the price at which they would sell their candles. They also allocated the amount of spermaceti that each member of the group might buy. This has sometimes been called the "Spermaceti Trust." It was not a trust or monopoly in the more normal sense of the term, for it was organized to exploit the raw material producer rather than the buyer of the candles. In any event it succeeded rather poorly; the price of spermaceti rose anyway, and so did the price of candles. New manufacturers entered the field despite efforts to prevent their doing so.[2]

Mineral Products. Since the Indians represented a Stone Age civilization, they could tell the colonists little about the location of mines. A few Indians owned some implements made of native copper; that was all. At the time of the Revolution not one of the great mines of today had been discovered, and no mine then in existence is of any importance today. Only three metals of any significance were produced in British America in colonial times. They were iron, copper, and lead, and among these only iron was important. Tin, which when mixed with lead makes pewter, was not found. Neither was zinc, which when mixed with copper makes brass. The colonists imported both tin and brass. Despite the early hopes of Virginians and Puritans that they would find gold and silver, they found neither. A few outcroppings of coal were known about 1750, especially around Richmond, Virginia, and were used locally.

[2] James B. Hedges, *The Browns of Providence Plantations* (Cambridge: Harvard University Press, 1952), pp. 90–96, 122.

The early efforts of the Virginia colonists to work an iron mine at Falling Creek, up the James River, were ambitious. Some 173 persons skilled in the manufacture of iron were sent out from London around 1619, and the works were said to have cost $25,000. An Indian attack in 1622 wiped out the colony and work was never resumed. In New England John Winthrop, Jr., son of the Massachusetts governor, started the Saugus Ironworks at Lynn, Massachusetts, in 1643 (see Fig. 3-1) and another at New Haven in 1662. In the latter seventeenth century Connecticut and Rhode Island superseded Massachusetts in the manufacture

Fig. 3-1. The Saugus Ironworks at Lynn Massachusetts as it appeared around 1650. (*Courtesy of the American Iron and Steel Institute.*)

of iron, and in the eighteenth century the Middle Colonies took over the leadership, especially Pennsylvania. The chief source of iron in New England was bog iron; elsewhere it was iron ore. Bog iron was found at the bottom of the many small ponds located in eastern Massachusetts and apparently was deposited by the chemical action of tiny forms of water life. It was dragged from the mucky bottom of the ponds "by an instrument similar to an oyster dredge, at the rate of about two tons per diem for each man."[3] Utensils made of it were esteemed for their toughness and lightness.

[3] J. Leander Bishop, *A History of American Manufactures, 1608–1860* (Philadelphia: Edward Young and Co., 1868), vol. I, p. 490.

The stone furnaces for the smelting of iron ore were never large, partly because charcoal could not carry a heavy weight and draw, partly because the market for the product was limited. The capacity of the Lynn furnace was 8 tons a week. Most so-called furnaces were bloomeries: the line of demarcation between a small bloomery and a blacksmith forge is a fine one. From bloomeries came blooms or lumps of iron which when hammered yielded wrought iron. Joseph Mallinson of Dusboro, Massachusetts, produced the first castings made in sand. The colonists made a little "blister steel" also, the biggest plant being in Trenton, New Jersey; but the quality of steel was poor and the cost high. The age of cheap steel had not yet come; wrought iron performed most of its functions. There were also a few rolling and slitting mills, the former making sheet iron and the latter slitting the sheets into rods from which to make nails. All ironmaking operations were carried on in shops except manufacturing nails. These were frequently cut, headed, and pointed in the evening at home beside the hearth. In general, ironmaking required a moderate amount of capital, especially for blast furnaces. The leading iron-manufacturer was Peter Hasenclever of New Jersey, who controlled six blast furnaces, seven forges, a stamping mill, and other equipment, the whole being worth about $250,000. Among the many articles made of iron were pots and kettles, anchors, chains, guns and cannon, parts of agricultural implements such as hoes and scythe blades, equipment for the hearth, and millions of nails.

Lead, always in demand for making bullets, was found near Jamestown in 1621 and at various times in other colonies. A mine at Southampton, Massachusetts, was worked for awhile after 1765. John Winthrop organized the first copper mining company at Simsbury, Connecticut, in 1700, but it was not profitable for long. Arent Schuyler started another mine at Hanover, New Jersey, in 1719, and Elias Boudinot one near New Brunswick, New Jersey, in 1750. However, the colonists had to import the bulk of their lead and copper.

One other industry deserves mention because of the important lesson in manufacturing it illustrates. Baron Stiegel built an enormous glass house at Mannheim, Pennsylvania, in the 1760s. It was so huge that allegedly a coach and four could turn around inside the brick dome of the melting house. Stiegel produced some very fine glass and tableware and was reported to have earned $13,000 a year from the project. Yet within five years he headed into bankruptcy; the reason was, according to contemporary belief, that he had exhausted his local market, had not developed more distant ones, and could not sell all he was producing.[4] This goes far to explain why most industry had to be on a small scale to suc-

[4] Victor Clark, *History of Manufactures in the United States* (New York: McGraw-Hill Book Company, Inc., 1929), vol. I, pp. 105, 169.

ceed and why the vast majority of it was on a household or, at most, on a shop or mill basis.

Government Regulation of Industry. Local and provincial governments granted land, abated taxes for a time, or made awards to encourage such projects as gristmills, fulling mills, ironworks, and the like. The British government operated on colonial industry on a grander scale. It did so in two ways: it encouraged some industries by bounties, and it discouraged others. The English wanted to encourage the production of raw materials that England herself did not produce and had to import from foreign nations. They wanted to discourage the manufacture of more finished products which would compete with existing British industries. Thus the British granted bounties for the production of naval stores, masts, and hemp in 1705, of indigo in 1748, and of various other commodities on other occasions. Legislatures frequently joined the mother country by enacting bounty payments of their own. On the other hand, the British forbade export and sale of woolen goods in 1699; they prohibited the export of hats from one colony to another in 1732; and they forbade the manufacture of iron products beyond the pig-iron stage in 1750. On the whole, the prohibitions of colonial manufacturing were not successful, for enforcement at that distance was difficult. What helped the English most was that the colonies were not as interested in manufacturing then as they later were, because they lacked capital and large or ready markets. It was much more profitable to develop raw materials.

CAPITAL

Basic Principles. At this point a side journey into an important economic principle is essential. Land, labor, and capital are called the three basic economic factors of production. Every occupation or industry uses some of each, and in a general way the amount of any factor used will vary with its scarcity in the economy. In colonial times land was plentiful but labor and especially capital were scarce, and so people used these last two more sparingly. Land and labor have already been studied in the first two chapters. It is capital, the least understood of the three factors, which concerns us here. Capital is sometimes defined as "produced goods intended for further production." That means that capital is tools, equipment, improvements on land, processed resources, and inventory. Capital stands in contrast to consumer goods, which are things like furniture, food, and goods in the hands of the consumer which he is in the act of using up. Capital is made not to be consumed for itself but to help make more consumers' goods or more capital. A basket to gather apples is capital; the apples in the consumer's kitchen are consumers' goods. To gather

apples more efficiently, a farmer must take time off to weave a basket, or else he must trade some surplus apples to someone else who has woven the basket. In either case, the basketmaker has given up immediate harvesting of apples to do something that will bring him more apples in the long run. This "doing without" in the present in the hope of getting more in the long run is called "saving." Saving is essential for the accumulation of capital. Saving may take two forms: A farmer who weaves a basket or fences a field is simultaneously saving and creating capital. A farmer who puts aside some of his surplus apples for sale is saving and accumulating capital, too. The apples in the form of inventory destined for sale are the capital. When he converts them into money by sale and saves the money, he is said to have "liquid capital." The money is an especially flexible sort of "capital," for he can swap it for any kind of surplus which someone else has to sell, with a minimum of effort in the bargaining. This last use of the word capital is more familiar to most students, but it is less accurate. Money, or liquid capital, is capital only in an economy where trading goes on. Of itself it helps in the production of nothing, whereas a hoe or a basket does. Thus money that is added to a nation's money supply, say, by a printing press, adds nothing to its capital supply and only dilutes the value of the existing units of money. Gold or silver coins that have come in from abroad to pay for a shipment of tobacco do add to the country's liquid capital, for if sent abroad again in exchange for, say, equipment, they can add also to its actual capital. This simplified economic theory is needed to understand the history of capital growth in colonial times.

Early Forms of Capital. Several of the colonies were originally established by trading companies. These hoped to make a profit from sending settlers to the New World, helping them establish homes and develop the resources of the region, and trading with them, and through them with the Indians. These companies were known to be speculative ventures, but judged by the success of earlier trading ventures in the East Indies, they seemed to be worthwhile. Scarcely one of them, possibly only the Plymouth colony, was profitable, however, and most of them did not even pay a dividend (see Chap. 1). The English investors thus put up many hundreds of thousands of pounds to establish settlements and equip and supply them for a time. Some of the early settlers brought over supplies and equipment of their own, especially in Massachusetts Bay and Connecticut, which attracted a moderately well-to-do class of people. As the colonies sold their tobacco, naval stores, grain, and fish and received supplies and equipment in return, they accumulated their own capital. When plows finally appeared in Plymouth, twelve years after the founding of the colony, these were an important accretion of capital. When a group

of men built the *Blessing of the Bay* at Medford, they added this to the Massachusetts Bay Colony's capital. Each barn, mill, shop, or cleared field likewise increased the capital supply.

The value of capital equipment to the welfare of the community was more obvious then than it is today, for people could see how new equipment and mills eased their labors and raised their standard of living. Town aid to mills was common all through this period. In 1643 Boston granted 300 acres to the builders of a tide mill to grind corn, and in 1683 Woodbridge, New Jersey, granted land to a person to put up a sawmill. Such examples could be multiplied hundreds of times. Colonial legislatures also helped start industries because privately owned liquid capital to get them under way was so scarce. Rhode Island loaned William Borden £500 to set up a sailcloth plant, and in 1753 Massachusetts loaned £1,500 to a company to manufacture linen.

The vast majority of mills and small industries, however, got little or no local or provincial help. They just grew by reinvesting some of their profits in improvements. Because mills were scarce and much needed, their rate of profit was frequently handsome. In general, manufacturing was joined very closely with merchandising; the two had not yet become such separate operations as they were later to be. For example, the Brown brothers started manufacturing spermaceti candles because they needed a product to sell on their trading expeditions to the West Indies that would yield cash to pay for their imports. Early in the eighteenth century English woolens were selling at from 100 to 200 per cent higher in America than in London. Interest rates were also high; 8 per cent was the legal rate in New England until 1693 when it was lowered to 6 per cent, but in other colonies 8 per cent remained common for many more years. Thus there was room to make generous profits, and the man who plowed these profits back into his business often saw that business grow rapidly. About 1670 there were said to be thirty Boston merchants worth between $50,000 and $100,000, and in the 1750s a pioneer glass manufacturer in New Jersey had accumulated a fortune from a business that was said to amount to at least $90,000. Probably the biggest manufacturing ventures were those carried out with foreign capital, largely from Britain or Germany, such as the ironworks of Peter Hasenclever in New York and New Jersey or the glassworks of Baron Stiegel, but these were far from being the most successful.

Industries required a larger portion of their capital to be working capital (including "liquid capital") then than they do now. On the one hand, equipment was simpler; and on the other hand, the process of manufacture, from the beginning until the finished product reached the consumer's hands and was paid for, was much longer. Transportation was slow and payment was even slower. Whereas now we pay on delivery or in ten or thirty days, then the buyer might be a year or more in paying. This was quite normal. Most customers were farmers or those who dealt with farmers. Farmers in turn sold what cash crops they had only once a year and often had to wait for their pay, too. Thus a great deal of a merchant's or manufacturer's working capital was tied up in long credits. There were no commercial banks in the colonies to ease this situation. The greatest help to the colonial merchant or manufacturer was the English merchant with whom he dealt. Because the English had banks and also more capital than this country, they often paid promptly for what they bought from Americans and at the same time they allowed long credits for what they sold to American merchants and consumers. They took the place of commercial banks and were an important source of working capital in colonial times.

CHAPTER 4

Mercantilism, Commerce, and Finance

The period of mercantilism lasted from about the time of the discovery of America until its independence. Mercantilism's basic aim was to make the state economically self-sufficient. A number of new national states were appearing in Europe at about this time: Spain, Portugal, France, Holland, and England. All pursued mercantilistic policies. The actual name *mercantilism* was invented at a much later date. At this earlier time each nation had its own peculiar name for this policy, such as Colbertism in France, after the famous Prime Minister, or the Old Colonial System in Great Britain. The outstanding characteristic of mercantilism was government regulation of business activities, usually in the interest of the merchant classes. The regulations that made up mercantilism principally affected commerce and finance, but they bore also on manufacturing, transportation, and agriculture. To understand why Great Britain behaved as it did and treated the colonies as it did, or for that matter why it even had colonies, it is essential to understand mercantilism. It was the master plan that the leaders of government were following.

MERCANTILISM

The Six Basic Points. Taken together, the six fundamental aims of mercantilism, if successfully executed, would make England rich, powerful, and self-sufficient. The six were as follows: (1) Accumulate as large a store of precious metals within the country as possible, partly in the Treasury, but mostly in the hands of the people where they would still be within the reach of the tax collector. Wealth in a liquid form was looked upon as especially valuable in time of war, for the king who had treasure at his disposal could quickly hire armies and navies and supply them with the means to wage war. (2) Develop a strong merchant marine so that the nation would not be dependent on foreign shipping and so that a hardy race of sailors would be developed to man the navy in time of war. (3) Encourage and protect agriculture so that the nation would always be self-sufficient in the matter of food and clothing. (4)

Acquire colonies and foster the production of raw materials in them, especially raw materials that the mother country would otherwise be obliged to purchase from other nations. This had the additional advantage of holding down expenditures of gold and silver. (5) Encourage and protect manufacturing so that the nation would be self-sufficient in this respect. This would reap the handsome profits that manufacturing often yielded at the outset. Mercantilists did not hesitate to press manufacturing at the expense of agriculture. (6) Encourage the colonies to become customers of the mother country, especially for manufactured goods. These six tenets of mercantilism evolved chronologically in about the order in which they have been recited. England did not consider the last one, for example, of much importance until about twenty years before the American Revolution. By that time the emphasis on accumulating gold and silver had fallen into disrepute in some quarters. Mercantilism was a somewhat changing doctrine.

Of chief interest here is by what laws and regulations England applied mercantilism to the American colonies and with what degree of success.

Colonial Legislation. England aimed its mercantilist legislation in the seventeenth century primarily at Holland. During the first half of the English Revolution of 1642–1660 the English were so busy fighting one another that they had scant energy left to dispute the rising commercial power and merchant marine of Holland. That revolution pitted the mercantile and middle classes of England, led by Oliver Cromwell, against the Stuart king, Charles I, his nobility, and others loyal to him. As soon as the fighting ended and Charles I was executed (1649), Cromwell and his mercantile-minded advisers turned their attention to this urgent matter. The so-called Navigation Act of 1651 was one result. Navigation referred to the countries which ships might visit and to the goods which they might carry. The aim of the act was to cripple the Dutch merchant marine, which was carrying much of the world's trade, including trade to the new English colonies in America, and at the same time to revive the neglected English merchant marine. The 1651 act had three main provisions: (1) All exports from the colonies to England were to be carried in ships owned and manned by Englishmen. (Note that colonial ships were not forbidden to carry goods directly to Europe.) (2) All European products destined for England or the colonies must be carried either in English ships or in the ships of the country producing the products. Since Holland produced largely woolens, this was a severe blow to its carrying trade. (3) All foreign ships were excluded from England's coastwise trade. The word English, it should be clearly understood, included English colonists. Although the English did not enforce this act very well against Dutch ships trading to Virginia, they enforced it elsewhere, and it helped somewhat in reviving the British merchant marine.

After Cromwell died in 1658 his son was not equal to the task of governing England. The eldest son of the late Charles I was recalled and became Charles II. In 1660 his Parliament reenacted the 1651 Navigation Act, strengthening it somewhat in the process. The chief added feature was that England was to be the distributing point for an "enumerated" list of colonial staples. These goods could not be sent directly to, say, Holland, but must be landed in England, perhaps pay duties, and certainly be subject to some handling costs and middlemen's profits. English manufacturers would have the first opportunity to buy them. At first there were six enumerated goods, namely, sugar, raw cotton, indigo, ginger, speckle wood and other dyewoods, and tobacco. Only tobacco was a mainland product; all the rest came from the West Indies. Actually, since 1624 the colonies had been obliged to send their tobacco to England. Ships carrying enumerated products were expected to give bond that the goods would be taken to England. In the course of the eighteenth century, Parliament added more items to the enumerated list, for example, molasses and rice in 1704; masts, naval stores, and hemp in 1705; beaver skins, furs, and copper in 1721; iron and lumber, potash and pearlash, whale fins, raw silk, pimento, coffee, and cacao in 1764; and all colonial exports in 1766–1767. There were occasional changes and exceptions made to the enumerated list; for example, it was permissible to export some of the items, like rice and sugar, directly to southern Europe.

In 1662, 1663, 1673, and 1696 Parliament made further amendments to the Navigation Acts. English ships, with rare exceptions, had to be built by Englishmen as well as to be owned and manned by them. By the 1663 act all goods coming from Europe to the colonies had to pass through England except for certain items such as salt, wine from the Madeiras, or servants, horses, and food from Scotland and Ireland. In 1673 the British even required enumerated commodities sold from one colony to another to go through England and pay duties. The 1696 act gave jurisdiction to the faster moving and stricter admiralty courts over cases involving the shipment of enumerated goods.

The Molasses Act of 1733 and the Sugar Act of 1764 were somewhat akin to the Navigation Acts. The Molasses Act imposed a prohibitive duty on molasses imported from the foreign West Indies into the colonies. This act protected the sugar planters of the British West Indies, many of whom were absentee landowners living in England where it was easy for them to bring considerable pressure upon Parliament. The trouble lay in the fact that these British planters demanded a higher price for their molasses (the raw material from which rum is distilled) than the French West Indian planters did. France, being a wine-drinking nation, at first had little use for molasses (a by-product of sugar) and threw it away. When the Yankee traders offered to pay a small price for it, the

French were glad to sell it and some of their sugar as well. Since such a trade of English colonies directly with French ones contravened the spirit as well as the letter of mercantilism, Parliament imposed a duty of sixpence a gallon upon molasses from the foreign West Indies. If the English had actually collected the duty, it would have taken all the profit out of this business for the New England colonies, who needed the rum exports to balance their trade with England. Fortunately, the duty was rarely collected. In 1764, however, Parliament changed its approach by reducing the molasses tax to threepence a gallon and raising the tax on foreign refined sugar. The English then vigorously enforced both measures. This antagonized the colonists so much that in 1767 Parliament cut the molasses tax to onepence, at which point it was a significant revenue producer for the Crown.

Other pieces of mercantilistic legislation, already mentioned in the previous chapter on manufacturing, should be recalled at this point. They were the three severe limitations on colonial manufacturing, namely, that of 1699 on woolens, that of 1732 on beaver hats, and that of 1750 on processed iron.

The details of monetary developments will be described later. These will show that the British authorities were opposed to the colonies' having any money of their own. They forbade the colony of Massachusetts to issue lightweight coins of its own after 1683; they forbade the colonies in 1708 to overvalue British or foreign coins; they insisted after the mid-1720s that the colonies obtain the Crown's permission before issuing any legal tender paper money; in 1751 they forbade the New England colonies to issue legal tender paper money; and finally in 1764 they forbade all colonies to issue legal tender paper money. In short, the rules governing the colonies' having any money of their own creation became constantly more stringent.

How Mercantilism Affected the Colonies. To stimulate an inflow of precious metals into Britain, the Navigation Acts tried to make the British and colonial merchants less dependent on the Dutch merchant marine, on Spanish tobacco, and on Swedish naval stores. They also made the colonies buy most of their foreign merchandise through England. If foreign goods would have to be bought through England anyway, it might seem better to many an American buyer to buy English goods from an English firm, but in either event the English merchants would make a profit on the transaction. An effort was made to stop any trade and accompanying payment of coin to the people of the French West Indies. The colonies were forbidden to have a mint of their own which might compete for silver that would otherwise flow to England. They were also forbidden to hold on to English and other coins by setting an extra-high value on them.

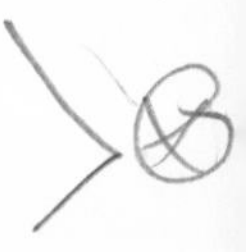

As for letting the colonies have paper money, the English should have agreed to that if they really wanted to drain the colonies of gold and silver coins, for excessive issues of paper money cause Gresham's law to work. Gresham's law is that overvalued money (which paper money certainly is when issued to excess) will drive undervalued money (which gold and silver coins are when treated as equal to such paper money) out of circulation. The coins are shipped abroad to pay for exports, because people in other lands will not accept the paper money, and the paper money stays in circulation at home because that is the only place where people will take it. The fact that the English did not encourage paper money was not in keeping with the desire to attract gold and silver to Britain.

The Navigation Acts of 1651, 1660, and 1662 obliged the British and the colonists to cease patronizing Dutch and other foreign ships and to use their own. It encouraged the building of new ships not only in English but in colonial shipyards. Indeed, at one point when the English shipyards complained of colonial competition, the British quashed the complaint on the ground that the more ships and shipyards Britain and its colonies had, the better. Reserving the coastwise trade for the English and forbidding it to foreign shipping likewise stimulated English and colonial shipping.

Other laws kept England self-sufficient from an agricultural point of view. The New England and Middle Colonies were not permitted to ship their fish and their grain and breadstuffs to the mother country. England preferred to do its own fishing and grain growing.

The British stimulated the production of various colonial products both by assuring them a market in England, as in the case of the enumerated articles, and by paying bounties on them, as in the case of products like hemp, naval stores, and indigo. England was especially anxious to encourage the production of naval stores and masts. When some ambitious farmers in southern Britain threatened to cultivate tobacco, the English put a stop to it, since this might upset the existing trade balance between England and the colonies.

The laws restricting colonial manufacturing were all designed to protect profitable industries in England. Wool and woolen goods especially had been England's staples for centuries. The manufacture of finished iron products typified the industrial revolution then getting under way.

Finally, for a long time the English looked upon the Northern Colonies as the least valuable of their American possessions. The West Indies and the Southern Colonies produced much that Britain did not possess and would otherwise have to buy elsewhere. The Northern Colonies offered chiefly fish and grain and breadstuffs which England already produced. Gradually these Northern Colonies learned to market their commodities in the West Indies and in southern Europe and found various ways to acquire enough bills of exchange and hard money to buy English manufactured goods. Thereafter the British merchants saw the Northern Colonies in another light. When Americans boycotted the English merchants, first on account of the Stamp Act in 1765–1766 and later on account of the Townshend Acts in 1768, the English merchants brought pressure on Parliament to get the obnoxious legislation repealed or largely amended so as to regain this valuable export trade.

It may be asked whether many of these mercantilistic aims would not have been achieved without this elaborate legislative effort. Abundance of land and of virgin resources encouraged the colonies to produce raw materials. They would naturally concentrate on producing those for which there was a market. At the same time, lack of capital and lack of sizable markets would discourage them from concentrating on manufactures. The fishing resources of New England would logically attract these people to become seafaring and probably commercially minded as well. Finally, the distance of the colonies from Britain and the difficulties of communication made it very difficult to enforce most of this legislation. In short, the colonists were not very much deterred from doing what they wanted to do. The fact that they seemed to be obeying the Old Colonial System, alias mercantilism, was largely because it was in their economic interest to do so anyway.

COMMERCE

Regional Specialties. The basis of commerce is exchanging the goods that a region has in abundance for those which it has in short supply. The colonies vis-à-vis England had a surplus of raw material commodities and an insufficiency of manufactured goods, especially of equipment and of luxury items. The Northern Colonies vis-à-vis the West Indies had a surplus of partly processed raw materials like flour, biscuits, and barrel staves, and an insufficiency of other raw materials and of cash. Looking at the picture on a regional basis, the New England Colonies had fish and lumber and later whaling products, horses, and ships; the Middle Colonies had flour, biscuits, grain, barrel staves, and other lumber products; and the Southern Colonies had tobacco, rice, naval stores, deerskins, and wheat. In addition, the New England Colonies, whose traders roamed the western world, brought in molasses from the West Indies from which they made rum to reexport. Two other products, conspicuous for their absence in Table 4-1 (p. 60), deserve mention. Furs were important exports in the seventeenth century but less so later. Indigo, produced in Georgia after the 1740s, actually did not rank high in value among exports.

Balance of Trade. Any region should be expected to export about as much as it imports, for that is how it raises the money, for the most part, to pay for its imports. At the same time, no region should be expected to maintain a perfect balance of exports and imports with every other region with which it trades. Regions trade unequally in their dealings with one another. Looked at on a region-to-region basis, trade is generally unbalanced, but looked at on a total exports to total imports basis, trade is more nearly balanced.

The Southern Colonies carried on the bulk of their trade with England, partly because tobacco constituted two-thirds of their exports. As an

Table 4-1
Exports of Three Regions, about 1763
(000 omitted)

Export	New England	New York, Pennsylvania	Virginia, Maryland
Dried codfish	£100.0		
Whale and cod oil	127.5		
Masts, boards, staves	75.0	£ 60.0	£ 55.0
Potash	35.0	14.0	
Beef, pork, and hams	28.5	63.0	15.0
Flour and biscuit	......	600.0	
Wheat	......	170.0	40.0
Other grain, beans, peas	......	52.0	30.0
Horses and livestock	37.0	37.0	
Ships	49.0	31.5	30.0
Copper and iron	......	55.0	
Tobacco	......	......	768.0
Other	33.0	159.0	132.0
Total	£485.0	£1,241.5	£1,060.0

SOURCE: Harry J. Carman (ed.), *American Husbandry* (New York: Columbia University Press, 1939), pp. 44, 91, 129, 182. See also pp. 247, 313.

enumerated commodity, that had to go to England. The trade of the Southern Colonies with England was generally in balance or close to it. The case of the Northern Colonies, that is, the New England and Middle Atlantic ones combined, was different. In 1769, the imports of the Northern Colonies from England were twice their exports to England. England did not want their fish, breadstuffs, and grain, although those colonies bought large amounts of English manufactured goods. The Northern Colonies had to find a market elsewhere for their fish and breadstuffs and obtain either bills of exchange, cash, or other goods to take to England to exchange for the desired manufactured imports. The resourceful traders of the Northern Colonies found three regions which needed their goods and had surplus products of their own to offer that the Northern merchants could in turn sell in England.

The Triangular Trade Routes. The British West Indies in 1770 exported three times as much to England as they bought from England. Their

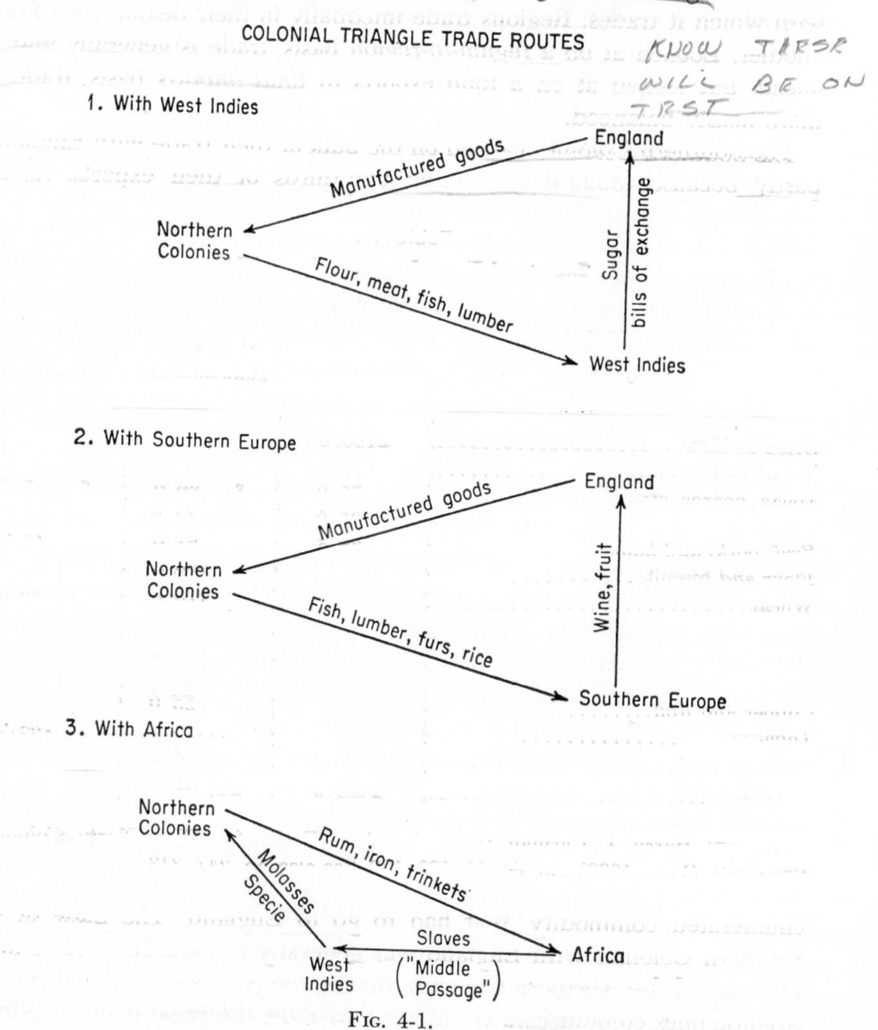

FIG. 4-1.

sugar was in great demand in the mother country. At the same time the islands, being so limited in size and so valuable for sugar production, lacked adequate food supplies and ran out of lumber to be used for housing and for barrel staves. These were just the articles which the Northern Colonies had in abundance, and so a brisk three-cornered trade sprang up between the Northern Colonies, the British West Indies, and

England. The Northern traders carried fish, flour, biscuits, meat, lumber, and barrel staves (a sugar barrel could be used only once) to the islands. There they picked up sugar, specie, and bills of exchange and carried them to England. In England they sold the sugar and cashed the bills of exchange and bought manufactured goods to take back to the Northern Colonies. Bills of exchange were essentially "checks" written by the islanders asking an English importer to pay the person presenting them. The islanders had money coming to them for sugar they had previously sold the English importing house. These importing houses served also as the islanders' banks in England.

A second triangular trade route took in the Catholic countries of southern Europe, which were large consumers of fish. A number of mercantilistic rules limiting colonial trade to England made exceptions of these regions south of Cape Finisterre (the northwest corner of Spain), and goods shipped to them did not have to pass through England. Among the goods sent to southern Europe were fish, rice, whale oil, and lumber. From these areas the colonial traders picked up wines, fruits, and spices, took them to England, sold them, and bought manufactured goods to carry back to the Northern Colonies (see Fig. 4-1).

Still a third fairly common triangular trade route involved the west coast of Africa where the traders exchanged rum, bar iron, and trinkets for slaves. These they packed almost like sardines into the shallow between-decks of their ships and transported to the West Indies. Sanitary conditions on this second leg of the ship's voyage were sometimes frightful, and many slaves died, hence the phrase often associated with this trade, "the horrors of the Middle Passage." The slaves were sold for use on the sugar plantations in the islands, and the northern traders picked up molasses and specie. The islands visited were frequently French or Spanish where the molasses was cheaper and the Spanish silver dollars more plentiful.

Two of these triangular trade routes were quite legal; the third one, involving the foreign West Indies, was not, especially after the Molasses Act of 1733. All three, however, enabled the Northern Colonies to buy manufactured goods from England and so stimulated England's industrial progress.

Piracy and Privateering. There were still other ways of obtaining specie to ship to England in exchange for manufactured goods. This was an age of piracy, privateering, and smuggling. Piracy was fairly rampant during the seventeenth century but was gradually eradicated during the first third of the eighteenth century. Pirates who brought their spoils to coastal ports had usually carried on their sea robberies in one of two areas. One was off the east coast of Africa, and the other was along the Spanish Main, that is, along the northern mainland of Spanish South

America and in the West Indies. Spices, silks, and the like were the booty seized off Africa, and coin was sometimes taken on the Spanish Main. Pirates sold their goods cheaply, then spent their coin in America because many colonies placed a higher value on coin than the English did.

Privateering was little better than piracy but had legal niceties added. Whenever England and France, or England and Spain were at war, which was half the time after 1689, the King of England would grant "Letters of Marque and Reprisal" to armed merchantmen to prey on merchantmen flying the flag of the enemy. The privateers were entitled to keep part of the booty captured, and of course sell it as best they could. Smuggling also was rather widespread, especially in New England and in the West Indies, since it was impossible to do very effective policing so far from England. Most of the colonists thought it no particular sin to evade rules and duties that they regarded as an unreasonable interference with their business. How much cash pirates and later privateers brought into the colonies, to what degree stolen and smuggled goods affected the merchandise balance of trade will never be known, but at times the amounts must have been substantial. Once in 1704, for example, a band of pirates brought £10,000 of booty into Boston, half of it in coin which was seized by provincial officials.

Organization of Foreign Commerce. In a region as sparsely populated as the colonies, most articles destined for export tended to be funneled toward one of the chief regional ports. The leading colonial ports were Boston and Newport for New England, New York and Philadelphia for the Middle Colonies, and Baltimore, Norfolk, Charleston, and Savannah in the South. The business of importing and exporting was more formally organized in the South where one staple, tobacco, constituted two-thirds of the business. In London certain importers specialized in tobacco and other southern staples, either selling these goods on commission or buying them outright. Many became the bankers and buying agents for their colonial planter customers, handling their mounting debts and executing their orders for everything from milady's wardrobe to equipment for the plantation. Another set of specialists, generally known as factors, appeared in the colonies, and they likewise either bought tobacco or handled it on consignment. They also delivered cargoes, collected debts for the merchants in England, and performed other duties. A number eventually became planters themselves.

In the North where there was less trade with England and a greater variety of exports, the organization of trade was not so clear-cut. As has been shown in the case of the triangular trades, the trade of that region was thinly disguised barter. The captain or supercargo (an agent of the owner-merchant) handled the trade of a ship that wandered from port to port for months or years, picking up what he could at a bargain and selling it in the most likely market. The triangular trades were merely the more frequently used routes of these tramp-ship operations. The merchant-owners or co-owners of these ships sometimes built up very respectable fortunes: as early as about 1670 there were reported to be thirty Massachusetts merchants worth between $50,000 and $100,000. Merchant families dominated politics and society in the Northern Colonies during most of the colonial period.

Internal Trade. Most internal trade between the colonies was coastal, with the Northern Colonies taking the initiative of sending out small trading vessels. Activity was considerable as far south as Pennsylvania. New Jersey, for example, lying between New York and Pennsylvania, was likened to a "keg tapped at both ends." Farther to the south, where settlements were more scattered, there was less trade, although greater concentration on cash crops required that some necessities be imported. Also, the climatic differences between North and South created the opportunity for some exchange of different products. New England sold fish and whale oil all along the coast; New York and Pennsylvania sold breadstuffs, iron, and ironware both in New England and to the South; and the South sent out deerskins, naval stores, tobacco, and ham and bacon.

The greatest amount of retail specialization was found in the larger port towns. It appeared in Boston first and then in Philadelphia. The specialty shops found in the seventeenth century in Boston were apothecaries, tobacconists, bookshops, stationers, grocers, milliners, and even a glass shop. Most stores, however, were general stores, carrying dry goods and an assortment of other articles. Goods were fairly commonly marked up 100 per cent over London prices; credit terms ran for a year to two years in this region dominated by farmers who sold their surpluses about once a year. In smaller places specialty stores were rarer and general stores more frequent. Public markets were common in the Northern Colonies. They took place twice a week in Philadelphia in the 1740s, beginning at daybreak and lasting until noon. Fairs, at which imported goods were sold, were held twice a year. Peddlers such as the Pattison brothers of Connecticut toured the less settled regions selling tinware and other light, useful, and not too costly items.

MONEY AND EXCHANGE

Any money that the first English settlers brought with them for use on the ship or on arrival probably did not remain very long in circulation in the colonies since it was the easiest means of payment for the additional supplies that were needed. Exchange was largely conducted on a barter or at least a credit basis. But barter, even when facilitated by credit, is cumbersome, particularly so for people who are used to money. Reliable money serves at least three very useful purposes: It is a measure of value, a yardstick by which one may compare, say, the value of a hogshead of tobacco with that of a suit of clothes. It is a store of value; that is, something which if laid away for one year or five or ten will still have about the same value when finally spent. And it is a medium of exchange, which means that the seller of a hogshead of tobacco who wants a suit of clothes does not have to find a clothes merchant who smokes a lot of tobacco and who agrees with him on the relative values of tobacco and suits. All he needs to find is someone who wants to purchase tobacco and can agree with him on a price for it, and then someone else who wants to sell clothes and can agree on a price. The latter undertaking is much the easier to accomplish.

The barter system which the colonists were at first forced to adopt soon evolved into a partial money system and then into a full money system. For example, the first East New Jersey tax law (1668) required that taxes be paid at the following valuations: "Winter Wheat at Five Shillings a Bushel . . . Indian Corn at Three Shillings, Rye at Four Shillings . . . Beef at Two pence Half penny, Pork at Three pence Half penny a Pound.[1] Such payment "in kind" was legal in New Jersey for thirty years. The practice also prevailed in other colonies. In time certain commodities came to be especially popular in business transactions because they were so readily marketable. Generally it was the staple product of the town or colony, such as tobacco in Virginia, codfish around Boston, beaver in New York, and later rice in South Carolina. Wampum, that is, strings of decorative beads made and prized by Indians, was another popular commodity money. Such single commodities were more practical than a variety of commodities. At the same time they were sometimes perishable, usually not very portable, and they generally varied a lot in quality. The colonists preferred a more modern kind of money.

Coins in Circulation. For some three centuries the Spanish peso or dollar was the most commonly used coin in the western world. It originated in Joachimthal in Bohemia about 1517, and Austria and Spain eventually adopted it. Mints in Mexico and Peru produced vast quantities of these coins. It required eight smaller coins called reals to equal a dollar. In terms of English money the peso or dollar was worth four shillings sixpence; thus the one-real piece was worth approximately the same as the English sixpence or six penny "bit." The dollar of eight reals, or about eight bits, was the well-known "piece of eight." A remnant

[1] Aaron Leaming and Jacob Spicer, *Grants, Concessions and Original Constitutions of the Province of New Jersey, 1664–1682* (1752), p. 31.

of this is the still current expression of "two bits" for a quarter. Although the piece of eight overshadowed all other coins, there were other moneys in circulation such as Portuguese johannes and moidores, French crowns and ducats, Austrian ducatoons and rix-dollars. For accounting purposes, all were converted into pounds, shillings, and pence.

Since all coins tended to leave the colonies rather soon, several of the provinces talked of coining their own money, but only Massachusetts Bay proceeded to do so. Its Pine Tree shilling, minted between 1652 and 1683, contained 22.5 per cent less silver than the English shilling and so was less apt to be shipped out. When traded from one part of the world to another, silver coins were weighed rather than counted, whereas inside Massachusetts they were counted rather than weighed. The people of Massachusetts were depending on the operation of Gresham's law to provide them with a lightweight metal currency. In 1683 the English government closed the Massachusetts mint on the ground that it infringed on the King's prerogative to coin the money of the realm.

Meanwhile many colonies came up with a simpler manner of keeping coins from being exported. Around the mid-seventeenth century several of them made the piece of eight legal tender for five shillings, although in England it was worth only four shillings sixpence. In 1652 Massachusetts upped its valuation to close to six shillings. Other colonies could also play at this game, and Virginia retaliated by valuing it at over six shillings. New York raised it to six shillings ninepence in 1676 and Pennsylvania shortly went still higher. There were other motives for doing this. It induced pirates to spend their ill-gotten coins in ports where coins commanded a premium, thus bringing additional money into the colony. Colonial debtors could also pay off their English creditors more easily. Most of these were temporary advantages, for the prices of goods soon rose proportionately. The British merchants complained to their government about these practices. The Privy Council responded in 1704, in the name of the Queen, by proclaiming that no coins circulating in America might be made legal tender for more than a third greater than their value in England. Thus a piece of eight, worth four shillings sixpence in England, might not have its value set higher than six shillings in any colony. But by the time this had been done, the upped valuation already exceeded one-third in some colonies. Enforcement would have meant lowering prices, that is, deflation, so the proclamation was widely ignored. In 1708 Parliament enacted the policy into law. All coins valued at the one-third higher rate were henceforth known as Proclamation money. Even so the regulation was not too well heeded. By now, however, other events were under way which would soon drive out most of this silver.

Paper Money. It is sometimes said that paper money originated in North America near the end of the seventeenth century. Massachusetts had launched an unsuccessful expedition against the French in Quebec in 1690 as its part in the War of the League of Augsburg. Because it did not have enough funds to pay the soldiers on their return it printed and distributed some £40,000 in bills of credit or treasury I.O.U.'s to the men with the understanding that these might circulate as money and would be retired within a few years. Retirement was slower than promised. The legislature had discovered that paper I.O.U.'s were an easy way of avoiding the odium of imposing taxes. The device was not only used again in Massachusetts but also in at least five other colonies before 1711. Eventually the paper money habit spread to all the colonies.

Soon a second type of paper money appeared which was more akin to bank notes in character than to treasury notes. These were called loan office notes when issued through government agencies, and land bank notes when issued through privately owned institutions. Generally they appeared in eras of peace, such as that between 1713 and 1739, and were intended to help the citizenry borrow, or at least to consolidate their debts at a reasonable rate of interest.

Both loan offices and land banks were representative of some of the banking theory of the time. About 1650 William Potter had published a book called *The Key to Wealth* in which he advocated land banks. Private land banks may have been briefly tried in Massachusetts in the 1680s. In England this was the era when goldsmiths carried on commercial banking by lending out in circulating notes more than they actually held in gold. It was an easy step to argue that if gold backing of paper gave it value, land back of other paper money should give it value, or commodities back of still other paper should give it value. Thus it was not necessary to have gold or silver to have money. Anything of value would do. All this was to a considerable degree the theory on which John Law would shortly build his disastrous scheme in France. The theory failed to recognize that it is the scarcity of money, not its backing, that gives money value. It is also essential that money be a stable measure of value and a dependable store of value as well as just a medium of exchange.

The loan office system was tried three times in New Jersey. An extreme shortage of specie gave rise to the first Loan Office Act of 1723. The situation was brought on in part by overissues of bills of credit, by foreclosures, and by the needs of a capital-starved frontier economy. New Jersey ordered that £40,000 in notes be made up for private loans. A farmer could go to his county loan office and mortgage his £200 farm up to half its value for a loan repayable in annual installments over a twelve-year period. Interest was at 5 per cent instead of at 8 per cent as on a private loan. If the borrower did not make payment within thirty days of grace, foreclosure took place. Repayment of the principal took care of the retirement of the original issue of paper money, and the interest payments provided the running expenses of the provincial government and thus reduced taxes or eliminated them entirely in some instances. The trouble with the New Jersey system was that it gave rise to cycles of inflation and deflation. The abrupt appearance of £40,000 in little New Jersey tended to push up prices. The retirement of notes then caused prices to fall, and this was accentuated by the fact that even New Jersey was an expanding economy. That made it harder for people to pay their debts, which led to a demand for another loan office issue.

The most famous private version of this system was the Massachusetts Land Bank of 1739. The original intention was to issue £150,000 of notes, although only £50,000 was ever put into circulation. As under the New Jersey scheme, borrowers gave a mortgage on their real estate, but they had twenty years in which to pay, reducing the principal by 5 per cent a year. The interest rate was only 3 per cent. Repayment might be in notes of the Land Bank or in manufactured articles. No clear provision was made for the eventual retirement of the notes; this was the big difference between it and the loan office plan. The notes would go on circulating indefinitely and thus represent a profit to the owners of the bank, who were also the original borrowers. Governor Jonathan Belcher and his provincial Council opposed the plan and some 150 merchants agreed not to accept the notes. Parliament ruled in 1741 that the so-called Bubble Act of 1720, which made such schemes illegal in Britain, applied also to the colonies, despite the fact that the attorney general had previously said it did not. This led to court cases for the next forty years and enduring resentment by some individuals against Parliament.

Inflation in the Colonies. When prices rose the dollar or pound would buy less; it had depreciated in value. This is commonly called inflation. Even before the paper money era there was already some inflation, chiefly because coins were being overvalued. Although New York, Pennsylvania, and New Jersey kept their bills and notes from depreciating more than about 40 per cent, most other colonies did not do as well. Rhode Island was the worst offender, with North and South Carolina, Connecticut, and Massachusetts showing up poorly too. For example, in 1702 it took 133 Massachusetts paper pounds to buy 100 pounds sterling. This was equal to the imminent Proclamation Money rate. In 1713 Massachusetts' rate was 150; by 1740 it had climbed to 550; and in 1749 it reached 1,100. In North and South Carolina paper money sank to one-tenth the value of sterling, and in Rhode Island to one twenty-third.

This much inflation in New England and in the Deep South had several consequences. The operation of Gresham's law drove whatever coins there were left out of the country or into hiding. One farmer wrote a public letter to the merchants of Boston in 1720 saying, "As to silver and gold, we never had much of it in the country; but we can very well remember that before we had paper money there was a sufficiency of it current . . . and as the bills of credit came in and multiplied, the silver ceased and was gone, and . . . especially merchants should be silent as to that matter, for you have shipped it off . . . ."[2] In the second place, the government officials, ministers, and any others who received a somewhat fixed or customary salary saw their real incomes decline. Governor William Franklin wrote in 1763, "all the Necessaries of Life in this country are increased in Price near Three fold what they were seven years ago."[3] Finally, anyone who saved was destined to see the value of his savings melt away. This discouraged saving and made creditors demand harsh terms of their debtors to ensure adequate repayment and thus protect themselves.

Among the creditors most affected by paper money issues were the merchants both in England and in the colonies. When the debts to English export merchants were payable in legal tender local currency instead of in sterling, the English exporters could be paid off in depreciated local currency. When the debts were payable in sterling, the final result was nonetheless damaging to the business of the British exporter. Debts to the local merchant by his customers were still payable in local legal tender paper money. The local merchant thus faced this difficult choice. Either he had to mark up his merchandise to an almost exorbitant degree to protect himself, or he bought sterling to pay off the British exporter at the high rates at which the provincial money was exchangeable for it. This sometimes meant that he was actually taking a loss, since what he had received would not buy an equal amount of new merchandise. Accordingly, he went deeper into debt and perhaps finally went bankrupt. Often the provincial merchant did not analyze this situation very well and looked with some favor upon paper money, believing that if his customers had more money, they would pay up their accounts. But the English exporters saw more clearly that paper money was a device that would either cheat them or ruin the American merchants with whom they dealt, thus hurting them indirectly.

From an early date British merchants brought pressure upon the British Board of Trade and Privy Council to examine every proposed paper money law and veto most of them. After the mid-1720s the English warned governors to send all paper money legislation home for final approval by the Crown before letting the money be issued. Parliament enacted a law in 1751 forbidding the issue of bills of credit in the four

[2] Joseph B. Felt, *An Historical Account of Massachusetts Currency* (Boston: Perkins and Marvin, 1839), p. 74.

[3] *Proceedings of the New Jersey Historical Society* (Newark, N.J.: April, 1906), p. 133.

New England colonies. Then the outbreak of the French and Indian War in 1754 obliged the English to relax their restrictions somewhat in order to obtain more generous appropriations from the colonial assemblies to pay the provincial troops and buy supplies. Considerable inflation ensued. Accordingly, in 1764 Parliament forbade all legal tender issues of paper money in the colonies. The colonial assemblies sought repeatedly but unsuccessfully to break through this act. Benjamin Franklin believed that English restrictions against colonial paper money laws were a major cause of resentment leading to the Revolution.

The majority of the testimony on the part of the colonists was that there was a shortage of money. It is relatively easy to persuade any group of people that there is not enough money; nearly every individual knows he could use more and believes he deserves to earn more. This is not the real test. If there is not enough money, prices will tend to fall; if there is too much, they will tend to rise. Prices were rising during most of the colonial period, which demonstrates that there was too much paper money. True, there was a dearth of coin, but in the early days this was because the colonists sent it home to buy equipment and supplies, and later on the operation of Gresham's law caused it to flow out.

Bad as inflation in the colonies was at times, it might well have been worse except for two factors. The economic growth of the colonies meant that they needed some additional money to carry on their expanding business; thus there was need for some of the paper money issues. And the restrictive regulations and acts of the British, resented though they were by the colonists, kept the inflationary situation from getting out of hand more than it did.

Colonial Taxation. The British colonies in America were taxed very lightly and conducted their business affairs much as they pleased. Collection of taxes was poorly enforced, and smuggling was widespread. These facts go a long way toward explaining the American reaction in the 1760s and 1770s toward British enforcement of trading regulations and British efforts to collect taxes. George Grenville had found in the 1760s that it cost Britain £8,000 to collect £2,000. The truth was that the colonists opposed not just "taxation without representation" but any appreciable taxation.

When the colonies were first founded in the seventeenth century, the poll tax was the most common tax. By the mid-seventeenth century Massachusetts and Virginia were collecting "rates" or property taxes, and after 1685 Virginia's quitrents went to the colonial treasury. The larger colonies with well-known seaports got considerable revenue from tonnage duties and import and export duties, and Massachusetts early developed a tariff system. Excise or internal revenue taxes were relatively rare, although Massachusetts and Virginia taxed wine and liquors and later carriages. The chief reason that the colonies needed any taxes in peacetime was to pay the governor, legislature, and judges. Governmental responsibility did not yet take in schools, roads, or institutions for the helpless. Even the colonial wars were paid for in considerable part by Britain. It is doubtful that more than 1 per cent of the colonists' incomes was paid out in taxes. Yet the existence of £8 million of paper bills in the colonies just before the Revolution indicates a sizable load of taxes which the colonists thought they had avoided. Issuing paper money to pay governmental bills, with inflation almost inevitably following, was only a delayed, costly, and unfair form of taxation, probably the worst kind of all.

CHAPTER 5

The Birth of a Nation

It is impossible to understand political history without looking at economic causes, and it is equally impossible to understand economic history and ignore major political changes. The United States changed successively from being a group of colonies, resisting political and military control by England, into a loose union of states bound together much as the members of the United Nations are today, to a more closely bound Federal union. Finally, after the War of 1812, it became a nation enjoying economic as well as political independence.

BACKGROUND OF THE AMERICAN REVOLUTION

Results of the French and Indian War. During most of the generation between the Treaty of Utrecht (1713) and the Treaty of Aix-la-Chapelle (1748), England and France were at peace and the colonies were under the general supervision of the easygoing Duke of Newcastle. In this period of so-called "salutary neglect," England made less effort than usual to enforce mercantilistic regulations and the colonies prospered. The Duke of Bedford, who succeeded the Duke of Newcastle in 1748, had just started enforcing the mercantilistic rules when the French and Indian War broke out in 1754 and postponed enforcement for another decade.

In America the central issue of the war was whether or not France should control the Ohio and Mississippi Valleys and prevent westward expansion of the English colonies. Although France won in the early stages of the war, England decisively defeated it from 1757 on, and in the end deprived it of all its major possessions in America—most significantly, Canada. For seventy-five years previous to this, the French and their Indian allies had stood as a constant threat on the frontier of the Northern Colonies, and more recently of the Southern Colonies as well. This made the British colonies and Britain mutually dependent upon one another for military asssitance. The removal of French control of Canada largely ended the colonies' need for English military protection.

In the course of defeating the French and Indians with colonial aid the English reached several conclusions concerning the American colonies: (1) The colonies profited from the victory as much as England. (2) The colonies were wealthier than the English had realized and were well able to afford a larger share of the heavy war burden. (3) The colonies had become too independent, not only in the attitudes of their assemblies toward the governors, who were usually appointed by the King, but also as regards their obedience to laws regulating commerce. The colonies needed to be brought back into line. In 1760 George II had died and his grandson, George III, a willful young man of twenty-three, came to the throne. In 1763 George Grenville became prime minister, assisted by the Duke of Bedford.

The Grenville Acts. The policies toward the colonies inaugurated in the three ministries of George Grenville, Charles Townshend, and Lord North led to the American Revolution. It was not that these ministers were trying to impose so many new rules, but rather they were trying to enforce existing laws which the colonists had ceased to observe or never had observed. It was once said of Grenville that he "lost America because he read the American dispatches which none of his predecessors had done." His policy consisted of three parts: (1) He would enforce the Navigation Acts. For example, the severe Molasses Act of 1733 had been ignored; in its place he now put the milder-appearing Sugar Act of 1764 and enforced it. Without the trade arising from selling sugar and molasses obtained in the foreign West Indies, the Northern merchants would have remained hopelessly in debt, or would not have been able to purchase nearly as many British manufactures. (2) He would maintain an army of 10,000 men in America, supported in part from the proceeds of the Sugar Act. The army was supposedly intended to protect the colonists from Indian uprisings. (3) He would impose a stamp tax on legal documents and playing cards and turn the proceeds over to the Crown. This was a slap at the colonial assemblies, which for years had been using their power of granting or withholding funds to wring concessions from the governors or the King. Also about this same time the Crown issued the Proclamation of 1763, which in part forbade the colonists to venture west of the headwaters of rivers flowing into the Atlantic. This was to keep the Indians from rebelling. A serious Indian uprising in 1763–1764 under a chief named Pontiac is evidence that this was no idle fear. However, to the colonists, keeping them out of the Ohio Valley, with its profitable fur trade, seemed to deprive them of the fruits of victory over the French.

The colonists were especially incensed over the Stamp Act. Eight colonies sent representatives to an unofficial congress in New York to protest the imposition of *internal* taxes, such as the Stamp Act, without the colonies having representation in Parliament. *External* taxes, such as import duties, had long been imposed, of course. Agreements were made not to import English manufactures unless Parliament repealed the Stamp Act. In 1766 Parliament rescinded the Stamp Act, partly upon the urging of British merchants, whose business was being hurt.

Fig. 5-1. Patriots burning stamps in Boston as a reaction to the Stamp Act. (*Courtesy of the Library of Congress.*)

The Townshend Acts. Young Charles Townshend, who became acting prime minister in 1767, also felt that the colonists were behaving too independently. Townshend imposed *external* taxes to get money so that the Crown could both reduce taxes in England and also pay its governors in America and free them from dominance by the assemblies. Townshend's duties on glass, paper, red and white lead, and tea were collected at the colonial ports. It was hard to defeat Townshend's logic that these taxes were reasonable because they were external instead of internal. Nevertheless, the colonists again resorted to a nonimportation agreement and in 1770 got Townshend's successor, Lord North, to repeal all but the tax on tea. It was from this last tax that the incidents leading to the American Revolution were to develop over the next few years.

The North Acts. The East India Company was in financial difficulties, partly because it could not sell tea in America. Lord North had an English export tax on tea rescinded but refused to remove the colonial import duty. That was all that was left of the Townshend acts, and North kept it to demonstrate England's right to tax the colonies. The colonists stood firm and everywhere refused to accept the company's tea. The situation incensed some merchants because it enabled the East India

Fig. 5-2. The Boston Tea Party. (*Courtesy of the Library of Congress.*)

Company to undersell even the tea they bought from smugglers. In Boston where a firebrand leader named Sam Adams held sway, a band of fifty men, disguised as Indians, boarded company ships and tossed 342 casks of tea into the bay. Lord North could not let this challenge to Britain's authority go unnoticed.

Parliament reacted to the Boston Tea Party by passing five acts which the colonists branded "The Intolerable Acts": (1) Parliament closed the port of Boston by a naval blockade until the tea was paid for. (2) It remodeled the charter of Massachusetts to give the Crown more power and the people less. (3) It authorized transfer of trials for capital crimes to England. (4) It renewed a law for quartering troops in Massachusetts and made the garrison commander governor of the colony. (5) It organized Quebec into a colony with boundaries extending south to the

Ohio Valley and recognized the Catholic Church as the established church in Quebec. This last was probably not intended as a punishment for Massachusetts, but its timing was unfortunate and most colonies regarded it as part of the punishment. The colonists now had the choice of giving in or of resisting.

Massachusetts chose a policy of resistance and was encouraged by most of the other colonies. All but Georgia sent delegates to a Continental Congress in September of 1774 to consider a course of action. For a third time the colonists resolved to boycott English manufactures; they would bring the English to terms by a method that had worked twice before. It was the moderates, hoping to avoid war, who most favored the third boycott. But this time the British refused to capitulate before economic sanctions.

THE AMERICAN REVOLUTION, 1775–1783—POLITICAL INDEPENDENCE

The Decision to Seek Independence. At first only a few radicals talked of "independence," for most people preferred to remain British. They believed that the King and his government could be made to see how unreasonable they were being. In fact, the decisive word "independence" remained almost taboo all during the year 1775, despite the pitched battles at Lexington and Concord in April, the battle of Bunker Hill in June, and the siege of Boston all during the year. The moderate group in the Second Continental Congress of 1775 still hoped to find a solution short of independence. But as the news of Bunker Hill spread and its implications became realized, the inevitability of a war for independence became more apparent. The Continental Congress formally declared American independence on July 4, 1776. Congress declared that "all men are created equal" and were entitled to enjoy "life, liberty and the pursuit of happiness," that when a government ceases to guarantee these privileges, the people were justified in overthrowing it and in setting up one that would do so. Although most of the long list of acts of tyranny which Congress attributed to George III were political in nature, at least three were economic: (1) He had forbidden his governors to sign "Laws of immediate and pressing importance" without a suspension clause, and then he had neglected to attend to these laws (this clearly meant paper money legislation). (2) He was guilty of "cutting off our Trade with all Parts of the world." (3) He was also guilty of "imposing taxes on us without our consent."

The Odds against and for Winning Independence. At the time of the outbreak of the Revolution, there were 2½ million persons living in the thirteen colonies, whereas the population of England and Wales was three times that figure. Historians of the Revolution state that about one-third of the colonists wanted independence enough to fight for it, one-third were loyal to the Crown, and one-third wanted primarily to keep out of trouble. The thirteen colonies were suspicious and jealous of one another and had a record of constant bickering in past wars. The nation was primarily agricultural and lacked industries to provide it with gunpowder, muskets, cannon, and many other war supplies. There was a lack of officers trained to direct sizable armies and almost no tradition of discipline among the soldiers. The problem of financing the war was particularly thorny since the colonists were fighting against taxation by a central authority and also since most of the wealth was in the hands of the loyalists. The chances of the colonists looked poor. There seemed little likelihood of finding allies in Europe where England, however much disliked, was respected as a military and naval power after its recent defeat of France.

The colonies, however, had more factors on their side than were immediately apparent. They were fighting for a cause they thought right and for their homes on terrain that was known to them. The English had to operate with supply lines extending across the Atlantic Ocean. Moreover, the English were by no means of one mind about this war. Lord Jeffery Amherst, whose brilliant direction won the French and Indian War, refused to take command against the colonists. The great William Pitt felt there was much to be said on the colonial side. England was obliged to hire Hessians to do much of its fighting. George Washington, Nathaniel Greene in the South, and Benedict Arnold (until he turned traitor) were more brilliant and dedicated leaders than their English opponents. Even so, the colonists could never have succeeded without the courageous and steadfast leadership of Washington, especially when the outlook was darkest, as before the battle of Trenton on Christmas, 1776, or at Valley Forge the next winter. In between, General Horatio Gates's smashing victory near Saratoga made the French realize that the colonial cause was by no means hopeless; clearly this was a heaven-sent opportunity to take revenge on their recent conqueror. The French signed a treaty of alliance in 1778 and followed it by assistance in the form of troops, supplies, and money and at an opportune moment in 1781 a naval squadron. All this encouraged the colonists to hold out until the English finally became weary of the war. The defeat of Cornwallis by General Washington and Admiral De Grasse's fleet at Yorktown on October 17, 1781, virtually ended the war. In one sense the colonists had the easier task to perform, for a stalemate meant they had won, whereas the English had to gain a clear victory.

Economic Aspects of the War. The outbreak of hostilities stimulated the repressed and slow-developing industries. Slitting mills and forges were set up in greater numbers, gunsmiths found their products in constant and growing demand, and powder mills were encouraged by provincial assemblies and Continental Congress. The textile industry, whose product was needed for uniforms, grew up from a homespun occupation to a household one, in which merchants came around to buy up cloth previously ordered. The Revolution, like most wars, was a stimulus to industrial advancement because numerous industries had an opportunity to sell all they could produce upon rather favorable terms. Unfortunately, this industrial progress was short-lived and faded after the war ended.

Financial difficulties might well have lost the war. There are three ways of financing any war, namely, by taxation, by borrowing either abroad or at home, and by creating money. The three ways are desirable and difficult in just the order given. Needless to say, all three are nearly always used to some degree. In the Revolution, however, taxation produced little revenue, for the war was being fought to a large degree over the issue of taxation by a distant authority. The Continental Congress had no power to tax; the provincial assemblies were reluctant to impose burdensome taxes. The colonies were able to borrow $7.8 million from France, Spain, and Holland, but chiefly from France. Some of this, which arrived in the form of specie, was used to found the Bank of North America in 1781. As for borrowing internally, bond issues were virtually unknown in this age, and anyway most of the wealthy men were loyalists. Only about $12 million was obtained by domestic loans. That left only one way of raising funds—by issuing paper money—and the colonists had plenty of experience along that line and considerable desire to make further use of it. The Continental Congress authorized forty-two issues amounting to $242 million by the end of 1779. And the states issued paper money also until 1777 when Congress urged them to stop. The issues of the Continental Congress were so depreciated in 1780 that an association of merchants agreed to convert them into specie at 100 to 1, but soon the rate exceeded this figure. The expression, "not worth a Continental," referring to the value of a paper dollar, originated at this time. Although it is hard to see how the colonies could have financed the Revolution without resort to paper money, it is equally hard to see how they succeeded with it in view of its serious depreciation. Robert Morris of Philadelphia, the "financier of the Revolution," managed to limit paper money issues to some degree; he founded the Bank of North America which helped in the closing years of the war, and he put what order there was in the Congress's finances. Finances were but one of several weaknesses of the Continental Congress, operating under the Articles of Confederation.

THE ARTICLES OF CONFEDERATION

Nature and Weaknesses of the Articles. The Articles of Confederation were comparable to the rather loose charter that today binds the members of the United Nations. At this point the thirteen colonies felt not much more kinship for one another than thirteen nations menaced by a common foe. The United States had not yet been forged into one people and it would take a generation to do so. But the Continental Congress felt the need of a written constitution from the moment independence was contemplated. The delegates reached agreement on the Articles of Confederation on November 15, 1777, and sent them to the states for ratification. Supposedly the Articles would not go into effect until all states signed them, but nine states had agreed by July 9, 1778, and thereafter the Articles tended to be followed. Officially they went into effect March 1, 1781, when the last state, Maryland, ratified them. One of the chief difficulties was whether or not Congress should fix the western boundaries of states. Seven states—Georgia, the two Carolinas, Virginia, New York, Massachusetts, and Connecticut—claimed ownership of lands beyond the Appalachians, but the six other states felt this would make the landowning states too powerful in the Union. Besides, all were fighting a common enemy; why should some get prizes in the form of lands and others not? Maryland refused to ratify until all the larger states had yielded on this point. The land-claiming states were to give over the western land to the central government with the idea that it would eventually develop into new states.

The Articles of Confederation established a United States of America and provided for a "firm league of friendship" and a "perpetual union." The union, however, was a loose one that lasted only about a decade. Each state remained sovereign but appointed delegates to the Continental Congress. There each state voted as a unit. The United States had no president unless it was the speaker of this unicameral congress. What power the Union had rested in the hands of the legislative body. It had the power to manage foreign affairs, make war, borrow money, issue bills of credit, operate the post office, and conduct Indian affairs. A majority of states had to agree to reach a decision on all issues, and nine out of thirteen on some matters.

The Articles had five major weaknesses from an economic point of view: (1) Congress had no power to tax but was obliged instead to indicate the amount desired, apportion this among the states according to population, and wait for the states to impose and collect the taxes and hand over the money. (2) Congress did not have the sole power to levy import duties, and the states might even levy them against one another's trade. Between 1780 and 1789 Pennsylvania enacted fifteen tariff laws. (3) Congress had to share with the states the power to issue money. (4) The Articles did not safeguard the obligation of contracts or offer adequate protection of property rights. (5) The Articles were too cumbersome to amend, for all thirteen states had to agree to any amendment. In 1781 all but Rhode Island agreed to grant the Continental Congress the right to impose a 5 per cent tax on imports so that Congress might have some tax revenue of its own. Rhode Island's veto killed the amendment. In addition to these weaknesses, the nation also faced other difficulties of an economic nature.

A Hollow Economic Victory. Dislike of the Old Colonial System, or British mercantilism, was one reason for the American Revolution. The colonists, however, failed to take into account that they derived numerous advantages as well as disadvantages from this system. For example, world-wide respect for the British navy protected colonial ships on the high seas and in many parts of the world. The colonists had a virtually assured market for their "enumerated" articles such as tobacco, rice, and indigo. The colonies received bounties from the English government on products like indigo, hemp, and naval stores. They were permitted to trade with other British colonies. Now that the thirteen states were, by their own actions, outside the British family, they ceased to enjoy these various advantages. The states now began to realize how valuable some of these privileges were.

When the war ended, the colonial merchants hastened to resume business relations with English firms. English styles, sizes, and materials were more dependable and to the liking of the colonists; also, the British offered more favorable terms of credit. Business boomed for a while, but soon the colonists had bought far more than they could pay for. Some of the old triangular trade arrangements no longer worked, and it took time to develop new ones. Trade with the British West Indies was illegal—Britain would not let a foreign nation trade directly with its colonies—and this broke up two of the favorite triangular trade routes (see p. 61). True, the colonies carried on a sizable clandestine trade, making special use of the Danish West Indies and of St. Eustatius and Saba of the Dutch West Indies as transfer points for smuggled merchandise. The old triangular route to southern Europe was still available, but pirates from North Africa had little respect for ships flying the American flag. The colonies had hoped for free trade with France and other nations of Europe after the war, but it simply did not materialize. American ships explored the possibilities of previously unvisited areas like the Baltic Sea, the East Indies, and China. The *Empress of China*, out of Boston, reached Canton in 1784. Unfortunately, the total of this did not produce enough bills of exchange to pay for all that Americans had bought from

England and wanted to buy. In 1784 the United States had imported five times as much from England as it had exported to it. In 1786 it halved this ratio: the imports from England declined; American exports remained about the same. When the United States sought special trade concessions from Britain, it received none. It really had nothing to offer.

Lord Sheffield, a member of Parliament in 1783, wrote a brochure, "Observations on the Commerce of the American States," in which he opposed granting any consideration to the United States to regain its trade. Some Englishmen feared that France and others would run off with the American trade, which England had once had largely for itself. Sheffield answered that England should not modify its Navigation Acts to please America. England owed its superiority in world trade to those Navigation Acts and if it granted favors to America, it would impair its own commercial supremacy. It would win nothing that it would not gain without concessions. He emphasized that American merchants could get the credit they needed only in Britain. Also "No American articles are so necessary to us as our manufacturers are to the Americans" and "It will be a long time before the Americans can manufacture for themselves." He said there was no need to fear combinations among the American states, whose interests disunited them to the point that it was even impossible under their Articles to make a single treaty binding on all of them. Sheffield's observations, though unfriendly and bitter medicine, were true and showed that the United States had not yet gained economic independence.

Shays' Rebellion. The end of a war brings numerous economic readjustments. The flood of English manufactures at the war's end served to kill off some of the budding manufactories that had sprung up. The tapering off of wartime inflation led people to spend less freely, and it became harder for debtors to pay their creditors. The failure of merchants to sell enough of their imports ruined many of them. The United States fell into a depression in the years 1785 and 1786. As often happens, some economic groups wanted to be relieved of the obligation to meet contracts which, under the circumstances, bore rather heavily on them. Others demanded new issues of paper money so that they could pay their debts more easily.

In western Massachusetts in the summer of 1786, many farmers were being sued in courts for payment of overdue debts and delinquent taxes. Some were even ejected from their homes. The farmers reacted by demanding reforms in the courts, changes in tax laws, and above all the issuance of more paper money. Since most of them were not entitled to vote, they gathered in mobs before courthouses and threatened to halt convictions for nonpayment of debts and taxes. Daniel Shays, who was a war veteran and a local politician in Pelham, became the leader. Eventually the insurgents became so well-organized, so vocal, and so violent that the militia had to be called out. A pitched battle ensued and the rebels were put down by force of arms. Yet in state elections soon afterward many of the candidates elected were sympathetic to Shays' views, and the legislature enacted several measures looking to the relief of debtors.

In Rhode Island the postwar issues of paper money had depreciated, and creditors were reluctant to accept settlement of their debts in depreciated paper. State law, however, imposed heavy fines for such refusal plus the loss of a man's rights as a freeman. Some merchants closed their shops and refused to do business, and many farmers ceased bringing their produce to town. Creditors fled from their debtors. The situation eventually came to a head in the case of *Trevett v. Weeden.* John Weeden, a butcher, refused to accept payment of a debt in paper money. He was brought to court, and acquitted on the ground that the state law requiring him to accept the money at par was unconstitutional. This aroused the wrath of the legislators, who called the judge before them and denounced him.

The Weeden case, Shays' Rebellion, and other incidents, such as a mob storming the New Hampshire legislature when the lawmakers refused to enact a paper money law, aroused the fears of men of property in many parts of the country. These realized that they must do something soon to give the new nation a stronger and more effective government.

ADOPTION OF THE CONSTITUTION

Meanwhile several states sought to rewrite the Articles of Confederation. In 1785 Virginia and Maryland sent commissioners to a meeting to reconcile their differences in navigation laws and tariffs on the Chesapeake Bay and Potomac River. One state had lower tariffs than the other, so that goods tended to be landed in a low tariff port in order to be smuggled into the neighboring higher tariff area. Virginia invited its neighbor states to send delegates to a meeting held in Annapolis in 1786; five states were represented at that meeting. They decided to invite all the states to a meeting to be held in Philadelphia the next spring to look into the much broader question of overhauling the whole framework of government. All but Rhode Island responded enthusiastically and sent some of their most able citizens as delegates.

The convention got under way on May 25, 1787, with George Washington presiding, and by September the Constitution was ready. The new document provided for a central government based on the principle of a balance of power among the legislative, executive, and judicial branches. The legislature had two houses: the Senate gave equal representation to each state, large or small, and the House gave nearly equal representation to every 30,000 persons. The legislative branch did not overshadow the executive and judiciary as under the Articles of Confederation. Indeed, the fact that there now was an executive branch, a president, strengthened the government. Whereas a legislative body is inclined to debate and delay, one man entrusted with the direction of a government will make decisions, execute them, and in emergencies take action which the legislature subsequently must approve. The American president was given great powers: for example, he was commander-in-chief of the army and navy which Congress was empowered to establish. The judicial branch was to interpret laws enacted by Congress, treaties, and any state laws in conflict with the Constitution. In many respects, however, the states still retained their sovereignty. The Tenth Amendment, offered at the time of ratification, said, "The Powers not delegated to the United States by the Constitution, nor prohibited by it to the States, are reserved to the States respectively or to the People."

The Constitution remedied the more troublesome economic weaknesses of the Articles of Confederation: (1) Congress as well as the states now had the power to tax, which made it much less dependent upon the states. (2) Congress alone had the power to impose tariffs and to regulate interstate and foreign commerce. (3) Congress had the sole power "to coin Money and regulate the Value thereof." The Constitution forbade any state to "make any Thing but Gold and Silver Coin a Tender in Payment of Debts." Legal tender paper money was outlawed. (4) The Constitution also forbade any state to pass any "Law impairing the Obligation of Contracts." As if to show good faith on the obligation of contracts, the Constitution specifically said that the new government would assume the debts of the Confederation. (5) The Constitution could be amended by a vote of three-quarters of the states. Although it is not easy to amend the Constitution, it was easier to amend than the Articles had been. In reality, amendments on many points have been supplied by judicial interpretation. The "implied powers" clause has given the Constitution a high degree of flexibility. That clause says Congress shall have the power "to make all laws which shall be necessary and proper for carrying into execution" any powers specifically assigned the Federal government or any of its officers.

The Constitution provided a framework of government under which a modern capitalistic system could thrive. It set up a strong central government which would not only supply military protection but which would also protect the propertied classes against subtle invasion of their rights by paper money laws and laws impairing obligations of contract. If the Constitution could be adopted and then be put into actual operation, the economic future of the propertied classes would clearly brighten. The supporters of the Constitution were a minority when they sought its adoption. Since they had much to lose if they failed, judged by such recent incidents as Shays' Rebellion and *Trevett v. Weeden,* they went at their job of persuasion with great diligence and intelligence. Two men were especially influential. James Madison of Virginia and Alexander Hamilton of New York wrote most of *The Federalist* papers, a now-classic group of essays in support of the Constitution. Their essays together with skillful political maneuverings in their states tipped the balance. Five states—Delaware, Pennsylvania, New Jersey, Georgia, and Connecticut—ratified the Constitution promptly and without much hesitation. Matters then proceeded more slowly. By June 21, 1788, Massachusetts, Maryland, South Carolina, and New Hampshire had also ratified, making nine, enough to adopt. But such important states as Virginia and New York had not yet decided, and as a practical matter their cooperation was vital. Virginia agreed late in June and New York, with reluctance, a month later. The Constitution was put into effect and George Washington was elected President and took office March 4, 1789. A month later North Carolina joined the Union; Rhode Island came in in May of 1790.

THE PERIOD OF FEDERALISM

The Basic Issue. It is one thing to set up a desirable form of government; it is another and more difficult matter to make it work. Three men were most responsible for making a central government that was strong on paper equally strong in fact. These were George Washington, Alexander Hamilton, and John Marshall. Elected unanimously to the Presidency, Washington was the one man who could hold the union of states together in peace as he had in war. Yet popular as he was, by the end of his first term even he was regarded as a member of the Federalist party and was subjected to much criticism. The aim of the Federalists was to develop a strong central government. They interpreted broadly the powers granted by the Constitution to the Federal government and made much use of the doctrine of "implied powers" in doing so. Thomas Jefferson and after a time James Madison, both of Virginia, preferred to interpret the Constitution narrowly and to leave to the states all powers not clearly assigned to the Federal government. This was the great issue in the early years of the new government. Although Jefferson and his Democratic party eventually defeated the Federalists decisively, the latter meanwhile had been able to establish a strong Federal government. Hamilton did so with important legislative measures, and Marshall as Chief Justice continued the work with his judicial interpretations until his death in 1835.

Hamilton's Financial Program. Alexander Hamilton, the first Secretary of the Treasury, a young man of thirty-four when he took office, was both brilliant and brash. He got things done but he made enemies, especially Secretary of State Thomas Jefferson. Hamilton believed in an even stronger government than had been established. He believed that to succeed and to improve, the new government must have the backing of the men of wealth and influence. Hamilton's philosophy appears clearly in his three-part financial program which consisted of (1) refunding and paying off all governmental war debts, (2) establishing a tax system to pay these debts and to run the government, and (3) setting up a large bank to help the Treasury and to promote commerce and industry.

Hamilton urged that the Federal government pay off its domestic debts in full. These amounted to about $56 million and had been selling as low as 25 cents on the dollar. James Madison and others felt that paying them off at par would unduly enrich the speculators who had bought them at bargain prices. Hamilton's motive was that paying off the debts at par would enhance the government's credit. Also, it would cause the holders of these debts to make more strenuous efforts to help the new government succeed. As soon as the refunding bill was passed, some congressmen and their friends sent out fast couriers by land and sea to buy up any of these debts which they could still find. Hamilton himself was honest and had no part in this.

The Secretary of the Treasury also wanted the Federal government to assume the state debts since, after all, they had been incurred largely in the war for independence. Some states, chiefly Southern ones, which had already paid off much of their war debts, objected to sharing the burden of other states which had thus far made less effort. The opponents of assumption held a slight majority. Assumption of state debts would not have taken place if Hamilton had not arranged a political deal at this point. The Southern states, especially Virginia, wanted the national capital located on the Potomac, whereas the Northern states leaned toward Philadelphia or New York as the capital city. Hamilton and Jefferson struck a bargain that each would work to achieve the goal of the other. So Washington city was located on the Potomac, the national debt was augmented by another $18 million, and the national credit was improved.

The second main point in Hamilton's program dealt with establishing an adequate tax system. At Hamilton's request, Congress passed an excise tax in January of 1791, consisting of a 9- to 30-cent tax on distilled liquor. This was an obnoxious tax to many people. In the first place, it was regressive, that is, it bore more heavily on the poor than on the rich. Many frontier farmers got cash for their surplus corn by distilling it into whisky, slinging a few kegs over the back of a mule, and trudging to market with it. Thus a whisky tax was a tax on their cash income. In addition, the idea of an excise tax was relatively new in America and not popular. As time went on the farmers in western Pennsylvania refused to pay the hated whisky tax. In a skirmish with a tax collector named Neville, six were wounded and one person killed. This aroused Hamilton's ire and he dispatched an expedition to the rebellious region. The rebellion subsided, but he rounded up some insurgents and herded them ahead of the returning army on its triumphal march through Philadelphia. It was not a pretty sight, but it demonstrated for all to see that the new government was strong: when it levied taxes, it meant to collect them.

The third point in Hamilton's program was the establishment of the first Bank of the United States. This was to be the fiscal (financial) agent of the Treasury to help supply the nation with currency and to provide funds to lend to commerce and industry. Washington consulted his cabinet on the project and found them equally divided on the question. Jefferson opposed it because the Constitution gave no power to the Federal government to found a bank. Hamilton pointed out that the government had the power to borrow money, to coin money and regulate the value thereof, and to make all laws "necessary and proper" for carrying these powers into execution. A bank was necessary and proper to this end. This was the doctrine of implied powers. Because the bank lay in Hamilton's area of activity, Washington decided in his favor and signed the bill creating the Bank of the United States on February 25, 1791. Its capital was to be $10 million, one-fifth subscribed by the government. The bank was an enormous institution for its day. Other banks were fearful and jealous of it because it was so huge and had special privileges of serving the government. Its charter lasted for only twenty years and Jefferson, who never abandoned his suspicions of it, lived to see it fail to be rechartered. Nevertheless, the bank was a most valuable arm of the Treasury during its life and also helped to keep the other banks in the nation from overlending.

Federalist Influence of John Marshall. One of the last acts of President John Adams, the second and last Federalist party president, was to appoint John Marshall as new Chief Justice of the Supreme Court. Marshall held the office from 1801 to 1835 and exercised a strong influence toward increasing the authority of the central government. His decision in *Marbury v. Madison* in 1803 made it really clear for the first time that the Supreme Court might declare void an act of Congress that was in conflict with the Constitution. In other words, this established the custom of judicial review under the Constitution. In *McCulloch v. Maryland* (1819) Marshall wrote the decision that a state might not tax and destroy a Federal agency (a branch of the second Bank of the

United States). In *Gibbons v. Ogden* (1824) his decision underlined that only Congress, not the states, might enact laws regulating interstate commerce. These and other decisions all had the effect of strengthening the power of the Federal government. It was highly important that some branch of the government exert its influence in that direction if the Federal government were to survive, for after 1801 the Democratic-Republicans (the Democrats of today) under President Jefferson took power and they were then opposed to a strong central government.

Jefferson's Influence. Jefferson represented a desirable counterforce to Hamilton. Too much democracy had weakened the young nation in the 1780s. Similarly too much power in the hands of the aristocracy of wealth and intelligence which Hamilton favored might have produced a different America than that which finally emerged. Hamilton's influence was essential to launch the nation; Jefferson's was needed to keep it democratic. Whereas Hamilton distrusted the common man, Jefferson had implicit faith in him. Jefferson had grown up in a near-frontier community of sturdy pioneer folk and trusted their basic good sense. At this stage in America's growth, such people were numerous and they instinctively gave Jefferson their support. Jefferson wisely preached that education was vital to make democracy work. He contended that government is a natural enemy of man; therefore, its power at the top should be held to a minimum. Most governmental functions should be carried on at the state and local levels, within easy reach of the people. Thus he stressed a strict interpretation of the Constitution that would leave most government powers to the states. He also distrusted aristocrats and the creditor classes. He wanted the nation to remain agricultural and feared the growth of industry. Such views counterbalanced those of Hamilton's followers who wanted to foster the industrial growth which was beginning to take form. Yet Jefferson's beliefs could not serve as the basis for an industrial economy any more than Hamilton's would have been suitable on the expanding frontier.

THE WAR OF 1812 AND ECONOMIC INDEPENDENCE

The War of 1812, which was but an ancillary action to the Napoleonic Wars in Europe, placed the United States on the side of the Emperor Napoleon. It is nevertheless important in American economic history. The French Revolution began in 1789 with the fall of the Bastille and in January, 1793, the French guillotined their king and queen. Other monarchies, incensed by this treatment of royalty (most royal families were related), attacked France. The French ably defended themselves and in doing so produced a master strategist, Napoleon Bonaparte, who eventually made himself emperor. Although the British defeated his navy at Trafalgar in October, 1805, and thenceforth ruled the seas, Napoleon remained master on the Continent. His armies overran one nation after another, and he handed out kingships and other royal titles to his brothers and favorite marshals.

How could the war resolve itself, how could a sea power defeat a land power? The English declared a blockade of the Continent from the river Elbe in Germany to Brest in France in May, 1806, by an Order in Council. Napoleon retaliated in November with the Berlin Decree declaring England under a state of blockade. England countered with further Orders in Council in 1807 declaring all ports belonging to France and her colonies to be under blockade. Meanwhile the American merchant marine had been doing a thriving business, since the English and French were busy fighting and it was dangerous to ship goods under their flags. The tonnage of American ships engaged in foreign trade grew from 368,000 to 848,000 between 1793 and 1807. While England and France were fighting one another, the United States, the leading neutral, was running off with the prize. Especially was the United States gaining in trade from some South American countries which were seeking their independence from Spain. This aroused the jealousies of the English. The Orders in Council and the French Decrees made it more hazardous for American ships to sail to English or French ports. A French privateer might seize an American ship sailing to England, declare all its cargo contraband, and keep it. English privateers and vessels of war handed out similar treatment to those bound for France. Privateers and others working for the two belligerent powers seized some 1,600 American ships and $60 million of property. This was both costly and humiliating.

During this final conflict between England and France, American ships were unfairly seized by both European powers. In addition, the English often impressed sailors found on American ships, saying that they were English deserters, which sometimes they were. When the Federalist party was in power, the leaders made it appear that the French were the worse offenders, and in 1798 the United States had an undeclared sea war with France. Then the Democrats took office and tended to judge the English more harshly. After a number of serious provocations Congress passed the Embargo Act in December of 1807, forbidding American vessels loaded with cargo to leave American ports for a foreign one. It may be recalled that this manner of saying to England, "Behave yourself or we will stop trading with your merchants," had been tried three times before the Revolution, twice with success. Jefferson, being essentially a peaceful man, preferred to avoid war if he possibly could. The embargo proved, however, to be too strong a measure of self-denial on America's part. This time the English were not displeased to see American merchant ships withdraw from the scene. And American businessmen, who had been doing a thriving business despite some losses, were extremely annoyed at the Embargo Act. They soon complained that "grass has begun to grow upon the wharves." Congress relented and substituted the Nonintercourse Act of 1809, which cut off shipping trade only with England and France. Despite repeated efforts to reach an agreement with the English, seizures and impressments continued until American patience finally snapped. At least this was the explanation for many years, but it was not an accurate one.

The section which finally sought war was not New England, whose ships and men suffered the most indignities. Rather, it was the West, for another element had entered the picture. Congressmen from the South and West, like John C. Calhoun of South Carolina and Henry Clay of Kentucky, believed that in the event of war Canada could be plucked like a ripe plum and Florida could be taken as well. It was these men who voted for war, while New England congressmen opposed it unsuccessfully. Congress declared war on June 18, 1812.

It was the most paradoxical of wars. Allegedly fought to preserve the freedom of the seas for neutral shipping and to end impressment of sailors, it was least popular in maritime New England, which almost threatened to secede from the Union because of dislike of "Mr. Madison's War." Canada proved to be no ripe plum at all: the Canadians defeated American forces repeatedly. The greatest American victory, Andrew Jackson's defeat of the British at New Orleans, took place after peace had been signed. And the Treaty of Ghent contained no mention or concession by the British that they would no longer seize neutral shipping in wartime or impress sailors. What then did this second war against Great Britain accomplish?

The chief result of the War of 1812, from the American point of view, was that this country now gained its economic independence from Britain. Nearly nine years elapsed from the time of the Orders in Council and the Berlin Decree of 1806 through the Embargo Act, the Nonintercourse Act, to the end of the War of 1812 in December, 1814. A much-reduced supply of imports reached this country from England and from other parts of Europe during this period. To supply the market, American shops and mills and small factories appeared and prospered. The impediments to imports acted like a highly protective tariff and gave the new industries ample opportunity to build up their clientele, to improve their methods, and to become well established. As soon as the war ended, Congress put on a mildly protective tariff to provide the new industries with further protection. To a lesser degree Americans weaned themselves from dependence on English credit too. Finally, the second war against England welded the states into even more of a nation than had the Revolution, New England's dislike of the war notwithstanding.

SUMMARY OF PART ONE

The discovery and development of America shifted the center of European commercial activity from the Mediterranean Sea to the west coast of Europe. This was sometimes called the commercial revolution. America offered many attractions for colonization: it abounded in resources such as fish, furs, naval stores, and lumber, and there were vast stretches of arable land. The climate was pleasant and similar to that of Europe. The chief handicaps were the partial hostility of the American Indians and the great distance over a dangerous ocean to reach America. After hesitating for well over a century, England began to plant colonies, and continued to plant them, some sixteen in all, until 1732. At first Holland and then France established competing colonies, but the English eventually drove both of these rivals out of North America. Ironically, just at this point, the British colonies themselves tired of domination by England and declared their independence.

The economic model or plan which England and other nations of this era followed was later given the name of mercantilism. Its basic aim was to make the mother country strong and self-sufficient economically. To the degree that colonies played a part in this plan, they were to provide the mother country with raw materials that she lacked and with a market for her manufactured goods. Mercantilism contained many petty regulations, nearly all of them in the interests of the merchant class of the mother country. However, the great distance from England made it difficult for the English to enforce their mercantilistic rules. In general, mercantilism was successful to the degree that it required the colonies to do what was to their economic profit in any event. For example, mercantilism encouraged colonial agriculture.

From the time that there were a few dozen colonists in Virginia in 1607 until there were 2½ million colonials 170 years later, farming was the chief activity. Even the Indians were primarily farmers, and the many crops which they introduced to the colonists added much to the eating pleasure of the western world. Indian corn, squash, pumpkins, potatoes from South America, and tobacco for smoking were the chief items. The colonists, like the Indians, appeared to be rather sloppy farmers, but that was because fertile land was abundant and labor was very scarce; this was just the opposite condition from that prevailing in Europe. The colonists were farming primarily for themselves; to the extent that they had surpluses to offer, these were tobacco from the South, grain from the

Middle Colonies, and codfish from the North where people "farmed" the sea rather than the land. Of these the English wanted only tobacco.

Manufacturing in the colonies was hardly more than a step beyond agriculture; in fact, much that was called manufacturing was simply the processing of some farm crop or forest product, such as grinding grain into flour, making linen out of flax, or making potash, collecting naval stores, or fashioning barrel staves and ship timbers. On the whole, manufacturing was extractive and small scale. It was extractive because the colonists lacked the capital equipment and skilled labor to process their raw materials very far and therefore limited themselves to the first easy steps. They were merely skimming the cream off their rich new continent. Manufacturing was on a small scale because markets were small and often far away as well.

Most people stayed close to home except for a few trappers and traders, some businessmen, and soldiers in time of war. Transportation within the colonies was by water, by canoes and keelboats; between the colonies it was by sloops, schooners, and ships up and down the ocean which was at the front door of every colony. Because large settlements were few and people were busy, they constructed few roads and overland transportation was poorly developed.

Commerce was chiefly in the hands of the northern colonists who had ships because of their interest in fishing. Also, if they were to import the manufactured goods they desired from Britain, they had to sail far away to find markets for their fish and grain which the English would not accept. The northern colonists developed various triangular trade routes taking in the West Indies and Africa, or southern Europe and England, or the West Indies and Europe. Always it was with the view of selling their fish and grain, obtaining something that the English wanted, and then buying English manufactures. The Southern Colonies did not have such a complex problem, for they produced tobacco which the English would take in unlimited amounts. The kind of retail establishment most often seen was the general store.

The colonists complained continually that they lacked money. Pounds sterling were scarce; America was starved for capital and used every piece of money it obtained to buy more from Europe. To make up for their supposed lack of money, the colonists first used staple commodities; then they raised the value of the coins they received—the one most often seen being the Spanish dollar; and finally they began to print paper money. Most of the colonies experienced serious inflations as a result of issuing paper money. They probably would have been hurt even worse if England had not made strenuous and partially successful efforts to limit their paper money legislation, forbidding it in New England after 1751 and everywhere after 1764. Instead of being grateful, the colonists were resentful, attributing their difficulties to not enough money, whereas in reality they had too much, the inflations being proof of that. There were no commercial banks in colonial times; what short-term credit the colonial merchant got, he obtained usually from the exporting house that he did business with in England. Bills were generally payable about once every year or two.

If Britain had continued to govern the colonies with a loose rein, it might have kept them, but instead Parliament tried to enforce its mercantilist restrictions and to collect heavier taxes after the French and Indian War. Twice the colonies showed their displeasure by boycotting English merchants and England backed down, but the third time England did not retreat and the colonists rebelled. Britain had the difficult task of bringing the rebellious colonies under control again, and it failed. France, seeing its old enemy in difficulty, aided the colonies to win their freedom.

Even after the colonies had won their independence, they held together only in a loose and precarious union for several years. It was the conservative classes, fearing for the safety of their property, who finally managed to obtain a stronger central government under the Constitution, adopted in 1789. Three men, George Washington, first President, Alexander Hamilton, first Secretary of the Treasury, and John Marshall, Chief Justice, made the new Constitution work, and this led people in this country and overseas to respect the new republic. Even so, the United States remained agricultural and was still dependent on Britain for credit and for her manufactured goods. It was not until the time of the second war with England, the War of 1812, that the United States began to build up its own manufactures and to achieve economic independence to go along with its political independence.

PART TWO

An Era of Fundamental Economic Change

INTRODUCTION

For centuries the western world's economy had been primarily agricultural, varied by a little commerce and even less manufacturing. Although there was economic change from one century to the next, it was gradual; for example, if a person living in 1500 could have been transplanted forward to 1700 he would not have been unduly shocked and mystified by the new way of life that he found. Yet between 1790 and 1860 probably more profound changes took place than in any previous two centuries. Moreover, the rate of change was accelerating all the time.

There were a number of reasons for this transformation. People in the Northeast embarked upon the industrial revolution which Great Britain had first tried half a century earlier. Conditions were ripe for this technical and economic development, and it proceeded at a rapid pace. Simultaneously there took place also revolutions in transportation, agriculture, finance, commerce, and labor-management relations. The new factory system was characterized by greater specialization within the factory and greater output from the factory. Like the widening waves from a pebble dropped into a pool of water, the new factory system led to ever-greater specialization in all walks of life and thus to greater dependence of man upon his fellow man. To dispose of the increasing output of the factories, businessmen in the Northeast had to devise new methods of marketing.

As for the West, American pioneers had pierced the Appalachian wall and American diplomats had removed the restraining influence of major nations such as England, France, or Spain in the abundant land beyond. Within half a century these settlers planted and raised a new civilization.

The South underwent the least immediate change, in fact, the people resisted change so much that when adjustment came it was explosive. The economy remained not only agricultural but retained a labor system that characterized only backward parts of the world. The South sought first, unsuccessfully, to maintain political equality with the more progressive Northeast and West; failing in that, it seceded to escape outright domination. The rest of the nation was reluctant to permit its own dismemberment and the Civil War resulted.

CHAPTER 6

The Westward Movement

Nearly everyone has read of gold rushes or oil rushes which created boom towns in the space of months. And many persons have witnessed the mushroom growth of a town or some part of a city which happened to have an especially thriving industry. People flock into such boom communities like ants drawn to honey. Jerry-built housing and a degree of lawlessness are early characteristics of such places; if the industry lasts, then more permanent buildings and homes are erected and life in the community eventually becomes normal and orderly. The United States was a boom nation. With its millions of acres of fertile but largely untilled lands and its untapped timber, mineral, and other resources, it offered extraordinary opportunities between the Revolution and Civil War to millions of Americans and persons in overcrowded Europe as well. It was "manifest destiny" that this virgin territory should be subdued and that the vigorous people of the nation closest by should do it. The optimism, enthusiasm, and brash assurance with which these people went about their task were the spirit of the Westward Movement. They knew that nothing could stop their onward rush, nothing could prevent their building a great nation.

The statistical record of population and territorial growth reveals the magnitude of this movement. Within a period of eighty-five years the population increased from 2.5 to 31.5 million, or about thirteen times, and the territorial size of the United States grew from 393,152 to 3,022,387 square miles, or about eightfold. The existence of this vast territory made it inevitable that the population would increase; the increase in the population made it equally inevitable that they would occupy any vacant or thinly settled territory. The ease with which people might gain legal possession of their lands was also an important factor in the population growth and in its westward expansion.

TERRITORIAL GROWTH

The Nation Doubles Its Size. The thirteen rebellious colonies were all located on the Atlantic coast. Although some of them claimed lands from sea to sea, they had no settlements of consequence beyond the Appalachian mountains in 1775, the British government having forbidden these by the Proclamation of 1763. The approximately 400,000 square miles held by the United States at the start of the Revolution consisted of the present-day holdings of the thirteen original states, plus those of Vermont and Maine which were already somewhat settled, plus West Virginia which was then part of Virginia. As a result of the Treaty of Paris, concluding the American Revolution, the United States more than doubled its territorial holdings. Credit for this doubling goes to Colonel George Rogers Clark, who in the late winter of 1779 captured Vincennes, Indiana, the most significant fortified place between the Appalachians and the Mississippi River. Since the peace treaty was signed on a *status quo* basis, the United States kept what it held at the time—all the land north of Florida, south of Canada, and east of the Mississippi River. This doubled the size of the nation to 888,811 square miles.

The Nation Redoubles Its Size. The next great increase came in 1803 when the United States bought Louisiana, which redoubled the territory of the nation to 1,626,003 square miles. Louisiana encompassed all the lands lying between the Mississippi River and the crest of the Rocky Mountains except Texas; had the government wished, it might well have included Texas too. The story of the Louisiana Purchase is a dramatic one.

By the 1790s there were several hundred thousand persons living west of the Appalachians, but it was not easy for them to communicate with the eastern seaboard. The chief route west was the crude Wilderness Road, leading in a southwesterly direction down the Appalachian Mountain valleys and into Kentucky through the Cumberland Gap. The people living in Kentucky and Tennessee shipped their produce down the Ohio and Mississippi Rivers to New Orleans. That was the most effective way they had of reaching the outside world. Accordingly, they protested vigorously when the Spaniards, who owned Louisiana from 1783 to 1800, imposed tariffs on goods passing through New Orleans. When Congress paid slight heed to their complaints, they talked of seceding and setting up a nation of their own in the West. George Washington was much concerned and felt that better communication between East and West was vital to hold the nation together both economically and politically. From 1795 to 1802 the Spanish, by Pinckney's treaty, granted the Americans the "right of deposit," as it was called, at New Orleans. Because Spain was already a weak nation and not likely to withdraw this privilege, the arrangement was for the time acceptable.

However, France under Napoleon had taken over Spain, and Spain had secretly ceded Louisiana to France in 1800. The right of deposit was withdrawn late in 1802, and soon the secret was out that France owned

Louisiana. The western frontiersmen threatened to seize New Orleans by force. Even such a friend of France as Thomas Jefferson could see that a powerful France on the west would be a menace. He remarked that if Napoleon persisted, "we must marry ourselves to the British fleet and nation." Meanwhile Napoleon was becoming discouraged about Louisiana. He had hoped, in acquiring it, to restore the glories of France's once great colonial empire. But one of his best generals, with 10,000 men, had just been defeated in Santo Domingo by a brilliant Negro guerrilla leader, Toussaint L'Ouverture. Napoleon decided that if France could not control the island of Santo Domingo, it would have even greater difficulty doing anything with Louisiana. There was also the powerful English fleet standing between France and faraway Louisiana. When President Jefferson sent three envoys to France with authority to buy the island of New Orleans from Napoleon, Napoleon's minister, Talleyrand, asked them, "What would you give for all of Louisiana?" It was beyond their authority to buy so much, and such an expenditure to enhance the holdings of the Federal government was contrary to Jefferson's principles. Nevertheless, the Democrats made the most of this unexpected opportunity: the United States paid France $12 million in cash and assumed $4 million of claims of Americans against France.

The Nation Re-redoubles Its Size. The final expansion of the United States came in six major steps, all but one successful. These were: (1) the abortive attempt to take Canada in 1812; (2) the acquisition of Florida in 1819; (3) the annexation of Texas in 1845; (4) the settlement of the Oregon dispute in 1846; (5) the acquisition of California and other Mexican territories in 1848; and (6) the Gadsden Purchase in 1853. The total of these amounted to an increase of 1.4 million square miles which, on top of the 1.6 million square miles the nation already possessed, made a grand total of 3,022,387 square miles. During the century since 1853 the addition of Alaska and Hawaii represents the chief permanent boundary change. The main task has been peopling and developing the territories already acquired.

The support in Congress for the War of 1812 came from the West and the South, the areas least affected by seizure of neutral shipping and impressment of sailors. Already there were about a million persons living west of the Appalachians and, strange as it may seem, some of them felt "crowded." There was some basis for that: the Indians, incited in part by the British in Canada, made frequent forays on the western settlements. The most famous of these uprisings was quelled when General William Harrison defeated Tecumseh and his warriors at Tippecanoe in Indiana in 1811. Some young congressmen from the West, called the "War Hawks," advocated a war to drive the British from Canada. When war came, it did not work out that way. American military strategy was poorly devised, communications were difficult, the Canadians and British regulars fought valiantly, and this most imperialistic of all American wars was unsuccessful.

Several efforts to acquire Florida, especially eastern Florida, took place between 1803 and 1819. In 1818 General Andrew Jackson invaded Florida to punish the Seminole Indians who had been raiding settlements, and he captured and hanged two Englishmen who had been encouraging the Indians. Spain was annoyed but it also recognized the difficulty of holding on to Florida. In 1819 Spain negotiated a treaty ceding Florida for some $5 million and formally handed it over in 1821. Florida added some 58,560 square miles to the United States, and other areas acquired at the time added another 13,443 square miles.

Texas, the state of many flags, belonged to Spain when Americans first obtained permission to migrate there in 1820. Mexico shortly won its independence and then Texas was part of Mexico. In time the Mexican government began to fear the growth of several thriving American settlements in Texas. When it tried to enforce some unpopular Mexican laws, such as the one outlawing slavery, and also questioned American ownership of lands, the Texans rebelled and gained their independence in 1836. Texas next asked to be admitted to the United States, but several Northern states objected; this would increase Southern power in the Senate too much. About 1842 Americans began to fear that England had designs on Texas. In 1845 Congress admitted Texas to the Union but Mexico, which had always hoped to regain Texas, objected, and the Mexican War ensued in 1846. Victory confirmed the addition of 390,144 square miles of what was then Texas to the United States, a region as large as pre-World War II France and Germany.

During the 1840s Americans had also been moving into California. In 1845, while relations with Mexico were already uneasy, the United States sought to buy California and some other Mexican territories. The Mexicans refused to consider the offer. As soon as hostilities began, Americans in California took over in one settled area after another. After its defeat, Mexico not only gave up its claims on Texas but also ceded California, Nevada, Arizona, New Mexico, and parts of Utah, Colorado, and Wyoming. The Mexican Cession contained a total of 529,017 square miles, a region double the size of modern Texas but also quite arid.

Meanwhile, a long-standing dispute over the Oregon territory in the far Northwest was settled. Oregon then included what is now Washington, Oregon, Idaho, British Columbia, and parts of Alberta, Montana, and Wyoming. At one time Russia, Spain, England, and the United States all laid claim to the region, but in 1819 Spain gave up its rights and in 1824 Russia agreed that its claim did not extend south of latitude 54°40′. For a time England and the United States jointly ruled the unsettled region. In the late 1830s Americans began to move into Oregon. The United States suggested to the British that extending the 49th parallel to the Pacific would be a satisfactory boundary compromise. The British refused, for they wanted the area south to the Columbia River. Increased American interest led to a cry of "54°40′ or fight"—the United States was now asking for all of Oregon, too. In June of 1846 England suggested the 49th parallel as a compromise and the United States accepted, glad to settle the dispute peacefully because of the war with Mexico then in progress. This added another 285,580 square miles to the United States.

The last large piece of land added was the Gadsden Purchase, negotiated by James Gadsden, American minister to Mexico, in 1853. This 29,640 square mile area in what is now southern Arizona contained the best route for a much-discussed southern transcontinental railroad into California. President Santa Anna was in need of funds and the United States paid him $10 million for this territory. It was about half the size of the state of Illinois.

THE CREATION OF NEW STATES

The Ordinance of 1787. Placing so much new territory in the hands of the central government from 1781–1783 onward posed the problem of how to give the people living in it representation when it became settled. Would the government of the recently rebellious colonies soon have western colonies of its own? Or should new states be created, and if so, how? Should they enjoy equality with the older states?

The solution to this problem was one of the most far-reaching decisions that the Continental Congress made. Actually the directors of the Ohio Company of America, a New England land company, prepared the rules of government in the Northwest for the Congress and Congress wisely accepted them. The Ordinance of 1787 applied to the Old Northwest Territory, that is, the region west of the Appalachians, north of the Ohio River, and east of the Mississippi River. The ordinance provided that there be no less than three and no more than five states in this area, that temporary government be by agents of Congress until the number of adult males exceed 5,000, and that a province be permitted to apply for statehood when the population reached 60,000. It guaranteed the basic Anglo-Saxon rights of freedom. Once admitted to the Union, each new state was to have equal rights with all other states, except that slavery was forbidden in the Old Northwest. The five states of Ohio, Indiana, Illinois, Michigan, and Wisconsin, and a part of Minnesota eventually came out of this territory. Later, a similar Southwest Ordinance, without the slavery prohibition, provided for setting up new states in the Old Southwest, chiefly Alabama and Mississippi. (See Map 6-2A.) As a consequence of this legislation, the United States has taken its present form, with the possibility always of adding new states. It has avoided very largely the complaints from newly settled areas of "colonialism" and "taxation without representation."

Admission of New States. Between 1791 and 1859 twenty new states entered the union. Vermont, carved from upstate New York, was the first, admitted in 1791. Next came Kentucky (1792) and Tennessee (1796), the first states west of the Appalachian Mountains. Earlier they had been

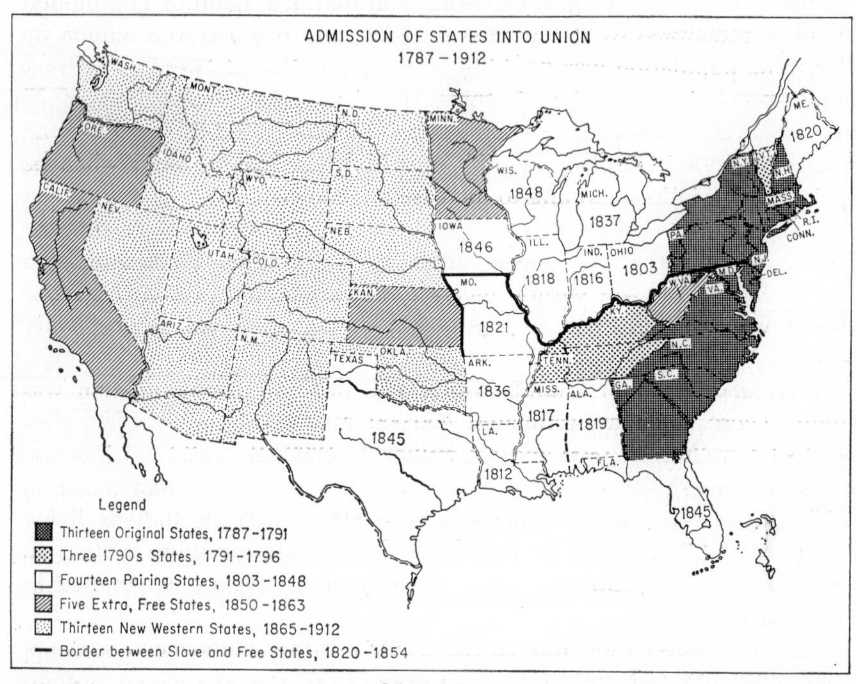

MAP 6-1.

looked upon as large western counties of Virginia and North Carolina, respectively. The first representative of the Northwest Territory was Ohio in 1803. Louisiana, already well-settled at the time of its purchase, especially around New Orleans, entered in 1812. Henceforth, up to 1848, the states entered in pairs, one Southern state and one Northern state. Indiana (1816) entered with Mississippi (1817); Illinois (1818) with Alabama (1819); and Maine (1820) with Missouri (1821). There followed a fifteen-year period during which the new regions became more settled. Then an era of internal improvements gave rise to heavy speculation in land and brought in two more states, Arkansas in 1836 and Michigan in 1837. Another period of quiescence followed, after which four states, Florida, Texas, Iowa, and Wisconsin, were admitted between 1845 and 1848. During the 1850s three more states, all free, however, came in, namely, California (1850), Minnesota (1858), and Oregon (1859). See Map 6-1.

POPULATION TRENDS, 1775–1860

The Increase in Population. The population of the thirteen colonies and their western settlements in 1775 was not far from 2.5 million. This had doubled to 5.3 million by 1800, more than doubled again to 11.3 million by 1825, redoubled to 23.3 million by 1850, and reached 31.5 million by 1860. The population was doubling every generation of twenty-five years (more precisely, every twenty-three years) or growing at a rate of 35 per cent every decade. It was the example of the United States which the English economist and divine, Thomas Malthus, had in mind when he spoke of populations tending to increase in geometric (1, 2, 4, 8) progression if not hampered by a lack of food. When reading the biographies of famous men of this era, one is struck by the number of families of a dozen children. It was natural increase that accounted primarily for this almost explosive growth in population; immigration was a secondary cause.

Racial and National Characteristics. The bulk of this population was white. There were an estimated 450,000 Negroes here in 1775; they reached 1 million in 1800 and 4.4 million in 1860: they did not increase quite as fast as the whites. Other racial groups were unimportant in 1860; there were 35,000 Chinese and 45,000 American Indians living among the whites. There were perhaps close to half a million Indians on reservations or beyond the frontier, but these could not be counted in the census.

The white population was on the whole a rather homogeneous group. They were predominantly Anglo-Saxon in origin, that is English, Scotch-Irish, or German, and predominantly Protestant in religion. This continued to be true until the Civil War except for the large inflow of Catholic Irish after 1846 because of the Irish potato famine.

Immigration. Immigration statistics were kept from 1820 on, but immigration was small in the 1820s and amounted to about 55,000 a year in the 1830s. After 1846 it averaged 260,000 a year, with close to 400,000 entering each year from 1850 to 1854. This inflow, which was huge relative to the population of that time, caused grave concern in some quarters and a sort of emotional panic in others. In the mid-1850s the *proportion* of the population that was foreign-born relative to that which was native-born was higher than at any other period in American history. A secret political party, the American or Know-Nothing party, was formed in 1849; its members agreed to vote only for native Americans and to demand a twenty-one-year probationary period before a foreigner might attain citizenship. When questioned about the party's aims, members were sworn to answer "I know nothing." By the middle 1850s it had become a third party of major importance. It did not, however, succeed in restricting immigration.

Nine out of ten of these immigrants came either from Great Britain or one of its dependencies, or from Germany. Of the others, about half came from France. Switzerland, the Scandinavian countries, and China each made a meager showing and no other nation's immigrants were important at all. Of the vast numbers coming from Great Britain, almost three-quarters were Irish. A blight struck the potato crop in Ireland first in 1846 and repeated its ravages in several of the following years. Since the potato was the chief food of the Irish peasants, many were forced to leave. Those who could manage to do so departed for America, selling their property, drawing on hoards that had been set aside for such an emergency, or borrowing from friends or from anyone who would lend. They poured into eastern port cities, especially Boston and New York, their funds exhausted, took the cheapest lodgings they could find, and offered their services for what they could get. Since their customs and religion were different and they worked for less than native Americans, they were often heartily disliked.

The Germans, only a little less numerous than the Irish, were driven to the New World by two forces. In the first place, many of them were also dependent on the lowly potato and blight destroyed their crops, too. On top of this, a political revolution in 1848 led many to feel that they would be safer and happier to leave Germany. Others left to avoid the compulsory military service that was now required in many of the German states. The English, and to a lesser degree the French also, came over to escape the changes in economic status imposed on them by the industrial revolution. For example, Andrew Carnegie's father was a hand-loom weaver, and when he could no longer compete with the power loom and make a living, he brought his family to America rather than work in a factory in Scotland. The lure of gold in California after 1849 likewise drew many immigrants to America. Finally, the possibility of owning a farm was an attraction to hundreds of thousands of Europeans who only rented land and had always dreamed of owning their own property.

The occupations of the 5½ million immigrants who came in between 1820 and 1860 are significant. Of those who reported their occupations, presumably the heads of families and single adults, 900,000 were laborers, 800,000 farmers, 400,000 mechanics, and 200,000 merchants. Other occupations numerous enough to mention were servants, miners, mariners, and weavers and spinners. Two-thirds of the immigrants were between fifteen and forty years of age and three-fifths were men. Immigration was a great help to the labor market, since such a large proportion were men in the most productive years of their lives, many of them already trained in some skill. If a value can be attached to them, as it was to slaves, the immigrant population should be valued at least as highly as the slaves. In fact, most observers agreed that free white labor was more efficient than slave labor. In this period 5½ million slaves would have been worth close to $3 billion.

Age. The United States was known as a young nation. The people were young as well as the nation, although one might not think so, looking at the bearded faces of the men and the untouched, often careworn faces of the women, who were frequently haggard by their forties from bearing large families and from household drudgery. The average age of an American in 1800 was sixteen, and by 1860 it was twenty; by the 1950s it was a trifle over thirty. In 1860 only about 4 per cent of the population were over sixty years of age and only 18 per cent were over forty; earlier those percentages had been smaller. The largest single segment of the population was children of fourteen and under (40 per cent). An average family had five to six members, and there were many exceptions on the high side. The second largest segment of the population was adults of fifteen to thirty (30 per cent). With 70 per cent of the people under thirty, it is small wonder that the people had tremendous youthful vitality, that they often attempted the seemingly impossible and sometimes succeeded, and that they were guilty of many acts of immaturity.

Urbanization. As population increased, some people moved westward and some moved into cities or helped build towns into cities. Although the Westward Movement was more dramatic, involving as it did pioneering and fighting Indians, and was very important before 1860, nevertheless, in the long run it was no more important than the growth of cities. A considerable degree of urbanization had taken place by 1860; 20 per cent of the population was urban (living in places of over 2,500) whereas in 1790 it had been only 5 per cent. In 1790 the largest city was New York with about 50,000, and there were only five places altogether of over 10,000 and only twenty-four of over 2,500. By 1860 New York had a population of 1,200,000 and small skyscrapers of seven stories. Philadelphia had half a million people, and Baltimore, Boston, New Orleans, Cincinnati, St. Louis, and Chicago, in descending order, all had over 100,000, and the number of urban centers had mushroomed to 392. Even some relatively new states such as California were surprisingly urbanized.

Diffusion. The density of population was about 6 per square mile in 1775 and it reached 11 by 1860, but the rise was not steady, since the country had increased almost eightfold in size. (See Maps 6-2A and 6-2B.) The density declined after the Treaty of 1783, then rose gradually,

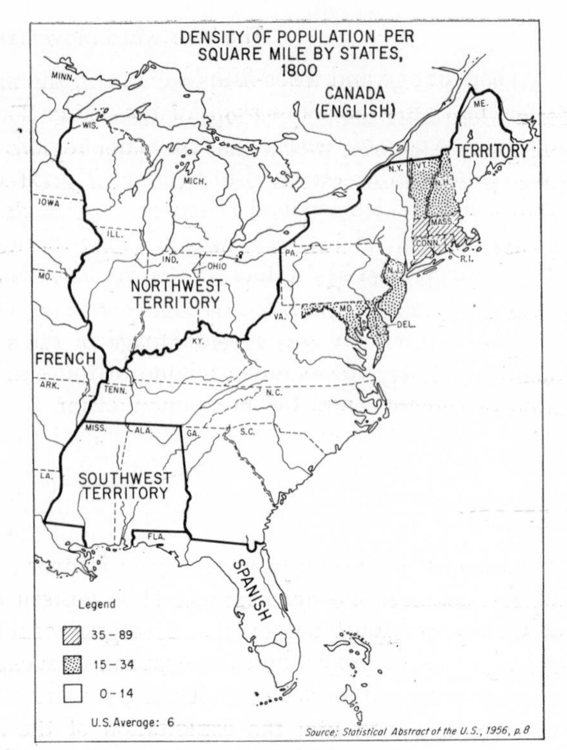

Map 6-2A.

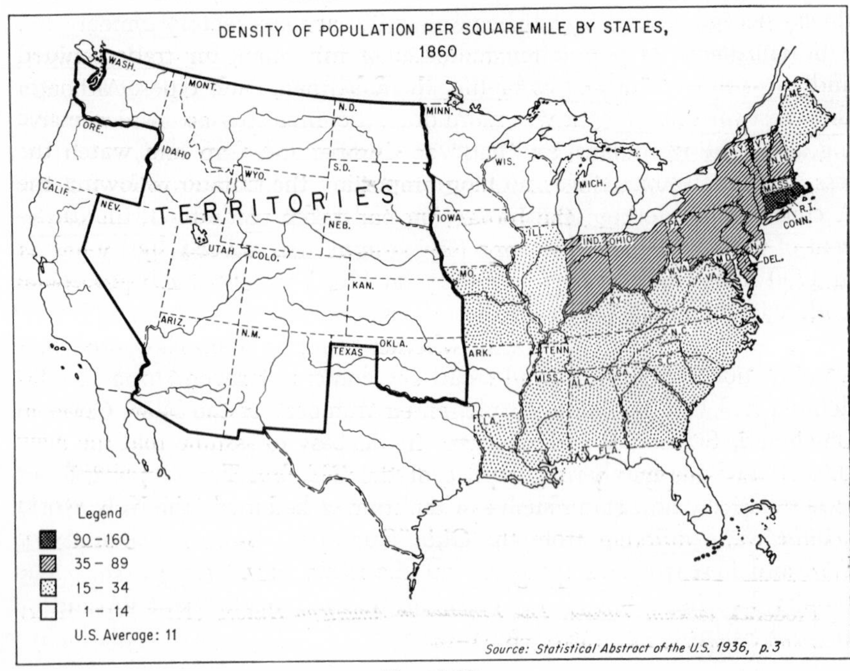

Map 6-2B.

declined again after the Louisiana Purchase, rose once more, and then declined again for a while after the acquisitions of 1845–1848. The additions of each of these great territories meant that the older regions to the east would spill their populations toward the west with greater ease and would themselves become urbanized less rapidly than might otherwise have been the case. This may well have handicapped the development of the nation from the short-range viewpoint. It may have caused fewer large markets, less adequate yet more costly transportation, fewer laborers and hence higher labor costs, less careful tillage of the soil because land was so plentiful, slower development of industries, and longer life for the institution of slavery. Diffusion of the population is synonymous with cheap land.

CIVILIZATION REBORN

Heredity or Environment. Frederick Jackson Turner, historian interpreter of American history, likened the development of a western community to a rebirth of society, a "social evolution." "It begins with the Indian and the hunter; it goes on to tell of the disintegration of savagery by the entrance of the trader, the pathfinder of civilization; we read the annals of the pastoral stage in ranch life; the exploitation of the soil by the raising of unrotated crops of corn and wheat in sparsely settled farming communities, the intensive culture of the denser farm settlement; and finally the manufacturing organization with city and factory system. . . . The Atlantic frontier was compounded of fisherman, fur trader, miner, cattle-raiser, and farmer. Excepting the fisherman, each type of industry was on the march toward the West. . . . Each passed in successive waves across the continent. Stand at Cumberland Gap and watch the procession of civilization marching singlefile—the buffalo following the trail to the salt springs, the Indian, the fur-trader and hunter, the cattle-raiser, the pioneer farmer—and the frontier has passed by. Stand at South Pass in the Rockies a century later and see the same procession with wider intervals between."[1]

The question is bound to arise whether the new civilization was more affected by the institutions and customs which it inherited from its Old World parent or by the uncultivated environment of the New World in which it developed. For a long time it was easy to assume that the New World was simply a young replica of the Old, but Turner pointed out that the environmental influence of the frontier had made the New World society quite different from the Old. "Our early history is the study of European germs developing in an American environment. . . . The

[1] Frederick Jackson Turner, *The Frontier in American History* (New York: Henry Holt and Company, Inc., 1920), pp. 11–12.

wilderness masters the colonist. . . . It strips off the garments of civilization and arrays him in the hunting shirt and moccasin. . . . Before long he has gone to planting Indian corn and plowing with a sharp stick: he shouts the war cry and takes the scalp in orthodox Indian fashion. In short, at the frontier the environment is at first too strong for the man. He must accept the conditions which it furnishes, or perish. . . . Little by little he transforms the wilderness but the outcome is not the old Europe, not simply the development of Germanic germs. . . . The fact is that

FIG. 6-1. A pioneer home in the wilderness. (*Courtesy of the Library of Congress.*)

here is a new product that is American."[2] The need to work hard to survive had caused successive generations of Americans to skimp on their education and culture; common dangers and shared privations made Americans more democratic, a steady stream of new situations made Americans ingenious and self-reliant, obvious opportunities made them a mercurial and optimistic folk, and the need to develop and fill up the country kept them forever on the move.

Three Stages of Settlement. The westward migration of the American people was an irregular and spasmodic movement. It was greater in the North than in the South, greater in prosperity than in depression, greater near navigable streams than away from them, greater in wooded areas than on the prairies. According to J. M. Peck, a writer of the time, the settlement of any locality took place in three fairly distinct stages.

[2] *Ibid.*, p. 4.

"Generally, in all the western settlements, three classes, like the waves of the ocean, have rolled one after the other. First comes the pioneer, who depends for the subsistence of his family chiefly upon the natural growth of vegetation, and the proceeds of hunting. His implements of agriculture are rude, chiefly of his own make, and his efforts directed mainly to a crop of corn and a 'truck patch.' . . . A log cabin, and occasionally a stable and corn-crib, and a field of a dozen acres, the timber girdled or 'deadened' and fenced, are enough for his occupancy. . . . The pre-emption law enables him to dispose of his cabin and corn field to the next class of emigrants; and to employ his own figure he . . . 'clears out for the New Purchase' . . . to work the same process over.

"The next class of emigrants purchase the lands, add field to field, clear out the roads, throw rough bridges over the streams, put up hewn log houses with glass windows and brick or stone chimneys, occasionally plant orchards, build mills, school-houses, court-houses, etc., and exhibit the pictures and forms of plain frugal, civilized life." The frontier shopping center of New Salem, Illinois, where Abraham Lincoln lived from the time he was twenty-one until he was twenty-seven, is an example of this. It had an inn, several stores, a cooper, blacksmith, hatmaker, wheelwright, two doctors, a sawmill and gristmill, and a carding mill. The town served the farmers within a radius of perhaps 20 miles.

"Another wave rolls on. The men of capital and enterprise come. The settler is ready to sell out and take advantage of the rise in property, push farther into the interior and become himself a man of capital and enterprise in turn. The small village rises to a spacious town or city, substantial edifices of brick, extensive fields, orchards, gardens, colleges and churches are seen." This happened to Cleveland and Chicago, for example.

"A portion of the first two classes remain stationary amidst the general movement, improve their habits and conditions, and rise in the scale of society."[3]

In the South the pattern was somewhat different and in the end less progressive. After the first wave of pioneers had cleared the land and built a few cabins, the plantation owner moved in. He was ineffective as a pioneer and so let the professional frontiersman do this heavy preparatory work. Thomas Dabney of Virginia was such a planter in 1835. As his lands had worn out he prospected for some new lands in Alabama and Mississippi, finally finding some to his liking in Hinds County, Mississippi. There he bought 4,000 acres from several small farmers, and moved south with his family, his wagons of equipment and household furnishings, and a retinue of slaves. Since the cotton planter was wont to

[3] J. M. Peck, *A New Guide for Emigrants to the West* (Boston: Gould, Kendall and Lincoln, 1837), pp. 119–121.

plant cotton year after year, cotton land tended to be somewhat exhausted within a generation. The really smart planter sold out while his plantation was still near the peak of its production, but not many were that smart. The hopeful buyer, the old planter, or the old planter's son then saw the soil wear out, the profits decline and the debts pile up, and the decadent plantation become a gaunt and shabby caricature of its former self.

Migrations Generally Short. When most American families decided to migrate, they moved only about 100 or 200 miles. The Superintendent of the Census reported in 1860, "In thirty States out of thirty-four it will be perceived that the native emigrants have chiefly preferred to locate in a State immediately adjacent to that of their birth." Thus Indiana was peopled chiefly by persons who began their lives in Ohio or Kentucky, and Illinois by persons from Indiana and Kentucky. Two of the four exceptions were Texas and California, and obviously these had to be settled from greater distances, by means of long overland treks.[4] It should be kept firmly in mind that the migrations to Texas, Oregon, Utah (not a state until 1896), and California in the pre-Civil War period were dramatic exceptions to the short migration rule. Much more typical was the migration of Tom Lincoln, father of Abraham Lincoln, and his family from Knob Creek, Kentucky, to Little Pigeon Creek, Indiana, to near Decatur, Illinois, to close to Charleston, Illinois. The early life of Abraham Lincoln is representative of that of the American pioneer.

FAR WESTERN SETTLEMENTS

Traveling to Oregon, Utah, or California necessitated crossing difficult arid stretches. Such a trip was usually made in a covered wagon, or "prairie schooner," and was to be undertaken no more lightly than an ocean voyage; in fact, the hardships were probably greater. Wagon trains were organized in early spring and set forth from such jumping-off places as Independence, Missouri, or Council Bluffs, Iowa, about the end of April, as soon as the grass became green on the prairies. They proceeded at a rate of about 15 to 20 miles a day, staying close to river beds for water, wood, and forage and making the passage over the hot and dangerous desert stretches between rivers as expeditiously as possible. Such a caravan might expect to reach California or Oregon in September or Utah in midsummer. (See Map 6-3.) It was the cheapest way to reach a Pacific coast destination.

[4] *Census of 1860—Population* (Washington, 1864), p. 35. The other two exceptions were Massachusetts getting most of its out-of-state migrants from Maine, and Ohio drawing its from Maryland.

Oregon. The first of the three regions to attract Americans in any numbers by the overland route was Oregon. The only vestige of civilization there in the 1820s was the trading post of the English Hudson's Bay Company at Fort Vancouver, presided over by the kindly but efficient Dr.

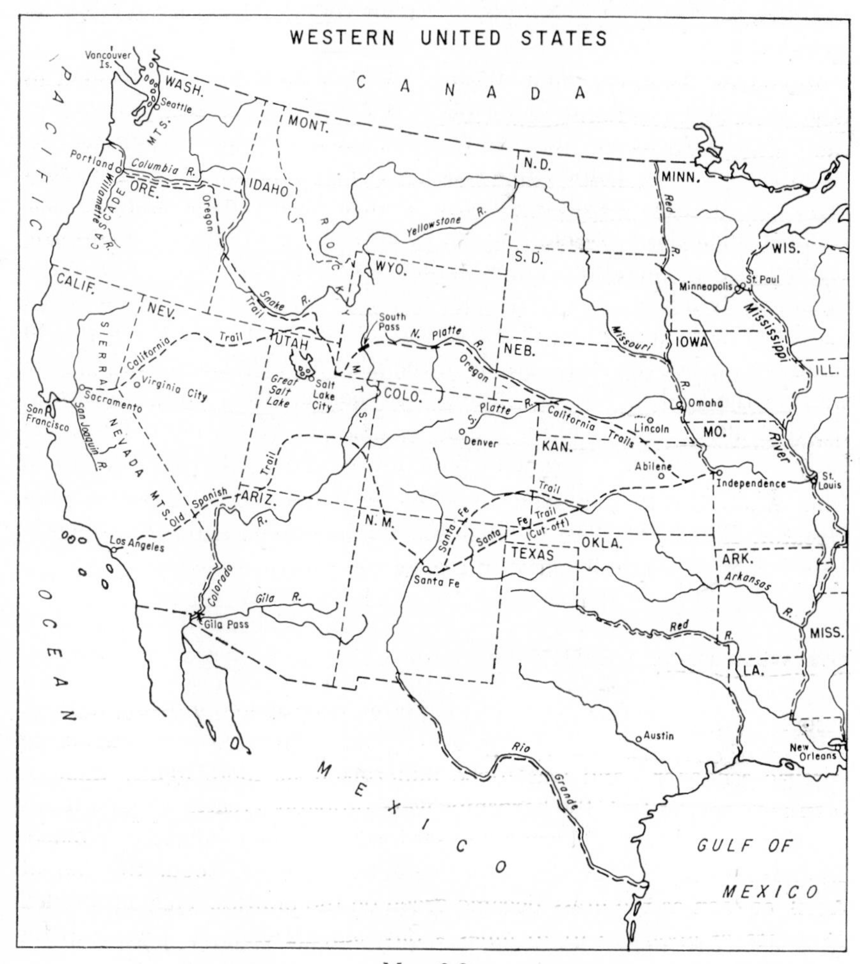

Map 6-3.

John McLoughlin. Fur trading was the chief occupation until the late 1830s. American public interest in Oregon began with an attempt by Hall J. Kelley, a Boston schoolmaster, to organize an expedition of emigrants in 1828 to this faraway territory, which he maintained belonged to the United States and not to England. The expedition did not materialize, but the publicity was a success. One result was that Nathaniel J. Wyeth, a shrewd Boston businessman, tried to break the Hudson Bay Company's monopoly but failed, partly owing to bad luck. The real entering wedge was made by missionaries. The progressive Flathead Indians sent word east that they wanted someone to teach them how to worship God, and the Methodist Church responded by sending out Jason Lee and his nephew, Daniel Lee. The Methodists settled up the Willamette Valley, however, far from the Flatheads, and their endeavors to Christianize the local but less advanced redskins were ineffectual. Their farming success, however, was considerable and attracted other Americans to that region. A second plea from the Flatheads was answered by the Presbyterian Church, which sent out Marcus Whitman and his wife. Their mission, located farther east, helped the Flatheads a little but they too devoted more attention to agriculture. Eventually a Catholic group led by Father DeSmet filled the Flatheads' needs; meanwhile, glowing accounts of the fertility of the general region found their way back east.

Emigrants might have come sooner and in larger numbers if Oregon had been more accessible. The discovery of South Pass in 1828 helped to some extent, but the steep ascent of the Blue Mountains and the canyon walls of the Snake River discouraged the pioneers from using wagons on the difficult Oregon Trail for a number of years. (See Map 6-3.) In the early 1840s emigrants began to pour into Oregon, 125 in 1842, 875 in 1843, 1,800 in 1844, and 3,000 in 1845. As noted previously, the United States took over that part of Oregon below the 49th parallel in 1846 and Britain kept the rest.

Utah. A little more than halfway to Oregon but not far from the Oregon Trail lay the Great Salt Lake, near which another outpost of civilization arose. This was the Mormon state of Deseret. The Mormon religion was conceived in 1829 in New York State by a youth named Joseph Smith. The religion took hold of people's imagination and the number of converts grew. First in Ohio, then in Missouri, next in Nauvoo, Illinois, the Mormons took up their abode, but they never stayed long for they were not popular. They believed they were destined to inherit the earth and some of them, it was said, undertook to inherit somewhat prematurely. When Joseph Smith himself was murdered, the Mormons determined to move far enough west to avoid religious persecution. An advance party under the new leader, Brigham Young, picked out an unprepossessing spot south of the Great Salt Lake and immediately set to work irrigating the soil and preparing for the main body of Mormons who came on later in 1847.

Under the energetic and efficient leadership of Brigham Young the community prospered. The settlement was a welcome halfway station for those traveling overland to California in 1849, and the Mormons acquired much valuable equipment in trade from the weary gold seekers. Next they began offering prizes for the discovery of coal and iron deposits and encouraged artisans from the outside world to come. Plain but effective announcements were sent out, such as "We want a company of potters; we need them. The clay is ready and the dishes wanted." Agents of the church contacted immigrants in England and Denmark as well as the eastern United States, helped arrange their passage to America, often lending them money for the trip, and assisting them at intermediate transfer points. To the miserable factory workers of England and Wales Mormonism promised an opportunity to "secure earthly prosperity and eternal salvation at one stroke." By 1859 there were twenty-eight settlements

FIG. 6-2. An early wagon train crossing the plains. The Rocky Mountains are in the background. (*Courtesy of the Library of Congress.*)

and 43,000 persons in Utah. Utah was not a scandalous polygamous settlement; it was probably the most efficiently developed colonization project in America's long history. But because public opinion was shocked at the thought of polygamy, Utah was admitted to the union (1896) only after it had abolished that practice.

California. California's history has been full of the romantic and unusual from the first Jesuit missions in the seventeenth century to present-day Hollywood. After 1822 California became a Mexican province famous for its huge cattle ranches; its ports were a source of hides and tallow to American trading ships. Overland emigration to California from Kansas and Missouri commenced in the spring of 1841 and by 1846 the parties were numerous; California's population reached 10,000. During the Mexican War Americans easily conquered California.

James Marshall found gold near Sutter's Fort (now Sacramento) early in 1848, and by the year's end an enthusiastic report on its abundance by California's Governor Mason had electrified the world. People of all walks of life came from the Eastern states, some by ship via Cape Horn or the Isthmus of Panama, others overland by "prairie schooner." From abroad flocked Germans, Frenchmen, Englishmen, Australians, and Chinese; it is estimated that 80,000 arrived in 1848 and 1849, and by 1852 the population reached 250,000. Nearly all were in a hurry to reach the gold fields, fearing they were just one ship too late. There was no scientific method of locating deposits; some miners worked all day with meager results while others "struck it rich" within a short while. Veins were found in the most improbable spots and nuggets were occasionally picked up under bushes. On the whole, the work was hot and tedious, the discomforts numerous, and the average pay for all men and all days amounted to little more than a living wage. Yet prices skyrocketed because of shortages of equipment and essentials for living. Miners paid as high as $15 for a pick, 50 cents for a loaf of bread, and $100 for good boots. Saloon proprietors and storekeepers made the real profits. Moreover, from a very early date California's population was urban, a large part being found in the four "S" towns of San Francisco, Sacramento, Stockton, and San José. Ever since the mid-century California has remained a magnet attracting people toward the west, but it has also, to some extent, been a point of origin for a lesser frontier moving eastward into Nevada and Arizona.

PUBLIC LAND POLICIES

Land Sales and Land Legislation before 1800. The great majority of people migrating to this country or moving westward were impelled by a deep desire to own their own land, for relatively few Europeans achieved the status of landowner. There was much land to be settled, and it was desirable that the settlement take place in as orderly a fashion as possible. This need for proper procedure is underlined by the fact that disputes over land titles were by far the largest category of law cases in court. In addition, the western lands were the chief asset of the impecunious Continental Congress, which sought a simple and not too costly way of marketing them. In 1785 Congress passed an ordinance providing for a system of rectangular surveys based on meridian lines in the western territories. Townships of 6 miles square were surveyed; each township contained thirty-six sections of 1 square mile or 640 acres. (See Fig. 6-3.) Land was to be sold at $1 an acre in minimum amounts of 640 acres, and after 1787, one-third was paid at time of sale and two-thirds within three months' time. Half the townships were to be sold as whole townships, the idea being that settlements would be concentrated, as in New England. In anticipation of sales the government laid out some of its first grants, called the Seven Ranges, along the Ohio River.

Congress's plans did not work out well. People did not want to settle in townships, the government did not get much income from land, and few persons had as much as $640 to pay virtually all at once for land; or at least they thought they knew less costly ways of gaining title to

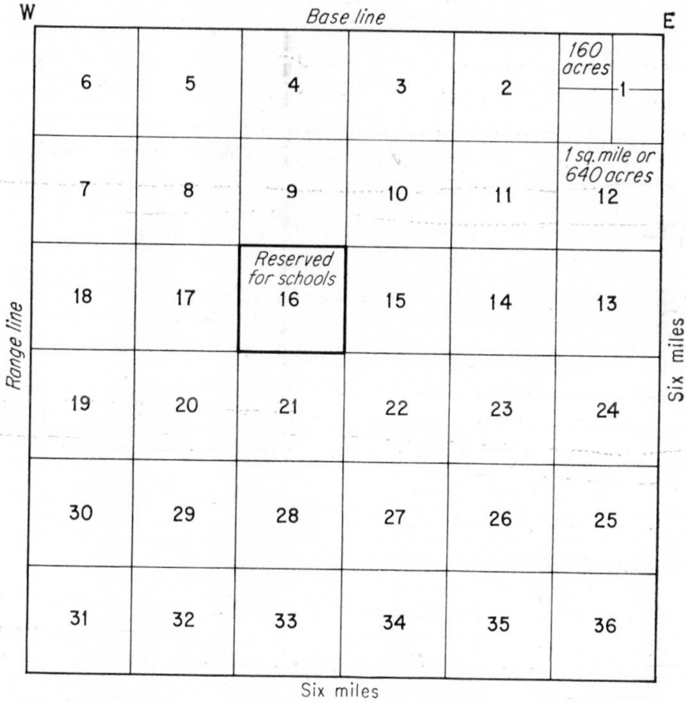

W — Base line — E

6	5	4	3	2	160 acres 1
7	8	9	10	11	1 sq. mile or 640 acres 12
18	17	Reserved for schools 16	15	14	13
19	20	21	22	23	24
30	29	28	27	26	25
31	32	33	34	35	36

Range line — Six miles — Six miles

FIG. 6-3. Survey of a township under the Ordinance of 1785. (*Drawn by D. L. Kemmerer.*)

land. Thus before 1800 government sales averaged only 100,000 acres a year, and there were many "squatters" on government land. The chief lands that were bought and settled were those belonging to various land companies which had bought in southern Ohio along the Ohio River, and lands in new states like Kentucky and Tennessee. These had not been ceded to the Federal government largely because title to them had been disposed of by Virginia and North Carolina after the close of the Revolution.

Land Sold on Credit, 1800–1820. The frontiersman, who was after all the customer, had a voice in drafting the Act of 1800. William Henry

Harrison, delegate from the Ohio Territory, introduced a new philosophy and several new features into the method of disposing of the public lands. The government was now to sell its land in minimum 320-acre blocks, it was to open up more local land offices, and most important, it was to offer more generous credit terms. The buyer was to make a down payment of one-quarter within forty days of sale, the second quarter within two years, and the balance in two annual installments. The minimum price was $2 an acre. Sales were on an auction basis, although anyone who had built a sawmill or gristmill on his land was entitled to buy it at the minimum price. This last was the first appearance of the preemption laws in public land policies. In 1804 Congress reduced the smallest-sized purchase to 160 acres and in 1817 it cut it again, under some circumstances, to 80 acres.

Granting long terms of credit, the most heralded feature of the Harrison Act, certainly increased sales of Federal lands; yet in the long run it was a failure. Frontiersmen were generally optimistic about the future of their locality and often with reason—Morris Birkbeck tells of land values rising ten to fifteenfold in twelve years in a representative Ohio village. Consequently, the new settler ventured most of his cash to purchase as large a tract as possible at the outset. Most settlers were, it should be realized, small-scale land speculators. When the time for later payments came, some could not raise enough cash to pay for all they had "bought." But it was difficult to evict them, and no neighbors wanted to bid in a fellow townsman's land. Thus from 1806 on Congress passed one relief act after another giving additional time or special terms to these debtors. Still the debts rose, especially in the hard times before the War of 1812. After the war began, the government accepted depreciated paper money in payment, but this just fed the fires of speculation. From 1812 onward sentiment grew in Congress in favor of cash sales. In 1817 payments in specie were required. Yet speculation kept mounting until the Panic of 1819. By 1820 private persons owed the government $21 million for land, and the pressure for relief, especially in Alabama and Mississippi where over half the debt lay, was heavy. Between 1821 and 1832, through a series of acts offering special terms to landholders, this debt was liquidated, and the government took back some 4.6 million acres for which people had not been able to pay.

Land Sold on a Cash Basis, 1820 on. The necessity for selling public lands on a cash basis was obvious. Also the sentiment was growing that land should be made available to the growing segment of the population living beyond the Appalachian Mountains. This was despite increasing opposition in the East, which looked upon cheap land in the West as a cause of rising wages. In the East industrialization was making more persons wage-conscious. This aspect of the debate was destined to continue for years. In 1820 Congress overhauled the basic Federal land act and provided that henceforth land should be sold for cash only, with a price minimum of $1.25 an acre and a tract minimum of 80 acres. In 1832 the tract minimum was reduced to 40 acres, so that now a pioneer with $50 could buy a modest homestead. Although land was still auctioned, the minimum price was not often exceeded; the average price of land from 1823 to 1837 was $1.31. For a long time only the most choice lands sold for $1.25, which suggests the price was none too low.[5]

The Preemption Laws. From the outset settlers had gone west far in advance of the surveyors and land offices, squatted on government land, cleared fields, built cabins, and made local improvements. Some did this for their own convenience and expected to remain on the land they had improved; others expected to sell the improved land at a profit to later arrivals. A Federal law in 1807 authorized the dispossession of such squatters, but it was not vigorously enforced, especially after 1814. As time passed, the contributions of the squatters to opening the West came to be more and more appreciated. Or looked at another way, it was manifestly unjust to permit some recently arrived speculator with cash to buy up the improved lands of a long-established squatter when the land office opened. Admittedly, the squatters did not often permit this to happen. They formed "claim clubs," appeared in force at auctions, and sometimes displayed ropes to would-be buyers of improved lands in a manner that was unmistakable. But this too, although understandable enough, could and sometimes did lead to excesses; a better solution was called for.

In 1828 the Public Lands Committee of the House reported, "It is right and proper that the first settlers, who have made roads and bridges over the public lands at their own expense and with great labor and toil, should be allowed a privilege greater than other purchasers." Several state legislatures and numerous petitions asked that squatters be permitted to buy their lands at the minimum price whenever a land office opened in any region. This became temporarily the law in 1830, was re-enacted in 1834 and again in 1838 in a modified form, and was finally made general and permanent in 1841 (see Table 6-1).

The preemption law was sometimes called a disguised form of selling land on credit. Since the squatter was often several years ahead of the land office, by the time the land office opened he had enough profit from the land to be able to pay for it. This merely demonstrated that Congress had discovered a better way of granting credit to the pioneer.

Agitation for a Homestead Act. As time passed, Congress was increasingly inclined to favor legislation that would get the lands into the hands of settlers in an equitable and orderly fashion. In the 1840s a growing

[5] Benjamin H. Hibbard, *A History of Public Land Policies* (New York: The Macmillan Company, 1924), p. 154.

demand developed to give the land to would-be settlers. Opponents of slavery saw in small homesteads a device to stop the spread of slavery, which required large blocks of land to work most profitably. Southern legislators opposed a homestead law for this reason. Champions of the workingman, like the land reformer George Henry Evans, saw in it a way

Table 6-1

Major Legislation Affecting the Disposition of the Public Lands, 1785–1862

Year and title	Minimum and maximum acreage	Minimum price	Purchase terms
Ordinance of 1785	640—no maximum	$1.00	Cash; after 1787, one-third down, balance in 3 months
1796	640—no maximum	$2.00	One-half in 30 days; balance within one year
Harrison Act of 1800	320—no maximum	$2.00	One-fourth in 40 days, one-fourth in 2 years, one-fourth in 3 years, final one-fourth in 4 years
1804	160—no maximum	$2.00 (credit) $1.64 (cash)	Credit as in 1800
1817	80—no maximum	$2.00 (credit) $1.64 (cash)	Credit as in 1800
Cash Sales Act of 1820	80—no maximum	$1.25	Cash after auctioning
1830	80—160	$1.25	Cash; preemption basis on maximum of 160 acres
1832	40—160	$1.25	Cash; preemption as in 1830
1834, 1838	40—160	$1.25	Cash; preemption as in 1830
Preemption Act of 1841	40—160	$1.25	Cash; preemption as in 1830
Graduation Act of 1854	40—no maximum	$0.12½	Price graduated downward to $1.00 for land unsold for 10 years; to $0.12½ for land unsold 30 years
Homestead Act of 1862	160 only	Free	Filing fee of $10 and 5 years' occupancy

SOURCE: Benjamin H. Hibbard, *A History of the Public Land Policies* (New York: The Macmillan Company, 1924), *passim.*

to counteract the centralizing effects of the industrial revolution. Still others saw in free homesteads a way of raising wages—if a worker did not get enough, he could always go West and work on his homestead for himself. Some Eastern legislators, such as Daniel Webster, saw in cheap lands a threat to wage scales in Eastern factory towns. Among the leading members of Congress favoring a homestead law were Thomas Hart Benton, senator from Missouri and close friend of President Jackson, and

Congressman Andrew Johnson of Tennessee, who became President in 1865 after Lincoln was assassinated. As long as the planter South opposed homesteads, the law had no chance of passage: it was not enacted until after the Civil War began. Partly as a makeshift in 1854, Senator Benton sponsored the Graduation Act, which made available at bargain prices lands that had been on the market for many years and were still unsold. The cut prices ranged downward from $1 an acre for land that had been available for ten years to 12½ cents an acrea for land that had been available for thirty or more years. There was no maximum limit on the amount a person might buy. Land sales rose sharply as a result of this act; land sold under it at an average of 32 cents an acre.

Despite the argument in favor of cheap land as an alternative way of life which would enable any employee to force his employer to raise wages to hold him, this was not the way things worked by the 1840s. Most of the industrial laborers worked in eastern villages, towns, and cities, whereas most of the cheap land was 1,000 or more miles away, near or beyond the Mississippi River. Iowa entered the Union in 1846, Wisconsin in 1848. To farm this frontier land required a collection of skills and half skills and a willingness "to live alone and like it" that an Eastern factory worker and his family were not likely to possess. Besides it took some capital to move all that distance and to go into farming even in a simple way. In short, from this time on, cheap land had less and less influence on industrial wages.

CHAPTER 7

The Transportation Revolution

The technical advances of the eighteenth century, such as new ways of using steam power, brought about changes in industrial methods which in turn wrought even greater changes in American economic and social life. The industrial revolution signified the coming of the factory system, but it was accompanied by an agricultural revolution, which made it possible to feed the factory worker. There was also a transportation revolution, which made it possible to bring in raw materials from afar and to distribute the finished products over ever-widening markets. Then there were revolutions in finance, labor, and commerce, too, which are just beginning to be discussed in those terms.

Which of these revolutions came first? The standard answer, and probably the best, is that they all came at about the same time. Without improvements in transportation, permitting the better marketing of goods, the industrial revolution could not have gone far; contrariwise, without factory goods and farm products to carry, transportation improvements would not have paid for themselves. Yet, if preference had to be allocated to some one of these developments, it might well go to transportation. England in Europe, and Japan in Asia, were the first to industrialize: both were blessed by nature with excellent transportation facilities in the form of the nearby ocean. The improvements in transportation in this country around 1800 are more striking than those in industry; contrast developments in turnpikes and early canals with a few thread factories.

The changes in transportation fall into three categories: first, those involving more efficient use of water; second, those involving more efficient use of land routes; and third, those involving air, the last not coming until after the 1930s. The oldest is water; in this case, nature provided the roadbed and man had only to supply and propel the vessel. Most of the early improvements in transportation were in canals, steamboats, and ships. However, an exception must be noted in the case or turnpikes.

TURNPIKES

One of the significant developments late in the colonial period was greater use of pack trains of horses for transporting goods. A logical next step was improved roads and greater use of wagons. In an age when capital was scarce, either the government had to pay for better roads or some new ingenious financing device had to be found. Businessmen used the corporate device to collect the initial capital to construct roads. These were put on a toll basis to reward the corporate investors.

The first important turnpike ran from the port of Philadelphia to the fair-sized town of Lancaster, lying 60 miles west along the Conestoga River in a prosperous agricultural region. The opportunities for trade between a commercial and industrial town and an agricultural region were obvious. Work was begun in 1792 and the road was opened to traffic in 1794. The next year a stagecoach company offered twelve-hour service nightly. Much of the traffic on the road, however, was Conestoga wagons, which were the trucks of this era. The Lancaster Pike was such a great success that it was widely imitated: seventy-two turnpike corporations were established before 1800.

President Washington in the 1790s and Jefferson's Secretary of the Treasury, Albert Gallatin, a decade later, both urged better lines of transportation, especially between the east coast and the regions beyond the Appalachians. In 1808 Gallatin proposed an ambitious four-part program by which the Federal government would construct: (1) several north-south canals between Massachusetts and Georgia to give coastal vessels protected passage; (2) four highways connecting the upper waters of Atlantic coast and Middle Western rivers; (3) a series of canals connecting the Hudson River, the St. Lawrence River, and the Great Lakes; and (4) a network of interior roads and canals. He thought the government could accomplish the whole program for $20 million and urged Congress to appropriate $50,000 immediately for a survey. The program was widely discussed and Jefferson believed it was unconstitutional. Although the War of 1812 ended the debate, subsequent developments showed how farsighted Gallatin was. Either public or private organizations eventually carried through in a piecemeal fashion much of his elaborate program.

One of its most important features was the trans-Appalachian highways. As early as 1802 Congress granted Ohio 5 per cent of the proceeds of all Federal lands sold within the state to build roads. It was subsequently decided that 2 of this 5 per cent would go to build a road over the mountains from a suitable starting place on an east coast river. Ohio chose Cumberland, Maryland, on the upper Potomac River, as the place.

Construction began in 1811 but little was accomplished immediately. Then the War of 1812, in which American forces were repeatedly defeated in the West, partly for lack of supplies, demonstrated the need of better communication with the East.

The Cumberland Road, as it was called, was completed to Wheeling, Virginia, in 1818 at a cost of about $13,000 per mile. This was the first improved communication completed from the east coast to the new West. It was basically a gigantic portage trail from the highest point of navigation on the Potomac River, which was Cumberland, over the Appalachians in southwest Pennsylvania to a fort town, Wheeling, on the Ohio River.[1] At this point much of the freight coming from the East took to water again and went down the Ohio on flatboats. In the mid-1820s Ohio extended the road farther across Ohio to Zanesville, and then on to Columbus in 1833. Still later, after 1838, it was built across Indiana and it finally ended at Vandalia, previously the capital of Illinois, about 1850. How rough this road was in its early days may be gauged from specifications for construction in 1829, stating that in the central 30 feet of the road all trees over 18 inches in diameter should be cut to within 15 inches of the ground. Nevertheless, the roadbed was steadily improved, and from an early date a large amount of traffic flowed over it, especially over the eastern section. Conestoga wagons, stagecoaches, private carriages, people on horseback, and flocks of hogs or sheep made up the busy traffic.

The turnpike period came to an end with the Panic of 1837. It might have been more intensive if the Democratic leaders in the Federal government had not been fearful of infringing on states' rights by too great activity in promoting internal improvements. When the second Bank of the United States paid a bonus for its charter, President Madison vetoed a bill in 1817 to use the money to carry out internal improvements. President Monroe also vetoed a bill for the collection of tolls on the Cumberland Road in 1822, which made it necessary to turn over parts of the road to the states to operate and maintain. And in 1830 President Jackson likewise vetoed a bill authorizing the Federal government to subscribe to stock to build a toll road starting at Maysville, Kentucky. The road was entirely within the state of Kentucky and had no particular connection with any national system of roads. This was Jackson's response to the "American System" (see "The Tariff Controversy," Chap. 14) program of his rival, Henry Clay of Kentucky, who had proposed, in part, to bind the East and West with numerous federally supported "internal improvements." These vetoes took the Federal

[1] This road did *not* go through the Cumberland Gap, which lies some 300 miles to the south at the junction of Virginia, Kentucky, and Tennessee. Daniel Boone's Wilderness Road entered the West via the Cumberland Gap.

government out of further road building. Meanwhile, several states were showing greater interest in canals and some even in railways.

CANALS

Extensive use of rivers led next to building canals around falls, rapids, or other obstructions. This in turn caused the building of longer canals, virtually artificial rivers, connecting two important bodies of water. An early canal of this sort, one on which the first canal builders learned by experience, was the Middlesex Canal, completed in 1803. It connected Boston and the Merrimac River flowing southeast from New Hampshire so that boats from that river would not have to venture out to sea to reach Boston.

The Erie Canal. The public really focused its attention on canals, however, when the Erie Canal project got under way in 1817. Parts of it were such an obvious success even before the whole was completed that people in other states talked of building canals, too. The state of New York financed the Erie Canal: the Federal government would not construct an internal improvement within a state, and the canal was too grandiose for private financing. The man who worked endlessly to further the project and finally made it a political reality was DeWitt Clinton, who became governor while it was under construction. The canal began at the mouth of the Mohawk River, which empties into the Hudson River near Albany, 150 miles above New York. It ran along the sea-level trough which breaks through the Appalachian range at this point, to Buffalo, 362 miles to the west, on the shores of Lake Erie. The initial justification for the canal was not so much to reach the Great Lakes area, which was largely unsettled at this time, but rather to tap the fine agricultural region of the Mohawk Valley and beyond. Even so, the promoters might well have let the canal terminate at Lake Ontario, which was certainly handier, if they had not been thinking of the future. Lake trade would have to get around Niagara Falls (between Lakes Erie and Ontario) to reach Lake Ontario. More important, ships that had come that far east would very likely continue down the St. Lawrence and do business in Montreal, New York City's rival. Thus it was essential to divert this traffic toward New York City at a point farther west, namely, Buffalo. The merchants of New York had a keen "mercantilistic" interest in the project, for they gave far more attention to imports than to exports. They hoped to sell more of their imported merchandise in the hitherto inaccessible markets of upstate New York.

The original canal was a success, both as a state project and as a very valuable transportation system. The project cost $7 million, the announced cost, it was finished on time, and it made a profit: few govern-

FIG. 7-1. The Erie Canal at Lockport, N.Y., in 1836. Notice series of locks on right and teams of horses towing canal boat in lower right corner. (*Courtesy of the Library of Congress.*)

ment projects can boast such a record. Whereas before the canal existed it cost $100 to move a ton of freight, partly by wagon, from Buffalo to New York and took twenty days' time, now it cost only $10 and took but eight days' time. Admittedly, canal boats and barges, towed by horses or mules, and moving only 2 to 3 miles an hour, still left much to be desired in the way of speed (see Fig. 7-1). But the canal did much to open up central New York State. Some villages and towns along the route like Schenectady, Utica, Rome, Syracuse, and Rochester grew very rapidly in the next twenty years. By the 1830s and 1840s the effects of the Erie Canal were felt still farther west, along the shores of the Great Lakes, as towns like Cleveland, Toledo, Detroit, and Chicago grew into cities too.

Feeder Canals. Regions and states bordering on the Erie Canal system early sought to tie into this highly successful transportation network. New York State opened a canal connecting the Hudson River and Lake Champlain in 1822. This was the most-used route of trade between the United States and Canada. Ohio constructed two north-south canal systems. The Ohio and Erie Canal in the eastern part of the state connected Cleveland on Lake Erie with Portsmouth on the Ohio River. Opened in 1833, it enjoyed a small degree of success for a time. A second canal, the Miami and Erie, opened ten years later, ran from Toledo in the north to Cincinnati on the Ohio River, and chiefly served local needs. A third system, the Wabash and Erie, was set up by Indiana and made some use of the Wabash River. It connected with Toledo, Ohio, in the north and had Evansville on the Ohio as its southern terminus. Still a fourth system, the Illinois-Michigan Canal, was completed in 1848, connecting Chicago on Lake Michigan with the headwaters of the Illinois River at LaSalle (see Map 7-1). None of these western canals was profitable from a purely business point of view. Indiana and western Ohio especially were not yet ready for such costly and intricate systems: they were still sparsely settled frontier regions. Yet despite their shortcomings these canals, working in conjunction with the Erie Canal, probably aided materially in developing the region between the Ohio River and the Great Lakes and thus in feeding traffic into the original Erie Canal. In the 1830s the Erie Canal began to attract toward New York traffic that formerly went south via New Orleans to the outside world.

Rival Canals. Even before construction began on the Erie Canal, New York was the most important east coast port: the success of the Erie Canal put it even further in the lead. Merchants in other east coast cities did not accept this without a struggle. The Philadelphians, for example, came forth with a system which was very ingenious, considering the geographical obstacles to be overcome, but not very practical. Pennsylvania, unlike New York, had no low-level trough cutting through the

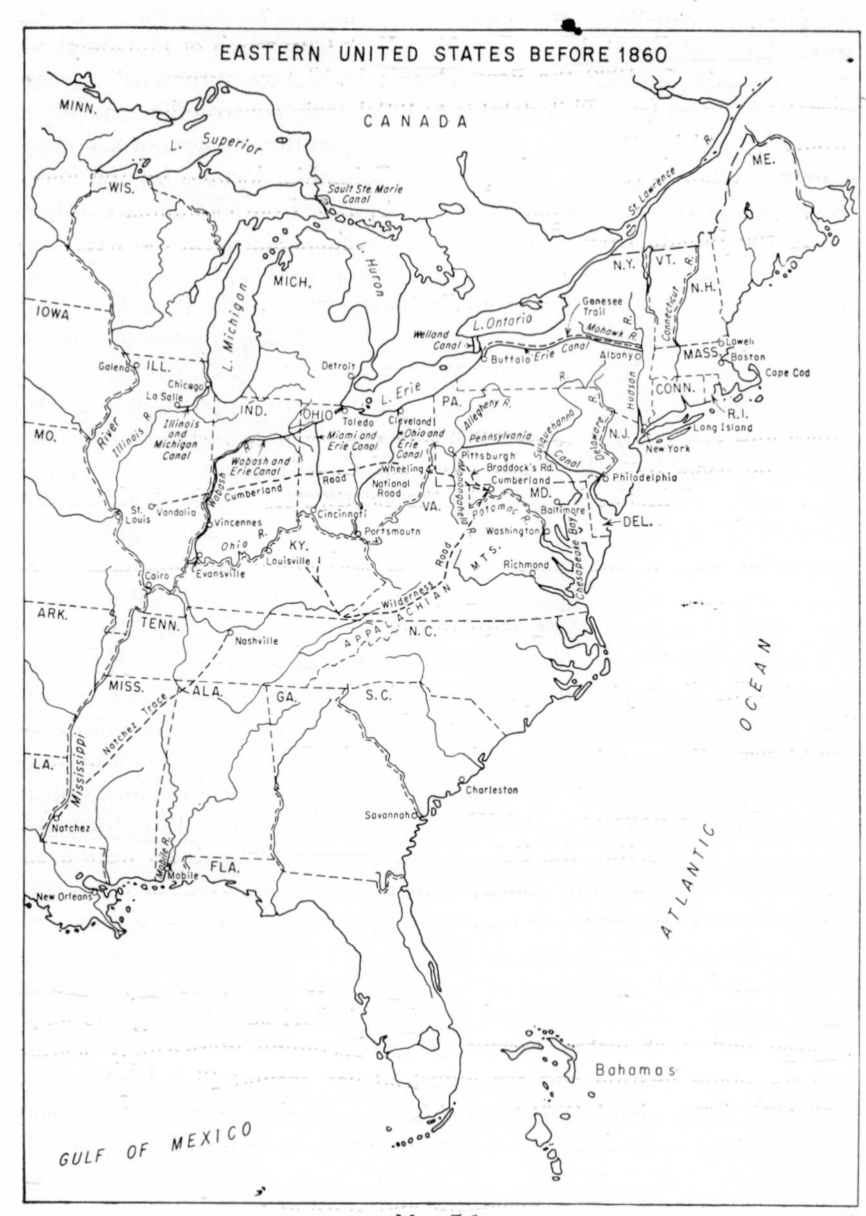
EASTERN UNITED STATES BEFORE 1860
CANADA
MINN.
L. Superior
WIS.
Sault Ste. Marie Canal
L. Huron
MICH.
L. Michigan
IOWA
ILL.
Galena
Chicago
La Salle
Illinois and Michigan Canal
Illinois R.
River
MO.
IND.
OHIO
Detroit
L. Erie
Toledo
Cleveland
Miami and Erie Canal
Ohio and Erie Canal
Wabash and Erie Canal
Wabash R.
Cumberland
Road
National Road
Wheeling
St. Louis
Vandalia
Vincennes
Cincinnati
Portsmouth
Ohio R.
KY.
Louisville
Evansville
Cairo
L. Ontario
Welland Canal
Buffalo
Erie Canal
Genesee Trail
Mohawk R.
Albany
N.Y.
St. Lawrence R.
VT.
N.H.
ME.
Connecticut R.
MASS.
Lowell
Boston
Cape Cod
CONN.
R.I.
Long Island
New York
N.J.
Hudson R.
Delaware R.
Susquehanna R.
PA.
Allegheny R.
Pennsylvania Canal
Pittsburgh
Braddock's Rd.
Cumberland
Monongahela R.
Potomac R.
MD.
Baltimore
Philadelphia
DEL.
Washington
VA.
Richmond
Chesapeake Bay
MTS.
APPALACHIAN
Wilderness Road
ARK.
TENN.
Nashville
N.C.
MISS.
ALA.
GA.
S.C.
Natchez Trace
Mississippi
LA.
Natchez
Charleston
Savannah
Mobile R.
Mobile
FLA.
New Orleans
ATLANTIC OCEAN
Bahamas
GULF OF MEXICO

MAP 7-1.

Allegheny Mountains. Yet Pennsylvania had to do something or else watch the Erie Canal draw off to New York City much of Philadelphia's western trade. In 1826 the Pennsylvania legislature authorized a transportation system from Philadelphia to Pittsburgh; construction was begun promptly, and by 1834 the system was in operation. It was, of necessity, a hybrid affair. From Philadelphia to Columbia, located on the lower Susquehanna River, transportation was by rail; from Columbia north, to where the Juniata River flows into the Susquehanna from the west, and some distance west on the Juniata as well, a canal was the mode of transport. But the boats and goods finally had to go over the mountains, and to accomplish this the canal engineers devised an intricate system of inclined planes. They used divisible canal boats, each part of which could be fastened into a cradle on wheels. They hauled these cars by cables and stationary engines up a series of inclined planes to the summit, some 2,000 feet above sea level, and then lowered them down another series of inclined planes to the headwaters of the Kiskiminetas River on the western side. There they reassembled the canal boats, which proceeded west to the Allegheny River and finally to Pittsburgh (see Map 7-1). So much engineering gadgetry was costly and the system had a hard time competing with the Erie Canal. Eventually the Pennsylvania Railroad took it over when that was sufficiently developed to do the job. The Pennsylvania system was further handicapped by the fact that other parts of the state wanted the state to pay for branches that would serve them and connect them with the "main line." All that augmented the cost of the program and contributed to its ultimate collapse.

The efforts of Baltimore and Washington to build the Chesapeake and Ohio Canal connecting the Potomac and several Ohio rivers were even less successful because of construction problems and right-of-way suits. The canal was completed to Cumberland, Maryland, but never got over the mountains.

Profitable Canals. Aside from the original Erie Canal, the only successful canals were some of the coal canals and short ones linking two long or large bodies of water. Firewood was becoming increasingly scarce both for home heating and for industrial use around Philadelphia and New York. From about 1820 onward increasing reliance was put on coal, most of which came from the anthracite fields of eastern Pennsylvania, especially the very famous one at Mauch Chunk. One of the successful anthracite canals was the Delaware and Raritan Canal, across central New Jersey, from Bordentown on the west to New Brunswick on the Raritan and thence accessible to New York. There were three outstanding examples of profitable short canals. One was at Louisville, Kentucky, around the falls of the Ohio, which interrupt navigation there except during high water. The second was the Welland Canal, a Canadian project around Niagara Falls, opened in 1830. And the third was the Sault Ste. Marie Canal connecting Lake Superior and Lake Huron. It was first opened in June, 1855, and was absolutely essential if iron ore were to be brought east from the recently opened Marquette range.

Canals suffered from serious handicaps in an age when fast, direct, year-round transportation was becoming increasingly essential. Canal boats could not easily cross mountains, traffic through locks was bound to be slow, and canals were generally frozen several months a year. With the coming of railroads, the days of canal and river transportation as the chief mode of transportation were numbered.

RIVER STEAMBOATS

Invention of the Steamboat. Robert Fulton is widely credited with inventing the first commercially practical steamboat, the *Clermont*, which made the 150-mile run from New York to Albany in thirty-two hours in August, 1807. Actually, at least sixteen steamboats had been built and operated before Fulton's, some of them with considerable success. James Rumsey, Oliver Evans, and John Fitch were among the earlier inventors. Fitch had built several boats and run a regular steamboat service between Burlington, New Jersey, and Philadelphia in 1790 and received a patent on his invention in 1791. Yet Fulton still got the credit. It was several more years, however, before Fulton achieved his original aim and produced a steamboat, the *Aetna*, strong enough to run upstream on western rivers. Meanwhile the *Enterprise*, designed and built by Daniel French and captained by Henry Shreve, had made a successful trip up the Mississippi in 1815. What finally convinced the western public that steamboats were practical was the trip of Henry Shreve's own *Washington*, a large vessel for her day, from New Orleans to Louisville in twenty-five days in 1817. Her use of high-compression engines was also novel.

To appreciate the full significance of the steamboat to the West, one must note the method of transportation in use before it. Traffic was largely downstream, and mostly in flatboats which were broken up for their lumber on arrival in New Orleans. Flatboats could not be navigated against the current (see Fig. 7-2). Only keelboats moved upstream and then with difficulty. For the most part they were poled. It took thirty men three months to make the run from New Orleans to Cairo. It is not surprising, therefore, that few boats went upstream, and that the coffee, tea, sugar, and molasses which arrived in this manner brought high prices. The people of the West got their supplies either this way or perhaps by pack train from the East, or they made them themselves or did without. So far as bringing in goods from the outside world, the Middle West was rather effectively isolated. The steamboat changed all this in a short span of time for towns along the Mississippi, Ohio, and Missouri. It even led villages on small streams, such as Abe Lincoln's New Salem, Illinois, on the Sangamon, to dream of someday having steamboat service. Goods now poured in from the outside world. Persons who floated their produce down to New Orleans in flatboats no longer had to brave the hazards of the brigand-ridden Natchez Trace as they walked back north. Instead they could ride home in comfort on a steamboat and perhaps lose their hard-earned coin to "card sharks."

FIG. 7-2. Emigrants descending the Tennessee River on a flatboat. (*Courtesy of the Library of Congress.*)

Breaking the Monopoly. Both New York and Louisiana had granted Fulton and his partner, Robert Livingston, a monopoly on the operation of steamboats within their boundaries. Thomas Gibbons in New Jersey and Henry Shreve out west were not content to accept this situation. For some years Cornelius Vanderbilt, one of Gibbons's captains on a boat running from New Jersey into New York, ignored this special privilege and artfully dodged process servers. But Aaron Ogden, who represented the Fulton-Livingston interests, finally sued Gibbons: the Supreme Court of the United States settled the case in 1824. Chief Justice Marshall ruled that such traffic between states was part of the commerce between the states, and according to the Constitution only the Federal government might regulate interstate commerce.[2] Therefore, state laws granting these steamboat monopolies were unconstitutional. Once freed of such trammels, steamboat traffic grew even more rapidly than before.

Growth of Steamboating. The number of steamboats operating on western rivers increased from 17 in 1817 to 187 in 1830 and 740 in 1850. The decade of the 1850s was the heyday of steamboating. Boats grew in size from an average of 150 tons to about 200 tons. Altogether the internal steam-propelled merchant marine was very substantial.

Steamboating was a highly competitive business. Because of the many dangers of river navigation—sand bars, concealed underwater tree trunks, shifting channels—the average life of a steamboat was about five years. Since a boat cost about $25,000 on the average, it stood to reason that the owners must do enough business to pay for their boat within a rather short time. One form of advertising was steamboat racing—one of the great sporting events of the period. Races attracted attention and brought much business to the winner. The most famous race of all time was that between the *Robert E. Lee* and the *Natchez* in 1870, in which the two vessels made the run from New Orleans to St. Louis in under four days. Most races, however, were informal skirmishes. Such contests placed a great strain on steamboat boilers, which were not always new anyway. Engines could often be salvaged and used again when shattered superstructures or hulls of wrecked vessels had to be abandoned. Thus a corollary of keen competition and racing was a shockingly large number of explosions which took the lives of scores of deck passengers and crew members. This was not a period in which safety measures were widely demanded or vigorously enforced. But the result of this unbridled competition was ample low-priced service for a growing West which demanded just that. Most boats, however, served only local "trades" or sections along the river. There were few successful "packet" or regularly scheduled service lines; if anything, steamboats were famous for their unreliability in keeping schedules.

Decline of the River Steamboats. It was inevitable that the railroad would eventually take over the business done by the steamboats, just as it had cut into the canal business. The railroad was faster and could deliver freight directly to its destination. Its speed was further accentuated by the fact that steamboats, following the tortuous route of the rivers, nearly always had a greater distance to travel. For example, it was 1,164 miles by river from Pittsburgh to St. Louis but only 612 miles by rail, about half the distance. In the late 1850s a steamboat required seventy hours to make the run, a freight train thirty hours, and a passenger train sixteen hours. Fast packets even advertised themselves as "going through with railroad speed." In addition, the weather, especially in so far as it

[2] *Gibbons v. Ogden*, 9 Wheaton 1.

caused droughts and freezes, interfered more with steamboat service than with train service. Low water on the Ohio during several years in the early 1850s forced many shippers to turn to railroads. Once they had enjoyed the convenience of rail service, many of them did not come back to the rivers. As the steamboats declined in importance, so did river cities like Cincinnati and Louisville, which were superseded by railroad centers like Chicago.

Steamboats on the Great Lakes. Steamboats appeared later on the Great Lakes than on the rivers. Until the Middle West felt the effects of the Erie Canal in the 1830s there were very few settlements along these inland seas. Most of the population in Ohio, Indiana, and Illinois was concentrated in the southern parts of those states, especially along the Ohio River. The first lake steamboat was the *Walk-in-the-Water* (1818), which made a regular two-day run between Buffalo and Detroit, with intermediate stops. It had no steamboat competition, but even so, traffic was so light that it earned no dividends. When it was wrecked in 1821, no effort was made to replace it. As late as 1836 there were only forty-five steamboats in service on the Lakes, most of them passenger vessels. After canals were built between the Lakes, steamboats increased in popularity, for they could negotiate these narrow waters more easily than sailing vessels. Even though total tonnage on the Lakes increased from 7,000 in 1830 to 450,000 in 1860, two-thirds of it at the latter date was in sailing vessels. Speed was not important in carrying iron ore, copper ore, lumber, and grain, the chief products of this region. After 1857 lake boats lost ground in another important respect: railroads drew off more of their passenger business.

RAILROADS

Beginnings. The railroad, in the original sense of the term, began somewhere back in the sixteenth century; it was used then to keep heavily laden wagons carrying ore from mine shafts to barges from sinking too deeply into muddy ruts. Parallel planks, metal-plated planks, flanged rails, and flanged wheels were successive improvements, but the wagons or carts were always horse-drawn. In 1803 Richard Trevithick operated a steam-powered vehicle which ran on a highway near London. But it was not until 1825 that George Stephenson put an engine on a track and the first railroad, the Stockton and Darlington, went into operation in the north of England.

Meanwhile in America John Stevens of Hoboken and a few other farsighted individuals had been urging, to little avail, that if large sums were to be expended for improved transportation, they should be on railroads rather than on canals. Three railroads claim to be the first in the United States. The Mohawk and Hudson, between Albany and Schenectady, was the first chartered, in 1826, and eventually constructed, although it was not put into operation until August, 1831 (see Fig. 7-3). The Baltimore and Ohio, running from Baltimore to Ellicott Mills, 13 miles out, was the first to go into operation as a common carrier, in May of 1830, but its cars were horse-drawn and, except for experimental runs, continued to be horse-drawn for another year. The first to be built with steampowered locomotion in mind was the Charleston and Hamburg, running from Charleston, South Carolina, to Hamburg, 125 miles

FIG. 7-3. The *DeWitt Clinton* 1831, the third locomotive built in America. Note the passenger cars, which were little more than stage coaches on iron wheels. (*Courtesy of the New York Central System.*)

away, at the fall-line point on the Savannah River, across from Augusta, Georgia. Regular service began in January, 1831, with a locomotive, *The Best Friend of Charleston*, built in New York State.

American railroading was very primitive at first. Among the ideas suggested were providing power by hoisting sails or selling the right to run one's own train on the company tracks, as if it were a toll road. Horses easily could haul the trains, which after all were just converted stage coaches on wheels. Sleeping cars and dining cars were at first unknown, and accidents were few because the trains were so slow and light. It was some time before the freight business surpassed the passenger business in importance.

The first railroads were fundamentally just links in existing transportation systems. The Mohawk and Hudson enabled passengers to omit the slow first part of the trip westward on the Erie Canal, there being many locks between Albany and Schenectady. The Philadelphia to Columbia rail section of the Pennsylvania Canal System was a rail link over a countryside not suitable for canalization. As a matter of fact, the canal supporters were fearful of the competition of railroads and tried to limit their development. New York forbade railroads paralleling the Erie Canal to carry goods except in winter. By 1840 there were about 3,000 miles of railroad in the country, nearly all of them short lines. By 1850 there were about 9,000 miles of railroad, and the so-called "trunk lines" were appearing; by 1860 there were about 31,000 miles.

Trunk Lines. Trunk lines were railroad transportation systems that were all railroad, and in most cases they crossed the Appalachian range. About 1850 seven such lines came into operation. Three of them were the Pennsylvania from Harrisburg to Pittsburgh (but still using inclined planes over the mountains) in 1852; the Baltimore and Ohio from Baltimore to Wheeling, Virginia, in January, 1853; and the New York Central from Albany to Buffalo in May of 1853, with a connection to New York by the Hudson River Railroad. The New York Central affords a classic early example of forming a trunk line by consolidation, or of forging numerous links into a chain. During the 1830s and 1840s, promoters built at least seven little railroads from town to town across upstate New York, such as the Mohawk and Hudson, the Schenectady and Utica, the Utica and Syracuse, the Syracuse and Auburn, etc. These did not operate on any cooperative plan and often pointedly ignored one another, to the distress of the passenger or customer. Erastus Corning brought them together in 1853 and formed the New York Central.

Railroads grew up in other ways, too. The freight business had surpassed the passenger business by the 1840s; the telegraph became a part of railroading about 1852; the first sleeping car appeared about 1837 and the first Pullman about 1858. In the 1840s Americans began to manufacture their own rails instead of importing them from England, and iron bridges supplanted wooden ones. Overbuilding of railroad lines was the chief underlying cause of the financial panic of 1857.

Midwestern Railroads. Once the Appalachian range had been pierced, laying the lines in the more level country beyond went on fairly rapidly. Chicago was reached in 1853 and East St. Louis in 1855. There was very little railroad construction west of the Mississippi River before the Civil War. However, one of the longest railroads in the world, 700 miles, was completed in Illinois in 1856. It ran in the shape of a giant Y the length of the state, from Dubuque, Iowa, in the northwest and Chicago in the northeast, joined at Centralia, and continued to Cairo in the southern tip. This Illinois Central Railroad was the first to enjoy the railroad land grant system, later used on the transcontinental roads. The Federal government was relenting somewhat on its determination not to assist internal improvements: it decided that it was all right to give lands to a state to hand on to a railroad to help finance itself. The Illinois Central Railroad was a great success. It opened to farming the fertile but hitherto neglected prairies of central Illinois.

By the 1850s the railroads had unquestionably become the leading form of transportation. The Panic of 1837 slowed down the pace of canal building and the success of the trunk lines brought it to a stop. The railroads took from river and lake steamboats much of the traffic which they once had had. This development, in fact, changed the whole complexion of commerce between the East, the West, and the South. Formerly the West had shipped the bulk of its commodities downriver to the South with some destined for the East by a long sea voyage; now the West sent most of its produce directly east by rail. Commercial ties were made between East and West that no doubt bound these two regions more closely together when the Civil War broke out.

OCEAN SHIPPING

The pre-Civil War era was the heyday of the American merchant marine. During much of the time American shipping was second in importance only to England's. In the decade 1820–1830, for example, American ships carried about 90 per cent of all United States imports and exports. In other words, not many ships flying foreign flags were to be seen in American ports. In the period up to the Civil War the United States initiated packet-line service to Europe, pioneered in steamships, and made startling contributions to ship design in the form of the speedy, graceful clipper ship. Nonetheless, by the outbreak of the Civil War American ships were carrying only 66 per cent of American foreign trade, and by the end of the century, the figure had slipped to 10 per cent. What was going on, at least before the Civil War, to explain this steady decline? Apparently, when America had the advantage, it did not exploit it sufficiently.

Packet Ships. Until the early nineteenth century ships rarely ran according to any published schedule. This was for various reasons such as uncertainties of wind and weather and market limitations. But after the War of 1812 the amount of freight carried between America's largest import port and England's, that is, between New York and Liverpool, appeared to justify an experiment. The Black Ball Line announced that every month beginning in January, 1818, a ship would sail for Liverpool. Shipping people doubted that the first vessel would sail if it did not have an adequate cargo; after all, it would hardly be worth spending many hundreds of dollars to send off a half-empty ship just to carry out the schedule. What would the company gain? The critics thought the company would gain a reputation for pigheadedness. The company thought it would gain a reputation for promptness and would attract business willing to pay a higher rate to be assured of prompt service. The company was right. Although the *James Monroe*, the first vessel, took on a cargo of apples as ballast and lost money, soon the ships were sailing with sizable passenger lists and valuable cargoes. After four years the packet-line idea began to have imitators, one of the first being the Red Star Line in 1822. By 1824 there were four packet sailings every month for Liverpool, two to Le Havre, France, one to London, and several in the coastal service. The benefits of packet service were becoming increasingly obvious. Of course arrival time could not be guaranteed until later on (the 1840s) when the steam packet replaced the sailing packet. From Liverpool to New York an average sailing crossing was thirty-nine days.

Steamships. The *Savannah* was the first American ship to use steam in a trans-Atlantic crossing in 1819. It had what would today be called an auxiliary engine, which was used only during a small part of the voyage. Two British vessels made the first crossing entirely under steam: a small converted river boat, the *Sirius*, and an ocean vessel built for the purpose, the *Great Western*. Both arrived in New York on April 23, 1838. It seemed as if this success stimulated the British to experiment further with a view to regaining supremacy of the trans-Atlantic trade which the Americans had enjoyed as long as vessels were of wood and driven by the wind. In 1840 the British built and operated the *Great Britain*, 3,500 tons, made of iron and using a screw propeller. This ship was revolutionary in size, material, and method of propulsion. Although it was successful, not until about 1850 were many ships built with iron hulls and screw propellers. The two went together, for it took an iron hull to stand the vibration of a screw propeller.

The success of steamships led the British government to offer a profitable mail contract to a steamship line that would run between England and America by way of Halifax. The Cunard line won the contract and thus received its start. Toward the end of the 1840s the Cunard steamships began to beat the mail packets across the Atlantic. In 1845 Congress awarded mail contracts to an American line operating two ships between New York and Bremen. In 1847 a newly formed company, the Collins line, also obtained a generous mail contract from Congress. It had four ships, costing $3 million each, faster and more luxurious than the Cunard liners. However, in maintaining the speed and luxury required to outdo the British, they consistently lost money.

On top of that, the *Arctic* had a collision in 1854 with serious loss of life and a total loss of the ship, and the *Pacific*, with 288 passengers aboard, vanished at sea in 1856. Meanwhile, the same Southern congressmen and senators who opposed high tariffs for Northern industry also opposed the granting of a subsidy to a Northern steamship company. When Congress withdrew the subsidy in 1858, the Collins company, already suffering from its misfortunes at sea, discontinued operations. This left the field of ocean steam packets largely to the British. The Black Ball Line had made an effort in 1848 to provide steam service, and so later had the Livingston Line and a line owned by Cornelius Vanderbilt, but all were short-lived and unsuccessful.

Clipper Ships. Successful American competition with the British lay in a different direction, one in which Americans had done well in the past, namely, the improvement in design of wooden sailing ships. Yet the end result was unfortunate despite brilliant initial success. John W. Griffiths in 1841 designed a ship with a sleek hull, characterized by a knifelike concave bow, with the greatest width amidships and a narrow stern. The vessel was capable of carrying an amazing amount of sail. The new design stirred up a lot of controversy, and a New York merchant had such a ship built for him. This first clipper ship, the *Rainbow*, cost $45,000 and was launched in January, 1845. On her first trip to China she earned $90,000, paying for herself and making as much in profit as well. On her second voyage she went out and back in six months, the normal time for a one-way trip. The *Sea Witch*, Griffiths' second ship, made the trip to Hong Kong in 73 days. The *Memmon* cut the New York–San Francisco run record from 180 days to 120 days. After 1848 clipper ships rapidly became popular. In 1850 Donald McKay, a Boston shipbuilder, entered the competition. His *Flying Cloud* made the 16,000-mile run from New York to San Francisco in 89 days, an all-time record. Wherever the clipper ships went, they set new records; if the winds were at all favorable, they scudded past the slower steamships of the period. The clipper ships, emphasizing speed rather than capacity, were best-suited for carrying high-class freight and passengers, and frequently reaped fabulous returns. They brought the first tasty tea harvest each year from China. They carried impatient gold seekers to the gold fields of California, troops to suppress the Sepoy rebellion in India in 1857, and high-priced goods anywhere when time was of the essence. Yet the glorious days of the American clipper were over by 1860, having lasted a scant fifteen years. The British could build and buy clippers, too, but more important, the always-improving steamship was more dependable, especially when winds were unfavorable.

Decline of the Merchant Marine. All things considered, the American merchant marine paid dearly for this burst of glory. It made Americans believe that they could, with the aid of superior ship design and more daring seamanship, pit wooden sailing vessels against iron steamships. The Americans could proudly boast of the beauty and romance of the graceful clippers and the courage of the masters and crew. Yet in the long run the ugly iron steamships of the British earned the greater profits. America fell behind in the race by trying to succeed with out-of-date materials and methods. In this era, whether on land or sea, human muscle, wind power, and wood were no match for steam power and iron. Anyone who thought so paid with his economic well-being.

As ships grew in size and complexity, they grew in cost. Sailing vessels cost a few thousand dollars, the *Savannah* $50,000 in 1819, and the Collins line ships $3 million each in the 1850s. A merchant, the captain, and a mate, and perhaps a few others could as partners share in the ownership and operation of a sailing ship, even a $45,000 clipper, but it took more capital than an ordinary merchant and a few seafarers could muster to own an iron steamship, and especially to own a line of them. To a growing degree, ships were owned by corporations. The company had to keep the expensive vessels busy, earning their keep, or it would go bankrupt. The large companies had the best and fastest ships, they handled the highest-class freight and passenger business on the most traveled shipping lanes, and they pushed the sailing vessels and tramps off the highways onto the byways of commerce. The most successful companies got ship subsidies from their governments as well. Since American shipowners stayed with wooden ships for the most part, and the American government did not long pay subsidies, the American merchant marine lost ground in the race. Another reason, however, was that the most alert American businessmen of this period saw more profit-making opportunities in manufacturing, railroads, and commerce. They had turned their attention away from overcrowded Europe toward the opportunities of the growing West. Also they tended to abandon businesses which required much labor and offered little hope of economizing on labor costs for those which were more mechanized. There was always one important part of the shipping business, however, that was set aside for Americans.

Coastal Shipping. From the outset Congress virtually reserved American coastwise trade to American shipping. In 1789 Congress imposed a duty of 6 cents a ton on American-built and -owned ships entering American ports, payable once a year; foreign-built and -owned ships had to pay 50 cents a ton at every entry. In 1793 Congress excluded foreign ships from the coastwise trade. The tonnage of the coastwise merchant marine was 120,000 in 1793, over 500,000 in 1816, and 2,340,000 by 1860. After 1831 the coastwise and internal merchant marine exceeded that engaged in foreign trade. Because the ships ran closer to shore than ocean ships, the coastal trade was actually more dangerous. Stormy Cape Hatteras, off North Carolina, especially was a graveyard of ships. This situation was somewhat improved by the opening of the Chesapeake and Albemarle Canal in 1860 which enabled vessels to go inside instead of outside the dreaded cape.

COMMUNICATION

There were revolutionary developments in communication along with those in transportation. In fact, ideas, being lighter than goods, can be carried more cheaply and are among the first customers of new fast forms of transportation. Communication is just as important as transportation in the widening of markets since goods must be advertised, ordered, and the terms of financing and delivery discussed before they are delivered. Communication is sometimes divided into two categories, personal and mass; there are several varieties of each today. Until the invention of the telegraph there was but one personal means of communication, the post office, and one mass method, newspapers and magazines.

Postal Service. The British had begun a postal service to the colonies in 1707 and put Benjamin Franklin in charge in 1753. At the time of the Revolution there were seventy-six post offices handling 250,000 pieces of mail a year. The first contract for sending mail by rail was in 1835. About that time express companies were competing with the post office and were successfully undercutting the government's high-priced and "odious monopoly." Popular sympathy was with the express companies and their cut rates. It took a cheap postage law in 1845 to save the government service, and the post office generally lost money thereafter. By 1850 there were some 18,400 post offices handling 100 million pieces of mail annually.

Newspapers. The first American newspaper appeared in Boston in 1704. There were 150 newspapers before the Revolution. About 1,200 more appeared, some very briefly, in the forty years after the Revolution. The first western one was published in Pittsburgh in 1786. Most papers appeared weekly and were printed on one large sheet and then folded to make four medium-sized pages. Philadelphia had the first daily paper in 1783. Early newspapers contained little advertising and almost no local news. Rather they concerned themselves with published reports of foreign correspondents (not theirs), reprints from foreign papers, new laws and ordinances, and after about 1800 they carried much partisan editorial comment. Their circulation was limited to a few hundred copies because of the difficulties of printing with hand presses, the problem of a limited market, and the high cost of paper. The modern era of newspaper publishing began in the 1830s with the wider use of steam-power-driven presses. Rotary presses appeared before the Civil War. The penny newspaper, hawked by a raucous-voiced urchin, also came first in the

1830s. As railroad and telegraph networks were laid out in the 1840s and 1850s and cities expanded, newspapers gave more attention to advertising although it was almost exclusively of the classified sort. Newspapers, and some magazines, like *Niles Weekly Register* and *Hunt's Merchant Magazine* (the *Business Week* or *Fortune* of its day) exercised considerable influence on the markets of the economy.

The Telegraph. With the invention of the telegraph by Samuel F. B. Morse in 1837, man had a practical way of sending messages faster than he himself could travel. Morse persuaded Congress to appropriate $30,000 and strung wire 40 miles from Washington to Baltimore. In 1844 one of the first messages transmitted announced the nomination of Henry Clay for the Presidency by the Whigs. Morse hoped that Congress would make the telegraph a government monopoly like the post office, but after some debate Congress decided against that. Numerous private companies, some leasing Morse's patent, some relying on other patents, erected telegraph lines in various parts of the country. Cooperation between the companies in transmitting long-distance messages was poor and many messages were garbled or even lost with no one willing to admit responsibility. This damaged the reputation of the early telegraph business and hampered its progress. Nevertheless, newspapers and especially railroads soon realized the great value of the telegraph. Many early lines were built along railroad right-of-ways.

By 1857 almost all telegraph lines were within one of six great telegraph networks, called "The Six Nations," each serving its own region and supposedly not invading that of its neighbor. By 1866 the number of big companies had been reduced to two, the American and the Western Union. Rather than compete and perhaps lose, the Western Union, the weaker of the two, offered advantageous terms to American and absorbed it in that year. Morse's dream of a monopoly had been realized, although this one was privately controlled. Western Union Telegraph was the first nationwide private monopoly, the first trust.

The telegraph accomplished much even before the Civil War. It informed merchants of the whereabouts of better marketing opportunities, it speeded up purchase and delivery arrangements, and it reduced risks of extending credit to unknown persons. In 1858 for a brief time a trans-Atlantic cable was in operation, but this was not a permanent convenience until 1866.

CHAPTER 8

The Agricultural Revolution

In 1789, an overwhelming percentage of Americans were farmers. At least nine out of every ten persons lived and worked on farms and agriculture produced about 40 per cent of the realized national income. In spite of its dominant economic position, farming was backward and primitive. It was essentially on a subsistence basis, except on the staple-producing farms of the coastal regions. With but few exceptions, the farmer continued to imitate the techniques of his colonial ancestors. After 1800 agriculture underwent substantial changes; commercial farming became more commonplace.

Why did American farming improve so little in the two centuries prior to 1800? The answer, stated simply, was the lack of markets for farm products. Agricultural improvements occurred in the Old World long before 1800, but their adoption usually required an extra expenditure of money and effort. The farmer regarded such additional outlays as foolish since he probably could not sell any produce in excess of his family's needs. In the underdeveloped America of 1790, inadequate transportation and a predominantly rural civilization prohibited extensive exchange of farm commodities. Furthermore, labor was scarce and land was plentiful; this combination of circumstances encouraged wasteful and inefficient practices.

In the South, commercial farming might well have caused the use of better methods. The Southern planters had good markets; yet, they too failed to adopt improved techniques before 1800. Southern cash crops—tobacco, rice, and indigo—required much hand labor, performed by Negro slaves. Slavery led to wastefulness and inefficiency, especially where good land was abundant (see "Improved Tillage"). This explains why the agricultural revolution occurred first in the Northern states.

THE AGRICULTURAL REVOLUTION

Viewed in perspective, progress in farming from 1800 to 1860 was definitely revolutionary. Characteristics of the American agricultural revolution included (1) a shift from subsistence to commercial farming, with a steady increase in regional specialization; (2) better methods of crop production; (3) better breeding and care of livestock; (4) more efficient implements and increased mechanization; (5) the Westward Movement of farming.

The primary cause of the revolution was the growth of commercial markets. These emerged with the earliest signs of town life; but domestic markets, except near a few seaports, remained small and unimportant until after the Revolutionary War. That conflict had caused a brief flurry of cash farming, but it was not until the era of the Napoleonic Wars (1792–1815) that the proper stimulus was present. These wars caused a rapid increase in agricultural exports during the 1790s. The foreign shipments benefited the coastal farmers and those fortunate enough to live near a navigable stream flowing to the Atlantic or Gulf of Mexico. But most farmers still needed domestic markets to engage in commercial agriculture. Such markets developed during the trade disputes between the United States and the chief warring nations of Europe, namely, France and England. Those nations, in maneuvering to gain a strategic advantage, interfered so greatly with American shipping in the 1790s and 1800s that Congress finally stopped foreign trade by the Embargo Act of 1807. In the intervening years before the end of the War of 1812, the United States had to rely increasingly upon its own manufactures. The resultant industrial growth stimulated transportation and urban developments, and these in turn called forth commercial agriculture.

The Berkshire Agricultural Society. The growing markets aroused interest in new ideas. In this respect, agricultural societies proved useful. Some of these societies dated back to Revolutionary War times, but the early ones were primarily for "gentlemen" farmers and did not appeal to the "dirt" farmers. It was not until Elkanah Watson founded his Berkshire Agricultural Society in 1810 that societies began to exercise a marked influence. Watson's organization was the first one directed primarily toward the interests of the common farmer.

Elkanah Watson was prominent before 1810. He had been a successful businessman and banker in Europe and America in the years following the Revolutionary War and achieved public notice as a canal promoter. At the age of fifty he decided to become a farmer, buying a farm near Pittsfield, Massachusetts. There he showed neighboring farmers that agriculture could be profitable, beginning in 1807 by exhibiting a pair of Merino sheep on the village green. While Watson was not the first American to acquire these fine animals, he was certainly among the first to popularize them. For generations, they had been raised in Spain exclusively, their export restricted by royal decree. Napoleon's invasion of Spain made it possible for American diplomats, Robert Livingston and

David Humphreys, to ship several head to America. The Embargo of 1807 stimulated American production of woolen goods and ensured the immediate popularity of Merinos. The Merino was a great improvement over the native American sheep, being larger in size and yielding more wool. In addition, the fleece was longer and more silky in texture, making it more valuable.

After introducing the Merino sheep, Watson exhibited improved breeds of hogs and cattle and encouraged better crop production. He deliberately appealed to the ordinary farmer through agricultural exhibits and farmers' conventions, which evolved eventually into the county fair. Farmers learned better methods, exchanged ideas, and equipped themselves to participate in the agricultural revolution. After 1810, farm progress gained momentum. Numerous advances occurred, especially in soil tillage, livestock raising, and farm implements.

Improved Tillage. American farmers were slow to adopt better methods of tilling the soil. To the small subsistence farmer, who had few opportunities to sell any surplus output, it generally seemed easier to bring new, more fertile land under cultivation than to apply more labor and fertilizers to older wornout soil. "Soil butchery," that process by which land was carelessly farmed until exhausted, had been the general rule since early colonial days. In fact, it continued as a fairly common practice through the nineteenth century until good arable land became scarce.

A few American farmers practiced improved tillage before 1800. Englishmen like Jethro Tull, Charles Townshend, and Arthur Young wrote about and practiced advanced techniques in soil tillage; much of this knowledge reached America and appealed to educated, wealthy farmers such as Jared Eliot, John Beale Bordley, Thomas Jefferson, and George Washington. These men in turn wrote about or practiced better farming, urging others to follow their examples. Gradually, crop rotation to preserve soil fertility and to increase productivity—especially the use of legumes and turnips in place of weed fallow—became more commonplace in the East. In the 1820s and 1830s, application of fertilizers and soil rebuilding elements—manure, guano, limestone—gained acceptance among more progressive farmers. This was particularly true in the exhausted regions of Virginia, where Edmund Ruffin led the way. At the same time, farmers used more effective means of breaking and tilling the ground. Instrumental in the dissemination of information about these newer, more profitable methods were the agricultural societies and the growing list of agricultural publications. *The American Farmer* (1819), *The Ploughboy* (1819), *The Cultivator* (1834), and the *Prairie Farmer* (1840) were early farm journals which carried ideas and suggestions to the practical farmer. By 1840, more than thirty such periodicals reached perhaps 100,000 readers.

Breeding and Care of Livestock. A logical accompaniment of better soil tillage was improvement in livestock raising. The farmer had normally kept a few head of swine, cattle, and sheep to provide food, power, and clothing for his family farm. The swine and sheep were scrubby, mongrel-type stock yielding poor quality meat and wool. The cattle, used as draft oxen, were likewise of low quality. Horses were not widely utilized for draft purposes because oxen were more suited to the leisurely pace of subsistence farming. Oxen were easier and cheaper to manage and feed, were more powerful and gentler than horses, and finally, when too old to work, could be slaughtered for beef.

As progress continued, improved breeds of livestock appeared. The importation of the Spanish Merino sheep after 1800 was followed by the Saxony breed in the 1820s. Shorthorn cattle from England and the Continent became more numerous, with most of the common breeds having been introduced by 1840. Beef cattle included Herefords and Improved Durhams or Shorthorns; Alderneys, Guernseys, and Devons were milk cows. In the 1840s and 1850s, Ayrshires, Jerseys, and Holsteins, also primarily dairy stock, gained prominence. Especially after 1850, imported cattle became more than mere show animals for the well-to-do; in fact, high-quality stock was widespread by 1860. Swine breeds also underwent striking improvement. The long-legged "razorback" native hog had virtually disappeared from the commercial farm by 1860, replaced by European hogs, often bearing the title of a county in England. By 1830, Berkshires, Suffolks, and Chester County (Pennsylvania) Whites were well known on Eastern farms.

Somewhat later, horses were imported from Scotland (Clydesdales) and France (Percherons), taking their place on American farms with the native-bred Morgans. Outside of New York, Pennsylvania, and Vermont, they did not receive much attention on farms before 1840. Lighter plows and harrows, reapers, and other horse-drawn implements finally created greater demand for horses; although the horse was smaller and less powerful than the ox, he was swifter and more adaptable to the newer machines. In New England, where oxen were commonly used, around 1790 they outnumbered horses by about 20 to 1; the ratio gradually fell to 12 to 1 by 1812 and to 3 to 2 in 1850. By 1860, horses far exceeded oxen for draft purposes. Mules, used sparingly before the Revolution, became popular in the South after 1800. That small, hardy animal came to be preferred on Southern farms because he was economical and well suited to the kind of work required. He did not trample young cotton and corn plants as much as horses or oxen. Mule breeding, popularized by George Washington in Virginia, developed into a sizable industry in Kentucky, Tennessee, and Missouri. The importation of European jacks made possible quality breeds of mules.

Farmers took better care of these superior, costly breeds of animals. They devoted more attention to supplementing pasturage with hay and grain and providing effective shelters during winter weather. They no longer turned the livestock loose to roam at will over the countryside. As livestock raisers recognized the advantages of selective breeding, they erected more and better fences.

Advances in Farm Implements. A third general advance took place in agricultural implements. Progress was greatest in plows, harvesting implements, and grain threshers, although there were other significant contributions. Before 1800 the plows used by American farmers were crude, unwieldy instruments made of wood; better models had pieces of iron to

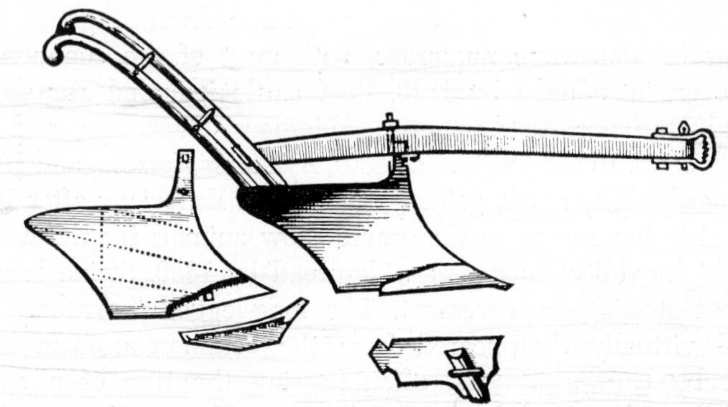

FIG. 8-1. An early three-piece iron plow. The large disassembled part on the left is the moldboard. (*Courtesy of Minneapolis-Moline Co.*)

serve as a plowshare. It has been estimated that with such a plow, "two men or a man and a boy, using 2 or 3 horses or 4 or 6 oxen, could scratch over 1 or 2 acres a day."[1] Early improvements in the plow came in the late eighteenth century when Thomas Jefferson applied mathematics to the design of moldboards to improve performance. In 1797, Charles Newbold of New Jersey constructed an iron plow, casting in one piece the moldboard, share, and landside, but it was not widely adopted. It was expensive and farmers realized that the entire plow had to be replaced if any part should break; further, many farmers erroneously believed that cast iron poisoned the soil and encouraged weeds.

Other inventors experimented with better plows after 1800, with Jethro Wood and John Deere making significant contributions. Wood patented in 1814 and 1819 a three-piece iron plow consisting of separately cast replaceable parts (see Fig. 8-1). This was one of the earliest applications

[1] Percy W. Bidwell and John I. Falconer, *History of Agriculture in the Northern United States, 1620–1860* (New York: Peter Smith, 1941), p. 124.

of Eli Whitney's principle of interchangeable mechanisms to farm equipment. Wood's plow, with later improvements, was adopted generally in the East. In the western regions, however, farmers found that the heavy soil stuck to the porous moldboard of the cast-iron plows; further, the densely matted grass roots of the prairies required a cutting edge finer than that of a cast-iron plow. John Deere, a Vermont blacksmith who had moved to Grand Detour, Illinois, observed the difficulties and produced a steel plow in 1837. The chief advantage was that the steel moldboard could be highly polished and would thus scour (clean itself) in

FIG. 8-2. Cradling wheat. (*Courtesy of U.S. Department of Agriculture.*)

the prairie soil. By 1850 the steel plow was widely used on the prairies and Deere, who established a factory at Moline, Illinois, in 1847, was turning out 13,000 annually by 1858. Meanwhile, Southern farmers clung to a crude, one-piece iron "shovel" plow; this produced the effect of "dragging a cat by the tail." Only rarely, as in Virginia, did improved plows find popularity in the Southern states.

Of possibly greater importance than improved plows were the laborsaving devices for harvesting grass and grain crops. Farmers cut these crops with a sickle or a scythe until the cradle was introduced into the Middle Colonies some time in the eighteenth century. A cradler could cut two to five times as much as a man with a sickle; even so, farmers continued to use the sickle for harvesting small grain until around 1840, especially in New England. This was primarily because the less delicate stroke of the cradle shattered much of the grain, causing it to fall on the ground and be lost. The development of a horse-drawn reaper heralded the greatest progress in harvesting.

Two Americans developed such a reaper almost simultaneously; Obed Hussey and Cyrus H. McCormick patented implements in 1833 and 1834, respectively. There had been numerous prior patents issued in the United States and Europe, but the earlier machines were not successful. McCormick generally has been regarded as the first American to succeed, since he successfully cut wheat in Virgina in 1831. Further, his reaper resembled later harvesters more closely than did Hussey's. The latter sold his first reaper in 1833 and by 1840 had about forty-five reapers in use throughout the nation. McCormick did not begin selling until 1840, but he was the more successful businessman and by 1850 had clearly established himself as the leader in this field. By that year, McCormick had distributed approximately 4,500 machines, whereas Hussey had sold but 500 since 1833. The production and sale of reapers increased rapidly after 1850. On the eve of the Civil War an estimated 73,000 reapers harvested about two-thirds of the wheat crop grown west of the Appalachian Mountains, or about one-half of the nation's total.

Mechanical harvesting represented much labor saved. From the standpoint of time saved in cutting wheat, the reaper was capable of doing the work of four to five cradles. Furthermore, owing to the manner in which the grain was cut and raked, fewer binders were needed to follow machines than was the case with cradles. Without the reapers, farmers could scarcely have met the greatly increased demands for wheat during the Civil War.

While Hussey and McCormick were perfecting harvesting machinery, others were at work on laborsaving devices for separating grain from the straw and chaff. As late as 1830, most grain was obtained by the laborious method of using a flail to beat the kernels out of the husk. After raking off the straw, workers then winnowed or fanned away the chaff. By such a method, a man could at best produce 6 to 8 bushels of wheat in a ten-hour workday. Progressive farmers such as John Beale Bordley in Maryland constructed expensive treading floors in the late eighteenth and early nineteenth centuries; horses or cattle were led around the treading floor to thresh the grain. Mechanical threshers had been experimented with in Scotland as early as 1732; but such machines were hand-operated and did no more than shell the grain from the head. A few wealthy American farmers purchased such machines before 1800, and John Pope of Boston patented one in 1802, probably the earliest American model. The early threshers did not solve the problem, however, since more energy was required to turn the crank than to swing a flail.

Demand for a power-driven thresher developed after the reaper inventions. In 1834, Hiram and John Pitts of Maine patented the first practical thresher which combined the three operations of threshing, separating, and winnowing. The horse-powered machines were too expensive for the ordinary farmer to purchase; nonetheless, nearly all of the grain produced in the United States in 1860 was threshed mechanically, mostly by itinerant custom threshers moving through the grain-producing regions.

Threshing machines of the type developed by the Pitts brothers compared favorably with the reaper in respect to time and labor conserved. In 1852, at an official trial held at Geneva, New York, a Pitts machine operated by seven men and eight horses threshed 270 bushels of wheat in one day, a rate five to seven times more effective per man-day than hand methods. The application of steam power to threshing machines and other farm implements, basically unsuccessful before 1860, further increased labor efficiency on American farms in the post-Civil War era.

Improvements in the plow, harvesters, and threshers were merely the most outstanding; other mechanical inventions further aided the American farmer in increasing his productivity before 1860. The reaper was also important in hay mowing; in fact, not until around 1850 was a great distinction made between mowing and reaping machines. Cyrenus Wheeler patented a two-wheeled mower with a flexible cutting bar in 1856, divorcing the reaper and the mower entirely. Already a horse-drawn hay rake had been perfected to lighten the farmer's burdens in this important work. Although most small grain was sown broadcast as late as 1860, mechanical seed drills were introduced in the 1840s for planting wheat, oats, barley, and rye. Corn planters came rapidly into use in the 1850s. Cultivating implements also underwent considerable changes. Harrows, so essential in proper seedbed preparation, were improved in design and made more efficient by the use of steel teeth. Multiple-bladed plows for cultivating row crops, especially corn, appeared in the form of the straddle-row cultivator by 1860. These mechanical innovations served primarily to overcome the shortage of labor. Although some of the inventions contributed indirectly to higher crop output from a given amount of land, a higher yield per acre was not a major consideration. It is noteworthy that most important innovations in farm equipment dealt with the production of small grain. As in textile manufacturing, widespread demand and a standardized product led to mechanization.

REGIONAL SPECIALIZATION

As the agricultural revolution progressed after 1800 under the stimulus of an expanding market for farm products, there was a marked trend toward greater regional specialization. In colonial days, Southerners had produced tobacco, indigo, and rice commercially, and the Middle Colonies had cash grain farms. Those regions had specialized, however, solely because they had good water transportation and available markets abroad. The vast interior country, more than a few miles removed from any adequate means of shipping its produce, remained on a self-sufficient basis until the steamboat, canal, and railroad era. With each succeeding improvement in transportation, geographic specialization grew apace. The Westward Movement contributed greatly to the trend, as did the mechanization of wheat production.

Yet, in spite of more specialization and exchange among the regions of the United States, no single area ever ceased to have diversification in its agriculture. Writers have too often emphasized the prominent staple crops of a section and neglected the role of lesser products. It was true that the staple crops, being the "money crops" of farmers everywhere, dominated the thinking and practices of large and small producers alike; however, this does not alter the fact that the Northeast, West, and South each grew a great variety of products.

The Northeast. That area north of Maryland and east of central Pennsylvania and New York developed in a manner to permit classification as an agricultural region. There were some basic differences between the farming in eastern Pennsylvania and New York and that in New England, but the differences were more in the nature of methods rather than of products. At the beginning of the 1789–1860 era, the Northeastern section of the United States was dotted with small farms growing a variety of products for local consumption. The typical Northeastern farm, especially in New England, ranged from 100 to 200 acres in size, with rarely more than 10 to 12 acres under cultivation at any time. Corn was the principal crop raised on such farms; mixed with rye, it served as the common bread for the people and was highly valued for fattening livestock and poultry. Rye, oats, barley, and buckwheat were usually sown in small quantities. Wheat, though highly desired as a breadstuff, could not be grown in all parts of the Northeast. Insect pests, chief among which was the Hessian fly, and wheat "rust" so reduced the profitability of wheat growing that the crop was all but abandoned in much of New England. Newer soils of western Vermont and Maine were found suitable for wheat growing between 1800 and 1820; but shortly after that Western wheat began to reach the Eastern markets in increasing amounts, causing a further decline in Northeastern production. Northeastern farmers also raised livestock and a few crops, such as potatoes, pumpkins, peas, and beans, for their own consumption.

With the advent of commercial agriculture, farming in the Northeast changed substantially. Between 1810 and about 1840, there was an increased output of most of the crops common to the 1800 era. Rye growing was stimulated by the development of distilleries in the larger towns and cities, and the breweries of New York and other cities provided excellent markets for barley. Potatoes from Maine and tobacco from the Connecticut River Valley became widely known for their quality by 1840. Around the more densely populated areas, market gardening, fruit growing, and dairying developed after 1820. Wool production emerged as a leading pastoral industry in northwestern New England after the importation of better breeds of sheep. Beef cattle, swine, and horses were raised commercially in some localities, although by no means universally.

The initial phases of the revolution in Northeastern farming unfolded within three or four decades; then further changes appeared. Around 1840, several significant trends were observable. Cattle grazing and dairying became more profitable than wool growing and grain production. Wheat raising continued to decline, and decreasing swine output occurred at about the same time. Hay, always an important crop, became even more so with the growth of the beef and dairy cattle industries. Fruit and vegetable production further increased throughout the region. Probably the most important factor causing these developments was the increasing competition from the West. With improvements in transportation, highlighted by the opening of the Erie Canal in 1825, ever-increasing amounts of Western produce entered Eastern markets, underselling the grain, pork, and wool produced on the worn lands of the older region. Other factors changing the nature of Northeastern farming were the rapidly advancing industrial revolution and urbanization, both of which had profoundly affected the East by 1840. By 1860, the self-sufficient farm household of the earlier era had all but disappeared from the Eastern countryside as the rise of the factory system hastened the decline of household industries.

The West. What the Northeast lost by way of advantages in farming between 1825 and 1840 the newer lands to the west gained. The spread of settlement across western New York and Pennsylvania, down the Ohio Valley, into the Missouri River country, and along the Upper Mississippi carried with it the centers of agricultural production. Even before 1800, some commercial farming existed in the Ohio Valley. Farmers who were located favorably along navigable streams were able to float grain, salt pork, whisky, tobacco, and hemp down the Ohio-Mississippi system to New Orleans for reshipment to the South, the East, and to Europe. Stock raisers in the bluegrass regions of Kentucky and the fertile cornlands of the Scioto Valley in Ohio were driving cattle across the mountains to Baltimore and Philadelphia. But the prevailing pattern of farming for the majority of Westerners before 1800 was that of the pioneer, whose small patch of corn and vegetables in a forest clearing made up the greater amount of his farm production. He hunted and fished to supplement the diet of his family until such time as he could bring enough land under cultivation to produce a surplus now and then.

Prairie farming did not improve appreciably until after the extension of canals and railroads in the 1830s and 1840s and the advent of better plows, reapers, and threshers. Then the West came into prominence as a more specialized region. While many farmers continued to raise a variety of foodstuffs for family consumption, the West became the center of grain and livestock production for the nation between 1840 and 1860. The cornerstones upon which such preeminence rested were corn, wheat, beef, and pork.

Corn, the leading crop quantitatively, had little commercial value except when converted into a readily marketable product such as whisky or pork. But because it was easily grown and could be fed to livestock, farmers of the West came to depend upon corn to a great extent. Kentucky, Tennessee, and Ohio rapidly became leading states in corn production, with the last gaining national leadership by 1849. After 1840, prairie sod was planted to corn and by 1860, Illinois led the country in its output.

Wheat was the most important cash grain crop in the West, even though that region produced more corn than wheat. Farmers fed corn to their livestock but milled most of the wheat into flour. As adequate transportation facilities became available, wheat growing centralized in eastern Ohio and western New York and Pennsylvania. By 1840, those states produced nearly half of America's wheat. Wheat growing continued to spread westward during the next twenty years; in 1860, Illinois, Indiana, and Wisconsin ranked as the three top states, with Ohio, the 1840 leader, a close fourth. The West yielded more than 50 per cent of the nation's crop in 1860. Better plows, improved harrows, seed drills, reapers, and threshers made possible this rapid growth of the western wheat industry.

The *beef cattle* industry, which actually preceded commercial grain and swine production in the West, also grew rapidly throughout the era. Permanent farm settlement pushed cattle raising westward from the Kentucky and Ohio feeding areas. The industry spread into the Miami Valley of Ohio, thence to the Wabash range in central Indiana, and later onto the Grand Prairie of central Illinois. The coming of the railroads and the turning of the prairie sod transformed the beef cattle industry of the mid-continent after 1850. Instead of open ranges and overland drives to the East or to Chicago or St. Louis, the former range-feeding areas became producers of pen-fed cattle which were shipped by rail to slaughterhouses in Chicago.

Pork production followed the Westward Movement of corn and wheat. Pioneer farmers kept a few hogs for home use and often had a small surplus to dispose of as salt pork. Westerners devoted little effort to swine production at first, allowing the animals to forage for themselves in the fields and forests. As population increased in the West, commercial hog raising came to be associated with corn growing in Kentucky and Ohio, then later in Indiana, Illinois, Missouri, and Iowa. Common practices in hog raising pointed up the dearness of labor in early America; farmers generally gave as little time and effort as possible to feeding and caring for the animals. Where good summer pasture was available, hogs were allowed to roam freely over the grasslands until fall. Then frequently the two-year-old animals were fattened by turning them into an unharvested cornfield. This required a minimum of labor and had as a virtue the returning of some fertility to the soil in the form of manure. Another common method of fattening was to have hogs "follow" cattle in the feeding lots, two hogs for each well-fed steer. Swine grew fat from corn and fodder left by the beeves.

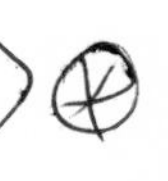

Unlike cattle, hogs fared poorly on long overland drives to market. Generally, the swine were driven to markets in nearby towns or fairs or sold to drovers who regularly passed through the countryside in search of cattle and hogs. The drovers were of great importance in the marketing of livestock in the West before the rise of an extensive meat-packing industry in that region. There were hundreds of towns throughout Ohio, Indiana, and Illinois with slaughterhouses and packing plants by 1850, dealing almost exclusively in pork products. Cincinnati, appropriately nicknamed "Porkopolis," was the leader until 1860. By that date, Chicago had risen to prominence and soon took over the leadership; Louisville, Alton, St. Louis, and Quincy also had prosperous packing establishments.

Western farmers, while specializing in corn, wheat, cattle, and hogs, grew a variety of other crops such as hay, oats, rye and barley for livestock feed, fruits and vegetables for local consumption, and hemp, flax, and tobacco for marketing. This diversity in Western agriculture gave the Northern economy a degree of stability which the South lacked.

The South. Southern agriculture developed somewhat differently from that of the Northeast and the West. In spite of progressive farmers like Edmund Ruffin of Virginia and David Dickson of Georgia, the South did not experience great advances in methods and equipment. Cotton and the other leading commercial crops in the South—tobacco, sugar cane, and rice—demanded detailed attention, supplied for the most part by Negro slaves. Such work did not lend itself to mechanization, as did wheat growing. The Negro hands, being generally uneducated, inefficient, and lacking motivation for improving their working methods, were not well suited to improved techniques of farming. Furthermore, cheap lands encouraged wasteful practices in land utilization, while constant planting of row crops tended to deplete the soil.

Cotton. Cotton was the leading commercial crop of the South during the nineteenth century. Although the South did not grow it to the exclusion of other products, cotton took on increasing importance in the Old South after 1786. In the decades following the War of 1812 it came to dominate the lives of most farmers, small and large alike, from the Carolinas to Texas. Production doubled every decade up to 1860.

Commercial production of cotton began about 1786, when a small amount of long-fibered, silky cotton was produced along the Georgia coast and sold at an attractive price. The variety, later to be called Sea Island cotton, had been imported from Brazil and the Bahama Islands. The high quality of the fiber and the relative ease with which the smooth black seeds could be removed caused a rapid expansion in the production of Sea Island cotton. Its culture spread to the islands and coastal regions of South Carolina and by 1801 Charleston alone exported some 8.3 million pounds of the lint. Further expansion was limited, however, since the cotton could not be successfully produced in the interior. There, a short-staple cotton grew well, but the problem of extracting the rough, green seeds from the lint stifled extensive production.

Conditions were such just after the Revolutionary War that a solution to the problem of removing seed from short-staple cotton was imperative. A series of inventions in England had revolutionized the textile industry and had created an unprecedented need for raw cotton by the middle 1780s. Overseas sources could not fill the insatiable demands of the faster spinning and weaving machines in Great Britain. That fact, plus the decline in the profitability of raising indigo, accounted for the rapid increase in the growth of Sea Island cotton after 1786. Then, too, America's economic situation had badly deteriorated following the Revolution, and the young nation needed an export staple such as cotton to revive its sagging economy. In this environment, Eli Whitney invented a simple machine which revolutionized Southern agriculture within a decade.

Whitney had accepted a teaching position in South Carolina upon his graduation from Yale in 1792; en route to his new job, he met the widow of General Nathaniel Greene of Revolutionary War fame. The widow and her business manager, William Miller, persuaded Whitney to go with them to their plantation in Georgia for a few days, and while visiting there, Whitney learned of the difficulties in ginning cotton. Schoolteaching faded from his mind as he turned his attention to the building of a workable model. Inventiveness was not new to the transplanted Yankee. He had established himself as an inventive genius even as a boy on his father's Massachusetts farm; there he had mass-produced nails for the surrounding countryside during the Revolutionary War at the youthful age of 15. Once the need for a new type of cotton gin became clear to Whitney, he quickly produced it, basing his invention on the commonplace roller gin.

Roller gins had been used for many years before Whitney's time to remove the smooth black seeds from certain strains of cotton; in fact, some unsupported claims have been made that the short-staple variety had been ginned successfully. However, green-seed cotton could not be cleaned satisfactorily in a roller gin. The rough-textured seed often went through the rollers, was crushed, and became mixed with the fiber in such a way as to reduce the value of the lint.

Whitney's first machine was a modification of the roller gin. It contained a revolving roller equipped with metal teeth which forced the lint through a wire screen while extracting the seed; a second cylinder with a brush freed the fiber from the teeth of the first roller. Whitney built an improved larger gin that permitted one man to clean up to 50 pounds of cotton per day, which was about ten times as much as he could clean in any other manner. The inventor entered into a partnership with William Miller and returned to Connecticut to manufacture gins. Whitney and Miller decided not to sell their machines but to operate them on a toll basis, charging 40 per cent of the cleaned cotton as a fee. The attempt at monopoly, plus the rather heavy toll, aroused much hostility among farmers who were clamoring for more gins. Since the machine was so simple in its construction, it could be easily duplicated, and imitations appeared in many places. For a number of years, costly lawsuits over patent rights deprived Whitney of any financial return worthy of mention.

Whitney's failure to profit from the cotton gin was inconsistent with the invention's influence upon Southern farming. After 1793, cotton production moved across the Georgia and South Carolina uplands and thence to adjacent areas. In southeastern Virginia and in North Carolina wornout tobacco lands were planted to cotton; cotton growing spread to the hills of Tennessee and the Lower Mississippi Valley. By 1820, the whole of the lower South, from the Atlantic Ocean to the Sabine River, was producing cotton. Shortly thereafter, Americans carried the culture into Mexican-owned Texas. Savannah and Charleston, the leading cotton-export ports before 1820, surrendered their primacy to Mobile and New Orleans as the center of production moved west.

Cotton was grown on small farms and large plantations alike. Although there appeared to be some advantage to growing cotton on large tracts of land with slave labor, the crop was also profitable to the independent yeoman farmer working with his family or possibly alongside a slave or two. In the lower South, cotton became the primary cash crop, while farther north, small farmers produced a bale or two along with tobacco, wheat, corn, and livestock. The great emphasis placed on the growing of cotton revived the slowly dying institution of slavery, hastened the settlement of the Southern parts of the nation, bolstered America's foreign trade, and helped to cause the Civil War.

Tobacco. Cotton dominated the lower South, but tobacco, the nation's biggest export product until 1803, was the leading cash crop in the upper South. The Tidewater plantations, so important in colonial tobacco production, lost their fertility, causing the Tobacco Kingdom to shift to the Piedmont region of Maryland, Virginia, and North Carolina. At the same time, pioneer farmers carried tobacco culture across the mountains into Kentucky, Tennessee, and Missouri, where tobacco became a main source of cash income for many farms. Tobacco farmers in South Carolina and Georgia turned their attention almost exclusively to cotton after 1800.

Tobacco farming had certain distinctive characteristics. The most basic trait was the small amount of land devoted to the crop. No matter how large the farm, farmers planted only a few acres of tobacco each year; in fact, they usually spoke about the number of plants rather than the number of acres. In Virginia and North Carolina, small and large farms averaged 3 and 13 acres of tobacco, respectively. The main reason was that tobacco required so much detailed attention; one man could tend no more than two or three acres per year. If slaves did the field work, they required constant and costly supervision which reduced the profits from large plantings. Most farms combined tobacco raising with general farming, a condition which further discouraged large-scale tobacco production. General farming was particularly desirable to reduce the soil exhaustion which resulted from constant cropping of tobacco. Progressive Southern farmers learned that diversification and rotation of crops were effective barriers to soil depletion and erosion. A common crop sequence was tobacco or corn, wheat, and one or two years of clover; farmers using such a plan found it necessary to put tobacco on a given plot of ground only once in five or six years.

A tobacco field hand had few slack seasons; in fact, the crop required attention "thirteen months out of the year." Late January, or shortly thereafter, was the time for seedbed preparations. During March and April, farmers readied the fields for transplanting the seedlings. In May or June, when sufficient rainfall permitted, workers transferred the young plants to the fields. Then followed the chores of hoeing or plowing the rows of tobacco to keep the soil loose and free of weeds, "topping and suckering" to produce large, broad leaves, and "worming" to protect the quality of the leaf. When the plant had ripened and before the first killing frost, workers cut the tobacco stalks and allowed the leaves to wilt on the ground. Soon, they put the stalks on laths or sticks which were placed across beams in curing barns. There the tobacco remained until spring when it was taken down, the leaves stripped from the stalks and packed into hogsheads. The tobacco was then ready for market. Meanwhile, the seedbed for the next crop had already been completed and the transplanting season was at hand.

Other Products. Rice production on the tidelands of South Carolina and Georgia remained important up to 1860, although just before that, production began to shift to the lower Mississippi Valley. Sugar cane, grown commercially in Louisiana from 1796, was limited in its importance to the South because of restrictions from climatic conditions and capital requirements. The crop could not be grown extensively except in the Gulf Coast area; and the large labor force required for harvesting, plus the expensive equipment for refining the sugar, meant that the number of plantations engaged in producing sugar cane was small. Nonetheless, as a cash crop, sugar cane ranked high.

Corn was the leading crop in the South before the Civil War in terms of weight, value, and acreage harvested. It represented food for livestock, slaves, and farm families, and it was distilled into whisky. Cultivation and harvesting of the crop dovetailed perfectly with cotton growing, enabling a more profitable use of slave labor on plantations. Little of the South's corn was marketed, however, and consequently the importance of the crop has been greatly overlooked. Except for the output of Kentucky and Tennessee (and to a lesser extent Virginia and Missouri), corn was consumed in the localities where it was produced. In fact, considerable quantities of corn were imported by the plantations of the Lower Mississippi Valley from the border states of Kentucky, Tennessee, and Missouri.

In addition to corn, of which the South produced more than half of the nation's total in 1859, Southern farmers grew more than one-quarter of the nation's wheat, nearly one-fifth of the rye and oats, over nine-tenths of the sweet potatoes, and about four-fifths of the peas and beans. Furthermore, the South raised over 60 per cent of the swine, about 50 per cent of the beef cattle, almost 45 per cent of the horses, 90 per cent of the mules, and 30 per cent of the sheep in 1859. While the South was anything but a one-crop section in the pre-Civil War era, it still lacked diversification in its *commercial* farming. For the most part, farmers rarely relied upon more than one staple as a cash crop, especially in the Cotton Kingdom. Thus entire regions tied their economic well-being to the price of cotton or tobacco or sugar, risking everything on the vagaries of nature and of the market place.

CHAPTER 9

The Industrial Revolution

In the United States the industrial revolution began in the Northeast about the start of the nineteenth century. In Britain it had begun a half century earlier; in the American South, it began after the Civil War; in China and India in the early twentieth century; and in some parts of the world it has not yet begun. It is fairly easy to determine when it began, but whether it has ever ended is more difficult to decide. Certainly, significant changes in industrial methods have been taking place almost continually in this nation during the last 150 years and presumably will continue for a long time.

BACKGROUND AND NATURE OF THE INDUSTRIAL REVOLUTION

In studying the industrial revolution three basic questions come to mind: (1) What were the methods of production before the industrial revolution began? (2) What is meant by the industrial revolution? (3) What are the necessary or favorable background conditions that must exist before an industrial revolution is likely to take place? The first two can be quickly answered.

The methods of production in use for centuries involved making goods by hand or with simple tools, either for one's own personal use or on customer's order or for a chiefly local market. Goods were produced in the home, or in small shops, mills, or forges; the workmen usually owned their own tools and the power was provided by human beings or animals, or by windmills or watermills. Little, if any, technical knowledge of steam, electricity, or chemistry was needed. The employer generally worked beside his laborers.

The industrial revolution was characterized by the appearance of the factory and the factory system. Early factories were hardly distinguishable from mills, but the philosophy governing their operation was different. As time went on, it became even more different and eventually made the factory a revolutionary type of operation when compared with the home, mill, or shop. Bogart has defined the factory system as "the concentration of all the processes of manufacture in a factory, involving their withdrawal from the household or shop where they had previously been carried on; it involves also the use of specialized machines, driven by non-human power, and the organization of the workers under skilled management, for stipulated wages and fixed hours, with production for the general market and not upon order."[1]

Before a nation can make much industrial progress most of the following eight conditions must prevail. In the case of the United States about 1800, all of them obtained.

1. There must be some technical progress. This was the outstanding difference between the economy of the mid-eighteenth century and that of the early nineteenth century. For centuries there had been little technical progress in industry, agriculture, or transportation. Now long strides began to be made. No longer did son use the same methods as those used by father, grandfather, and great-grandfather. One of the most outstanding developments was the invention by the Englishman James Watt, between 1765 and 1782, of a steam engine that would do more than pump water out of a mine. This one could turn a wheel. It gave the world a new source of power, one that could be employed when streams ran low, or even in towns where there were no streams. It put greater energy into the hand of man and freed him from some of the vagaries of nature. Indeed the sciences of physics and chemistry made more rapid advances from this time forward. Engineering, which was previously almost unknown, except in the military sense, began to develop rapidly. Formerly the file and chisel were the chief instruments for shaping metals; there was no adequate way of making one machine the exact replica of another except through the skilled eye and hand of the workman. Tooling to within 1/32 inch was considered a high degree of accuracy. The English manufacturer Matthew Boulton spoke with pride of his chief mechanic who could bore a 50-inch cylinder so accurately that it did not "err the thickness of an old shilling in any part." In England, thanks to men like Henry Maudslay, accurate copying tools such as the slide rest came into being, and other inventors like Bramah and Nasmyth came forth with their machine tools. In this country one man, Eli Whitney, drew somewhat on Old World skill and somewhat on his own ingenuity to fashion the tools and dies to turn out thousands of gun parts as "like as peas" and thus introduce the concept of interchangeable parts to the American industrial world. The American patent registration office, which went into operation in 1793, encouraged the technical progress that was so essential to industrial innovation.

2. Capital too is essential to operate a factory. Capital, strictly speak-

[1] Ernest L. Bogart, *Economic History of the American People* (New York: Longmans, Green & Co., Inc., 1935), p. 384.

ing, is tools, equipment, inventory, and plant. Money or liquid capital is essential to buy this equipment or to pay the workers while they make it. By the early nineteenth century there was a sufficient supply of savings in the hands of American merchants and others to acquire the capital needed to establish the first simple factories. With England and France at war, American merchants made handsome profits for a while. Then blockades and embargoes began to hurt trade. So Francis Lowell and his brother-in-law, Patrick Tracy Jackson, who until then had been in foreign trade, decided to divert their liquid capital to what appeared to be a more lucrative line, textile manufacturing, at Waltham, Massachusetts, in 1813.

3. Business must have confidence in the strength and good will and justice of their government before they will put their savings and capital in large amounts into long-range ventures such as textile mills, iron forges, or gun factories. The protection given property holders and creditors by the Constitution, the steps taken by Alexander Hamilton to pay off old government debts, and the continuing efforts of Chief Justice Marshall to strengthen the authority of the Federal government, all gave businessmen confidence in the future of their government and of their country. Without this confidence, that is, under conditions such as prevailed at the time of Shays' Rebellion, it may be doubted that as many of these businessmen would have risked their savings in investments that would take years to pay off.

4. Adequate markets were absolutely essential to dispose of goods produced in large quantities. These presupposed reasonably cheap transportation, or concentrations of population in towns or cities, or conditions of free trade (no tariff barriers) between states. The building of turnpikes and then of canals did much to cut transportation costs. Several developments improved the market situation, such as the doubling of the population every generation and the increasing number of towns of over 2,500, from twenty-four in 1790 to sixty-one in 1820, for example, and the adoption of the Constitution, which threw out tariff barriers between the states. Adam Smith, the Scottish economist, had commented a few years before that "Specialization is limited by the extent of the market." Making goods in a factory, where one man did the same thing day after day, turning out a large number of the same product, was clearly specialization; the amount of this kind of business that was profitable depended on the extent or size of the market.

5. An adequate labor supply was likewise essential for the factory system to succeed. In colonial times labor had been scarce and dear, which was one of several reasons why America lagged behind England in industrial progress. At the other extreme, labor can also be so plentiful and cheap, as in China and India, that machines, which are primarily

laborsaving, must be very efficient to be worth the investment. That is one reason why the industrial revolution has come so late to those lands. In the United States about 1810 labor was neither too scarce nor too plentiful, although the employment of children and of part-time workers suggests that if anything, labor was on the scarce side.

6. A protective tariff may also be essential to defend infant industries from the ruthless competition of older and more efficient foreign producers. This was clearly true in the United States where knowledge of textile machinery was less advanced and wages were higher than in England. Although the protection was not in the form of a tariff, it was the equivalent of a highly protective tariff. From 1806 until the end of 1814 the entrance of English textiles into American markets was either hampered or prevented by French privateers trying to enforce Napoleon's blockade of England, or by the Embargo Act, the Nonintercourse Acts, or by the War of 1812 itself. Behind this protection new industries were able to thrive, despite fumbling experimentation and high prices which otherwise would have cost them their economic lives. By 1816 some had become efficient enough to stand on their own feet. Thenceforth the government began enacting tariff laws to protect them.

7. Raw materials can be imported, but it is a great advantage if they are at hand. New England, which had the first textile factories, had to import raw cotton, but cotton was light enough to stand the cost of transportation from distant points. As for wool, plenty was available. The Middle states, but not New England, had ample iron. The small amounts of copper and lead sufficed for the needs of the time. Early machinery was in large part of wood; there was plenty of this, including sturdy hickory and oak.

8. As for power, that too existed in adequate amounts. Water was the chief source of power at the beginning. Since the mountains lie nearer the ocean in New England than farther south, the streams come tumbling down a little faster and the falls lie closer to the coast. Many of the streams were also small enough to be easily dammed. Fuel power came from the then ample supplies of wood, from which charcoal could be made, and later from coal, which existed in quantity in eastern Pennsylvania.

THE COTTON TEXTILE INDUSTRY

In one newly industrialized nation after another, cotton thread or cloth has been the first product to be manufactured under the factory system. There are reasons for this. Just about everyone wears some cotton clothing and wears it out, so that the demand for cotton textiles is tremendous and continuous. The spinning of thread, the weaving of cloth, and the other steps in clothmaking, when done in the home, are tedious and time-consuming; accordingly, the women or "distaff side" of the household were glad to let the factory take over this responsibility. From the manufacturer's point of view, the fact that he could satisfy his customers with a few weights of thread and cloth enabled him to put spinning and weaving on a large-scale power production basis at an early date. Finally, since raw cotton, thread, and cloth are relatively valuable for their weight, both raw materials and finished products could be sold over a wide market. Two systems of manufacturing cotton textiles appeared in America: one was English in origin, one native American.

Samuel Slater and the Providence System. Samuel Slater, a twenty-one-year-old English immigrant, is credited with setting up the first factory to make cotton thread or yarn at Pawtucket, Rhode Island. In 1790 he formed a partnership with William Almy and Moses Brown, who provided the capital and agreed to handle the marketing side of the business. Slater was the production expert and manager. Orphaned in England at fourteen, he had been apprenticed to his father's friend, Jedediah Strutt, who in turn was a partner of Richard Arkwright. The name of Arkwright was famous in late eighteenth century England because of his inventions of spinning machines and his success in cloth manufacturing. Young Slater was so able that he became a foreman while still an apprentice and helped supervise the building of a new mill and the installation of modern machinery before he was twenty-one. Thus he knew intimately the details of installation and operation of the most modern-type textile factory of the time. Meanwhile, he had seen advertisements for textile machine experts in America and had heard reports of handsome prizes given for machines already obsolete in England. America seemed to offer opportunity. But the English, whose industrial supremacy depended on superior technical knowledge, had laws against the export of machine blueprints or the emigration of mechanical experts. Slater sewed his apprentice papers, which he needed to prove he was no imposter, in his clothing but carried all other information in his head and, disguised as a farm boy, slipped out of England and came to America.

Within a year Slater formed his partnership with Almy and Brown. His factory produced only thread; he operated it by water power; and he employed only a few men and several apprentices, that is, child labor. This was the system under which Slater himself had grown up. At times when he produced too much thread he "put out" (subcontracted) some of it to be made into cloth which he could more easily sell. Slater was successful and set up other mills and went into other partnerships. His plants were small but he made a fairly high-grade product. His profits he poured back into his business—sometimes so fast that he was short of cash—and when he died in 1836, he was worth about $635,000. Slater was conservative in his methods; it was years before he made cloth as well as yarn, and he did not install power looms until 1823, many years after his American competitors began using them.

Francis Lowell, Patrick Tracy Jackson, and the Lowell System. Francis Lowell of Boston was also mechanically inclined, but in his younger years he was a successful importer. In 1810 he went to England, allegedly for a rest cure, but his relaxation took the form of visiting textile factories which he regarded as the secret of Britain's industrial supremacy. Upon his return he persuaded his brother-in-law, Patrick Tracy Jackson, to go into partnership with him and to turn their capital to setting up a factory to make cotton cloth. Lowell designed the machines, no doubt drawing on his observations in England, but he also made substantial contributions of his own. Lowell and Jackson's factory, which went into operation in 1813, was the first in America to make cloth under one roof. Located at Waltham, on the Charles River near Boston, it was such a success that within a few years it outgrew its building and site. Meanwhile Francis Lowell died in 1817.

In 1822 Patrick Tracy Jackson founded a town called Lowell, after the deceased inventor, at Pawtucket Falls on the Merrimac River, some 30 miles outside of Boston. He incorporated the company, for the concept of its operations was grandiose. Jackson and his associates bought the land at Pawtucket Falls, not only with the idea of using some of it themselves, but also with the thought of leasing the rest to machine-making plants and to other manufacturing firms. It was a public utility and real estate as well as a textile manufacturing project. To obtain an adequate labor supply, Jackson encouraged farmers' daughters to work in his mills, setting up boardinghouses for them and installing house matrons. His mills produced large amounts of cloth, but its quality was not as high as that put out by Slater's mills.

Lowell grew rapidly. In 1830, realizing that the town needed better transportation to its chief market, Boston, than its road, river, and canal facilities offered, Jackson sponsored the building of the Boston and Lowell Railroad, one of New England's earliest. By 1836 Lowell was a city, and by 1850 it was the second largest in the state. Furthermore, it was the nation's leading cotton textile center. Its success of course encouraged imitators: Jackson himself helped to found Lawrence. Other Boston capitalists founded other textile towns at Manchester and Nashua in New Hampshire, and at Saco, Biddeford, and Lewiston in Maine. All followed much the same pattern. Capitalists bought a water-power site along a river and built a textile mill. Other mills sprang up to serve the community or to use the power site too. These towns, fast-growing and wild as mining camps at first, in time became well-run cities.

Improvements in textile manufacturing machinery took place quite rapidly in this period. Machinery generally became obsolete before it was worn out. Companies that discarded out-of-date equipment often made good profits; competition usually killed off the others. Under the circumstances, more and more cotton cloth was produced by the larger mills, and the worker productivity, thanks to the better machinery, advanced sharply. In 1815 a girl could earn in one week enough money to buy 2½ yards of calico; by 1850 her week's earnings would buy 39 yards, or sixteen times as much. Perhaps this is one reason why nineteenth century women wore so much more clothing than eighteenth or twentieth century women. When cloth became cheaper, they could not resist the bargain.

The Lowell or Boston method of operation differed from that of Slater in Providence in at least four respects. Lowell and Jackson were capitalists running million-dollar corporations with many stockholders, whereas Slater and his associates were small entrepreneurs using the partnership device. The Lowell-type capitalists built whole towns; Slater and his kind erected a small mill in a small town already supplied with adequate power and labor. Lowell and Jackson found a new source of labor, farmers' daughters; Slater depended on the English system of a few skilled workers assisted by child apprentices. The less-skilled operatives in the Lowell mills turned out a medium-quality product cheaply and abundantly, whereas Slater and his imitators produced a higher quality yarn and cloth in smaller quantities. The very best quality material still came from England, however. Slater brought the textile industry from England to America; Lowell and Jackson gave the industry a new and what was destined to be a characteristically American form.

THE SHOE INDUSTRY—MODEL OF THE RISE OF THE FACTORY

The industrial revolution developed gradually. The factory system was the logical result of many barely perceptible changes. Although the factory first appeared in the production of cotton textiles, the clearest picture of the rise of the factory system is found in the shoe industry. Familiarity with it will help to understand developments in other industries, even though they follow the pattern less perfectly. There were four stages in the rise of the factory system in shoe making.[2]

The Home Stage. In colonial New England and in later frontier areas also, shoes were generally made in the home. Under frontier conditions

[2] Most of the material in the next few pages is based on Blanche Hazard, *The Organization of the Boot and Shoe Industry in Massachusetts before 1875* (Cambridge: Harvard University Press, 1921). A shorter version appeared in the *Quarterly Journal of Economics,* February, 1913.

the father of the household was of necessity a jack-of-all-trades. His shoemaking equipment was simple—a knife, an awl, needles, and several lasts or foot forms. On an autumn evening, when the season for going barefoot had about ended, he would take the foot measurements of one of his sons, choose from his supply of lasts the one nearest the proper size, cut the leather he had tanned himself, and make the boy a pair of shoes. The shoes were crude and might pinch the lad's toes, or he might seem to take several steps before starting to walk, but they protected his feet from the cold hard ground. If someone in the community developed skill at shoemaking, the neighbors were glad to let him make their shoes in exchange for rendering him some other service. But if a man were to put in all his time making shoes, he would soon run out of orders if he stayed in one small village. Hence the early shoemaker became an itinerant craftsman, moving from village to village, boarding at the homes of his customers, and accepting food, clothing, or other produce in exchange for his services. Since he made better-fitting shoes and brought gossip from other villages and stories of adventure and political news from the outside world, families always welcomed his arrival. In time the shoemaker tired of the wandering life and yearned to settle down in a community large enough to support him most of the year. At this point the home stage ended and the handicraft stage began.

The Handicraft Stage. The chief characteristic of the handicraft stage was that the shoemaker still met his customer face to face, but now it was in the shoemaker's shop, for the customer came to him. The shoemaker made most shoes on order—called "bespoke work"—and he usually supplied the leather. Occasionally a customer failed for some reason to take the shoes he had ordered, and sometimes when business was dull the shoemaker made up a batch of average-sized shoes to have on hand. These he could sell from his shop or he might trade them to the local general store for groceries or other supplies, or he might even take them to a larger town and dispose of them to a merchant there. It is at this point, when the shoemaker ceased to deal directly with his customer, that the handicraft stage ended and the domestic stage began.

The Domestic Stage. In the domestic stage the middleman appeared. Usually he had been a shoemaker himself but sometimes, like Ephraim Lincoln of Braintree, he was a local storekeeper. Whoever he was, he left orders with various shoemakers throughout the countryside, supplied them with leather, picked up the shoes periodically, and sold them in town or even shipped them to points as far distant as New Orleans or the West Indies. This system of distribution and collection was known as "putting out." Most of the shoes were still plain in appearance—before the 1850s lefts and rights were made only on special order. Shoes were often displayed in a general store in a barrel from which the customer picked out two of about the proper size. In fact, shoemaking standards declined during the domestic stage because the shoemaker no longer dealt directly with his customer. Instead his chief interest was the income he received—the more shoes he made, the more pay he got, and the middleman would generally take them as fast as he could make them. To fatten their incomes some of the less scrupulous shoemakers cut wastefully the leather that was furnished them and disposed of the leftover pieces to traveling scrap-leather dealers. To speed up production the shoemaker taught members of his family to perform some of the simpler tasks while he did the more difficult ones.

This idea appealed to the middleman, too. In order to avoid paying master craftsman rates and to eliminate the scrap-leather racket, the middleman set up his own "central shop" where he cut his own leather and then portioned it out to workers to do the "fitting"—the work on the uppers. Then he brought it back to the central shop, from which he again distributed it to the "makers" along with the proper number of rough-cut soles and the right amount of thread to assemble the shoe. This involved much lost motion, wide variation in the quality of the work done, shoe parts left a long time in the hands of slow workers, and other inconveniences. Delays became especially exasperating when hundreds of crates of shoes were being prepared for shipment to California or Australia in the early 1850s. It was this urgent need to save time and gain efficiency that resulted in the final concentration of shoemaking in one building. Thus the domestic stage ended and the factory stage began.

The Factory Stage. With the whole operation in one building, machines, such as the recently invented sewing machine, could be used most profitably, for they could be kept in almost constant operation. Operations could be more minutely subdivided, the foremen could maintain the quality of the work and enforce a respectable pace of production, and the enterpriser knew whether or not he had enough shoes to fill a large order and could add extra hands to complete the order if he needed to. Workers of course no longer owned the tools, they worked increasingly on a time rather than a piece-rate system, and they worked a set number of hours, say twelve, per day. The factory owner, of course, had to face the problem of selling this stream of shoes that his workers were producing.

The evolution of the factory system has been going on ever since the eighteenth century and is still in process. In general, the older and more populous parts of the country reached the factory stage first. Shoemaking remained in the handicraft and domestic stages in the Middle West for some time after it reached the factory stage in New England. Even today the preliminary stages may be found in some occupations not yet ready for the factory system. In most homes the mother is the "jill-of-all-trades" so far as food preparation is concerned; everyone is familiar with tailors who do custom work, and in big cities cheap dresses are still being "put out" for completion. The products that reached the factory stage first were those which could be easily standardized, hence made by machine methods, and for which there was a fairly large and steady demand. At the same time, it should be pointed out that not all industries have passed through every stage outlined above; ironmaking did not, for example.

14

THE IRON AND STEEL INDUSTRY

Up to approximately the 1840s the situation in iron and steel was much as it had been in colonial times. Ironmaking was an industry of numerous centers of production, each with its local mines and wood preserves to provide charcoal and its local or regional market. True, Pennsylvania was the best endowed for iron production: as early as 1817 Morris Birkbeck described Pittsburgh as the Birmingham of America. Blacksmith shops and small bloomeries made many finished wrought-iron products during this period.

There were two basic types of iron in use, cast iron and wrought iron. Cast iron, containing about 2 or 3 per cent carbon, was hard but brittle; wrought iron, with almost all the carbon pounded out or burned out of it, was softer but malleable and did not break. The carbon content of steel lies in between these two irons; it has their two advantages—but lacks their bad characteristics. Steelmaking was a delicate operation requiring experience, technical skill, and patience, with the result that steel was a costly product. Yet cheap steel was increasingly needed for the machines of the advancing industrial revolution, which could not function much longer with hickory and oak, brittle cast iron, and wrought iron that wore out fast. In fact, even the iron industries could not supply all the wrought-iron rails needed to build the growing number of railroad lines and to replace rails that wore out.

Advances in Ironmaking. By the 1840s the demands of the industrial revolution for iron had to be met. Within a few years' time, a number of new discoveries were made, or good but hitherto little-used methods were adopted. For example, the hot blast oven was invented and anthracite began to replace charcoal as a smelting fuel; puddling was more widely practiced; America began to make its own railroad rails and large engine parts; and finally the principle of cheap steel was discovered.

As the demand for iron grew, iron furnaces exhausted their readily available supplies of wood convertible into charcoal. Either wood had to be hauled long distances, or the furnace itself must find a new location, or a new fuel had to be found. Anthracite coal existed in quantity near the iron mines of eastern Pennsylvania which, in turn, were near the Eastern iron-consuming markets. Yet a furnace charged with iron ore, limestone, and anthracite coal would yield an iron that was definitely inferior to iron made with charcoal as fuel. The discovery of the hot blast oven about 1833 made possible the use of anthracite coal for smelting equally good iron because it heated the hot gases away from the iron. The hot blast also made possible higher temperatures and economized on fuel. Thus "anthracite iron" came into increasing prominence after about 1840 and anthracite was the chief smelting fuel from 1855 to 1875. This nation was slow to make much use of coke.

An Englishman, Henry Cort, discovered puddling as a method to purify iron in 1784 but it first came into widespread use in this country about 1840. Hitherto ironworkers had hammered the final impurities out of the "bloom." By the puddling process the molten iron was run into a furnace with an iron oxide lining. The oxygen in the lining and the carbon in the iron united and escaped in a gaseous form. Even so, the "puddlers" who stirred the hot fluid with long bars had a very hot, heavy job to perform which required much skill, strength, and endurance. Puddling made possible the production of more wrought iron in a day's work than before.

Almost from the outset railroads had a ravenous appetite for wrought iron. All the mills accessible to the Baltimore and Ohio Railroad could not supply it with the 15,000 tons of iron needed to face its wooden rails. Although Congress was trying to protect and develop the iron industry, which was not very progressive before the 1830s, the need for rails was so great that Congress took the tariff off on any imported iron rails that were put into use within three years. During the ensuing decade railroads relied largely on imported rails. After 1842 Congress imposed the tariff on rails again. This encouragement, and even more, the use of new methods, stimulated iron production to grow from 300,000 tons in 1840–1841 to 650,000 tons in 1846–1847. After 1845 the United States also supplied most of the rails for its own railroads. By 1847 sixteen mills were turning out 100,000 tons of rails a year. Merchant mills, that is, iron plants that rolled other shapes, also appeared. Trenton had the nation's largest plant in 1845, and Fall River, Richmond, Cincinnati, and Pittsburgh were also well-known as rolling-mill centers. Eastern Pennsylvania, however, led the nation in iron production. Scranton, because of its furnaces and mills, mushroomed from a hamlet of five houses in 1840 to a bustling city of 15,000 in 1860. In the early 1850s Reading Forge fashioned a 34-ton shaft for the Collins liner *Arctic,* and the Morris foundry in Philadelphia cast a 65-ton bedplate for the Collins liner *Baltic.* By 1860, 256 establishments were rolling 500,000 tons of iron, almost half of it for railroads.[3]

[3] Victor Clark, *History of Manufactures in the United States* (New York: McGraw-Hill Book Company, Inc., 1929), vol. I, pp. 514–515.

The Invention of Cheap Steel. At the rate that industry was growing, wrought iron could not satisfy its needs much longer. The industrial sector of the economy desperately needed cheap steel. Steel was expensive to make because it required great skill to add just the right amount of carbon and diffuse it properly. Because it has a medium amount of carbon, steel is both hard and malleable. Steel has the good qualities of both the irons and the bad qualities of neither; carbon is the key to its virtues. Two men share the fame of having simultaneously discovered a way to make steel cheaply. They were Sir Henry Bessemer, an Englishman, and William Kelly of Eddyville, Kentucky, who manufactured large kettles for boiling cane sugar. Kelly discovered by accident that if he blew cold air through molten iron, it would remove the carbon: the oxygen in the air united with the carbon, leaving pure or wrought iron. The process was simply that of creating a fire. For years Kelly's neighbors and competitors would not believe that he had invented anything of value; rather, they thought he was turning out an inferior iron. Actually, the converter or container that Kelly used did not do as good a job of purifying the iron as the one that Bessemer invented. Each man obtained a patent in his own country in 1856. Kelly, however, had a compensating advantage over Bessemer: he had the American rights to the so-called Mushet process. After all, the converters just made pure or wrought iron, whereas cheap steel was the ultimate goal. Robert Mushet, also an Englishman, had a patent on the use of spiegeleisen, which is an alloy of manganese and carbon in known amounts. The manganese takes off any remaining oxygen, and the carbon builds the wrought iron into steel. Thus by charging a converter with molten iron, blowing out the impurities, adding a known amount of carbon in the form of spiegeleisen, and mixing well, steel could be made easily (see Fig. 9-1). Like many inventions, the idea was simple once it was found. For nearly ten years Bessemer and Kelly engaged in a patent dispute which kept the country from enjoying the benefits of their discovery. Cheap steel was not generally available until after the Civil War.

OTHER INDUSTRIES AND THEIR CONTRIBUTIONS

Most of the major industries of this era were based on organic or agricultural raw materials. Textiles were based on cotton, wool, or flax, shoes on leather, flour milling on grains, meat packing on hogs, cattle, and sheep, and all the wood-using industries on lumber. As the industrial revolution progressed, more articles were made of metal. Also the assembling process, as in the case of guns, clocks, or machines, became more intricate. The beginnings of industrial methods that were to become increasingly important in later years appeared quite early. The principle

FIG. 9-1. Early bessemer-type converters (about 1870). (*Courtesy of the American Iron and Steel Institute.*)

of interchangeable parts and "tooling up" before going into production, the assembly line, and even a concept as modern as automation are all discernible.

The Principle of Interchangeable Parts and Eli Whitney. Eli Whitney, inventor of the cotton gin, made a second contribution to American industrial development that was probably more far-reaching in its importance than his first. It all began in 1798 when this country was engaged in an undeclared war with France that looked as if it might grow more serious. Congress voted an appropriation for 50,000 rifles. Whitney offered to manufacture 10,000 of them, 4,000 to be delivered in fifteen months, and he got a contract of $134,000. The government distributed the rest of the 50,000-rifle contract among twenty-six gunmakers. Whitney's offer was an amazing one and probably only a person as famous as Whitney could have obtained the contract. No more than 750 rifles had ever been made in one arsenal before, each one largely handmade by a skilled gunsmith. Whitney proposed to employ a method that seems natural and normal today but was a revolutionary departure at the time; it took some convincing arguments to persuade the government men that it would work. He intended first to make the machine that would make or fashion each part of the rifle. Thus every part would be the same size and shape as every other part; the parts would be interchangeable. He also had to train the workers who were to carry out these processes. Then after all these preparations were made, he would go into production on a large scale. Whitney estimated that most of the first fifteen months would be devoted to getting ready—today it would be called "tooling up." Only the last few months would be devoted to turning out his rifle parts and assembling them. Whitney's method of procedure was quite successful, although he did not allow enough time for unforeseen delays. Fortunately, the war petered out and the government officials were patient.

Whitney's invention had many important implications. Once the contract was completed, he had to find other orders to keep his plant, equipment, and workers busy or else he would lose heavily on the idle investment. Whitney had found a road to depressions as well as to efficient large-scale production. What Eli Whitney could do with guns, other inventors and manufacturers could do with other goods, such as clocks, locks, and plows. A great advantage of interchangeable parts was that when one part broke, an order to the factory for a replacement was all that was needed. The customer did not have to send in the whole piece of equipment to be made over or to have the new part fitted to it exactly. Today the principle of interchangeable parts is employed in making almost any good that has more than one part.

The Disassembly Line in the Cincinnati Meat-packing Industry. The assembly line, albeit in reverse form as a disassembly line, was in existence before the Civil War. For example, in the establishment of Milward and Oldershaw in Covington, Kentucky, across the Ohio River from Cincinnati, the slaughtering and packing of hogs was carried on in 1850 much as it is today. The hogs were driven up an inclined runway to the hogpens located on the roof of the three-story establishment. Slaughtering took place on the top floor and then the cleaning processes were carried out on the second floor. Cutting and packing were done on the first floor and finally the meat was stored in "lofty and well ventilated cellars . . . so excellently adapted . . . that spoiled meat is comparatively unknown on these premises."[4] This 2-acre establishment was said to be the largest of its kind in the nation. Thus the assembly line idea was already present in America in its incipient form.

Inventions of Oliver Evans. One of the most remarkable inventors of the late eighteenth and early nineteenth centuries was Oliver Evans, sometimes referred to as the American James Watt. He invented the high-compression engine, produced a land vehicle propelled by steam and an early steamboat, improved textile machinery, and made numerous other mechanical contributions. Perhaps his most remarkable invention was the Brandywine flour mill, in which grain moved from grain bag to flour barrel almost without being touched by human hand. True, he used principles already known, but in an ingenious way and to accomplish a new purpose. His mill went into operation in September, 1785. All the machinery was moved by water power. There were buckets on an endless conveyor to carry grain to the top floor of the mill, a revolving rake or arm to push it to the chute which fed it to the grinding millstones, more buckets and conveyors to carry the ground product back up to the meal loft, another revolving rake, called a "hopper-boy," to spread the meal out evenly so that it would cool and dry, and another device to feed it into the hopper of the bolting (sifting) machine. He had practically eliminated all the heavy mill work of lugging heavy bags and shoveling grain (often trampling it with dirt in the process). This was a laborsaving device of the first magnitude. Where formerly a mill needed four men and a boy, Evans's mill needed only two men, and their chief function was to put the tops on the barrels of flour. A few millers were grateful to Evans, but most of them did not care to change their methods, because of the expense of installation. Evans was ahead of his time.

As business and industrial historians probe into the methods of the more advanced businessmen of a century to a century and a half ago, they find the clear beginnings of a number of very modern practices.

[4] Charles Cist, *Sketches and Statistics of Cincinnati in 1851* (Cincinnati: William H. Moore and Company, 1851), pp. 228–229.

DEVELOPMENTS IN POWER AND FUELS

James Watt of England invented the steam engine as a power device about 1769 and Oliver Evans contributed to its improvement in America, but the chief sources of power for industry until shortly before the Civil War were water power, animal power, and human muscles. Likewise, although some coal was used in the eighteenth century, the chief fuel was wood. Coal did not come into prominence until the 1830s or 1840s. Oil was not discovered in quantity until 1859 and was used then as an illuminant and as a lubricant but not as a fuel.

Water Power. There were all kinds of water mills, depending on how much power was needed, how much the miller had to invest, the nature of the site, the speed of the current, and other considerations. Usually, the more power that was desired, the greater the preparations and hence the greater the investment that the miller had to make. Oliver Evans put out a manual, *The Young Mill-wright and Miller's Guide,* in 1795 to instruct persons intending to build and operate water mills. It was widely used. The simplest mill to construct was one using a "float wheel." Although it required no expensive building of dams or millraces, it turned the wheel only as fast as the current ran and posed problems when the water level was unduly low or high.

To get more power, it was essential to build a dam and thus make use of the force and height of the contained water. It was unthinkable to dam large streams because of the engineering problems and expense involved. A dam over the Merrimac at Lowell in 1832 was a success, but one over the Connecticut at Holyoke in 1847 broke two hours after completion. Most dams were erected on small rivers or streams. Where there was a dam, the mill builder had a variety of wheels to choose from. An overshot wheel provided considerable power but the water had to be led to it by a wooden trough or flume. The miller opened the gate to this flume only when he desired to turn the wheel and operate the mill. In using the undershot wheel, the water was shot down a flume at a sharp angle against the bottom of the wheel, the impact of the water rather than its weight providing the power. In the case of the popular pitch-back wheel, the weight of the water, falling on the wheel from overhead, supplied the impetus. Which wheel was used depended also to some extent on its purpose. Most mills were gristmills: many doubled as sawmills and sometimes as fulling mills as well. A fulling mill pounds woolen cloth after it has come from the loom and thus softens and stretches it. Water mills as suppliers of power to factories were prominent between 1813 and 1860.

In the 1850s turbines replaced water wheels to some degree. Uriah Boyden in 1844 designed turbines for the Appleton company at Lowell. Within twelve years they displaced most of the company's pitch-back wheels. Turbines receive their greater power from the "kick" that is generated when water changes direction.

Steam Power. Steam as a motive power in factories was not prominent until about the 1840s. It enjoyed greater success in transportation than in manufacturing during the first half of the century. One of the earliest mills driven by steam was a New York sawmill. About 1812 Oliver Evans's high-pressure type of engine gained some popularity: he soon had ten in operation. This engine wasted fuel, but fuel was plentiful and the engine was simple to build. By 1817 a cotton factory, a woolen factory, and a wireworks were operated by steam in Pittsburgh. Yet progress was slow, as evidenced by the fact that out of 421 manufacturing plants in New England in 1831, only 43 used steam and most of these were printing offices. Water power was favored in New York and New Jersey although about a third of Pennsylvania's plants were steam-propelled. Steam engines were expensive in this country for another two decades. Meanwhile water-power advocates constructed larger dams over bigger rivers and managed to generate sizable quantities of horsepower.

By the 1840s the end of the water-power expansion was in sight. A controversy now broke out between the defenders of water power and the advocates of steam power. General Charles T. James, mill superintendent and engineer, was the leading champion of steam power. He spoke and wrote frequently in favor of it and was responsible during the 1840s for starting twenty-three steam mills, most of them in New England. He particularly favored seaports as sites because coal could be brought to them so cheaply. Writing in 1849 he said, "There are many things in favor of steam power, compared with water power. You can have steam where you please; and you can have, as you choose, much or little. However inconvenient, you must take water where it is, and, at some times have much more than you want, and at other times, not near as much as you want—perhaps none at all. With steam power you may go into a city, town or village, where dwellings for operatives, and other requisites, are at hand; and thus avoid a heavy outlay for them. With water-power, you will have a village to build, and roads to make, and dams, raceways, flumes, wheels, and wheel-pits, to construct, and heavy foundations to lay, before you can apply the water to use. Thus you will have to divert a large amount of capital from the business of manufacturing . . . ".[5] Among James's mills were large ones at Salem and New-

[5] Article by Charles T. James in Freeman Hunt (ed.), *The Merchant Magazine and Commercial Review* (New York, 1849), vol. 21, p. 500.

buryport, Massachusetts, and at Portsmouth, New Hampshire. Steam mills were increasingly successful and gained at the expense of water-power ones. As soon as mills could locate near their labor supply or nearer their markets, they appeared in greater numbers in other than strictly textile towns and in greater numbers outside New England, especially in the Middle Atlantic states. Steam power gave manufacturing more flexibility than it had had with water power.

Coal as a Fuel. From colonial times on, coal had been known and where available was used by some blacksmiths. In 1792 Colonel Jacob Weiss and others formed the Lehigh Coal Mine Company to mine and market the anthracite deposits at Mauch Chunk in the Lehigh Valley in eastern Pennsylvania. Success came slowly, for few knew how to handle anthracite as a fuel, and fewer cared to try. But in 1813 White and Hazard Company, located near Philadelphia and manufacturing iron and wire, found quite by accident how to burn anthracite effectively in their furnaces. This company soon joined forces with the Lehigh Coal Mine Company to transport coal more effectively by water to the Philadelphia and New York markets. A century or more ago the Mauch Chunk coal pits vied with Niagara Falls as one of the sights visitors to America had to see: they were as famous as the Mesabi iron pits are today. Coal production grew from 50,000 tons mined in 1820 to 14,334,000 tons in 1860. The demand for coal was stimulated by railroads after the 1830s, by iron mills after the 1840s, and by steam-driven textile mills after the 1850s. Some coal was also imported; it was often called "sea coal" for this reason. It came from England at first, later from Nova Scotia and from the bituminous fields around Richmond, Virginia.

PROGRESS IN MINING METALS

As the industrial revolution progressed and manufacturing became more complex and invaded more fields of production, the demand for metals grew. The chief industrial metals mined were few in number: iron, copper, and lead. Gold did not affect industry directly.

20

Until about 1850 the mediocre local iron deposits in western New England, northern New Jersey, eastern Pennsylvania, and upper New York had sufficed, along with some imported iron. They could not be expected to last in view of the growing demands for iron. Fortunately, a rich deposit of iron was discovered in 1844 in the Marquette range on the northern shores of Lake Michigan, although it was another decade before any significant amount could be shipped east. Rail lines had to be built to this remote region, the first Sault Ste. Marie canal had to be opened in 1855, and a system of ore boats and rail lines to eastern smelting centers, especially Pittsburgh, had to be worked out. By 1857, however, the local railroad serving the Marquette range was sending out 1,000 tons of ore daily during the season.

Next in industrial importance was copper; at first the United States imported most of its needs from England and western South America. After the 1840s and especially the 1850s, increasing amounts came from the rich mines on the Keeweenaw Peninsula some distance west of the Marquette iron mine in Upper Michigan. By the early 1860s these deposits supplied 14 million pounds of copper a year, or 60 per cent of the domestic needs. Copper was especially valuable for sheathing wooden ships and also found uses in the engineering trades. These mines even exported copper after 1855.

The biggest lead-mining area likewise was in the West, at Galena in northern Illinois, which is on the Fever or Galena River, a tributary of the Upper Mississippi. It had been known and operated by the Indians and French since the late seventeenth century. Americans leased mines here and began working them after 1822. Production grew from 100 tons in 1824 to 7,000 tons in 1829, then sloughed off for a few years as the market became glutted. The period from 1835 to 1848 was the heyday of these mines, the annual production going from 5,500 to 27,000 tons. Lead was the chief cargo of steamboats plying the Upper Mississippi. After 1848 production declined and America again stepped up its imports of lead. Lead was chiefly used for bullets and in paints.

LACK OF LEGISLATION AFFECTING INDUSTRIES

In this early period of manufacturing development there were few regulations or laws affecting industries, and what few there were were more of a help than a hindrance. Manufacturers sometimes requested local and state governments to enact legislation exempting their factories from taxation during their early years of growth, or to grant them favorably located pieces of land; legislatures frequently acceded to such requests. The help that some companies received from being allowed to incorporate will be discussed in the next chapter; this was of considerable assistance in obtaining funds.

As had been done during colonial times, state governments enacted inspection laws to guarantee the quality of such commodities as flour, nails, pork, and potash. Some people disliked what they heard about industrial conditions in England and looked with misgiving upon the spread of industry to America. Apparently at the instigation of General David Humphreys, one-time minister to Spain and European traveler, Connecticut enacted a law requiring factory owners to give children employees a minimum of education and moral training. Little progress was made in this matter, however, before the 1830s.

The realm in which government affected industry the most was in that of protective tariffs. That helps to explain why tariffs seemed so much more important to people then than they do now. Suffice to say at this point that industries got only incidental protection in the form of tariff laws up to 1816, mild protection from the 1816 act, rather substantial protection from the legislation in effect from 1824 until 1846, and again mild protection thereafter. The cotton textile industry, the woolen industry, and the iron industry were among those especially favored by early tariff laws.

On the whole, this was a period in which governments interfered very little with industry: it was an era of *laissez faire*.

CHAPTER 10

Growth of Long-term Capital

There are various reasons why the United States, even this early, became more prosperous than many other nations. The relatively larger amounts of capital that Americans possessed was one of the most important. Workers with new equipment generally produce more in a year than those with old-fashioned tools. Tools, equipment, raw materials, inventories are all capital. Capital is basic to the productivity and thus to the prosperity of a nation.

Economists measure a nation's material welfare in terms of its national income (taken yearly). It is made up primarily of the consumers' goods produced in the past year plus the new capital accumulated plus the services performed. The national income divided by the population gives the per capita national income. Some economists believe that it is more realistic to divide by the number of family units and get the per family national income. Neither figure, however, is very meaningful if only a few persons receive the bulk of the income, as has sometimes been the case in Oriental kingdoms. In the United States, per capita or per family income figures both have meaning. An economist should also quote the figures in dollars of the same value when making comparisons between different eras. Even this does not take into account, however, that in most cases manufactured goods are constantly improving in quality; $100 of cotton cloth produced in 1850 was of better quality than $100 of cloth produced in 1815.

Historians of national income are only now starting to find out what the national income was before the Civil War and how much capital accumulated each year, or at least in certain key years. The available estimates are far from reliable; they give us only orders of magnitude to compare. Although the country was expanding its total output fairly rapidly before the Civil War, the per capita income, in terms of dollars of the same value, was making only modest advances. The average citizen of 1859 had a 40 per cent larger real income than his grandfather of 1799.[1]

[1] National Industrial Conference Board, *The Economic Almanac, 1956* (New York: Thomas Y. Crowell Company, 1956), pp. 423, 443. Simon Kuznets believes that the

It is fairly safe to guess that before the Civil War the nation saved and invested approximately 7 or 8 per cent of this national income. This is the figure for net capital formation between 1869 and 1888, the earliest period for which such data have been gathered. Also the census gathered data on manufacturing capital before the Civil War. It was $50 million in 1820, $250 million in 1840, $500 million in 1850, and $1 billion in 1860. When manufacturing capital doubles every ten years, it is increasing at an average rate of 7 per cent a year.

It took several years for a water mill and a dam to earn enough to pay for themselves, but raw material like cotton, when made up into cloth, would pay for itself as soon as it was sold. The mill and dam were long-term capital; raw materials and inventory were short-term or working capital. In general, one kind of institution, such as a commercial bank, helped supply working capital and another kind, such as an investment bank, supplied the long-term capital. All businesses use both kinds of capital, but the relative amounts needed vary from industry to industry. Business also had to find new ways of organizing itself now that it needed large amounts of either kind of capital. The problems of mobilizing long-term capital will be dealt with in this chapter and those involving short-term capital in the next.

Although a capital growth of 7 to 8 per cent a year was very respectable, nevertheless capital was not plentiful before the Civil War. The Westward Movement constantly opened up new lands and resources for exploitation and thus created new demands for capital. Interest rates on loanable funds or "liquid" capital were higher in America than in Europe, a fact which attracted European capital. Loanable funds were especially scarce on the frontier. In Edwardsville, Illinois, in 1820 long-term borrowers paid 50 per cent a year.[2] There were many risks in moneylending, but those who had surplus funds to invest or who owned manufacturing capital often got handsome returns.

INSTITUTIONS FOR MOBILIZING CAPITAL

Many persons with idle funds have them because they lack the energy or imagination to put those funds to work. Likewise, many who are blessed with energy and imagination and have projects to promote lack adequate funds to carry them out. Up to the start of the nineteenth

---

often-quoted figures of Martin understate the progress made, but unfortunately he has provided no estimates of his own to use in their stead. "National Income Estimates for the United States prior to 1870," *Journal of Economic History*, vol. 12 (1952), pp. 115ff.

[2] Theodore Carlson, *The Illinois Military Tract*, Illinois Studies in Social Sciences, vol. 32, no. 2 (Urbana, Ill.: University of Illinois Press, 1951), p. 53.

century most promoters obtained outside capital by forming partnerships. They accomplished with the funds of two or more persons what those of one would not suffice to do. The trouble with the partnership was that if one partner died or wanted to withdraw, the others had to prepare new articles of agreement. Also the business was likely to be pressed for funds to pay off the heirs of the deceased or to retire the dissatisfied partner. And if one partner incurred debts on behalf of the company, creditors could sue any or all of the other partners. A partnership was easy to set up, but it was hazardous and inconvenient as well as inadequate when it came to financing large projects. Thus promotors began to utilize two hitherto neglected agents for mobilizing capital. These were private corporations and governments.

The Private Corporation. A corporation is sometimes defined as a legal entity, established with government permission to carry on specified kinds of business. The persons constituting the corporation, whether they be three or many dozens or thousands, are one artificial person in the eyes of the law. These persons may sue, or be sued, as if they were one indivisible person. If one shareholder dies or becomes dissatisfied, his shares may be transferred and his departure does not disrupt or inconvenience the whole company. Unless given a definite period of years to exist, the corporation, through its salable shares, can exist almost indefinitely as long as it is successful in business. The most important feature of a corporation, however, is the limited liability of the shareholders. Once the shareholder has paid in full for his share or shares in the company, he is not liable any further. If his company goes deeply into debt and goes bankrupt, he cannot be sued to pay off the creditors. The company's assets consist of what the stockholders paid in, plus what the company has earned and saved; after these assets are used up, the company has nothing else to fall back upon. All these peculiar features of the corporation—the right to sue or be sued as one person, indefinite life, and limited liability—are logical consequences of the fundamental fact that the corporation is a legal entity. The chief difference between corporations and the earlier joint stock companies lay in the fact that corporations had state-granted charters and joint stock companies were often informally organized. In general, then, joint stock companies were enlarged and somewhat streamlined partnerships whose shares were transferable, which afforded them continuity of existence.

Corporations, however, did not enjoy all the above-mentioned features when businessmen first used them. In the decade of the 1790s, the Federal and state governments chartered 335 business corporations. Almost two-thirds of them were turnpike, toll-bridge, canal, water, insurance, and banking companies. Only eight were authorized to engage in manufacturing. Thus most of the first business corporations were either public utilities or financial institutions. The governments hesitated to grant corporate powers to other undertakings. It was not until about 1815 that many manufacturing corporations came into being. Maryland, a leader in granting corporate charters, had only five manufacturing corporations before 1815. Between 1800 and 1823 eight states incorporated 557 manufacturing companies; most of them appeared after 1814 in the two states of Massachusetts and New York.

The legislatures freely granted corporations the right to sue and be sued as one person. They generally took the precaution, however, of limiting the life of a corporation; Maryland for a time set a forty-year limit. Congress limited the charters of both the first and the second Banks of the United States to twenty years. And the early legislatures were most hesitant of all about granting the privilege of limited liability. For a while some refused altogether to do so; others left the matter vague and unsettled, allowing the courts to decide; still others resorted to various compromises. Among the compromises were double, triple, and proportional liability. In the case of double liability the shareholder stood to lose, at worst, what he had paid for the stock plus an assessment equal to its original par value. That is, if John Brown bought a $100 par share in the Tracy Manufacturing Company for $75 on the market and the Tracy Company went into bankruptcy, Brown would lose his $75 original investment plus as much as $100. Under the triple liability plan, the shareholder might be assessed double the par value, in addition to the loss of his original investment. Under the proportional liability plan, the shareholder whose shares constituted one one-hundredth of the capital stock would be liable for one one-hundredth of the debts. Yet any of these kinds of limited liability gave wealthy men more protection than if they had invested in a partnership. When a partnership went bankrupt, the creditors sometimes found it easier to sue one wealthy person for all the debts.

States gradually clarified their position on the question of limited liability during the 1820s and 1830s. Angel and Ames's treatise on *The Law of Private Corporations Aggregate,* published in 1832, stated "no rule of law we believe is better settled, than that, in general the individual members of a private corporate body are not liable for the debts, either in their persons or in their property, beyond the amount of property which they have in the stock."[3] This statement was somewhat optimistic. Maryland clearly granted limited liability in 1839, on condition, however, that the company had not declared dividends in excess of profits. Massachusetts retained unlimited liability until 1830 and New Hampshire insisted

[3] Quoted in Joseph G. Blandi, *Maryland Business Corporations, 1783–1852,* The Johns Hopkins University Studies in Historical and Political Science (Baltimore: Johns Hopkins Press, 1934), p. 29. See also p. 50.

upon it as late as 1842. Two facts appear to have influenced states to grant limited liability. One was the fact that states which refused to grant this privilege saw those corporations seek charters in states which did. The other was the fact that states themselves sometimes invested in corporations, and their legislatures did not want the state to be liable for more than its investment. Some states, however, retained the double liability feature for banks and insurance companies. Legislatures believed that shareholders in this type of business should be made to feel a heavier responsibility for the proper behavior of their companies since they dealt with the savings of many citizens and provided much of the actual circulating money in the community. Under many state laws the directors of corporations, who after all directed its policies and knew its secrets, were subject to greater liability and severe penalties if they mismanaged the corporation.

In the early days of business corporations the state legislature had to pass a special law to grant them a charter. The legislators determined what corporate privileges the company should enjoy and what sorts of business it should carry on. This afforded an opportunity for corrupt legislators to be deaf to promoters' wishes until the clink of coin made them hear better. The system had other faults. As these private bills became more numerous, they cluttered up the legislative agenda. Yet each time a charter was proposed, the committee on corporations tended to follow the pattern adopted in granting previous charters. New York in 1811 was the first to pass a somewhat general law to streamline the whole procedure. It permitted *manufacturing* corporations with capital stock not greater than $100,000 to obtain a charter by filing certain basic information with the proper state official. New Jersey enacted a similar law in 1816. In 1837 Connecticut enacted a general law permitting incorporation "for any lawful business." Maryland in 1853 did likewise. Most states, however, did not have general incorporation laws until after the Civil War. The Northern and Western states were the most progressive and the Southern ones the least.

As the nineteenth century progressed, and especially from about 1820 onward, the corporate device became increasingly important for mobilizing capital. With it, promoters were able to draw upon the savings of people who otherwise would have hoarded their money, or at least would not have taken part in large manufacturing, transportation, or financial projects. Hundreds of persons subscribed to shares in the first and second Banks of the United States, in 1791 and in 1816.

The so-called giant corporations of a century ago were the Lowell corporations. The Merrimac Company of Lowell in 1845 had a capitalization of $2,500,000 and 390 stockholders, of whom 52 were retired businessmen, 68 were "females," 46 were merchants, 23 were lawyers, 45 employees of the company, and 80 administrators, guardians, and trustees.[4] The savings of many of these individuals would not have been employed in as large, and probably not in as productive, an enterprise if the investors had not been protected by the limited liability feature of the corporation. Moreover, it is impossible to conceive of 390 partners operating an enterprise successfully. The corporate device concentrated power in the hands of a board of directors, who in turn entrusted a manager and his staff with responsibility for directing operations. This gave the business both the advantages of a small-scale enterprise, in which a decision could be quickly reached and carried out, and at the same time the advantages of a large-scale enterprise with its larger capital and greater degree of specialization.

Government Projects. There was of course an upper limit to what a corporation could undertake. Also businessmen sometimes doubted that certain public improvements would yield enough profit to justify the risk. Under such circumstances promoters appealed to the government, either Federal, state, or local. Local governments were rarely stronger than corporations, although they would sometimes undertake more risky ventures. The Federal government helped finance the first two Banks of the United States and the Cumberland Road. After about 1816, however, little help could be expected from the Federal government. The Democrats' increasing emphasis on "states rights" kept the Federal government from participating in internal improvements. That left the responsibility to the state governments, who shouldered it up to the Panic of 1837.

One of the outstanding early examples of state financing was New York's Erie Canal: this cost the state $7,000,000. The rival project of Pennsylvania on which construction began about 1826 cost $10,000,000. Up to 1830 state projects were relatively few in number; after 1830, and especially between 1835 and 1838, state expenditures for such projects increased sharply. "By 1839 American states had issued, or authorized to be issued, state stocks amounting to $69,000,000 for canals, $43,000,000 for railroads and $7,000,000 for turnpikes."[5] Maryland, Ohio, Indiana, Illinois, Michigan, Alabama, Kentucky, and Tennessee had joined the parade, and New York and Pennsylvania had contracted for a number of subsidiary canal and rail lines feeding into their main systems. Only governments as yet could be expected to finance these large and risky undertakings. Even the Erie Canal, the only one that succeeded financially, looked bad enough beforehand. That canal was to run 350 miles, much of it "through a wilderness" as President Jefferson remarked.

[4] Malcolm Keir, *Manufacturing* (New York: The Ronald Press Company, 1928), p. 300.

[5] Reginald McGrane, *Foreign Bondholders and American State Debts* (New York: The Macmillan Company, 1935), p. 6. (Figures rounded off.)

It was to be ten times as long as any canal heretofore built. It was to cost seven times as much as the most expensive previous canal, the Middlesex. Even with the State of New York backing the project, the wonder is that enough banks and people were willing to buy the bonds. Within a few years, and before it was completed, however, the Erie Canal began to pay for itself. In the following years many investors apparently believed that if New York could do it, so could other states. They made a big mistake in thinking this.

FACTORS IN CAPITAL GROWTH

The small to medium-sized merchant or manufacturer resorted to a number of devices to add to the capital which he, or he and his partners, had invested in the business. They could sometimes borrow money locally on rather reasonable terms, if there were people of wealth at hand. Such individuals would often prefer to invest in a business that was nearby and which they could watch, rather than invest in a more distant operation. Also manufacturers, especially textile manufacturers, sometimes got capital from the merchants to whom they sold their finished products. A Boston wholesale merchant supplied John Waterman with capital in 1808 to put up a cotton mill in Canton, Massachusetts, and then took repayment, at a prearranged price, in the products of the mill.[6] The chief clerks and more skilled employees also would sometimes invest in a business which they knew something about. Then there was an indirect way of making the workers provide some capital. That was to make them accept part of their pay in kind: they then had to sell the goods they had made to get the balance of their wages. Payment in kind is considered unfair today, but it was somewhat more justified then. That was an era of barter, of small shops and mills, and of direct dealings between producer and consumer. This practice economized considerably on working capital, both on the money that the employer had to pay in wages and on the funds tied up for months in unpaid bills until the consumer paid him.

Plowing Back Profits. However, by far the most important way in which capital increased was by the so-called "plowing back" process. Every time a manufacturer employed some of his profits to enlarge his plant or to add new and better machines, he enlarged his capital. The farmer did the same thing when he set aside a bigger fraction of his crop for seed corn for the next year's planting and then cleared, plowed, and planted a larger acreage. In many lines of business all during the nineteenth century and even to this day, a rule of thumb in the distribution of profits has been "a dollar for dividends, a dollar for improvements." In other

[6] Victor Clark, *History of Manufactures in the United States* (New York: McGraw-Hill Book Company, Inc., 1929), vol. I, pp. 371, 378.

words, "keep the stockholders happy, but keep the business growing as well."

The examples of plowing back are legion. The life of Samuel Slater illustrates the practice for this period. He arrived in America with no capital and with only the knowledge of how to build textile machinery; as his business prospered he participated in the construction and operation of one textile mill after another, and when he died in 1836 he was worth $635,000. Thomas Barrows, in woolens, had nothing in 1820 and built up a fortune of $500,000 in the next thirty years. These and many other manufacturing projects could not have grown so rapidly if they had not made handsome profits. During its first ten years the profits of the Boston Manufacturing Company (Lowell's and Jackson's company) averaged 19 per cent. Another Lowell company, the Merrimac, averaged 12 per cent profits from its founding until 1860. During one decade the $20 million invested in manufacturing in New England averaged dividends of 10 per cent. Iron furnaces, foundries and machine shops, leather, lumber, paper, and other manufacturing companies also reported earnings of between 10 and 20 per cent. In a growing country with an expanding market, it was logical to plow back many of these profits into enlarging plants. This was especially true in the manufacturing segment of the economy.

Selling Securities to Get Capital. Promoters of privately owned canals and to a lesser extent those of railroads and turnpikes were more inclined to obtain capital from the sale of securities. They used two basic types of securities for such financing, namely, bonds and stocks. The bondholder is a creditor of the company; the company has borrowed money from him which it agrees to pay back later. The bond is a long-term I.O.U. The stockholder is a part owner of the company. As such he normally has a vote for each share of stock he owns in electing the board of directors, who in turn help determine company policies and select the manager. Bondholders receive a fixed return on their investment and if the company fails they, as creditors, share in the distribution of what is left. Stockholders get dividends, or a share of the profits. If the company prospers, their dividends increase and so does the value of their stock or shares. If the company fails, they lose heavily, perhaps all they have invested. Governments which financed canal projects sold only bonds. The very fact that a government had undertaken such a project instead of leaving it to private capital to manage ruled out the sale of stock for such a project. A governmentally appointed committee generally managed such operations.

From the moment that business corporations appeared, that is, from the 1790s onward, they offered and sold stocks and bonds. The first Bank of the United States disposed of $8 million of stock within two hours. By the 1830s the American capital market (for securities) was made up of several wealthy families living in cities like New York, Boston, and Philadelphia, some large insurance companies, numerous banks, and finally a growing number of manufacturers and merchants who invested some of their surplus profits in securities. Several brokerage houses, such as Prime, Ward, and King, knew who these potential buyers were and got in touch with them whenever they had some good issues to sell. By the 1850s this informal way of selling had largely disappeared. The capital market had become larger and better organized, similar in many ways to what it is today with its well-organized stock exchanges and other investment institutions. The majority of stocks and bonds were at all times disposed of in the domestic capital market. In certain periods, however, large blocks of them were also sold abroad.

As early as 1803 Samuel Blodget estimated that foreign investors held almost half of the $130 million of American securities then in existence. The absolute amounts of American securities in foreign hands grew during the century, especially in the 1817–1837 period and in the 1850s. But Americans bought an ever-larger proportion of their own securities as the century progressed. About 1817 several factors gave English investors confidence in American securities and made them willing to buy. Among these were the recollection of Alexander Hamilton's program for the assumption of state debts, the good record of the first Bank of the United States, the steady repayment of the national debt, and the immediate success of the Erie Canal. The British, for their part, had had their fill of military loans to foreign nations which had not always been repaid. They preferred to invest in productive enterprises, especially in ones in a rapidly growing nation like the United States. Furthermore, good English securities paid only 4 or 5 per cent, whereas good American ones paid at a rate 2 or 3 per cent higher. The problem was to distinguish the good American securities from the bad ones.

Investment Banking. A number of British investment houses began to specialize in the sale of American securities. The most famous was Baring Brothers and Company. The Rothschilds on the Continent took a somewhat lesser interest in American securities. At a later date George Peabody, originally an American dry goods merchant from Baltimore, specialized in American securities and founded the investment selling house that eventually became J. P. Morgan and Company. On this side of the ocean some large banks engaged in the business of buying securities in America and reselling them to individuals, financial institutions, and others in Europe, especially in Britain. Nicholas Biddle of Pennsylvania, head of the second Bank of the United States, reportedly arrived in London on one occasion in the late 1830s with his valise bulging with American securities to sell.

A number of investment dealers began to acquire some of the characteristics of a modern investment banker. An investment banker is not really a banker at all; he is a merchant of stocks and bonds. Before buying securities the investment banker should examine their quality; that is, he should consider carefully the ability of the management, their past record of success, and what the prospects of profit are. He then buys the stocks or bonds at as favorable a price as he can. Like a merchant of dry goods or of any other commodity, he may have to borrow money from a commercial bank to finance his purchase. In the third step, he sells the securities at a profit to his customers. To do this well, he has to have a large list of customers and know their tastes in securities. Also he must take care to sell his customers, in so far as he is able to do so, only good securities, or else he will soon lose their confidence. Before the Civil War a few individuals, banks, and brokerage houses had already ceased being mere dealers in investments or "loan contractors." The better ones investigated their offerings carefully and felt a sense of responsibility for their success.

For a number of years the sale of state securities in Europe, especially in England, went very well. New York State bonds, to finance the Erie Canal, appeared in 1817. The success of this project led to others. Pennsylvania began to sell bonds to finance her rival canal project in 1824, Virginia did the same for her Chesapeake and Ohio Canal, and Ohio for the Ohio and Erie Canal in 1828. Between 1820 and 1830 state debts climbed from a modest $12.8 million to $26.5 million; yet state borrowing was just getting under way. The states found it increasingly easy to obtain funds abroad for worthy projects: the English investors learned that state bonds were apparently good; they paid well and on schedule. Both parties, and the investment firms as well, now grew ambitious or careless. As early as 1829 Pennsylvania borrowed to build new public works and to pay interest charges on an earlier loan which had not done well. This was already a danger sign.

Between 1830 and 1835 the various states' debts climbed from $26.5 to $66.5 million, and by 1838 they had risen to $170.4 million. The largest part went to build canals and railroads, especially canals. Although private corporations had ceased investing in canals by 1831, sensing already that the railroad rather than the canal was the transportation form of the future, state authorities discounted this viewpoint and went on a canal building spree. Canal building was expensive, with costs at $30,000 per mile and sometimes higher. Yet past successes were great—the Erie Canal was bringing in $1 million of revenues a year. Also present pressures were strong—Western farmers saw no other way of reaching markets, so that state legislatures threw precautions to the winds. Thinly populated Western states undertook huge programs and Eastern states like New York, Pennsylvania, and Maryland ordered the construction of little-needed subsidiary canals. Early in the 1830s Ohio proceeded with the Miami and Erie Canal in the western part of the state; Indiana, after debating the matter for a decade, voted to expend the first $10 million on the Wabash and Erie; Illinois projected a canal to the Illinois River and also a series of rail lines crisscrossing the state; and Michigan likewise had an ambitious program of canals and railroads in mind. Meanwhile, both Pennsylvania and New York at great expense built second locks on their systems so that boats could proceed two ways simultaneously. By 1838 Europe had invested some $200 million in America, most of it in internal improvement projects.

States Default on Bonds. The Panic of 1837 in various ways made it difficult for several states to meet payments on their loans. Indiana, Illinois, and Michigan had placed large blocks of state bonds with brokerage houses. These firms sold the bonds but went into bankruptcy shortly thereafter; thus the states derived only limited funds from the transaction but still had to meet the obligations. The tax incomes of the states also dropped sharply during the 1837–1844 depression. This long and severe depression was delivered to the country in three blows. The 1837 punch staggered several states financially; a second in 1839 felled even a greater number; and that in 1841 leveled several more. By 1842 nine states: Arkansas, Florida, Mississippi, Michigan, Louisiana, Pennsylvania, Maryland, Indiana, and Illinois had defaulted either on all or on some of their obligations. The first three of these states finally repudiated payments; the fourth, Michigan, paid in part; and the other five, prodded by Baring Brothers, eventually paid in full.

Meanwhile the British investors urged the United States government to assume the states' debts, as Hamilton had done fifty years before. To the anger and dismay of many British, the Federal government said these debts were the sole responsibility of the separate sovereign states. Europeans found it hard to understand how states could be sovereign and still be subject to a Federal government; they looked upon that government's refusal as a feeble excuse. When an agent of the Federal Treasury in 1842 sought a loan, the head of the House of Rothschild in Paris told him curtly, "You may tell your government that you have seen the man who is at the head of the finances of Europe, and that he has told you that they cannot borrow a dollar, not a dollar." In London Baring Brothers said the Federal government would get no loan there unless it assumed the states' debts.[7] During most of the 1840s American credit in Europe was poor. The Barings devoted less attention henceforth to han-

[7] Cleona Lewis, *America's Stake in International Investments* (Washington: Brookings Institution, 1938), p. 28.

dling American securities. American internal improvements, primarily railroads, now had to be financed by corporations rather than by state governments. For several years the promoters had to raise their funds almost entirely in this country.

STOCK EXCHANGES

A stock exchange is a market where stocks and bonds may be bought and sold, that is, after their original sale by the investment dealer to the customer. It is a market for secondhand securities. The stock exchange quotations are simply a factual reporting of the prices paid for certain stocks on a given day. Investment dealers and stock exchanges appeared almost simultaneously in the financial development of the country. Without a stock exchange in the picture, investment dealers would have found it more difficult to sell their securities. The existence of stock exchanges assured the customer that any time he wanted to obtain cash for his securities, he would have a market at hand in which he could find buyers. This opportunity, accordingly, encouraged more people to invest in stocks and bonds. That in turn made it easier for corporations and governmental agencies to obtain funds to expand their operations. It all stimulated the growth of capital.

The first informal stock exchange in America was in New York in 1791. This was a time when there was considerable trading in the stock of the first Bank of the United States, in refunded debts of the Federal and state governments, and in the stocks of various corporations, especially banks and insurance companies. Nearly all these latter institutions were located on Wall Street. Since some of them paid as much as 15 or 18 per cent dividends, their stocks were in great demand. The men of wealth who bought and sold these securities, and their representatives (their brokers), formed the habit of gathering every weekday at a certain time of day under the shade of a buttonwood tree on Wall Street. Twenty-four brokers in 1792 agreed on what the commission should be when they bought and sold securities for customers. After 1793 they met at the Tontine Coffee House. In 1817 the brokers set up a more formal organization called The New York Stock and Exchange Board, and a month later they rented a second-floor room at 40 Wall Street. Meanwhile the brokers of Philadelphia, as early as 1800, set up a more formal stock exchange than that in New York (for this reason, they claim to have had the nation's first stock exchange). Philadelphia, containing the main offices of the first Bank of the United States, was then as much of a financial center as New York. In the 1820s and 1830s there were increasing numbers of canal bonds (of states) and stocks (of private companies) traded on the exchanges. Railroad securities came into vogue too during the 1830s and mining ones in the 1850s. By 1857 the New York exchange could boast the sale of 71,000 shares on a record day.

NEW FINANCIAL INSTITUTIONS

Enough has already been said to suggest that there was a "financial revolution" accompanying the industrial, agricultural, and transportation revolutions. Merely mentioning some of the new financial institutions demonstrates this. In addition to investment houses, brokerage houses, and stock exchanges, there were commercial banks, which will be discussed more fully in the next chapter, savings banks, trust companies, fire and marine insurance companies, life insurance companies, and land banks. Each one, in its way, stimulated the accumulation of savings. The system functioned like a tree gathering moisture and nourishment from its capillary roots which in turn fed them on and upward through larger roots to make the tree grow. These financial institutions loaned the savings they had gathered to customers who put the money in capital projects which made the economy flourish.

Long-term Lending of Commercial Banks. Commercial banks are supposed to be institutions for the lending of funds on a short-term basis (up to six months) since they must pay depositors or noteholders on a moment's notice. Early in the nineteenth century this rule was not as strictly enforced as it was later on. Early banks were general stores of finance and performed a variety of operations. Also it must be admitted that commercial banks have nearly always made more long-term loans than might seem desirable because there were not enough good short-term loans available. Thus commercial banks either made outright long-term loans to industrialists, merchants, and farmers or else they made short-term loans with the expectation on everyone's part that the loans would be renewed repeatedly. Although banks did not buy stocks of industrial corporations or even their bonds, they accepted them as collateral on loans. Long-term lending is more properly the function of institutions such as savings banks whose depositors may be required to give warning before withdrawing deposits.

Savings Banks. Savings banks began in Boston and Philadelphia in 1816. The Provident Institution for Savings of Boston was the first to receive a charter. By 1860 nine such banks had been chartered and their deposits were $150 million. They had over half a million depositors with an average deposit of $215. These savings contributed to capital improvements in housing and agriculture, for savings banks invested heavily in mortgages.

Trust Companies. The business of a trust company is to invest and safeguard the legacies left to widows, orphans, and others. The first trust company was the Massachusetts Hospital Life Insurance Company, which despite its name was chiefly a trust company, founded in 1823. Others, such as the New York Life and Trust Company, appeared in the 1830s. The Massachusetts Hospital Life was the largest financial institution of any kind in New England in the 1830s: it administered $4.8 million of trusts. By 1858 the figure had climbed to $8.6 million. Its minimum trust account was $500 and the average account in 1860 was $5,600. In its earlier period the company invested chiefly in mortgages, both urban and rural, but after the mid-1840s it loaned also to large textile companies.[8]

Insurance Companies. The early ways of insuring against loss by fire and shipwreck and of getting life insurance on a short-term basis contributed little to capital accumulation. In 1800 there were thirty-one insurance companies operating with American charters, most of them insuring against fire and marine disaster, although five sold life insurance. Insurance companies with premiums to invest thus appeared about the end of the eighteenth century, but life insurance was not significant until the 1840s and 1850s. Life insurance is basically a discipline submitted to by its "buyers" to force themselves to save. Since death comes eventually to all, the insurance company must have collected enough in premiums to pay death benefits. Meanwhile the insurance company must safely invest these savings.

A new type of insurance company, the mutual, appeared about 1843–1847. The persons being insured shared in the profits of the company. An outstanding company of this sort was The Mutual Life Insurance Company of New York. Mutual insurance penetrated south of New York with the founding in 1847 of the Penn Mutual Life Insurance Company. By 1850 there were forty-seven life insurance companies in business. By 1860 fire and marine insurance policies totaled about $3,000 million and life insurance companies' policies some $200 million. That does not mean, however, that the various companies had collected that much and had it to invest. The amount available for investment was but a fraction of all this. It seems probable, however, that all insurance companies in all states must have had invested funds amounting to as much as $60 million. They invested much of this in mortgages, although some companies invested in textile industries.

Mortgage Banks. For a while during the 1830s mortgage banks or land banks were institutions of some prominence in the South. Their loanable funds, however, were not the savings of thrifty individuals in this country but rather came from the proceeds of bonds sold in England. Most mortgage banks loaned to planters. They did not make their loans care-

[8] Gerald T. White, *A History of the Massachusetts Hospital Life Insurance Company* (Cambridge: Harvard University Press, 1955), pp. 39, 46, 86–90.

fully, and they soon went bankrupt. The Union Bank, set up in Mississippi in 1838 with $5 million of capital, was bankrupt within two years, and then the state defaulted on the bonds. This kind of institution contributed little if anything to the capital growth of the nation.

Lotteries. Lotteries constituted another way of raising capital. The proceeds of lotteries helped finance roads, river improvements, and even colleges. In 1832 Boston did a million-dollar lottery business, and the value of all lottery tickets sold in Eastern states in that year was estimated to be $53 million. Thereafter states began passing laws prohibiting lotteries.

In summary, the amount of liquid capital mobilized for long-term investment by all these institutions was relatively modest. Commercial banks probably contributed the largest part despite the fact that this was a dangerous function for them to perform. Savings banks, trust companies, and insurance companies had their beginnings at this time, but their contributions were small. Mortgage banks and lotteries did more harm than good, either by their poor example or by the mania for gambling which they encouraged.

TAXATION

Governmental agencies were among the largest money-collecting and money-dispensing agencies in the economy. The Federal government spent $10 million in 1800, $37 million in 1837, and $63 million in 1860. That was between 1 and 2 per cent of the national income. Much of this expenditure was for current operations, but part went into capital expenditures. Leaving out those for military and naval equipment, some of the more important items were the building of the Cumberland Road, post offices, and other government buildings. The chief sources of income of the Federal government were import duties (usually yielding 85 per

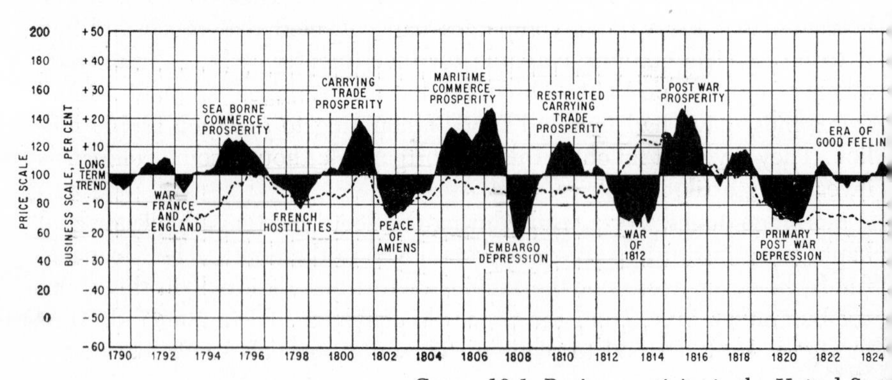

CHART 10-1. Business activity in the United Stat

cent or more), sales of public lands (important only during ten scattered years, and most notably 1835–1837), and some internal revenue taxes on such things as liquor and carriages. The income tax was unused.

The activities of the states compared to those of the Federal government were fairly important. They spent about a third of what the Federal government did. This was a period when the Democrats were generally in office, and they stressed states' rights and tried to restrain such activities as Federal investments in internal improvements. State debts climbed from almost nothing in 1800 to $257 million in 1860, which was four times the national debt. States were called upon to build and operate penitentiaries, reformatories, and institutions for the aged and mentally unfit. They helped in establishing schools, and some established state-supported universities and normal schools. For a time they also built canals, roads, and railroads, although generally with borrowed money rather than with taxes. Early in the century states got money from lotteries, dividends on bank stock, and a few taxes. After about 1842 the general property tax produced their chief revenue.

Large cities spent twice as much per inhabitant as the Federal government did. The cost per person tends to rise where the population is more closely crowded together. Cities had to pave their streets, provide water and sewage systems, and establish hospitals and schools. New York's reservoir, built in the late 1830s, cost over $8 million. The chief municipal tax was the property tax. Cities borrowed heavily and by 1860 they had debts of some $200 million, almost as much as the states had.

BUSINESS CYCLES

The business cycle was a product of the industrial revolution. It was closely associated with the activities of the new capital-accumulating in-

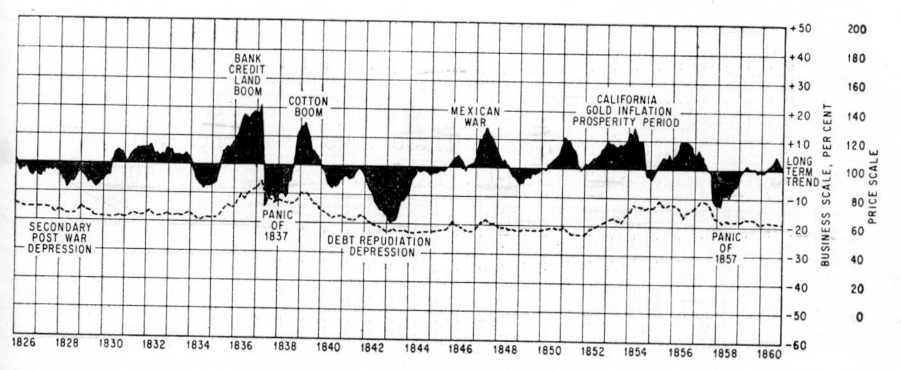

1790–1860. (*Courtesy of the Cleveland Trust Company.*)

stitutions. Although there had been famines, instances of overproduction, and panics over the course of many centuries, the more clearly discernible modern business cycle began in Britain in the mid-eighteenth century and in this country not long afterward.

The word "cycle" suggests the appearance of a similar situation again and again. There are four parts of a business cycle, namely, prosperity, panic and liquidation, depression, and recovery, and they always follow one another in that order. In prosperity businessmen, wage earners, and the general public become highly optimistic: they expect too easy profits or too generous wages; they borrow to speculate on land or in securities; or they expand their business plants too rapidly. They raise their standard of living in the expectation that the existing happy situation will continue or even become better. Eventually their hopes are dashed by rising costs, saturated markets, and slimming profit margins. At first a few alert persons realize what has happened, and then the great majority sense it. Panic ensues as many try to sell lands or securities for which they have gone into debt. Obviously these will not now yield the hoped-for profits and may cost them some frightening losses. By this time potential buyers are few and can be tempted only by remarkable bargain prices. The public is extremely pessimistic, and while this attitude lasts, depression reigns. In time, though, the business of a few individuals improves, perhaps because of favorable bargains they drove, or hard work, or intelligent merchandising, or simply the needs of a reawakened buying public. Recovery is under way. Optimism grows once more, and eventually it leads to a new prosperity and the cycle repeats itself.

As early as the 1830s some businessmen recognized in a general way the existence of the business cycle. Leaders in a financial house like Barings in London could read its danger signals and prepare to some extent for the hard times ahead.

The most noticed features of the business cycle are the most painful parts, namely, either panic and liquidation or the sometimes long depression that follows. The most readily recalled early depressions were those of 1764–1765 and 1784–1786 following major wars and inflations, and the embargo depression of 1808. The modern major ones were those of 1819–1822, 1837–1844, and 1857–1858. There were lesser ones, too, in 1828, 1848, and 1854 (see Chart 10-1). All the major ones grew out of business expansion financed by capital-accumulating institutions, especially by banks. Yet no two were exactly alike. The 1819–1822 affair was characterized by war-induced inflation and then bank-financed speculation in lands; the 1837–1844 episode, by overbuilding of internal improvements and bank-financed speculation in lands; and the 1857–1858 panic, by excessive railroad building. The expansion was always premature or overdone, such as elaborate canal systems in western Ohio and Indiana. The losses consequent upon these panics were tremendous and painful. The 1835–1844 "boom and bust," which was the worst of all, discouraged many Americans from investing soon again; it also led many English investors to foreswear entrusting their savings to American state governments again.

Yet discouraging as these financial holocausts were, they did not prevent the nation from growing. At each round of prosperity or of depression the country was richer and stronger than at the equivalent time in the preceding cycle. An economy, like any living organism, seems to live and grow by a series of pulsations.

CHAPTER 11

Money and Banking

MONEY

It is virtually impossible to cite an example of a progressive nation in modern times that has not had a reliable money system. If money is subject to counterfeiting or inclined to depreciate, this increases the risks and costs of doing business. Unsound money discourages people from saving, without which capital cannot grow; that keeps the standard of living from improving and holds back the nation's progress. This helps to explain why the American industrial revolution did not occur until after the adoption of the Constitution and of Hamilton's programs for a dependable money system. As the industrial revolution progressed, as manufacturers turned the selling of goods over to merchants, and as economic activity became more specialized, the role of money became increasingly important. More transactions were effected with cash and fewer by barter. Money, a medium of exchange, was the lubricant that made the close-fitting gears of a more intricate economy function smoothly.

The American Dollar. Alexander Hamilton, Thomas Jefferson, Gouverneur Morris, Robert Morris, and others concerned themselves with giving their new nation an up-to-date and reliable money system; they profited from the mistakes of the past and planned well. The Constitution took the regulation of the currency from the states and put it into the hands of the Federal Congress. It also forbade the states to make anything but gold or silver legal tender. Thomas Jefferson brought back from France the decimal system, which is easier to use than the eighths characterizing Spanish money or the twentieths and twelfths characterizing pounds, shillings, and pence. Alexander Hamilton was responsible for the adoption of the bimetallic system which, despite its imperfections, was about the best money system of its day. As for the American dollar, this was but a slightly smaller variation of the Spanish dollar or "piece of eight," the most common silver coin then in circulation. Shifting to it was not difficult for the American people.

Hamilton followed an ingenious procedure in setting up the bimetallic standard. Weights of worn silver dollars varied so widely that he did not want to take a rough average of them. Instead he began with the amount of gold at which a dollar was commonly valued, namely, 24.75 grains of pure gold. A grain is a very small weight for measuring precious metals: there are 480 grains to the troy ounce. Since gold was currently considered fifteen times as valuable as silver, he multiplied 24.75 grains by 15 and took the result, 371.25 grains, as the pure silver weight for the silver dollar.[1] Actually there was no gold dollar for many years; the gold unit was the eagle, or ten dollars. Gold and silver are soft metals, and so the mint had to add a harder alloying metal to them, making the coins actually nine-tenths pure. At first the mint did not make many coins; molding, stamping, and cutting gold and silver coins were a delicate manufacturing operation, and manufacturing was in its infancy in the 1790s. In addition to the silver dollar, it put out gold quarter eagles, half eagles, and eagles, the silver half dollars, quarter dollars, dimes and half dimes, and some copper pennies and half pennies. For years there were not enough American coins to meet current business needs, and Congress repeatedly reenacted a law making foreign coins legal tender. These remained in circulation until mid-century.

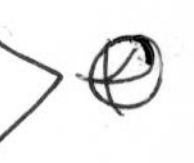

Bimetallism. Under a silver coin standard, a certain weight of silver, in this instance 371.25 grains of pure silver called a dollar, is the basic measure of value. In addition, four fundamental rules must be observed. (1) All other moneys are eventually redeemable in silver dollars. (2) There is free coinage of silver; that is, anyone may bring any amount of silver to the mint and ask to have it made up into coin so that it will be handier to spend. (3) The owner of coin may melt it or export it if he wishes. (4) Silver coins are legal tender; that is, if a debtor offers a creditor silver dollars in discharge of debts and the creditor refuses to accept the money, he has no legal recourse against the debtor because silver is the standard money. Under a gold coin standard, these same four rules apply to the gold money. Under a bimetallic standard the rules apply to both metals, but neither metal should be regarded as superior to the other.

Complications enter the picture, however, as soon as two metals are standards. Two ratios necessarily exist between them: one is the mint ratio, the other, the market ratio. The mint ratio is the relative pure metal content of the coins. The United States started off by putting fifteen times as much silver in ten silver dollars as it put gold in the gold eagle ($10). Thus 15 to 1 was the mint ratio. The market ratio is the relative value placed on the two metals in the metal markets of the world; that in turn may be much influenced by the mint ratio of some major nation. At the outset the United States government used the world market ratio to fix its own mint ratio. Bimetallism works only as long as the two ratios remain

[1] Neil Carothers, *Fractional Money* (New York: John Wiley & Sons, Inc., 1930), p. 57.

identical. In the next few years gold rose in value in the European metal markets. By 1799 the (market) ratio quoted in Hamburg and London was 15¾ to 1. Under the circumstances, anyone owning much gold tended to sell it to the nearest bullion dealer, who sent it abroad. Similarly, owners of silver brought it to the United States Mint, which was the better place to sell silver. This situation continued for nearly half a century.

In 1834 Congress reduced the size of the gold eagle to 232 grains but left the silver coins unchanged in size. In other words, Congress made gold sixteen times as valuable as silver, since 232 is almost exactly one-sixteenth of 3,712.5. Various explanations have been advanced for this step. One is that some small gold mines were discovered in North Carolina; their owners were men of political influence who, desiring a handy, unlimited market for their product, induced Congress to change the mint ratio from 15 to 1 to 16 to 1. Since the French ratio remained at 15½ to 1, the effect was now to attract gold to the American mint and drive silver abroad to the French mint, just the opposite of what had happened before. Another explanation is that President Andrew Jackson and some of his close advisers, such as Senator Thomas Hart ("Old Bullion") Benton of Missouri, preferred gold to silver as the standard money metal and urged this step to attract gold to the mint. Actually, the change in the size of the eagle and thus in the mint ratio had little effect on the coining of gold coins for almost ten years. Although the mint manufactured some $20 million of coins in 1834 instead of the usual $5 million, its output declined again until 1843 when suddenly it minted some $50 million. Thereafter the flow of gold coins into circulation was high, especially after the gold discoveries in California in 1848.

The minting of silver coins, chiefly half dollars anyway, did not noticeably decline; it merely ceased to grow and keep pace with the expansion of the economy. Nor did silver coins promptly disappear from circulation; that began only after about 1843, and more particularly after 1848. By 1834 most silver coins were so old and worn that they were worth more as money in America than as bullion abroad. Thus the bimetallic system, thanks to a coincidence, actually worked again for about ten years, from 1834 to 1843.[2]

After 1848 the discoveries of gold in California, supplemented by others in Australia in 1851 and 1853, greatly increased the world's supply of gold. How enormous these discoveries were may be seen from the fact that the world's supply of monetary gold, accumulated through the ages, doubled in a decade. This was bound to cheapen gold, which the American mint ratio favored anyway, and so silver flowed out. This was an example of Gresham's law.

[2] *Ibid.*, p. 101.

The serious aspect of the outflow of silver was that it drew away the small change. To remedy this situation, Congress passed the Subsidiary Coinage Act of 1853. This law reduced by 6 per cent the amount of pure silver in coins below one dollar and took all these coins off the "free coinage" list. It was not worth while to melt down the new silver coins of less than one dollar for export. That solved the problem of a shortage of small change but left on the free coinage list only one coin, the silver dollar, of which the mint was coining rather few. The nation had virtually adopted the gold coin standard. That was the monetary standard that England was on and the standard to which most progressive nations of the world would be aspiring during the rest of the century.

Actually coins of silver, gold, and copper were not the chief money in circulation. Per capita circulation of these in 1800 was $3; this was not enough money to do the nation's business. True, many transactions were concluded on a barter basis, especially in rural areas and near the frontier. However, the most important money in circulation, quantity-wise, was paper money, namely, the notes of dozens of privately owned banks. A bank note is a bank's demand I.O.U.; it is a promise to redeem the note in specie, that is, gold or silver coins, on a moment's notice. No bank notes were legal tender, but they were generally acceptable in business transactions.[3] At times some of these notes were in denominations of less than $1, called "shinplasters," as during the War of 1812, in the 1830s, and in the early 1850s when small change was scarce. Table 11-1 (p. 201) shows that during the pre-Civil War period the circulation of bank notes was from two to three times that of specie.

The Quality of American Money. How satisfactory was the money in use in the United States before 1860? How well did it perform, not only as a medium of exchange but also as a measure of value and a store of value? Or, put another way, did people have confidence in the money which they used to pay the local storekeeper, and did the storekeeper have confidence in it? Did the price level remain reasonably stable, or was there too little money during long periods, leading to falling prices (deflation), and was there too much at other times, leading to rising prices (inflation)? Did the bimetallic system break down often and with little provocation, or did it work fairly satisfactorily?

Bank notes varied greatly in quality. A bank note was as good as the bank that issued it, and there were numerous fraudulent and shaky banks. A bank note that was far from the bank that issued it was almost certain to pass at a discount. All during this era counterfeiting was rampant. Two types of publication appeared which by their very existence reflected on the money in use. One was a semiannual or annual publica-

[3] Notes of the first and second Banks of the United States were by law acceptable in payment of Federal taxes, however.

tion called a *Bank Note Detector.* Several companies published them. They explained in detail how to detect fraudulent notes such as raised notes, or notes of nonexistent banks. The second publication appeared weekly and was called a *Bank Note Reporter.* It was a specialized newspaper which cited the current rate of discount on all bank notes and reported recent bank failures. Usually when the discount on a bank's notes exceeded 30 per cent, the bank failed. *Bank Note Reporters,* along with *Bank Note Detectors,* were essential tools for all who handled very much money during a business day. Even with these two aids, however, the businessman faced losses from counterfeits or discounted notes that somehow slipped by, and the small merchant was especially exposed to these hazards. Accordingly, businessmen simply had to allow for this risk in pricing their goods and the customer paid to support these fraudulent or badly managed banks. During the 1850s there was increasing demand for a dependable national currency that would pass at par all over the nation.

The price level did not vary markedly in the sixty-year period between 1800 and 1860. On a 1913 base of 100, wholesale prices rose from 85 in 1808 to 127 in 1814, which was the worst year of the War of 1812 inflation, and then dropped back by 1821 to 74, partly as a result of the 1819–1822 depression. This was a 50 per cent rise and a 42 per cent decline in wholesale prices within thirteen years' time. It represented the most disruptive price swing of the whole era. During the boom period of 1834–1836 wholesale prices went up 18 per cent; during eight years of depression that followed, they fell by 27 per cent. The lowest point of the whole era was 1849, the year of the California gold rush which yielded such vast amounts of gold as to cause prices to advance all over the world. By the boom year of 1857 wholesale prices had gone up 23 per cent, but the panic of that year lowered them again. To sum up, wholesale prices were 87.5 in 1800 and 71 in 1860.[4] The cost of living index varied within a somewhat narrower range for the period for which it exists, 1820–1860, except that the price climb of 40 per cent between 1834–1837 was more pronounced. Altogether the bimetallic system, whether resting more heavily on its gold leg or on its silver leg, gave the nation a rather stable level of prices in the sixty-year period.

Several times the banking system broke down. Banks, and later the Independent Treasury System, were expected to pay their obligations in specie, that is, gold or silver coins, when requested to do so. Early in the century when a bank did not redeem its notes in specie, such failure injured the bank's reputation but did not ruin it. After the War of 1812 states imposed financial penalties on banks that did not redeem in specie,

[4] U.S. Bureau of the Census, *Historical Statistics, of the United States, 1789–1945* (Washington, 1949), pp. 231–236.

and after the 1830s states became increasingly severe and eventually made such refusal to redeem the equivalent of failure of the bank. Specie payments were suspended on at least five occasions: in 1814 by all but the banks of New England; in 1819–1822 especially by western banks; and also in 1837, in 1839–1841, and in 1857. In no instance did every bank in the country suspend. In 1814 there was the excuse of a war and the burning of Washington, D.C., by the enemy; the 1857 suspension was short-lived. The other three suspensions, growing out of two major depressions, were less excusable. These were bank suspensions, however, and not abandonment of bimetallism by the Treasury or by Act of Congress.

In summary, then, bimetallism provided a reasonably stable price level, especially in the 1840s and 1850s. It broke down only a few times, although with rather frightening results on those occasions. The most common money in use, bank notes, was not very satisfactory in the newer parts of the nation. Reported bank losses totaled many million in the 1837 crash.

BANKING

Modern commercial banking appeared in this period in America, although it had been known in Europe for 175 years. A commercial bank performs three basic functions: first, it accepts money on deposit for safekeeping; second, it makes loans to customers; and third, it makes most of those loans in the form of its own credit. This last point requires fuller explanation, for it is the essence of banking. Banks have two ways of loaning credit, either by printing and lending bank notes or by granting customers deposits against which they may write checks. The bank note method was developed first, and during most of this pre-Civil War period it was the more widely used. An individual would hardly have dared to do business and pay his bills by handing out his own I.O.U.'s to circulate through the community. Yet banks did just this and thereby made their profits. People borrowed bank notes from the bank and the community accepted them as money. With these bank notes the customer could pay his bills. He paid the bank interest for substituting its superior credit for the individual's inferior or less well-known credit. Back of the bank notes were the general credit of the bank, some specie reserve, some mortgages, but chiefly the customers' promissory notes. Of course, if the public became suspicious that the bank was unsound and started demanding specie for bank notes and deposits, the bank probably could not redeem them all promptly and in full. But the banker could guard against this situation by a conservative lending policy. He thus tried to steer a middle course between safety and profit, that is, to keep enough reserve so that

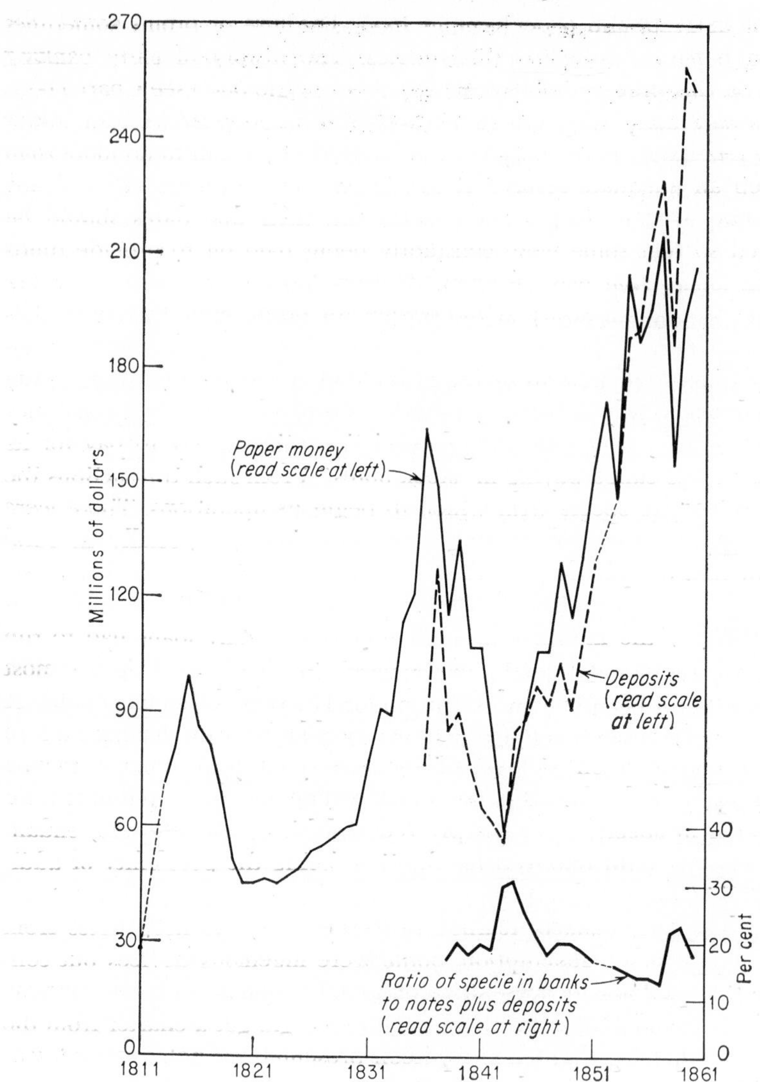

CHART 11-1. Paper money (chiefly state bank notes) and deposits, 1811–1860, and specie reserves. (*Adapted from A. B. Hepburn, A History of Currency in the United States, The Macmillan Company, New York, 1915, pp. 87, 129, 141, 159–160, 177–178.*)

he could meet all likely demands for specie; yet he printed and loaned enough bank notes so that he could receive considerable income from interest. The more notes he had out, the greater the profit but also the greater the danger. The early banker had to learn by experience how many notes he dared issue on a given specie reserve. Massachusetts banks averaged 33 per cent specie behind notes and deposits in 1803, 15 per cent in 1825, and 5 per cent in 1835. The lure of profits sometimes tempted banks to issue too many notes. The history of early banking centers on this problem more than any other single one (see Chart 11-1).

Banks had many other difficulties, too. Since a commercial bank might have to redeem its notes in specie on short notice, it had to do more than just keep an adequate reserve of specie on hand. In addition, its loans should not run for too long a period, and their due dates should be staggered so that some were constantly being paid off to provide funds for fresh loans. That was the ideal situation. Economic conditions in the period as well as the desire of the banker for profit made this ideal difficult to achieve. Also the nation's supply of specie was scanty. Even wealthy individuals able to invest in bank stock frequently lacked ready cash and made only token payment for the stock. Sometimes the very bank which they were founding loaned them the money to pay for its stock. This was called paying in "stock notes." From such transactions the bank received no specie with which to begin its operations. There were limited opportunities for making short-term loans, especially in rural areas. In that era people paid their bills once or twice a year when they sold their crops. When the farmers paid the merchants, the merchants in turn could pay the manufacturers or importers. Many loans had to run for a year or more and then be renewed. As for collateral, the most common form was land; in fact, mortgages loomed high on the list of loans made by banks. Land varied considerably in price, selling high in boom times and low on other occasions. Consequently, if a bank were well "loaned up," the banker did not relish seeing his notes presented for redemption in specie. That sharply reduced his specie reserves, endangered the bank, and removed for the time being the possibility of additional profit from new loans.

Over the years, bankers learned of various ways to keep notes from being brought in for redemption. Some were ingenious devices but contrary to the spirit and purpose of commercial banking; some were simply fraudulent. In 1818 the Bank of Darien in Georgia got a charter from the legislature requiring that when a person presented his notes for redemption in specie, he had to take an oath in writing that the notes were his and that he was not redeeming them for another bank or company. He had to take this oath before a justice of the peace and in the presence of five directors of the bank. One may imagine with what willingness all these people let themselves be assembled for the purpose. In other towns strangers presenting notes for redemption were sometimes threatened with violence by the local citizens. These knew that their bank could make them fewer loans if strangers took away its specie. Some North Carolina banks in 1819 stipulated that persons borrowing their notes must repay in specie. Still other banks made it a practice to buy up their own notes when these fell to a discount, thus making a profit out of their own dubious reputation. Banks also loaned "post notes" which looked like ordinary bank notes but carried a provision in fine print to the effect that the bank would not redeem them in specie until another thirty or sixty days after presentation, or after some date printed on them. In Michigan so-called "wildcat banks" existed in the 1830s. This was a branch banking system under which any branch could make or collect a loan but only the "main office" was "authorized" to redeem notes in specie; that main office was hidden deep in the woods, where only wildcats lurked, if indeed it existed at all. It should not be assumed that these kinds of deception were characteristic of all or even of a majority of banking. They did exist, however, and they reflected the problems of an age when specie and loanable funds were scarce and the demands were heavy for liquid capital to develop the economy.

Because banking was in its infancy in this country, virtually all bankers were amateurs, learning about banking by practicing it. Many made honest mistakes, but unfortunately other amateurs repeated them. "What New England did in the first decade of the century is what the Middle states did in the second and the Southwest in the fourth and the Ohio states in the sixth."[5] It was not until the Civil War that Congress, profiting from many of these costly experiences, enacted a national law setting forth rules of sound banking.

The First Commercial Banks. The first real commercial bank in the United States was the Bank of North America, founded by Robert Morris in Philadelphia to help finance the closing years of the Revolutionary War as well as to do a banking business. It received its specie reserve from a loan made to the United States by France. The second and third banks were the Bank of Massachusetts and the Bank of New York, both founded in 1784. A fourth was chartered in Baltimore in 1790. There were 29 banks in the nation by 1800, 89 by 1811, 713 by 1836, and 1,562 by 1860. Table 11-1 shows the tremendous growth of this necessary business.

The periods of great growth were the boom periods during and after the War of 1812, during the first part of the 1830s, and during the 1850s. There were nearly three-quarters of a billion dollars of loans outstanding by the eve of the Civil War. Deposits exceeded bank notes after 1855 and checking accounts were of growing importance in the larger eastern cities. So much banking activity needed some coordinated supervision and help as by a central bank, but the banks did not have that during half of the period.

[5] William G. Sumner, "A History of Banking in the United States," in *A History of Banking in All the Leading Nations* (New York: Journal of Commerce and Commercial Bulletin, 1896), p. 37.

Table 11-1
Commercial Bank Statistics, 1790–1860
(Dollars in millions)

Year	Number of banks	Specie held	Note circulation	Deposits	Loans outstanding
1790	4	....	2.0		
1800	29	....	15.5		
1811	89	....	28.1		
1815	208	16.5	100	.....	150
1820	307	16.7	40.6	31.2	157*
1836	713	40	140	115	457
1849	782	44	115	91	332
1860	1,562	84	207	254	692

* 1819.

SOURCE: A. B. Hepburn, *A History of Currency in the United States* (New York: The Macmillan Company, 1915), pp. 87, 127, 159, 178.

Functions of a Central Bank. A central bank is a banker's bank; it does for banks what banks do for their customers. It may lend them money in time of need if they have adequate collateral or good credit; it may keep some of their reserves in its vaults for them; and it creates its own credit to lend to banks. A central bank usually works closely with the Treasury too. A central bank keeps the nation's commercial banks from overlending in good times, and it comes to their assistance in bad times. Its managers should be more concerned with the welfare of the economy than with making a profit for the central bank. The central bank of some 150 years ago was not this highly developed. It disciplined the commercial banks more than it helped them; it engaged in commercial banking itself and was regarded more as a powerful competitor; and it sometimes set some rather bad examples. The United States had two of these banks.

The First Bank of the United States. The first, called the Bank of the United States, was founded in Philadelphia in 1791, largely by the efforts of the Secretary of the Treasury, Alexander Hamilton (see "Hamilton's Financial Program," pp. 85–86). It was to serve as a fiscal (financial) agent of the Treasury and was also to be one of the major commercial banks of the nation. Its capital of $10 million made it by far *the largest business institution* in the country and aroused the suspicions and fears of many democratically minded people. Jeffersonian Democrats disliked the fact that the Federal government not only chartered the Bank but also subscribed to one-fifth of its stock, thus making it partly a government institution. Its charter ran for twenty years, at which time it was to come before Congress for renewal. Its specie reserve was probably a third of all the specie in the country.

The Bank was of great service to the people in providing a safe currency and in furnishing banking facilities for commercial transactions through its eight branches. Unfortunately, these public services were not promptly appreciated. This was a period of war prosperity in which commerce and agriculture were greatly stimulated. Each year saw more state banks chartered; each year heard more protests over the strictness

Fig. 11-1. The first Bank of the United States (1791–1811) in Philadelphia. This building, finished in 1797, was purchased by Stephen Girard in 1812. (*Courtesy of the Library of Congress.*)

of the first Bank. As fiscal agent for the Federal government, the Bank was custodian of import duties and other tax moneys. By refusing to accept the notes of non-specie-paying banks it also became the regulator of the currency, thereby incurring the enmity of all slovenly and fraudulent banks and sometimes even of better-grade banks. It lessened their opportunity for profit by obliging them to stand ready at all times to redeem a quantity of their own banks notes. When the question of renewing the Bank's charter came up in 1810, several state banks brought pressure on Congress to oppose recharter. In addition, many Democrats, like Thomas Jefferson, who interpreted the Constitution literally, believed Congress had no right to charter a bank and that it was an undemocratic institution. The recharter bill in 1811 failed by a narrow margin. Thereupon the Bank wound up its affairs, paying $434 on each $400 share of stock, in addition to its annual dividends. Stephen Girard bought the building (see Fig. 11-1). The state banks now had the field to themselves.

The withdrawal of millions in bank notes and the return of $7 million to Europe to pay off European stockholders left a vacuum for the state banks to fill. They made the most of the opportunity to expand. Between 1811 and 1816 the number of state banks grew from 88 to 246; in their enthusiasm, doubtless stimulated by the demands of wartime finance,

Fig. 11-2. The second Bank of the United States in Philadelphia. (*Courtesy of the Library of Congress.*)

they made far too many loans. Note circulation rose from $45 million in 1812 to $100 million in 1817, specie reserves declined, and the price level went up by some 50 per cent. In 1814 all but the New England banks suspended specie payments; that is, they refused henceforth to redeem their bank notes at face value in silver or gold coins. Although there was a war to blame it on, most people realized that the real explanation was that there was no longer a central bank to police the state banks and restrain their excesses.

The Second Bank of the United States. By the war's end the public had come to appreciate the services once performed by the first Bank. In 1816 Congress established the second Bank of the United States, and once again the head office was in Philadelphia (see Fig. 11-2). It was similar in organization to the first Bank. Chartered also for twenty years, it had a capital of $35 million, of which the Federal government subscribed one-fifth. Note circulation was limited to the amount of the capital, notes were receivable in all payments to the United States, and they were payable in specie on demand. Within a short time after the bank opened early in 1817 commercial banks went through the motions of resuming specie payments. Actually, the second Bank, in its desire to have the resumption succeed, did not press commercial banks to redeem their notes. This was partly because its own specie reserves were slender, too.

The first president of the Bank, William Jones, had little conception of the responsibilities of a central bank and concentrated on having the Bank make as much money as possible. That was not difficult. The wartime inflation had started a boom in business, especially in the West; there was heavy migration there and land speculation was rife. Of the Bank's eighteen branches, six were west of the Appalachians (Lexington, Cincinnati, Chillicothe [Ohio], Louisville, Pittsburgh, and New Orleans). The demand for loanable funds was heavy in the Middle West; there is some evidence as well that local banks encouraged people to borrow, assuring them that their promissory notes could be renewed if need be. In any event, many customers borrowed from their local commercial banks to import goods from the East or from Europe. The local banks in turn borrowed from the nearest Western branch of the second Bank, and it in turn requested the Philadelphia head office or another branch office in an Eastern city to pay for the Westerner's purchase. "The effect was similar to that which would have been produced by making Western bank notes current in New York and Philadelphia."[6] In addition, the notes of many Western banks which had been accepted for payment of land from the government were deposited in Western branches. As a result of all this, specie was being drained off to Europe, for Eastern branches had advanced much of their loanable funds on behalf of the Western branches. "The East was drained dry so that the West might live high."

A change of policy was essential, and it came in 1818. The head office forbade Western branches to borrow any more from Eastern ones, ordered them to reduce their loans, forbade them to accept notes of non-specie-paying Western banks, and ordered them to send $700,000 of specie to pay off their obligations to the Eastern offices. The fast moving Western economy came to a sudden stop and the shock was tremendous. The Western branches demanded payment from Western banks, which in turn forced their customers to pay up. Loans that customers expected to have renewed were not renewed. Forced sale followed forced sale, and land

[6] William M. Gouge, *A Short History of Paper Money in the United States* (Philadelphia: T. W. Ustick, 1833), vol. II, p. 128.

values plummeted. Corn was reported selling at 10 cents a bushel and wheat at 20 cents in some parts of Kentucky to obtain specie to pay debts to the banks. State banks contracted their note circulation from $100 million in 1817 to $45 million in 1819. Many persons were badly hurt financially by all this, among them Andrew Jackson of Nashville, Tennessee, the future President, and a number of his friends. Thomas Hart Benton of Missouri lost out on a land speculation. Elected senator in 1820, Benton later described his journey to Washington as "one long ride amidst the crashings and explosions of banks, and the cries and lamentations of a deceived and plundered people. The National Bank was then in the third year of its age; and so far from affording a remedy for the evils, it was itself the mother of the evils. . . ."[7]

The public reacted violently against the Bank. Several states passed laws to tax out of existence branches within their borders. Only the decisions of Chief Justice Marshall in *McCulloch v. Maryland* (1819) and *Osborn v. United States Bank* (1824) saved the branches from their wrath. William Jones resigned as president of the Bank and in March, 1819, Langdon Cheves of South Carolina took over. He saved the second Bank and put its affairs in order but many commercial banks, particularly in the West and South, failed in the process. It was several years before banks in the West resumed specie payments. Hatred of the second Bank lingered for a long time.

The "Bank War," or Nicholas Biddle v. Andrew Jackson. In 1823 Nicholas Biddle succeeded Langdon Cheves in the presidency of the Bank. Biddle was an intellectual and a genius. He had graduated from Princeton as valedictorian of his class at the age of fifteen and had been editor of the nation's leading literary magazine before he was thirty. Biddle's early administration of the Bank was model: when a small panic broke out in 1826, the second Bank was able to help the commercial banks, as a central bank should, instead of having to save itself at their expense. Biddle was not able to handle politicians, however; some of them bore grudges against the Bank for the 1819 affair, and some of them wanted to borrow more than they should or find jobs in its branches for their friends. Honest and forceful, Biddle thought it was obvious to intelligent people that the Bank was now performing a valuable service. His lack of political acumen handicapped him increasingly.

A change in the political complexion of the country was taking place as state after state removed the property qualification for voting. Presidents were no longer cultured Virginia gentlemen or intellectual Bostonians, but instead less-educated men of the people. Andrew Jackson had fought in the American Revolution at the age of thirteen; he was

[7] Quoted in William M. Meigs, *The Life of Thomas Hart Benton* (Philadelphia: J. B. Lippincott Company, 1904), p. 126.

loyal to his friends and expected them to be loyal to him; he was frequently in debt and thus sympathetic to the debtor classes; he was honest and blunt in speech; and he had strong prejudices. One of these was against banks. President Jackson was critical of the second Bank in his inaugural address in 1829 and in annual messages thereafter. On one occasion when Biddle endeavored to placate him, Jackson frankly told him, "I do not dislike your Bank any more than all banks. But ever since I read the history of the South Sea Bubble I have been afraid of banks."[8] If there had to be banks, he had earlier shown that he wanted them to be obliged to redeem their notes in specie, but he preferred to have no banks at all. He wanted instead to rely on dependable gold and silver coins for money.

Biddle's greatest problem was that the Bank's charter would expire in 1836, and he was responsible for keeping this essential institution alive. He had assurances from close friends of the President that Jackson would eventually approve a recharter if the issue were not pressed. Still, he hesitated to rely on the none-too-friendly President. Whig party leaders, whose candidate was Henry Clay of Kentucky, told Biddle he must make up his mind whether to entrust the future of his bank to his sure friends or to his probable enemies. Biddle finally decided to force the issue and let Clay's party introduce a bill in Congress to recharter the Bank. It passed, Jackson vetoed it, and the question of a recharter for the Bank became the central issue of the presidential campaign of 1832. In view of the experience following the dissolution of the first Bank, Biddle and Clay thought the people would surely support the Bank and that Clay would defeat Jackson. They guessed wrong; Jackson won, and thereafter the days of the Bank were numbered. After 1833 the Treasury stopped putting its deposits in the second Bank or in its branches and gradually paid out what was there. The second Bank took out a state charter in 1836 and became the Bank of the United States of Pennsylvania.

The "Pet" Banks. When the government stopped depositing its funds in the second Bank and its branches, the Treasury selected state banks in various parts of the country for this purpose. Those chosen, often for political reasons, were known as "pet" banks. These banks, now favored with sizable government deposits, were in a good position to expand their loans and had strong inducement to do so. No longer was there a second Bank to police them by presenting large batches of their notes for redemption, and the pet banks quickly took advantage of the opportunity. The nation was in the throes of a speculative boom from about 1834 onward because of the building of canals, railroads, and turnpikes. The opening of the Erie Canal had demonstrated for all to see that whoever

[8] Ralph C. Catterall, *The Second Bank of the United States* (Chicago: University of Chicago Press, 1903), p. 184.

owned land near a projected or newly built means of transportation would almost certainly see his land rise sharply in value within a short time. Each time that speculators borrowed bank notes at pet banks to buy government land, the land office put the payment money back in the pet bank, which could then make another round of loans. It seemed that this might go on almost indefinitely. The number of acres sold by the Federal government jumped from 5 million in 1834 to 20 million in 1836.

The most spectacular boom town of the period was Chicago, a fort in 1833, a small metropolis in 1836. Single lots near the projected site of the Illinois-Michigan Canal sold for $9,000 to $21,400. Harriet Martineau, an English visitor, said of Chicago, "There streets were crowded with land speculators hurrying from one sale to another. A negro dressed up in scarlet, bearing a scarlet flag and riding a white horse, with housings of scarlet, announced the times of sale. At every street corner, where he stopped, the crowd flocked around him; and it seemed as if some prevalent mania infested the whole people. . . . As the gentlemen of our party walked the streets, storekeepers hailed them from their doors, with offers of farms and all manner of land-lots, advising them to speculate before the price of land rose higher. . . . [A] friend had realized in two years, ten times as much money as he had before fixed upon as a competence for life. Of course this rapid money-making is a merely temporary evil. A bursting of the bubble must soon come. The absurdity is so striking, that the wonder is that the fever should have attained such height as I witnessed."[9] Bank loans in the United States expanded from $324 million in 1834 to $525 million in 1836.

Panic of 1837. Andrew Jackson and some of his advisers, especially Senator Benton, had seen this kind of thing happen once before, and they became thoroughly alarmed. At the urging of Benton, who believed that payment in specie offered the only sound solution, President Jackson issued the so-called Specie Circular on July 11, 1836. This order required that henceforth all purchasers of government lands must pay in specie. Purchasers of land withdrew specie from banks, and banks with reduced specie reserves made fewer loans. True, the government land offices put their specie receipts for land sales right back in the pet banks which, it might seem, were still in a position to lend as freely as ever. But another factor broke the circular flow of funds. By 1836 the Federal government was out of debt and had built up a surplus. Congress decided to distribute this to the states and the pet banks had to pay it out in specie. Thus, with this drain on their specie reserves, even the pet banks made fewer loans to land buyers. The demand for land sloughed off and smart speculators tried to sell out and pay their debts before prices fell too

[9] Harriet Martineau, *Society in America* (Paris: Baudry's European Library, 1842), vol. I, p. 180.

much. Soon the rush to sell was as mad as that to buy had recently been. Lands worth $1,000 in Chicago in 1836 could be had for $100 a year later. Unable to collect on their loans, many banks failed. In May, 1837, they suspended specie payments generally.

It has sometimes been said that the Depression of 1837–1844 was caused by the success of the Erie Canal and the Federal government's refusal to recharter the second Bank. This latter was owing to the inability of President Jackson and Senator Benton to recognize that commercial banks were here to stay and that the second Bank was the most practical device available to keep them from overexpanding their note issues.

15 The period of failure, liquidation, and readjustment brought on another effort at reappraisal of the need for a central bank. A bill for a third Bank of the United States failed in 1841, but Jackson's followers could not be expected to admit that they had been wrong. They adopted instead, at first temporarily in 1840–1841 and then more permanently in 1846, a compromise measure called the Independent Treasury System. It established subtreasuries in six major cities to collect and disburse Federal funds. All collections and disbursements had to be made in specie. This system was in no sense a central bank, however, for it could not assist banks in distress or perform other helpful functions of a central bank. One of its disadvantages was that in seasons or years when the government had a surplus, the system's holdings of specie made bank reserves scarce so that it was especially difficult to obtain loans.

Some Sound Banking Systems. The responsibility for sound banking was 16 now largely in the hands of the states, and some of them performed their duties rather well. There were good state banks in Ohio, Indiana, Missouri, and Iowa. The large private banks in Massachusetts, especially in Boston, were sound: the Suffolk Bank was a sort of regional central bank for New England after about 1818. New York's Safety Fund System, under which banks insured their notes in case of bankruptcy, was also a success despite one breakdown in 1837. Probably the best banking system was in Louisiana. The Louisiana state law of 1842 required all banks to hold a specie reserve equal to one-third of their liabilities and to cover the other two-thirds with customers' promissory notes and drafts due within ninety days. Bank directors were fully liable for losses resulting from loans and investments made contrary to law, and the state provided effective supervision of the banks. Some of these provisions foreshadowed reforms found in the present-day Federal Reserve System. It was the public's preference for these reliable Louisiana notes that is presumed to have given the name "Dixie" to the South. Some of the New Orleans banks printed one side of their notes in French, the $10 note having DIX in large letters across it. River traders and boat captains heading south with merchandise were wont to remark that they were going to get a lot of "dixies." Thus Louisiana became "Dixie Land," a name popularized by a song hit just before the Civil War and then applied to the whole South.

Free Banking. Another important banking reform, known as "free" banking, was tried with varying success in fourteen states. There had been frequent complaints that the only persons who could get a bank charter were those with the right political connection and some cash to offer their sponsors in the legislature. This was undemocratic, to say the least. Once established, a banker occupied a position of privilege and power in the community and could make or break many a business venture. This, too, was undemocratic. To cure this situation the states of Michigan and New York passed free banking laws in 1837–1838. They granted a free charter to anyone with the necessary funds to start a bank; the would-be banker simply turned his cash into acceptable state or Federal government bonds which he deposited with the state's comptroller of banks in exchange for bank notes. Now he was ready to do business. If he made wise loans, he received interest on them and on his bonds and was a successful banker. If he made unwise loans, he soon went bankrupt and forfeited his bonds to redeem the bank notes, which by now were in the hands of the general public. Thus the plan had the democratic, albeit dubious, merit of giving anyone with capital an opportunity to be a banker, and at the same time of protecting innocent noteholders from his mistakes. Congress later incorporated the basic principle of this plan into the National Currency Act of 1863.

Some Banking Abuses. Yet there continued to be too many unsound banks, especially in the West. It was not so much the system employed that caused this as it was the lack of integrity of the men in charge of the banks. The "free" banks succeeded in New York but were terrible failures in Michigan, Indiana, Illinois, and some other states. The standards for the list of securities required to back the bank notes were low, with the result that would-be bankers could buy depreciated state bonds at as low as 20 cents on the dollar and obtain about 100 cents on the dollar in notes to lend out. If the bank failed, the sale of bonds paid off only a fraction of the notes outstanding. In Indiana bankers used another trick: one free bank would lend to the promoters of a second to buy bonds to start a bank, and the second would in turn create a third until the state was "shingled" with banks, most of which soon failed.

Likewise some state banks, as in Illinois, Kentucky, and Tennessee, were quite unsuccessful. Several states then went to the opposite extreme and forbade the establishment of banks altogether. Arkansas, Texas, California, and Oregon did so. In several instances this created a void into which flowed notes from out-of-state banks over which they exercised no control. Fraudulent operations were easier in frontier states, witness the famous case of several Michigan banks sending the same specie reserve ahead of the bank examiner as he made his rounds. Even it consisted of broken glass and nails below the top layer of coins.

The Agrarian Attitude toward Banks. Because capital was scarce on the frontier and in the agricultural West and South, many persons there were in favor of easy money, lax banking, and inflation. Creating money is all too often resorted to as a remedy when there is a lack of capital. After the Panic of 1819 the number of persons favoring lax banking declined, but their numbers grew again in the 1830s until the 1837 panic taught the country a second lesson. As a result of these experiences there was a large element who opposed banks in general, special privilege, corporations, and paper money. Several states prohibited banking altogether; others insisted that it be put under state jurisdiction if it had to exist; and still others removed the hated aspect of privilege in banking by adopting free banking. Men like Andrew Jackson and Thomas Hart Benton not only opposed the most privileged bank of all, the second Bank, but disliked all banks. "The Jacksonian agrarians were fanatically opposed to paper currency." They preferred a simple return to silver and gold coins. Yet in destroying the hated "money power" of the second Bank which had kept state banks under control, they hurt their own cause. The Western agrarians "nevertheless produced in Indiana, Missouri, and Iowa, some of the best banking in American history—restrained, conservative and untouched by the enthusiastic belief that credit was the font of every blessing."[10]

Type of Loans Made. Walter Bagehot, English mid-nineteenth century economist, once observed that the first thing that a banker must learn is the difference between a promissory note and a mortgage, for his business should be limited to the former. This is because notes and deposits are payable on demand whereas lending on mortgages ties the banker's funds for a long period of time; it "freezes his assets." Hugh McCulloch, once head of the State Bank of Indiana, remarked that in his bank before 1837 "a large part of the loans were necessarily to men who were buying or improving lands. . . . These loans . . . were sluggish and unreliable, and . . . might become dangerous. . . . This fact and the lesson which it taught were so sharply impressed upon them [branch managers] by the financial crisis of 1837 and the terrible depression which followed that from the time when business began to revive, the loans which they made were mainly confined to bills of exchange, based upon produce shipped, or to be shipped to Eastern or Southern markets. . . What the bank needed, in order at all times to meet its liabilities was what was called

[10] Bray Hammond, "Banking in the Early West: Monopoly, Prohibition and Laissez-faire," *The Journal of Economic History*, vol. 8 (1948), pp. 20–24.

prompt paper."[11] The bank adopted this policy in 1843 and pursued it henceforth. This was likewise the policy provided by law for Louisiana banks in 1842, and the one followed by the state banks in Missouri and Iowa and by the Wisconsin Marine and Fire Insurance Company (a bank). Sound banks increasingly concentrated on the purchase of prompt or "self-liquidating" paper. They sought to provide the working capital of merchants and manufacturers. Many banks, however, continued to lend against mortgages or make other long-term loans too, for most banks remained "general stores of finance" and offered a variety of services to customers. This was to be expected in view of the great need for long-term capital and the scarcity of specialized institutions to supply it. Nevertheless, banks that loaned heavily on mortgages or other long-term paper were likely to pay for doing so with their financial lives when a periodic depression appeared.

Interest Rates Charged. The interest charges for the use of bank funds differed widely. Eastern banks charged less than Western and Southern ones because the supply of savings was greater in the East. One reason was that Easterners formed the habit at an earlier date of depositing their savings in banks. Checking accounts first appeared in Eastern cities. For short-term loans 6 per cent was a fairly common rate in the East. A customer of the Bank of Alexandria, Virginia, unsuccessfully sued that bank in 1806 for trying to charge him about 6½ per cent on an $800 sixty-day loan, alleging it was above the 6 per cent usury limit. The State Bank of Indiana, chartered in 1834, was permitted to charge 6 per cent and to exact 8 per cent on judgments following nonpayment at maturity. In frontier areas, however, the interest charges were much higher. In Edwardsville, Illinois, in 1820 short-term borrowers paid 10 per cent a *month*.[12] In 1857 the Sidle Bank in the frontier town of St. Anthony's Falls (Minneapolis) charged the usual rates of 3 per cent a *month*, increased to 5 per cent a month when the debts were not paid at maturity.[13] All this emphasizes that liquid capital was scarce and in great demand while the western United States was still an "underdeveloped country."

[11] Hugh McCulloch, *Men and Measures of a Half Century* (New York: Charles Scribner's Sons, 1888), pp. 116–117.

[12] Theodore Carlson, *The Illinois Military Tract*, Illinois Studies in Social Sciences, vol. 32, no. 2 (Urbana, Ill.; University of Illinois Press, 1951), p. 53.

[13] Marion E. Cross, *Pioneer Harvest* (Minneapolis: The Farmers and Mechanics Savings Bank of Minneapolis, 1949), pp. 18, 50.

CHAPTER 12

Labor Awakens

There was a scarcity of workers, both skilled and unskilled, in America during the years following the Revolution. Virtually everyone in the new nation engaged in some type of farming; the few nonagricultural workers tended to be self-employed. As late as 1820, after industrial expansion was well under way, there were only about 800,000 nonfarm workers, representing approximately 28 per cent of the total gainfully employed. By 1860, the percentage had increased to 41; but this nonagricultural labor force amounted to only 4.3 million. Fewer than two million of them could be considered industrial workers.

Accordingly, in the early decades after 1789, the status of American laborers was somewhat higher than that of workers in England or Europe, a fact which encouraged immigration. While hours worked per day were about the same on both sides of the Atlantic, working conditions and wages differed. The factory system did not dominate the economy as it did in England, and conditions in the homes and shops of American workers were better. As for wages, unskilled laborers in America drew from one-third to one-half more than those elsewhere; payments to skilled workers varied less.

THE LABOR MOVEMENT TO 1820

The earliest organizations of workers were primarily philanthropic and social. While they continued to exist up to 1800, the forerunners of modern trade unions were more properly the societies formed to raise wages and reduce hours in the 1790s. These were a product of the changing commercial environment.

The Organization of Production and Distribution. Before the Revolutionary War, production had been either in the home or handicraft stage. There, the craftsman was essentially his own employer and most finished goods passed directly from the producer to the consumer. As the domestic stage of production developed (as in the shoe industry discussed on page 161), two things frequently happened to the skilled worker, first, he no longer came in direct contact with the purchaser of the product, and second, he became a dependent wage earner rather than an independent craftsman. Some master craftsmen became "merchant employers" who devoted increasing attention to selling in wholesale markets. There was no distinction between merchant and employer functions; one person served in both capacities and in most cases also furnished the capital for the business. As these merchant employers ranged over broader market areas, they came into competition with each other. Competition forced prices down; the merchant employer, in order to hold his business, had to cut costs. Reducing his employees' wages was the most effective method. This led the men, in self-defense, to set up trade organizations and created a breach between the master and the journeymen.

The expanding economic order which gave birth to the domestic system produced a further refinement in the organization of production and distribution. The merchant employer gradually gave way to the "merchant capitalist"—a bargaining specialist and sometimes an organizing genius. The merchant capitalist arose when the horizons of commerce widened beyond the reach of the merchant employer, who often had little marketing ability and even less capital. The new merchant capitalist had "the ability to size up markets for raw materials, for producing the finished product, and for disposing of it. Only such a person could command the capital necessary to finance a business on a large scale. . . . Here occurs the separation of the merchant-function from the employer-function."[1]

Just as the merchant employer had forced down wages to meet competition, so did the merchant capitalist. He did so by paying less for the finished product. Workers bore the brunt of the price reduction, because employers were caught squarely between the levels of prices and wages. Since they could not hold up prices, they tried to force down wages, using two principal methods. Employers either reduced wages directly by paying less per hour or per unit output, or they hired women, children, and prison labor, all of whom worked for less than skilled workers. In some cases, employers hired additional apprentices instead of journeymen or master craftsmen. Such apprentices were frequently green or inexperienced hands who, despite their older years, masqueraded under the guise of "apprentices." These various cost-cutting devices forced the skilled workmen to organize to protect their living standards. The journeymen were the first to organize successfully, turning their efforts against the masters who had become merchant employers. Later, after the rise of the merchant capitalist, the attack shifted toward the capitalist. In a Boston

[1] John R. Commons et al., *History of Labour in the United States* (New York: The Macmillan Company, 1921), vol. I, p. 101.

strike for a ten-hour day, led by carpenters in 1835, the workers even showed sympathy for the employers' plight. They declared in a circular that "We would not be too severe on our employers; they are slaves to the capitalists, as we are to them."[2]

Early Trade Societies. The shoemakers of Philadelphia formed a successful journeymen's organization in 1794. The Federal Society of Journeymen Cordwainers, established to maintain wages, staged an organized strike in 1799; it survived the strike but disbanded after 1806. New York printers followed the example of the shoemakers by organizing in 1794. During the next decade, craftsmen in most seaboard cities took similar action.

These early trade societies were closely restricted craft unions, operating on a local basis. Their primary objectives were to maintain or advance wages, reduce the hours of labor, improve working conditions, and establish the closed-shop principle. The last, when successful, prevented employers from using green hands to replace skilled workers. To achieve these objectives, the workers relied upon peaceful strikes and collective bargaining. Occasionally, strikes tended toward violence when employers ignored the workers' demands; on the whole, however, labor was not militant in the early years.

Opposition by Employers. The flurry of organizational activity by workers drove employers to the counterattack. They sought protection through associations of their own; where possible, they combined along trade lines and tried to destroy the trade societies. Employers in Philadelphia and New York attempted to flood the labor market by advertising for workers in nearby cities. When associations failed to break up the workers' organizations, employers asked the courts for assistance.

For centuries, English common law had held that organizations of two or more persons to attain some objective were combinations or conspiracies prejudicial to the public interest. That was the case even if the actions taken by the group were perfectly lawful when practiced by an individual. Americans debated whether or not the English common law applied in United States courts; the judicial system around 1800, under the Federalists, ruled that it did. Probably the most important of the early conspiracy cases involved the cordwainers of Philadelphia, who in 1806 were found guilty of combining to raise their wages. The court ruled that the journeymen's society was formed either to benefit its members or to work harm on those who did not join the movement; in either case, the common law condemned the action. A subsequent decision involving the shoemakers of Pittsburgh in 1815 likewise declared that an attempt by workers to raise wages was harmful to employers and to the

[2] Selig Perlman, *A History of Trade Unionism in the United States* (New York: The Macmillan Company, 1929), pp. 22–23.

community interest. Although these decisions did not prevent the continuation of trade societies and strikes, harassment from the courts definitely limited the effectiveness of labor organizations.

Frequent economic depressions were even more damaging to the success of the early labor movement than employers' associations or court actions. Workingmen's societies increased in prominence from 1794 until the severe business depression of 1819, but then falling prices and unemployment submerged them until 1822. This was the pattern for more than a century: union activity and membership rose during prosperity and declined sharply during depressions. Unions were successful in obtaining wage increases during periods of high employment and rising prices, but during depressions workers did not remain loyal to their organizations when doing so meant starvation and deprivation. Employers who had to cut wages to compensate for falling prices always turned to nonunion help; if unemployment existed, former members of trade societies deserted their fellow craftsmen in order to find work at any wage. Thus trade unions foundered on the rocks of economic distress in all the major panics before the Civil War.

THE MILITANT ERA AFTER 1820

The return of prosperity in 1822 brought a resurgence of unionism, generally stronger and more militant than what had gone before. The earlier trade societies re-formed and newer groups appeared, including the earliest organizations among millworkers in New England. The latter was highlighted by a strike of female weavers at Pawtucket, Rhode Island, in 1824.

Also during the 1820s, city-wide federations of several craft unions appeared for the first time. The first successful one stemmed from a strike for a ten-hour workday by Philadelphia carpenters in 1827. They were joined by several other trades and became the focal point for the formation of the Philadelphia Mechanics' Union of Trade Associations. Through the *Mechanics' Free Press*, founded in 1828 as the federation's official organ, labor sounded a new note in its struggle for recognition and strength. The organization raised the broad issue of equality for the producing element of society, arguing that merchants and capitalists did not contribute anything to the welfare of society. The Mechanics' Union protested the loss of social status among craftsmen and vowed to uphold the dignity of honest toil. The laborers of Philadelphia then moved into the political arena. They formed a workingmen's party and demanded full equality before the law. Workingmen's parties sprang up in most of the larger cities along the Atlantic coast and spread to the interior of Pennsylvania, New York, and Massachusetts.

The Workingmen's Parties. The primary contention of these political parties was that a nonproductive aristocracy was exploiting the poor laboring class. Capitalists enjoyed special privileges and entrenched themselves through control of capital and government. Long workdays of twelve to fifteen hours, low pay, and other indignities were cited as evidence of exploitation. An important cause of the laborers' concern was the fall in real income after 1822. Wages during the 1820s had failed to keep pace with rising prices; to make matters worse, many employers paid wages in depreciated state bank notes. On some occasions wages were not paid at all, in which case the workers had no means of recovering what they had rightfully earned. Employees who could not satisfy their creditors often wound up in debtors' prisons. The workingmen's parties concluded that their best chance to correct these evils was to gain participation in government. For some time suffrage qualifications had been growing more liberal; the workingmen saw a champion in the 1828 Democratic presidential nominee, Andrew Jackson. Accordingly, they entered candidates in state and local elections.

Demands of Workingmen's Parties. The political demands of labor in the late 1820s were radical for that era; yet, viewed in retrospect, their objectives were basically in keeping with the goals of a democratic society. The principal aim was free public schools. Labor's leaders agreed with Thomas Jefferson that widespread education of the masses was the best way to establish a true democracy, but free, tax-supported public schools were virtually nonexistent in 1828. Labor also demanded abolition of imprisonment for debt. In the 1820s as many as 75,000 persons were placed in penal institutions each year for nonpayment of debts. The condition was even more appalling because a great many owed less than $25. One prison held thirty-two persons whose debts were under $1 each. Such people had no chance to repay their obligations.

Closely associated with the abolition of debtors' prisons was the drive for mechanics' lien laws and for revision of state militia systems. Labor demanded laws which would enable a worker to collect wages in the event of nonpayment by placing a lien (or legal claim) on the finished work; under such a system, the employer could not sell the product until he had paid his laborers. Workers also asked for a revision of state militia regulations. Most states required participation in militia activities for a number of days each year; any person who declined to serve was subject to fine or imprisonment. For the worker, military duty meant a loss of earnings for the time spent in service plus traveling expenses. Furthermore, he had no assurance that he would have a job when he returned home. The fact that wealthy individuals escaped their militia obligations simply by paying the necessary fine further irked working people.

Other less important aims of the workingmen's parties included the direct election of all public officials in order to lessen graft and corruption in local and state politics; greater equality in regard to taxes; complete separation of church and state; and elimination of all special privileges, especially chartered business monopolies. The common people disliked the privileged position of state-chartered banks and frequently suffered from the depreciated bank notes issued by such banks. Organized labor gained the support of Western farmers in many of their demands and backed Jackson in 1828.

Results of Political Action. The workingmen's parties were short-lived. They nominated candidates for local office and campaigned vigorously in state and national elections in 1828 and 1829. In the elections of 1832, the movement merged with the Democratic party and tended to vanish from the national scene. The brief period of activity left its imprint on society, however, because both major parties of the era, Whig as well as Democratic, harkened to the cries for reform. The workingmen's parties achieved success in most of their basic aims. Pennsylvania inaugurated educational reform in 1834 by founding a free tax-supported school system; other states fell rapidly into line. Ohio led the way in eliminating imprisonment for debt in 1828; debtors' prisons were virtually nonexistent by 1840. After 1830, most states severely modified or ended compulsory militia service. Mechanics' lien laws gained wide adoption in the years following 1828. New York inaugurated "free banking" in 1838 as a means of democratizing the state banking system (see Chapter 11). While success in other respects was less obvious, at least the workers' protests had called attention to existing evils.

This political agitation for reform did not generally reach the extreme of "class warfare" as it sometimes did in Europe. America's social structure differed from that of the Old World in that there were no clear-cut class barriers to prevent movement up the social scale. In the United States, class solidarity did not exist. The influence of the frontier and the democratic heritage kept society more fluid and preserved opportunity for economic and social advancement. There were a number of leaders in the labor movement around 1830, however, who were dissatisfied with American society, and they continually agitated for reforms. The experience of the Workingmen's party of New York demonstrated the role of these reformers.

Radical Reformers of the Jacksonian Era. At least four zealous reformers came to be associated with the New York City Workingmen's party after 1828: Thomas Skidmore, George Henry Evans, Robert Dale Owen, and Frances Wright. Skidmore controlled the party from the beginning and influenced its policies to a great extent by his radical philosophies. A machinist by trade, he was a firm believer in social and economic equality and offered extreme proposals for guaranteeing the well-being of everyone. He proposed canceling all existing debts and property titles and selling the total wealth of the country at public auction; every citizen should have equal purchasing power. Also he wanted to abolish inheritance in order to maintain the equality thus established. Skidmore's ideas received some support from George Henry Evans, a New York printer. Evans founded the *Workingman's Advocate* as the official organ for the New York labor party and through its pages agitated for equality in education, property, and civil rights. He never endorsed all of Skidmore's extreme views, although he proposed that Congress divide all land equally among the people. He was unsuccessful at first, but he renewed his drive for land reform in the 1840s, after the influence of Skidmore and others had waned.

Robert Dale Owen and Frances Wright had won reputations as reformers before affiliating with the New York party. Both of them had tried in vain to establish utopias at New Harmony, Indiana, and Nashoba, Tennessee. Their failure led them to New York City where they began publishing a radical newspaper, the *Free Enquirer.* Owen, son of an idealistic Scottish industrialist, and Miss Wright, a woman of striking beauty and high intellect, used the Workingmen's party as a sounding board for their radical views. Owen was particularly interested in free education and offered a revolutionary idea of state guardianship for children. He proposed placing all children in national schools as wards of the government, regardless of the social or economic status of the parents; such a system would remove all vestiges of class distinction and foster a true democracy. Owen voiced other extreme views in regard to property ownership, religion, and divorce laws. Frances Wright, one of the few women of her day who dared speak her views in public, voiced unconventional ideas on education, religion, and marriage. Her opponents accused her of advocating free love and called her the "Red Harlot of Infidelity." But her natural beauty and sparkling wit enabled her to captivate and dazzle her audiences, and she quickly became a renowned leader of the reform movement.

Extremists like Skidmore, Evans, Owen, and Wright wrecked the New York labor party. After a modest show of success in 1829, the party disintegrated. The leaders fell out of harmony, and the workers rejected their more radical proposals. Skidmore's communistic program for property distribution and Owen's state guardianship for children had no appeal to workers. Frances Wright's avowed disdain for established religious and marital mores was equally distasteful.

Trade Unionism in the 1830s. The political interlude from 1828 to 1832 was followed by a revival of trade unionism. The spirited revival centered about demands for higher wages and shorter hours. The mounting prosperity and inflation from 1834 to 1837 placed workers in a position to press for better terms of employment. They possessed a better bargaining position owing to the high demand for laborers; at the same time, rising prices caused employers to attempt to hold down costs. As the cost of living ascended, real wages fell. Employers resisted the demands for adjustment in pay scales and turned to cheaper sources of labor, including more women, children, and convicts. As in the early 1820s, the older trade societies came to life and many new ones appeared. The upsurge of activity carried over into textile mills and shoe factories, which had heard little worker protest heretofore.

A wave of city-wide federations accompanied the revival of these organizations. The General Trades' Union of New York, consisting of fifty-two associated trade societies, was an example of this type of union. Similiar groups formed in Philadelphia, Boston, Cincinnati, and other cities; by 1836 there were at least thirteen. A noteworthy effort toward nationalization of the trade union movement came when the National Trades' Union formed in New York in 1834. Local societies from several Eastern cities combined, with purely economic objectives in mind. Their enthusiasm faded, however, in the Panic of 1837; the resulting depression halted the drive toward permanent national unions.

Further evidence of the strength of the union movement of the 1830s was the outbreak of strikes. Work stoppages occurred in virtually every large city in the country, there being an estimated 168 strikes from 1833 to 1837, mostly over wages and hours. The pressure for a ten-hour day gained momentum. Workers argued that leisure time was necessary for self-improvement; employers opposed them, claiming that leisure promoted idleness, intemperance, and degradation of society. Labor scored a notable victory in Philadelphia in 1835 by winning a general strike for a ten-hour day. Meanwhile, the movement had spread from Boston to Baltimore, where it influenced the Federal government to establish a ten-hour workday in 1840. In spite of these gains, the ten-hour day was the exception rather than the rule in the 1840s.

During the 1830s, employers made concessions to workers only when necessary. They again formed protective associations and combatted unions through the courts, obtaining favorable court decisions for the most part, as in the case of the New York tailors' union. In 1836, twenty striking tailors were arrested on conspiracy charges and found guilty by a jury which deliberated for only thirty minutes. The judge fined the workers $50 each, except their president, who paid $150. The public reacted strongly in favor of the defendants: a crowd estimated at 27,000 gathered and burned the judge in effigy. Such public sentiment brought forth an important modification to the conspiracy theory as applied to organized labor. In 1842 Chief Justice Lemuel Shaw of the Massachusetts

Supreme Court ruled in *Commonwealth v. Hunt* that an association of workers to regulate conditions of labor or to raise wages was not in itself illegal. He declared that "the legality of such an association will therefore depend upon the means to be used for its accomplishment. . . ."[3] Shaw upheld the right to strike for a closed shop, which was the central issue in the case. Although the decision did not immediately free unions from court harassment, it did establish an important precedent in labor law.

LABOR IN THE TEXTILE INDUSTRY

Factory production steadily gained prominence in America. Because unions and factories developed at the same time, it might be assumed that factory workers formed the first labor unions. Actually, there was slight organizational activity among millworkers before 1860; successful union efforts occurred among skilled artisans who worked in their own shops or on contract jobs. Most factory jobs required little skill and permitted the hiring of cheap labor from among women, children, and newly arrived immigrants, none of whom were suitable union prospects. Thus, as factory production grew in importance, unskilled labor accounted for an increasing amount of manufacturing output.

The Rhode Island System. The textile industry of New England provides two examples of the type of labor utilized in the early factories of the United States. Different systems of factory organization developed in the cotton mills located at Providence, Rhode Island, and at Waltham and Lowell, Massachusetts. The Rhode Island system originated in the thread mills built and run by Samuel Slater. Slater and his business associates adopted the British method of hiring entire families to work the machines. They set up their factories near villages, where the workers frequently lived in company-owned tenements. This allowed millowners to hire much female and child labor at extremely low wages. Pay for children averaged about $1.37 per week, while women earned on the average $2.37 for the same period. Male workers, relatively few in number, received about 65 cents a day. Workers labored from sixty-eight to seventy-two hours every week. Strikes were frequent under such conditions but usually failed owing to poor leadership.

The Lowell System. The labor used by Francis Lowell and Patrick Tracy Jackson was in sharp contrast to the Rhode Island system. At their textile mills at Waltham and Lowell, these men devised a unique plan for recruiting and maintaining a work force. The Lowell system, as it came to be called, was a boardinghouse plan for young female workers, most of whom came from New England farms. Lowell and Jackson

[3] Massachusetts Reports, 4 Metcalf 45 (1842).

recognized the need for a dependable and stable supply of workers. Many girls lived on nearby farms, but the men had to find a way to attract the young ladies to the mills. They solved it by establishing closely supervised boardinghouses. Lowell and Jackson provided an environment which would overcome the moral objections to factory work away from home. They succeeded so well that factory operators in other parts of New England soon copied the plan. Imitators, however, never achieved the degree of perfection found at Waltham and Lowell.

The Lowell girls submitted to a rigorous discipline in keeping with their Puritanical heritage. They had to be in bed by 10 P.M. and had to attend church. They might not use profanity, and supervisors also forbade dancing or any other displays of "feminine immodesty." Departure from the code brought dismissal. The pay was generally better than that of laborers under the Rhode Island system, although the girls worked about the same number of hours. Each girl earned around $2 a week in addition to board and room; $100 a year was an important sum to farm families accustomed to little cash income. Then, too, there were social advantages in working under the Waltham or Lowell system. It was somewhat fashionable for young ladies to work in the mills for a few years, accumulate a few hundred dollars, and then settle down to married life. The boardinghouses were not unlike college dormitories. The girls formed literary societies, produced their own periodical, the *Lowell Offering*, and found time to enjoy the sociability of group living. Several European travelers commented enthusiastically on the system.

One such visitor was Charles Dickens, who in his travels through the United States was harshly critical of what he saw. His observations of Lowell, however, were mostly laudatory. He noted a sharp contrast between England and America in respect to factory labor and remarked that after a day of visiting in the mills he could not "recall or separate one face that gave me a painful impression." Harriet Martineau and Michael Chevalier, other renowned foreign visitors, also praised the system.

At least one American observer did not bestow such lavish praise. Writing in 1846, an anonymous traveler claimed that the Lowell factory work was tedious and monotonous, leaving the girls utterly exhausted at the end of their thirteen-hour day. The writer also condemned the conditions under which the girls worked and lived, stating that the factories were poorly ventilated and conditions were conducive to poor health; the dormitories were little better. "The young women sleep upon an average six in a room; three beds to a room. There is no privacy, no retirement here; it is almost impossible to read or write alone. . . . "[4]

[4] Ray A. Billington et al. (eds.), *The Making of American Democracy: Readings and Documents* (New York: Rinehart & Company, 1950), vol. I, p. 254.

Undoubtedly, around 1840, conditions had deteriorated in the Lowell mills. Intensive competition in the industry and the influx of immigrants from Ireland brought lower standards for the workers. Wages fell and the hours of work lengthened; workers were required to tend more machines with no increase in pay. After the Panic of 1837, another wave of reform sentiment, not unlike that of the first Jackson administration, swept the country.

REFORM MOVEMENTS OF THE 1840s

During the Depression of 1837–1844, idealistic reform movements attracted the attention of the working class. Perhaps reformers could succeed where trade unions had failed. After all, laborers needed help more in a depression than during prosperity, yet trade unions were powerless to cope with unemployment and low wages after 1837. The reformers promised to alter the existing social and economic order.

Fourierism. One of the foremost reform movements was Fourierism. The ideas of the French socialist, Charles Fourier, appealed most forcibly to a Genesee Valley New Yorker, Albert Brisbane. Brisbane attracted attention in 1840 with his book, *Social Destiny of Man,* and gained no less a disciple than the famous newspaper editor, Horace Greeley. Brisbane believed that Fourier's new social organization, built around small compact cells called "phalanxes," was the answer to the quest for a better America. According to the Frenchman's "blueprint," each phalanx was a self-sufficient community of 1,620 members in which work and rewards followed an established pattern for each individual. Much as in the transcendentalist experiment at Brook Farm, no person was to do unpleasant manual labor except under the stimulus of special rewards. Grand tabernacles of labor, surrounded by orchards and flowing fountains, would keep everyone blissfully happy. Brisbane convinced a starry-eyed Horace Greeley of the merits of Fourierism; Greeley contributed several thousand dollars and an even greater number of inches of newspaper space in the *New York Tribune.* Together the two men generated enough enthusiasm to start more than forty phalanxes throughout the United States. Brisbane realized his own dream of a "North American phalanx" in 1843 on 700 acres near Red Bank, New Jersey. Instead of 1,620 individuals, however, only 112 ever took part in the endeavor, and they abandoned it in 1854. The disillusioned Greeley found on a visit to Red Bank no gleaming colonnaded tabernacles. Instead he saw a bleak, unattractive communal building with a rickety front porch where "dedicated men wore long beards while their elderly women took to bloomers." Greeley realized, as others have before and after him, that utopia was indeed a distant land.

Agrarianism. Shortly after Brisbane founded his North American phalanx, George Henry Evans began the publication of the second *Workingman's Advocate* in New York. Following the Panic of 1837, Evans had given up his first journal and moved to a New Jersey farm. He came out of retirement in 1844, more firmly convinced than ever that agrarianism offered salvation from the evils of an industrial society. Evans argued in his paper and at labor meetings that the land belonged to all men. He urged Congress to make available 160-acre farms for all who wanted them. Workers would then move to the West in sufficient numbers to raise industrial wages in the East. To press his views more forcefully, Evans helped to organize the National Reform Association in 1845, a group dedicated to the principles of agrarian reform until its collapse a few years later. Agrarianism proved of little value to the workingmen in the 1840–1860 era, but it played a part in the ultimate passage by Congress of a homestead law in 1862.

Other Movements. Two other reform movements, motivated primarily by humanitarian impulses, claimed attention in the 1840s. The pressure for a shorter working day and the formation of producers' and consumers' cooperatives became part of the drive for social and economic progress. The attempt to reduce hours worked per day was basically a renewal of the ten-hour-day sentiment of the previous decade. The most concerted effort was that of the New England Workingmen's Association, organized in 1844. Humanitarians and labor leaders participated in the first meeting at Boston, and for the five years of its existence the association clamored for the passage of laws limiting the length of the working day. Success came in 1847 when New Hampshire adopted the first state law fixing the normal number of working hours at ten; a loophole permitted longer days by special contract. Pennsylvania passed a ten-hour law for certain industries in 1848 and within a few years a number of other states enacted similar legislation.

Toward the close of the 1840s, labor also turned to cooperation as a means of improving its lot. Greatly influenced by European thought, reformers created a number of associations to enable workingmen to derive greater benefits from their labors. The iron molders of Cincinnati enjoyed a degree of success in their cooperative foundry which they erected in 1848. They organized a stock company by pooling some $2,100 of personal funds and drawing upon the generosity of two city philanthropists who paid for their building. Within a year and a half, the molders accumulated additional capital of nearly $5,700. Numerous other producers' groups set up co-ops with varying success. The Philadelphia tailoresses sought financial aid from tradesmen in other cities in order to start a co-op so "that the rewards of industry may reach the hands which accomplish the task." Yet on the whole American workmen did not respond favorably to the idea of cooperation. The nation was too greatly under the influence of private enterprise and individualism for such schemes to make much headway. The German immigrants in the larger cities were active in forming cooperative societies, but most of their efforts failed because of inadequate capital resources and poor business management. Workers learned the hard way that entrepreneurs and capitalists truly performed an essential function in productive enterprise.

Consumer cooperatives fared somewhat better. This was especially true in New England where the reformers found a better environment for action. Workers organized "protective unions" to purchase groceries, clothing, and the like; outside New England, however, the absence of wholehearted support from the laboring class generally caused failure.

TRADE UNIONISM, 1840–1860

The inadequacy of the reform movements prompted another revival of trade unionism. Unions showed some signs of life during four years of gently rising prices between 1843 and 1847. But a recession in 1848, which lasted through 1849, plus preoccupation with the humanitarian reform movements, caused further delay. With the price increases of 1850, however, the craftsmen shed the cloak of humanitarianism and returned to simple trade unionism. They concentrated on the "cold business of getting more pay for themselves by means of permanent and exclusive organizations." They demanded strict rules governing apprenticeships, the closed shop, better terms of pay and employment, exclusion of employers from their unions, and a sharper separation of skilled and unskilled labor.

A wave of strikes in 1850 grew out of this resurgence of trade unions. Most strikes were for higher pay to offset rising prices. During the strikes, some unions rented "hiring halls" where striking and unemployed artisans could register and seek employment. Labor disturbances continued sporadically through 1852, and then another upsurge in the number of strikes followed. In the two years, 1853–1854, about four-hundred strikes, mostly over wages, occurred. Wages in some trades soared to levels of $15 to $30 per week. In San Francisco, under the influence of the gold rush, pay reached even higher ranges; bricklayers commanded as much as $8 to $10 per day! Union success was short-lived. In 1855 prices sagged, and, although early 1857 brought a temporary reversal, the Panic of 1857 shattered the new unionism. In one sense, this was not a total loss, for it forced on the unions a recognition of the acute need for relief funds, essential in enabling unions to survive depressions. Later on, labor benefited from this painfully learned lesson.

LABOR'S PROGRESS

Between 1789 and 1860, workers made significant progress in wages and hours. After 1820, *money* wages rose by 23 per cent to 1860, while *real* wages increased 39 per cent. The primary reason for the more rapid increase in real wages was the greater output per worker. As production expanded, the cost of living fell 7 per cent between 1820 and 1860 (see Table 12-1). Actually, real wages did not increase as rapidly as production. This is perhaps one reason for the greater organizational activity among workers after 1820. They resented the increasingly larger

Table 12-1
Indexes of Money Wages, Cost of Living, and Real Wages, 1820–1860
(1913 = 100)

Year	Money wages	Cost of living	Real wages
1820	36	88	41
1825	37	78	47
1830	37	72	51
1835	39	81	48
1837	40	97	41
1840	41	80	51
1845	41	72	57
1850	43	73	59
1855	46	90	51
1860	47	82	57

SOURCE: Alvin H. Hansen, "Factors Influencing the Trend of Real Wages," *American Economic Review*, vol. 15, no. 1 (March, 1925), p. 32.

share of output which went to the owners of capital. Technological innovations which preceded most of the increased production required unprecedented capital outlays in an age when capital was scarce. The owners of that capital extracted a generous share of the proceeds, which left a declining *relative* share of increased production for the worker.

Of course, all workers did not benefit alike from the increase in real wages. Earnings varied according to geography, industry, and level of skill involved. Especially after 1840, as the use of machinery increased and the influx of immigrants speeded up, workers in skilled trades such as weaving, needlework, and cabinetmaking failed to benefit as much as unskilled laborers. Factory operators forced wage reductions on many workers, as in the textile mills of New England. The reductions were in the form of lowered *piece rates*, which did not necessarily result in lower total earnings. The workers avoided a decline in money wages by speeding up their daily output. Speed-ups in the textile mills became more and more of a problem as competition in the industry increased.

Loss of economic status, relative to unskilled workers, was not the only problem for the skilled workers. The factory system also brought on the general degradation of the laborer. It increased "the strain and discipline under which the work was carried on." With the greater use of cheap immigrant labor, especially after 1840, the dignity of human labor lessened appreciably. Immigrants replaced the New England farm girls in the Lowell mills.

Perhaps labor's most significant economic gain, other than the increase in real wages, was the steady shortening of the working day. The number of hours, which measured "from sun to sun" in the beginning, averaged eleven in 1860. Some workers achieved a ten-hour day, but it is interesting to note that workers still spent twelve hours on the job. The two-hour difference was usually the time allowed the workers for breakfast (midmorning) and dinner (midafternoon).

Progress for labor unions was slight. Although unions appeared as early as the 1790s, they had but little impact on American economic life. Since the unions were confined to the bigger cities, they affected few people; only 1 or 2 per cent of the labor force belonged to unions at any time. In short, labor unions were essentially experimental and evolutionary and did not emerge from their embryonic stage until after 1860.

CHAPTER 13

Domestic and Foreign Commerce

The role of the merchant in the nineteenth century was one of growing importance. The new factories could continue to operate only to the degree that merchants performed their function of finding new markets and selling the ever greater stream of goods being produced. The more rapid the turnover of goods, that is, the faster they were sold, the larger the factories could become. The more that factory management could employ the economies of specialization, the lower they could price their goods, and the higher the standard of living could rise. Such merchandising required special skills, knowledge, and experience, with the result that early in the history of many factories the selling department was separated from the manufacturing. In Samuel Slater's first factory, Almy and Brown kept the merchandising end of the business and put Slater in charge of manufacturing.

In the history of American commerce, domestic trade has never commanded as much attention as foreign trade. This may be because overseas voyages to distant ports are more romantic, or because customs regulations require that records be kept of goods entering and leaving the country. Contrariwise, the sale of goods within the country has always been less accurately recorded, so that less is known about the details of domestic trade. Yet foreign trade has long been less important than domestic. In 1799 foreign trade was about a third of domestic trade; statistics for 1850 show that foreign commerce was $300 million compared to $2 billion for domestic commerce, or about one-seventh. As the economy has grown, foreign commerce has fallen still farther behind, perhaps because the United States is enormous in size, and there is free trade across state lines. In smaller nations such as Holland, Belgium, or even England, foreign trade is relatively more important than it is in America. Domestic commerce may be examined from the viewpoint of retailing, wholesaling, and selling, or from the viewpoint of regional specialization.

RETAILING

Public Markets. In villages and towns public markets were held once or twice a week or even every weekday. For many years farmers around

Philadelphia offered fruits, vegetables, and sometimes meats for sale on High Street (later called Market Street); housewives came there to buy. As villages and towns grew in size, consumers had to walk farther with their shopping loads and farmers had to rise earlier in the morning to travel the greater distances. Some farmers found it easier to sell to wholesale buyers and, likewise, housewives preferred to buy from neighboring grocery stores and butchers. From a sanitary point of view, the farmers' markets were often dirty and unpleasant. Local storekeepers made the most of this objection, for markets cut into their business, and some wanted to eliminate them entirely. By 1860 the public market was declining in importance, although many towns and cities continued to hold them well into the present century.

Peddlers. Away from towns and cities pioneers and many farmers lived simply. Most of what they produced they consumed themselves, so there was no selling problem for these products. They exchanged skills with neighbors and bought a few things from itinerant peddlers. The peddler brought such useful knickknacks as thread, needles and pins, tinware, baskets, spices, and perhaps articles as large and complex as clocks. Many of these items had originated in New England, and the peddler himself was frequently a Yankee. He brought news and stories of the outside world, and people looked forward to his arrival with pleasure. He was nearly always a smart trader; he had to be to survive. Only part of the time did farmers have the cash to pay for the useful and fascinating objects that he offered, and accordingly they paid him in farm produce. That generally meant that the peddler had to barter to sell his goods; then when he carried the produce to town, he had to barter again to dispose of it. At first peddlers traveled afoot or on horseback and were obviously limited in what they could carry on their backs or in saddlebags. As soon as roads improved somewhat, they drove wagons. A peddler's wagon was a wonder of efficiency with its many compartments, each with an outside door or lid for easy access and sale, and many items neatly packed or nested within. It was amazing how much a good packer could stow in a small space (see Fig. 13-1). Even so, the peddler had to stock up occasionally, which created a problem if he had ventured a long distance from his source of supplies. In time peddling became so well organized that there were chains consisting of a New England manufacturer, peddlers' depots at various central points, and peddlers with their carts, each working in a specific territory.

By the time this occurred the region was usually sufficiently settled that the people preferred a more dependable form of merchandising. A general store had the advantage of being always at hand, it had a greater variety of goods, and complaints could be made to the storekeeper if the merchandise was faulty. Storekeepers, for their part, felt the competition of peddlers, whose overhead was negligible, was unfair and that their practices were sometimes unethical. Communities levied taxes on peddlers and discouraged them in other ways. Also, peddling was a young man's occupation. When he grew older and married and wanted to settle down, many a peddler set up a general store in a well populated area that he had served and let his customers come to him. With improved roads, canals, and the coming of railroads, peddling began to die

FIG. 13-1. The peddlers' wagon. (*Harper's Weekly.*)

out. Some of the peddlers' depots in time became wholesale warehouses for retail establishments.

General Stores. A certain number of customers in an area was needed to keep a general store in business. In contrast to the peddler, these stores carried various heavy items such as plows, ox yokes, harnesses, chains, and iron kettles. Also, some of the farm products which they accepted in trade from one customer, they could dispose of to others; especially was this true in the West where new settlers had just arrived or were passing through and did not have any food of their own. Even so, the operations of many a Western general store were but slightly larger than those of a peddler. Gross sales for the year might average about $10,000, and the storekeeper would be on duty at his store from seven in the morning until ten in the evening. Every transaction involved some higgling—this was before the time of the one-price system. The customer paid according to his ability as a bargainer, whether he paid in cash, offered goods in barter, or asked for credit. If he asked for credit, the price also depended on his credit standing. Much business was done on a credit basis, and the inability to judge the credit worthiness of customers was a major reason for many store failures. To compensate for this additional risk and for transportation as well, the same item that sold for 50 cents in New York or Philadelphia would sell for $1 or more in, say, New Salem, Illinois.

Many Western storekeepers made annual journeys all the way to Philadelphia or New York to restock their stores: they found that more satisfactory than buying in Western wholesale centers. True, the merchant had to be gone for at least six weeks, but he could advertise that he had goods fresh from the East, which appealed to his customers. Occasionally a merchant would seize the opportunity to urge his customers to pay up their accounts, for everyone knew that the trip was both necessary and costly. More important, he could buy recently imported goods at bargain prices from those who had attended the New York auctions. Eastern terms of credit were also generous—six months' time to pay and 6 per cent on the second six months was generally allowed. Finally, there was an excuse for a trip to the big city and the chance to tell about it when he got back. The smart merchant sometimes accompanied his wagon of goods on the return trip to make sure that it came through safely and on time. The amount of commerce moving from East to West may be gauged from the fact that as early as 1820, 3,000 wagons with $18 million worth of goods arrived in Pittsburgh from Philadelphia. Then they were shipped down the Ohio River. It usually took several weeks to deliver the goods: in 1837 a shipment that reached St. Louis from Baltimore in two weeks warranted comment in the newspapers.

Disposing of Bartered Produce. Local storekeepers had a wholesale selling as well as a wholesale buying problem to solve. They traded much of their merchandise for local produce, or accepted produce in payment of debts. Some of this they were able to sell or trade to other customers, but they had to dispose of much of it in distant markets. Among the commodities which they shipped out in quantity were wool, beeswax, honey, flour, tallow, whisky, and pork. In time the handling of these became well organized, with commission merchants competing vigorously for the business. A New Orleans house, Renfro, Breedlove, and Richeson, in 1825 sent out an analysis of the likely price range of various crops during the coming season.[1] Samuel Hill of New Salem, Illinois, set up a card-

[1] Lewis Atherton, *The Pioneer Merchants in Mid-America* (Columbia: Missouri University Press, 1939), pp. 90–102.

ing mill in 1835 and advertised for wool: nearly everyone in that area kept a few sheep. He charged his customers for carding their wool and took care of all surplus which they wished to sell, crediting their accounts in his store. They then bought goods at his store in order to use up those credits. His store was the only one to prosper while the village lasted, and he became the only person in the village to own a two-story house. It was farm produce of this kind that flatboats and steamboats carried in great quantity to St. Louis and New Orleans. There it was sold for consumption in the South or for shipment by water to the East.

The Specialty Stores. As villages grew into towns, there were enough customers for certain products to justify the founding of specialty stores. One of the early specialty stores was the saloon. Men preferred to do their tippling where women were not constantly entering to shop, and the women preferred not to buy in stores whose habitués were town roisterers. The dry goods store appeared early for the same reason that textiles were the first factory-made goods: there was a large and steady demand for cloth. Hardware and farm implement stores developed early, too. Larger towns might also support a drugstore, a jewelry store, a furniture store, a men's clothing store, and a dress shop; groceries would be found in a specialty shop of their own. The specialty store had several advantages. Since the merchant had to be familiar with only one kind of goods, he could be much better informed about his merchandise. He not only bought with more discrimination and had a greater variety to offer, but he bought in larger lots and thus at lower cost. By the time a town reached a certain size, roughly 2,500 people, its general stores were declining and its specialty stores were growing in importance. By 1840 there were 131 towns and cities of over 2,500 and by 1860, 392; the specialty store was a well-established institution.

WHOLESALING

Shipping Merchant. One of the earliest wholesale merchants was the so-called shipping merchant. He owned his own vessels, exported and imported merchandise, and often engaged in retail trade too. Stephen Girard was a highly successful shipping merchant. Of French origin, he came to Philadelphia about the time of the American Revolution. He dispatched his ships to various parts of the world, especially to the French West Indies, although these were forbidden to trade directly with America. He imported sugar from the West Indies and wines from France, which he sold in Philadelphia. Girard's ships were well-outfitted, he paid his men good wages, and he let the captains carry on a limited trade of their own on the side. However, he demanded strict obedience and hard work of everyone; he put in a fifteen-hour day himself. No sooner did Girard hear that, say, flour was in great demand in Martinique, than he sent off a shipload to the island. In one case a vessel took out a cargo worth $68,000 and brought one back that sold for $248,000. It is noteworthy that Girard was a wholesale importer and exporter, a shipowner, and a retail merchant, all at the same time. He later became a banker as well and in his last years devoted most of his attention to that occupation. He died in 1831, one of the richest men in America.

Importers. Specialization appeared in importing before it did in exporting. Too many uncertainties were involved in relying on independent suppliers. A proprietor or partner in an importing house sometimes journeyed to London once a year or even took up residence there to obtain the best quality of goods for his firm at the lowest cost; for example, George Peabody of Baltimore, a dry goods importer, went to London to live in the 1830s.

Wholesale Merchants and Other Middlemen. Wholesale houses were important first in New York. They dealt primarily with imported merchandise and to a lesser degree with domestic goods. Dry goods, which after all were the first factory-made goods, were an early specialty. There were also wholesale houses in boots and shoes and in groceries soon after the War of 1812. By 1850 there was a clear distinction between wholesaling and retailing. In fact, other middlemen besides the wholesaler had appeared between the manufacturer and retailer. Just as the manufacturer could not be bothered with selling to individual customers, neither could he be bothered to sell to small stores which wanted only a dozen or a few dozen of certain articles. It was the function of the wholesalers and others to gather and deliver these relatively small orders and sometimes to help the retailers finance them too.

Auctions. In most Eastern seaports, auctions took place fairly frequently, but they achieved their highest development in New York. The auction grew into prominence as a way of disposing of merchandise right after the War of 1812. British textile merchants were loaded with goods which they had made but had been unable to market during the last years of the Napoleonic Wars. When peace with America was again achieved, they literally "dumped" large quantities of these goods on New York and put them up for auction. Some merchants picked up remarkable bargains, and the fame of New York spread. When other cities like Boston and Philadelphia also began featuring auctions, the New York auctioneers sought to do something unusual to keep New York's position as the leading auction city. Abraham Thompson secured a special law from the state legislature in 1817 requiring that once a merchant put up a piece of goods for auction, he could not withdraw it if the bidding were unsatisfactory, but must let it be sold. As auctions in other cities did not have this rule, the effect was to draw bargain hunters to New York, where they knew there would be bargains whenever bidding was light. This attracted more buyers and most of the time kept the bidding spirited. The auction law was almost as important in making New York a great importing port as was the building of the Erie Canal. During the years 1821–1830 auction sales of imported goods amounted to $160 million, or 44 per cent of all New York's imports.[2] Auction sales declined relatively after 1830, for many merchants disliked the uncertainties they caused in the cost of merchandise. A piece of cloth might sell for 65 cents a yard in the morning and 43 cents in the afternoon. Despite growing efforts to discourage auctions, New York auctioneers sold as much in 1831–1840 as in the decade before, although now it was only a fifth of all New York's imports. Wholesale merchants were the chief buyers at these auctions. It was the lower prices made possible by the auctions which explain why country storekeepers traveled such long distances to buy in New York City.

Marketing Cotton. A planter had three ways of marketing his cotton. He might consign it directly to a Northern or European market and have his agent there sell it for him, a method that was used less as the century progressed. Or a planter might ship it to the nearest cotton port and have a factor there sell it for him. Or he might have a cotton factor sell the cotton for him at a nearby inland assembly point located on some river or rail line. The factor was the business representative of the planter in the outside world and often maintained close personal as well as business relations with planters. The factor served the planter in three fundamental ways. He not only sold the cotton but took care of such details as storing it, repacking it, shipping it, and insuring it. He also acted as the buying agent for the planter, often buying not only plantation supplies and equipment but tending to the personal shopping needs of the planter and his family. And he provided the planter with funds and credit to operate his plantation while the cotton was growing. Factors would even lend on cotton in the ground, but they charged a good rate of interest and demanded the privilege of handling the entire crop. Factors not only got a commission on the sale of cotton but made a profit on other services. Factors sometimes found it easier to deal with planters who were in debt; the Southern planters usually obliged them in this respect, for many lived beyond their means. Since most cotton factors were from the North and since debtors often cherish a grudge against their creditors, this was another basis for sectional ill feeling.

Produce Exchanges. About the middle of the century produce exchanges made their appearance. The Chicago Board of Trade was founded in 1848, the Merchants Exchange of St. Louis in 1850, and the

[2] Robert G. Albion, *The Rise of New York Port* (New York: Charles Scribner's Sons, 1939), pp. 13, 61, 276–280.

Produce Exchange of New York in 1851. All began informally. In New York, "the flour dealers were the first to progress through the cycle which dealers in cotton, coffee and other commodities would follow later—first gathering in the open air on a street corner; then acquiring an awning for shelter; then renting quarters and incorporating as an exchange, and finally erecting a building."[3] These exchanges, like the earlier stock exchange, were auctionlike offerings of flour in one part of the exchange, cotton in another corner, and tobacco in still another. Newspapers reported the amounts sold and the prices paid.

ADVERTISING AND SELLING

Advertising. Before the Civil War advertising had made slight headway. Most advertising was in newspapers, although probably less than half of the Western merchants advertised at all. The advertisements were of the classified kind—strictly informational. They gave the name of a store, its location, and what goods it currently had on sale. They almost never mentioned any prices and rarely praised the goods. There were no pictures until about 1830, when newsprint became less expensive. Then certain occupations adopted standard ways of attracting attention to themselves, such as displaying a boot for a shoemaker or a mortar and pestle for a drugstore. There were relatively few brand names in merchandise; to the extent that these existed, the manufacturer let the local merchant do the advertising. Almost no national advertising of brand merchandise existed except in the patent medicine field.[4] Handbills were another form of advertising in this era.

The Extension of Credit. Although there have been glib salesmen in all times, the art of "selling" had not yet been formally developed. To many buyers the most convincing sales argument was a low price and a long time to pay. Before the Civil War it was normal for store accounts to run six months or more before the customer paid. After all, cash was scarcer then and the majority of people were from farm families, who sold their crops only once or twice a year. Poor judgment in granting credit caused many merchants to fail. Yet the merchant had to grant credit; otherwise he simply did not attract enough business, or at least he did not hold it for long.

Collectors, Drummers, and Traveling Salesmen. Since customers paid at long intervals, the storekeepers were only occasionally in funds. Moreover, many of them lived at a great distance from the Eastern seaboard where the wholesaler or importer was. By 1840 a third of the population

[3] *Ibid.*, p. 283.

[4] Fred Jones, *Middlemen in the Domestic Trade in the United States, 1800–1860* (Urbana, Ill.: University of Illinois Press, 1937), pp. 54–55.

lived beyond the Appalachians, and the states lying farthest west were Arkansas and Missouri. Wholesale houses sent out bill collectors to dun storekeepers who were slow in their payments. While these collectors were seeing various interior customers, it was logical for them to try to sell some new merchandise as well. Thus the collectors became some of the earliest traveling salesmen.

Traveling salesmen did not have just one origin, however. Some peddlers took up the profession, carrying samples and taking orders. Also in the cities the competition to curry favor with out-of-town merchants was becoming steadily sharper. When country storekeepers arrived in New York, alert representatives met them at the hotels which the storekeepers frequented and sometimes had displays of their firm's products as well. So persuasive, or at least so persistent, were these people that they acquired the names of "borers" and "drummers." If it were effective to meet potential customers at their hotels or even at the station, some energetic drummers thought it might be even more so to travel out and board the train or stagecoach a few stops short of the city and ride in with a likely prospect. Even before the Civil War, the practice had started for drummers, or traveling salesmen as they were now called, to travel all the way out to the customer's store and take orders; many more storekeepers could be contacted in that way.

Credit Agencies. Collectors were not solving the bad debt problem which the Depression of 1837–1844 in particular had highlighted. Clearly there was need for some kind of organization to inform Eastern importing houses, wholesalers, banks, and others as to the credit reliability of purchasers in distant parts of the country. It did not suffice that a Western storekeeper bring a letter of introduction from the local minister or even banker; these could be faked, and one loss would eat up profits on many successful sales.

In 1841 Lewis Tappan founded The Mercantile Agency to supply credit rating information to subscribers to his service. While in the silk importing business in New York with his brother Arthur, Lewis Tappan had made it a practice to quiz almost every out-of-town customer on the credit standing of businessmen in his locality. He then recorded this valuable credit information in books: over the years he had accumulated an enormous knowledge of the reliability of business firms in all parts of the country. After the Panic of 1837, he decided to make a living by selling this unusual information. He persuaded lawyers and friends in various sections of the country to become his correspondents and keep him up to date. Their reports were copied by hand in huge sheepskin ledgers. Subscribers could get credit information on stores in Indiana, Alabama, or Missouri simply by calling at the office and having it looked up. In 1843 he opened his first branch office in Boston and then one in

Philadelphia in 1845. By 1851 Tappan had offices in seven cities; some thirty clerks worked in the New York office on over a hundred ledgers of some 700 pages each.[5] Thus was born the firm that today is Dun and Bradstreet. By exposing dishonest and inefficient businessmen, this firm and others like it did much to reduce the risk in doing business. They also reduced the number of failures by limiting the amount of credit that an honest but overoptimistic storekeeper might obtain. In the long run, it meant fewer losses, lower markups on goods, lower prices for customers, and a higher standard of living because a dollar would buy more.

INTERREGIONAL TRADE

Internal trade was largely triangular in nature until the 1850s, at which time an increasing proportion of it moved along only one side of the triangle. The East sent greater value in goods to the West than it received in return; the West sent greater value down the Mississippi than it got in return; and the South sent greater value to the East than it got in return. During the 1850s the East-West side of the triangle became the most important, and the West-South side the least important (see Fig. 13-2).

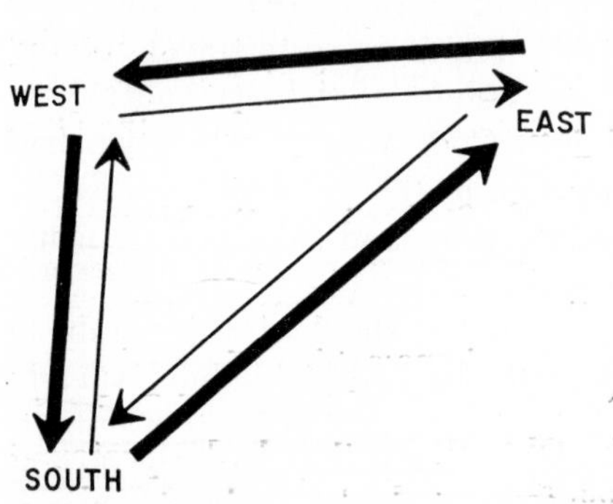

FIG. 13-2. Diagram of internal triangular trade, 1815–1855.

The East-West Trade. At first poor transportation seriously handicapped trade between the East and West. Merchandise had to be valuable for its weight and bulk to stand the cost of transportation by pack train over mountain roads and trails; only furs, hides, and ginseng (a root prized as an aphrodisiac) were valuable enough to be brought east by pack horses. Cattle, sheep, and pigs to a lesser degree could transport themselves, and travelers reported seeing large herds en route. Most of them came from Ohio and Kentucky and were destined for slaughter and packing in Baltimore and Philadelphia. The first improved road over the Appalachians, the Cumberland Road, was completed to Wheeling, on the Ohio River, in 1818. This facilitated transportation considerably, and soon hundreds, even thousands of Conestoga wagons were traveling each year over that road in both directions. The cost of transportation was estimated to be $10 per ton per 100 miles; only fairly valuable goods could bear such

[5] Roy Foulke, *The Sinews of American Commerce* (New York: Dun and Bradstreet, 1941), pp. 290–291.

high freight charges. It was unprofitable to transport grain by wagon more than 150 miles. This was a major reason why merchandise sold for two or three times as much in Indiana or Illinois as on the Eastern seaboard.

The opening of the Erie Canal in 1825 had little immediate effect on East-West trade because the shores of the Great Lakes were sparsely settled. For the first ten years the canal's influence did not extend beyond upstate New York, but by 1840 large amounts of grain and flour were flowing eastward from the Middle West, as well as some pork and bacon and considerable lumber. Buffalo, Cleveland, Toledo, Detroit, and Chicago, all on the shores of the Great Lakes, started to grow; Cleveland and Toledo had canals reaching south and tapping Ohio's grain-growing region. The more valuable commerce moving to the West continued to be either imported or Eastern merchandise. New York was always the nation's leading port for imports. The westward-moving merchandise was smaller in bulk but greater in value than the eastward-moving agricultural commodities. Up to the 1850s a large amount of this westward traffic went overland to Pittsburgh or Wheeling and then down the Ohio River by steamboat. The chief Ohio River ports and distributing points were Cincinnati, Louisville, and Portsmouth. St. Louis, on the Mississippi, was strategically located not only to distribute goods in its immediate area but also to ship them south or farther west up the Missouri River.

About 1850 several railroads crossed the Appalachian Mountains and soon afterward established through connections to Chicago and St. Louis. Since they more or less paralleled the Ohio River, they had a profound effect on East-West trade. Goods which formerly had gone by steamboat, or even by flatboat, down the Ohio and Mississippi Rivers and had then been transferred at New Orleans to a vessel bound for an Eastern port were now put on an eastbound freight train and went much more directly and quickly to their destination. In the early 1850s a series of drought years caused low water on the Ohio and periodically disrupted steamboat service, which encouraged shippers to make use of the new railroads. The bulk of the eastward shipments still consisted of grain and livestock, packing products like pork and bacon from Cincinnati, and after about 1855 some iron and copper ore from Upper Michigan. By 1860 most of the livestock and two-thirds of all grain shipments went eastward by rail. The Erie Canal still carried more tonnage than the railroads, but its freight was chiefly bulky items like lumber. A considerable part of the grain was destined for Europe after England repealed her Corn Laws in 1846.

The Western farmers and merchants were enlarging their business contacts with Eastern businessmen and carrying on relatively less business with those of the South. This strengthened the economic and political bonds between the East and West. The importance of this fact could not then be foreseen; later historians, with the benefit of hindsight, consider it a significant factor in uniting the East and West against the South in the Civil War.

The West-South Trade. Heavier shipments down-river than up-river characterized the trade between the West and the South. This was especially the case in the flatboat and keelboat period before the 1820s. Large numbers of flatboats loaded with farm products floated down to New Orleans, the goods being sold either en route or at the Southern port and the flatboat disposed of for its lumber. Even after the introduction of steamboats, flatboat traffic remained heavy for many years. As late as 1846, 2,000 flatboats arrived at New Orleans. Just after the War of 1812 a few ocean-going vessels, such as the 50-ton schooner *Maria* built at Marietta, Ohio, sailed down-river and out to sea, never again to visit their port of origin.

The only early vessels coming downstream that could also go up again were keelboats. Probably no more than twenty keelboats went up the river each year before 1817. Poling or "warping" these heavy craft upstream was very arduous. It was easier to bring supplies into the West by wagon from Philadelphia to Pittsburgh and then float them down the Ohio. In whatever way the West chose to solve the problem, before the appearance of the steamboat it was limited in its ability to get merchandise from the outside world.

Steamboats gained success on the Mississippi by 1815 and they achieved popularity very rapidly: by 1825 they carried over half of all river traffic. All kinds of agricultural products, especially grain, flour and pork, continued to go down-river to be sold in New Orleans or to be sent east or overseas to Europe. At lower Mississippi landings, steamboats picked up bales of cotton, largely for overseas shipment from New Orleans, the chief cotton export city. The principal product coming from the upper Mississippi during the 1830s and 1840s was lead from the mines around Galena in northern Illinois. Up-river traffic never amounted to half of that going down-river but it was very important. With the coming of the steamboat, all kinds of merchandise could come upstream at more reasonable rates, and some heavy machinery was brought in to supply the first industries of the West. A considerable part of the upward traffic on the lower part of the river was food products and merchandise which had gone to New Orleans for distribution and then returned part way upstream again. Steamboat traffic reached its zenith in the 1850s. Steamboat arrivals in New Orleans grew from 250 bearing merchandise worth $15 million in 1819–1820 to 3,500 arrivals carrying almost $200 million worth of merchandise in 1859–1860. By then railroads paralleling the Ohio River offered severe competition to steamboats.

The South-East Trade. Coastwise shipping carried most of the trade between the South and the East. Cotton was the leading commercial crop of the South as early as 1803 and by 1851 it constituted 60 per cent of all American exports. Large amounts of cotton went to Northern textile mills as well. Although the majority of these cotton exports went directly from a Southern port of Europe, an important minority traveled the other two sides of a so-called "cotton triangle." They went from, say, New Orleans to New York, where they were transshipped to another vessel going to Liverpool or Havre.[6] There was good reason for sending cotton some 200 miles out of its way and changing ships—to provide a return cargo for the vessels bringing European imports into New York. It was also a profitable business from the viewpoint of shipowners, most of whom were Northern. "The transportation of that portion of the crop . . . coastwise to eastern cities, employs upwards of 1,100,000 tons of *American* shipping in the Gulf and Atlantic coasting trade, and upwards of 55,000 American seamen engaged in such trade. As no foreign vessel can participate in the trade, the freights are highly profitable."[7] The fact that Northern shipowners, merchants, and financiers bought, transported, and sold most of the Southern cotton and other staples, and financed Southern planters at good rates of interest as well, was a matter of increasing annoyance to Southerners. Northerners took about 40 cents out of every dollar paid for cotton.[8] Although no other Southern product was in a class with cotton, the South sent out significant quantities of sugar from Louisiana, naval stores from North Carolina, rice from Georgia, and tobacco and lumber products from the Chesapeake Bay region. The value of the goods going east exceeded that of those moving south.

In the early part of the century, much of the goods carried south from Northern ports was imported merchandise, but "as time went on, it seems likely that the cargoes carried southward from New York to the cotton ports contained an increasing amount of northern domestic manufactures, which gradually took the place of previous similar wares from Europe."[9] New York's coastal trade was equal to the combined total of her two chief rivals, Boston and Philadelphia. Much of this trade was carried in schooners.

Other Internal Trade Routes. Several other types of internal trade at least deserve mention. There was the coastal trade within the northeastern area between Portland, Maine, and Philadelphia. There, for example,

[6] Albion, *New York Port,* pp. 95–96.

[7] Israel D. Andrews, *Trade and Commerce of the British North American Colonies,* Senate Executive Document no. 112, 32nd Cong., 1st Sess. (Washington, 1853), pp. 833–834.

[8] Albion, *New York Port,* p. 96.

[9] *Ibid.,* p. 117.

New York imported large quantities of coal from Philadelphia, and Boston sent its shoes and textiles up and down the coast and bought much flour from New York. New York also imported large amounts of building materials from New England, including lime from Maine; this was a rather dangerous cargo, since it would burst into flame if drenched with water.

After the discovery of gold in California, many ships made the long voyage, some 16,000 miles, around Cape Horn to San Francisco. They carried not only hopeful seekers after gold but also all kinds of food and clothing, picks and pans, and more elaborate gold-mining equipment. Merchants shipped to California just about everything they thought a man in the wilderness might need. It is notable that the so-called "Big Four" (Leland Stanford, Collis Huntington, Charles Crocker, and Mark Hopkins), who some years later financed the western end of the first transcontinental railroad, made their initial fortunes in merchandising.

In the South there was the internal slave trade. Slaves frequently sold for $100 more in the New Orleans market than in Norfolk, Virginia. Slaves were more profitable on the virgin soils of the Deep South than on worn-out Virginia farms; accordingly, Virginia sent thousands southward for sale.

Finally, the trade to Santa Fe from St. Louis and Independence, Missouri, in the 1820s was unique. It was from here that the Spaniards and others living in New Mexico (then Mexico) obtained the manufactured products of the outside world. Each spring merchandise sent by boat from Pittsburgh or New Orleans would be loaded into covered wagons. The caravans left as soon as the grass was up and traveled some 700 miles across the plains to Santa Fe. Supposedly Mexico forbade this commerce, but there were ways of solving that problem. In exchange for the much-desired merchandise the traders received coin, skins and furs, and large numbers of the mules for which Missouri became famous. At the peak some 230 wagons engaged in this trade, which averaged about $300,000 a year from 1822 to 1843. Although not large, it was the most outstanding commerce on the edge of the frontier. Until the Mexican War, it was really foreign trade.

FOREIGN COMMERCE

Between 1791 and 1860, merchandise exports and imports of the United States increased more than twenty times. They doubled in the period before the War of 1812, made good progress in the four years right after that war, but made only modest headway during the 1820s and early 1830s. Foreign commerce then picked up about 1834 and was not affected by the long depression of 1837–1844. During the next sixteen years foreign trade quadrupled, showing especially rapid progress during the 1850s.

Major Trends in Foreign Trade. The outstanding trends in foreign trade throughout the history of the United States have been the steady relative increase in exports of manufactured goods and an equally steady relative decrease in imports of them. Correspondingly, there have been relative increases in imports of semimanufactured goods, food, and crude materials, and a relative decrease in their exports. The greatest changes took place after the Civil War when industrialization went forward at a more rapid pace; even before the Civil War, however, the direction of the trends was evident.

In 1821 manufactures constituted only about 5 per cent of all American exports, chief of which were cotton textiles. By the Civil War period, 1861–1865, manufactures made up about 18 per cent of all American exports. Textiles were still the major item, but iron products, tobacco manufactures, carriages, wood manufactures, and boots and shoes were also significant. Meanwhile, imports of manufactured goods declined from 55 to 40 per cent of all imports. Exports of semimanufactures, food, and crude materials declined and imports of them grew. Until the Civil War the chief crude material export was cotton, with flour and wheat second but far less important.

Another trend in foreign trade was for exports to Europe to increase, not only absolutely but relatively. In 1821 exports to Europe were two-thirds of the total and by 1860 they were three-quarters. Cotton going abroad went to Europe almost entirely. Trade to Canada and to South America made some slight relative gains, but that to Mexico and Central America fell off sharply. Asia remained unimportant: the long voyages to Asia of the *Empress of China* in 1784, the first American ship to visit that part of the world, or of the speedy clipper ships shortly before the Civil War were romantic adventures and generally profitable, but they did not add appreciably to the nation's total exports.

Europe, especially Britain, was also the most important source of American foreign trade. In 1821, 64 per cent of all American imports came from Britain; by 1860 the figure was down slightly to 61 per cent, which indicated correctly the trend for the future. The other three sources of consequence in 1860 were South America (10 per cent), Asia (8 per cent), and Canada (6 per cent). Both South America and Canada had shown a substantial relative growth, but Asia had declined slightly since 1821. From England came manufactured goods of all kinds, especially textiles, haberdashery and hats, rails during the 1830s and 1840s, crockery, lead, tin, brass and copper, and glass. Brazilian coffee was South America's great contribution, for Americans were becoming coffee drinkers. Canada contributed lumber and Asia sent silks and tea.

The United States was a debtor nation all during the nineteenth century. Americans were borrowing to buy foreign equipment, like rails, to build the nation. This meant that most of the time before the Civil War, American merchandise imports exceeded merchandise exports, and the balance was met largely by borrowing, that is, by the export of securities. The only times that merchandise exports exceeded merchandise imports were about the time of the War of 1812 and in years following depressions. The most devastating depression was the one starting in 1837. For the decade, 1838–1847, merchandise exports exceeded merchandise imports. The bankruptcies of several states and many private companies damaged American credit standing, making it more difficult to borrow.

Chief Ports. Just as there was rivalry between the merchants of various nations, so also there was rivalry between the merchants of the major seaports. Some cities were primarily import ports, and some were primarily export ports. Each tended to specialize in the export of the commodity of its hinterland. To enlarge that hinterland, merchants sometimes made strenuous efforts to promote the building of turnpikes, canals, or railroads. New York merchants were staunch backers of the Erie Canal.

New York was by far the nation's leading port in the pre-Civil War era. Back in the eighteenth century first Boston and then Philadelphia had held the leadership at different times. About 1800 New York gained it, never again to lose its primacy, although Boston and Philadelphia pursued it closely until about 1817. The measurement is the total imports and exports at the ports. New York handled 70 per cent of all imports by 1870. That meant that New York merchants were more interested in what they could sell in the interior than in what they could buy there. Nevertheless, New York was also the chief export port, up until 1834, and held the second position thereafter. There were several reasons for New York's supremacy. To begin with, it had certain natural advantages such as a large, deep, and well-protected harbor, the Hudson River navigable 150 miles into the interior, and a central location. Sailing ships going to Europe all tended to take the Gulf Stream, which brought them within a few hundred miles of New York. Since they were that close, many planned to stop and load or unload some cargo. What really pushed New York so far into the lead, however, was a series of improvements instituted by forward-looking businessmen about 1817. One was the building of the Erie Canal, which enlarged New York's hinterland; a second was the inauguration of scheduled sailings, beginning with the Black Ball Line packets; a third was the passage, on the same day that the Erie Canal bill was passed, of the auction law forbidding withdrawal of goods put up for auction; and a fourth was the development of the "cotton triangle."[10]

In varying degrees the merchants in rival ports attempted to copy the practices which were giving New York its great success. The Erie Canal especially impressed them. Philadelphia developed its hybrid rail and canal system across central Pennsylvania, and Baltimore pinned its hopes on the success of the Cumberland Road, the Baltimore and Ohio Railroad, and the never-completed Chesapeake and Ohio Canal. Boston built the Western Railroad, completed in 1841, to the New York boundary near Albany, which made it a competitor with New York for the area served by the Erie Canal. None of these projects was as good as the Erie Canal; also, by the time they were in operation, New York was even farther in the lead.

In contrast to the Northern ports which were import-minded, the Southern ports were export-minded. About 1815 Charleston was the leader, with New Orleans and Savannah close behind, in that order. South Carolina and Georgia were then the leading cotton states, and they produced rice as well. As cotton growing moved west toward Louisiana and Mississippi, New Orleans assumed the leadership. Not only did New Orleans handle the Mississippi's downward traffic, but it also was accessible to the most productive parts of the Cotton Kingdom and handled Louisiana's sugar as well. New Orleans passed New York as the nation's leading export port in 1834. Meanwhile Mobile, Alabama, also overtook the two older cotton ports of the east coast to become the second-ranking Southern port.

Tariff Trends. The Constitution did not permit the states to levy tariffs, and it forbade export duties. Only the Federal government levied tariffs, which were solely import duties. Within the United States trade was free; in fact, the United States was one of the largest free-trade areas in the world. This made possible large markets, hence large-scale production, one of the keystones of American business success.

Congress at first imposed tariffs more for the revenue they produced than for the protection they gave. Under the first law of 1789, rates averaged close to 5 per cent: protection was obviously nominal. The nation was largely agricultural, and although Alexander Hamilton in his *Report on Manufactures* in 1791 made a strong plea for protecting and encouraging manufactures in order to increase the national wealth, his advice had little immediate effect. Tariffs remained low for another twenty-five years. True, America's new industries enjoyed great protection for about ten years, 1806 to 1814, but this was the result of accident, not of a conscious tariff policy. English and French blockades, American embargoes,

[10] *Ibid.*, chap. 1.

and the War of 1812 effectively barred the entry of foreign goods. Most economists agree that tariffs are normally undesirable because they prevent the consumer from buying from the lowest-priced and presumably most efficient producer. Only under special circumstances are tariffs in the public interest. For example, new industries sometimes need protection from older foreign competitors until they mature to the point where they are equally as efficient. Young American industries needed such protection during the very early part of the nineteenth century.

By the time the War of 1812 ended, British mills and factories had accumulated a large surplus of finished goods which they were anxious to turn into cash, even at sacrifice prices. Furthermore, some individuals believed that dumping these goods on the American market might kill off the young but promising American textile industry, which, if allowed to develop, would probably give the English severe competition. The British goods arrived in time for the spring sales and auctions of 1816 and sold at bargain prices. The New England textile mills promptly asked for tariff protection; the whole nation, including the South, joined in granting them protection against the economic attack of the recent enemy. The degree of protection was rather mild; the law put a duty of 25 per cent on textiles and one of 30 per cent on a few other articles. Industry had won its point, however: most parts of the country had accepted a tariff for protection, and various industries next sought to increase the tariff rates which they enjoyed. A tariff bill in 1820 failed, but in 1824 Congress enacted substantially higher rates. This was a protective tariff beyond any doubt. The peak was reached in 1828 with the so-called Tariff of Abominations. The Southern congressmen, who were now opposed to tariffs, conspired to offer a bill with many abominable features, such as high rates on raw materials like wool, so that the East itself would oppose the bill and kill it. Candidate Andrew Jackson could then pose as a friend of protection and thereby gain votes without his party's having to have a tariff law. The plan "backfired," for the East accepted the bill rather than none at all. The high tariff of 1828 annoyed Southerners, and a more moderate law in 1832 did not appease them. Henry Clay then proposed a Compromise Tariff in 1833, to lower rates gradually over a ten-year period until they reached 20 per cent. Two months after the 20 per cent low point was reached in 1842, however, a Whig Congress reenacted a high tariff. It lasted only four years because the Democrats won the 1844 presidential election. Congress enacted a moderate bill, called the Walker Tariff, in 1846, and in 1857 Congress lowered duties still further.

Thus before the Civil War tariffs rose up to 1828 and then fell (except for 1842) until the Civil War. The tariff was a much more discussed political issue during that period than it is today, for it was one of the few areas where government interfered with business. The tariff was probably less important in encouraging infant industries, except possibly about 1816, than it was in annoying the South and in laying the ground for the Civil War (see "The Tariff Controversy" in Chapter 14).

Trade Treaties. In the western world mercantilism, including high tariffs, was dying out and *laissez faire*, featured by low tariffs, was coming into fashion. Britain was the leader but the United States, France, and other nations followed its example until the 1860s. Three important trade developments stand out: First, in 1815 the United States offered to repeal discriminating duties on the direct trade of any nation that would remove duties against American goods and ships. In 1828 it repeated this offer. A dozen European nations and city-states and a number of South American countries availed themselves of the opportunity. In 1830 Great Britain officially opened the West Indies to American shipping, although American ships had actually been trading there illegally for many years. Second, Great Britain repealed its Corn Laws in 1846 and its Navigation Acts in 1849. Now American grain could enter the British market more often, and American ships could enter British and colonial ports with greater freedom. And third, in 1854, the United States negotiated its first reciprocal trade agreement, with Canada. It contained a sizable list of commodities which might cross the border duty-free in either direction.

CHAP 15 FOR
+ HURS.

CHAPTER 14

Slavery and the Civil War

Slavery occupies a prominent place in pre-1860 American history. It was important as a system of labor and it was a basic cause of the Civil War. Historians have had difficulty in evaluating slavery as an economic force because of moral, social, and political considerations; but no one denies the essential role which slavery played in Southern agriculture. Slave labor and the plantation system dominated staple-crop production; the slaveholders exercised an influence on social, political, and economic thinking out of all proportion to their numbers. Southerners, whether slaveholders or not, regarded slavery as indispensable to the successful functioning of their economic society; they defended their "peculiar institution," even with their lives, against attacks from outside.

SLAVERY

Negro slaves in the United States numbered approximately 700,000 in 1790; nearly all of them were in the South. Most Northern states had provided for eventual abolition of slavery in the decade following the Revolution. The 40,000 or more slaves in New England and the Middle Atlantic states were primarily household servants. Meanwhile, slavery had declined in importance in the South as well.

Decline of Slavery before 1790. The reasons for the decline of slavery in the United States were largely economic. In the North, Negro slaves were not well suited to general farming and manufacturing; furthermore, an increase in the number of free white laborers helped alleviate the labor shortage. In the South, exhaustion of tobacco lands in Maryland, Virginia, and North Carolina, plus the loss of indigo markets, the westward exodus of a number of planters, and low tobacco prices, made slaveholding an "intolerable burden" to many owners. Some Southern sentiment developed in favor of ending slavery.

The feeling for abolition was strongest in the upper South. In Delaware and Maryland, a diminishing use of Negro labor led to a decline in the number of slaves in the decades after 1790 and an increase in the number of free Negroes. Opponents of slavery in Virginia, perhaps the firmest in their denunciation of the practice, were not so successful in reducing the number of slaves. Thomas Jefferson and George Washington both objected to the inhumane aspects of slavery, but their attitudes on outright abolition reflected the general philosophy of their region. Jefferson advocated freedom only in conjunction with deportation and colonization in some distant land where the Negro would be "beyond the reach of mixture." Washington favored "slow, sure and imperceptible" emancipation. The prospect of thousands of Negroes suddenly released upon society did not appeal to either man. South of Virginia, no substantial body of public opinion supported the freedom movement. North Carolina's leading spokesmen tended toward conservatism without being adamant, but in South Carolina and Georgia, where the ratio of Negro slaves to white population was greater, a strong proslavery attitude prevailed.

Even in the North, abolition remained incomplete until long after 1800. There, emancipation came about gradually through laws which granted freedom at a specified age to children born of slave parents. It was not until New Jersey's 1829 law, resulting in complete freedom for Negroes in 1846, that the last legal vestiges disappeared in the North. Meanwhile, state laws ended the importation of slaves from foreign sources between 1776 and 1798, and Congress prohibited slavery in the Old Northwest Territory in the Ordinance of 1787. The African trade reopened briefly when South Carolina repealed her import prohibition in 1803, an event which influenced Congress to exercise its constitutional privilege of regulating the slave trade after 1808. In that year, a Federal law made illegal the further importation of Negroes, and although some illicit activity continued, the number of slaves entering the country was never high enough to have an appreciable influence on supply or price.

Revival of Slavery. The South revived its lagging interest in slavery after Eli Whitney invented the cotton gin. Immediately following 1793, the slaveholders of the seaboard areas sought out the best upland acreage for cotton growing and established plantations which were vitally dependent on slavery for their existence. The spread of the Cotton Kingdom across the lower South eventually encompassed most of the available farm lands from South Carolina to Texas. The result was a greatly increased demand for field hands (see Table 14-1). Plantation owners did not pause to weigh the social, moral, or economic consequences of reviving slavery. They had to get laborers wherever they could find them. In the absence of a supply of free workers, the South again used Negro slaves to meet the critical labor shortage.

The number of slaves rose steadily from about 700,000 in 1790 to nearly 4,000,000 in 1860. The rate of increase varied from 25 to 33 per cent each decade. The growth resulted primarily from the natural increase of the slave population in the older Southern states.

Table 14-1 shows the growth of the slave population, along with cotton output, cotton prices, and slave prices. Up to 1850, both slave and cotton

Table 14-1
Cotton Output and Slavery Statistics for Selected Years, 1800–1859

Year	Cotton produced (thousand bales)*	Price per pound (weighted annual average, New Orleans), cents†	Estimated slave population (thousands)‡	Approximate price of prime field hands (New Orleans), dollars§
1800	73	14.7‖	895	500
1805	146	23.3	1,040	600
1810	178	14.7	1,190	900
1814	146	16.9	1,330	550
1817	271	29.8	1,420	1,000
1819	349	14.3	1,530	1,100
1822	438	11.5	1,620	700
1823	387	14.5	1,670	650
1826	731	9.3	1,810	850
1831	805	9.0	2,050	950
1834	961	15.5	2,200	1,100
1837	1,427	9.0	2,340	1,300
1844	2,077	5.5	2,730	700
1850	2,134	11.7	3,205	1,100
1851	2,796	7.4	3,280	1,150
1856	2,871	12.4	3,650	1,400
1859	4,541	10.8	3,950	1,700

* Lewis C. Gray, *History of Agriculture in the Southern United States to 1860* (New York: Peter Smith, 1941), vol. II, p. 1026.

† *Ibid.*, p. 1027.

‡ U.S. Bureau of the Census, *Historical Statistics of the United States, 1789–1945* (Washington, 1949), p. 27.

§ Ulrich B. Phillips, *American Negro Slavery* (New York: D. Appleton-Century Company, Inc., 1940), chart between pp. 370–371.

‖ 1802.

prices tended to move up and down with changes in the general price level, although slave prices usually lagged a year or so behind cotton prices. In the 1850s, however, slave prices moved rapidly upward while cotton prices remained essentially lower for the decade. The sharp rise in slave prices after 1850 probably resulted from a mounting labor shortage in the South. In this respect, it is important to note the decreasing ratio of slaves to bales of cotton: in 1800, it was 12 to 1; in 1817, 5 to 1; in 1831, 2½ to 1; in 1850, 3 to 2; and in 1859, less than 1 to 1. The 2,400,000 bale increase after 1850 was obtained primarily through the application of additional labor to new lands. Cotton acreage and output increased many times faster than the slave population, however, causing slave prices to rise sharply. Only planters with highly productive land could afford to purchase prime field hands at the top prices.

Performance of Slave Labor. Contemporary observers and writers often debated the comparative advantages of slave versus free labor. The majority apparently concluded that slavery by its very nature was less efficient and thereby more costly. Some commentators did not speak from firsthand knowledge, never having witnessed the operation of a Southern plantation. Much of their opinion was undoubtedly conditioned more by moral and ethical considerations than by economic analysis. They contended that slave labor was inherently less efficient and more costly because it was given reluctantly and lacked the stimulus of self-interest. Critics like John E. Cairnes, a British economist, tended to attribute the inefficiency to the workers' status as slaves, largely ignoring the more important fact that most slaves had been but recently primitive savages in western Africa. Any discussion of relative efficiency should have included an examination of the cultural traits of the Negro. He was primitive, ignorant, unskillful, and lacking in versatility because of his background rather than because he was a slave. In fact, the progress made by many slaves, when given proper guidance and training, deserved far more notice than it ever received.

Negro slaves were quite capable of acquiring special skills for field work and handicrafts. This was amply demonstrated on the plantation of David Dickson in central Georgia. Dickson, a highly efficient manager, insisted that all his hands be efficient, capable operatives; he developed a relationship between himself and his slaves which resulted in much personal pride on the part of the workers. Dickson's slaves were better fed, clothed, and sheltered than most. They responded to his treatment in such a manner as to allow him to build a $500,000 fortune from a $25,000 investment between 1845 and 1860. While most of the credit for his success must go to Dickson's managerial talent, still he proved conclusively that slave labor could be efficient.

Conditions Favorable to Slavery. David Dickson's experiences, while exceptional, were not unique. Even without expert guidance, slaves were employed profitably wherever favorable economic conditions existed. Generally, the combination of cheap fertile land and a staple crop which admitted to year-round work made slavery economically feasible. An adequate supply of cheap land could be maintained only by a continued expansion of acreage, either at the expense of small, free farmers from whom planters purchased land or by opening new lands farther to the west.

Slavery lost its profitability in the older parts of the South whenever the soil wore out or conditions became crowded. The farm depression and poverty along the Eastern seaboard after the War of 1812 testified to this. Four staple crops, cotton, sugar cane, rice, and tobacco, lent themselves to profitable production under the slavery system. Cotton, by far the most important of the four, was exceedingly adaptable to the use of slave labor, since seedbed preparation, planting, cultivating, and harvesting occupied most of the months of the year. Furthermore, the work could be "routinized" and geared to the tempo best suited to Negro needs. Tobacco production also permitted the employment of slaves, requiring attention for "thirteen months out of the year." Such staples as corn and wheat, important in the Southern economy for food, were primarily outputs of general farming. Sometimes slaves were used successfully for such work, especially since corn growing dovetailed with cotton production. Slavery was most profitably utilized, however, in the production of cotton and other cash crops. The need for more supervision, the lack of home markets, and the higher profits in cotton, sugar, rice, and tobacco were the main hindrances to the use of slaves in general farming.

5

Management of Slaves. Whatever the type of crops produced, slaves worked under one of two commonly practiced systems of management. Most of the farming was done under the gang system, although in the rice fields, and to a lesser degree in tobacco production, the task system was employed. In the gang system, crews of slaves, varying from a few to more than a hundred, worked under the direction of a driver or leader. The driver of large gangs was sometimes a white man hired for the purpose, although often a Negro "drove" the other slaves in the fields. For the most part, the hands worked from sunup to sundown, or until dark if circumstances required longer hours. They took time out for meals, served in the fields, and for rest at midday. Sundays belonged to the slaves for their own domestic work and leisure, and some plantation owners granted free time from noon Saturday to Monday morning.

The tasks system, when used, was more popular with the Negroes. The overseer assigned each hand a particular job, such as cultivating one acre of ground in a day; when the slave finished his work, he was through for the day. The system was flexible in that allowances were made for the difficulty of the job assigned and for the varying skills and capacities of the slave in question. Critics claimed that the method was wasteful since it encouraged slaves to do shoddy work in order to gain more leisure time. Under unskillful management, this was undoubtedly true; but apt supervision assured the success of the task system on many plantations.

In addition to the gang and task organization of slave labor, there was some hiring of Negro hands for both farm and factory work. This was especially prevalent in the older regions where owners did not have enough work to keep their slaves busy. Negroes liked the practice of "hiring out," since they received more freedom and were sometimes able to earn personal "spending" money. Virginia and North Carolina tobacco factories successfully employed as many as 13,000 slaves under such an arrangement in 1860.

The Business Aspects of Slavery. How profitable was slavery? Opponents of slavery argued that it was more expensive than free labor because it

FIG. 14-1. Negro slaves picking cotton. (*Courtesy of the Library of Congress.*)

was generally wasteful and inefficient. Further, they felt that most planters did not use proper methods in figuring costs and profits. Most slaveowners were guilty in this last respect. Still, evidence shows conclusively that slavery *was* profitable, else plantation operators would hardly have continued the business right up to the Civil War in the face of rising slave prices and falling cotton prices.

Enough plantation accounts and general operating information were recorded to permit a realistic estimate of costs and profits. A major item of expense, and one which more often than not was ignored by the planter, was interest on money invested in slaves.[1] Assuming the average

[1] It is necessary to charge this interest, even if money has not been *borrowed* for the purpose, because the funds could have been loaned out for some other use at the going rate of interest. In economics this is called the opportunity cost.

price of a field hand to be $500, interest at 8 per cent per annum was therefore about $40 per slave. In addition, there were the costs of maintaining slave children in their early years, caring for Negroes rendered unable to work through old age, sickness, or accident, and replacing the labor of slaves who died or ran away. Where slave families existed, these costs were amply offset by the natural increase in slave population, from which the owner reaped the entire benefit. Maintenance costs included food, clothing, shelter, and medical care. Most of these items were supplied

Fig. 14-2. Slave cabins on a Southern plantation. (*Courtesy of the Library of Congress.*)

as cheaply as possible by the use of simple, easily provided commodities. The diet of slaves consisted primarily of coarse, wholesome foods such as cornmeal, molasses, and salt pork, often supplemented by fresh produce from the Negroes' own gardens. Most planters provided only the barest essentials in clothing and erected crude shacks to house the slaves. An Alabama operator reported that total cost of food, clothing, medical care, and taxation amounted to $34.70 annually per hand.[2] A further expense was wages paid to overseers. An overseer received a salary of about $500 per year to manage twenty-five to fifty hands—an average of $10 to $20 per slave. The total of interest, maintenance, and super-

[2] R. W. Smith, "Was Slavery Unprofitable in the Ante-bellum South?" *Agricultural History*, vol. 20 (January, 1946), p. 63.

visory expense was somewhere between $80 and $95. Some miscellaneous expenses such as insurance (not widely utilized) and taxes added a little more.

The income from a slave's labor, when compared to these costs, indicates that slavery was undoubtedly profitable. According to contemporary sources, cotton selling at 8 cents per pound in the 1840s yielded a profit of about $60 for each hand on South Carolina plantations and $110 to $140 in the Southwest.[3] Best estimates showed that the South as a whole averaged around 500 pounds of cotton per acre; each field hand tended from 3 to 10 acres. On the poorest lands, a slave did not as a rule produce in excess of 1,000 pounds of ginned cotton; on fertile lands in Alabama, Mississippi, and Texas, 1,000 pounds per field hand *per acre* were not unusual. There one slave was capable of tending several acres. The owner of a 120-slave cotton plantation in Alabama, which produced most of the food consumed by the slaves, estimated his annual monetary outlay at $900; interest on capital investment amounted to $5,800.[4] Considering that a goodly number of the slave force was unproductive, probably no more than sixty hands figured in the actual production of cotton. Assuming a yield of 4,000 pounds per hand (4 acres at 1,000 pounds each), such a plantation would bring a gross revenue of $24,000 with cotton at 10 cents. Hence, profits of more than $17,000 would accrue; when divided by the labor force of 120, they would amount to just under $142 per slave. This figure was undoubtedly above average for the entire South, but it was by no means exceptional, as some planters realized far greater profits. For example, David Dickson "netted an income of $59,000 in 1859 from the labor of 59 'hands' who 'made and gathered' 657 bales of cotton and produced $100 each of corn, meat, and wheat. In 1860, he produced 810 bales . . . with 60 'hands.' "[5]

Many plantations did not have skilled managers, however. Waste and inefficiency inevitably occurred in the absence of careful supervision. On such plantations, owners failed to profit from the use of slaves.

Even though slavery was apparently profitable to the Southern planter, much historical literature, especially in the pre-Civil War era, contended that free labor would have been *less* costly. Such spokesmen often ignored a basic fact: free labor simply was not available. Even had a planter believed that free white labor was preferable (and some undoubtedly did), he could not have found enough workers to fill his

[3] Gray, *History of Agriculture in the Southern United States to 1860* (New York: Peter Smith, 1941), vol. II, p. 709.

[4] *Ibid.*, vol. I, p. 543.

[5] Chester McArthur Destler, "David Dickson's 'System of Farming' and the Agricultural Revolution in the Deep South, 1850–1885," *Agricultural History*, vol. 31 (July, 1957), p. 33.

needs. Thus his choice was not between free *white* and slave labor but rather between free *Negro* and slave labor. And since the relative inefficiency of slave labor rested on the fact that the worker was a Negro as well as a slave, planters would have gained nothing of substance by freeing the Negroes and hiring them as freemen. The decades following the Civil War showed clearly that freedom did not mean greater efficiency and productivity for the Negro field worker. In fact, he was noticeably less productive for some time.

9

Economic Effects of Slavery on the South. Whatever the costs to the individual planter, slavery most certainly represented an economic loss to the South. The foremost drawback was the manner in which slavery retarded the over-all economic development of the region. In the pre-Civil War decades, most Southern capital tended to flow into land and slaves; planters used any increase in wealth "to buy more land to grow more cotton to buy more slaves." The result was that the South failed to establish a diversified economy. A dearth of manufacturing, commerce, and other nonagricultural activity prevailed, as not only capital but labor, natural resources, and managerial ability went to promote and expand the plantation economy. The retarding of general economic growth was not readily apparent in the years up to 1840; after that time, the North outdistanced the South in terms of accumulated wealth. Furthermore, population increase was far greater in the North since immigrants were reluctant to settle in an area where slavery existed. Both the causes and the ultimate outcome of the Civil War are traceable to the failure of the South to develop a more diversified economy.

Summary Critique of Slavery. No criticism of slavery should ignore the basic consideration that the institution developed in response to a specific need for a working force. Despite the obviously distasteful aspects of enslaving human beings and the harmful effects on the Southern economy in general, slavery was not without its advantages. It assured the employer of a readily available supply of workers and eliminated most of the labor disputes common to free societies, such as strikes, bargaining over wages, and the right to form unions. Furthermore, for the slaves themselves, there was no problem of unemployment. There was some merit to the arguments of pro-Southern spokesmen who claimed that most slaves were far better off than many of the exploited free workers in the industrial North. It would be erroneous to conclude, however, that all Southerners defended slavery. Many non-slave owners recognized the harmful effects, both social and economic, and advocated an end to the system. An outspoken advocate of abolition was a North Carolinian, Hinton R. Helper, who blamed slavery for the South's economic subservience to the North. In his book, *The Impending Crisis* (1857), Helper expressed full faith in the South's capacity to foster and maintain a well-rounded economy if it could only free itself from the ignominy of slave labor.

The arguments for and against slavery, however valid, obscured another essential fact. Slavery was not universal in the South in terms of the number of persons who owned Negroes. Even with all the heated defense by Southerners, the truth was that in 1860 only 26 per cent of the 8 million white population lived on farms which used slaves. Furthermore, a small percentage of the slaveowners controlled most of the slaves. Families owning ten or more slaves constituted only 7.4 per cent of the South's free population; ¾ of 1 per cent held fifty or more. Still the large plantation owner stood at the top of the social structure and dominated political and economic thinking in the South. Non-slaveholding small farmers aspired to own slaves, since this was the most direct path to social and political success. At the same time, Southerners feared the consequences of freeing the slaves and allowing them to remain in the United States.[6]

ECONOMIC CAUSES OF THE CIVIL WAR

Northern hostility to slavery was a primary cause of the Civil War. In fact, many historians, writing in the postwar decades, regarded it as the *sole* cause of the conflict. They believed that Northerners, inflamed by fanatical abolitionists, had grimly determined to wipe out slavery because it was incompatible with democracy and Christianity. This drove Southerners to a staunch defense of their labor system, making war inevitable.

Historians in the twentieth century have viewed slavery in a different perspective; they see it as one of several related problems, all of which led to war. Broadly speaking, the war resulted from the fact that the Northern and Southern economies developed along highly divergent paths. Their distinctive systems stood in such sharp contrast to each other that peaceful coexistence under the same political roof became untenable. The Southern states seceded in 1860–1861 in order to preserve their economy; they felt that survival of their cherished institutions depended upon political independence from the North and they were prepared to fight to uphold their right to secede. In order to understand the economic causes of the Civil War, it is necessary to look briefly at the patterns of Northern and Southern growth.

The Northern Economy. The North built a diversified economy almost from the first settlement at Plymouth. The Pilgrims immediately took up farming, but New England's climatic and physical characteristics pre-

[6] Southern hostility toward freeing the slaves solidified after the Nat Turner insurrection in 1831. Turner, a trusted Negro preacher, led a Virginia slave revolt in which fifty-seven whites died. This intensified Southern fear of abolition.

cluded the development of an extensive commercial agriculture. New Englanders turned to the sea and the forests for their riches; colonial shipbuilders, sea captains, men of commerce, and fishermen rolled back the economic frontiers of the north Atlantic coast. In New York, Pennsylvania, and New Jersey, a thriving grain trade kept farming in the forefront; but these Middle Colonies also supported much commerce and were leaders in colonial glass and iron manufacturing. After 1800, the industrial revolution invaded the Northern states and manufacturing increased in importance. Manufacturing growth at no time threatened to smother other economic activities, however. On the contrary, the industrial revolution accompanied revolutions in transportation and agriculture. Under the stimulus of expanding markets, Northern seaboard merchants invested heavily in much-needed transportation projects. This in turn fostered a commercialization of agriculture and pushed the farming frontier westward across the Appalachian Mountains.

The Southern Economy. Meanwhile, south of Pennsylvania, Americans lavished much attention on staple-crop farming. The first Virginians had found the natural environment conducive to raising tobacco, and within a few years they devoted a major portion of their energies to producing it for export. Settlers in Maryland and the Carolinas imitated their Virginia neighbors and earned the bulk of their cash incomes from tobacco farming throughout the seventeenth and eighteenth centuries. After about 1740, rice and indigo were major staples in South Carolina and Georgia, although indigo faded into insignificance before 1790.

After 1793, Eli Whitney's cotton gin made possible commercial production of short-staple cotton in the lower South. And almost simultaneously, commercial sugar cane production in Louisiana added another item to the short list of major Southern staples. Each of these crops—tobacco, rice, cotton, and sugar cane—necessitated much detailed hand labor; in the absence of enough free workers, planters bought Negro slaves to perform the work. Southern agriculture developed around the plantation system, with slave labor an integral part of the economy. This absorbing attention to agriculture relegated commerce and industry to insignificant places in the economy. Furthermore, blessed with many navigable streams, the South tended to lag behind the North in internal improvements, building fewer improved roads and canals from 1790 to 1830 and far less railroad mileage from 1830 to 1860. For example, the South had 9,000 miles of railroads in 1860 compared to 22,000 for the Northern states. Thus, excessive emphasis on plantation farming retarded general economic growth and prevented diversification.

The Politics of Sectionalism. Such divergent patterns of growth caused political views to contrast sharply in the two sections. The North wanted protective tariffs except for the merchants and shipping interests engaged in foreign trade. Northern congressmen, especially after 1840, supported liberal land legislation. And Northerners favored Federal aid for internal improvements and subsidies to shipping. The South, on the other hand, tended to oppose each of these policies. Southerners endorsed the Jeffersonian doctrine of states' rights as the best defense against Northern domination of Federal politics and blocked the passage of laws favorable to the North whenever they could.

Any discussion of sectionalism must include a reference to the West as a separate entity. Especially before 1840, the area west of the Appalachians and north of the Ohio River maintained a degree of political independence. Its representatives in Congress frequently appeared as "fence sitters" on important questions like the tariff and were ready to lend their support to whichever section offered the West the best bargain. Westerners always wanted liberal land laws and Federal aid to internal improvements; their lack of basic concern over tariffs and shipping subsidies placed them in a strategic position to trade votes. After the opening of the Erie Canal in 1825, the West increasingly supported the North; by 1840, the economic bonds between the two sections tended to bring them together politically. This isolated the South and left that section politically vulnerable. Politicians realized that they could protect the South's economic interests only by maintaining numerical equality between Northern and Southern states. This explains why states entered the Union in pairs between 1816 and 1848.

Southern Economic Subservience. The South became economically subservient to the North because of its lesser degree of diversification and development. This was painfully apparent to Southerners in three basic respects. First, Southern planters marketed most of their crops through the factor system (see "Marketing Cotton," Chap. 13). The factors often loaned money to the planters and were in a position to require the production of certain amounts of cotton or tobacco annually. This made plantation operations inflexible. Although the factors generally lived in the South, they sold the staples through commission men in New York or England and depended upon Northern banks and Northern merchants to supply their credit needs. Accordingly, middlemen's commissions and interest payments flowed northward, drawing off Southern funds. Second, the South produced practically no manufactured goods, buying needed merchandise either from the Northeast or from England. But even imports from England passed first through the hands of Northern merchants, whose profits added to the prices paid by Southerners. Thus, indirect buying as well as indirect selling hurt the South financially. Third, tariffs, levied to protect Northern manufacturers, also added to the South's financial troubles and increased the outflow of money. On a number of occasions before 1860, the Southern states considered secession as a means of throwing off their economic bonds. But before secession became a reality, Southern politicians ably defended the South's economic interests in Washington.

Among the several controversial issues leading up to the Civil War, four merit special consideration. These are (1) the tariff, (2) Federal land legislation, (3) Federal aid for internal improvements, and (4) the extension of slavery into newly acquired Western territories.

The Tariff Controversy. Southern opposition to tariffs rested on solid economic ground. The South sold its cotton and other staples largely abroad; Southerners either bought European goods, on which they paid import duties, or they bought Northern goods which cost more partly because of tariff protection. Whichever choice the South made, it bought less goods than if no tariff had existed. Southerners accordingly wanted tariffs reduced to a very low level—in their eyes, a tariff's only justification was to produce income for the government. On the other hand, Northern manufacturers who wrested political control from the Northeastern merchants after 1824 favored tariffs to protect their young industries from foreign competition.

Both the North and the South sought the support of the West, whose people were generally open to persuasion on the tariff issue. In this connection, Henry Clay of Kentucky proposed in 1824 his "American System" which he hoped would unite the Northeastern manufacturing region with the West and make him President. He suggested that the Northeast vote for internal improvements which would give the West better access to Eastern markets; he urged the West to support high tariffs. He favored distributing tariff revenues to the states to build the internal improvements.[7] All this would free the country from dependence on foreign markets and provide an insulated home market for both Western farmers and Northern manufacturers. Admittedly, this offered nothing to the South and intensified Southern hostility toward tariffs.

The high tariff of 1828 annoyed Southerners intensely, and the slightly lower tariff of 1832 failed to appease them. South Carolina, through her leading spokesman, John C. Calhoun, declared the two bills null and void and forbade Federal officials to collect customs at Charleston. Congress responded, at President Jackson's urging, by authorizing him to call out the Army to enforce Federal laws, if need be. Henry Clay then proposed a compromise tariff in 1833 to lower rates gradually until they reached a general level of 20 per cent in 1842. This staved off an outbreak of hostilities between North and South and momentarily quieted

[7] Actually, if Clay's tariff were completely protective, it would keep competing foreign goods out and thus yield no revenue. Contrariwise, a purely revenue tariff provides no protection, for goods must enter in order to tax them. Most tariffs were partially protective and so produced some revenue.

secession talk in South Carolina. But the tariff continued to be a major political issue in the years before 1860 and the hard feelings which it generated were a major cause of the Civil War.

Federal Land Policy. Sectional attitudes toward Federal land legislation depended on certain other considerations. The Northeastern politicians tended to oppose liberal policies like preemption and free homesteads down to about 1840, because industrialists feared that easily obtained land would drain off their labor force and push wages higher. Two developments caused a change in this Northeastern view: (1) the transportation revolution opened up the West as a potential market for manufactured goods; and (2) a heavy influx of immigrants in the 1840s reduced the fear of a labor shortage. Thereafter, the Northeast supported Western demands for cheap and easily accessible lands.

The South at first wooed Western support on tariffs by favoring liberal land laws. Also, Southerners were anxious to expand their land holdings in the newly opened Gulf states. But after about 1840, when the movement for free homesteads began making headway, Southerners became resolutely opposed to a homestead law and prevented its passage until after they seceded from the Union. Their opposition was based on both political and economic considerations. First, they knew that the Northern population was larger and more mobile than that of the South; free homesteads would cause Northern small farmers to settle the West. Southern planters with their slaves could not easily move. The second consideration had to do with the tariff question. The South argued that if the government gave away rather than sold its land, this would make the Treasury more dependent upon tariffs for income.

Federal Aid for Internal Improvements. As noted earlier, the West and the Northeast favored the use of tariff receipts for building internal transportation projects. Since the South did not expect to benefit very much from such proposals, it stood firmly against them. Southern spokesmen reasoned that the South had good navigable streams and did not need so many roads and canals as did the North; furthermore, the South paid the largest proportion of the import duties which would be used to build the projects. Why should they vote Southern taxes to improve Northern transportation?

Southerners took much the same position in regard to Federal land grants to finance proposed transcontinental railroads. They refused to allow Congress to provide for a railroad from the Mississippi Valley to the Pacific coast unless the route traversed the Southern states. Since there was no apparent need for more than one railroad to the coast before 1860, Northern politicians would not sanction Federal aid for a Southern railroad. The stalemate lasted until after the start of the Civil War, when the Northern Congress chartered the Union Pacific Railroad in 1862 and provided huge subsidies to the Union Pacific and Central Pacific companies.

Slavery in the Western Territories. Slavery of itself was a highly controversial issue. As a cause of the Civil War, its greatest importance lies in the attempt by Northerners to block the extension of slavery into newly acquired Western territories. The South felt that the containment of slavery east of the Mississippi River meant loss of political equality with the North. Many Southerners argued forcefully that Congress had no right to exclude slaveholders and their property from Federal territories and that under no circumstances could Congress dictate to a state whether or not slavery was legal within its borders. Northern lawyers replied that Congress had every right to legislate on all matters concerning territories of the United States. When Missouri applied for statehood in 1819, with a state constitution permitting slavery, Northern congressmen demanded that Missouri eventually free her slaves. This set off the first of several major disputes over the expansion of slavery. The Missouri Compromise of 1820 settled the immediate question by permitting Missouri to enter the Union as a slave state; at the same time, it forbade slavery north of 36°30′ north latitude (Missouri's southern border) in the remaining portion of the Louisiana Purchase territory. The North agreed to accept Missouri as a slave state because Maine joined the Union as a free state in 1820; the South permitted the ban on slavery north of 36°30′ because its congressmen believed that the lands north of that line were not suited to settlement—slave or free.

The Missouri Compromise tempered the heat of sectional animosity for a time. Hostility over the tariffs of 1828 and 1832, however, plus the feeling of economic subservience to the North, kept the South discontented and wary. The argument over slavery in the West flared again in connection with lands acquired from Mexico in 1848. Northern congressmen wanted to exclude slavery from the Mexican Cession territory and to admit California to the Union as a free state, an action which would upset the balance of political power in the Senate. Henry Clay and Daniel Webster narrowly averted Southern secession by engineering another compromise through Congress. The Compromise of 1850 brought California into the Union as a free state but it did not bar slaveholders from the Southwestern territories; instead, it left the legal status of slavery for later court determination. This agreement calmed both Northerners and Southerners until Congress organized the Kansas and Nebraska Territories in 1854. The Kansas-Nebraska Act allowed the settlers in those territories to decide for themselves whether or not to exclude slavery. It repealed the Missouri Compromise and thoroughly aroused Northern antislavery sentiment. In fact, the law led to open warfare on the plains of Kansas as free soilers and advocates of slavery both tried to win Kansas politically. Repercussions of the Kansas struggle had not died when the Dred Scott decision[8] drove deeper the wedge between North and South. In that case, Chief Justice Roger Taney, a pro-Southerner of long standing, ruled that slaveholders were free to take their slaves into *any* Federal territory; the Missouri Compromise of 1820 had been unconstitutional; and the Fifth Amendment to the Constitution of the United States gave full protection to slaveholders as well as to

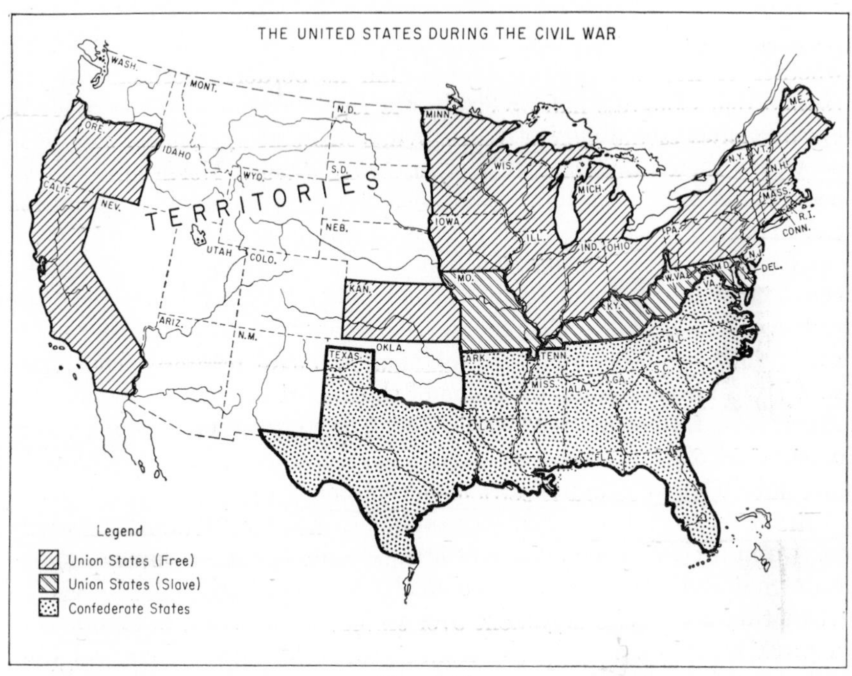

MAP 14-1.

other property holders. The Dred Scott decision eliminated any remaining hope of a peaceful settlement and helped to elect Abraham Lincoln in 1860 as the first Republican President of the United States.

Secession. Lincoln's victory placed the Southern economy in jeopardy; the Republican platform opposed the extension of slavery in the West and advocated higher tariffs and a homestead law. The admission of California (1850), Minnesota (1858), and Oregon (1859) as free states had ended forever the chance of equality in the Senate; the loss of the Presidency to Lincoln was too much to bear. Accordingly, on December 20, 1860, South Carolina broke its bonds with the Union. Before February

[8] *Dred Scott v. Sanford,* 19 Howard 393 (1857).

1, 1861, Mississippi, Florida, Alabama, Georgia, Louisiana, and Texas had withdrawn; on February 8, the seven states formed the Confederate States of America. Fighting between North and South began in April. Immediately, Virginia, North Carolina, Tennessee, and Arkansas joined the Confederacy. The border states of Delaware, Missouri, Maryland, and Kentucky remained with the Union. In Virginia, the northwestern counties refused to secede with the rest of the state and became the Union state of West Virginia in 1863 (see Map 14-1).

ECONOMIC ASPECTS OF THE CIVIL WAR

Comparative Resources of the Rivals. The final outcome of the Civil War depended upon the ability of the Union and the Confederacy to muster and utilize their resources. Of course, the availability of certain critical resources, in a war of four years' duration, was vitally important. In nearly every respect, the North possessed superiority. At the start of the war, the twenty-three states which made up the Union had 22 million people, compared to some 9 million (including nearly 4 million slaves) in the eleven states of the Confederacy. Even more striking was the maldistribution of material wealth. The Union commanded 75 per cent of the nation's wealth (excluding the value of slaves), 81 per cent of the manufacturing establishments (see Map 17-1A), 74 per cent of bank deposits, 70 per cent of the railway mileage, and 67 per cent of the improved farmlands. Thus, the South was in an extremely disadvantageous position from the very beginning. Her problems of raising and provisioning troops appeared insurmountable at first. Yet the feeling of righteousness in defending their economic, political, and social systems, plus the fact that most of the fighting occurred on their own land, gave Southerners great incentive. The excellence in training and performance of the Confederate cavalry also played an important part in prolonging the conflict and giving hope at times of a Southern victory.

The Logistical Problem. Securing and distributing war supplies was quite naturally one of the most critical aspects of the war. It was in this respect that the North's diversified and larger economy held its greatest advantage. The Union at no time had a serious problem of obtaining sufficient supplies; the principal concern was the effective mobilization, coordination, and distribution of materials and men. Blessed with superior capital resources, Northern producers generally met the government's demands after a slow start. A labor shortage naturally followed the call to arms, but a sizable flow of immigrants and the adoption of laborsaving devices (especially in farming) did much to eliminate hardships. The North also reaped the fruits of extensive railway building in the 1850s; her transportation facilities were reasonably efficient in distributing troops and materials.

The Confederate states did not fare so well. The failure to develop manufacturing severely handicapped the region in providing arms, clothing, medical supplies, and other munitions of war. The South was not unaware of this condition when it seceded, but it had erred greatly in evaluating the outcome of its action. Leaders in the South doubted seriously that the North would fight to hold the rebellious states in the Union and were willing to risk being wrong. They based much of their thinking on a strong belief that "Cotton is King." Neither the North nor England, said many Southerners, could withstand an interruption of the cotton trade. The Confederacy was quite certain that England would recognize the independence of the new government rather than lose her supply of cotton. It was true that Northern businessmen greatly disliked the disruptions in trade which war brought with it and that British millowners preferred American cotton. But an oversupply of cotton in British factories in 1861, plus a serious British wheat shortage from 1860 to 1862, lessened the importance of cotton. Middle Western farmers supplied over 40 per cent of England's wheat imports from 1861 to 1863. Soon other nations were supplying British textile factories with raw cotton.

A Union blockade of the seven important Southern ports added to the South's supply problem. The Confederacy managed to get some goods past the Union ships, primarily from West Indies ports. Also, trade went on with Mexico until the fall of Vicksburg in 1863 cut the South in half. Basically, however, the South had to rely upon its own productive capacity for the bulk of its needs. The penalty for overspecializing in staple-crop farming became increasingly apparent as the Confederacy exhausted its meager supply of machinery, skilled labor, and managerial talent. Although the labor source remained largely intact (most slaves remained on the plantations until the end of the war), virtually all adult male whites served at one time or another in the Confederate Army. Equally critical was the poorly developed transportation system of the area, for the South had lagged in railroad building in the 1850s. As a consequence, the Confederacy was frequently unable to mobilize men and materials effectively. Thus it was not merely a shortage of resources but the lack of an adequate distribution network which hampered the military effort.

Effects on Economic Activity. The North experienced the usual reactions attendant upon a major war. There was a brief, sharp business recession which ran its course within a year, followed by a period of sharp inflation. (See Chap. 19 for an account of Union and Confederate financing in the Civil War.) Manufacturing flourished, agriculture expanded, and business in general profited. Workers did not benefit, however, as the cost of living advanced faster than wages. The war left its imprint on the economy as a whole in that postwar readjustment and Southern reconstruction required the major efforts of the next generation. In the South, complete economic disorganization accompanied the war. The loss of markets meant that the chief economic activity—staple-crop agriculture—had to give way to war-sustaining efforts. A runaway inflation, the devastation of farm lands, and the ultimate surrender at Appomattox left the South economically destitute after 1865.

SUMMARY OF PART TWO

Tremendous growth and revolutionary change characterized the period between the American Revolution and the Civil War. The United States increased its land area eightfold and acquired most of its national boundaries within seventy years. Population increased somewhat more and pioneers settled all but the arid Great Plains and Rocky Mountain regions. This was primarily an era of territorial acquisition, and to a lesser degree of settlement. Development of the West would assume greater importance in the post-1860 period. In the East the industrial revolution began, keynoted by the rise of the factory. There were significant changes in the other major areas of the economy: there was an agricultural revolution, a transportation revolution, a financial revolution, a labor-management revolution, and a commercial revolution. Finally, there was a major political revolution, the Civil War, which shifted control of the government from the hands of slaveholding planters (whose peculiar institution was a holdover from the past) to the hands of the tycoon of industry (whose methods were the basis of America's future growth). It is difficult to say which of the economic revolutions came first. All progressed more or less simultaneously, for advances in one area could not proceed very far without parallel ones in other areas. A summary of the main developments may make this more apparent.

During the last quarter of the eighteenth century pioneers settled in the region just west of the Appalachian Mountains. In the next quarter century they moved into the region east of the Mississippi River, opening up the Northwest Territory and the Southwest Territory. In the succeeding twenty-five years they settled the first tier of states west of the Mississippi River, and meanwhile most of the long migrations to the Pacific coast occurred during the 1840s and 1850s. In general, the people who settled the West did not travel long distances to found their new homes. It took a young people to do all this moving, clearing, and building: the average age in the United States about 1840 was eighteen. Likewise, class distinctions broke down on the frontier, where all lived in log cabins and feared the dangers of Indian attack. Property qualifications for voting were swept aside, and the trend to greater democracy spread eastward to the older states. People were also too busy clearing the forest, improving farms, and building a new nation to have much time for formal education; accordingly, pioneers relied heavily upon ingenuity to solve their problems. The frontier environment helped to develop a new civilization that differed in many ways from that of the Old World.

Improved transportation made this an era of growing specialization. As Adam Smith said, "Specialization is limited by the extent of the market," and transportation widened the market. Most of the early advances took the form of better uses of waterways, which nature had already provided. The transportation revolution began with turnpikes, the Lancaster Turnpike (1794) and the National Road (1818) achieving the greatest prominence. Canals, most of them state-constructed, appeared next and dominated the period 1817 to 1842. The first important one and the best known one was the Erie Canal (1825) whose success no other project was able to duplicate. Steamboats able to navigate upstream on western rivers appeared about 1816 and did much to speed up the development of the Middle West, whose people could at last import from the outside world. Likewise about 1818 regular ocean service to Europe began. The year 1817 was a key one in transportation developments. In the 1840s and 1850s ocean steam vessels appeared, although the United States, relying on clipper ships, resisted this innovation for a while. Last and most important came the railroads. At first they were links in existing systems of transportation, but by about 1850 they were becoming the major highways of transportation. Their rise altered some of the old avenues of commerce. There was progress in communication too: it became easier to produce newspapers in the 1830s, and the telegraph and low-cost government postal service appeared in the 1840s.

An evolution from subsistence to commercial farming took place in the northern half of the nation, brought about by the development of better transportation and urban markets. Under the stimulus of greater demand, improved implements helped to overcome the traditional labor shortage. Agricultural societies and publications assisted in the spread of better methods of farming and in the adoption of improved breeds of livestock. In the Southern states, the invention of the cotton gin caused the rapid expansion of cotton cultivation across the lower South, although the use of slave labor and the emphasis on row crops hampered progress in Southern farming. Accordingly, patterns of economic growth tended to vary somewhat between North and South. In the North, the small holding of farm land predominated in the absence of a slave labor system, and in comparison with the South, there appeared to be more diversification in commercial agriculture and in the economy as a whole. The South, on the other hand, was characterized by the large plantation and the slave labor system, although the small farmers greatly outnumbered the owners of large plantations. The tendency of the lower South to depend so heavily upon "King Cotton" retarded economic growth.

The industrial revolution began in cotton textiles in the United States just as it had done in England almost a century before. An Englishman, Samuel Slater, introduced English techniques at the outset, but soon Francis Lowell and Patrick Tracy Jackson devised methods that would henceforth characterize American manufacturing, namely, integration and large-scale production. Other important American innovators were Eli Whitney, who developed the principle of interchangeable parts, and Oliver Evans, whose high-compression engines and other inventions made him the American counterpart of the Englishman James Watt. In the realm of iron and steel, progress was slow until the 1850s when William Kelly's method of producing cheap steel paralleled, if it did not antedate, the more famous bessemer process. The power to run the new mills and factories came at first from water mills, but after the 1840s Colonel James popularized the steam engine, which gave factories a wider choice of location. From about 1830 on anthracite coal from eastern Pennsylvania began to replace charcoal as fuel, especially in the manufacture of iron. Americans also made progress in the manufacture of fairly intricate machinery such as railroad locomotives. The government interfered very little with the progress of industry: this was an era of *laissez faire.*

So many innovations required large amounts of capital, not only to construct factories and railroads but also to carry on day-to-day operations. Those who provided capital in large amounts were either governments or private corporations. Investors increasingly demanded the protection of limited liability, which the corporation could provide but which the partnership and joint stock company could not. Investment dealers and a few investment bankers found buyers for corporation stocks and bonds. Stock exchanges in New York and Philadelphia were the markets where investors could subsequently trade these securities on short notice. Most businesses got their additional capital from plowing back a part of their profits. Various new financial institutions began to supply some as well, for example, commercial banks, trust companies, savings banks, and insurance companies. The commercial banks provided much of the working capital. Had these banks restricted their financial operations to meeting that need, the nation might have been better off. Instead, many invested heavily in real estate loans as well and thus helped to produce several severe panics. Thus the business cycle came into prominence along with the new financial institutions mentioned above. The commercial banks also provided most of the nation's money supply in the form of bank notes; however, the standard moneys were gold and silver coins. Although the price level was remarkably stable, in certain regions and at certain times the bank currency was very unreliable and caused severe losses.

Now that mills and factories were turning out more goods, the owners separated the functions of producing and selling, and selling in turn became increasingly specialized. Peddling gave way to general stores and these to specialty stores. Wholesaling became separated from retailing. Factors, auctions, produce exchanges, commission merchants, and mercantile credit agencies were among the mercantile specialties that came into prominence. The northeastern part of the nation was the first to industrialize and was also the most advanced commercially. The East sent its own and imported goods in quantity to the Middle West and took some raw materials in return; the Middle West sent large amounts of foodstuffs down the Ohio and Mississippi Rivers and received some imports in return; and the South sent its cotton, tobacco, sugar, and other staples to the East and to Europe and took lesser amounts of manufactured goods in return. This internal triangular trade became more and more a two-way trade between East and West in the 1850s because of better railroad connections between those two regions. Domestic trade was three times as important as foreign trade in 1799 and seven times as important in 1850. Cotton was the nation's chief export and Europe the chief market place. Europe was also the main source of imports, most of which were manufactures. Tariffs had little effect on foreign trade until the 1820s; they reached their peak in 1828 and then drifted downward until the Civil War. Southerners deeply resented tariffs, and the tariff became a sectional issue of importance between the North and South.

Labor was relatively scarce during the larger part of the pre-Civil War period, and so manufacturers in the North used children and farm girls in their mills and Southerners revived the dying institution of slavery. After the 1840s, improved mechanical techniques and a rising tide of immigration made labor more plentiful in the North, at least. Unions appeared in the domestic stage of manufacture, with the appearance of the merchant employer and the merchant capitalist. Skilled workers formed unions to preserve their status as independent craftsmen. Conservative courts interfered with the early unions, which were generally short-lived and only local in character. Indeed, in the late 1820s and early 1830s local workingmen's political parties probably made more progress toward achieving labor's goals than unions did. These included such reforms as free public schools, mechanic's lien laws, and abolition of imprisonment for debt. A Massachusetts Supreme Court decision in 1842 recognized the legality of unions, and their heretofore fitful growth became more regular. This was also a period of humanitarian reforms, some of which were quite unrealistic. Unfriendly critics called it a "hot air" period but friendly ones designated it a time when the public conscience awoke and protested against man's inhumanity to man.

The most violent protest was against the archaic institution of slavery in the South. There one family in four owned at least one slave, and the successful cultivation of the chief crop, cotton, was thought to depend squarely on slavery. Northerners saw chiefly the evils of slavery, Southerners thought chiefly of its necessity. The South feared that the North would limit the further expansion of slavery and succeeded, until 1850, in preventing this. When the North won the political victory essential to end further expansion of slavery, the South tried to withdraw from the Union. But since that agricultural region was only a quarter to a third as strong as the industrialized North, the South lost its war for independence. Perhaps had the South husbanded its military power and sought merely to stand off the Union armies until the stronger North wearied of the fight, it might have gained its freedom. That was essentially how the weaker colonies had won their independence from stronger England in the previous century. After the Civil War, the tycoons of Northern industry displaced the Southern planters in political power.

PART THREE

Problems of Plenty—Private Solutions

INTRODUCTION

The period before the Civil War was an era of growth and change, characterized by several economic revolutions. Following the Civil War, an expanding population settled and developed the West and began to reap the fruits of industrial progress. It was a rich harvest, so much so that in one industry after another the major problem was how to dispose profitably of all the goods that the factories were turning out. Similarly, railroads and shipping lines had their problems of overcapacity, and farmers theirs of overproduction.

There were four chief ways of solving these new problems of plenty. One was to find new markets; a second was to keep foreign competitors out of American markets; a third was to cut costs of production as much as possible; and the last was to form a monopoly and limit output to keep prices up. In short, if none of the first three worked, if a businessman could not beat his competitors, then perforce he must join them. Pursuit of all four of these policies characterizes the period leading up to 1914. Cheaper transportation widened markets, making them nationwide for many products. Merchants and manufacturers invented new retail institutions such as department stores, chain stores, variety stores, and mail-order houses. They also devised new ways of garnering the consumers' dollars through installment selling and more imaginative advertising. This was likewise an era of high tariffs to exclude foreign competition. To cut costs, manufacturers pursued the economies of large-scale production: they subdivided operations so as to substitute unskilled for skilled labor and then found ways of substituting machines for certain tasks performed by the unskilled. But if capacity was still too great, if they still could not dispose of all the output at a profit, they formed monopolies, generally called trusts, which restricted output and held prices at a profitable level.

In time, the trusts antagonized the public. Workers formed national labor unions and farmers combined to combat the national monopolies. In response to public protests, the Federal government took action to restore competition. *Laissez faire*, by not automatically correcting the  situation, had shown that it was less practical than many had supposed. The government again assumed a more significant role in economic affairs.

CHAPTER 15

Population Growth and Westward Expansion

The period between the Civil War and World War I saw the United States further settle and develop the area that it had acquired in the first half of the nineteenth century. By the end of the century there was no longer a clearly discernible frontier. Except for Alaska, new permanent additions were meager. Population growth also slackened, despite a large flow of immigration; even so, by 1914 the total population was 100 million and the United States was reckoned among the major powers of the world.

POPULATION AND IMMIGRATION

Population Growth. The rule of thumb that the population doubled every twenty-five years is reasonably applicable up to 1900, although the rate of growth began to decline in the decade of the 1860s. Up to that time it had been close to 35 per cent per decade, in the 1860s it dropped to 27 per cent, and by the 1890s to 21 per cent. Thus in the fifty years between 1860 and 1910 the population tripled from 31 million to 92 million, instead of quadrupling as it did in the previous half century. Several facts explain the slower growth: As the country filled up, more people lived in cities where large families are less useful than on a farm and harder to raise. The standard of living was rising: people who have a high standard of living, or who seek to raise their standard of living, generally have small families. As improvements took place in medical science and infant mortality declined, it required fewer births to produce the desired family size. The birth rate fell from an annual average of 41 per 1,000 in 1860 to 26 in 1912. The average size of the American family was just over five in 1860, it was just under five in 1890, and it was four and a half in 1910. The rate of population growth might have decreased even more had it not been for the arrival of some 27 million immigrants between 1860 and 1914. Most of them remained. These immigrants were largely young and middle-aged and their birth rate was extraordinarily high for the first generation. Great strides in medicine and sanitation also cut the death rate from 21 per 1,000 in 1865 to 13 in 1914, and kept the rate of population growth fairly high. There were other population trends of significance besides the simple fact of continued growth.

The Westward Movement continued although it was no longer as obvious as when the West was still unsettled. The Superintendent of the Census pointed out that by 1890 there was no longer a clearly defined frontier, that is, he could no longer draw a north-south line, on one side of which the population was less than two persons per square mile and on the other side of which it was two to six persons per square mile. The "frontier" was an arbitrarily chosen population per square mile. Had that figure been, say, ten per square mile, the so-called end of the frontier would have come at a later time. The basic fact is that population growth continued to be faster in the West than in the East or South. The population of the Rocky Mountain and Pacific coast states combined was eleven times as great in 1910 as it had been in 1860, whereas for the nation as a whole it was three times as great and little better than twice as great for New England or the South Atlantic states.

The most striking shift in population was the growth of large cities. Between 1860 and 1900 "twenty farmers moved to town for each industrial laborer who moved to the land."[1] It was the cities which absorbed the major portion of the immigrants and in some states the growth of cities even occasioned an absolute decrease in the rural population. The number of towns and cities over 2,500 increased from about 400 to 3,500 between 1860 and 1910; three cities passed the million mark, with New York City boasting nearly 5 million. The movement toward towns and cities occurred in all parts of the nation, but it was most pronounced in the industrial regions of the East and the Middle West. Living conditions in the slums of many of these cities were appallingly bad and gave rise to all kinds of social problems.

A change of a different sort was the aging of the population. The United States was still a nation of young people, but this situation was drawing to an end. The median age rose from nineteen in 1860 to twenty-four in 1910. One reason for the aging was the declining birth rate. If it had not been for the sharp increase in immigration—most immigrants were between the ages of fourteen and forty-five—this aging would have been more marked. In 1860 about half the population was under twenty years of age, only about 14 per cent were over forty-five, and 2 per cent were over sixty-five. By 1910 half the population was under twenty-five, about one-fifth were over forty-five, and the percentage over sixty-five

[1] Fred A. Shannon, "A Post-mortem on the Labor-safety-valve Theory" in *Agricultural History,* vol. 19 (January, 1945), p. 34.

had doubled. While this age shift did not have significant economic effects at the time, it was destined to produce some in the next generation.

The nonwhite population decreased from about 13 per cent in 1860 to 11 per cent in 1910: the great majority of these were Negroes. The Negro population little more than doubled in the half-century period compared to a tripling on the part of the whites. About 90 per cent of the Negroes were still in the South in 1910 just as they had been in 1860, but they were free men now. As for other nonwhite races, the Indians had been "tamed" to the point that they could now be counted: some 200,000 were living on reservations in the far West. There were also about 150,000 Orientals, chiefly in California, about half of them Chinese and half Japanese. The economic status of the nonwhite races had probably improved more than that of the general average of the nation, but there remained many problems to be solved in dealing with these groups.

Immigration. Absorbing the new arrivals from Europe constituted a more immediate problem. Just before 1914 they were pouring in in especially large numbers. Immigration fell off early in the Civil War, but it picked up sharply before the war ended. The need was great for labor to build railroads and to work in factories. Congress passed a contract labor law in 1864 which remained in effect until 1868 to encourage immigration; several Western states set up immigration bureaus, and a number of Western railroads offered inducements to European farmers to buy farms and settle near their rail lines. The long depression of 1873–1878 checked the flow of immigration temporarily, but in 1882 it reached a peak of nearly 800,000. The tide slackened again during the depression years of the 1890s but then attained an all-time record of nearly 1,300,000 in 1907. In six out of ten years before World War I immigration exceeded the million mark. In general, its tide flowed and ebbed with periods of prosperity and depression much as the Westward Movement had done earlier in the nineteenth century.

In general, it was higher wages and the hope of raising their standard of living that attracted the immigrants. Up to about 1880 nine-tenths of the immigrants were from Germany, Ireland, Great Britain, Canada, and the Scandinavian countries. They are frequently described as the "old immigration." During the next generation the character of immigration changed, large numbers coming from Austria-Hungary, Russia, Poland, Italy, and the Balkans. These are often referred to as the "new immigration."

There were several reasons for this change. As long as transportation costs were high, most of the immigrants came from the near side or west coast of Europe. However, as transportation cheapened and as steamship companies undertook extensive advertising campaigns, more people came from eastern and southern Europe. Once started, the flow grew in intensity, for the first comers wrote home and encouraged others to follow. The higher American wage scales were even more attractive to the peoples of eastern and southern Europe than to those of northern and western Europe, whose living standards had improved and were more comparable to those of America. Furthermore, the Anglo-Saxon and Teutonic peoples felt superior to the Slavic and Latin peoples and disliked having to compete with them. Their higher living standards, moreover, made it hard for them to do so successfully. Hence the "old immigration" declined and the "new" supplanted it.

Just as the "old immigration" had comprised, in part at least, the unskilled laborers and had taken the lower places in the industrial system while the native workers moved up into higher ones, so now the "new immigration" took the heavy and unskilled jobs and the children of the "old immigration" moved up to better-paid jobs.

Between 1881 and 1914 about 16 million immigrants entered this country and stayed. Nearly 75 per cent of them were males, and over 80 per cent were between the ages of fourteen and forty-five. Most of the cost of raising them had been paid for and they were arriving in the most productive years of their lives. They came to a country that was making rapid progress industrially and that needed ever larger supplies of reasonably priced unskilled labor to man its expanding mines and factories. It is obviously difficult to measure with any accuracy how important this immigration was to the nation's economic development. Dr. Farr, an English government statistician writing in 1877, calculated that every emigrant leaving England represented a loss of $875, and Thorold Rogers, an English economist, writing in 1888 valued European immigration to America at the somewhat higher rate of $500 million a year, or $1,000 a head. If these admittedly rough estimates are accepted, then the immigrants who came between 1881 and 1914 were worth between $14 and $16 billion to this country. That is six to seven times the value of the slaves freed as a result of the Civil War.

However, this enormous immigration had its disadvantages as well as its advantages. While the new immigrants were probably just as hardworking, thrifty, and intelligent as the old immigrants had been, one-third of them were illiterate and they were unfamiliar with democratic government. Their racial and social background was different and their standard of living decidedly lower. Many of them were mere sojourners, especially the Italians, and expected to return to the land of their birth with their savings after a brief stay in this country. These differences led to a social stratification which, for one thing, complicated the trade union movement by making common action more difficult. On various counts, the new immigrants were more difficult to amalgamate with the native population.

There was little legislation limiting immigration in this period. Early state laws regulating immigration were declared unconstitutional. The first significant Federal law limited Chinese immigration. When Congress passed it in 1882, it was for ten years; in 1884 it became permanent. Another law enacted in 1882 forbade entry of undesirable persons such as convicts, idiots, lunatics, and others likely to become public charges. The ship company that brought them over had to take them back at its own expense. Subsequent laws in 1891, 1893, and 1907 strengthened the provisions of the 1882 law and added a few more categories of undesirables. Meanwhile, organized labor increasingly disliked the competition of immigrants willing to work for wages below those considered acceptable in America. They especially resented individuals who, before leaving Europe, had made contracts to work for a certain time at a low fixed rate and got their passage to America paid as part of the bargain. There were marked similarities between this system, called "contract labor," and the colonial system of indentured servitude. The crowded condition of the labor market in the 1880s, the vigorous voice of organized labor, and the higher regard for human liberty now altered the public's outlook. In 1885, the Knights of Labor persuaded Congress to forbid the importation of contract laborers. Organized labor felt that it was merely demanding for itself a protection against foreign competition that was analogous to what industry asked when it sought protective tariffs against cheaply made foreign goods.

GROWTH OF THE UNION—RENEWED STATES, NEW STATES, AND TERRITORIES

Just before the Civil War began, the Union consisted of thirty-four states; eleven seceded to form the Confederate States of America. After the war each of the seceding states had to undergo a political trial period before regaining equality with other states, and economically they required extensive rebuilding. Political reconstruction lasted until 1877; economic reconstruction went on longer. Meanwhile, between 1863 and 1912 Congress admitted fourteen new states to the Union, all but one of them west of the Mississippi River. The country also made three territorial acquisitions which were likely some day to achieve statehood, namely, Alaska, Hawaii, and Puerto Rico.

Reconstruction in the South. There were several theories about the secession of the Southern states. One was that they were part of an indissoluble union; they could not secede and therefore had not. A second was that they had in fact committed suicide as states and had then been conquered by the North. It was up to Congress to determine the conditions under which they might achieve statehood again. A third was a compromise view, denying the right to secede but nevertheless withholding full equality during a trial period. This third and least logical view was the one actually followed. Lincoln had wanted to readmit the Southern states with a minimum of penalties. President Andrew Johnson, who was a less persuasive person, tried essentially to carry out such a program. Several leading Northern senators, however, had come to hate the South. They suspected that the recent enemy would send its leaders to Congress, try to regain the political power it had enjoyed before the war, and then deny the newly freed slaves the freedom which the North had won for them. Two events seemed to justify this fear, namely, the enactment of the so-called "black codes" to penalize the newly freed Negroes for becoming tramps and vagrants, and the appearance at an early date in Congress of some recent Confederate generals. President Johnson antagonized his Congress, and they passed a Reconstruction Act over his veto in 1867 which divided the Southern states into five military districts. It stipulated further that each state might be restored to its place in the Union, with military government withdrawn, only after it had ratified the Fourteenth Amendment. The Thirteenth Amendment, adopted in 1865, freed the slaves; the Fourteenth Amendment, adopted in 1868, assured them the rights of citizenship except to vote in Federal elections. Excesses of Negroes elected to Southern state legislatures and the arrogance of some Negroes led the Southern whites in some areas to retaliate. They organized what they called the Ku Klux Klan and disguised themselves in white sheets and bore burning crosses. Thus outfitted, the whites easily terrified the ignorant and superstitious Negroes into submission. This in turn aroused the friends of the Negro in the North and resulted in reestablishment of military rule in some sections. The Fifteenth Amendment, adopted in 1870, gave the Negroes voting rights. Military government finally ended in the South in 1877. By this time the whites had largely regained control and the activities of the Klan had subsided. However, the Southern whites were numb with hate for the North and united in their determination to keep the Negroes forever under control.

Economically, the war left the South in a shambles. The military plan of the North had seemed to be to cut the South in half, down the Mississippi, and then carve the eastern half into smaller pieces, first by Sherman's march across Georgia to the sea, and then by his next march north to Columbia, South Carolina, which he burned. Northern armies, especially Sherman's, left a trail of pillage and devastation behind them. Since General Lee drew his supplies and provisions largely from Georgia, General Sherman applied a "scorched earth" policy wherever he went. His men gave particular attention to railroads. "The bridges and trestles were burned, the masonry of the culverts was blown up. . . . The chief engineer designed a machine for twisting the rails after heating them in the fires made by burning the ties. . . . About 265 miles of railroad were thus destroyed in Georgia." In his report to General Halleck, Sherman boasted, "We have consumed the corn and fodder in the region of country thirty miles on either side of a line from Atlanta to Savannah as also the sweet potatoes, cattle, hogs, sheep and poultry, and have carried away more than 10,000 horses and mules as well as a countless number of their slaves. I estimate the damage done to the State of Georgia and its military resources at $100,000,000; at least $20,000,000 of which has

FIG. 15-1. The Civil War left much of the South in ruins. Note the large number of railroad cars destroyed. (*Courtesy of the Library of Congress.*)

inured to our advantage and the remainder is simple waste and destruction."[2] (See Fig. 15-1.)

Laying waste the country and turning the political and social structure upside down was not exactly the equivalent of "giving the country back to the Indians" and going back to the seventeenth century and starting over. Yet the war undoubtedly set back the progress of the South several decades. The South had to do a vast amount of rebuilding. Gradually the more enterprising elements found ways of earning much-needed dollars by trading their crops and products to the North and to the outside world. By 1877 cotton output was permanently back to the 1859 level.

[2] James F. Rhodes, *History of the United States* (New York: The Macmillan Company, 1928), vol. 5, pp. 20–22.

The cattlemen of southern Texas drove numerous herds of $4-a-head cattle north to railheads at Abilene, Ellsworth, and Ellis, Kansas, to sell them in the Chicago market, where they commanded as much as $40 a head. After about 1881 the eastern South turned its attention increasingly to cotton textile production—the industrial revolution now began in the South. Yet rebuilding this part of the nation and trying to catch up with the rest of the United States was slow and painful.

New States. Between 1863 and 1912 the United States acquired fourteen new states. The last two territories within the continental boundaries became states in 1912. The average size of each of these states was greater than that of Great Britain. Yet up to 1910 only four of them—Oklahoma, West Virginia, Nebraska, and Washington—had as many as one million inhabitants and none had two million. From the viewpoint of settlement vast sections in most of these states were unattractive, although each boasted some very attractive regions too. Most of the fourteen states entered the union in one of three periods. West Virginia, Nevada, and Nebraska were products of the Civil War era. When Virginia seceded from the union, the mountainous western section of Virginia seceded from Virginia and became a separate state in 1863. West Virginia had been settled from the North, it had few slaves, and the people's mode of life and outlook were more northern. Nevada, the nation's outstanding example of a "rotten borough" state, was admitted with the motive of getting the vote of one more state so as to ratify the Thirteenth Amendment freeing the slaves. In 1910 Nevada still had less than 100,000 inhabitants. Nebraska, destined to be a free state at the time of the Kansas-Nebraska controversy, was large enough to become a state in 1867. No more states came in until 1876 when Colorado entered; in that era it was her mines more than her colorful scenery that attracted inhabitants.

The years 1889–1890 witnessed the greatest influx of states that the United States had experienced in exactly a century. During the 1870s there were rushes of gold seekers and homesteaders into the Dakota Territory and other territories of the Northwest. The application by these territories for statehood was repeatedly laid aside during the 1880s because the would-be states were Republican in complexion. The Democrats, always controlling at least one house of Congress, blocked their admission. Then in 1888 the Republicans won the Presidency and both houses. They promptly admitted Washington and Montana and split the Dakota Territory into two states, thus gaining four states in one year. Idaho and Wyoming came in the following year. These half dozen states occupied over a million square miles but mustered only about a million inhabitants. Utah, which for a generation had merited statehood, remained a territory because of the Mormon practice of polygamy. When the Mormons outlawed it, Congress admitted Utah in 1896 (see map, p. 100).

The next three states were Oklahoma (1907), New Mexico (1912), and Arizona (1912). Since the 1820s the Federal government had been moving such relatively civilized Indian tribes as the Cherokees, Creeks, Choctaws, and Chickasaws into the Oklahoma region. Five of them had little republics; the four tribes mentioned above even had written constitutions and laws. After the Civil War they had to share their lands with other tribes which the government moved in with them. And from the 1880s onward, bands of white settlers known as "Boomers" sought to locate on Indian lands or at least on a few enclaves of unclaimed lands. Although soldiers repeatedly threw them out, they kept returning; the clamor for Oklahoma lands mounted, both in the region and in Washington, D.C. Congress finally gave in and on April 22, 1889, the government staged the first of several famous "runs." On the stroke of noon some 100,000 persons in wagons, trains, and even on bicycles and on foot rushed into a 2-million-acre tract and in a few hours had staked out claims to all of it. A few "Sooners" who had sneaked in earlier and concealed themselves got the choicest tracts. In the next few years there were other "runs" as many of the Indians were bought out or otherwise shoved aside. Oklahoma became a territory in 1890 and a state in 1907. Oklahoma has always had a large Indian population. Meanwhile, Congress offered New Mexico, with strong cultural ties to Mexico, and Arizona, with strong Anglo-Saxon leanings, joint statehood in 1905, but they turned it down. In 1912 they came in as separate states.

EXPANSION OVERSEAS

Neither the Gadsden Purchase of 1853 nor the "closing of the frontier" in 1890 ended American expansion. Since mountain ranges, hostile Indians, and vast semiarid plains had not done so, it was hardly to be expected that an expanse of salt water on the west and south would either, especially with transportation methods continually improving. By 1914 the United States had acquired seven new territories and possessions covering 710,700 square miles, an area roughly equal to all the states east of the Mississippi River.

Alaska. Alaska with 586,400 square miles, or over twice the size of Texas, was the first and largest overseas possession. Russia offered to sell it in 1867 and Secretary of State William H. Seward, who envisioned his country eventually occupying the entire continent, gladly agreed. For a generation Alaska was derisively known as "Seward's Ice Box" and many considered the $7,200,000 paid for it a waste. After the discovery of gold there in 1896, the attitude changed. The fisheries early proved to be of great value, too, and rich coal and oil reserves were discovered as well. Although Alaska lies largely south of the Arctic Circle, most of it is useless: the best regions are the coastal plains and the lower reaches of the valleys along the southern coast and on the west below Nome. These have plenty of rain and a relatively moderate climate because of the warm Japan Current. In that area near the Arctic Circle, the winter nights and summer days are long, and so crops grow rapidly and luxuriously in June and July when the sun shines most of the time. Up to 1910, however, only 55,000 persons had settled there, chiefly during the gold rush at the end of the century. Catching seal and salmon were the principal industries other than mining.

Failure to Annex the Dominican Republic. In 1868 the dictator of Santo Domingo, Buenaventura Baez, fearing revolution, offered to sell his country to the United States. Apparently he expected to keep most of the proceeds. Santo Domingo, the western portion of the island of Haiti, is 19,325 square miles, or about twice the size of Massachusetts. President Ulysses S. Grant became very interested in the project and on two occasions sent his personal secretary to visit the Negro republic: the second time the envoy returned with a treaty of annexation. Despite Grant's repeated attempts, the Senate would not approve the deal, and the matter was dropped in 1871.

Hawaii. The Sandwich Islands, or Hawaii as it is called today, were the next American acquisition, being formally annexed August 12, 1898. About this time the world's major powers were busily engaged in hoisting flags, provoking incidents, or marking out "spheres of influence," all with the intention of taking possession of whatever remnants of the world were not yet under the white man's domination. The United States was not immune to this imperialistic fever. During the nineteenth century Hawaii had succumbed successively to the influence of American traders, whalemen, missionaries, sugar planters, and finally naval strategists. A crisis arose in 1893 when Queen Liliuokalani ("Queen Lil" to the public) tried to eliminate American influence and rule the islands herself. Planter interests engineered a revolution and set up a republic. The demonstrated value of Hawaiian harbors during the 1898 war with Spain and fear of Japanese designs led the United States to annex the islands. The twenty Hawaiian islands occupy 6,419 square miles and are about the size of Connecticut and Rhode Island combined. They lie 2,400 miles southwest of San Francisco, in the same latitude as Cuba. In 1910 they had a mixed population of 256,000, largely Orientals.

Cuba, Puerto Rico, and Guam. The war against Spain further enlarged American overseas holdings. The war had a number of causes. These were American sympathy with Cuban revolutionists fighting since 1895 for independence, and anger at the brutal Spanish methods in dealing with the rebels, no doubt exaggerated by a sensational press. (The Hearst and Pulitzer newspapers were engaged in a circulation race.) The "last straw" was the mysterious destruction of the battleship *Maine* in Havana harbor on February 15, 1898. The United States virtually ordered Spain to grant Cuba her independence; Spain refused, and Congress declared war on April 25. Within a week Commodore George Dewey, halfway across the world, had won the battle of Manila Bay in the Philippines, and within eight weeks Commodore Winfield Schley destroyed the Spanish fleet off Cuba. That virtually ended the war, although peace was not signed until December 10, 1898. The United States momentarily acquired Cuba (the size of Indiana) but gave it independence with several strings attached. One was that Cuba should not grant any territory to a foreign power and would permit the United States to intervene to maintain order if necessary. This was the Platt amendment, always unpopular in Cuba: it was used three times before being repealed. The United States also gained outright possession of Puerto Rico (3,435 square miles), half the size of the Hawaiian group and the fourth largest island in the Caribbean, and secured Guam (206 square miles) in the Pacific, as a coaling station and steppingstone between Hawaii and the Philippines.

The Philippine Islands. The most important fruit of victory was the Philippine Islands, for which America paid Spain $20 million. It required three years of fighting the Filipinos, however, before they abandoned their own immediate hopes of independence. There are over 7,000 Philippine islands covering 114,000 square miles, an area equal to that of Arizona or Italy. The population in 1910 was 7,600,000, largely native, and the leading export was sugar.

Samoa. The United States took a growing interest in the Samoan Islands from 1872 on. These fourteen islands, 1,200 square miles, or the size of Rhode Island, represented a valuable naval and coaling station in the southwest Pacific. Germany and Great Britain also coveted them, and from 1889 to 1899 the three nations exercised virtually a tri-nation protectorate over them. By a treaty of December 2, 1899, the United States and Germany divided them: Great Britain withdrew, accepting concessions elsewhere. American Samoa is 75 square miles.

The Panama Canal Zone. Probably the most reprehensible piece of imperialism in modern American history was the seizure of the Panama Canal Zone. The idea of an interoceanic canal, a break through the American continent, is as old as the centuries-long search for a Northwest Passage around North America. The United States first began to take a real interest in an isthmian canal after the California gold rush. A railroad was completed across the Isthmus in 1855. The French engineer, Ferdinand de Lesseps, confident from the success of the newly finished

Suez Canal, began work on a sea-level Panama canal in 1881. Yellow fever, engineering difficulties, and financial corruption defeated his project. When the United States took up the idea under Theodore Roosevelt in 1903, the Colombian government wanted $40 million to approve the transfer of the defunct French company's rights to the United States. Panama belonged to Colombia, so Colombia was within her rights, although the price was high. The United States had for some time considered building a canal through Nicaragua. When Panama rebelled and set up its own government to deal with the United States, the United States prevented Colombia from suppressing the revolt and immediately recognized Panama. The new little nation ceded America a zone 10 miles wide along the route of the canal. It was necessary to wipe out yellow fever before the Panama Canal, the greatest engineering feat of its day, could be completed. The United States opened it on August 15, 1914; henceforth a ship going from New York to San Francisco no longer had to round South America and had only 6,000 instead of 16,000 miles to travel, a saving of about 63 per cent.

PUBLIC LAND POLICIES

Between 1785 and the outbreak of the Civil War the United States disposed of 163 million acres of public lands to settlers and speculators. Although this was a veritable empire, the government still had almost a billion acres on its hands, a far vaster empire. There had already been many complaints that the public lands had all too often fallen into the hands of big speculators. The Homestead Act of 1862 is sometimes cited as evidence that the government had turned over a new leaf in its public land policies and was henceforth favoring the small settler. He, after all, was the man who really opened the West; he was the backbone of the nation. Any such hope was largely mistaken. The big landowner, even more than before, got possession of lands before the small man did despite the Homestead Act.

The Homestead Act of 1862. One of the planks in the Republican platform of 1860 had been a homestead law. The secession of the South, which had always opposed such an act because it was not compatible with slavery, now made it possible to pass the law. The Homestead Act provided that any person twenty-one years of age or head of a family, who was a citizen or had declared his intention of becoming a citizen, might file claim for any 160 acres of land that were open to purchase under the Preemption Act. After he had paid a registration fee and had lived on the land for five years, he might receive full title to it. A soldier in the Union army might count his period of army service as part of the five years. A soldier in the Confederate army, since he had borne arms against his country, was until 1866 denied the right of acquiring land under the act. The gist of the act lay in one man's statement that "The government bets you you can't live on the land for five years and if you can, you win the land." If a settler decided after six months that he preferred to buy the land at $1.25 an acre under the Preemption Act and gain title immediately, the law permitted him to do so. This was called "commutation"; the settler generally employed this right when he had found a buyer. Nearly every landowner in the West was a speculator to some degree. Up to 1900 settlers took up some 80 million acres of land under the Homestead Act but the government disposed of 500 million acres in other ways.

Railway Land Grants. Between 1850 and 1871 the Federal government gave 174 million acres to railroads in the form of land grants to encourage them to build across the Western Plains.[3] Where railroads had to precede settlement, west of the Mississippi, their promoters needed some special encouragement. The Illinois Central Railroad, back in 1850, had been the first to receive such an imperial grant. Others so favored included the Union Pacific–Central Pacific lines, the Northern Pacific, the Southern Pacific, the Atcheson, Topeka and Santa Fe, and the Burlington. Altogether, about 8 per cent of all railroads, in terms of mileage, received land grants. The practice was for the Federal government to grant the railroad alternate sections, say, 6, 10, 20, or even 40 miles each side of the track. With the passage of time, the grants became more generous. Buyers under the Preemption Act had to pay a minimum of $2.50 per acre and received only 80 instead of 160 acres of such choice lands. Homesteading was not permitted in railroad land grant areas. When a considerable portion of the lands had been taken up along a proposed railroad right of way before the grant was made, the government made up for the shortage by offering the railroads substitute or "lieu" lands farther out. The government expected the railroads to use the lands in two ways, as collateral for mortgages against which they could borrow to finance construction, and to sell to settlers who would become customers of the railroad by virtue of living near it. When some of the early land-grant railroads began to charge seemingly high and sometimes discriminatory rates, the public and Congress turned against them and made no more land grants. Of course some railroads still had several years within which to complete their trackage across the continent before their land grant offers would expire. Some barely completed their track laying in time to keep their lands. Railroads generally sold their lands at several

[3] Eventually the railroads returned about 43 million acres and kept 131.4 million acres. But this much land, 174 million acres, was withheld from circulation for many years so far as settlers were concerned. "Notes and Documents," *Mississippi Valley Historical Review*, vol. 32 (March, 1946), p. 559.

times the preemption price. Altogether there was far more justification for the railroad land grants than there was for some other land grants.

Other Opportunities for Speculators. There were several ways in which speculators might buy large blocks of land directly from the government or at least very cheaply. The small settler rarely had an opportunity to acquire these lands. In the years after 1862 the various states disposed of 140 million acres; the Federal government offered 100 million at auction, mostly in large blocks for cash. It also put up for sale lands wrested from the Indians by treaty to the extent of another 100 million. With Federal and state railroad land grants of 181 million, this adds up to 521 million acres.[4] For example, under the Morrill Act of 1862, enacted to encourage the founding of state colleges and universities, every state was offered 30,000 acres per senator or congressman it had. The lands were to be sold on the most advantageous possible terms; this excluded homesteaders. Subsequent amendments to the Morrill Act increased the supply of lands sold under these conditions. The states, anxious to turn this asset into cash with the least inconvenience, preferred to sell to large buyers. "Probably no other scrip or warrant act was used so extensively by speculators to build up large holdings as was this Agricultural College Act."[5] Speculators moreover bought shrewdly, buying up fine agricultural and timber lands. One such buyer, William S. Chapman, acquired 650,000 acres (equal to the state of Rhode Island) with cash, scrip, and warrant in the five years between 1868 and 1871. As a result of such activities tenancy appeared in the United States at a surprisingly early date. As early as 1880, 16 per cent of the farmers in Kansas and 18 per cent in Nebraska, were tenants, compared to 25.5 per cent in the nation as a whole.

Still another hunting ground for the speculator was a series of acts passed in the 1870s, which paid lip service to the principle of conservation. In 1873 Congress passed the Timber Culture Act. Any person who would plant a certain number of trees on 40 acres of land, tend them for ten years, and save a quarter of them would receive 160 acres of land free. The Desert Land Act in 1877 offered 640 acres at $1.25 per acre to anyone who would undertake a certain amount of irrigation within three years in stipulated arid regions. There were also the Timber Cutting Act (1878) and the Timber and Stone Act (1878) which mining and lumber companies sometimes used cleverly to acquire large blocks of fine timberland at bargain prices. It was possible for a shrewd operator to acquire 160 acres under the Homestead Act, 160 under the Preemption Act, 160 under the Timber and Stone Act, and 640 under the Desert

[4] Paul W. Gates, "The Homestead Law in an Incongruous Land System," *American Historical Review*, vol. 41, no. 4 (July, 1936), pp. 657–665.

[5] *Ibid.*, p. 665.

Land Act, show enough effort to satisfy outward appearances, and wind up with 1,120 acres of land for a very modest total payment.[6]

Eventually Congress began to introduce a degree of order into the hodgepodge of land acts. In 1891 it repealed the Preemption Act so that a settler could no longer obtain two 160-acre tracts simultaneously, one under the Preemption Act and one under the Homestead Act. Congress also repealed the Timber Culture Act in 1891 and at the same time improved the Desert Land Act. In 1904 and 1909 the government at last recognized that 160 acres might be a fine homestead east of the Mississippi where farming was moderately intensive, but it would not suffice west of the Mississippi. There farming was either very extensive or consisted of cattle raising. In either case the settler needed a minimum of 320 acres. The Kinkaid Act of 1904 allowed a homestead of 320 acres in Nebraska, and the Enlarged Homestead Act of 1909 allowed the settlers 320 acres in any of nine different western states and territories. Settlers took up twice as much land under the Homestead Act between 1891 and 1914 as they had up to 1891.

Choices of a Settler in Acquiring Land. If most settlers did not acquire their land under the Homestead Act, there must have been reasons. A settler in Nebraska in the 1870s had four basic choices. He could get his land from the government by the Homestead Act or the Preemption Act or both; he could buy it from a foresighted speculator; he could rent his land from a frontier landlord; or he could buy it on an installment plan from a land grant railroad.

If he got his land from the government, it would more than likely be far from any railroad line, perhaps as much as 100 miles, for the big speculators had usually snapped up the best lands. Traveling at a rate of 20 miles a day was good time in horse and wagon days. Thus the settler might get his land cheaply, but he would have to pay for it in other ways. He would have to live an austere and isolated life, very frequently in a sod house. Notice the bleak living conditions shown in Fig. 15-2.

If he bought his land from a speculator, he probably got it in a choicer location, say, nearer a railroad line. But he had to pay a price of several dollars an acre and probably he had to pay it in cash or else mortgage his land at a high rate of interest. Frontier mortgages usually carried rates of at least 12 per cent.

Another way of obtaining land was to rent it from a frontier landlord like William Scully. Some renters optimistically hoped to use tenancy as a steppingstone, in time, to ownership; others simply had never been able to save enough to buy their own land. Whichever it was, they could expect little assistance in getting started. Also, the settler would have to pay all the taxes on the land—landlords insisted on this to prevent ten-

[6] *Ibid.*, p. 652

ants from foisting the costs of schools, roads, and other public improvements on them. And he might have to pay his rent in cash. Some landlords, but not Scully, accepted a share of the crop, normally a third, in settlement of the rent. In general, the farmers who ended up on lands like Scully's were inclined to butcher the land and to move on to something better as soon as possible. Any that stayed paid a good rent year after year and, even so, ended up not owning the land.

If the settler got his land from a railroad, such as the Burlington, he acquired less land and he paid a higher price—a purchase of 120 acres at

FIG. 15-2. A Western pioneer clearing land in 1880. (*Courtesy of U.S. Department of Agriculture.*)

$8 an acre was representative in Nebraska in the 1870s. But in just about every other respect, he was better off. The lands were reasonably near the railroad, hence he was not far from his market, his supplies, and civilization. The Burlington helped him to get settled by hauling in his household effects at a nominal charge. The railroad gave him advice on cultivating his land and took an enlightened attitude toward his success, for the more he produced, the more freight business the railroad enjoyed. Most important of all, it allowed the settler ten years in which to buy his land. Interest was at 6 per cent, a very reasonable rate on the frontier, and he did not have to start payments until the fourth year, which gave him ample time to become settled. If he were diligent, thrifty, and lucky and wished to pay off his debt sooner, he got a discount for doing that.

Despite the initial high price, buying railroad land was the best deal of the four. Not everyone was in a position to do this, however. The railroad preferred to sell to individuals who had farming experience and who had brought about $1,000 along, to buy supplies and equipment in the early years and to tide them over the hard times which they would face sooner or later.[7]

THE SOD-HOUSE FRONTIER

Just as the log cabin in a forest clearing is associated with the pre-Civil War frontier, so the sod house on a treeless plain most nearly characterized the post-Civil War frontier. The sod house was found in Kansas, Nebraska, and the Dakotas and in eastern Colorado, Wyoming, and Montana during the last half of the nineteenth century and even into the present century. People lived in sod dugouts or sod houses because lumber was scarce. A few boards for a roof, door frame, and window frame were all the wood, other than crude furniture, to be found in a sod house. The walls were built of "bricks" that were 3-foot slices of prairie sod, turned and cut with a spade. The roof was often very crude: a forked post at each end held the ridgepole; rafter poles ribbed in each direction from the ridgepole to the parallel walls. The sheeting was of brush, covered with prairie grass and topped with sod, grass side down. The whole contraption was "made without mortar, square, plumb or greenbacks." When it rained the roof invariably leaked, and sometimes it soaked up so much water that it collapsed on the occupants. On the other hand, crude as the dwelling was, it had the advantage of being cool in summer and warm in winter.

Life on the Plains was often cruel. Driving blizzards in winter would bring temperatures well below zero, and the south winds of the summer carried temperatures to over 100 degrees and parched everything they touched, or occasionally a plague of locusts destroyed the crops. Just as the pioneers solved the shelter problem with sod, so they solved their other living problems in equally crude fashion. To get water they sometimes had to resort to muddy buffalo wallows. At best they had deep wells, which they had to dig themselves, sometimes 200 feet deep. Fuel for heating came from buffalo chips while these lasted; later the settlers used hay twists which they fed into a special type stove. Gathering and twisting the hay to refuel the stove was a full-time job. Corn cobs were another favorite fuel. Many settlers lived far from one another and even farther from town. Frequently it took several days by wagon to reach

[7] Richard C. Overton, *Burlington West* (Cambridge: Harvard University Press, 1941), pp. 340–350.

town to market the corn or wheat or to get supplies. Doctors were rare, and persons who could not do without them were unlikely to survive.

We may well ask why anyone chose this life. One answer is that some perished and others changed their minds and turned back east. Yet many hardy ones remained who gradually made these treeless plains into fields of waving wheat, in good years, and erected handsome towns and cities. Outwardly, this frontier had a different appearance from the one east of the Mississippi of pre-Civil War days. Yet the frontiers were quite similar in terms of their effects on the men who lived on them, and on the nation of which they were a part.

CHAPTER 16

The Age of Railway Transportation

After 1865, rapid expansion of transportation and communications facilities created serious problems. A methodless enthusiasm gripped these industries, threatening them with ruin and affecting the entire economy. Businessmen sought to protect their interests by consolidating their holdings. Such actions brought a degree of order out of the chaos but made government regulation inevitable.

BUILDING THE RAILWAY NETWORK

Railroads were in a youthful stage in 1860. The nation had about 31,000 miles of first track, mostly east of the Mississippi River. By 1914,

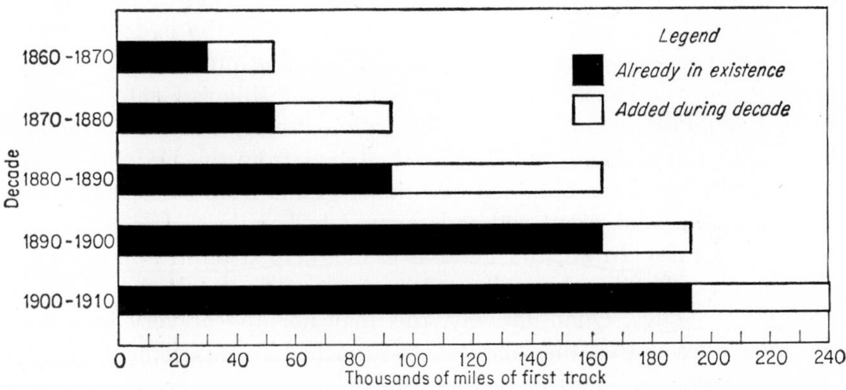

CHART 16-1. Expansion of railway mileage in the United States, 1860–1910. (*Adapted from U.S. Bureau of the Census, Historical Statistics of the United States, 1789–1945, Washington, 1949, pp. 200, 202.*)

total mileage was 252,000 and an integrated railway network was completed. Chart 16-1 shows the growth of mileage by decades, indicating the heavy construction of new roads from 1870 to 1910. A slight increase followed until 1916, after which railroad companies abandoned more track than they built.

Geographically, the greater building occurred in the trans-Mississippi West, where rail mileage increased by 110,000 miles in the fifty-five years before World War I. The regions east of the Mississippi almost matched the accomplishment by building 100,000 miles. By 1914, the West's share of total mileage, which had been 6 per cent in 1860, reached 48 per cent. The West was at last obtaining a transportation system while the East was integrating its own and filling in between the trunk lines.

Railway Financing. The rapid expansion of the railway network required unprecedented capital outlays. The sources of these funds were roughly similar to those of the pre-Civil War era, with private investors in the Eastern cities and in Europe playing prominent roles. The size of the fund-raising operations even exceeded that of Jay Cooke's Civil War government bond sales; new railroad securities appeared at an annual rate of $500 million in the early 1870s and reached $800 million in 1882. The huge issues were major factors in the speculation and the financial instability of the period. The common stock of many companies was "watered," as they carried assets on their books at inflated values. Many firms overburdened themselves with bonded indebtedness. Sharp operators like Jay Gould manipulated railroad securities for quick personal profits; the same practices spread into other industries.

Private capital did not immediately flow into railroad projects in the thinly settled areas. For example, when Congress chartered the first transcontinental line in 1862, it was necessary to offer a generous subsidy to attract sufficient private investment. By that time, the Federal government had committed itself to a policy of granting public lands to assist railway construction. It initiated the plan in the Illinois Central grant of 1850. Eventually, companies like the Union Pacific, Central Pacific, and the Burlington claimed over 131 million acres from the Federal government, and some lines obtained additional grants from states like Texas. In return, the land grant railroads agreed to handle government traffic at reduced rates. In all, the Federal grants helped build approximately 18,700 miles of railroad, or about 8 per cent of the total construction in the United States. Quantitatively, this may not appear very important; the main idea is that the land grants furnished an inducement for individuals to pour millions of dollars into railroad developments, which of necessity preceded settlement in most of the Western states. The grants were particularly vital in building the transcontinentals (see Map 16-1).

The Transcontinentals. The most spectacular phase in the growth of the railroads was the building of the transcontinental lines. The first practical proposal for a railroad to the west coast had come from Asa Whitney, who petitioned Congress in 1845 to sponsor a line from Lake Superior to Puget Sound. Whitney, a New York merchant engaged in the China trade, hoped to funnel much of the world's east-west trade through the heart of North America. His urgings fell on deaf ears until the California gold rush and the organization of the Oregon Territory left thousands of Americans cut off from the East by a 1,500-mile, landlocked, uncivilized expanse. Meanwhile, the Mexican War had demonstrated the strategic importance of adequate transportation.

It was with some urgency that Secretary of War Jefferson Davis of Mississippi directed a survey of five possible routes for a transcontinental railway in 1853. The northernmost one lay south of the 49th parallel; there were four other choices, with the central or Platte River route

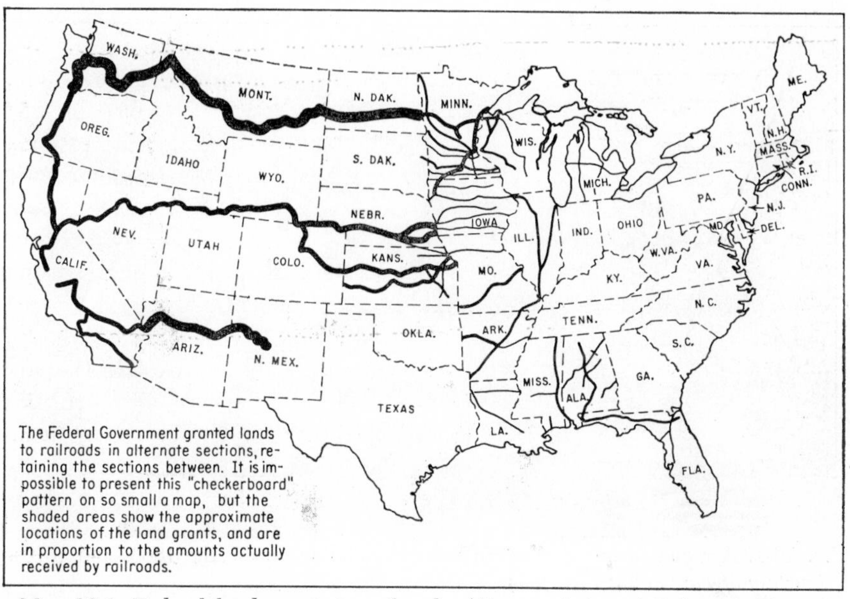

MAP 16-1. Federal land grants to railroads. (*By permission of Robert S. Henry.*)

through the South Pass offering the most advantages. Southerners, for obvious reasons, insisted that the southern route from Vicksburg or New Orleans be given first consideration. To make this possible, they influenced Congress to authorize the Gadsden Purchase, because the best access to southern California was through Mexican territory in the Gila River Valley. For ten years Congress debated the choice of routes, with the South effectively blocking Northern attempts to push through a road from Chicago or St. Louis along the Platte. No one considered seriously building both a Northern *and* a Southern line, because the nation in the 1850s did not anticipate a need for more than one railroad to the west coast. The stalemate ended when the Confederate states seceded and Congress selected the central or Platte route.

In 1862, Congress chartered the Union Pacific Company and authorized it to construct a line from Fort Kearney, Nebraska, to the Great Salt Lake, Utah. A previously incorporated California company, the Central Pacific, built eastward from Sacramento, California. On May 10, 1869, the Central Pacific's Leland Stanford drove a golden spike into a silver-bound laurel tie to join the rails of the two companies at Promontory Point, Utah, just northwest of Ogden. The harmonious incident, marred slightly by Stanford's poor aim on the first swing of the sledge hammer, concluded the feverish competition which had prevailed between the Union Pacific and Central Pacific.

FIG. 16-1. A reenactment of Western railroad building during the 1860s and 1870s. (*Courtesy of Paramount Pictures.*)

The competition resulted from the terms of the 1862 congressional action. To attract private capital, Congress had granted a 400-foot right-of-way plus 10 square miles of land for each mile of road plus a first mortgage loan of $16,000 to $48,000 per mile, the amount varying with the harshness of the terrain. Such generosity failed to attract investors, however, and Congress doubled the land grant in 1864 and altered its claim on railway property to that of a second mortgage. With 12,800 acres of land per mile,[1] plus bountiful loans, the companies had less diffi-

[1] One should not suppose that the railroad simply sold the land and used the proceeds to build the line. Virtually all Federal land grants to railroads provided that actual construction had to precede title to the land; however, after construction of a segment of 40 miles, the acreage adjacent to the completed line passed to the company. Most companies sold mortgage bonds, with the land as collateral, and used these funds for construction. They retired the bonds with proceeds from the later sale of the land or from company profits.

culty raising money. Unfortunately, the government had not specified where the tracks would meet. Consequently, each company hurried its building, with much shoddiness and waste, in order to pluck the rich plums of land and loans from the plains of Utah. Congress had classified that level terrain as "mountainous" and allowed a loan subsidy of $48,000 per mile. When the rival crews met, they graded parallel roadbeds. Only an order from Congress stopped the race and forced the junction at Promontory Point.

The joy with which the nation greeted this achievement temporarily obscured the attendant waste and corruption. Then during the presidential campaign of 1872, the *New York Sun* rocked the country with its exposé of the Union Pacific fraud. The newspaper charged that prominent public officials, including Vice-President Schuyler Colfax and Congressman James A. Garfield (later President of the United States), had exchanged political influence for shares of stock in the Credit Mobilier Company. This firm, organized in 1864 by the Union Pacific's directors and owners, obtained the contract to build the Union Pacific. It padded construction costs, diverting Union Pacific funds to the Credit Mobilier. The money returned to the Union Pacific directors in the form of dividends on their Credit Mobilier stock. A congressional investigation revealed that corruption had invaded high places. Railroad officers had distributed free stock in Washington in order to avoid criticism for their conduct. Congress censured two of its members, but a generous coat of whitewash covered up most of the dirt. The Republicans won the election of 1872 in spite of this scandal.

The Credit Mobilier scandal merely foreshadowed further revelations of wasteful and inferior construction on the Union Pacific and other Western roads. Haste and laxity had been responsible for improper grades, poor quality of materials, and washed-out roadbeds; much of the work had to be done over. The Union Pacific floundered haplessly amid recurrent business depressions, its badly watered stock and its bonded indebtedness imposing an intolerable burden. For its customers, this meant poor service and high charges for years to come. These frauds and inept performances were major factors in bringing on government regulation of railroads.

Even before the completion of the Union Pacific–Central Pacific, Congress had authorized a number of other transcontinentals. Three additional lines linked the Mississippi Valley with the Pacific coast by 1883. The Southern Pacific–Texas Pacific belatedly fulfilled the South's wish for a road from New Orleans; Asa Whitney's dream of a northern route came true with the completion of the Northern Pacific from Duluth to Portland; and the Atchison, Topeka & Santa Fe provided a diagonal or southwesterly tie between Kansas City and southern California. In 1893, James J. Hill's Great Northern reached Seattle from St. Paul. Hill proved that Western railroads did not have to be poorly built and operated. He painstakingly eliminated grades and curves, sought cost-cutting routes, built solid roadbeds, laid good rails, and ran his company with wisdom and foresight. Success rewarded his efforts. His company made profits during the depressed 1890s, while companies like the Union Pacific went bankrupt.

Influence of the Transcontinentals. The transcontinentals bridged the gap between the Missouri-Mississippi frontier and the Pacific coast. Even more important, the railroad builders opened a vast landlocked interior to settlement and exploitation. The railroads of the West generally preceded settlers in the Great Plains and Rocky Mountain country; they stimulated the growth of the Cattle Kingdom and the mining industry. Furthermore, the railroads spread the farmer's frontier across the 98th meridian onto the High Plains—not just by their mere presence but as a result of conscious efforts to attract settlers and build a business. They also contributed to an atmosphere of frenzy in railroad extension, which led to excess capacity. This in turn led to ruinous competition, which was resolved first through integration and consolidation and later by government regulation.

Southern Railroads. Southern railroad construction lagged behind the national trends, especially between 1860 and 1884. In 1860, the South's 9,000 miles of road were not proportionately out of line with the North's 22,000 miles. The Southern population bore the same relationship to the national total (9 million to 31 million) as did its rail mileage. Furthermore, the South had excellent natural waterways, which lessened the need for extensive railroad building in the pre-1860 era. Following 1860, however, Southern rail facilities deteriorated rapidly. Northern armies destroyed tracks, bridges, and equipment while the South did not possess adequate rolling mills and machine shops to keep the railroads in repair. After the war, political and economic reconstruction prevented immediate rebuilding of the roads. Between 1860 and 1880, the Southern states managed to build 11,000 miles of new road, most of which was in the border and western parts of the South. Meanwhile, other parts of the country laid nearly 52,000 miles of new main track.

Following the depression of the early 1880s, an influx of Northern capital stimulated much more Southern railroad construction. Southern mileage grew by 57,000 between 1880 and 1910, compared to an increase of 90,000 for the remainder of the United States. Again, in proportion to population, this was an adequate performance. Much of the new construction was in short stretches, many of which were later combined into large operating units. The biggest consolidation movement in Southern railroads followed the Panic of 1893 when J. P. Morgan & Company applied its financial reorganization techniques to several bankrupt lines;

the end product was the Southern Railway system. By 1914, the South had made sufficient progress in railroading to permit a modest industrial revolution to take place.

Consolidation and Control. Meanwhile, railroad companies in the East expanded their systems. The New York Central, the first line to connect Chicago with the east coast, enjoyed its initial advantage only momentarily as the Pennsylvania, the Erie, and the Baltimore & Ohio also built to Chicago. Under the stimulus of thriving trade and rugged competition, the Eastern trunk lines built spurs and branch and main lines wherever necessary to gain a share of freight traffic. Sometimes rival companies constructed parallel lines where only one line was needed.

A dramatic episode in this unbridled competition was the Erie war (1869–1872) between Commodore Cornelius Vanderbilt and the Erie Railroad "crowd"—Jay Gould, Jim Fisk, and Daniel Drew. Gould and his associates sought to prevent Vanderbilt from buying control of the Erie and gaining a monopoly on railroad transportation in upper New York State. They had no noble motive; their sole objective was to bleed Vanderbilt of his millions and operate the Erie for personal profit. Their prime weapon was the printing of an endless stream of stock, which kept Vanderbilt from ever acquiring a controlling interest. When Gould subsequently sold out his Erie stock at a tremendous profit in 1872, it was not to Vanderbilt. He left the Erie with a bonded indebtedness of $64 million, much of it accumulated in the struggle with Vanderbilt. The Erie gave poor service for generations and its common stock did not earn a dividend until World War II. The public and the small investors were the real losers in the Erie fight.

The Inevitability of Monopolies in Railroads. Railroad executives recognized the waste and futility of jungle warfare of the Erie type. They knew that cooperation, not competition, was the normal relationship among rival companies. They generally agreed with J. P. Morgan that cutthroat competition was ruinous and that they should act in harmony with one another. To the onlooking public, such cooperation was monopolistic and therefore evil. People who condemned the elimination of competition in railroading rarely considered that railways are natural monopolies. The basic nature of the industry made railroad monopoly inevitable. A railroad had a large investment in durable capital which produced a relatively high ratio of fixed to variable costs; this caused competing companies to make such strenuous efforts to gain more business.

Railroads had to make exceedingly large initial investments in roadbed, track, freight-handling facilities, terminals, and rolling stock. Since much of this was financed through the sale of bonds, interest payments were regularly recurring expenses which the company had to meet without regard to the amount of business. Other fixed costs (those which do not vary with changes in the level of operation) included depreciation, certain taxes, rents, and some wages and salaries; these remained fairly stable so long as the railroad's plant size did not change. And, as a practical matter, conscientious management also regarded a *normal* return to stockholders as a nonvariable cost of doing business. Variable costs, such as fuel, fluctuated directly with the volume of freight and passenger traffic. The profitable employment of capital depended upon obtaining sufficient income to cover both the fixed and the variable costs. To accomplish this, railroads had to attract enough business to keep the rails, engines, coaches, and freight cars constantly in use. The greater the traffic, the lower the per unit fixed cost.

This is why railroads became so competitive in the early years. They were seeking to spread the fixed costs over a greater volume of traffic. Rate cutting became commonplace. Where two roads vied for the same business, one would frequently reduce its rates to induce customers away from its rival. The other followed suit and a rate war resulted. The outcome of such "wars" was nearly always the same; either one company finally went bankrupt or the warring factions, following J. P. Morgan's prescription, called a truce. In either event, competition between them disappeared. In the first case, the stronger company took over the bankrupted rival, leaving but one firm in an area. In the second circumstance, the competitors combined in some way. In the 1860s and 1870s, the pooling agreement predominated. Later, holding companies and interlocking directorates followed, in that order, each device emerging to fill a void created by the legal demise of its predecessor.

Whatever the technique utilized, the "community of interest" provided stabilized rates at a level considerably above that of the cutthroat struggles. These developments occurred wherever railroads were constructed in excess of need. In Iowa, Kansas, and Nebraska, where Federal land grants encouraged building in advance of population, railroad operators frequently found it necessary to "cooperate" to protect their capital. In so doing, they discovered and used practices which ultimately led to governmental regulation.

Abusive Conduct in the Railway Business. Railroad rates caused the most trouble. Traditionally, a businessman has had the privilege of charging whatever price he pleased for a product or service which he produced. The consumer has been equally free to accept or reject the price. Railroad operators at first enjoyed the freedom of establishing their own rates. Where canals, river steamboats, and rival railroads offered a shipper an alternative method of getting his goods to market, railroad rates were competitively determined. After the Civil War, railroads expanded westward beyond the bounds of canal and river competition. Also, technological advancements gave trains a great advantage over water transportation. Railroads then did not always need to consider rates set by others: they found many occasions on which it was possible "to charge all that the traffic would bear." This was especially true where they had a monopoly and where the company needed to make up losses incurred in rate wars in competitive regions. Rate setting came to be extremely arbitrary; high rates and discriminatory charges became commonplace.

High freight rates were not always without justification. A line which served a purely agricultural area which imported very little freight often had to raise charges on outgoing farm products to levels high enough to cover the costs of operating the trains in both directions. While farmers complained of the high freight charges on wheat and livestock, they rarely realized that it cost the company almost as much to run a train of empty cars in as it did to operate a loaded one out. Still, there is much evidence that railroads often levied unreasonably high charges. The record of the Southern Pacific when it was under the direction of the "Big Four"—Leland Stanford, Collis P. Huntington, Mark Hopkins, and Charles Crocker—is particularly damning. The Southern Pacific held a virtual monopoly on transportation in California and its officials had ways of learning exactly how much the traffic could bear. For example, the company forced a quartz mining firm to make its business accounts available to the railroad so that rates could be fixed as high as possible, without bankrupting the mining concern.

Discrimination took three basic forms: (1) between commodities, (2) between places, and (3) between persons. The first form existed because of differences in classes of freight; bulky, low-value goods cannot support as high a transportation charge as can more valuable products. The other two types of discrimination appeared most often where competition was lacking. Long-short haul discrimination, a special kind of place discrimination, was fairly widespread. This occurred most frequently where there was keen competition for business between two rail terminals. A good example was the Omaha-Chicago traffic. Between those two cities, there were at least three major routes; this caused the various railroads to take their competitors' actions clearly into account before setting exorbitantly high rates. On the other hand, towns between Omaha and Chicago often were served by only one of the three lines. It regularly cost more to ship a ton of freight the shorter distance from Omaha to Des Moines than from Omaha to Chicago. In only isolated cases did conditions justify this type of discriminatory rate setting.

The granting of rebates or refunds to certain shippers was especially prevalent in the East. The practice originated from the fact that there are economies in large-scale freight handling which permit lower charges.

An early example was when John D. Rockefeller guaranteed to ship sixty cars of oil per day in return for rate reductions. Rather than set a lower rate, the railroads preferred to collect on a standard basis from all customers and then give a refund to large shippers. Shippers soon began to apply pressure to obtain rebates. The outstanding episode of this sort involved Rockefeller's Standard Oil Company. Seeking to eliminate rival refineries, Standard chose the rebate system as its most potent weapon. Rockefeller and his lieutenants wrung from three Eastern lines (the South Shore belonging to the New York Central, the Erie, and the Pennsylvania) gigantic concessions in the form of preferential rate treatment. Although this particular scheme operated only a short while, Standard profited enormously from rebates on its oil shipments—a privilege not so fully enjoyed by its rivals. The practice frequently harmed the railroads' earnings as well as those of Standard's competitors.

Railroads also aroused antagonism through questionable financing operations. It has been proved that officials of companies like the Erie and Union Pacific manipulated corporate securities for personal gain; small stockholders and the public suffered. Equally reprehensible was the way railroad promoters sometimes fleeced residents in sparsely settled regions. The "slick" promoter went into rural areas and exchanged stock in his company for farm mortgages, taking advantage of the farmers' urgent need for improved transportation. Farmers, eager to assist the proposed projects, willingly mortgaged their farms to purchase stock, since they had little cash. The promoters then sold the mortgages to Eastern bankers, often pocketing the proceeds. In many cases, the railroad lines were never built, leaving farmers with worthless stock. Antipathy toward railroad promoters became strong in the West; in fact, such sharp practices gave all business a bad reputation. Farmers particularly resented Eastern bankers who tried to foreclose on mortgages so obtained. Other railroad men distributed stock to influence legislators and judges who were in a position to help or hinder the railroads. Few operations achieved the notoriety accorded the Credit Mobilier scheme, but similar bribery and corruption frequently appeared at state and local levels.

Two qualifications to this generally unfavorable view toward railroads are necessary. First, not all railroad companies behaved so abominably; second, the conduct of some of the railway officials, while unethical and illegal by twentieth century standards, was largely a product of the age. In regard to the first point, the antics of a Jay Gould have served to overshadow and obscure the able management of men like Charles E. Perkins of the Burlington Railroad and James J. Hill of the Great Northern. Scandals generally make more headlines than exemplary behavior. Furthermore, the twentieth century historian has often added to the distortion by judging past events in the light of his own environment and by failing to place the railway and business executive of the late nineteenth century in the proper setting. After the Civil War, the nation anxiously resumed the task of developing the vast resources of the interior; the prevailing philosophy of *laissez faire* offered few legal barriers to exploitation and waste. An expanding people, eager to accomplish the task at hand, became overzealous. For the most part, the general public did not disapprove of the conduct of its business leaders until after 1900. By that time, much of the physical plant for industrial supremacy had been established: a railway network, a steel industry, an oil-refining business, and other vital accomplishments provided the United States with the greatest industrial potential on earth. Hence, the people could afford the luxury of reviewing and criticizing the methods their fathers had used in building such a framework.

REGULATION OF RAILROADS

The Granger Laws. Shortly after the Civil War, certain pressures were brought to bear on the railway industry. Farmers, speaking primarily through the Grange (see Chap. 22), became quite vocal in demanding that railroads be publicly controlled. The Grange attacked business in general, singling out railroads in particular because of high transportation charges and abusive practices. By 1870, the Grangers had captured the state legislatures in the Upper Mississippi Valley and passed laws designed to curb the "monsters" which were exploiting the farmer.

Western farmers had welcomed railroads as a blessing. They had believed that better transportation would make accessible Eastern markets where attractive prices prevailed. They overlooked the fact that farmers in other territories would gain the same benefits. Railways enabled producers in distant regions to compete in the same markets. They made the market for products like wheat national. *High* freight charges, however obnoxious, were not the primary problem; *low* rates brought Montana wheat into contention with Wisconsin wheat. This depressed the price in Eastern markets, lessening the expected benefits of low rates. Therefore, the farmer's plea for lower freight rates was not a carefully reasoned one.

Nonetheless, state legislatures responded to the farmers' demands. Illinois adopted one of the first Granger laws in 1869. It required railroads chartered in Illinois to keep rates "just, reasonable, and uniform." A new law in 1873 outlawed *unjust* rate discrimination and provided a commission to determine maximum rates. Meanwhile, Wisconsin, Minnesota, and Iowa passed similar laws. The Granger laws reflected the basic philosophy that railroads were public service companies and should be treated differently from other businesses. Since railroads had received much public aid, they "owed" the public something better than high rates and poor service. Railroad men denied the legitimacy of the Granger laws. Railways were private concerns, built primarily with private capital; the owners were privileged to run the roads as they saw fit. Accordingly, they refused, for the most part, to obey the early laws. Within a decade, repeal or judicial ruling rendered state regulation largely ineffective. The railroads did not hesitate to bribe or intimidate legislators and judges in achieving this victory. In Illinois, however, farmers hung on tenaciously and gained success when the United States Supreme Court upheld the right of the state to regulate railroads in the public interest.

The Supreme Court reached this crucial decision in *Munn v. Illinois* (1877).[2] Although the Munn case concerned grain warehouse charges, the court applied the same doctrine to several Granger railroad cases at the same time. In the Munn case, the court denied the contention that the Illinois law deprived Munn, a warehouse operator, of property in violation of the Fourteenth Amendment. Chief Justice Morrison Waite held that "when private property is devoted to a public use, it is subject to public regulation." Warehouses and railroads clearly affected the public interest and could therefore "be controlled by the public for the common good. . . . " The decision also refuted the plaintiff's claim that his business was interstate in nature and therefore outside the jurisdiction of the state of Illinois. It held that the grain elevators in question were located "exclusively within the limits . . . of Illinois." The business might "become connected with interstate commerce, but not necessarily so. . . . Until Congress acts in reference to . . . interstate relations, the state may exercise all the powers of government over them. . . . " For the next ten years, this was very important.

The Illinois law then ran afoul of the courts again. In 1886 the Supreme Court upheld the Wabash, St. Louis and Pacific Railway Company in its suit against the state. The Illinois courts had found the railroad guilty of rate discrimination, basing the state's right to regulate rates on the *Munn v. Illinois* decision. The Wabash appealed the case to the Supreme Court. The court ruled that a different set of circumstances were involved than in the Munn case. The Wabash operated across state boundaries; if every state regulated rates as Illinois had done, "the embarrassments upon interstate transportation . . . might be too oppressive to be submitted to." The court reiterated the right of a state to regulate a business wholly within state boundaries, but it stated that any regulation concerning the transit of goods across state lines "should be done by . . . Congress . . . under the commerce clause of the Constitution." Only

[2] 94 U.S. 113.

Congress had the "enlarged view of the interests of all the states" and it alone could "establish just and equitable rules."[3] Considering that about four-fifths of all railroad traffic was *interstate*, this ruling had far-reaching implications.

The Interstate Commerce Act of 1887. The failure of state regulation, already evident before the Wabash decision, led to congressional action. As early as 1873, the House of Representatives had studied a bill to regulate commerce. In the Senate, the Windom Committee Report of 1874 exposed many abusive practices among railroads and recommended a Federal law "to enforce fair competition." The report proposed Federal construction and operation of a railroad between the Atlantic Ocean and the Mississippi River to serve as a "yardstick" in measuring the performance of privately operated companies. Senator Windom further recommended greater improvement of waterways to provide competition for railroads; he believed strong competitors would be the "most effective regulators of railway transportation." In 1878, Congressman John H. Reagan of Texas also introduced a bill to outlaw many railway evils; it passed the House but failed in the Senate. Numerous proposals followed in both houses with no decisive action until Senator Shelby Cullom of Illinois headed a Senate committee to investigate transportation regulation. The ensuing Cullom report, in January, 1886, along with the Wabash ruling, prompted the passage of the Interstate Commerce Act in February, 1887.

The Interstate Commerce Act applied solely to railway companies which served as common carriers across state lines. It provided that the rates of such railroads "shall be reasonable and just." It outlawed all discrimination between persons as well as "long-short haul discrimination," although a commission, established under the law, was empowered to allow exceptions. The act made pooling agreements illegal and required railroads to publish and post their rate schedule, from which they might not depart without ten days' advanced public notice. It created a five-man commission with the authority "to inquire into the management of" interstate railroads, including the right to examine accounts and records. Persons with complaints against railways could ask the Commission to investigate. If the complaints appeared reasonably founded, the Commission was to hold hearings and might issue "cease and desist" orders to the offending parties; however, enforcement of the orders rested with the Federal courts. At first, the Interstate Commerce Commission successfully adjusted rates and settled disputes, but within ten years weaknesses in the act and adverse court decisions had made the Commission practically useless.

[3] *Wabash, St. Louis and Pacific Railroad Company v. Illinois*, 118 U.S. 557.

Weaknesses of the Act. The law was vague and indefinite, leaving final interpretation to the courts. This was especially true with regard to the meaning of "reasonable and just" rates. It was in this connection that the Supreme Court delivered the first crippling blow to the Interstate Commerce Commission. In cases involving the Cincinnati, New Orleans and Texas Pacific Railway Company, the ICC found that the railroad's rates were unreasonably high and specified maximum rates for the company. The Supreme Court, in 1896 and 1897, overruled the Commission. It declared that the Commission did not have the power to fix rates and that no fair interpretation of the act of 1887 "would tolerate a grant of such power by mere implication."[4]

Another ruling in 1897 left the Commission even more powerless. The Supreme Court upheld the Alabama Midland Railway Company in a long-short haul ruling by the ICC, contending that long-short haul discrimination was legal where substantially different circumstances and conditions existed between two towns.[5] This nullified the effectiveness of the long-short haul clause, for the railroad could always argue that conditions were "substantially different." It also impaired the Commission's function as a fact-finding body. The Commission expected the courts to accept the commissioners' findings as conclusive evidence, but the Supreme Court refused to do so. It admitted new evidence and reversed the Commission's order. The 1896–1897 decisions stripped the Commission of most of its power. Court delays, refusal of witnesses to testify before the Commission, and evasive tactics by railroads and shippers further weakened the law. The ICC was powerless to stamp out rebate practices and had inadequate machinery for enforcing its powers to inspect accounts and records. The Commission lost sixteen of the seventeen cases heard by the Supreme Court between 1897 and 1906.

Amendments to the Interstate Commerce Act. Around 1900, the climate of public opinion grew more hostile to big business. A wave of reform swept over the country, leaving in its wake a number of amendments to the Interstate Commerce Act. The first was the Elkins Antirebate Act of 1903, sponsored by railroads. It made receiving (as well as granting) rebates a Federal offense. Up to 1903, large shippers, having no fear of the law, had successfully forced carriers to give rebates.

The second major change was the Hepburn Act of 1906. It brought other transport agencies (express companies, sleeping car companies, pipelines) under the control of the Commission; it gave the Commission

[4] *Cincinnati, New Orleans and Texas Pacific Railway Co. v. Interstate Commerce Commission,* 162 U.S. 184 (1896); *Interstate Commerce Commission v. Cincinnati, New Orleans and Texas Pacific Railway Co.,* 167 U.S. 479 (1897).

[5] *Interstate Commerce Commission v. Alabama Midland Railway Co.,* 168 U.S. 144 (1897).

the positive power to set *maximum* freight and passenger rates; it provided the ICC with adequate powers over accounts and records; it placed on the carriers the burden of appeals to the courts; and it increased the number of commissioners to seven. Almost immediately, the Illinois Central Railroad tested the new rate-making powers, but the Supreme Court upheld those powers and laid down the principle of "administrative discretion." It recognized the Commission as a technically expert group of responsible administrators and announced that it would no longer judge the "expediency or wisdom" of ICC findings. The Court would henceforth confine its judgments to matters of legal procedure.[6]

By 1910, Congress and the Supreme Court had largely reconstructed the Interstate Commerce Act. Still lacking, however, was the ability to control *new* rate increases by the carriers. Earlier laws had required carriers to file advance notice of rate increases with the Commission; after thirty days the new rates became effective. The Commission then had to order reductions if the increases were excessive. Another unsolved problem was long-short haul discrimination, which had gone on unabated since the Alabama Midland Case in 1897. The Mann-Elkins Act of 1910 corrected these two deficiencies. It gave the Commission power to suspend new rates for 120 days, or longer if necessary, beyond the usual effective date. Furthermore, the law placed on the carriers the burden of proof that a rate increase was necessary. It reworded the long-short haul clause of the Act of 1887, eliminating the phrase "under substantially similar circumstances and conditions." This closed the loophole which had long permitted place discrimination. Finally, it gave the Commission a more positive power to initiate investigations on its own, without waiting for complaints from shippers.

The Hepburn and Mann-Elkins Acts greatly clarified the rate-making powers of the Interstate Commerce Commission. But Congress still had not defined "reasonable and just" rates. The Supreme Court attacked the problem of definition in *Smyth v. Ames* (1898),[7] ruling that a railroad was entitled to a reasonable return on its investment. This decision led to the Valuation Act of 1913, which directed the ICC to determine the fair value of the property of each railroad in the United States. Unfortunately, the Commission took twenty years to complete the task, by which time a new philosophy of rate making made this herculean task less useful. Still, the principle that "reasonable and just" rates are related to a fair return on investment is highly important to railroads.

16

[6] *Illinois Central Railroad Co. v. Interstate Commerce Commission,* 206 U.S. 441 (1907); *Interstate Commerce Commission v. Illinois Central Railroad Co.,* 215 U.S. 452 (1910); *Interstate Commerce Commission v. Union Pacific Railroad Company.* 222 U.S. 541 (1912).

[7] 169 U.S. 466.

Two other laws imposed additional regulations on the railroads. The Panama Canal Act of 1912 forbade any railroad to own or control a competing water carrier operating through the canal. This was to prevent railroads from stifling competition via the Panama Canal, which was soon to open. The Clayton Antitrust Act of 1914 also included provisions which affected railroads. It set an annual limit of $50,000 on a common carrier's payments (for "securities, supplies, or other articles") to a firm in any way connected with the carrier. This was to prevent any recurrence of frauds like the Credit Mobilier episode. The Clayton Act also outlawed interlocking directorates and purchases by one carrier of the stock of another when the action would lessen competition.

The Supreme Court further strengthened the Interstate Commerce Commission in the *Shreveport Cases* (1914),[8] when it extended the Commission's jurisdiction to include *intrastate* rates. The cases arose when Texas, through a state commission, established intrastate rates below the level of ICC rates. Justice Charles Evans Hughes had ruled the year before[9] that interstate and intrastate commerce are "inextricably blended" and that the Federal government could regulate intrastate traffic under certain conditions. The Interstate Commerce Commission might regulate intrastate commerce whenever it affected interstate commerce directly. This broadened the scope of the Interstate Commerce Commission's jurisdiction and expanded Federal sovereignty to a hitherto unknown degree.

Declining Railroad Rates. Railroad rates declined drastically in this era from 1860 to 1914, without regard to government regulation. After a 25 to 50 per cent increase from 1860 to 1865, freight charges fell off sharply to the middle 1870s and then more slowly to 1900. Rail revenue per ton-mile dropped from an average of about 1.9 gold cents to around 0.7 gold cent, or to about one-third of the 1865 level. Competition and technological progress caused the decline. Railroad rates undoubtedly responded somewhat to the insistent clamoring for public regulation, but effective control was largely lacking before 1900. By then, the decline had stopped and rates remained relatively stable up to 1914.

INNOVATIONS IN RAILROADING

Railroad companies adopted new techniques and equipment to make railroading more efficient and more economical. Railroads made technological progress in rails, rolling stock, automatic car couplers, signaling devices and systems, roadbed maintenance, wooden tie preservation, and

[8] 234 U.S. 342.

[9] *Minnesota Rate Cases*, 230 U.S. 352 (1913).

a host of other respects. Two in particular stand out: the substitution of steel for iron rails and the automatic air brake. Iron rails had serious limitations from the viewpoint of endurance and ability to withstand heavy loads. The bessemer process for making cheaper steel, adopted widely after 1870, solved both problems: bessemer rolled-steel rails were eight to fifteen times longer-lasting than iron rails and could support much heavier weights. This meant great savings in maintenance of tracks. Furthermore, the railroads could economize by operating longer and heavier trains. Freight cars, which had averaged 15,000 pounds capacity at the time of the Civil War, were from two to three times that size by 1914. Locomotives became larger and more powerful; the number of driving wheels increased from four to eight; and various types of engines were developed to handle the different kinds of service (passenger, freight, switching, etc.). Passenger accommodations improved when George M. Pullman put his first sleeping car in use in 1859. Pullman's dining cars and parlor coaches, along with heavier and larger passenger cars, also made rail travel more comfortable and attractive.

19

Another major technological improvement was the automatic air brake, perfected by George Westinghouse in 1907. The first air brake, patented in 1869, did not stop all cars in a train simultaneously. The result was that passengers and freight in the last cars were sometimes thrown forward violently by the delayed action. The improved Westinghouse brake, with air reservoirs in each car operated from a master control on the engine, contributed both safety and comfort to railway operations.

Nontechnological improvements kept pace with rail and brake innovations. A major step toward integrating the rail network occurred in the 1880s when most companies adopted the standard gauge (distance between tracks) of 4 feet 8½ inches. Almost simultaneously the railroads' General Time Convention of Railway Managers (predecessor of the American Railway Association and the Association of American Railroads) established "standard time." On November 18, 1883, the railroads abolished nearly 100 local times and set their clocks and watches on four standards: Eastern, Central, Mountain, and Pacific, each one hour apart. "The advocates of 'God's time' were outraged, but time tables were regularized."[10] Competing lines gradually developed full interchange of business. Freight and passenger terminals for cooperative usage sped through traffic. Companies exchanged freight cars on a per diem basis, whereby one company paid a certain fee per day for the use of another's cars. Car interchange eliminated much extra handling of freight when it passed from one company to another. By 1890, the American railway network, in the true sense of the word, had been established.

[10] Edward C. Kirkland, *A History of American Economic Life*, 3d ed. (New York: Appleton-Century-Crofts, Inc., 1951), p. 358.

THE RAILROADS' COMPETITORS—OLD AND NEW

18 **Decline of River and Canal Traffic.** The ascendancy of railroads caused the decline of transportation by rivers and canals. The speed, directness, and year-round service offered by railroads placed the slower water carriers at a serious disadvantage. Mississippi traffic, which reached a peak about 1880, fell off sharply. In 1879 St. Louis received or shipped

FIG. 16-2. A cargo of cotton aboard a Mississippi steamboat. (*Courtesy of National Cotton Council.*)

over 1 million tons of freight by river; by 1905, the total had fallen to 141,000 tons, which was only one one-hundredth of that city's rail traffic. The lower Mississippi, which had little or no rail competition before 1860, lost most of its cotton trade to railroads after 1880. The Ohio and its source river, the Monongahela, alone remained important. There, coal shipments kept tonnages from declining significantly. Steamboats, pushing flotillas of barges laden with coal, sand, or gravel, continued to ply the Ohio between Pittsburgh and Paducah. Coal could be delivered in New Orleans, 2,000 miles from the mines, for 60 cents a ton. Interest in river traffic revived somewhat after 1900 and an Inland Waterways

Commission studied possible river improvement projects in 1907–1908. Little was done, however, until World War I demonstrated the inadequacy of railroads to cope with the heavy wartime traffic.

Canals experienced a similar fate. By 1880 the states had abandoned nearly 2,000 miles, built at great costs to them. Of the remaining 2,500 miles, another 1,000 had succumbed to competitors by World War I. The Erie Canal was one of the few to survive. Its business increased up to 1880, when it handled over 4 million tons. From that time on, it too lost traffic to the railroads, in spite of the elimination of tolls after 1882. In 1914, the Erie moved less than 1.4 million tons. The Illinois-Michigan Canal, opened in 1848, also competed successfully with the railroads until 1882; by the end of the century, it was no longer important.

Growth of Great Lakes and Coastwise Shipping. Shipping on the Great Lakes and along the coasts offered a marked contrast to the decline of river and canal commerce. The opening of the "Soo Locks," connecting Lakes Superior and Huron in 1855, permitted the low-cost shipment of iron ore to the Pittsburgh and Great Lakes steel centers. After the Federal government took over the canal and rebuilt it, the volume of traffic on the lakes increased rapidly. Lumber, copper, grain, and flour moved eastward, while coal was the chief item of the less important westbound commerce. Great Lakes tonnage amounted to 25 million in 1889, the first year for which statistics are available; by World War I, it had increased fivefold.

Coastwise shipping, protected from foreign competition, also grew, although to a lesser degree. Registered tonnage engaged in this trade rose from 2.4 million in 1860 to 4 million in 1914. Chief commodities were bulky items like coal, cotton, lumber, stone, ice, and grain. After 1865, the coastwise merchant marine became larger than that engaged in foreign trade.

New Agencies of Transportation. Railroads carried nine-tenths of all freight and passengers by 1900. Their monopolistic position encouraged experimentation and progress in new forms of transportation. Consolidation of rail interests and high freight rates led oil companies of Pennsylvania and Ohio to construct the first pipelines. The first long line was opened in 1878 and by 1914 a 10,000-mile system linked the oil-producing regions with Middle Western and Eastern markets. The lines saved transportation costs and facilitated handling. Electric railways, an outgrowth of the street railways introduced just before the Civil War, also gained prominence after the adaptation of the electric dynamo to railway traction in the 1880s. After 1895, the electric railways escaped the confines of the large cities and competed with the steam railroad between cities in Illinois, Indiana, Michigan, Ohio, New York, Pennsylvania, and California. Before the rapid rise of highway travel in the post-World

War I era, the electric railway did much to break the isolation of the rural areas. Two other important twentieth century transportation agencies were born in the pre-World War I period. The first practical automobile in the United States appeared in 1892, and in 1903 the Wright brothers made their flight at Kitty Hawk, North Carolina, to inaugurate the aviation industry. Although the automobile stimulated the "improved roads movement," launched in 1890 by bicycle enthusiasts, neither the automobile nor the airplane played important roles in transportation before World War I.

COMMUNICATIONS

While steel rails bound the nation into a single market area, strands of copper wire formed a communications system. It consisted of two main networks: the telegraph and the telephone. In 1866, there were 75,000 miles of telegraph lines and Western Union became the first nationwide private monopoly. The industry expanded through improved methods and equipment. Thomas A. Edison and others perfected techniques which permitted the simultaneous sending of an ever-increasing number of messages over the same wire. Perforated tape increased the rate of transmission to 400 words per minute, ten times as fast as a manually sent message. The telegraph became important to businessmen as it provided up-to-the-minute information on market conditions, allowed same-day contact with distant places, and after 1870 assisted in the transfer of money through local telegraph offices. Bankers of New York used a telegraphic device known as a "bank printer" to keep in constant touch with the clearing house until the telephone replaced it within a few years' time. The stock ticker, originated in 1867, was first used to indicate the price of gold; more complex tickers replaced the army of messengers which had previously linked the brokerage offices with the stock exchanges.

The telephone, dating from Alexander Graham Bell's first success in 1876, further revolutionized communications. Businessmen adopted it from the start for local convenience; within a decade, trunk lines widened the range of immediate communications. Lines opened between Boston and Providence in 1880, Boston and New York in 1884, and New York and Washington in 1885. The first line from New York to Chicago went into service in 1892 and one between New York and San Francisco in 1915. At first, only the wealthy could afford telephone service, with rates in cities as high as $200 or more per year. Rural service spread slowly at first, but after 1900, the telephone became more commonplace. The telephone industry, because of the high cost of transmitting equipment, quickly became a "big business." Under the direction of Theodore N.

Vail, the American Telephone and Telegraph Company (dating from 1885) had become a $250 million corporation by 1900.

Communications by mail kept pace with progress in transportation and communications. Postal revenues rose from $8.5 million in 1860 to $288 million in 1914; postal service became more extensive and prompt. There were numerous improvements in service: free city delivery (1863), postal money orders (1864), special delivery service (1885), rural free delivery (1896), and motor vehicle service (1914). The railroads were confronted with a strong competitor in 1912 when the government launched its parcel post system.

Newspapers. The growth of newspapers paralleled achievements in transportation and electronic communications. The perfection of power printing presses and the mechanization of cutting, folding, and counting newspapers made possible mass production. In 1884, Ottmar Mergenthaler of Baltimore invented the linotype machine, which permitted the casting of a line of type from molten lead in one operation. Publishers began using it commercially in 1886. Cheaper newsprint resulted from the more widespread use of wood pulp in the manufacture of paper. There was a fivefold growth in the number of newspapers between 1860 and 1893, by which time the total was 20,000. There were some 1,300 foreign language papers by 1914. A major development in newspaper publishing was integration within the industry. Following the trends in manufacturing and transportation, publishers combined for wider news coverage and greater efficiency. News syndicates provided "readyprint" for local papers after 1861. The Associated Press, first formed in 1848, became more effective after its reorganization in 1900. The United Press failed in a brief trial from 1882 to 1893, but the second United Press operated successfully after its founding in 1907. Meanwhile, newspaper chains began to appear. The Scripps-McRae League of Newspapers, started in 1897, had thirteen papers by 1914. In 1913, William Randolph Hearst originated his chain and acquired thirty papers and two wire services within twenty years.

CHAPTER 17

Large-scale Manufacturing

Relatively few industries had left the mill and shop stage before the mid-nineteenth century. From that time on, factories rapidly increased in number, many became quite large, and they made a greater variety of products. Progress in manufacturing was now more marked than in any other segment of the economy. Between 1859 and 1914 the value of manufactured goods increased twelvefold (see Table 17-1), and income

Table 17-1
Growth of Manufacturing

Year	Number of establishments (thousands)	Wage earners (thousands)	Value of products ($ in millions)	Value added ($ in millions)
1849	123	957	1.0	0.5
1859	140	1,311	1.9	0.9
1869	252	2,054	3.4	1.4
1879	254	2,733	5.4	2.0
1889	355	4,252	9.4	4.2
1899	512	5,306	13.0	5.7
1899*	205	4,502	11.0	4.6
1904	213	5,182	14.3	6.0
1909	265	6,262	19.9	8.2
1914	268	6,603	23.3	9.4

* Henceforth, figures exclude "hand and neighboring" industries.
SOURCE: U.S. Bureau of the Census, *Historical Statistics of the United States, 1789–1945* (Washington, 1949), p. 179.

from manufacturing grew from 12 to 22 per cent of total national income, whereas income from agriculture shrank from 30 to 20 per cent. Income from manufacturing passed income from agriculture in 1901. Likewise, by 1914 there were three-quarters as many persons employed in manufacturing as in agriculture, whereas in 1860 the number of persons engaged in agriculture had been half again as great as the number *in all other* pursuits combined.

FACTORS FAVORING INDUSTRIAL PROGRESS

There were strong reasons for this startling industrial growth. They may be treated under the same eight headings used in Chapter 9 in order to explain why the industrial revolution began when it did.

Technical progress went forward at an even more rapid pace after the Civil War than before. In this era the scientist achieved tremendous prestige because he made great contributions toward bettering mankind's economic welfare and health. Chemistry and physics became important tools of industrial progress: chemistry gave the world cheap steel in the 1850s by the bessemer process, even cheaper steel in the 1860s by the open-hearth process, low-cost newsprint in the 1870s, reasonably priced aluminum in the 1880s, and the cyanide process for treating low-cost gold ores in the 1890s. Physics and its applied field, engineering, increased understanding of steam power. Engineers really harnessed electricity for the first time, thus bringing the world better lighting, rapid means of communication, and smoother-running power devices. Also, they developed the internal-combustion engine, which is the basis of automobiles, tractors, motor boats, and many kinds of pumps. Recognition of the importance of engineering is seen in the Morrill Act of 1862 to establish the land grant colleges, which were institutions to teach the agricultural and mechanical arts. From this came most state universities, notably those which today carry the word "State" or "A. and M." in their titles. Private engineering colleges also appeared and prospered. Professional engineers founded their learned societies, such as the Civil Engineers in Boston in 1852, the Mining Engineers in 1871, and the Electrical Engineers in 1884. The natural sciences likewise contributed to improvement in health: the Frenchman Louis Pasteur (1822–1895) demonstrated the need for cleanliness in the handling of foods like milk.

Much of this progress is attributable to the inventive genius of the American workman, who loved to tinker, who had to find out for himself why a machine broke down, or who was curious to devise some easier or better way of making things. However much he would have done anyway, the patent system rewarded his cupidity as well as his ingenuity. The number of patents granted for inventions grew from 4,400 in 1860 to 40,000 in 1914; the Civil War especially stimulated inventiveness. Among some of the noteworthy inventions upon which important and prosperous industries were erected were the following: telephones, gramophones, electric lights, typewriters, cash registers, adding machines, streetcars, automobiles, airplanes, refrigerators, cream separators, and oil drilling and refining machinery. In addition, Americans continually improved railroad equipment, steamships, metal making and cutting machinery, textile equipment, rubber goods, newsprint, photographic devices, harvesting machinery, and many others. This was a period of rapid industrial progress.

Capital became less scarce. In 1850 each worker used $550 worth of equipment, but by 1910 he was using $2,800 worth. The supply of loanable funds or liquid capital was also increasing sharply and financial institutions were improving the methods for mobilizing it and getting it to those who could use it most profitably. This will be discussed in Chapter 18.

The strength of their government no longer worried businessmen as it had at the start of the nineteenth century. The Civil War had demonstrated its durability. Businessmen, however, on three occasions lacked confidence in the stability of the dollar—during the Civil War, afterward when there was agitation to issue more greenbacks, and during the era of 1893–1896 when there was a strong demand for the "free coinage of silver at 16 to 1." An index of their concern is the fact that tens of thousands inserted a "gold clause" in their contracts. According to this, the borrower agreed to repay his debt in "United States gold coin equal to the present standard of weight and fineness." The creditor did this to protect himself against being repaid in depreciated currency in case the nation went onto a paper standard or a silver standard.

Markets were improving all the time, making possible ever-larger factories. The Civil War especially gave much impetus to industrial development. Wars frequently have this effect, for during a war governments place large orders for standardized goods—uniforms, shoes, guns, ammunition, processed food—and do not argue too much about cost, since winning the war is their chief aim. This is an ideal situation for the factory system. It was a large demand for a standardized product that caused the industrial revolution to begin in textiles in one nation after another. It was a war with France that gave Eli Whitney his opportunity to develop and demonstrate the principle of interchangeable parts. In the half century following the Civil War, improved transportation opened wider markets to one industry after another. Between 1865 and 1900 freight rates fell by two-thirds. That meant that a shipment of goods that could barely pay its transportation beyond 300 miles in 1865 could be marketed perhaps as much as 900 miles away a third of a century later. This type of development put many businesses on a nationwide selling basis. The movement of people to cities also made it easier to sell the output of the factories. Marketing institutions improved their selling and distributing methods. Finally, the American manufacturer was especially fortunate that he lived in a nation in which there were no tariff barriers between states.

Tariffs, however, protected the American manufacturer very effectively from foreign competition. This was an era of high and rising tariffs, and an industry of any importance that wanted protection could get it.

The labor supply was more adequate than at the start of the century, probably more plentiful than at any other time in American history. Immigrants were pouring in by the hundreds of thousands. During the 1850s a quarter of a million entered per year, during the 1900s, a million. The labor supply was also more concentrated in large cities, hence more accessible. Furthermore, the breakdown of skills had the effect of rendering a worker employable in a greater number of occupations. Whereas in former times a shoemaker could not readily become a weaver, now an employee in a shoe factory could fairly soon learn all he needed to know to work in a textile mill.

Vast new supplies of raw materials were discovered in this era. There were new iron mines in Michigan and Minnesota, new coal mines in the Middle West, oil wells in Texas and California, and copper mines in the Rocky Mountain states. Cheap transportation brought these raw materials to factories from greater distances than had previously been practical. There were all kinds of agricultural raw materials, too—wheat, pork and beef, wool, cotton, sugar beets—to be packed, canned, or otherwise processed. Finally, chemists and others developed a variety of new raw materials with special attributes. Some of these now became quite important, for example, aluminum, oil, various alloy steels, Portland cement, and sulfur. Larger and faster ships and cheaper freight rates made it possible to import raw materials from overseas, too, such as rubber from Brazil, sugar from Cuba, tin from Malaya, copper from Chile, and new as well as already known foods from all over the world.

Power no longer constituted a major problem, for the factories had ceased to be dependent on water power. Coal, first for steam-driven machinery and later to generate electric power, existed in abundance.

The bulk of the nation's industries were located in the northeastern portion of the nation. Cheap transportation and all the other favoring factors had caused manufacturing to break out of the New England and Middle Atlantic states area, where it had chiefly been located before the Civil War. Now it spread to the large quadrant north of the Ohio River and east of the Mississippi. True, there were industries elsewhere, but they were generally not as highly developed. The industrial revolution was just beginning in the South in this era. See Maps 17-1A and 17-1B.

Likewise there was a strong tendency for competing industries to concentrate in the same locality. If one textile mill found a certain area suitable, other mills were likely to find it similarly attractive—witness the migration of cotton mills to North Carolina. It may appear that an industry has located in a place purely by accident, and sometimes that is true, but usually there is more reason for it than meets the eye. Certainly, if

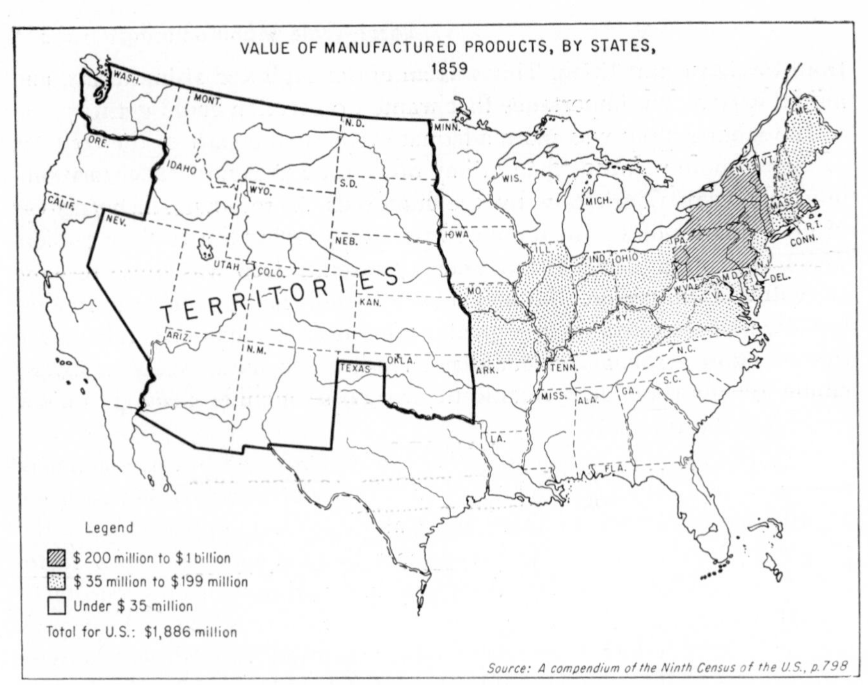

MAP 17-1A. (*Adapted from U.S. Bureau of the Census, A Compendium of the Ninth Census, 1870, Washington, 1872.*)

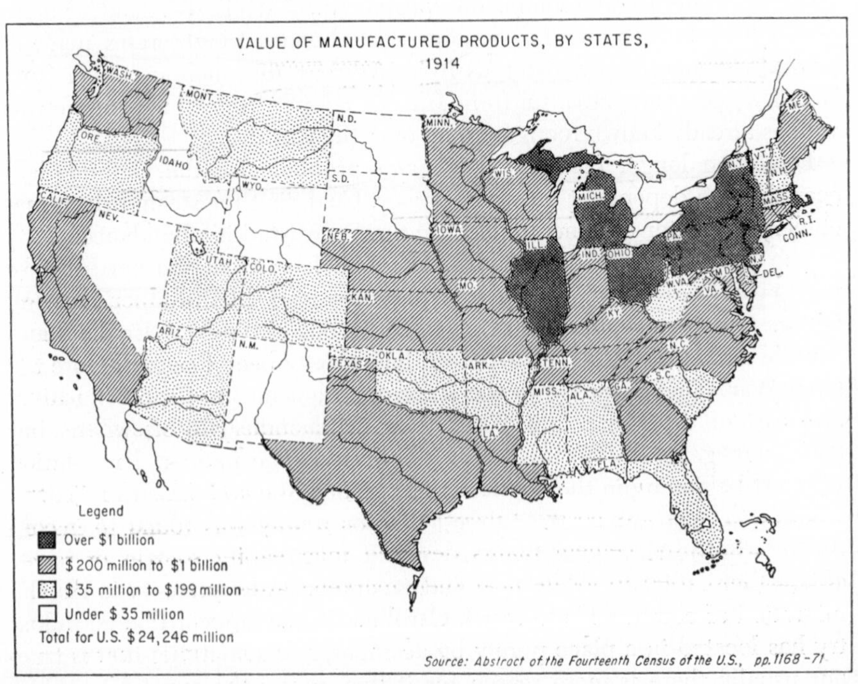

MAP 17-1B. (*Adapted from U.S. Bureau of the Census, Abstract of the Fourteenth Census of the United States, 1920, Washington, 1923.*)

basic economic conditions in any locality do not favor an industry, it is quite likely to fail. Once well-established, however, only powerful countervailing attractions will cause it to leave.

There are four basic factors that draw an industry to any location: they are accessibility to raw materials, to markets, to power, and to labor supply. Which one of the four is the most important depends on the individual industry. The cement industry around 1900 was quite heavily concentrated in eastern Pennsylvania because the best raw materials were there. Likewise the meat packing industry moved westward in the wake of its raw materials. Markets are of primary importance in determining the location of other industries. These include dairy products,

Table 17-2
Eight Leading American Industries, 1859 and 1914
(Dollars in millions)

Rank	Industries in 1859	Product value	Industries in 1914	Product value
1	Flour and meal	$218	Slaughtering, meat packing	$1,674
2	Cotton goods	107	Foundry and machine-shop products	1,373
3	Lumber, planed, sawed	104	Lumber products	1,119
4	Boots and shoes	92	Iron and steel	919
5	Clothing, furnishings	88	Printing and publishing	901
6	Leather	76	Flour milling	878
7	Iron forgings	73	Cotton goods	677
8	Woolen goods	66	Automobiles and parts	632

SOURCE: Secretary of the Interior, *Manufactures of the United States in 1860 Compiled from the Original Returns of the Eighth Census* (Washington, 1865), pp. 733–742; Bureau of Foreign and Domestic Commerce, *Statistical Abstract of the United States, 1920* (Washington, 1921) pp. 194–212.

bulky low-cost materials like gravel, and even some iron products. It was water power which first drew textile mills to the banks of small New England rivers. It was a nearby supply of excellent coking coal that helped to make Pittsburgh an important steel center. On the other hand, when textile mill owners began to drive their machinery by steam, then a second factor, cheap labor, became their prime consideration. This eventually pulled cotton textiles out of New England and into the South where labor was less costly. Likewise, when a way was found to make cement artificially, cement plants deserted their earlier sources of raw-materials and tried to locate near their markets: after about 1910, every large city began to have its nearby cement mills.

There was also a tendency for manufacturing to lose its close dependence on agricultural raw materials and to make greater use of minerals, metals, and chemicals. Table 17-2 shows the nation's eight leading industries in 1859 and in 1914. Two of the main industries of 1914 based on agricultural raw materials and two based on metals exhibit important characteristics of these later stages of industrialization. These will now be discussed.

LEADING INDUSTRIES

Meat Packing. Meat packing was the leading industry just before World War I. Even before the Civil War it had begun to use assembly-line methods, and following that war it developed this technique to a high degree. The industry had also contributed significantly to industrial progress in other regards such as refrigeration, sanitation, and use of by-products.

From a fairly early date the meat packing industry tended to locate in or near fairly large cities. This was partly because its markets were there but also because the packers needed banks from which to borrow the money to pay the farmers. Cincinnati on the Ohio River lost its primacy in meat packing to Chicago about 1861 because railroads superseded rivers as the chief means of transportation. By 1864 Chicago had fifty-eight packing houses. About this time the industry also became more integrated: the same establishment did both slaughtering and packing. In the 1870s, and especially after the advances in chemistry in the 1880s, packing houses processed more and more by-products. Refrigeration was another major cause of the localization of the industry in Chicago and of the rise of some very large establishments there.

Refrigeration revolutionized the meat packing industry. Gustavus Swift, one of the last of the great packers to reach Chicago, was largely responsible for putting over this innovation. Ice-cooled warehouses were the first step in the latter 1860s and 1870s. Mechanical refrigerating machinery followed these, but it was not significant until the 1870s and it did not displace ice until the 1880s and 1890s. Meanwhile, G. H. Hammond and Gustavus Swift experimented with ice-laden refrigerator cars. In so far as these early cars had any icing mechanism, it was simply brine in pipes. Swift saw in refrigeration an opportunity to make some important economies. A beef carcass, for example, weighs only 50 to 60 per cent as much as the live steer—why pay freight to send all this extra weight east where the local butcher would throw most of it away? Meat packing has always been an industry in which the margin of profit was narrow but the turnover rapid. Thus a few pennies once saved would be many times earned.

Swift had to convince three skeptical groups of people. First, there were the railroads which preferred to haul the whole animal and receive more freight revenue. Also, railroads did not want to experiment with untried refrigerator cars. Although Swift supplied his own cars and agreed to pay somewhat higher freight rates on dressed beef, he still encountered resistance. He made his first contract with the Grand Trunk Railroad, whose roundabout route to New York made it willing to take risks to win business from other roads. Second, Eastern butchers did not like the idea of Chicago establishments taking over the slaughtering part of the business, which reduced the Eastern butchers to the status of mere cutters of meat. Swift, who came from Cape Cod and had many friends in the East, broke down this opposition by taking a hundred butchers in different localities into partnership with him. Third, Eastern consumers of beef were skeptical of his ice-cooled product, partly because Eastern butchers had spread the word that "Western" beef was inferior. Swift countered that one by offering Western beef at bargain prices; housewives tried it and found it good. Soon other packers began to follow Swift's example. Although the packers had to supply their own refrigerator cars, all the railroads now accepted this business.

Refrigeration made it possible to center the bulk of the slaughtering and packing business in Chicago. Many Eastern butchers became mere meat dealers and many small packing establishments went out of business because they could not compete with the low prices of the big Chicago packers. These could charge less because of economies of large-scale production and profits on the by-products which the Eastern butcher or small packing plants had to pay freight upon and then throw away.

In Chicago, slaughtering and disassembling the animals, especially hogs, became a smooth-flowing series of operations. These began with the hog hanging helplessly by one hind leg awaiting the knife, and they continued until the hams or other parts were stored in the cooler. Many dozens of workmen, each performing his appointed task, cleansed the animal, removed the entrails, and made the proper cuts as the carcass moved on a trolley from one worker to the next. Simultaneously, in adjoining rooms or buildings other workmen prepared the numerous by-products, which varied from soaps to pharmaceuticals to fertilizers to baseball mitts. Nothing went unused, it was said, except the squeal of the pig, and a later version has that being made into a whistle. Inspection to eliminate the carcasses of sick animals and a high degree of sanitation were also early characteristics of this industry.

Refrigeration substituted cold and dressed meats for salted and smoked meats, which meant that the Chicago packers' products were better tasting than before. The bulk of the business was in hogs at all times, with pork the principal meat, although beef grew in popularity as the century advanced. By 1914 the packers were putting forth 5 billion pounds of pork annually, 4 billion of beef, and 1 billion of mutton and veal. Five great packing houses in Chicago handled the bulk of the business: Armour, Swift, Morris, Wilson, and Cudahy.

Cotton Textiles. Once the leader, the cotton textile industry was in second place in 1859 and in seventh place in 1914. There continued to be significant advances in textile manufacturing and good profits in the business, but textiles never became concentrated in the hands of a few giant companies as meat packing, steel, and automobiles did. The two outstanding characteristics of cotton textiles were this resistance to concentration and the fact that the industry grew most rapidly in the South, which entered upon its industrial revolution in this era.

Among the significant technical improvements in cotton textiles were the introduction of ring spinning in the 1870s and of the Northrop loom in the 1890s. Ring spinning employed a lighter-weight, faster-moving spindle and economized greatly on fuel and also on attendants. The Northrop loom automatically supplied new spools of yarn to exhausted shuttles, thus saving time and dispensing with an attendant to reload the machines. The loom also stopped instantly, the moment a thread broke. Within a decade the number of looms that one weaver could attend increased from eight to twenty-four. There was nothing in these or other textile developments, however, that made a wealthy individual or a medium-sized corporation hesitate to enter the textile field. Accordingly, the industry remained on a very competitive basis.

The necessities of war had obliged the South to industrialize during the Civil War. Although Northern armies destroyed many Southern factories, a knowledge of industrialization remained. Southern economic historians dispute as to what class of people developed the textile business. Some say it was old Southern families who after the war shouldered the burden of running a new type of economy. Some contend that it was a cooperative determination of people in certain Southern towns to pull themselves out of the economic lethargy. And others explain that it was the work of a few energetic individuals, some coming down out of the North, some from the South itself. Whoever the promoters were, the rise of cotton textiles in the South is usually traced to the Atlanta International Cotton Exposition of 1881. By 1877 the quantity of cotton produced in the South had returned to its prewar volume, but the quality still left much to be desired. A New England businessman, Edward Atkinson, urged Southern legislators to hold an exposition to demonstrate better methods of producing and ginning cotton. The Southerners, however, added a wing to the exposition hall devoted to textile manufacturing machinery as well. This last was the "eye catcher" of the exposition and stimulated the establishment of a number of small mills in the Piedmont area of North Carolina and Georgia in the next few years. Cheap labor was the great advantage that the South had in cotton manufacturing.

Closeness to the raw material was actually a minor consideration, for cotton is light and valuable enough to stand transport a long distance. But the chance to earn some cash income was a great attraction to the poor whites of the pine barrens and hills of that region, many of whom lived in extreme poverty. Also, it was a way of making a living from which, by early custom, Negroes were excluded. The Southern mills generally produced a lower-quality cloth than the New England mills.

Growth in Southern textiles came fairly fast, as Table 17-3 shows. The number of spindles is a measure of a mill's producing capacity. The South made a modest beginning in the 1880s; by 1900 it had one-third as many spindles in operation as New England, by 1910 two-thirds as many,

Table 17-3
Growth of Cotton Textile Mills in New England and the South, 1860–1914
(000,000 omitted)

Date	Spindles in New England	Spindles in the South	Total spindles in the nation
1860	3.9	0.3	5.2
1870	5.5	0.3	7.1
1880	8.6	0.6	10.7
1890	10.9	1.6	14.4
1900	13.2	4.4	19.5
1905	14.2	7.6	23.7
1910	15.7	10.5	28.3
1914	17.4	12.7	32.1

SOURCE: U.S. Bureau of the Census, *Statistical Abstract of the United States, 1931* (Washington, 1931), p. 866. These figures are for spindles in actual operation. Figures for other regions have been omitted, except in the total.

and in 1925 the South finally caught up with and passed New England. In terms of pounds of cotton consumed, the South passed New England as early as 1905, but that is because coarse weaves required more weight than fine ones. The Southern cotton textile industry of this era was largely in the Piedmont region of four states—the two Carolinas, Georgia, and Alabama.

Iron and Steel. Meanwhile, the North was in a more advanced state of industrial development. The United States had reached the Steel Age. Railroads were the greatest consumers of steel, for steel rails replaced wrought iron ones in the 1870s and 1880s, and the decade of the eighties saw American railroad mileage (all track) double, this being the period of greatest growth in American railroad history. Steel or sometimes iron was also used in structural pieces for bridges and high buildings, in steamships, railroad equipment other than rails, wire fencing, pipes, household equipment, farm equipment, and all kinds of machines found in factories. The growth in steel production between 1867 and 1914 appearing in Table 17-4 testifies to the very startling advances in this segment of the economy. Old-fashioned methods accounted for the bulk of steel production until the end of the 1860s: it was in this period that Andrew Carnegie refused to listen to the advice of his technicians, saying, "Pioneering doesn't pay." In the 1870s the bessemer process became by far the most widely used, although already there were devotees of open-hearth steel. After 1880 total production approximately tripled every decade, with production of open-hearth steel advancing faster than

Table 17-4
Output of Steel in the United States, 1867–1914
(In thousand long tons)

Date	Total	Bessemer	Open-hearth	Crucible
1869	31	11	1	
1875	390	335	8	35
1880	1,247	1,074	101	65
1890	4,277	3,689	513	71
1900	10,188	6,685	3,398	101
1907	23,399	11,668	11,550	131
1908	14,023	6,117	7,837	64
1913	31,301	9,546	21,600	121
1914	23,513	6,221	17,175	90

SOURCE: *Historical Statistics*, p. 187. Figures for other types of steel omitted except in the total.

that of bessemer steel and finally passing bessemer in 1908. Throughout this era the steel industry seemed to enjoy either a "feast or a famine" in the matter of orders. In prosperity, orders for such a prime capital material as steel were large in this growing nation; whenever a depression took place, as in 1908 or 1914, orders and production fell off sharply.

There were two basic steps in the manufacture of steel: first, the producer made iron from iron ore in a blast furnace; and second, he made steel from iron, usually either by the bessemer process or by the open-hearth process. The blast furnace heated the iron ore, and the molten iron then flowed out into prepared hollow forms, called pigs. This pig iron was cast iron. There were significant improvements in blast furnaces in this era; perhaps the major one was their capacity. Between 1876 and 1896 the annual capacity of the average blast furnace increased from 7,000 to 37,000 tons. By 1910 twenty-two modern furnaces had an annual capacity of 160,000 tons.[1] It was the use of coke instead of charcoal as fuel which was largely responsible for the improvement. With the development of the coking coal deposits at Connelsville, Pennsylvania, in the 1860s, Pittsburgh grew rapidly as a blast furnace center. Another important innovation was the Whitewell hot-blast stove which came into use about 1875. It created higher temperatures and yet reduced fuel consumption. Using it involved considerable redesigning of the interior of blast furnaces and the stacks became higher. In 1877 the best American furnaces were turning out 600 tons a week, whereas the best English ones produced 800. Fifteen years later, single American furnaces were turning out 3,000 tons a week. By 1890 the United States surpassed Britain in pig-iron production, and by 1914 the United States produced a third of the world's pig-iron output. By 1907 American per capita consumption of pig iron was double that of Britain or Germany, reflecting the rapid rate of construction and progress going on in America. Moreover, by 1900 four-fifths of the pig iron was being processed into steel.

Using the bessemer process, a steel mill could turn out a medium quality of steel cheaply in fair-sized batches. Much of the steel went into rails, but bessemer rails, although longer-lasting than wrought-iron ones, showed a disturbing inclination to crack, especially in cold weather. Moreover, bessemer steel was not easy to manufacture for special purposes. Very soon after the bessemer method came into use in America, the open-hearth system was also introduced, and during the decade of the 1890s it grew rapidly in popularity: in 1908 open-hearth production passed bessemer and by 1914 was three times it. The open-hearth process consisted of recooking the molten iron in a large receptacle with a lining of limestone. The new process had several advantages. It permitted the use of iron having more impurities than the bessemer process was able to eliminate. It could handle smaller or larger amounts of metal at one time. Finally, it permitted more accurate control of the iron brew so that faults were less likely to occur in the steel.

The manufacture of crucible steel required a further heating process to achieve its still greater degree of purity; crucible steel went into cutlery, springs, and high-grade tools. A lot of crucible steel was imported. Electric steel achieved no prominence until World War I. Crucible steel manufacturers preferred to work with wrought iron from puddling furnaces rather than with bessemer steel, and this kept the wrought iron industry alive many years after the coming of the bessemer process. Alloying elements were not much used in steel before 1890, although it was known that chromium or nickel would harden or toughen steel. From the 1890s on, manufacturers of special-purpose steel made increasing use

[1] Victor Clark, *History of Manufactures in the United States* (New York: McGraw-Hill Book Company, Inc., 1929), vol. II, p. 221; vol. III, p. 30.

of these elements. Of the alloy steels produced in 1910, three-fifths used titanium and one-fifth nickel, with chrome, manganese, vanadium, and various combinations making up the rest.

19 The manufacture of iron and steel required a large investment. When the Bethlehem Iron Company became the Bethlehem Steel Company in 1899, its capital of $5 million was tripled to $15 million. It was about this time that Andrew Carnegie asked $158 million for his steel empire,

FIG. 17-1. Open-hearth furnaces in Chicago at United States Steel, 1900. (*Courtesy of United States Steel Corporation.*)

and he subsequently tripled the price. Blast furnaces, bessemer converters, and open-hearth furnaces were expensive equipment. Yet they made possible the economies of large-scale production; manufacturers could put out iron and steel at amazingly low cost. In 1897 it cost $9.50 to produce a ton of iron at Pittsburgh, compared to $12 in Britain, nearly $13 in Germany or Belgium, and $14 in France.[2] Andrew Carnegie stated in 1903, "There have been made and sold without loss hundreds of thousands of tons of four-inch billets at three pounds for a penny. . . . To make that three pounds of steel, at least nine pounds of material were required—three pounds of coke, mined and transported sixty miles to

[2] *Ibid.*, vol. III, p. 92.

the works, one and one half pounds of lime, mined and transported one hundred and fifty miles, and four and one half pounds of iron stone, mined at Lake Superior, and transported nine hundred miles to Pittsburgh, being transferred twice, once from the car to the ship and again from the ship into the railway cars."[3]

No longer did limited deposits of iron from various parts of the East suffice to feed this ravenous industry. The Marquette range in upper Michigan was sending ore east via the Sault Ste. Marie Canal by the late 1850s. During the next half century, five more iron ranges went into operation in that part of the country. They were the Menominee, opened about 1870, containing Iron Mountain's Chapin mine, and the Gogebic (1886), both in Upper Michigan; the Vermilion (1884) and Mesabi (1892) both in northeastern Minnesota; and finally the Cuyuna (1905) in east central Minnesota. The best known of these was the Mesabi, whose ore of 60 per cent purity and whose enormous open pits represent in many minds the American iron-mining industry. The great bulk of iron ore mined in America came from these six ranges. It moved eastward in huge ore boats to mill cities in Pennsylvania, Ohio, or New York, or southward to Illinois and Indiana to be manufactured into iron and steel. In addition, the Great Lakes made is possible to transport the ore long distances without undue expense. The steel mills of the Eastern states were near coking coal deposits and not too far from their markets; therein lay their locational advantages. The United States Steel Company chose its mill site at Gary, Indiana, with scientific care to reap maximum location advantages. Steel production also grew rapidly around Birmingham, Alabama, in the 1880s because there, in close proximity, were excellent deposits of iron, coking coal, and limestone, the three chief ingredients for producing iron. The so-called tidewater mills in eastern Pennsylvania and Maryland imported their ores and scrap iron by ocean vessel; rail transportation costs on Western ores were too high. Mills located near big cities also had access to a secondhand iron supply of ever-growing importance, namely, scrap iron. After all, iron ore, once mined, could be used repeatedly; only a part rusted away or was lost beyond recovery. Junk collectors and scrap iron dealers gathered and sold the rest to steel mills for reuse. Iron and steel were the basic materials for a growing number of products in an expanding and ever more complicated American economy.

The Automobile Industry. In the census of 1900 the automobile industry does not even appear; thirty years later it was the nation's top-ranking industry, and by 1914 it was already eighth. Credit for inventing this twentieth century product belongs to many persons, as is true of most major inventions, but if one person is to be singled out, it is Gottfried

[3] *Ibid.*, vol. III, p. 91.

Daimler, a former employee of the Otto Engine Works in Germany. Joseph Lenoir, a Belgian, developed the internal-combustion engine about 1860 and Dr. Nikolaus Otto improved it in 1876. An engine that runs by exploding compressed gas is very powerful for its size and weight. In fact, the faster it runs, the more power it generates and the lighter it can be made. An automobile became possible as soon as man could devise an engine light enough to place in a carriage and powerful enough to move that carriage at a practical rate of speed. An early problem was how to make the engine rotate the carriage's wheels. In 1885 Daimler made a motorcycle, soon after a motor tricycle, and finally a four-wheeled machine that he named Mercedes after his daughter. In America George Selden experimented with a gas-engine vehicle as early as 1877 but purposely delayed taking out a patent until 1895. Other Americans had similar ideas, and in 1895 Charles Duryea won an automobile race between Waukegan and Chicago on Thanksgiving Day, his average speed being 10 miles an hour. It gained him considerable publicity. In this early period the auto interested those who liked to tinker, and they drew attention by racing. At first, however, there were three ways of moving a car; that is, with electric battery engines, steam-powered engines, or gasoline-powered engines. For a time the gas engines were considered the least practical. Although some people thought that horseless carriages had a bright future, this was still an era of stage coaches, sulkies, surreys with a fringe on top, and dusty roads.

It has been estimated that at least 1,500 companies have embarked upon the making of automobiles and most have failed. Ransome E. Olds, creator of the Oldsmobile, was one of the early successful manufacturers and made the first low-priced car. Henry Ford, a farm boy from Dearborn, Michigan, who loved to tinker with engines, also built a car for himself. He next engaged in small-scale manufacturing of cars before selling out to the Cadillac company, and he got publicity by winning some races. In 1903 Alexander Malcolmsen, a bumptious but shrewd Detroit coal dealer, who had his finger in numerous promotional pies, joined with Henry Ford and others to form the Ford Motor Company. Among the others were the two Dodge brothers, already well-known for the engine parts which they manufactured, and James Couzens, later senator from Michigan. They capitalized the company at $100,000, only $28,000 of which was cash; the rest was engine parts, a building, and other equipment. This was but one of many such companies to go into car manufacturing about this time: there was no special reason to expect that it would be fantastically successful. Yet it was from the start, producing 1,700 cars in the first fifteen months and declaring a cash dividend of $100,000.

At first Ford hired skilled mechanics to assemble purchased auto parts.

Ford managed the plant and he continued to race cars; it was good advertising. He also experimented with various models of cars, each new one bearing the next letter in the alphabet. Ford noticed that when he produced for the low-priced market, he did better than when he catered to a wealthier clientele. He and Malcolmsen differed on this and eventually he bought Malcolmsen out. In 1908 he designed a car which had little more than the essential equipment which a car of that era had to have, but which at the same time was well-engineered and easy to operate. This was the first Model T. It was made of new vanadium-treated light steel, weighed only 1,200 pounds, and was very compact.

FIG. 17-2. Model T Ford, 1916. (*Courtesy of Ford Motor Company.*)

Ford advertised, "No car under $2000 offers more, and no car over $2000 offers more except in trimmings." His price was $825 and up. His dealers said, "This car sounds the death knell of high prices and big profits." Within a very short time, fourteen dealers ordered 15,000 cars. A Newcastle, Pennsylvania, dealer wrote, "This [advertising] circular alone will flood your factory with orders," and one in Rockford, Illinois, said that until the factory was ready to make deliveries in quantity, he had carefully hidden the circular describing the Model T and locked the drawer. To serve his enthusiastic public, Ford had to go into quantity production.[4] See Fig. 17-2.

[4] Allan Nevins, *Ford, the Times, the Man, the Company* (New York: Charles Scribner's Sons, 1954), pp. 387–388.

Standardizing the product enabled Ford to turn out large numbers of cars and to sell them at a low price. Ford remarked that people could buy the car in any color they wanted it, so long as it was black. In the beginning, the men who assembled Fords were skilled mechanics. At an early date Ford hired stock runners to fetch additional parts from the stockroom to save time. Eventually, he broke down the assembling of cars into more and simpler steps. The workers became so specialized that it required little time to train them. Ford organized his factory carefully

Fig. 17-3. Old Ford assembly line. (*Courtesy of Ford Motor Company.*)

so that the growing car had to move only a short distance to the next group of men who worked on it. About 1911 he introduced gravity slides in one plant so that when a worker finished making a part, he could let it slide down to the next person in the process of assembling. That was all right for small parts; it sped up their progress. But it caused bottlenecks, for men had to be laid off while the heavier and slower operations caught up. Ford also used another method: he had gangs of men move from one car to the next. The car was stationary, the gangs moved. An axle gang did its job and moved on, then came a wiring gang, then a motor gang, and so on (see Fig. 17-3). By 1913 Ford could put a whole car together in about twelve hours. Still he was not satisfied.

In the summer of 1913 he tried a moving assembly line. He had the chassis pulled slowly along a 250-foot path by a rope and windlass. This broke bottlenecks and cut the time to produce a Model T by 50 per cent, but it was still a crude method. So in 1914 he installed an "off-the-floor" endless conveyor with smaller assembly lines feeding into the main stream from the sides. That greatly speeded up the time needed to assemble a car. The modern automobile assembly line had arrived. The "new industrialism" was here; some called it "Fordism." In 1914 Ford

FIG. 17-4. Modern assembly line. (*Courtesy of Ford Motor Company.*)

celebrated the production of his millionth car. Soon he was producing $100 million worth of cars a year, doing it at a terrific pace, and he was behind in his orders. No other automobile producer was in his class. Probably no other large manufacturer had his plant as carefully organized.

Scientific Management. Ford very likely owed some of his basic ideas on plant organization to Frederick W. Taylor, who lectured in Detroit on scientific management several times between 1909 and 1911, but Taylor is probably indebted to Ford, too. Taylor, an efficiency expert, first published his book, *Principles of Scientific Management*, in 1901. By this term he meant the careful analysis of any manufacturing operation to determine how the worker could do his job with the least effort and the greatest speed. What tools he needed, how he should grasp each one, how high the bench should be, from what direction the light should come, and hundreds of other considerations went into this new "science." Essentially, it was the application to industry of techniques commonly associated with coaching sports. The enthusiastic golfer has the golf instructor show him how to grip a golf club, how to swing it, at the same time pivoting his body properly, shifting his weight at the right moment, and following through in a prescribed way. A little man who follows directions properly can get tremendous distance and achieve a high degree of accuracy. In using almost any kind of tool, there is a right way, requiring a minimum of effort to get a maximum of result, and there are all kinds of wrong ways that use up energy and often spoil the product. There are "stars" on the assembly line and among craftsmen, as well as on the golf links and on the gridiron, although they do not make the headlines. Factories more and more gave attention to training their workers to get the most out of an hour's effort and a day's work, and they came to expect more production from the workers. Just as the record golf scores have gone lower, so the number of bolts a worker puts on a car in a day's time has increased. That did not happen, of course, without considerable resistance from the worker, which will be treated elsewhere.

FUEL AND POWER

Coal. It required a tremendous amount of power to operate all the new industries springing up in the United States, and most of this power came from coal. Coal was the chief fuel, too, in iron and steel plants, in most other kinds of industry, for running railroads and ships and to heat homes. The amount of coal mined grew from an average of 14.5 million tons in the decade of the 1850s to an average of 523 million tons in the five-year period, 1910–1914. Most of it was bituminous at the close of the period, with Pennsylvania, Ohio, and Maryland being the chief producers in the 1850s and Pennsylvania, West Virginia, and Illinois the leaders half a century later. In 1899 coal was the source of 89 per cent of the nation's energy, with petroleum providing 4.5 per cent and natural gas and water power dividing the remainder. There were only two types of coal that were in any sense scarce, namely, anthracite or hard coal, used primarily for home heating and found chiefly in eastern Pennsylvania, and coking coal, used to produce iron and found mainly in western Pennsylvania, near Connelsville.

Coke. Iron furnaces consumed a quarter to a fifth of all coal, but they had to have coking coal almost exclusively. Around the time of the Civil War they had used anthracite, but it did not yield as good a product as charcoal, and coke replaced it in the 1870s. Metallurgical coke is semibituminous coal, baked into carbon with most of its impurities removed. For a long time the methods of producing coke were crude and wasteful. At first piles of coal were set on fire and then quenched; this process yielded a baked inner portion of coke. Next beehive ovens came into use. Although cheap to construct, they were very smoky and yielded nothing but coke; they saved none of the gases, tars, ammonia, and other by-products. In the 1890s a few forward-looking companies built by-product ovens which would save all these valuable by-products; by 1914 such ovens produced 27 per cent of the coke. The shift to them would have been faster if they had not been so expensive to construct.

Steam Power. This was the era of steam power. True, water power was still in use in New England and in many small plants, but it was disappearing. Likewise, electricity was gaining popularity by the start of the twentieth century, and some modern ships had shifted to oil. Steam power stood first, however, whether in industry, transportation, or home heating. The trend was toward achieving higher steam pressure so as to economize on both space and fuel. This required reliably constructed boilers, for a bursting steam boiler unleashes highly destructive forces. The celebrated Corliss engine, the most modern of its day, which the great Centennial Exposition at Philadelphia featured in 1876, boasted a pressure of 15 to 20 pounds per inch and 1,400 horsepower. By 1893 boilers with 200 pounds pressure were in use. Moreover, expert construction and good lubrication now made it possible to operate engines at high speeds for many months, whereas in the 1870s two weeks without stoppage was regarded as a fine performance. All this time the consumption of coal per horsepower as well as the weight of the engine per horsepower were declining. In the decade before 1893 the cost of steam power was cut in half.

Electric Power. Although steam power was a great advance over water power, it was still short of ideal. It required much preparation to deliver it and delivery was sometimes uneven; how much better would power be if it flowed evenly and could be turned on or off with the flick of a switch! These qualities were the advantages of electric power, plus the fact that it could be delivered at moderate distances. Electric power, like steam power, was derived chiefly from coal. Electric power was first used extensively for lighting; textile mills turned to it rapidly in the 1880s. In the 1890s central power plants were supplying it to run street railways. Hydroelectric power began to catch the public's imagination at this time, too: the Niagara Falls Power and Construction Company was expanding its operations about 1891. The General Electric Company likewise dates from this period (1892). Textile mills were among the earliest industries to employ electricity for driving their machinery; one at Taftville, Connecticut, in 1893 led the way. The new cotton mills in the South also took to the idea quickly. "The new power, which could be delivered easily and economically at any point, made it possible to build single story factories of large floor area without employing long lines of shafting, to select mill sites with a view to cheap foundations, convenient access to transportation and good lighting, and to obviate much of the risk of fire or accident incurred in establishments of older design."[5] Iron and steel manufacturers liked electric power even better, or at least employed more of it. The new modern plant constructed at Gary about 1905 turned its furnace gases to generating electricity and drove its machinery with the current. Between 1890 and 1905 there was a hundredfold increase in the use of electric power. Other users were the aluminum, chemical, clothing, electrolytic copper, ferroalloy, paper, and printing industries. Yet ideal as electricity was, it could not be delivered long distances into isolated areas nor in small amounts unless there were many users whose combined consumption made operation of a costly generating plant worth while.

Internal-combustion Engines. The internal-combustion engine, chiefly associated with the automobile, could be installed cheaply, in remote places, and could supply small amounts of power. It offered the farmer and small producer an alternative to the large power plant. Such engines powered pumps and small machines of all kinds, especially after 1900. It was the only engine that could accompany a twentieth century frontiersman and help him open up remote parts of the country.

GROWTH AND CONCENTRATION

Two of the outstanding tendencies in manufacturing in this period were for manufacturing to become large and for the production of any commodity to be concentrated in the hands of a few producers. In other words, factories became larger in size and sometimes fewer in number. Table 17-5 shows these tendencies. They were especially marked in industries which employed a large amount of capital equipment. Such industries as iron and steel, oil refining, shoe machinery, sugar refining, and certain forms of tobacco manufacturing became concentrated to the degree of monopoly, which will be treated in the next chapter. In 1859 the average iron and steel plant turned out $10,000 of products, and in 1909 it was $200,000. The number of wage earners employed per plant was rising most of the time, and the value of products per manufacturing establishment almost doubled between 1859 and 1899 and then nearly doubled again by 1914. One reason for this growth was the economies of large-scale production.

[5] Clark, *Manufactures*, vol. III, p. 167.

Table 17-5
Growing Size of Industry, 1859–1914

Year	Number of establishments (thousands)	Wage earners in each	Value of products produced by each ($ in thousands)
1859	140	9.4	13.6
1879	254	10.7	21.3
1899	512	10.3	25.4
1899*	205	22.0	53.0
1914*	268	24.6	87.0

* Excludes "hand and neighboring" industries.
SOURCE: *Historical Statistics,* p. 179.

The Economies of Large-scale Production. There are numerous reasons why it cost less to produce many standardized type articles on a large scale than on a small scale. (1) The overhead cost was spread over a larger number of articles. (2) The manager could break manufacturing operations into a greater number of steps and substitute semiskilled workers, unskilled ones, or even machines for skilled workers. (3) These less-skilled workers not only received a lower wage rate, but they also turned out more goods. By performing one operation repeatedly, they became very adept at it; in fact, they were more skilled than the skilled workman at that one operation. (4) Where the factory was producing in quantity, it could afford expert purchasing agents to buy its raw materials and was in a position to obtain quantity discounts for large orders. In large-scale production, there were economies at just about every step in the productive process. With price competition keen and goods flooding many markets, manufacturers sought to cut costs wherever possible. The economies of large-scale production offered one of the best opportunities, so that, gradually, the big producers won a lion's share in many lines of business.

CHAPTER 18

Capital and Corporations, Trusts and Taxation

Between 1869–1878 and 1904–1913 the net national production of the United States grew from $6.5 billion to $28.7 billion—a more than four-fold increase. If the gain is reduced to dollars of constant value on a per capita basis, the gain is still 137 per cent. All this means that the nation was turning out more goods and the people were enjoying a higher standard of living. Between 1865 and 1914 real wages went up 164 per cent. Furthermore, these gains do not take into account the improved quality of many products and services rendered by the later date.

It was the new factories, warehouses, farm equipment, railroads, and ships that had come into being before and during this period which enabled the workers to produce and distribute more goods than before. Capital formed at the rate of about 13 per cent a year between 1869 and 1913. This was the secret of America's seven-league strides in material progress and of its high standard of living. The financial foundations for much of this had been laid before the Civil War and even earlier. Material growth now took place like the proverbial snowball rolling downhill.

The corporation was rapidly becoming a very important business device for mobilizing and directing large amounts of capital. The various governments helped out less than they had before the Civil War and less than they would in the period after 1914. The aggregate of capital created by myriads of small businesses was also extremely important. Corporations acquired their funds in the first instance from the sale of securities; many accumulated further capital by retaining about half of their profits in order to enlarge their plants. The savings to purchase securities came either directly or indirectly from thousands of thrifty individuals. Most of them came directly. If they came indirectly, it was through commercial banks, savings banks, trust companies, and insurance companies, all of which enlarged their operations in this era. More and more the hub about which all these other financial institutions revolved was the corporation.

THE CORPORATION

Businessmen increasingly appreciated the virtues of the corporate device. By the 1880s some states were frankly in the business of selling corporate charters. The Secretary of State of West Virginia announced in a New York newspaper that he was staying at the Fifth Avenue Hotel and had the great seal of his state with him. That was an open invitation to any would-be founders of a business corporation desiring a loosely drawn charter to come see him: for a price he could accommodate them. Unfortunately, there was little that honest states could do about it. Each state recognized whatever corporate charters, marriages, divorces, births, and other legal events the other had authorized. To do otherwise would cause endless confusion. This practice was called "interstate comity." The flaw in interstate comity was that the state with the laxest standards could set the standards for the nation. Several states, such as New York and Ohio, were trying to tighten up their incorporation laws in the late 1880s and to outlaw trusts. Moreover, they were making some headway. To get around these reformer states, all that a firm had to do was to obtain a charter from an easygoing state, such as West Virginia or New Jersey.

A New York lawyer, James B. Dill, set up a private company, the Corporation Trust Company of New Jersey, to handle all the details for firms wishing to incorporate in New Jersey. The governor, secretary of state, and other key officials of the state were among the company's stockholders. Its office was in Jersey City, just over the Hudson River from New York. According to a long plaque on the front of the building, in 1905 the head offices of some 1,500 corporations were inside. Some of the names were well known everywhere in the nation. Actually, all shared one office, which was their head office in name only. One of the chief functions of this company was to help its corporation customers to push bills which they needed through the New Jersey legislature. Some of those customers were trusts. One concession made by New Jersey will show what damage one state could do. Heretofore, with rare exceptions, no state let one corporation own the stock of another. After 1889 New Jersey permitted this and thus made possible the security holding company, for many years thereafter a favorite device of trusts.

It stood to reason that what New Jersey could do, other states also could do. In time, some of them equaled New Jersey in their desire to please corporations, and Deleware suppassed it. It should not be surmised from this, however, that most corporations were trusts; only a minute fraction of them became trusts. But most trusts were corporations, and virtually all corporations appreciated a loosely worded charter.

Despite the overgenerous policies of New Jersey and some sister states, the corporation was an absolutely essential type of business organization. It is difficult to imagine how large or even medium-sized businesses could have functioned on any other basis. By 1914 one-fifth of the 1,655,000 businesses of all kinds listed in Dun and Bradstreet were incorporated. They produced, however, far more than a fifth of the products and services and they hired many more than a fifth of the wage earners. Corporations were most important in manufacturing and in mining; they were common in merchandising, banking, and other areas of finance, and in transportation. Between 1904 and 1914 the proportion of incorporated manufacturing establishments grew from 24 per cent of the total to 28 per cent, their proportion of wage earners hired grew from 70 to 80 per cent, and the value of the total manufacturing product grew from 74 to 83 per cent. Virtually every big business was incorporated, for it took a corporation to attract and direct large aggregations of capital.

Before the Civil War the Federal, state, and even local governments sometimes undertook needed business operations that were too big or too risky for private enterprise. By the start of the twentieth century giant corporations were as powerful financially as governments; for example, in 1902 the Federal budget was $272 million, New York City's annual expenditures were $244 million, and the annual net earnings of the United States Steel Corporation were $122 million. Among the outstanding business operations of cities were street railways and water companies. The chief example of outright Federal aid to business was the land grants by the Federal government to help build the transcontinental railroads. In general, in this period, businesses became increasingly able to stand on their own feet.

SELLING SECURITIES

Before the Civil War the investment bank, which marketed securities when they were first sold, and the stock exchanges, where subsequent sales generally took place, were established institutions. Both grew tremendously in importance during the half century following the war.

Investment Banking. Now that railroads and industrial concerns were assuming great size and the wartime financing of government was on such a grand scale, the burdens and risks were more than one firm wanted to undertake by itself. Developing new markets for securities was also becoming a pressing problem. In solving these problems, the investment banking fraternity showed imagination and gained for itself tremendous power and prestige in the economy. Probably the outstanding name associated with the merchandising of securities in the 1860s was that of Anthony Drexel, a prominent Philadelphian with New York business connections. A lesser-known Philadelphia banker, Jay Cooke, came into prominence during the Civil War by virtue of his sale of hundreds of millions of Treasury bonds to the general public. He had some 2,500 salesmen working under him, and his efforts for the first time made the American public acquainted with securities. Following the war, he undertook responsibility for selling the bonds of the Northern Pacific Railroad, which seemed destined to be the second transcontinental. When the railroad contracted debts faster than the too optimistic Cooke could sell bonds, his firm failed, and that in turn triggered the Panic of 1873.

The disappearance of Cooke left the firm of Junius S. Morgan and Company, sometimes associated with the Drexels, as the nation's leading investment banking house. J. S. Morgan's son, J. Pierpont Morgan, then in his thirties, became the outstanding investment banker of the era until his death in 1913. His name appears repeatedly in the histories of railroads, manufacturing trusts, and financial institutions. Morgan had an extremely strong personality. "He was awe-inspiring to his close co-operators, and terrifying to many with whom he came into occasional contact . . . he had a goal which went far beyond mere money-making, a goal which was highly beneficial to the national economy. He meant to put an end to buccaneering, the robbing of enterprises by the entrepreneur, and to unbridled, cutthroat competition; he intended to replace these defects of contemporary business by orderly and responsible administration in a cooperative system of interlocking directorates."[1] Early in his career Morgan got the better of Jim Fisk and Jay Gould in a dispute over the control of a New York railroad. In 1885 he brought together the presidents of the Pennsylvania Railroad and the New York Central, each of whom was about to acquire a line parallel to the other's railroad, and he made them abandon their senseless war. In the next decade he was primarily responsible for reorganizing the Southern railroads, which had been in a sorry state ever since the Civil War.

Morgan devised a specific technique for putting a bankrupt railroad on its feet. He estimated its minimum earning capacity and then made bondholders accept stock for all but a minimum proportion of bonds that they held. This was so that the road could pay interest on its bonds under even the worst circumstances. He then assembled the stockholders —former bondholders and sometimes former stockholders too—and assessed them for enough to provide the railroad with working capital. Although he held the amount of bonds to a minimum, he arranged

[1] Fritz Redlich, *The Molding of American Banking: Men and Ideas* (New York: Hafner Publishing Company, 1951), vol. I, p. 389.

7

enough new shares of stock to keep all the stockholders happy. Morgan demanded a good fee for this operation, which required powers of persuasion that few but he possessed. After the railroad was on its feet again, he might establish a "voting trust" to ensure that it did not get into trouble for several years. Under a voting trust stockholders turned over their voting rights for, say, six years, to perhaps five financiers in whom Morgan had confidence. These elected the board of directors and thus chose the management. The whole came to be called "Morganizing" the company. Even after the period of trial was past, a Morgan man very likely remained on the railroad's board of directors. If he objected to some policy, the other directors usually listened very attentively; there was no knowing when the railroad might need the help of Morgan again.

From the viewpoint of business ethics and strict honesty, Morgan and many of his investment banker contemporaries stood high in an era of loose business morals. The reason simply was that "honesty was the best policy" for gaining and keeping the patronage of investors. Above all else, the investor did not want to lose his money, and Morgan catered to this main desire by preventing rival businesses, like the Pennsylvania and New York Central railroads, from injuring one another financially. After all, he had marketed the securities of both of them. He also kept faith with the investors in the Southern railroads: he saw to it that the management ran them honestly and did not divert earnings that belonged to trusting bondholders and stockholders who had stood by in the hour of need.

According to the Pujo Money Trust Committee of 1912, "An [investment] banking house that has organized a great industrial or railway combination or that has offered its securities to the public, is represented on the board of directors and acts as its fiscal agent, thereby assumes a certain guardianship over that corporation. In the ratio in which that corporation succeeds or fails, the prestige of the banking house and its capacity for absorbing and distributing future issues of securities is affected. If competition is threatened, it is manifestly the duty of the bankers, from the point of view of the protection of the stockholders, as distinguished from the standpoint of the public, to prevent it if possible. If they control the sources of credit they can furnish such protection. It is this element in the situation that unless checked is likely to do more to prevent the restoration of competition than all other conditions combined."[2] In short, Morgan's policies led to the formation of monopolies.

Powerful as the J. P. Morgan firm and other investment banks became

[2] *Report of the Committee Appointed Pursuant to House Resolutions 429 and 504 to Investigate the Concentration of Control of Money and Credit,* Feb. 28, 1913 (Washington, 1913), p. 160.

in the post-Civil War period, no one of them was generally willing to assume alone the risk of buying and selling any large issue of securities. Thus, about 1860, several began to join together to form syndicates to underwrite and often to sell large issues. Underwriting meant jointly assuming the risk. A syndicate was a partnership of companies buying or selling the securities. J. P. Morgan nearly always sought the cooperation of certain other large investment banks which he particularly trusted or favored. By the turn of the century Morgan and this group had a part in every issue of any real consequence. In 1912, testifying before the Pujo committee, one of this inner group could not mention one instance in ten years in which Morgan and his friendly rivals had not participated or cooperated in the sale of any issue involving $10 million or more. When a financial panic struck New York suddenly in 1907, it was Morgan whom the financial leaders chose to lead a rescue committee. He made his banker colleagues lend the committee $38 million and then became the final arbiter for the committee that determined which shaky institutions they should save and which not. The Pujo committee pointed to Morgan as the head of a "money trust." Indeed he was the leader of a group of bankers of all sorts that could determine whether or not any company might borrow money in large amounts or market its securities. He and his close colleagues held 341 directorships in 112 large corporations. Personally, he was worth "only" a few million dollars, but through his powerful influence on banks, investment banking houses, railroads, and industries, he had at his disposition the wealth of some $22 billion of business.

Stock Exchanges. By the time of the Civil War the New York Stock Exchange was well established. A vast amount of speculative trading went on under the stimulus of war, both in stocks and bonds. As early as 1868 it may have amounted to $20 billion per year. By the prosperous year of 1906 the exchange was doing $30 billion of business a year. Until about 1898 most of its highest-grade stocks were those of railroads; with the flowering of the trust movement between 1898 and 1903 industrial stocks assumed greater prominence.

The New York Stock Exchange and its more informal counterpart, the New York Curb Association (1910), together with exchanges in a number of other cities, performed an extremely valuable function in a capitalistic, private enterprise economy. By making it easy for investors to find buyers for their stocks and bonds whenever the investors wanted cash, the exchanges made people more willing to invest. It is easy to dwell on the misdemeanors of Wall Street speculators and overlook this far greater contribution. Without invested savings, capital accumulates more slowly and the pace of industrial progress slackens. All this means that the standard of living will rise more slowly.

INSTITUTIONS OF CAPITAL ACCUMULATION

The chief thing to remember about savings banks, trust companies, and insurance companies *before* the Civil War was that they had come into existence and had contributed a small amount of capital toward the nation's economic progress. But until then the major financial institution was the commercial bank. In the next half century these other institutions achieved greater importance and funneled substantial capital into the hands of persons who were creating new businesses or expanding old ones. The commercial banks, however, remained the principal institutional contributors of liquid capital, normally supplying about two-thirds of the total (see Table 18-1).

Table 18-1
Institutions with Savings to Invest, 1860–1911
(Dollars in billions)

Year	Number of commercial banks	National banks' assets	State banks' assets	Savings banks' assets	Trust companies' assets	Life insurance companies' assets	Total assets
1860	1,562	....	1.0	0.1	...	0.03	1.13
1865	1,643	1.1	0.2	0.2	...	0.1	1.6
1875	3,336	1.9	1.3	0.9	0.1	0.4	4.6
1890	8,201	3.1	3.3	1.7	0.5	0.8	9.4
1900	10,382	4.9	5.8	2.6	1.4	1.7	16.4
1911	24,392	10.4	13.2	4.7	4.7	4.2	37.2

SOURCES: For commercial banks, U.S. Bureau of the Census, *Historical Statistics of the United States, 1789–1945* (Washington, 1949), pp. 262–266; for savings banks and trust companies, A. B. Hepburn, *A History of Currency in the United States* (New York: The Macmillan Company, 1915), pp. 330, 341, 435; for insurance, Institute of Life Insurance, *1956 Life Insurance Fact Book* (New York, 1956), p. 60, and *The Insurance Yearbook, 1882–93* (Chicago: Spectator Company, 1882), p. 194, and *The Spectator Magazine*, vol. 72, p. 94, and vol. 94, p. 182.

These various institutions invested their funds in different ways. After 1870 close to half of all national bank assets were on loan to customers, and it may reasonably be assumed that much of it was to finance raw material purchases or holdings of inventory. State banks likewise loaned out half of their assets to customers but a considerable part went for farm improvements, for farmers were major customers of these banks. In both types of banks, the other half of the assets was either in cash, in other banks, or in government bonds. Savings bank assets consisted in considerable part of mortgages also; thus they contributed to buildings in cities, housing developments, and agricultural improvements. Insurance companies likewise favored mortgages, although after about 1900 some big ones invested considerably in the stocks of trust companies. The trust companies, which were not important until about this time, were the only institutions to invest heavily in industrial and mining stocks and bonds. In fact, the speculations of trust companies, and of insurance companies acting through them, caused a number to fail and precipitated the Panic of 1907. That in turn resulted in some investigations and legislation concerning their investments. By 1914 life insurance companies were receiving about $50 million a month in premiums and having to find safe and profitable ways of investing about half of this. Like the trust companies, they placed a part of their funds in corporation bonds.

All in all, financial institutions were not yet heavy investors in stocks and bonds; they much preferred mortgages. It was still wealthy individuals and the corporations themselves that held most of the corporate securities. That was true because the bulk of capital accumulation was the result of plowing back earnings. Just as in the first half of the century, the rule of thumb with many corporations when it came time each year to dispose of profits was "a dollar for dividends and a dollar for improvements." Corporations thus retained half their profits for further expansion and in time, profitable companies became enormously large. The responsibility for managing them properly weighed heavily on their owners or managers. That was one of the reasons why trusts appeared at this stage.

THE TRUST MOVEMENT

The word "trust" has two meanings. The narrow meaning is a nickname for "trustee device," which was an early way to combine several rival companies into a monopoly. It had limited usage and it will not be employed in this book, except as described under "Methods of Combination." The broad meaning of trust is a monopoly, usually in manufacturing, operating over a wide market if not the whole nation. John D. Rockefeller's monopoly in oil refining and Elbert H. Gary's in steel were trusts.

Why Trusts Appeared at This Time. The business leaders of any age will strive for the profits and the power that go with monopoly; that was not peculiar to this generation. If Rockefeller and Carnegie had never existed, other individuals would have done about what they did. There are four major reasons and several minor ones to explain why trusts appeared in the last third of the nineteenth century.

First of all, nationwide monopolies were impossible before there was a nationwide transportation network. Plenty of local monopolies, from gristmills to salt mines, had existed in earlier periods. Intersectional and nationwide monopolies had to wait for the building of trunk-line railroads. The appearance of trusts coincides roughly with the coming of the transcontinental railroads, although it is incorrect to imply that the west-coast trade had to be secured before a business could be considered a trust. Likewise, this was the period during which average freight rates dropped two-thirds, thus creating national markets for many products that had previously been confined to local ones.

A second major reason for the appearance of trusts was the sharp increase in investment in plant and machinery in many industries. Much of this represented a rise in fixed costs. Economists divide costs into two categories, variable and fixed costs. These are also known sometimes as operating and overhead costs. In the iron and steel industry, to take an illustration, the variable costs were labor, raw materials, and fuel. These costs would vary with plant output; that is, if the company were busy, it would use more ore and fuel and hire more men; if times were dull, the company would use less ore and fuel and lay off some men. The fixed costs were property taxes, wages of management, obsolescence, and interest on funds invested in plant equipment. Fixed costs would be the same whether the plant operated at full or fractional capacity. Before the industrial revolution, and even in its early stages, most costs were variable. As markets widened and increasing specialization made possible the use of more machinery, and as the machines became more complex and expensive, fixed costs became a greater portion of total costs. This in turn stimulated cutthroat competition.

Each manufacturer sought to operate as near as possible to full capacity. Unit costs were much less then, for the fixed costs were spread over a larger output. Thus, as transportation made it possible for companies to sell farther afield and to invade one another's markets, the competition that followed took a price-cutting form. Since no one company could long afford to operate at fractional capacity while its competitor operated near full capacity, and since large investments were at stake, the competition was sometimes bitter. The result of such competition was frequently combination and occasionally monopoly. One or the other of two things was likely to happen. Either one company would defeat and take over its rivals, or most of the competing concerns would tire of their costly battle and join forces. The conclusion of the Industrial Commission, after hearing the testimony of many businessmen in 1899, was that a principal cause of industrial combinations was "competition so vigorous that profits of nearly all competing establishments were destroyed." The combining companies anticipated not only greater profits from more stable prices, but also fewer marketing problems, for those multiplied with fluctuating prices. Stable prices can do much to reduce business risks.

A third significant reason was the presence of high tariffs. When big industries decided to combine to exploit the consumer public rather than fight one another, that public was not in a good position to defend itself. Consumers were often uninformed and generally disorganized. It was difficult to find substitutes for monopolized products like kerosene, steel, sugar, and tobacco. If consumers sought to import these from abroad, they found that avenue closed by high tariffs. As H. O. Havemeyer, president of the sugar trust, admitted, "the mother of all trusts is the customs tariff." A national monopoly is easier to obtain than a world monopoly. Big companies, through generous contributions, sometimes simultaneously to both parties' candidates, saw to it that tariffs were kept high, no matter who won the election. The years after the Dingley Tariff of 1897, the highest of this era, saw more trusts formed than ever before. 16

Fourth, the influence of investment bankers such as J. P. Morgan contributed to the formation of trusts. Morgan's attitude was that all businessmen in a given industry had a "community of interest" in stabilizing prices. He believed that there was enough business for all and businessmen would be happier if they would agree to share it. Some of his major accomplishments turned bitter competition into peaceful monopolies. Among them were settling the dispute between the Harriman and Hill lines when he set up the Northern Securities Company, and forming the United States Steel Company. 17

Among the lesser causes of trusts were the practices of states such as New Jersey in granting loose corporate charters that made it easier to set up trusts. The perfection of the telephone also played a part; it was known as the "little mother" of trusts because it made possible quick and unrecorded "deals."

Finally, pervading the atmosphere of the entire period was the spirit of *laissez faire*. This is the economic philosophy that the best government is the one that governs the least. The economist Adam Smith, back in 1776, explained that when individuals were free to apply their capital and labor without government interference, they would act in a way which would do both them and society the most good. An important corollary was that customers, colleagues, and society in general would virtually ostracize and so punish individuals who cheated or produced faulty goods. That was unrealistic. Scoundrels sometimes prosper a long time; unfortunately, the world never catches up with some of them. That became evident in this period; when the public saw the abuse of freedom allowed under *laissez faire,* the pendulum swung the other way. Yet it was in this period that *laissez faire* reached its peak and that businessmen had their greatest opportunities. Legislation was either favorable to big business, in the form of tariffs, corporation laws, and railroad land grants, or where regulatory legislation was needed, it simply did not exist. When the state legislatures and Congress first tried to regulate railroads and industrial monopolies, big business found a second line of defense in the courts. Corporation lawyers made shrewd use of the Fifth and Fourteenth Amendments to the Constitution and vitiated the effectiveness of early Federal legislation to curb big business. That has been discussed in connection with the Interstate Commerce Act; the same sort of thing happened in the case of the first antitrust laws. See pp. 415–416.

Methods of Combination. Even before the Civil War, businessmen had resorted to various devices to restrict competition. Starting about 1865 they employed them more frequently. These devices passed through three stages. At first, from about 1865 to 1880, they were informal; then in the 1880s and 1890s they became formal, and after 1904 they became informal again.

The first ones were simple agreements, sometimes called *gentlemen's agreements,* among competing producers to fix prices or to limit output; these existed, for example, among the anthracite coal operators and also the salt producers. The agreements were loose and members broke them under the temptation of higher profits. In effect, the "gentlemen" were not always gentlemen. Accordingly, they perfected a more complex method of combining called the *pool,* which remained the leading form of organization up to 1895. Railroads especially favored it until the Interstate Commerce Act of 1887 forbade its further use. In industry the pool might take any of several forms such as agreement by a group of previously competing businessmen to control prices by limiting their output, or to divide the market, or to pool their profits. Like the informal agreement, it often broke down under the temptation of higher profits. Moreover, the aggrieved members could not enforce it in a law court because under the common law a pool was a conspiracy in restraint of trade.

Meanwhile, one of John D. Rockefeller's legal advisers, Samuel C. T. Dodd, came up with a more ingenious and stronger form of combination. That was the *trustee device,* or "trust," in the original, narrow, now rarely used, sense of the term. The first one, upon which all later ones were modeled, was secretly organized in 1879. Called the Standard Oil Company, it actually consisted of an early Rockefeller company of that name and several chief competitors. The leaders selected a board of three, later nine, trustees to whom the stockholders of the various companies surrendered their stock in exchange for trustee certificates. The trustees, now in control of all plants, operated them in the most efficient fashion they knew and divided the profits among the holders of the certificates. So successful was the device that other groups, engaged in the manufacture of whisky, sugar, and lead, copied it. Legislation in a number of states outlawed the device about 1889–1890 and forced the dissolution of these trusts. It did not necessarily follow, however, that the component parts began to compete again.

During the 1890s the prevailing form of combination was the *merger*, either whole or partial. Sometimes two or more companies simply joined together to form one; sometimes one company sold part of its property to another. The American Tobacco Company of 1890 and the American Sugar Refining Company of 1891 were built up in this way.

After 1900 the *security-holding company* vied in popularity with the *merger*. This is a corporation organized to hold a controlling proportion of the stock in various operating concerns and thus to dominate their management. The security-holding company itself does not do any manufacturing. The United States Steel Company was a holding company and did not manufacture a pound of steel. The operating companies which it owned manufactured the steel. As the century drew to a close, industry, transportation, and mercantile groups in considerable number reorganized in this new and effective form.

Between 1898 and 1903 trusts and combinations were formed in rapid succession. Not every combination was a trust, but often they were preliminary steps to trusts. By 1904 there were an estimated 318 industrial trusts whose capital totaled 7¼ billion dollars. Trusts controlled 40 per cent of the nation's manufacturing capital. In that same year the Supreme Court found that the Northern Securities Company, a holding company monopoly set up by J. P. Morgan, was contrary to the Federal antitrust law. The decision made monopoly-minded business leaders realize that the holding company was not as safe as they had supposed. It marked the start of a vigorous campaign against trusts by Federal and state authorities. President Theodore Roosevelt earned the name of "trust buster" at this time.

This prosecution of trusts obliged the monopolists to conceal their agreements once more. One informal method of effecting a monopoly without making it unduly obvious was by *interlocking directorates*. The device is almost self-explanatory: the same men served on the boards of directors of several supposedly competing companies with the result that each company knew what the other was doing and all followed a fairly uniform policy and might even charge the same prices. Similar ends were also achieved by *trade associations* or statistical associations, which industries established ostensibly to exchange information on production, sales, prices, and other matters. *Pools*, arranged secretly, likewise regained some of their popularity. The steel industry and others invented the *basing point system*, which will be discussed in detail later on (Chapter 26). Such trusts were not so easy to detect and prosecute.

Among the industries in which trusts appeared were tobacco, steel, oil refining, sugar refining, shipbuilding, copper, starch, cottonseed oil, matches, whisky, farm machinery, sewer pipe, locomotives, chewing gum, rubber goods, glass, salt, and candles, and these by no means exhaust the list. To produce these goods in the most economical fashion required a large investment and that might lead to a trust. Perhaps the best example of this is in tobacco. A monopoly existed in plug tobacco and cigarettes, both made by machine, but one did not exist in cigars, which workers made by hand in thousands of little shops across the nation. Trusts did not appear because a group of men became greedy; nearly always they were the result of a logical train of circumstances which led more or less inevitably to the trust that resulted. The steel trust is an example.

The Steel Trust.[3] As late as the early 1890s the steel business was highly competitive. Few companies were "integrated"; that is, few had their own iron mines, ore-carrying fleets, railroads, and coal mines. The strongest and most efficiently run steel company of the time was Carnegie Steel, headed by a genial but canny Scotsman named Andrew Carnegie. Carnegie Steel made semifinished steel such as rails, plates, bars, and the like. It then sold some of these to other steel companies which in turn manufactured tin plate, wire, tubes or pipes, sheet steel, and other more finished steel products. During the 1890s several combinations and trusts were formed among these specialized companies. There appeared in rapid succession a tin-plate trust, a wire trust, a tube trust, and a sheet-steel trust.

Toward the turn of the century Carnegie began to talk of retiring. He gave a group of Chicago promoters a ninety-day million dollar option to buy him out for $158 million, one-third to be paid in cash. When the promoters were unable to raise the money on time, Carnegie coolly pocketed the million. Next he discussed selling out to the Rockefeller interests for $250 million, but this did not materialize either. Meanwhile, some of Carnegie's rivals and customers were investing considerable sums in expanding their operations. All seemed to be acting on Rockefeller's maxim of "pay a profit to nobody." Some of the specialized steel trusts were preparing to build their own steel mills to supply themselves with semifinished steel. Carnegie watched and waited until all were deeply involved and then set on foot operations of his own calculated to create panic in their minds. He started to build his own tube, wire, and other specialized mills. If carried through, all these operations would have enlarged the steel-producing capacity of the nation far be-

[3] Much of this material is drawn from John Moody, *Masters of Capital* (New Haven: Yale University Press, 1921), chap. 5, and from Eliot Jones, *The Trust Problem* (New York: The Macmillan Company, 1924), chap. 9.

yond its needs. Bitter competition would have ensued and the financial losses would have been tremendous. Carnegie had vast amounts of capital and could carry out his threats to build and could probably outlast the others in a price war. It was not safe to believe that he was bluffing. Other steel magnates are reported to have said, "We must get rid of Carnegie. He will wreck both himself and us—he is a business pirate."

The alarmed secondary steel producers engaged J. P. Morgan and Company to buy out Carnegie. He finally agreed to sell out for $447 million, which was approximately three times his price to the Chicago promoters some months earlier. But the damage that Carnegie could do to his steel rivals on a grand scale, other steel companies could now do on a somewhat smaller scale to those who had just bought out the Carnegie interests. It was necessary to bring most of the big steel companies and specialized steel trusts into one gigantic trust. Morgan had to induce each of the steel tycoons to join, and more or less had to pay him his price. It was essential to have a monopoly and be able to charge monopoly prices to support the bloated capital structure arising from the prices paid to Carnegie and all the others. The arrangement was a typical Morgan solution, and he and the syndicate he headed received $62 million for their services. A year or so later, according to one of Morgan's biographers, he and Carnegie met on shipboard; Carnegie remarked that he had made one mistake in selling out to Morgan—he should have asked for another $100 million. Morgan replied, "Well, you would have got it if you had."

This trust which Morgan founded in 1901 was the United States Steel Company. It was a security-holding company, capitalized at $1,403 million, roughly one-third in bonds, one-third in preferred stock, and one-third in common stock. Because of the inflated prices which Carnegie and others had received for their plants, all the common stock and about half the preferred stock was "water." In other words, securities supposedly worth $1,403 million had only about $682 million of assets behind them. Only the prospect of generous earnings from those assets could maintain the market value of all that watered stock. However, since the United States Steel Company controlled over 66 per cent of the steel production of the nation, it was in an excellent position to set prices and wage ruthless war on any independent company that threatened to undersell. With high prices it could make enough profit to pay dividends on all its stocks. The chairman of the board of directors of United States Steel was Judge Elbert H. Gary. For several years, at regular annual dinners, he set forth his company's basic policies in suave after-dinner addresses. The millionaires who headed the independent steel companies came and listened attentively to what the head of the billion dollar corporation had to say. Although Gary was careful to tell them that they were under no obligation to conform, still, most of them saw fit to do so. It was not only the most discreet course of action but also the most profitable one. By 1910 the independents had grown more than United States Steel had. The big company's control had slipped from 66 per cent to 55 per cent. However, United States Steel had earned 12 per cent a year on the average of its capitalization, and that included much watered stock. The stockholders received reasonable dividends but the company plowed most of its huge profits right back into the business so that by 1910 the company's assets had increased from $682 million to almost $1,200 million. United States Steel had "squeezed all of the water" out of the preferred stock and half of it from the common stock.

Criticisms of Trusts. The assumption has predominated so far that trusts are undesirable. There are four main criticisms of trusts: namely, they charge too high prices, they employ unfair methods of competition, they are slow to adopt newer methods of production, and they let plant capacity lie unused.

The price of steel rails varied every year from 1867 to 1900, falling, for example, from $28 a ton in 1896 to $17 a ton in 1898. The United States Steel company began operations in April of 1901 and set the price of rails at $28 a ton, and there it remained for a decade. Yet some companies had been making a profit at $17 a ton in 1896. Furthermore, improvements in methods, with resultant lowering of costs, took place between 1901 and 1910. Under monopoly none of the gains from improvements went to the consumer in the form of lower prices, whereas under competition, before 1901, they had. High prices for rails meant higher costs for railroads, higher transportation costs for industries, higher prices for merchandise, and finally a smaller return to each consumer for every dollar he spent. It has been by reducing prices that the American standard of living has improved, not by raising prices or keeping them level. Monopolies thus prevented the general public from sharing in the fruits of progress to the extent that they would have if business had been competitive.

The Standard Oil Company maintained its monopoly partly by means of unfair competition. Although it was an efficient producer of refined petroleum products, there were independent concerns that were equally efficient. The Standard killed off some of these independents by getting rebates secretly from railroads at points where it had plants but the independents did not.

The United Shoe Machinery Company illustrates a monopoly which did not keep its methods up to date. The company leased its machinery for making shoes instead of selling it. To use any machine of the machinery company, the shoe manufacturer had to agree to take a full line of the company's shoe machines. In this way the shoe machinery trust forced the shoe companies to use all its machines long after the patents had run out on most of them. This so-called "tying contract" device relieved the shoe machinery trust of making as many improvements as it otherwise would have had to make. A rival company at last appeared, with equally good machinery, owned by Thomas Plant. However, Plant was forced to sell out to the shoe machinery trust under mysterious circumstances. The banks suddenly refused to lend him money although his credit had previously been good. There was strong suspicion that J. P. Morgan's "money trust" was helping its protégé, the shoe machinery trust, to eliminate Thomas Plant's firm.

Finally, since a trust made its monopoly profit by restricting production, it left perfectly good plant and equipment idle that might have been used to produce additional goods, presumably at lower prices, for consumers who now had to go without these goods.

The chief argument usually advanced in favor of trusts was that they brought to the public the economies of large-scale production. The fallacy of this argument is that economies do not keep increasing with size. The most efficient or optimum size for an industry is frequently smaller than that of behemoths like United States Steel, for example. Besides, trusts do not generally pass on their economies to the consumer. A more genuine argument for the trust is that it eliminates much risk and worry for the owners and investment bankers. As has been shown competition between high fixed cost industries can be extremely wasteful.

Antitrust Legislation. Several states had passed antitrust legislation before 1890, aimed chiefly at the trustee device. Congress aimed the Interstate Commerce Act of 1887 at monopolies in railroads. By 1890 public opinion was so aroused against monopolies, especially in industry, that Congress passed the Sherman Antitrust Act. This was, and still is, the basic antitrust law. It provided that "every contract, combination in the form of a trust or otherwise or conspiracy in restraint of trade or commerce among the several States, or with foreign nations, is hereby declared to be illegal." The penalty was a "fine not exceeding five thousand dollars" or "imprisonment not exceeding one year" or both if the court saw fit. Although these may seem petty enough punishments for trying to make millions of dollars and very likely succeeding, the chief punishment involved was really the humiliation of being convicted and held up to public opprobrium.

The conservative Supreme Court of the 1890s at first nullified the Sherman Act, as it had its companion piece, the Interstate Commerce Act. The Department of Justice prosecuted the sugar refining trust first, in the case of *United States v. E. C. Knight Company*,[4] decided in 1895. The Department of Justice presented its case inadequately, however, and

[4] 156 U.S. 1 (1895).

the court ruled that purchase of the E. C. Knight Company refineries in Pennsylvania, which gave the trust 98 per cent control of the industry, was merely a contract for acquisition of a manufacturing plant within a state and "bore no relation to commerce between the States." The first successful prosecutions of trusts took place in 1897 and 1899 when the Trans-Missouri Freight Association and the Addyston Pipe and Steel Company, both pools, were ordered to dissolve.[5] In 1904 the government, in *Northern Securities Company v. U.S.*,[6] won a decision against a securities holding company controlling two parallel transcontinental railroads. This really began the era of successful prosecution of trusts.

Between 1901 and 1911 the Department of Justice instituted eighty-one suits under the Sherman Antitrust Act. In that year the Supreme Court indicated that the Department might be going too far. Chief Justice Edward D. White in the decisions against the Standard Oil Company and the American Tobacco Company laid down the "rule of reason" in an "obiter dictum." He said that in order for a combination to be illegal it had to act in "unreasonable restraint of trade." The following year in the case of *United States v. St. Louis Terminal Railway Association,* the Court went a step farther.[7] It added that a combination that was illegal because of unreasonable restraint of trade might achieve legality by modifying its by-laws. Since the Sherman Antitrust Act did not contain the adjective "unreasonable," critics have often pointed to the Court's obiter dictum as a case of judicial legislation, a usurpation by the Court of a congressional function. It should be observed, however, that the "rule of reason" was a principle of long standing in all law.

It was becoming obvious that further and more specific antitrust legislation was needed to supplement the loosely phrased and variously interpreted Sherman Antitrust Act. Under the urging of President Woodrow Wilson, who demanded a "new freedom" from monopoly, Congress passed two important pieces of antitrust legislation in 1914.

Congress created a Federal Trade Commission to administer the antitrust laws and to prevent unfair methods of competition. The Commission was to determine whether unfair practices were being used, and if so, to order their cessation; final enforcement of such an order rested with the Federal courts.

The other measure, the Clayton Antitrust Act, prohibited mainly certain practices which "substantially tended to lessen competition" or substantially tended to create monopoly. Five of these particularly deserve mention. (1) It forbade producers to discriminate in price between different purchasers of a commodity, if the result would be to create a

[5] 166 U.S. 290 and 175 U.S. 211, respectively.

[6] 193 U.S. 197.

[7] 224 U.S. 383 (1912).

monopoly. (2) It prohibited "tying contracts" which would prevent purchasers of one line of goods from dealing in competing goods. (3) It outlawed the acquisition by one corporation of the stock of another where the tendency would be substantially to lessen competition. (4) It forbade interlocking directorates between nonbanking corporations of $1 million or more capitalization which were in competition. (5) And it placed restrictions on ownership relationships between railroads and construction companies or supply companies.

The purpose of antitrust legislation and of the court decisions based thereon was to destroy monopoly and to restore competition. The antitrust movement rested on the ideas that competition was beneficial and that individualism and *laissez faire* were the best methods by which to achieve social well-being. Both theory and practice contained serious flaws. It was not clearly perceived that railroads and some large industries like steel were burdened with high fixed costs and must operate continuously to live. Thus competition from overbuilding or during a depression was likely to bring on either combination or receivership. Receivership would not cause the plant to be scrapped but only to be reorganized; some working agreement would eventually result which meant combination.

If trusts were evil, particular care should have been taken to see that they were effectively dissolved; but here the course of action was very muddled. In the dissolution of the Standard Oil Company after the 1911 decision, the Supreme Court merely ordered that the stock of the subsidiary companies be distributed pro rata among the stockholders of the parent company. This meant that those who had been prominent in running the trust were later prominent in running the thirty-four presumably competing successor companies. In other words, the Court ordered the holding company dissolved but established an interlocking directorate in its place. In dissolving the American Tobacco Company also in 1911, the Court so distributed the stock among three companies by brands that each enjoyed a monopoly in a distinct sales territory.

Alternative Solutions for Handling Monopolies. There were at least seven ways to handle the monopoly problem but the Federal government made use of only three of them. (1) The government could let the monopolies exist but could regulate their prices and income. That is what it attempted to do to the railroads by means of the Interstate Commerce Act and its successor acts. (2) It could prosecute and dissolve them. That was particularly the policy between 1904 and 1911 in dealing with industrial monopolies. (3) It could take no action, in the expectation that high prices and handsome profits would eventually create new competition for the monopoly. That was largely the practice up to 1904. The remaining four possibilities the government did not use. (4) It could set

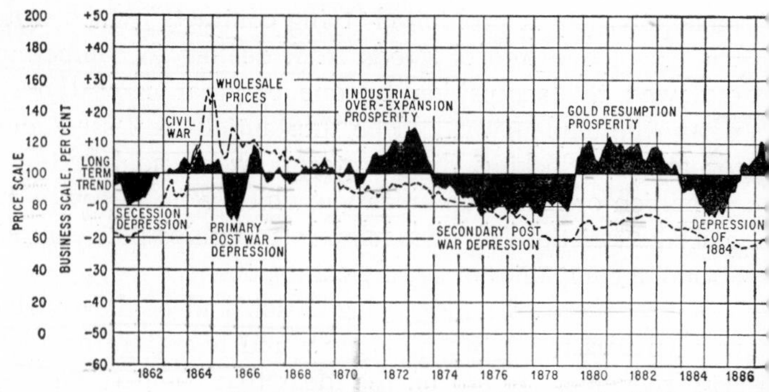

CHART 18-1. Business activity in the United State

up a yardstick railroad or industry which would compete with the private company and thus hold its prices down. That is what the Windom Committee of 1874 recommended for railroads. It was to be the principle in back of the later Tennessee Valley Authority. (5) It could remove tariff walls and let foreign competition keep the native monopolists from exacting too high prices. That was England's method. It had few tariffs and few trusts. (6) The government could nationalize monopolistic industries. England has adopted this policy in recent times. (7) It could let the monopolies exist but tax their profits heavily. The United States does this today to some degree. During most of this period there was no corporation tax and no income tax.

TRENDS IN TAXATION

In 1859 the average citizen paid to the Federal government $1.15 out of every $100 that he earned; in 1869 he paid $5.57; and in 1914 he paid $2.09. The Federal government collected over half of its income in the form of import duties during most of these years. During the Civil War internal revenue taxes were important, and from 1862 to 1872 the Federal government collected an income tax. The constitutionality of this income tax was challenged but the Supreme Court upheld it in *Springer v. United States.*[8] However, when Congress attached an income tax to the Wilson-Gorman Tariff in 1894, it was immediately challenged again. The conservative Court of 1895 declared it unconstitutional in the case of *Pollock v. Farmers Loan and Trust Company*[9] on grounds that necessitated an amendment to the Constitution if an income tax were to be possible in the future. By 1913 the required number of states had approved the Sixteenth Amendment and the first Democratic administration since President Grover Cleveland's time enacted an income tax law. Con-

[8] 102 U.S. 586 (1881).
[9] 158 U.S. 601 (1895).

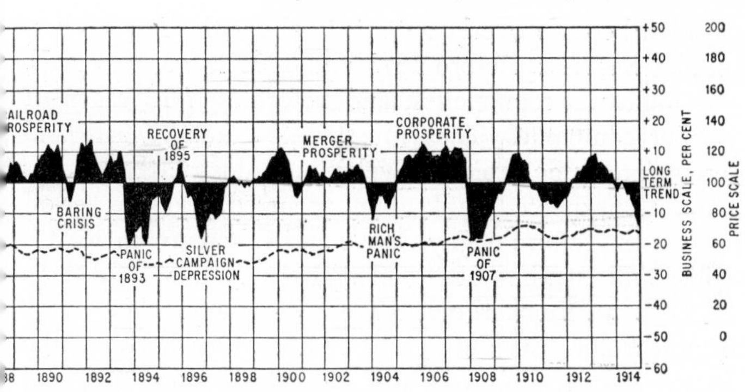

361–1914. (*Courtesy of the Cleveland Trust Company.*)

gress had, however, put a tax on corporations in 1909 that was virtually an income tax, although the Court declared it merely an excise tax.[10] Such tycoons of big industry as Andrew Carnegie, John D. Rockefeller, J. P. Morgan, and others had no income tax to pay during the time when they were accumulating most of their millions, and they paid comparatively minor property taxes. For its part, the chief worry of the Federal government was the Civil War debt, which was relatively huge in 1865. By 1914 it had declined to $1.2 billion, an easy load for a now larger and wealthier nation to carry. The per capita burden had been $75 in 1865; it had sunk to $12 by 1914. As yet the United States had not undertaken heavy international responsibilities nor expensive social welfare ones.

Expenditures by New York State and New York City quadrupled between 1860 and 1900. Other states and cities, however, did not increase their expenditures by as much. Those of all states and cities doubled between 1902 and 1913. Even so, the state burden in 1902 was only 1 per cent of the national income. States drew their revenue largely from the general property tax, but by the end of the period they were supplementing it by taxes on insurance companies and railroads, by liquor license taxes, and by inheritance taxes. Cities also relied on property taxes. States were beginning to establish asylums for the insane, to contribute more to education, and to build some roads after 1900. As for the cities, they had streets to pave, sewers to lay, water systems to install, and schools, especially high schools, to establish and maintain. New York City constructed costly bridges, great reservoirs, and municipal colleges.

PANICS AND DEPRESSIONS

The nation grew unevenly, jerkily, just as during the first half of the century. Every decade there was a panic, either major or minor. Never more than nine years went by without one, and usually one occurred after about seven years. The causes were basically similar. Bankers, in-

[10] *Flint v. Stone Tracy Company*, 220 U.S. 107 (1911).

vestors, or businessmen became overly optimistic about the future prospects of some kind of business. Before 1873 and 1893 it was railroads, before 1903 it was industrial monopolies, and before 1907 it was trust companies and copper companies. They invested too much; waste and even corruption crept into some rapidly developing industry; the returns were disappointing; an unexpected bankruptcy occurred, and that set off a panic. In 1873 it was the failure of Jay Cooke and Company; in 1893 it was the Philadelphia and Reading Railroad and the National Cordage Company; and in 1907 the Knickerbocker Trust Company. There were nine of these business holocausts during the half century between the Civil War and World War I. Only one was of major proportions, and that was the Depression of 1873–1878. It and the 1837–1844 Depression were the two worst in the nineteenth century. Each year for six years, from 1873 to 1878, more firms failed each year than had failed the year before. The memory of this financial setback colored the whole decade of the 1870s. Next in severity were the dual Depressions of 1893–1895 and 1896–1897, which made the years 1893–1897 such a grim period, and the Depression of 1907–1908, which was felt principally in New York and lasted but a year. Lesser depressions took place in 1866 and 1914, one at the end of one war and one caused by the outbreak of another. The 1884–1885 and the 1911 Depressions were short-lived. The 1903 one, known as "The Rich Man's Panic," occurred chiefly on Wall Street and was the culmination of the rapid formation of trusts between 1898 and 1903. See Chart 18-1 (pp. 352–353).

The attitude of the Federal government toward depressions during this era stands in marked contrast to that of today. The Great Depression of 1873–1878 called forth no relief measures. The violent railroad strike of 1877, a spontaneous revolt of the workers against pay cuts after several years of hard times, was put down by Federal troops. No congressional investigation of its causes ensued. The Haymarket Riot of 1886 was blamed entirely on the anarchists. The question was always "Who lit the match?" and not "Why was there so much loose powder lying about?" By the time of the Double Depression of 1893–1897 faint stirrings of the public conscience may be detected, although the administrations of the decade, Democratic as well as Republican, were characterized by extreme conservatism. As for the Panic of 1907 and the succeeding short depression, it was an outstanding private financier, J. P. Morgan, who directed rescue operations, albeit with the blessing of the Theodore Roosevelt administration. Out of it, at last, came the demand for an emergency-type currency to protect the financial public if another panic should occur, and the whole movement that led to the setting up of the Federal Reserve System. That was one of the first federally sponsored institutions to help soften the impact of panics and depressions.

CHAPTER 19

Money and Banking Problems

The nation's monetary and commercial banking systems provide the lubrication that lets the wheels of business spin smoothly. These systems must keep pace in efficiency with the other segments of the economy—such as manufacturing and commerce—or the whole mechanism will break down. The post-Civil War economy would have been greatly handicapped if businessmen had had to conduct most of their trade on a barter system or get most of their credit from English exporting houses. Yet that had been a common way of doing business a century earlier. The United States in this period made substantial progress toward establishing a better money system and toward improving its banking system. Probably at no other time in American history have American finances been in better shape than they were in 1914.

CIVIL WAR FINANCES

The improvements that occurred in this period in the areas of both money and banking were in considerable part consequences of the Civil War. During the war the price level more than doubled, which made many people conscious of the evils of inflation. Then after the war the desire to return to the prewar gold dollar made others equally fearful of deflation. Two great controversies developed between advocates of sound money and of easy money, namely, the Greenback controversy and the Free Silver controversy. Meanwhile, Congress had established the national banks in 1863 to provide an improved banking system. In time it became clear that that too had serious faults which would have to be remedied. The result was the Federal Reserve Act, passed in 1913, just half a century after the National Banking Act.

Greenbacks—Legal Tender Paper Money. At the outbreak of the Civil War almost no one foresaw how long and costly the conflict would be. President Lincoln called out 75,000 troops for three months, and Congress voted only meager appropriations even three months later. At this time the Federal budget amounted to about $65 million a year, and the public debt was also only $65 million. Virtually no one could foresee that within a year the war would be costing $1½ million to $3½ million a day, that it would go on for four years, and that by 1866 the public debt would reach $2,775 million. For the first time Americans would talk in terms of billions. Not foreseeing all this, Congress voted inadequate taxes and then had to resort to issues of paper money. The war cost more than it needed to, and the inflation was greater than necessary, even granted that some inflation will accompany any major war.

Secretary of the Treasury Salmon P. Chase was industrious, stubborn, and limited in foresight. His first plan was to use taxes to pay for ordinary expenses and interest on the debt, and to borrow the money to finance the suppression of the rebellion. In July, 1861, he told Congress that he would need $320 million, one-quarter in taxes and three-quarters in loans. Congress voted meager tax increases and authorized him to borrow $250 million and to issue $50 million in paper money (not greenbacks). When Chase tried to borrow from banks, he found that they had to strain themselves to the utmost to supply the amount that he needed. Only if things went smoothly could he expect any new loans. When the Treasury had spent these borrowed funds on the war effort, and soldiers and suppliers had put the money back in the banks, then Chase might borrow it again. If anything broke this circular flow of funds, if the people became frightened and held on to the money or demanded that banks redeem an abnormal amount of their notes in specie, then financial collapse would ensue. The banks would have to suspend specie payments and the government's source of funds would dry up. This is what happened following November 8, 1861, when a Northern ship intercepted a British mail steamer, the *Trent*, and took off two Confederate commissioners, James Mason and John Slidell. The British resented this and a war with Britain threatened. The banks had to suspend specie payments on December 30, 1861. The government's income now slowed to a trickle. By early February the war was costing $1 million a day, tax receipts were small, the Treasury had spent its $50 million of paper money, and the banks had little to lend. Unless Congress did something immediately, the Treasury would be out of funds within less than a month.

In desperation Congress passed the first Legal Tender Act on February 25, 1862. It provided for the issue of $150 million of legal tender notes; this paper money had no specie backing and was inconvertible. The law, however, permitted the public to buy government bonds with it, and the Treasury had to redeem these at maturity in gold dollars. The official name of the new legal tender notes was United States Notes, but since they were printed in a newly invented green ink (most bank notes were in black, brown, or red ink) they were known as "greenbacks." And because they were the first significant legal tender paper money since the adoption of the Constitution, they were also known as "legal tenders."[1] Congress also authorized Secretary Chase to borrow $500 million through the sale of bonds, but Chase was unable to sell many because he stubbornly insisted on too high a price for them. Consequently, he had to pay out his greenbacks and by July they were gone. Congress authorized a second issue of $150 million of greenbacks, and in January of 1863 a third issue. The Treasury never paid out quite all of this third issue: the greatest total amount out at any one time was $431 million.

As noted in discussing Revolutionary War financing, there are three basic ways of financing any war: namely, by taxation, by borrowing, or by creating money. They are desirable and also difficult in the order named. The Treasury financed the early years of the Civil War largely by issuing paper money; that is the easiest and the worst way. Fortunately, after 1863 it ceased to employ this manner of financing. It made greater use of taxation, and much greater use of borrowing. By the last year of the war the Treasury was paying for a quarter of the war by taxation. And from the spring of 1862 onward the Treasury had the valuable services of an able investment banker, Jay Cooke of Philadelphia. He did something that no one had ever done before in the United States: he sold war bonds to the general public. This freed the Treasury from dependence either on banks or on paper money. Cooke advertised the bonds in the newspapers, he employed 2,500 salesmen to ring doorbells and peddle bonds in every way imaginable, and before the war was over he had sold $1,200 million in bonds and his name was known in every household. The Treasury paid some 70 per cent of the cost of the war by the sale of bonds, another 18 per cent by taxes, and the last 12 per cent by greenback issues. Admittedly, Cooke had a mighty good bond to offer. The buyers could pay for it in depreciated greenbacks, up to January 21, 1864. Even after the government withdrew the right to

[1] From the time of the adoption of the Constitution until 1862, legal tender paper money had been looked upon as unconstitutional, although Congress issued a small amount to help finance the War of 1812. The constitutionality of the Civil War greenbacks was not tested before the Supreme Court until several years after that war had ended. In 1870 in *Hepburn v. Griswold* (8 Wallace 603), the Court found the issuance of legal tenders unconstitutional. Salmon Chase, now Chief Justice, wrote the decision outlawing what he had had to do while Secretary of the Treasury. It is sometimes alleged that President Grant packed the Court at this juncture; in any event, in the two *Legal Tender Cases* (12 Wallace 457) decided in 1871, the Court reversed itself and upheld issuance of the legal tenders as a necessay war measure. In 1884 in *Juilliard v. Greenman* (110 U.S. 421), the Court upheld the use of greenbacks in peacetime as well. It justified them under the implied power of Congress to borrow money. One way of borrowing money is to issue bills of credit, or noninterest bearing I.O.U.'s, that is, greenbacks.

convert greenbacks at par into bonds, bond prices rose but little.[2] Both interest and principal of the bond were payable in gold. Using these gold bonds substantially increased the cost of the war, although by how much it is impossible to say. If the bonds had been less of a bargain, presumably the Treasury could not have sold as many.

Inflation in the North. Between 1860 and 1865 wholesale prices rose from 61 to 132, or more than doubled, and the cost of living, based on retail prices, rose from 61 to 102, or by two-thirds.[3] There were several causes for this inflation. The greenback issues more than doubled the 1860 money supply; that is, $431 million of greenbacks were issued on top of $327 million of specie and state bank notes.[4] But the size of the nation over which this money circulated was smaller by one-third, for eleven of the thirty-four states seceded to form the Confederacy. The war was also very destructive; inflation resulted from the fact that the supply of goods decreased at the same time that the money supply increased. In the so-called Gold Room, off the main floor of the New York Stock Exchange, speculators sold gold dollars daily for greenbacks and the exchange reported the sales prices. The average price for gold dollars in 1864 was $2.03 and the highest price during the war, recorded in July, 1864, was $2.85. A great many people suffered from the pains and wrongs of this inflation, but even so, the financial sufferings of the people of the North were mild compared to those of the people of the South.

Confederate War Financing and Inflation. The South financed its part in the Civil War in somewhat the same manner as the Continental Congress had financed the Revolution, with paper money. The result was also similar—runaway inflation. Most Southern banks suspended specie payments within a few weeks of Lincoln's election. The South's efforts to raise money by taxes were feeble at first and never effective. The South had no Jay Cooke and no bonds payable in gold; Secretary of the Treasury C. C. Memminger sold his bonds with great difficulty. By 1864 the Confederate Treasury had issued about $1,000 million in paper money. The Treasury then tried to force the public to exchange these for a 4 per cent "culminating" $1,000 million loan on penalty of having all their notes declared worthless within a year. But the public did not

[2] Wesley C. Mitchell, *A History of the Greenbacks* (Chicago: University of Chicago Press, 1903), p. 197.

[3] U.S. Bureau of the Census, *Historical Statistics of the United States, 1789–1945* (Washington, 1949), pp. 233–235. The Bureau of Labor Statistics index (1926 = 100) is used for wholesale prices; the New York Federal Reserve Bank index (1913 = 100), for cost of living.

[4] At the outset of the war, there were $435 million of specie and state bank notes in the country. Since an estimated one-quarter was in the South, the North had about $327 million. In 1860 the South had 189 of the nation's 1,562 banks. Virginia had 65; Arkansas and Texas had none.

subscribe heavily to the loan and the Confederacy soon had to issue another $1,000 million of paper money. Near the end of the war Confederate dollars were worth only 2 cents in terms of their original value. In fact, the military departments were paying Confederate soldiers in greenbacks. At the war's end the Fourteenth Amendment pronounced all money and other obligations of the defeated Confederate government to be worthless.

THE FORCES OF DEFLATION VERSUS THE FORCES OF INFLATION, 1865–1896

During the generation between 1865 and 1896 one of the central political issues was whether the nation should adhere to a money system that very likely would lower prices, that is, cause deflation, or whether it should adopt a money system that quite likely would raise prices, cause inflation. Admittedly many a person hoped that prices would stay stable, but since they never did, the question was which a man minded less, deflation or inflation. Developments favored the deflationists; from 1865 to 1896 the index of wholesale prices (1913 = 100) fell from 190 to 66, or by two-thirds, and the cost of living index fell from 102 to 74, or by one-third (see Chart 19-1). Thus people living in the latter half of the nineteenth century suffered first the discomforts of inflation during the Civil War, and then the pains of deflation, more gradual but protracted over thirty years. Both inflation and deflation are evils because they favor some classes of society at the expense of others.

Evils of Inflation. Creditors lose and debtors gain from a period of inflation such as occurred during the Civil War. A price rise is the same as a fall in what the dollar will buy. For example, farm crops that sold for $1,000 in 1860 sold for $2,100 in 1865, and so $1,000 did not buy as much as it previously had. A storekeeper who had loaned his farmer neighbor $1,000 in 1860 would get back $1,000 that were less valuable in 1865. These dollars would not buy as much in farm crops or anything else as the ones he had loaned. His farmer neighbor would have to labor in the fields only half as long to pay off that debt in 1865 as he originally expected to do. Inflation would have cheated the lender or creditor, and it would have benefited the borrower or debtor. The creditor would be annoyed, the debtor quietly pleased. The example of a farmer borrower has been used purposely because during much of American history a large proportion of farmers have been debtors. Farmers have now and then welcomed inflation.

Farmers gained by inflation in another way, whether they were debtors or not. Farmers sell their crops on the wholesale markets. These markets are generally quite competitive and prices change on them quickly.

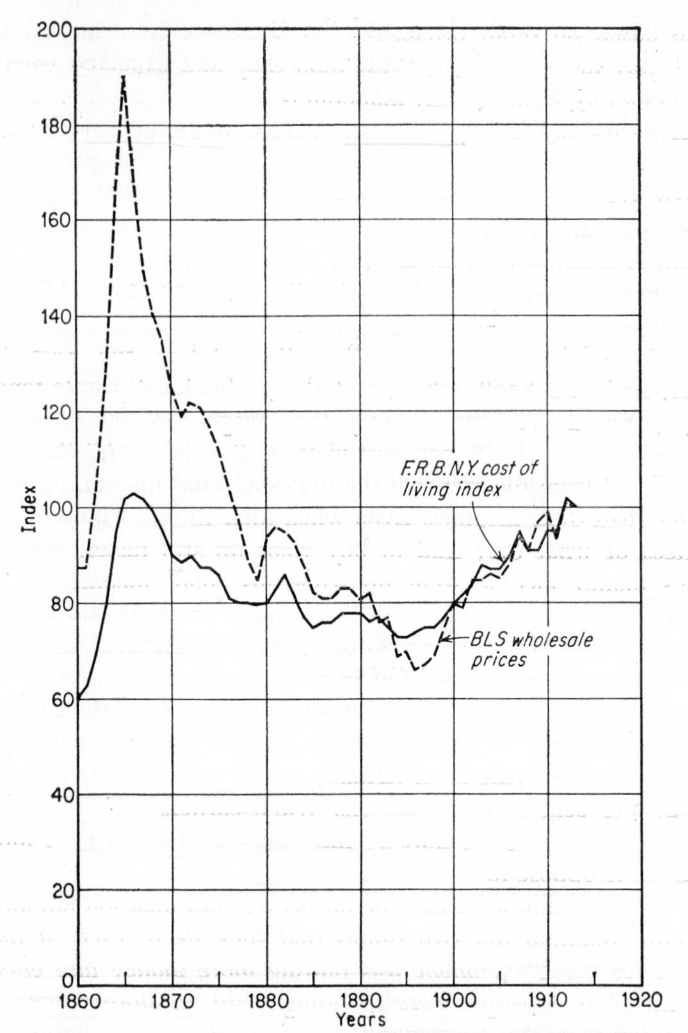

CHART 19-1. Price level indices, 1860–1913 (1913 = 100). (*Adapted from U.S. Bureau of the Census, Historical Statistics of the United States, 1789–1945, Washington, 1949, p. 235 [conversion of 1860–1889 wholesale price index to 1913 base by D. L. Kemmerer]; U.S. Bureau of the Census, Statistical Abstract of the United States, 1922, Washington, 1922, p. 503, new series.*)

Every indication or rumor of a surplus or of a scarcity affects these markets. Wholesale prices are thus more sensitive than retail prices. When the price level rose during the Civil War, wholesale prices usually led the way. Indices of farm commodities at wholesale in 1860 and in 1865 show them to have risen from 100 to 210, whereas the cost of living indices, based on retail prices, rose from 100 to 168. The farmers got considerably more for their wheat than they had expected whereas the price of clothing went up only moderately.

Laborers usually lose by inflation because wages do not rise as fast as prices do. That is less true today, but it was definitely so at the time of the Civil War. Labor unions then were not so influential. For example, between 1860 and 1865, the wages of farm laborers in general rose by 58 per cent, of machinists in the East by 46 per cent, machinists in the West by 67 per cent, and army privates by 46 per cent.[5] Meanwhile, the cost of living went up 68 per cent.[6] As a rule, wages rose more quickly in the West, where labor was scarce, than they did in the East. Salaried workers, such as schoolteachers, and also professional people tend to get their pay raised even more slowly than wage earners. Schoolteachers' salaries went up only 35 per cent in these five years. All these occupations suffered from the fact that the prices of what they had to buy went up faster than their incomes. Even when their incomes started going up, the prices of what they had to buy went up still faster. Actually, the worker's money income went up while his "real" income went down. "Real" income or "real" wages are the amount of goods and services that income or wages will buy. According to Wesley Mitchell, in nine industries the index of real wages fell from 100 to an average of 66 between January, 1860, and January, 1865.[7] In another study Alvin Hansen reached a similar conclusion.[8] Using the figures cited above, workers suffered *real* wage drops varying from virtually nothing for Western machinists to about 20 per cent for the teachers. Wage earners and salaried people were in different degrees hurt by inflation, but it was to the interest of all of them to oppose it.

Businessmen, somewhat like the farmers, found inflation not altogether distasteful. Inflation did two things that they liked. First, it increased business, for the government was putting more money into circulation, which meant that people were spending more. As storekeepers saw the demand for their goods growing and their supplies diminishing, they began to put up their prices. And when people saw prices rising and thought prices might continue to rise, they bought more for the future lest they lose by waiting. This further stimulated business. Second, businessmen made a good profit because they widened the margin between the original cost and the selling price. This could not go on forever, and many a businessman quickly realized that there was a fallacy somewhere.

[5] Mitchell, *Greenbacks*, pp. 320, 323, 331, 334.

[6] *Historical Statistics*, p. 235 (New York Federal Reserve Bank index).

[7] Mitchell, *Greenbacks*, p. 344.

[8] Alvin H. Hansen, "Factors Affecting the Trend of Real Wages," *The American Economic Review*, vol. 15 (March, 1925), p. 32.

When he came to reorder goods for his store, he found that the factory price had also risen; although he had made a profit on the original cost, it now cost more to replace the goods, so that he had to mark them up again. Increased sales and profits thus could last only as long as the inflation did. When customers with lower real wages began to economize and sales leveled off, the merchant could no longer raise his prices and expect to sell as many of his goods, and he began to suffer losses. Then the inflation seemed less attractive; but it was several years before this happened in the Civil War. On balance, the businessman remembered an inflation as he might a spree: the memory of the pleasant early effects was more lasting than those of the unpleasant morning after.

In short, inflation, such as happened during the Civil War, helped the debtor, the farmer, and the businessman at first, but it hurt the creditor, the salaried worker, and the laborer. It was unfair that some economic groups should be helped and others should be hurt.

Evils of Deflation. Under conditions of deflation, or falling prices, essentially the reverse takes place from what happens in an inflation. Deflation hurts debtors and helps creditors. During the long period of falling prices after the Civil War, wholesale prices were more than halved. A fall in prices is the same as a rise in what the dollar will buy. For example, wheat sold for $2.06 a bushel in 1866 and for $1.03 a bushel in 1876; obviously $1,000 bought twice as much wheat as it had previously. A farmer who had borrowed $1,000 on mortgage from the local moneylender in 1866 which he was to repay ten years later would have to pay back $1,000 that were more valuable than those he had borrowed. He would have to labor about twice as long in his wheat fields to pay off that debt. Incidentally, if it had been a thirty-year mortgage, payable in 1896, he would have had to labor four times as long to pay it off, for by then wheat was at 51 cents a bushel. The deflation would have cheated the borrower or debtor, and it would have quite undeservedly benefited the lender or creditor. Many tens of thousands of debtor farmers were hurt in this way during the generation after the Civil War.

Farmers lose from deflation because they sell their goods at wholesale and buy some of their supplies at retail. Wholesale prices fall first in a period of falling prices, and retail prices fall later on. In the period 1865 to 1891 the wholesale farm price index dropped from 100 to 45 but the cost of living index fell from 100 to 76.[9] The farmer of this period had two reasons for disliking falling prices: they hurt him as a farmer and they hurt him also to the degree that he was a debtor.

The laborer or salaried worker gains from falling prices if they are part of a long-term trend, as was true between 1865 and 1896. Real wages

[9] *Historical Statistics*, pp. 234–236. Aldrich Report, Weighted Farm Products Index (1860 = 100).

rose 182 per cent in this thirty-one-year period—they almost tripled, whereas they had lost ground during the Civil War; they lost ground again, although but slightly, after 1896 when the price level crept upward once more. This is not to imply that deflation alone raises real wages—obviously the workers must produce more to be able to receive more—but the workers are more likely to reap the gains of increased production in a period of falling prices. In a period of depression prices may also fall and the workers receive a gain in real wages. Yet under such conditions real wage increases are a dubious advantage, for the worker gains only *if he keeps his job,* and depressions bring unemployment.

The businessman is rather indifferent to a long-term trend of falling prices. On the other hand, the falling prices accompanying a depression hurt him very much. Often he is responsible for them: he must either sell at a lower price or not at all.

In conclusion, deflation helps the creditor and sometimes the salaried worker and wage earners, but it hurts the debtor and the farmer; if it is the product of a depression, it hurts salaried workers, wage earners, and businessmen. Inflation is generally the product of war and can only be excused as one of the costs of winning the war, but deflation usually happens in time of peace and there rarely seems any reasonable excuse for it. During the generation after the Civil War, politicians made two major proposals to stop the long-term deflation and thus escape the pains that it was inflicting. Both efforts, however, carried the implication that an inflation remedy, whose evils the Civil War generation already knew, would simply be substituted for deflation. One such effort was the Greenback movement; the other was the Free Silver movement.

Greenbacks or Resumption of Specie Payments. As soon as the Civil War ended, Secretary of the Treasury Hugh McCulloch took steps to enable the country to resume specie payments. To resume payments in the prewar gold dollar, he had to raise the value of the greenback materially. In 1862 the average value of the greenback dollar was 88 cents in terms of the gold dollar; by July, 1864, it had fallen to a low of 35 cents, and then it bounced back to 64 cents in 1865. McCulloch wanted to raise it back to 100 cents so that paper and gold would be interchangeable. The end of the war played into his hands, for it had a deflationary effect. The greenbacks now circulated over the entire country instead of over two-thirds of it, and the destructive activities of armies had ceased. Also the growing volume of business required more money each year. If the increase in money necessitated by the war had caused prices to go too high, it seemed clear that eliminating some of this money would bring prices down again and thus raise the value of the greenback dollar. McCulloch got permission to cremate (burn) some of the greenbacks collected as taxes so as to make those remaining worth more. He reduced the amount outstanding from about $400 to $356 million. By that time the greenback dollar had reached 71 cents, but the pinch of falling prices became so severe that Congress made McCulloch stop his "cremation" program.

The farmers of the West, especially in Ohio, objected to falling prices. It irked them to have to pay high taxes so that bondholders could collect on the fine bargain they had made when the nation was in peril. In 1868 it took $140 of taxes in greenbacks to buy the gold to pay off the 100 gold dollars the bondholder was entitled to receive. In response to this situation George Pendleton, a candidate for the presidency from Ohio, came up with his "Ohio idea" which was "The dollar that is good enough for the plow holder is good enough for the bond holder." In short, why not pay the bondholder off in greenbacks and spare the farmer some taxes? This would have broken faith with the bondholders and the government did not do it. The Democrats flirted with the greenback idea in 1868. Congress passed a bill in 1874 raising the amount of greenbacks outstanding to $400 million, but President Grant vetoed it. After that, Greenbackism became a minor party issue despite the serious depression which began in 1873 and lasted until 1878.

Meanwhile the trend toward eventual resumption was proceeding slowly. In 1870 the value of the greenback dollar reached 88 cents, where it remained for several years. In 1875, partly at the instigation of John Sherman, Republican senator from Ohio and brother of the Civil War general, Congress passed an act calling for resumption of specie payments by January 2, 1879. When President Rutherford B. Hayes took office in 1877, he made John Sherman his Secretary of the Treasury and Sherman prepared to carry out the Resumption Act. Sherman would stand for no delays, saying "The way to resume is to resume." Gathering a reserve of some $142 million of gold, he ignored the prophets of doom, who contended that banks and Treasury would be denuded of their gold the first day of resumption, and carried through the project. By December, 1878 the greenback was quoted at 100 cents, some banks were unofficially swapping gold for paper at par, and the Gold Room on the Stock Exchange was ready to close down. Resumption took place on January 2, 1879, without any difficulty; people deposited more gold in banks for safekeeping than they demanded in exchange for greenbacks. Meanwhile, in 1873 Congress had demonetized the silver dollar, which meant that when resumption took place it would be to the gold coin standard and not to the old bimetallic standard. Whether to adhere to this decision was the next major money controversy. Many persons believed that the country could put an end to deflation and its pains only by abandoning the new gold standard.

Free Coinage of Silver versus the Gold Standard. At first few persons other than some silver miners cared much whether the 1873 law obliged the mint any longer to coin all the silver brought to it. In time many farmers became concerned with this rather technical question. Congress had reduced the amount of gold in a gold dollar in 1834 but had left the silver dollar unchanged. This encouraged people to have gold minted. In 1853 Congress said it would no longer mint silver change in unlimited amounts; only silver dollars would be minted on request. Actually the silver needed to produce a dollar was at that time worth about $1.03, and few people brought in silver to be minted. In 1873, after debating the question for four years, Congress ended free coinage of the dollar. Since there was no longer free coinage of silver in any form, the United States had abandoned any intention to return to bimetallism; it could only return to the gold standard. Within a short time after this 1873 act, the price of silver relative to gold began to fall. This was partly because of recent new discoveries of silver in the West and partly because several nations in Europe were abandoning the bimetallic standard. An increase in the supply of silver and a decrease in the demand for it caused its price to fall. When the price of enough silver to make a silver dollar went below a dollar, the mining interests thought of taking their product to the mint, only to find that the mint would no longer accept silver in unlimited amounts.

After 1876 the miners began talking of the crime that Congress had committed in "secretly" repealing free coinage of silver in 1873; eventually this was dubbed the "crime of 1873." And about the same period farmers adopted the cause of "free coinage of silver at 16 to 1," or a return to bimetallism, as a way to augment the money supply. Silver seemed a more respectable means to this end than greenbacks. In 1878 the Silverites secured passage of the compromise Bland-Allison Act. That failed to restore bimetallism, as they had wished, but it ordered the mint to purchase monthly from $2 million to $4 million of silver, at the market price, and coin it into silver dollars. For the next twelve years the mint coined the minimum required. The big coins were so clumsy that they were not popular except in the West. In 1886 Congress permitted silver certificates in denominations as low as $1 (formerly $10 was the minimum). This enabled the silver coins to circulate by proxy; all dollar bills were and still are silver certificates, which means there is a silver dollar in the Treasury back of each one of them. The pressure to "do something for silver" continued. In 1890 Congress passed the Sherman Silver Purchase Act, which stipulated that the Treasury should buy 4.5 million ounces of silver a month; that was about the output of all American mines. This act became the central issue in the next scene of the silver controversy.

A depression that struck the country in 1893 threatened to push the United States off the gold standard, which it had struggled to achieve as recently as 1879. Imports increased, exports decreased, and gold flowed out, threatening to deplete the gold reserves of the Treasury. The administration blamed the situation on the Sherman Silver Purchase Act, which every month was causing more silver certificates to be pumped into circulation. It seemed a perfect example of Gresham's law in operation—cheap money (silver) was driving out dear money (gold). President Grover Cleveland, at the cost of considerable popularity, got the Sherman Silver Purchase Act repealed. However, gold continued to flow out. This was partly because when citizens presented greenbacks or silver certificates to obtain gold, the government turned about and reissued this paper money. It did so for two reasons. An old law forbade it to impound greenbacks, and in addition it was operating at a deficit and had to pay out all funds that it could lay its hands on. To maintain redemption in gold, which was essential to remain on the gold standard, the government had to float four loans, totaling $262 million, to replenish its gold supply. Repeatedly the gold reserve wasted away because of the operation of a so-called "endless chain." The government sold bonds to obtain gold, the public presented paper money for redemption to get gold to buy the bonds, and the government paid out the notes again to meet its bills. Importers or worried citizens presented notes again for redemption, the gold reserve once more declined, and the government had to float a new bond issue. On the third occasion the Treasury hired the services of the Wall Street investment banker, J. Pierpont Morgan, to bring in gold from abroad. His name was already anathema to all Western debtor farmers and it became doubly so now that he was doing his utmost to save the hated gold standard.

The Silverites pointed out that greenbacks and silver certificates were both legally redeemable in silver dollars; therefore the government did not have to use up its gold to redeem them. The Silverites were right, but if the government had made use of this technicality, the standing of the dollar would have been seriously damaged. The public would have employed every possible excuse to demand gold, the nation would have had to abandon its gold standard, and some inflation might well have ensued. Cleveland was not willing to see this happen. Yet the Silverites, pinched by a still falling price level, felt that Cleveland and others were asking too high a price of them to maintain the gold standard. They believed that some inflation was in order.

Whether to remain on the gold standard or to return to a bimetallic standard with a 16 to 1 mint ratio was the central issue of the presidential campaign of 1896. The market ratio was now 30 to 1; in other words, the world price of silver had dropped so low that the amount of silver needed to make a silver dollar was worth only 52 cents. To adopt bimetallism at 16 to 1 would have pushed the country onto a silver standard. Most of the major nations of the world were abandoning the silver standard and going over to gold. For the United States to adopt silver would have hurt the prestige of the dollar and have created unnecessary difficulties in carrying on international trade. The Republicans in 1896, with William McKinley as candidate, declared for gold.

The Democrats hesitated, although more of them favored silver than gold. To settle the question they scheduled a debate at the Democratic convention between the gold and the silver advocates. At the end of three speeches the gold supporters had had the best of the argument, to the annoyance of most listeners who favored silver. At this opportune moment the fourth debater, young, handsome William Jennings Bryan of Nebraska, appeared. He gave in a clear, resonant voice a speech that he had actually delivered many times before. Contending that silver was the money metal that would better serve the interests of the "struggling masses," he wound up with his memorable challenge to the businessmen and others advocating gold: "If they dare to come out in the open and defend the gold standard as a good thing, we will fight them to the uttermost. Having behind us the producing masses of this nation and the world, supported by the commercial interests, the laboring interests and the toilers everywhere, we will answer their demand for a gold standard by saying to them, 'You shall not press down upon the brow of labor this crown of thorns, you shall not crucify mankind upon a cross of gold.'" The convention went wild, and a few days later nominated Bryan as the Democratic candidate for the presidency. A spirited campaign ensued, but McKinley won the election and that assured maintenance of the gold standard for the immediate future.

If the price level had continued its downward trend, the silver party might have won the next presidential election. But meanwhile the price level began to climb. The depressions of the middle 1890s had ended and a successful war against Spain in 1898 and war prosperity turned the public's thoughts in other directions. In March of 1900, with Bryan looming as a probable repeat candidate for the Democrats, the Republicans passed the Gold Standard Act. It declared unequivocally that the United States was on the gold standard and installed safeguards to protect the cherished system in any future crisis. Bryan went down to defeat again, and the public heard no more of free coinage of silver. The price level continued to creep upward until World War I and then of course rose even more sharply.

All this attention to money suggests that gold or silver and some greenbacks were the most important money in circulation. As standard money into which all others were eventually convertible the two metals were

18

very important. But even before the Civil War most business was carried on with demand deposits in banks against which people wrote checks.

THE NATIONAL BANKING SYSTEM

At the outbreak of the Civil War there were some 1,600 commercial banks and each of the thirty-four states had its own banking regulations. The nation's banks varied widely in quality. The existence of *Banknote Reporters* and *Banknote Detectors* testified to the need for bank notes that would be equally good in all parts of the nation. Probably the most beneficial legislative legacy that Secretary of the Treasury Chase left was the National Currency Act of 1863. It is significant that that was the original name of the law which later was renamed the National Banking Act. Chase had a second motive for pushing through this reform in the middle of a war. He hoped that the new banks would absorb large amounts of government bonds: the Treasury needed all the bond buyers that it could find or create. Congress modeled the National Banking Act, as it will henceforth be called, on the free banking system in use in several states (see p. 209).

Provisions of the Act. The National Banking Act and its early amendments will be discussed here as a unit. National banks held their charters from the Federal government and thus operated under Federal law, which was the same everywhere. National banks carried the word "national" somewhere in their title. No national bank might be capitalized for less than $50,000. In medium-sized cities $100,000 was the minimum, and in New York, Chicago, and for a time St. Louis, $200,000 was the minimum. Stockholders had to pay for half of their capital stock immediately and the other half within six months; this provision was to lessen the stock note abuse. Each bank had to subscribe to $30,000 of bonds, or to an amount equal to one-third of its capital, whichever figure was larger; this of course was to stimulate the sale of government bonds. Banks might then deposit these bonds in Washington with the Comptroller of Currency (the head of the System) who would deliver to them up to 90 per cent as much in national bank notes to lend out to customers. The maximum of national bank notes outstanding was not to exceed $300 million, however. The banks received double interest, that is, interest on the bonds as well as interest on the loans to customers. This was less attractive than it appeared, however, for the interest on bonds was meager and there was a Federal tax to pay on bank notes.

If any bank failed, the Comptroller sold the bonds to pay off the notes, thus protecting innocent noteholders. This was the main principle of free banking. The law forbade the banks to have branches and required them to redeem their notes in legal money (specie after 1879). This was to eliminate any wildcat banking on the part of national banks. It virtually prohibited loans against real estate: there had been too many instances of banks tying up most of their funds in this type of loan and then going bankrupt. The new law was lenient in only one area, in regard to reserves against deposits. Few abuses had appeared as yet in connection with deposits. In short, the law sought to remedy the major evils of banking that had appeared during some eighty years of experience.

The law was excellent in many regards. Indeed, it was so excellent that it offered, so it seemed at first, only modest opportunity for profits. Accordingly, few state chartered banks applied for national banking charters and Chase sold disappointingly few bonds. There were only 638 national banks during the first year and a half of the act. Accordingly, in 1865 Congress said that after July 1, 1866, there should be a tax of 10 per cent per year levied on all state bank notes. Since such notes earned only about 6 per cent, this meant that state banks might no longer lend bank notes. The ratio of national banks to state banks changed from 1 to 2 within a year to 5 to 1.

It may well be asked why all state banks did not give up. The explanation is that there were, after all, two ways for a bank to lend its credit. With bank notes was one way; with created deposits against which the customer might draw checks was the other. The checking account method had been growing rapidly in importance, especially in Eastern seaboard cities, from the 1830s onward, and by 1855 the total of bank deposits exceeded the total of bank notes. After 1866 the American business public did an ever larger proportion of its business in this manner. It was more convenient; the state banks encouraged the practice since it was the only way in which they could stay in business, and even the national banks preferred it, for it was more profitable for them. In lending bank notes, national banks made double interest; in lending via deposits, however, they could do much better since the law required no government bond backing against deposits. By the end of the century the nation was conducting at least 85 per cent of its business by checks. After 1895 the number of state banks again exceeded the number of national banks, although national banks were generally larger and they performed the bulk of the nation's banking business.

In 1900 Congress revised the National Banking Act again. It reduced the minimum capital requirement from $50,000 to $25,000 and made additional bonds eligible as backing for national bank notes. Many new national banks, with capital of merely $25,000, appeared in the South and West. These are the kind that are most susceptible to failure, and failures increased too. The total number of national banks doubled between 1900 and 1914, and the amount of national bank notes in circulation nearly tripled.

Contributions and Weaknesses of Commercial Banks. Banks did far more than provide another kind of money for the people to use: banks supplied the working capital for a large portion of the nation's business concerns. This was essential if an increasingly specialized economy was to operate smoothly. Manufacturers borrowed from banks to pay for raw materials until they could process them into finished products to sell. Merchants borrowed to lay in a supply of store goods and paid off the loan after selling the goods. Banks took over more and more the function of providing credit, a function previously performed by English exporters and by wholesalers of the East or factors in the South. Such short-term, so-called self-liquidating loans were the ideal business from the bankers' point of view, for they involved little risk and the money was constantly coming back for relending. Total bank loans increased from $0.7 billion in 1860 to $3.9 billion in 1890 to $27 billion in 1914. Yet state banks also made a large part of these loans against real estate collateral, contrary to the admonition of economist Walter Bagehot that bankers should avoid real estate loans. National banks could not, of course, loan to farmers on real estate collateral. It was unfortunate that no nonbanking lending institution existed to take care of the long-term borrowing needs of the farmers. The chief security a farmer had to offer was real estate, and he sought a longer-term loan than it was safe for banks to take in any quantity. Since farmers were the chief customers that many state banks had, the banks had to lend against real estate or lose their customers. When times were bad or the chief crop in a locality failed, the local state banks sometimes collapsed.

Faults of the National Banking System. The test of experience revealed that the National Banking System had serious faults. That was despite the fact that it greatly improved the hybrid state system which it superseded and that it contributed appreciably to the economic advance of the nation after the Civil War. In addition to neglecting the farmers, the national banking laws carried restrictions that largely prevented importers and exporters from using its services. Also, the method of clearing checks was slow because banks could avoid extra charges by using roundabout routes. There were, however, three greater faults which eventually led Congress to overhaul the whole banking system.

The supply of bank notes was inelastic, or sometimes even perversely elastic; the amount available for lending did not readily expand at times when business was more active and then contract when a dull period occurred. The notes were backed by government bonds; if bond prices rose, banks were inclined to sell the bonds to make a profit and would then have to retire the notes. If bond prices were low, banks might invest in bonds and then have notes which they were anxious to lend. Bond prices and the possibility of lending notes sometimes had little relation to each other. Moreover, the steady retirement of the national debt, especially in the 1880s, reduced the supply of bonds available to back bank notes and so diminished the circulation of notes. The inelasticity of national bank notes would have created a vastly more critical situation than it did, had it not been for the silver certificates resulting from the Bland-Allison Act of 1878, and far more important, had not a checking system developed in this period.

Another important defect was the scattering of deposit reserves. The law provided for three classifications of banks, according to the size of the city in which they were located. The "country" or small city banks might keep part of their deposit reserves in the middle-sized city or large city banks. And the middle-sized city banks might keep part of their deposit reserves in the large city banks. Since the larger banks paid interest on these deposits, the result was that the lesser banks made the most of this opportunity and sent a large portion of their reserve funds to the cities, especially to New York City. In order to pay the interest, the large banks themselves had to lend the money, and they preferred to make short and well-secured loans. An obvious solution appeared to be the "call money market." In this market stockbrokers borrowed money, which they had to repay on a day's notice. They would protect the loan with their speculating customer's securities until the customer paid for them or ordered resale. In short, a considerable portion of the nation's banking reserves was being used to finance stock market speculation.

On several occasions the failure of some well-known business concern precipitated a serious panic. Outlying banks demanded their reserves, New York banks demanded early payment from brokers, call money rates soared, and speculation costs rose. Then stock prices dropped because many persons were offering shares and enough buyers could be found only at bargain prices. General panic spread over the land, leading to runs on banks. A run was a dramatic and horrible occurrence; frightened people gathered at the bank teller's window demanding their deposits, often the savings of a lifetime. A bank might have enough money on hand to pay the first comers and thus reassure the others and stop the run, or it might not, but one thing was fairly certain—the bank would find it hard to obtain help. No other bank would easily part with its own precious specie reserve, because it, too, might have to face a run. There was literally no lending institution to which harassed banks could turn. Under the circumstances, good banks as well as poorly managed ones sometimes suspended payments.

Third, the lack of a central bank, that is, a bankers' bank, was the crux of the problem; it was the most basic flaw in the National Banking System. This omission was purposeful. After the controversy over the second Bank of the United States in the 1830s, the idea of a central bank was unacceptable for a long time in many quarters. The Treasury managed its affairs through the Independent Treasury System. When panics took place in the post-Civil War era, as they did in 1873, 1884, and 1893, the New York City banks secured some relief through informal agreements centering around their membership in the big city's clearing house. This was no adequate solution. In the 1907 panic only the leadership of the nation's chief investment banker, J. P. Morgan, saved the banking system from a disastrous collapse. He persuaded the city's leading commercial bankers to contribute $38 million to a rescue fund. Then a committee of bankers, with Morgan seated in a damask-lined library as supreme arbiter, decided which faltering institutions they would save and which ones they would allow to collapse. Morgan was thus a one-man Federal Reserve System and Reconstruction Finance Corporation, to use an analogy more familiar today. Morgan's action saved the day and he used his great power wisely, on the whole. Nevertheless, it was clear that in a democracy no one private person ought to possess that much authority. A corrupt, selfish, or foolish man might do irreparable harm to the country; there were many people, like Bryan, who thought that Morgan was all those things. The frequent panics in this country and the haphazard way of dealing with them provoked a prominent European banker to call the United States "a great financial nuisance." By 1908 Congress felt that it was time to overhaul the banking system and perhaps to give the United States a central bank such as other modern nations had.

ESTABLISHING THE FEDERAL RESERVE SYSTEM

Nelson Aldrich and Bank Reform. In 1908 Congress passed the Aldrich-Vreeland Act with two basic purposes in mind. First, the act authorized temporary organizations of five or more banks to pool their assets in time of panic and obtain emergency government-backed currency to make money less "tight." The nation used such currency only once, to quiet the panic that broke out when World War I began. Second, the act set up a National Monetary Commission to study the American banking situation and the banking systems of other major nations and to propose suitable reforms. Nelson Aldrich was chairman of the Commission.

Aldrich was a senator from Rhode Island, the leader of the conservative wing of the Republican party, and a wealthy individual in his own right. The public thought of him as friendly to tycoons of industry or finance like Morgan, Carnegie, and Rockefeller, and in fact Aldrich's daughter was married to Rockefeller's son. Aldrich was a very able, forceful, and intelligent person. He worked hard to inform himself on banking methods. He sought the best advice he could get in America, traveled abroad to interview leading foreign bankers, and had outstanding American scholars prepare studies on American and foreign banking systems. Finally, he and his inner advisory committee came forth with the Aldrich plan or National Reserve Association. This proposed to superimpose on the National Banking System a central bank with power to influence general banking conditions, with authority to lend to banks in distress, and with numerous other desirable features. Congress later incorporated most of the Aldrich Plan into the Federal Reserve Act, which is more deeply indebted to Aldrich than is usually recognized. One feature of Aldrich's plan, however, bothered a great number of people. It provided for the election of the board of directors of his proposed central bank chiefly by the leading bankers of New York and other financial centers. Thus the new system would leave Morgan and his group in charge of the nation's finances: it would formalize what Morgan had done informally when he rescued the banking system in 1907. A congressional investigation early in 1912 made the public very much aware of this.

The Pujo Money Trust Investigation. A House subcommittee, with Arsene Pujo of Louisiana as chairman, investigated the question of whether there was a "money trust" in the United States. Admittedly Rockefeller had a monopoly in oil refining, Judge Elbert Gary headed one in steel manufacturing, and there were others. But did Morgan and a few financiers working in collusion with him have a monopoly in selling securities and in lending large sums of money?[10] The committee called Morgan on the witness stand and interrogated him. Morgan denied enjoying any such power, but the committee concluded that existing banking and credit practices resulted in a "vast and growing concentration of control of money and credit in the hands of a comparatively few men." Little might have come of all this if there had not been a change of political power some months later.

In the 1912 election the Republican party was split into the Regular and Progressive factions, with President William Howard Taft heading the Regulars and former President Theodore Roosevelt leading the Progressives. The Democratic candidate, Woodrow Wilson, former president of Princeton University, won the election. Supporting him was thrice-beaten William Jennings Bryan, who still feared and hated Wall Street and Morgan. The Democrats also won majorities in both houses of Congress and accordingly took charge of legislation reforming the banking system. Congressman Carter Glass of Virginia was responsible for the new bill in the House, but both Wilson and Bryan made their influence felt on

[10] J. P. Morgan and Company did an important commercial banking business also.

the question of where ultimate authority in the new central banking system should rest. It was in this respect that Glass's bill differed most importantly from the Aldrich plan. That bill became law on December 23, 1913, and the Federal Reserve System went into operation on November 16, 1914.

The Federal Reserve System. The Federal Reserve System was superimposed on the National Banking System. All national banks had to join it; state banks might do so if they conformed to Federal Reserve requirements. Only a handful of state banks joined at first. The law established twelve Federal Reserve banks, each of which served the member banks in twelve regions of the country. The Federal Reserve banks obtained their capital by selling stock to each member bank equal to 3 per cent of that bank's own capital and surplus. Thus the Federal Reserve was privately owned. At the head of the Federal Reserve System stood the Federal Reserve Board of seven men appointed by the President of the United States to administer the whole and give it a unity of policy.

The Federal Reserve banks can best be understood by regarding them as bankers' banks. To begin with, an individual rarely had dealings with them. More important, their relationship to member banks was, and still is, analogous to the member banks' relationship to customers. This was true in at least three major respects. First, customers deposited their idle funds in commercial banks for safekeeping; likewise, member banks were required after 1917 to keep all their legal reserves against deposits in their district Federal Reserve banks. Thus member banks' reserves were their deposits in the district Federal Reserve bank. Second, a customer with good security but insufficient cash funds might borrow from his bank; likewise, a member bank in the same circumstances might borrow from its district Federal Reserve bank. This gave the member banks a place to turn for help in times of panic, although it should be emphasized that the Federal Reserve banks helped only sound banks. And finally, just as commercial banks created credit to lend to their customers—at first in the form of bank notes and later in the form of deposits placed in their customers' names—so likewise a Federal Reserve bank created credit to lend to member banks. It did so either by issuing them Federal Reserve notes or by crediting the loan to the member bank's deposit in the Federal Reserve bank. The Federal Reserve notes issued by the Federal Reserve banks were an elastic currency. The member banks could obtain them in almost any amount by rediscounting their commercial paper (such as promissory notes of merchants or manufacturers to whom they had made loans). The supply of Federal Reserve notes thus expanded as business needs grew; it also contracted as business needs declined. This was because the Federal Reserve notes had to be backed at least 40 per cent by gold and the rest by commercial paper, or in the absence of commercial paper, entirely by gold. There was little profit for banks in circulating bank notes fully backed by gold, so when customers paid off their promissory notes, member banks generally retired an equal amount of Federal Reserve notes.

In summary, the Federal Reserve System overcame the three main evils of the National Banking System: inelasticity of notes, decentralization of reserves, and lack of a central bank overseeing the whole banking system. It gave the United States its third experiment in central banking.

CHAPTER 20

Expansion of Domestic and Foreign Commerce

In the period between the Civil War and World War I the country was plagued for the first time by many problems of plenty. Factories were producing more goods which merchants had to market in order to maintain production. This was not easy. Accordingly, merchants invented new methods of subdividing responsibility and a number of new selling institutions. At no other period in American history have so many new marketing devices been employed. At the retail level there were important developments in department stores, chain stores, variety stores, and mail-order houses. The one-price system replaced price higgling between merchant and customer, installment buying was developed, and consumer credit was put on a shorter term basis. Advertising became an art and nationally advertised brands came into prominence. At the wholesale level strides were also made as jobbers, commission agents, and brokers grew in importance. Produce exchanges appeared for a growing number of products. Markets were nationalized for an ever-widening range of products, thanks to falling costs of transportation—freight rates declined two-thirds between 1865 and 1900. Although foreign trade expanded substantially, it did not keep pace with the nation's enormous domestic trade, which by 1908 was nine times as great as foreign trade. Domestic commerce by definition is made up of the combined totals of the nation's retail and wholesale trade. In 1850 the total was $2 billion; by 1908 it was $28 billion. Approximately half of this was retail trade.

RETAIL TRADE INSTITUTIONS

The most important type of retail store, from the viewpoint of sales, was the specialty store. By 1910 there were 2,262 towns of 2,500 or more, and 46 per cent of the population was urban. It is reasonably safe to assume that general stores were disappearing from towns of that size and that such towns, as well as smaller ones, boasted several specialty stores.

General stores still existed in rural areas; in 1910 there were over 9,000 incorporated villages of under 1,000 inhabitants and many unincorporated ones too. Elsewhere the specialty store was the dominant type of retail institution. Among the more important types were those specializing in groceries, dry goods, stationery, harness, shoes, hardware, clothing, drugs, furniture, tobacco, and liquor. Dry goods stores were more important then than now and drugstores in that era limited their merchandise largely to medicines. The larger the town, the more a storekeeper could afford to specialize. By 1910 shops in large cities specialized in such things as fine foods, rare books, old stamps and coins, office equipment, pets, and auto supplies. But much as the city dweller at times appreciated the wide offerings and detailed information of the specialist, at the same time he, or usually she, did not like to visit many stores to do all her shopping. The department store and the variety store prospered in part because they gave the customer a wider selection and saved her steps.

The Department Store. Many early department stores grew out of dry goods stores. They developed in the large cities after the Civil War. Among the pioneers were A. T. Stewart's and R. H. Macy's in New York and John Wanamaker's in Philadelphia. Gimbel's, Arnold Constable's, and Lord and Taylor's in New York, Jordan Marsh's in Boston, and Marshall Field's in Chicago appeared after the war. By the 1870s and 1880s, medium-sized and even small cities had department stores. The virtue of the department store was that it combined the advantages of the general store and the specialty store. It had one building, one top management, and one set of accounts; yet each department manager was a specialist in his line of goods and could place large enough orders to get quantity discounts. Housewives liked department stores for their bargains as well as for their convenience. Macy's of New York, for example, boasted that its prices were the lowest in the city. Department stores were pioneers in various marketing techniques, especially in more aggressive advertising. They sometimes offered delivery service and maintained restaurants to attract their housewife clientele: Macy's restaurant in 1908 would seat 2,500 persons. Wanamaker's sold automobiles as early as 1903. Macy's departments grew from twelve in 1869 to thirty in 1887 and ninety-one in 1914, by which time the firm was selling $17.3 million of merchandise a year.[1] As early as the 1880s specialty storekeepers were resenting the vigorous competition of department stores to the point of labeling them monopolies and demanding their regulation.

Chain Stores. The chain store appeared at about the same time as the department store but had not developed so far by 1914. The earliest

[1] Ralph Hower, *History of Macy's of New York, 1858–1919* (Cambridge: Harvard University Press, 1943), pp. 103, 162, 330.

continuing chain was The Great American Tea Company. George Gilman and George Hartford founded it in New York about 1859, and by 1865 it had four stores. With the opening of the transcontinental railroad to the Pacific in 1869, whence came the world's finest tea, the firm changed its name to The Great Atlantic and Pacific Tea Company. Other early chains were Park and Tilford, whose second store opened in 1866, the Jones Brothers Tea Company (1872), and Woolworth's (1879). By 1881 the "A and P" had 100 stores and by 1911, 400. In 1913 the company inaugurated its "economy" stores in which the customer paid cash and carried out her groceries.[2] These and self-service stores belong primarily to the next era, however. Chain stores, like department stores, did a large enough business to buy at substantial discounts. They could offer the bargains which the housewife wanted. Almost from the outset independent grocers complained also of the chains' unfair competition and monopolistic practices.

Variety Stores. One of the fastest growing types of chain store was the variety store, perhaps better known as the "five and ten." Woolworth's was the leader, followed closely by Kresge's. Frank Woolworth began his merchandising career in Watertown, New York, where he did poorly as a store salesman but excelled in arranging window displays. It was logical that he seized upon and developed a type of merchandising in which the goods could be sold by display and without any personal selling effort. His first attempt in Utica failed because he chose a poor location; also his merchandise, mostly tinware selling for a nickel, was limited in its appeal. He promptly tried again in Lancaster, Pennsylvania, where he chose his location more carefully, offered a greater variety of goods, and put the store on a five and dime basis. Soon he established other outlets, either in partnership with his brother or others. By 1886 he had seven stores and by 1900 fifty-nine, and his sales were $5 million a year. Woolworth kept adding more items to his list of merchandise: Christmas decorations, kewpie dolls, candy, knives, toys, and many others. As long as he lived—until 1919—the top price was 10 cents. He would figure endlessly with manufacturers to help them find ways to produce at a low enough price so that he could sell at 10 cents and still make a profit. One unfulfilled dream was to be able to offer a watch for 10 cents. He sometimes arranged with a supplier to take all his output, thus eliminating the supplier's selling expense and substantially reducing his costs. Many suppliers eventually became millionaires.

Woolworth hired low-cost clerical help, relying on proper display to sell the goods. The goods were on open counters where the customer could see them, feel them, and choose them. All the clerk had to do was

[2] Paul Converse and Harvey Huegy, *Elements of Marketing* (Englewood Cliffs, N.J.: Prentice-Hall, Inc., 1946), p. 47.

wrap them up and make change. Woolworth watched carefully the merchandising methods of his store managers and insisted on every reasonable economy. He counted upon a low margin of profit, with a rapid turnover of his merchandise. His stores were popular with housewives, immigrants, and just about anyone seeking low-priced goods. Woolworth's did almost as well in depressions as in prosperity. Five and dime stores had much the same appeal to city people as the peddler's wares

Fig. 20-1. Woolworth's first successful 5 and 10 cent store in Lancaster, Pennsylvania.

once did to the country folk. By 1911 he and his family and partners had 594 stores and their sales had reached $50 million. They now formed a giant corporation capitalized at $65 million. Two years later Woolworth completed New York's tallest and most magnificent skyscraper of that day—the forty-two-story Woolworth Building.

Mail-order Houses. Meanwhile the desire of the American farmer, and many others, too, to circumvent the middleman and buy at lower prices suggested another kind of retail institution, namely, the mail-order house. This was, after all, a period when approximately two-thirds of the population lived in rural areas, and Western farmers especially lived an isolated life. They had the choice of paying high prices for a limited choice of goods at the local store or of postponing their shopping until the rare occasion of a trip to the city, which was an expense in other ways. For such people the mail-order house and its catalog filled an urgent need. The first mail-order house was Montgomery Ward, founded in 1872; it became the supply house for the Grange and advertised itself as such. Its later great rival, Sears, Roebuck, began in 1886 as a small watch-selling company. Richard W. Sears bought up discontinued lines and offered them by mail to farmers. He let his customers see the watches first, asked only a small down payment, and also guaranteed the watches and maintained a repair service. Alvah Roebuck was the original repair man. By 1893 the company had added other items and each year its catalogue grew larger; by 1895 it had 507 pages. (See Fig. 20-2.) In 1897 the company moved to Chicago. The mail-order house also was a form of retailing which prospered in depressions, for in such periods people are especially bargain-conscious. Sears Roebuck and Montgomery Ward were strictly mail-order houses in this era and not chain department stores as they later became. Accordingly their selling costs were low—their catalogs were their salesmen. Like Woolworth, they bought in quantity or even took a large amount of the products of selected manufacturing companies.

NEW RETAIL SELLING PRACTICES

It took more than new kinds of retail stores to dispose of the stream of goods pouring forth from the factories. Ingenious merchants sought to simplify the process of selling, to take some of the risk out of selling on credit, and to appeal to more customers. Important improvements in merchandising resulted.

The One-price System. Higgling over the price of every article purchased was logical as long as the customer was offering produce of his own in exchange or was buying on long-term credit or using bank notes of dubious value. As a matter of habit, it lasted long after customers began to pay in cash. The practice is still found in a great many underdeveloped parts of the world today and continues in large transactions such as buying a house or selling a car. The appearance of dependable national bank notes removed one reason for higgling. It disappeared first in the larger cities simply to save time. A one-price system enabled the merchant to sell more goods and to delegate selling to inexperienced clerks, and it permitted the shopper to buy more in a limited time. In cities, especially, people were putting a greater value on the use of their time. To the extent also that merchants offered money-back guarantees or offered price bargains in their advertising, the one-price system was

FIG. 20-2. A page from a Sears, Roebuck and Company catalog of 1910. (*Courtesy of Sears, Roebuck and Co.*)

absolutely essential. The Tappans used the one-price system in New York in the 1820s, and A. T. Stewart did so in the 1840s. Rowland Macy was unable to hold to it in his store in Haverhill, Massachusetts, in the 1850s but succeeded in New York after 1858. In Champaign, Illinois, a representative town of the Middle West, Scott and Willis department store successfully introduced it in 1872. The one-price system was the exception before the Civil War and the rule afterward.

Consumer Credit. Granting credit made it easier to reach a barter agreement with a customer but overgenerous credit was a major cause of business failure. Nevertheless, as long as most customers were farmers and sold their crops but once or twice a year, credit was necessary. Until the Civil War, merchants expected consumers to pay within six months to a year. In many instances customers simply kept running accounts, which they would reduce every so often when they were in funds. As more people moved to cities where factories, shops, and mills paid them monthly wages, merchants encouraged settlement of these accounts more frequently. Merchants sometimes offered their customers a discount or handed out a generous merchandise bonus for regular payments. Since many customers did not like to have debts weighing on their conscience, the eventual result was increasingly frequent settlement of accounts.

Installment Buying. The origins of installment buying must lie far back in history. Merchants on occasion must have suggested to customers that they pay off their debts in regular installments over a period of time. There are records of the sale of horses, carriages, and farm equipment on an installment basis in the latter eighteenth century. The Federal government sold land on the installment plan under the Harrison Act of 1800—the purchaser paid one-quarter down and the other three-quarters over four years. Building and loan associations from their outset offered a type of installment buying. In the 1850s and perhaps even earlier, McCormick reapers, Hale pianos, and Singer sewing machines were sold on the installment plan. Installment buying was likely to develop in connection with the sale of an article which would cost a worker a month's salary or more. The merchant had too much at stake to sell it on a simple book-credit basis, and he early learned the wisdom of requiring the buyer to pay a large enough part at the time of sale so that he would complete his payments. Merchants sometimes sold on an installment basis the mass-produced items for which the manufacturer was seeking a wider market. By the 1870s and 1880s stores were selling an increasing number of products this way. Also they were using the device to reach progressively lower income groups and the practice was spreading to more rural areas. To sell to lower-income persons, merchants had to take special safeguards in the matter of adequate security and interest charges. Some overdid it and exploited immigrants especially. In the 1890s installment selling received a bad reputation in certain quarters. Nevertheless, by 1914 the practice was well established and the first examples of automobile installment financing appeared shortly before World War I.

Advertising. Growing competition forced merchants and manufacturers to make more strenuous efforts than before to persuade the public to buy their products. More aggressive advertising and the rise of "salesmanship" bear witness to this trend. Before the Civil War advertising had been flatly informative; it told anyone who might be interested what merchant at what address had a new shipment of what merchandise for sale. Advertisements rarely mentioned price and seldom praised the products. It was the sort of situation which prevails when there is a "sellers' market," say, during a war when goods are in short supply. As factories increased production, the nation more and more found itself in a "buyers' market." It was necessary to tempt, persuade, and cajole the buyer to win and keep his patronage. The manufacturer needed that patronage to keep his factory operating at close to full capacity, which is where greater profits are made. Since local merchants often failed to appreciate the power of advertising or simply did too little about it, the manufacturers themselves began to give it their attention. The same era that witnessed the coming of national monopolies, almost nationwide railroad networks, and national labor unions likewise saw the development of national advertising. Patent medicines were among the first products to be nationally advertised; in fact, some had been advertised this way before the Civil War. Among the famous ones of the postwar era were J. C. Ayer's Sarsaparilla, and later Castoria and Lydia Pinkham's Compound. Manufacturers publicized soaps in the 1870s, "safety" bicycles in the 1880s, and breakfast cereals in the 1890s. About the turn of the century Eastman Kodak, Gillette razor blades, and Wrigley chewing gum increased their sales sharply because of their national advertising. Most of this advertising was in newspapers and magazines, but some also appeared on barns and billboards. By 1893 there were some 20,000 newspapers, five times as many as in 1860. National advertising meant that many more people knew the manufacturer's brand and demanded it. The merchant felt obliged to stock it and found it easier to sell. Since the manufacturer had relieved the merchant of part of his selling chores, he allowed the merchant a slimmer margin of profit on such nationally advertised merchandise.

Salesmanship. A variety of selling practices developed in this era or at least came into wider use. Among them may be mentioned the use of testimonials (of satisfied buyers of a product), the "canned" sales talk, the sales manual, training schools for salesmen, sales contests, sales conventions, sales managers, and the assignment of a quota and a guaranteed territory to each salesman. John H. Patterson, the ingenious and energetic head of the National Cash Register Company, has received credit for developing many of these practices. The significant point is that retail merchants saw many more traveling salesmen than they had seen earlier. These salesmen knew the virtues of their products and some had been trained in how to sell them. There was also around 1900 an increase in house-to-house selling of such things as brushes, magazine subscriptions, and stereoscopic slides of famous places.

WHOLESALE TRADE INSTITUTIONS

The word "wholesaler" has a broad and a narrow connotation. It includes those who take title to the merchandise as well as those who do not. The first are full-service wholesalers and the latter are agent wholesalers. The broad term includes all middlemen between retailer and producer. The narrow one may refer only to the proprietor of the wholesale house, that is, the middleman next back of the retailer. It is used in the broad sense in the title of this section, but it is used in the narrow sense in the two subsections just below. In general this period was the heyday of the wholesaler: his importance increased rapidly as markets broadened. Since World War I wholesalers have declined somewhat in importance. Wholesalers are less important where the product is expensive, where retailers place large orders, where the product is industrial rather than agricultural, and to some degree where the manufacturer has generously advertised the product. In the post-Civil War period most retailers were small independent merchants and national advertising was only beginning. Under these circumstances, wholesalers performed many valuable functions.

The Full-service Wholesaler. The wholesalers (in the narrow sense) maintained warehouses with a considerable stock of their particular line of goods, whether it was dry goods, hardware, packaged goods, or household equipment. They maintained salesmen on the road selling their goods to numerous retail stores. They bought outright from manufacturers and sold on credit to retailers, thus bearing most of the losses that arose from the failure of retailing establishments. Wholesalers even provided credit to manufacturers on occasion. Finally, they gathered all kinds of information on customer preferences, market trends, and the like, which they passed back to the manufacturer to guide him in further production. In this period in particular, the nation had many small manufacturers as well as numerous small retailers. The manufacturer had to devote all his time and money to producing; the retailer needed relatively small quantities of many items. The wholesaler relieved both of many burdensome responsibilities and was expert adviser to both. In some lines, however, there were other middlemen between the wholesaler and the manufacturer.

Jobbers, Commission Agents, and Brokers. A jobber, also a wholesale merchant, is a dealer; that is, he takes title to the merchandise and must stand a loss if he cannot cover his various costs. The jobber, by the nature of his occupation, was often an opportunist. He bought odd lots of merchandise, called "jobs"—perhaps goods left over at the end of a season—from the manufacturer or importer, usually at a bargain; he sold them to a wholesaler, or possibly directly to a retailer.

The commission merchant did not own the goods; he was simply an agent of the manufacturer and received a commission depending on the amount of his sales. Like the jobber and the full-service wholesaler, however, he had the goods physically in his warehouse and thus could deliver them.

The broker, on the other hand, had no warehouse and no goods that he could deliver, although he received a commission. Many a broker's office was said to be "in his hat"; he simply brought large-scale sellers and buyers together.

By 1910 there were about 1¼ million retailers and wholesalers in the broad sense, of whom perhaps 175,000 were wholesalers. There were in this period four types of marketing channels, depending on the product, which varied in the number of middlemen involved. The first and longest, involving products such as hardware, included a manufacturer, a jobber or commission agent or broker, a wholesaler, and a retailer before the product reached the hands of the customer. The second eliminated the jobber or commission agent or broker. The third cut out the wholesaler and would involve, say, department store or variety store purchases from a manufacturer. In the fourth, even the retailer dropped out, and the manufacturer dealt directly with the consumer: selling a locomotive to a railroad company would illustrate this situation. Because the various middlemen developed largely out of the needs of the new industrial age, the public did not always understand their contributions and sometimes resented their share of the selling price of the merchandise.

Just as there were middlemen on the distributing side of merchandising, so also there were middlemen on the assembling side. Local buyers collected agricultural products and passed them up the line to city wholesalers, who sold them in turn to commission agents or directly to manufacturers. Agricultural cooperative marketing associations began to displace the commission agents toward the end of the century. A considerable part of the agricultural produce was marketed on the produce exchanges.

Produce Exhanges. Exchanges had appeared even before the Civil War and many more came into existence in the major cities afterwards. The New York Produce Exchange was established in 1862, the New York and the New Orleans Cotton Exchanges in 1871, and the New York Coffee Exchange in 1882. By 1910 numerous commodities were being bought and sold at auction on the various exchanges. The majority of these exchanges were "spot" or cash markets, but selling for "future" delivery had appeared on some of the larger exchanges. Before an exchange for a product could be established, several conditions were essential. There had to be a considerable year-round demand for the product; there had to be a dependable method of grading or classifying it so that anyone buying a certain grade would know what he was getting; and there had to be warehousing and storing facilities. The produce exchanges, by providing an ever-present market for these important commodities, introduced a greater degree of stability into the businesses using them. Where there were futures markets, the stability was even greater, because the buyer or seller knew what price he could figure on for any future date. And if, say, wheat or cotton were low-priced now but high-priced six months hence, it would encourage the storage of the produce now, to bring the two prices closer together and eliminate what might otherwise be a "feast or famine" tendency in the market. Like any form of business, however, the produce exchanges had their abuses. Many speculators "bet upon the price of grain" and a few endeavored to "corner" the market, sometimes with financially disastrous results to those using the exchanges as they were intended to be used.

REGIONAL SPECIALIZATION AND NATIONAL MARKETS

The internal trade of the pre-Civil War period had been characterized by many local markets, some regional specialization, and a noticeable interregional triangular trade. In the post-Civil War period improvements in transportation and a sharp reduction of freight rates had profound effects on the character of the internal trade. The number of local markets diminished, regional specialization increased sharply, shipments of goods crisscrossed the nation in almost every direction, and there were national markets for an increasing number of products.

Bulky, low-cost commodities and perishable goods continued to be limited to local markets. Building stone, sand, gravel are examples of one; truck gardening produce, milk and dairy products, of the other. As shipping costs fell, even these goods could afford longer journeys to market. The "milkshed' or area from which a large city might draw its milk became more extensive. Likewise, after the 1870s, refrigeration made it possible to ship meat, vegetables, fruits, and seafoods longer distances than had previously been possible.

Regional Specialization. Between 1860 and 1900 total production grew eightfold but total shipments by rail and water grew twelvefold; this is a clear indication of increased regional specialization. In the realm of agricultural specialization, the following developments are particularly significant. Twelve North Central states produced three-quarters of the grain in 1890 and most of it moved east rather than south. After 1880 Louisiana supplanted South Carolina as the nation's rice-producing state.

The livestock-raising sections were south and west of Chicago. Cotton continued to be the chief crop of the South but Texas was the leading state, with over a quarter of the total acreage.

As for regions specializing in certain types of manufacturing, Pennsylvania produced half of the country's iron and steel. Flour milling was located near the wheat fields, with Buffalo and then Minneapolis enjoying the leadership, and Duluth, Superior, St. Louis, Milwaukee, Chicago, and Toledo important also-rans. Cincinnati early gave way to Chicago in meat packing, another industry that remained near its source of supply. New England held its dominance in cotton textiles although the eastern South was making rapid progress. Half of the coal came from Pennsylvania, West Virginia, Maryland, and Ohio, and nearly all the anthracite coal from eastern Pennsylvania. Ohio, West Virginia, and Pennsylvania yielded five-sixths of the petroleum in 1900. The Lake states and the South led in lumbering, upper New England in granite and marble, and Pennsylvania, New York, and Ohio in Portland (artificial) cement. In 1900 somewhat over half of the population lived east of the Mississippi River and north of the Ohio. Thus most of these products moved in this direction, if they had not originated there. That region was also the manufacturing quadrant of the nation.

National Markets. The completion of numerous transcontinental railroads and the two-thirds cut in railroad freight rates between 1865 and 1900 made possible nationwide markets for many products. The existence of produce exchanges for numerous commodities, of trusts, of branded products, and of nationwide advertising are all evidence of national markets. National markets were one of the outstanding developments of the era. Without a constitutional prohibition of interstate tariff barriers, they would have been virtually impossible. Without national markets, the United States could hardly have taken advantage of the economies of large-scale production which did so much to give the American people a higher standard of living. Businessmen seemed to be paying progressively less attention, relatively speaking, to foreign trade; yet in an absolute sense, foreign trade grew substantially in this period.

16

FOREIGN TRADE

Although the foreign trade of the United States was by 1908 only one-ninth of its domestic trade, it was third only to that of Great Britain and Germany among the nations of the world. Between 1860 and 1914 merchandise imports and exports of the United States increased over sixfold, from $0.7 to $4.2 billion. They declined sharply during the Civil War, especially exports, but rose steadily thereafter until 1873, at which time foreign trade was double what it had been in 1860. Little progress took place in the depressed 1870s but by 1892, at the end of another period of growth, foreign trade had increased by one-half. During the Depression of 1893–1897, it declined somewhat and then once again embarked upon a period of growth, doubling itself by 1914.

Major Trends in Foreign Trade. The trends in foreign trade that were becoming apparent before the Civil War now became unmistakable. Exports consisted to a growing degree of manufactured products; imports were made up largely of semimanufactured goods, food, and crude materials. Europe remained of prime importance both as a market and as a source of imports. The United States relied increasingly on foreign shipping services and American tourists were already becoming commonplace in Europe. On balance the United States remained a debtor nation, but after 1900 it tended to become an important lender also. Nearly all these foreign trade trends were reflections of developments taking place within the country.

17

In 1860 cotton constituted some 60 per cent of all American *exports* and with tobacco, wheat, and flour amounted to 73 per cent. Manufactured articles and foods amounted to about 23 per cent; the chief ones were textiles, iron products, tobacco manufactures, and boots and shoes. By 1914 raw materials, crude food stuffs, and semimanufactures were 57 per cent of exports but manufactured articles and foods had grown in relative importance to 43 per cent of the total. The six chief exports in order of importance were cotton, machinery, petroleum and its products, copper and its manufactures, wheat and flour, and iron and steel mill products.

In 1860 manufactured articles and foods constituted 66 per cent of the nation's *imports*. These were chiefly wool and cotton manufactures. Semimanufactures, food, and crude materials made up the remaining 34 per cent, and the most important were sugar, coffee, hides and skins, and raw wool. Half a century later, imports of manufactured articles and manufactured foods had shrunk to 35 per cent of the total; only cotton manufactures were among the leading six imports and these were in sixth place. The categories of semimanufactures, crude foodstuffs, and crude materials now constituted nearly two-thirds of all imports. The leading five imports from the viewpoint of value were hides and skins, coffee, sugar, raw silk, and crude rubber.

Half of American imports came from Europe in 1865, and the same was true half a century later (Table 20-1). Canada as a source of raw materials had declined from 15 to 5 per cent, and southern North America, that is, Mexico, Central America, and the West Indies, had also lost ground. South America held to a steady 10 per cent, with Brazil's coffee and rubber making up a large part. Asia and other parts of the world now supplied the United States with 20 per cent of its imports; raw silk and to a lesser degree sugar and rubber were their main contributions.

Europe was the market for almost exactly 60 per cent of American exports both in 1865 and in 1914. There had been virtually no change in half a century in this respect. The changes had been in other markets. Exports to Canada had grown from 10 to 15 per cent of the total and those to Asia and the rest of the world outside America and Europe had doubled from 5 to 10 per cent. There was no change in exports to South America, which remained at a meager 5 per cent. Those to southern North America had fallen from 20 to 10 per cent.

Table 20-1
Percentage Changes in Origin of Imports and Destination of Exports of the United States, 1865 to 1910–1914
(to nearest 5 per cent)

Type of trade	Year	Europe	Canada	Southern North America	South America	Asia, Africa, etc.
Imports........	1865	50	15	20	10	5
Imports........	1910–1914	50	5	15	10	20
Exports........	1865	60	10	20	5	5
Exports........	1910–1914	60	15	10	5	10

SOURCES: U.S. Bureau of the Census, *Historical Statistics of the United States, 1789–1945* (Washington, 1949), pp. 250–251. Also, Louis Hacker and others, *The United States: A Graphic History* (New York: Modern Age, Inc., 1937), pp. 143–145.

International Balance of Payments. The comparison of a nation's merchandise imports with its merchandise exports is called its "balance of trade." Merchandise imports and exports rarely balance because in addition any nation buys and sells services, borrows and lends, and pays out or takes in gold. A table that takes into account imports and exports not only of merchandise but also of services, gold, bad debts, loans, and gifts is called a "balance of international payments." It must balance. A most important factor affecting the makeup of a nation's balance of international payments is the amount it has loaned or borrowed in the recent past. The United States had borrowed a lot over a long period of time. There are various ways in which a nation may increase its borrowings. For example, its people may import more than they export, or they may sell bonds to foreigners (which shows itself soon in an excess of merchandise imports), or many of its tourists may go to other lands where they buy the services of hotels and travel agencies. Also its citizens may hire more shipping services from others than they perform in return, or they may give to relatives and friends in other lands more than they receive, or they may buy insurance and financing services overseas. All these are imports: the merchandise is a "visible" import, the others are "invisible" imports. Throughout this period the American people owed more to people of other countries, especially to the English, than people of other nations owed to Americans. Moreover, the total indebtedness of the American people to the rest of the world increased in this period for all the reasons cited above, although the first ones were of greatest importance (see Table 20-2).

Table 20-2

Balance of International Payments of the United States, 1850–1914
(Dollars in billions, rounded to nearest 100 million)

Item	1850–1873		1874–1895		1895–1914		Total	
	Exports	Imports	Exports	Imports	Exports	Imports	Exports	Imports
Merchandise	6.6	8.1	17.2	14.7	32.1	22.9	55.9	45.7
Investments of capital	1.0	....	1.0	....	2.0	1.0	4.0	1.0
Tourists' expenditures	....	0.6	....	0.8	....	3.2	....	4.6
Payments on investments	....	0.9	....	1.9	0.8	3.8	0.8	6.6
Specie	1.4	0.3	0.8	0.7	1.2	1.4	3.4	2.4
Shipping freights	0.6	0.4	0.1	0.7	0.1	0.7	0.8	1.8
Immigrants' funds	0.3	....	....	0.4	....	2.9	0.3	3.3
Insurance, financing	....	....	....	....	....	0.6	....	0.6
Sale of ships	0.1	....	....	....	....	....	0.1	
Total	10.0	10.4	19.2	19.2	36.2	36.4	65.4	66.0

SOURCE: Charles J. Bullock, John Williams, and Rufus Tucker, "The Balance of Trade of the United States," *The Review of Economic Statistics*, Preliminary vol. 1 (Cambridge, 1919), pp. 223, 227, 231–232.

There are various ways in which a nation may pay off its debts and work toward a creditor status. Its people usually export more merchandise than they import, although the excess of exports could also take the form of "invisible" items. It did not in the case of the United States, however. From 1874 to 1914, American merchandise exports were larger than merchandise imports except in four years. The interest and amortized principal payments on past debts were responsible for most of the excess of merchandise exports after 1874. Another important development was that Americans were starting to lend large amounts to people in other parts of the world. (This may show itself in an excess of exports.) By 1914 Americans had loaned about $2.5 to $4.5 billion to various foreign countries, chiefly in the Caribbean area and to Canada.

Yet in 1914 American debts abroad still exceeded debts owed Americans by $2 to $4 billion.

Ports. New York remained by far the most important port in the entire nation; in fact, it handled somewhat over half of all imports and exports in 1860 and 60 per cent of them by 1914. New York had earlier excelled as an import port and continued to do so in 1914. However, by now New York had also taken first position as an export port from New Orleans, which lost its lead back in the Civil War. New York in 1914 handled half of the nation's exports, and her importing and exporting businesses were more nearly in balance. In 1860 New Orleans, Mobile, Boston, and Philadelphia, in about that order, had been New York's chief rivals in the matter of total imports and exports. By 1914 the order had changed and three new ports had appeared among this group. The also-rans were now Galveston-Houston, New Orleans, Boston, Philadelphia, Baltimore, and San Francisco in about that order. Galveston-Houston was primarily an export port with cotton the chief product, for Texas was the South's chief cotton-producing state. Boston was closest to New York in the matter of imports, receiving almost a fifth as many.

TARIFFS

In this era of keen competition and widening markets, alert leaders in major industries felt that the least they could do for themselves was to demand high tariffs to shut out foreign competition. It was difficult enough to keep their share against domestic competition. Circumstances played into their hands.

To help pay for the Civil War the government increased taxes both on goods produced within the nation and on those coming from outside. After the war, Congress removed most of the internal revenue duties but left the external ones in force. The Democrats, as they had done before the Civil War, favored lower tariffs and the Republicans higher ones. But now the Republicans were in office most of the time—forty-four of the fifty-four years between 1861 and 1914. The tariff moved steadily upward, with the exception of slight reductions for brief periods once a decade, in the 1870s, 1880s, and 1890s, until it reached its peak in 1897. Then it drifted downward until World War I (see Table 20-3).

Civil War Tariffs. With the departure of eleven Southern states in 1861 and the outbreak of war, the Republicans had both the opportunity and the best of reasons for increasing import duties. The Morrill Act of 1861 raised duties drastically from 21 to 36 per cent, higher than at any time within the previous 25 years. In 1862 Congress enacted a comprehensive set of excise or internal revenue taxes and a companion piece of legislation on imported goods. One congressman said, "We intended to impose an additional duty on imports equal to the tax which had been put on domestic articles," and another added, "If we bleed manufactures, we must see to it that the proper tonic is administered at the same time."[3] However, Congress needed still more taxes to finance the war and in 1864 imposed twenty-two new kinds. It felt obliged to impose similar duties on imported merchandise.

Efforts to Reduce Tariffs. As soon as the war ended, Congress began to remove the despised excise taxes but did not disturb their twins, the

Table 20-3
Tariff Laws, 1857–1913

Date	Name of law	Average ad valorem rate
1857	. . . .	21*
1861	Morrill	36
1862	. . . .	35
1864	War	48
1872	. . . .	39
1875	. . . .	44
1883	. . . .	40
1890	McKinley	48
1894	Wilson-Gorman	41
1897	Dingley	50
1909	Payne-Aldrich	41
1913	Underwood-Simmons	33

* Average ad valorem rate of duty collected on dutiable articles, starting first year after passage of act and taken, when possible, over three years. (Calculations by D. L. Kemmerer.)

SOURCE: *Statistical Abstract of the United States, 1891* (Washington, 1892), pp. 16–18; *ibid.*, 1924 (Washington, 1925), p. 424.

import duties. Thus, as Professor Taussig, historian of the tariff, has said, "The extreme protective system, which had been at the first a temporary expedient for aiding in the struggle for the Union, adopted hastily and without any thought or deliberation, gradually became accepted as a permanent institution."[4] Manufacturers were happy to see it that way; indeed, they worked hard to keep it. Their congressmen defeated an 1867 bill to reduce the tariff. In 1872, with virtually all excise taxes repealed, Congress at last cut duties 10 per cent on all protective industries such as "manufactures of cotton, wool, iron, steel, metals in general, paper,

[3] Frank Taussig, *Tariff History of the United States* (New York: G. P. Putnam's Sons, 1923), p. 162.

[4] *Ibid.*, p. 174.

glass, and leather." Simultaneously they abolished duties on tea and coffee—big revenue producers—so that the government would not be able to afford any more cuts on manufactured items. In 1875 Congress repealed the 10 per cent reduction to meet a Treasury deficit brought on by the Depression of 1873–1878. As soon as the depression ended, however, the government began to reap a $100 million surplus each year. To many people a tariff reduction seemed long overdue, but a protectionist-minded Congress did not view that prospect with enthusiasm. President Chester Arthur appointed a tariff commission, most of whose members were protectionists and whose chairman, John L. Hayes, was secretary of the Wool Manufacturers Association. The 1883 act reduced the general level from 44 to 40 per cent, but the protectionists eliminated a number of the bill's better features and resorted to some clever devices to raise duties that appeared to be lowered.

High-level Tariffs. Grover Cleveland, the first Democratic President after the Civil War, developed a keen interest in the tariff. Despite the counsel of his political advisers, he devoted to it practically all of his 1887 annual message to Congress. Not all Democrats favored a low tariff. Cleveland urged a drastic reduction in duties, especially in those on raw materials. The tariff was the central issue in the presidential election of 1888, and although Cleveland won a majority of the popular vote, he lost the election. Victory enabled the Republicans to enact the McKinley tariff of 1890, which boosted rates to about a 48 per cent average. The Republicans had pushed their advantage rather far. That, plus a panic, contributed to their defeat in 1892 and the reelection of Cleveland. His success, however, in reducing the tariff in 1894 was disappointing. There were several reasons for this. His victory at the polls had been a narrow one. There were some high-tariff Democrats, and Cleveland had to use up his major bargaining weapon—patronage rewards—soon after he took office, in order to repeal the Sherman Silver Purchase Act. The Wilson-Gorman Act of 1894 removed the duties on wool, cut rates on pig iron and tin plate, and reduced the average of all levies from 48 to 41 per cent. But Cleveland was still so dissatisfied that he let it become law without signing it.

The campaign of 1896 centered on the free silver question and not on the tariff, but when the Republicans won, they hastened to raise tariff rates. The Dingley tariff of 1897 was the high mark of the post-Civil War period: it raised the average of duties to 50 per cent.

Protectionists on the Defense. Another issue, the trust problem, now diverted public attention from the tariffs, until the public began to realize that the trust and tariff questions were closely related. H. O. Havemeyer, head of the sugar refining trust, frankly testified before the Industrial Commission in 1902 that "the mother of all trusts is the customs tariff."

Carnegie's huge fortune, which he had made in the tariff-protected steel industry, also illustrated the connection.

The Republican party in its 1908 platform promised to look into a revision of the tariff. The result was the Payne-Aldrich Tariff of 1909, which put the level of customs duties down to 41 per cent, about where the Democrats had them in 1894. Conservative Republicans, like Aldrich himself, resisted many of the reductions, but Republicans from Western farm states insisted, impelled by their constituents' growing fear of trusts. The new law made many insignificant reductions but left the important rates high. At least the advocates of protective tariffs were now on the defensive.

The split in the Republican party in 1912 enabled the Democrats, led by Woodrow Wilson, to win the election. The Democrats passed the Underwood-Simmons Act in 1913, which lowered duties to about 33 per cent, the lowest since just before the Civil War. The opponents of protection and of trusts never had an opportunity to see how their twentieth century experiment in low tariffs would work, for World War I broke out in 1914 and put an end to normal trade conditions. After the war the tariff was never again as burning an issue as it had earlier been, except possibly in 1930.

SUBSIDIES AND THE MERCHANT MARINE

Why tariffs were considered consistent with *laissez faire* and subsidies were not is impossible to justify. Perhaps the most logical explanation is that tariff-protected industries happened to be growing in power and those requiring subsidies, such as shipping or perhaps agriculture, were slipping. A subsidy is a payment by the government, out of tax moneys, to help pay the costs of some private industry. Governments sometimes subsidize essential industries that cannot meet foreign competition. In this era several nations subsidized their merchant marines, partly to encourage foreign commerce and partly because they felt it essential to have a merchant fleet in the event of war. But the United States gave its merchant marine little help. A laissez-faire philosophy prevailed, foreign trade was relatively less important to America than to other nations, and the prospect of war seemed remote. Yet if the American merchant marine was to hold its own with those of other nations, it needed a subsidy.

Decline of Ocean Shipping. The merchants engaged in foreign trade did not experience the growth in business enjoyed by other segments of the economy. While the value of imports and exports from 1860 to 1914 grew more than sixfold, the amount of trade carried in American ships fell from 66 to 10 per cent. Registered tonnage in foreign commerce decreased from 2,500,000 in 1861 to 726,000 in 1898. The Spanish-American War interrupted the downward trend, but total tonnage in 1914 was still only 1,000,000. Thus, from a world leader in ocean shipping, America dropped to a weak, second-rate contender.

The decline had begun before the Civil War, and the war itself made matters worse. The depredations of Confederate raiders like the *Alabama* raised Northern insurance rates and led many shipowners to put their vessels under foreign flags. Once there, American law forbade them to re-register later as American. Two general factors explain the further decline. One was failure to keep pace with the changing patterns in international shipping; the other was preoccupation with internal development.

The British had switched to steam power before Americans did. Their advantage became even more apparent after the opening of the Suez Canal in 1869. American sailing vessels could not operate through the canal. From this time on, European steamships took an ever-increasing amount of the world's trade away from American shipping concerns. The geographic orientation of trade routes shifted toward the Mediterranean Sea, leaving the United States somewhat on the periphery, although trans-Atlantic trade was always important.

Also great advances were being made in this period in the size, speed, comfort, and general efficiency of ocean steamships. Steel hulls were stronger and more buoyant than wooden ones, allowing for greater cargoes and more powerful engines. As a result, cargo-carrying capacity rose from about 4,000 tons in the 1860s to 20,000 tons by 1900. Increased horsepower and multiple screw propellers increased speeds. The British liner *City of Brussels*, built in 1870, crossed the Atlantic in less than eight days, steaming at 14½ knots. By 1900, express liners capable of making 24 knots reduced the crossing time to about five days. In general, the record crossing was reduced a day a decade from 1850 to the 1900s: the record fell from nine to four days. Most of the faster ships were used in passenger service, but tankers and refrigerator ships, along with improved freighters, contributed to the more efficient handling of ocean commerce.

All this meant that ocean vessels were becoming costlier. A first-class sailing vessel cost about $100,000 in America around 1865; steamships built of iron or steel were four or five times more expensive. Thus, the capital to operate a great shipping line ran into the millions of dollars. Ocean shipping became a large-scale industry, especially as customers demanded more regularized and dependable service. The English firms changed over to the corporate form after 1862, attracting more private capital because of the privilege of limited liability.

Americans failed to adjust to the changes in world shipping. They could not build iron and steel steamships as cheaply as the British, even had they wanted to do so. Just after the Civil War, England's metal-fabricating and engine-building industries were more advanced than those of the United States. Even more important, the British government did not hesitate to grant generous subsidies to its maritime companies. Consequently, United States shipping concerns could not compete profitably with the British. Construction costs were from 25 to 50 per cent higher in America, while operating costs averaged almost as much above the British levels. The United States' failure to develop a well-regulated, adequate subsidy policy was a major factor in the decline.

The Federal government gave only limited aid to two companies, beginning in 1864 and 1865. It granted $100,000 per year to the Brazil Steamship Company from 1864 to 1875. The inadequacy of the grant plus poor supervision led to failure: the company went out of business in 1893. The second subsidy went to the Pacific Mail Company to support an operation between the west coast and the Orient. The amount was $500,000 annually from 1865 to 1872, at which time the sum was doubled. For somewhat different reasons, this subsidy also did not enable the American line to succeed. Meanwhile the subsidized companies of various European nations were forming "conferences" or international shipping monopolies, dividing up the business and assigning "fighting ships" to undercut the rates of independent lines and drive them out. American shipowners were too weak financially to force their way into these conferences and could not compete against them.

Owners of capital, some of which had come from the New England shipping industry, found more remunerative employment in manufacturing, railroading, mining, and land development after the Civil War. Along with capital, the best managerial talent likewise turned its attention to the interior. Ironically, some American capital flowed into foreign shipping lines, indicating that there was no absolute shortage of funds. J. P. Morgan organized the International Mercantile Marine Company in 1902 and purchased the largest private fleet of ocean liners in the world. The company operated 136 ships with a registry of more than a million tons, but only 12 per cent of the ships carried the American flag; 85 per cent were registered in England and 3 per cent in Belgium. The Morgan concern did not succeed financially: it was overcapitalized because of the excessive prices it paid for its various properties in 1902. The experience shows, however, that a well-designed shipping policy might have saved the merchant fleet, if the government had desired, since capitalists would most certainly have invested in a profitable venture.

From a purely economic point of view, the decline of the merchant marine was not especially regrettable. The United States could produce cotton and later machinery cheaper than other nations of the world; other nations could produce coffee, sugar, raw silk, and rubber and sail ships cheaper than Americans could. This is a sound basis for trade. The chief economic objection was that Americans had to deal with a foreign shipping monopoly whose rates might have been more reasonable if this country had had a stronger merchant marine. That, however, would have cost the American taxpayer dearly. The real disadvantage was military—when the United States entered World War I and had to send troops and supplies overseas, it had an inadequate merchant marine and had to depend on England's.

CHAPTER 21

Labor's Problems and Progress

The change in industrial organization that had begun before the Civil War was carried much farther in the period before World War I. It had a profound effect on the workers in a number of ways. As more and more industries moved out of the handicraft stage and into the factory stage, the workers lost personal contact with their employer. Formerly he had worked at the bench or forge beside them or at least he was well known to all of them. Now he devoted an increasing amount of his time to administrative or selling problems and moved in a different social circle. The factory system meant more workers and the breakdown of production into more specialized operations. These required less training to learn, and consequently a growing number of the workers were only semiskilled. Yet it should be kept in mind that industrial technology not only destroyed the need for old skills but also created the need for new ones. While the Ford assembly line replaced skilled mechanics with semiskilled workers and some mere bolt tighteners, the coming of the automobile also created the need for many new skills in making, installing, and repairing complex plant equipment and in repairing cars in countless garages across the country.

Increased output meant that the factory owner had to turn the marketing of the final goods over to merchant middlemen whose function it was to convert the goods into cash as quickly as possible: a rapid turnover meant greater profits for everyone. The middlemen in turn played competing manufacturers against one another because the retailers were playing competing middemen against one another. From the customer back up the line, everyone was seeking to buy at a lower price. The result of this drive for lower prices, so far as the manufacturer was concerned, was that he endeavored to reduce wage costs in one fashion or another. If an outright wage cut was impossible, he might achieve the same end in other ways such as a speeding up of operations under the name of efficiency, the introduction of a new faster-moving machine with simultaneous cuts in piece rates, and the substitution of semiskilled workers for skilled ones or of machines for semiskilled workers. After the Civil War, a laboring class developed in America as workers became increasingly aware of the need to defend themselves against these pressures.

The United States was shifting rapidly from a nation in which there were more independent farmers than persons of any other occupation to one in which the wage earner, whether in a factory, store, or railroad, predominated. By voluntarily leaving a run-down farm to take a job in a factory town, even a dismal town, many a farm lad was bettering his standard of living in terms of earnings. Soon after 1910 the number of persons engaged in manufacturing exceeded the number in farming. Throughout this whole period the inflow of immigrants from Europe, nearly all without capital, added to the ranks of the working class. Although many of these came to America in the hope of rising out of the laboring class and some succeeded, a great many carried with them the European belief that such a rise was impossible. By the start of the twentieth century there was a distinct wage-earning class in America. These people had given up any thought of becoming employers and were content to accept wage-earning status and to try to improve their incomes as workers. This change is evidenced in the attitude of the twentieth century college student whose chief interest at graduation time is who will give him a job. In the early part of the nineteenth century most young men had expected to make their own jobs, probably as farmers. By the end of the century they had come to depend on some other person's capital and initiative to provide them with a job.

Another reflection of this class feeling was the progress of unions. They had begun before the Civil War, but they were local in character and rarely survived a depression. By 1914 a significant minority of American workers (7 per cent) had unionized, the larger unions were national in scope, and they were accepted. Also, they had survived several depressions, and strikes had become common occurrences. Employers too had long ago banded together, although their organizations were less known. The economic conflicts of the two groups called attention chiefly to the problems and aspirations of the laboring class, which was looked upon as the "underdog." Yet the laboring class far outnumbered the employers, and in a democracy that is important since the majority determines what shall be the law. Labor made great economic progress in this period, partly because of union organization. More important, however, were industry's technical progress and efficiency and the individual energies and skills of the workers. These produced the greater output necessary to pay higher wages and to pay for better working conditions as well. It is significant that nonunionized workers, who far outnumbered unionized workers, made substantial wage and other gains although, in general, they did somewhat less well than union members.

NATIONAL UNIONS

5 National unions appeared in this era. The main reason was that transportation had so improved that markets were nationwide for many products. That meant that stoves manufactured in Albany, New York, and in Detroit, Michigan, were not stopped by high transportation costs from competing against one another almost anywhere in the nation. Since the stove molders in Albany were unionized and those in Detroit were not, the Albany manufacturers had to pay higher wages and so were at a disadvantage in selling their product. In time, the Albany stove molders suffered from the fact that their employers' business was not doing as well. The remedy for the Albany stove molders' union was to see to it that the stove molders in Detroit and in as many other competing places as possible were all unionized.[1] These locals should all join in a national organization and exact as nearly as possible similar wage and working conditions everywhere. Five significant national labor unions or groupings of them grew up. In the history of each is to be found one or more lessons about the efficacy of various types of labor organizations. Their length of life is a reasonable gauge of their success.

The National Labor Union. The first of these national unions was founded in 1866 by William H. Sylvis, an iron molder and treasurer in 1859 of the short-lived Iron-molders International Union. Sylvis helped to pull together a national trades assembly of representatives of various local, state, and national unions. They consisted chiefly of workers in the building trades, iron foundries, machine shops, and shoemaking. By 1868 Sylvis was president of the union and its membership was said to number 600,000, but after his death in July of 1869 the union began to disintegrate and the Panic of 1873 swept it away. The union was deeply interested in various political and social reforms such as tenement house reforms, Greenbackism, adult education, and government lands for genuine settlers only. It also espoused labor reforms such as an eight-hour day—partly to relieve unemployment—arbitration of labor conflicts, rigid enforcement of the apprentice system, and encouraging cooperatives as an alternative to the wage system. The union had its own journal in 1869, *The Workingman's Advocate.* The organization received some help from Congress in obtaining an eight-hour law for Federal employees, and it won a similar law in six states, without means to enforce it. This union achieved nothing of lasting consequence except to be the first large national union. The chief lesson to be learned from its experience was that unions should not expect to make great progress, at least at this

[1] Selig Perlman, *History of Trade Unionism in the United States* (New York: The Macmillan Company, 1929), p. 109.

time, by seeking reform legislation. The next national union devoted greater attention to achieving economic goals.

The Knights of Labor. A Philadelphia garment cutter named Uriah Stephens organized the Knights of Labor in 1869 as a secret society. Considerable uneasiness was caused when the appearance in public places of strange hieroglyphics, including five stars ★★★★★ standing for the union's name, would bring hundreds of workmen together. Originally intended to protect the members, the secrecy caused so much misrepresentation that the Knights dropped it in 1878. Thenceforth its membership grew more rapidly. It became the best-known labor union of its era and Terence V. Powderly, who became its chief officer in 1878, was believed to possess great authority. By 1885 the union had two great accomplishments to its credit: it had survived the long depression of 1873–1878, and it had won a strike on the Wabash and Missouri Railroad against that redoubtable capitalist, Jay Gould.

One of the Knights' major aims contributed to the organization's downfall. The Knights wanted above all to abolish the wage system, something which people today take so much for granted that it is difficult to conceive of any serious group of men wanting to do away with it. But 150 years ago most people worked for themselves, and 90 years ago the wage system was still young. Many men resented having to submit to shop discipline, having to work a stipulated number of hours, and receiving modest wages whereas the employer took seemingly generous profits and lived apart. All these were humiliating to men who thought of the "good old days" as the period when employer and worker toiled side by side, took time to go fishing if they wanted, and shared their troubles and gains. The Knights stated that they wanted "to secure to the workers the full enjoyment of the wealth they create, sufficient leisure in which to develop their intellectual, moral and social faculties, all of the benefits, recreation, and pleasures of association." Their solution was to establish workers' cooperatives whose profits would be distributed equitably among the workers. They said they opposed to use of strikes.

The Knights' other aims are easier to understand. Among them were weekly pay days, mechanics' lien laws, equal pay for men and women, prohibition of child labor before the age of fourteen, and better measures to protect health and safety in mines and factories. Especially important was an eight-hour day "so that the laborers may have more time for social enjoyment and intellectual improvement and . . . reap the advantages conferred by the labor-saving machinery. . . . " To benefit the working public in a more general way, the Knights urged such reforms as the establishment of a bureau of labor statistics, reserving the public lands for the actual settlers, swift and equal justice in the courts, and the substitution of greenbacks for national bank notes.

Membership in the Knights of Labor was open to anyone who worked, whether he were employee or employer, with a few remarkable exceptions. Forbidden entry were lawyers, bankers, stockbrokers, professional gamblers, saloonkeepers, and (up to 1881) physicians. The fact that employers might join is evidence that some employers still did toil beside their employees and that the wage system was by no means yet taken for granted. To the Knights, all workers should belong to "one big union." The strength of the skilled should be used to improve the status of the unskilled, and the unskilled should be mobilized so that their competition would not hurt the skilled.

The organization of the Knights was cumbersome. The lowest unit was the local assembly, usually made up of about a dozen workers largely of one trade. Above this level the basis of organization was geographical and not by trade. The district assembly came next, in which numerous trades were represented; it had complete authority over the locals. Above that was the general assembly, the "highest tribunal." When it was not in session, its power rested in the hands of the General Executive Board, headed by a Grand Master Workman. After 1878 Terence V. Powderly, an ardent idealist, succeeded Stephens to this office and held it almost continuously until 1893. By that time the Knights of Labor had lost their importance in the labor world.

It was in the middle 1880s that the Knights exercised their greatest influence. Between 1880 and 1885 membership expanded from 28,000 to 100,000 and then in 1886 it mushroomed to an estimated 700,000. It has often been said that the success of the strike against Jay Gould caused this, but recent researches indicate a quite different explanation. There were high hopes that the labor unions might be able to obtain an eight-hour day for the workers. The organization that soon would become the American Federation of Labor was pressing for an eight-hour day much more than the Knights were. Nevertheless, the Knights were better known; according to Powderly, many laborers joined the Knights who did not know the difference between the two organizations. When the eight-hour movement collapsed and the hopes of hundreds of thousands of workers were dashed, the fair-weather membership of the Knights vanished as quickly as it had come.[2] There were other important reasons, as well, for the Knights' decline.

1. Many failures occurred in the cooperative enterprises of the order. Some 200 cooperative ventures were undertaken, chiefly in cooperage, shoemaking, and mining, the best-known being a coal mine at Cannel-

[2] D. L. Kemmerer and Edward Wickersham, "Reasons for the Growth of the Knights of Labor in 1885–86" in *Industrial and Labor Relations Review* (Ithaca: Cornell University Press, 1950), vol. III, pp. 213–220.

burg, Indiana. The average investment was $10,000 and the financial losses were heavy. It was most discouraging to union members to see their hard-earned dues and their best efforts expended to no avail on these projects. In pre-Civil War days when workshops were small and most of the work was done by skilled craftsmen, cooperation was possible. After the Civil War manufacturing called increasingly for expensive machinery, centralized control, large outlays of capital, and all the other accoutrements of large-scale production. Under such circumstances, cooperatives could not hope to compete and were bound to fail. The man at the bench who wanted a say in management had too little appreciation of the problems of a factory executive. His participation in mangement only ruined the business.

2. Despite their professed abhorrence of strikes, the Knights engaged in a number of large ones for which they were quite unprepared. This of course hurt them in the workers' eyes. Considerable blame for this falls upon the organization's officers, who often lacked a settled policy and showed poor judgment in exercising their large powers. Certainly the ease with which they called one sympathetic strike after another, with little regard to the strategic importance of the groups selected, did more harm than good.

3. The Knights' uncompromising attitude and sometimes violent methods also lost them public support. The sabotage connected with the Southwestern railroad strike in 1886 made an impression on the public mind second only to that of the destructive railroad strike of 1877, and this was merely the most outstanding of many Knights' strikes at this time. On top of that came the bomb-throwing episode in Haymarket Square, Chicago, during the eight-hour movement. Although it was not known who was responsible for the missile, eight anarchists were arrested for inciting the outrage. When one proved to be a Knight and his local assembly would not expel him, many persons condemned the whole order.

4. Most important of all was the breakdown of the feeling of solidarity among the different types of members. The district assemblies had too few really common interests; vague ideas of brotherhood and slogans of "an injustice to one is an injustice to all" were simply not enough to produce united action among men of widely varied crafts. Between the skilled and the unskilled, especially, there developed at times a positive animosity. The skilled workers realized that they were strategically more important in winning a strike than the replaceable unskilled workers and consequently resented sharing the gains if the strike was successful or were bitter if it failed. To this should be added the success of the compact craft unions outside the order in winning their strikes. It thus be-

comes apparent why after 1886 the skilled workers in both industrial and craft unions drifted more and more into the ranks of the new American Federation of Labor.

The American Federation of Labor. This union of unions was founded chiefly by Samuel Gompers, a cigar maker. The cigar makers were progressive from the nature of their trade, which offered much opportunity for discussion of the craft's problems. One problem of the day was what was the best way for labor to deal with management. For a time Gompers, who had grown up in London and early rose to leadership, espoused socialism, the European answer, but he soon gave that up. Then he watched with interest but saw the futility of the Knights' cooperatives in an industrial economy. Finally, he decided that the opportunistic business union offered the best hope of success. Accordingly, he determined not to oppose mechanization, for it was inevitable, and to employ the strike rarely and only when the union was prepared and the moment was otherwise favorable. He and his colleague, Adolph Strasser, had such success with their cigar-makers' union in the late 1870s that other unions began to look upon the cigar makers as a model union and to copy its methods. Gompers and Strasser had four outstanding rules. First, the national officers were supreme over the local unions. Second, they increased the amount of dues sharply to build up a real treasury for use during strikes. Third, the national officers had control of the fund and determined when to call strikes. Fourth, they began to offer sickness, accident, and unemployment benefits. The benefits made the men more willing to pay the heavy dues. Once they had paid very much in dues, they remained loyal to the union.

In 1881 Gompers and other leaders formed a loose organization called the Federation of Organized Trades and Labor Unions, comprising some 48,000 members. This is sometimes cited as the start of the American Federation of Labor. Actually, it was a rather weak grouping of unions which relied chiefly on legislation to achieve its ends. It was not until 1886 that the American Federation of Labor really came into being. At the outset some twenty-five trades were represented, including iron molders, miners, typesetters, furniture makers, carpenters, and joiners, and of course cigar makers. The federation grew to 200,000 in 1889, at which time the declining Knights claimed about an equal number. By this time the organization had enrolled most of the easily obtained workers. Also several major strike failures, such as the Pullman strike of 1894, together with hard times in the middle 1890s, made it difficult to attract additional members. Then between 1898 and 1904, the AFL membership mushroomed from 280,000 to 1,700,000, a sixfold increase in six years. This was precisely the period of most rapid consolidation in business, the high point of trust formation. It was also the so-called "honeymoon period" between labor and management. After that the union's growth slowed down; the AFL membership had reached only 2,000,000 by 1914. Doubtless the heavy inflow about this time of immigrants willing to work at low wages was one factor in slowing down the growth of the AFL. Perhaps the mounting resistance and hostility of employers was another. Much of the AFL's success must be attributed to the leadership of Gompers, who was president from 1886 to his death in 1924, except for one year—1894—when the socialist faction in the organization won the election.

The business sense of the AFL showed itself in the growing use after 1890 of written collective bargaining agreements. At last representatives of management and labor were working out together their agreements on wages, hours, working rules, and the like and writing them down.

The aims of the AFL resembled those of the Knights in a number of respects. They sought to unite working people to promote their common interests, by favorable legislation or otherwise. Both, for example, were in favor of the eight-hour day. But there were also important differences. The AFL was not opposed to the wage system, and it accepted the strike as a weapon that it must employ. By its skillful use the AFL hoped to increase wages, shorten hours, and better working conditions. The AFL was opportunistic and accepted the economy as it was, whereas the Knights had been idealistic and tried to remake the economy.

The AFL at first largely excluded unskilled workers; in fact, the organization was exclusive in other respects, keeping out women and Negroes as well. It gradually had to modify this viewpoint in an industrial economy in which semiskilled workers or even machine tenders could perform more and more tasks. Accordingly, unions organized along industrial lines, or amalgamated unions, that is, ones containing two or more related crafts, began to appear. One of the first industrial unions was the United Mine Workers, which adopted that form of organization in 1897. A chief fault of the AFL was its slowness to make this kind of adaptation to the changes in factory organization of the industrial economy.

In organization the AFL differed rather sharply from the Knights. The lowest unit was the local union, whose members were all of one trade, say, cigar making; then all the cigar-making locals were organized into one national union, and finally the American Federation of Labor united all the nationals. The system was modeled on that of the Federal government, with each national union playing the role of a state. True, there were city and state organizations, but they were of secondary importance and often temporary. The federation was thus merely a loose grouping of practically self-governing national or local unions, which were largely independent of one another. The members of one affiliated union might strike and those of another might continue at work in the same plant. Only matters of general interest came before the federation's officers. The authority was highly decentralized and the federation was held together largely by the recognition of each union's independence plus the assurance that the federation would admit no rival union of the same trade. This prohibition of "dual unionism" made national unions very loyal to Gompers and the AFL.

12 The AFL under Gompers seemed to profit from the mistakes of the Knights of Labor. For example, they did not attempt to make over the economy, they avoided cooperatives, they kept out of politics, they had as little as possible to do with unskilled workers, they struck only when the moment seemed opportune, and they endeavored to avoid violence.

The Industrial Workers of the World. One union became rather notorious for its violent efforts in behalf of the unskilled worker: that was the Industrial Workers of the World. It was founded in 1905 by Eugene V. Debs and Daniel DeLeon, both Socialists, and William D. ("Big Bill") Haywood of the radical Western Federation of Miners. Debs resigned after two years. It began with 14,000 members and rarely exceeded 50,000 because of the poverty of its supporters. It had a large turnover in membership, having issued 300,000 cards by 1916. The leaders believed in direct action and were opposed to arbitration, collective bargaining, trade agreements, or asking aid from political parties: their terms were unconditional surrender. They advocated a great general strike which would paralyze society and would cease only when control of the means of production had been turned over to the workers. Meanwhile, they practiced sabotage—destruction of property and loafing on the job—initiated boycotts, and conducted strikes. Internal dissensions weakened the IWW at an early date and its unpatriotic sentiments and methods wrecked it during World War I. Although never the serious rival to the AFL that the Knights of Labor had been or the recent and more moderate Congress of Industrial Organizations was to be, the IWW proved a useful stimulus. It mobilized and directed the strikes of unskilled workers in lumber camps in the Northwest, of migratory laborers in the wheat fields of the West, of miners in the Great Lakes and Rocky Mountains, and of textile workers in Eastern mill towns. The AFL realized their neglect of this stratum of labor and took some action to remedy the oversight. Thus the chief contribution of the radical organization was the attention that it brought the unskilled. Even here, however, success was short-lived because the IWW leaders refused to enter into trade agreements, and soon after their departure the gains were usually lost. Unquestionably its violence did the whole labor movement much harm in the eyes of the general public.

The Railway Brotherhoods. The best-known and most respected of large independent unions were the four Railway Brotherhoods. Oldest of these were the Engineers, who traced their origins to an organization to strike against the Baltimore and Ohio in 1854. This union had high standards of admission because of the physical, mental, and moral requirements exacted by the job. The union expected exemplary conduct of its members: it ousted thirty-six for "unbecoming conduct" in 1909. It pioneered in various types of insurance protection for its members and it has enjoyed high respect for its willingness to keep its contracts. The next oldest order was the Order of Railway Conductors founded at Amboy, Illinois, by conductors on the Illinois Central in 1868. This profession also required a high level of intelligence and integrity; the conductor is the captain of the train. The International Firemen's Union was founded on the Erie Railroad in 1873, and the Brotherhood of Trainmen began in September, 1883.

Types of Unions: Summary. All these unions may be classified as to structure or as to aims, and there are three sorts in each classification.[3] With regard to structure, there are: (1) the general labor union which takes in all skills, whether butcher, baker, or candlestick maker, and all degrees thereof—of which the Knights of Labor is an example; (2) the industrial union which seeks to organize all the workers in a given industry—of which the Western Federation of Miners, the United Mine Workers, and the IWW are examples; and (3) the craft or trade union which limits itself to a single occupation like cigar maker—of which many of the unions in the AFL and the Railway Brotherhoods are examples. Then with regard to aim there are also three kinds: (1) the welfare union, which has lofty ideals of social welfare—the Knights of Labor falls into this category because of its desire to abolish the wage system and to provide self-employment through cooperatives; (2) the revolutionary union with its hope of revamping the social order, by violence if need be—the IWW was of this sort; and (3) the business union, which seeks to benefit its own members by securing shorter hours, more pay, and better working conditions as opportunities arise—obviously the AFL and the Railway Brotherhoods fall in this category.

Certain truths concerning organized labor in this period stand out. None of the three unions which opposed the wage system lasted; the organizations enjoying the greatest success, the AFL and the Railway Brotherhoods, always accepted the wage system. Attempts to organize the unskilled usually failed, but unions were now able to survive major business depressions. They were also becoming national in organization

[3] Walter E. Spahr (ed.), *Economic Principles and Problems* (New York: Farrar & Rinehart, Inc., 1936), vol. II, pp. 277–278.

and scope. The period of most rapid and enduring union growth coincided with the great period of business consolidations: both labor and capital moved in the direction of monopoly at the same time. Only 3 per cent of the working force was unionized in 1900 and only about 7 per cent in 1914. Total membership in 1914 was 2.6 million workers. Besides the giant AFL, the four Railway Brotherhoods, and the colorful IWW there were numerous smaller independent organizations.

EMPLOYERS' ASSOCIATIONS

14

It would be surprising indeed if all this organization by labor had not called into being somewhat similar organizations of employers. An employer or a corporation had a great advantage in bargaining with the individual laborer or even with a shop union, but it was usually at a disadvantage in dealing with a well-organized and disciplined union. This was, in fact, one of the reasons for the success of early craft unions—they were bigger and better organized than the individual employer. There was, accordingly, only one course of action for employers to take: they must organize on a regional or national scale also. The employers in various crafts formed their national associations after the Civil War. In some cases they had already done this to promote the sale of their product, in which event these trade associations gave increasing attention to the problem of dealing with unions. In other instances, the employers' associations were formed from the outset primarily to deal with unions. Among the early associations were the National Potters Association (1875), the Stove Founders National Defense Association (1866), and the General Managers Association (railroads). In 1895 some of these, and other specialized associations as well, grouped together into a national federation of employers' associations called the National Association of Manufacturers. Thus the NAM was the employers' counterpart for the employees' AFL.

For a time some of these associations enjoyed considerable success in negotiating trade agreements with unions and in maintaining industrial peace, especially from 1898 to 1904. The high point in friendly and successful working relations between the two sides was the refusal in 1902 by John Mitchell, president of the United Mine Workers, to call a strike of bituminous coal miners before the expiration date of the old contract in order not to break faith with the employers. In time the employers became increasingly uneasy at the growing power of the unions and adopted a more aggressive attitude. Some hoped to crush the unions before it became too late to do so. The National Council for Industrial Defense, founded in 1907, contained 228 organizations. The aggressive employers' associations sometimes insisted on the "open shop" and refused to make trade agreements. But the growth of employers' associations did not prevent the growth of unions; on occasions it had the contrary effect.

WEAPONS OF LABOR AND CAPITAL

In the economic wars that took place between employees and employers, it would appear that the employers had the better equipped arsenal of weapons. Yet the refusal of the employees to be completely dominated, their dogged determination to have a larger slice of the economic pie, plus of course their vastly greater numbers, enabled them to gain ground despite the heavier firepower of the employers.

Before a strike actually began, the advantage lay largely with the employer. He could maintain an antiunion open shop and hire no union members. It was a rare union in this period that could insist on a closed shop—one in which only union members might work—and get it. The employer could make new employees sign an "iron-clad oath" or "yellow-dog contract," by which they agreed not to join a union and were subject to dismissal if they did. He might also have access to a "black list" passed around by fellow employers, giving the names of potential troublemakers, alias ardent union members. And he could keep apprised of any brewing difficulties through the reports of "labor spies." Whereas the employees had the power to strike, the employers possessed the lockout. A lockout occurs when the employer suddenly shuts down the plant and offers no employment for a period of time. An employer who senses that a strike is in prospect may call a lockout to upset the plans of the union and set the period of idleness to suit his own convenience. Finally, the employer held the initiative in hiring and in firing workers.

Once the strike had started, the contestants were more evenly matched. On the matter of advertising their point of view to the public, the unions relied largely on picket lines and boycotts, whereas the employers had greater access to newspapers. Few unions had large strike funds so as to provide the strikers with some economic aid while they were without wages, and this meant that there was a limit to the length of time the strikers could refuse to go back to work. On the other hand, the employer had a large investment at stake; every day of idleness meant lost profit opportunities, heavy overhead costs with no income to cover them, and probably lost customers. The employees might use social ostracism to keep their weaker-minded colleagues from returning to work, or resort to violence to prevent "scabs" (imported substitute workers) from taking their jobs and keeping the business going. Violence was illegal, for supposedly the right to strike was merely the right of workers to quit as a group to demonstrate to the employer how much he needed their services. The workers had no legal right to keep the employer from hiring substitutes. Just the same, violence often did accompany strikes, the strikers forcibly prevented "scabs" from keeping the plant operating, and the public sometimes sympathized with men seeking to protect their jobs. Most people, and especially the workers themselves, felt that a man had a sort of property right in a job that he had held for a long time—even though at the moment he might be on strike.

The employers more often had public opinion on their side, for the public was still not accustomed to strikes. A strike inconvenienced many people, and they blamed it on the aggressiveness of workers rather than on the refusal of the employer to make reasonable concessions. Still more important, after the Pullman strike of 1894 the employers used the injunction more and more. An injunction is a court order to refrain from causing damages which cannot be made good afterward, or to perform some act by way of correction. It is a preventive order and stands in contrast to a damage suit, which is for injuries already suffered. Failure to heed an injunction is contempt of court and may result in a prison sentence.

The Pullman strike was probably the most significant strike in this entire period, because it was the first major strike suppressed by means of the injunction. The history of the strike is revealing. The Pullman Palace Car Company built an apparently model town outside Chicago, but the workers claimed that the landscaping was an advertising stunt and that rents were higher and accommodations poorer than in a nearby town to which they dared not move lest they lose their jobs. The year 1894 was a depression period and, although the company had cut wages, it had not cut rents, so that the men sometimes received but $1 to $6 cash for two weeks' work. The recently formed American Railway Union organized several locals. When three of the committee who had presented the men's grievances to company officials were discharged, the men struck. Other affiliated unions followed in sympathy and refused to handle trains hauling Pullman cars. Such trains generally contained mail cars too. Other unions' support of the Pullman strikers was balanced by the aid brought to the Pullman Company by the General Managers' Association, representing twenty-four railroads serving the Chicago area. As the strike spread, hoodlums seized the opportunity to rob, pillage, and burn property. Governor John P. Altgeld of Illinois said he could handle the situation but President Grover Cleveland called out Federal troops to protect the mails. The General Managers' Association got a sweeping antilabor injunction from a Federal court ordering the American Railway Union to cease interfering with the mails, with interstate commerce, or with the business of the twenty-four railroads. Unable to comply, the union's officers, notably the president, Eugene V. Debs, were arrested and the strike was soon broken. Debs served a six months' prison term.

In the generation following the Pullman strike, the injunction became one of the most devastating weapons at the disposal of employers. Courts sometimes took the attitude that the employer had a right to carry on business without interruptions that might interfere with his ability to fill orders. They then enjoined boycotting, picketing, and even striking because of the loss of income or other property damage caused. The social philosophy of the judge determined how sweeping the injunction was. For years labor's attempts to outlaw the use of the injunction were unsuccessful; probably no legal device came to be more hated and feared by labor leaders. They felt that it had repeatedly barred their path when they attempted to better the lot of the workingmen.

Labor leaders were also much disturbed to find the courts were able to use the Sherman Antitrust Act against them. In 1901 the United Hatters of North America tried to unionize the plant of Dietrich Loewe in Danbury, Connecticut. The company resisted, a strike ensued, and the union instituted a nationwide secondary boycott of the company's hats—that is, they urged all union members not to buy the Danbury company's hats. Loewe and his partners thereupon sued the 191 members of the local union as a combination in restraint of trade under the Sherman law, and the Supreme Court upheld the company.[4] Damages and costs amounted to some $250,000; the 191 members had to sell their homes and draw on their life savings to pay off this staggering penalty. The episode, called the Danbury Hatters' Case, made an indelible impression on union leaders. When Congress passed the Clayton Antitrust Act in 1914, it inserted a clause, at labor's urging, intended to exclude the use of antitrust laws against unions. This was called labor's "Magna Carta." However, the Supreme Court interpreted the clause so narrowly that it did not help the unions much.

LABOR'S PROGRESS

Labor unions were able to benefit the workingman in two basic ways: one was by the political pressure that they exerted to obtain legislation favorable to the laboring man; the other was by economic pressure, through strikes, to win higher wages or better working conditions.

Labor Legislation. The competition from immigrant labor made it difficult for unions to organize in the early 1880s, or once organized, to maintain discipline on the occasion of strikes. Low-cost immigrant labor threatened the wage scales of native Americans, and immigrants served

[4] *Loewe v. Lawlor*, 208 U.S. 274 (1908).

as "scabs." The Knights of Labor was largely responsible for the congressional act of 1885 outlawing the importation of contract laborers.

Most labor legislation, however, sought to protect laborers against unsafe or unhealthy working conditions, or against being forced to accept harsh terms of employment. Such legislation appeared first in the Northeast where experience was the longest: it began by protecting children, women, and persons engaged in hazardous occupations.

Child labor was the most urgent problem. Between 1880 and 1910 one out of every six children ten to fifteen years of age was employed. The

FIG. 21-1. Child labor in an American coal mine, 1903. (*Courtesy of U.S. Department of Labor.*)

peak census year was 1910 when nearly two million children, or 18.4 per cent, were employed.[5] This handicapped their education and injured the healthy growth of a large number. (See Fig. 21-1.) Even before the Civil War, four states had made some effort to limit child labor, but after the war Massachusetts took the lead. By two acts, in 1866 and 1867, its legislature forbade factories to hire children under ten and limited the working time of children to no more than ten hours a day. The laws also provided for factory inspection and required a minimum amount of schooling for the child workers. In the 1870s and 1880s the Knights of Labor and the AFL agitated against child labor. During the early years

[5] Harry A. Millis and Royal E. Montgomery, *Labor's Progress and Problems* (New York: McGraw-Hill Book Company, Inc., 1938), p. 423.

of the twentieth century many state legislatures passed child labor laws, most of them prohibiting employment of children in certain hazardous occupations. There was also a movement for a Federal child labor law but it did not reach the statute books until 1916; even then the Supreme Court declared it unconstitutional. The most effective type of child labor law was compulsory attendance at school, but it was less successful in this era than one might have supposed. By 1890 some twenty-five states had compulsory education laws for children under about fourteen, but these required attendance only for two to three months a year. Only two states, Massachusetts and Connecticut, enforced their laws very effectively.

Whereas children constituted about 5 per cent of the total labor force, women made up between 15 and 20 per cent. There were remarkably few occupations in which some women were not to be found working alongside of men. Women were most numerous in 1890 in such occupations as servants, factory workers, agricultural laborers, teachers, and laundresses. Within the next twenty years they appeared in great numbers as stenographers and store clerks, but they withdrew somewhat from agriculture. It is significant that in 1910 one-quarter of all women workers were married. The social dangers in this situation should be clear. Women do not have the physical strength of men, women who are bearing children should not be doing heavy work, and women who are away from home all day cannot take care of their growing children.

Women thus needed protection against exploitation by industry. The New Hampshire legislature had realized this as early as 1846 and imposed a ten-hour law for women in industry, and Massachusetts did likewise in 1874. The Federal government was slower to recognize these truths, as were also states to the west which had industrialized at a later date. The Illinois Supreme Court said in 1895, "sex is no bar under the constitution and the law" to endowing women with the "inalienable rights of liberty and property which include the right to make her own contracts." That meant a contract on unfavorable terms because she was helpless to do any better. Therefore, it did not seem proper for the legislature, under the guise of exercising its police power, to limit her exercise of these rights unless it could find a "reasonable connection between such limitation and the public health, safety, or welfare." By the turn of the century more legislatures and courts saw the connection. The Nebraska Supreme Court declared in 1902, "Women and children have always to a certain extent been wards of the state" and although "the employer and the laborer are practically on an equal footing, these observations do not apply to women and children." Then in 1908 the Federal Supreme Court in *Muller v. Oregon*[6] upheld an Oregon law limiting to ten the working hours for women in mechanical establish-

[6] 208 U.S. 412 (1908).

ments, factories, and laundries. In 1910 the Illinois court reversed its earlier decision. In 1915 the Federal Supreme Court upheld a California eight-hour law for women.[7]

Women needed protection in other ways also. In general, they entered less skilled occupations, many were merely seeking to supplement the family income, and most of them expected to remain employed only a few years of their life. Rarely did they join labor organizations. In some occupations they were less productive than men, although in others requiring great attention to detail, they were more effective. In any event, they nearly always got a lower rate of pay; this was owing in large part to their poorer bargaining position. Yet little effort was made to enact minimum wage laws for women and virtually none to obtain equal pay for equal work.

Male workers received little attention or special protection in this era. The American worker was a self-reliant person: this was one of the sources of his effectiveness. The chief legal protection that he had or sought was factory safety legislation. By 1900 half of the states had such laws together with inspection provisions to see that they were carried out. Factory laws provided such safeguards as that there be adequate air space, that working conditions be sanitary and safe, that certain kinds of machines be caged, and that lighting be sufficient. In 1898 a change took place which promised greater protection for workers in dangerous occupations. The state of Utah had passed a law limiting the number of hours that miners should work underground. The Federal Supreme Court upheld it (*Holden v. Hardy*) as a proper exercise of the state police power.[8] However, when the State of New York some years later endeavored to limit the number of hours per week in a bakery, the Federal Supreme Court ruled (*Lochner v. New York*) that bakeries were not hazardous places of work and therefore bakers did not require special attention.[9] Nevertheless, the employee was all the while gaining ground in the matter of compensation for industrial accidents.

Newer legislation and court rulings required the employer to assume greater liability for accidents than previously. Under the common law, as it had developed in the nineteenth century, an employee had an infinitesimal chance of recovering damages from his employer. The employer had three chief defenses: (1) that the employee knew the dangers of the occupation and assumed the risks when he took the job; (2) that the employee himself was at least partly responsible for the accident; and (3) that a fellow worker had been responsible and damages should be recovered from him. Moreover, if the employee died, his widow might

[7] Millis and Montgomery, *Labor's Progress*, pp. 528–529.

[8] 169 U.S. 366 (1898).

[9] 198 U.S. 45 (1905).

be told that any right of action expired with her husband. But even assuming the employee got past all these and several more defenses, it would require a long, expensive lawsuit at the end of which his lawyer's fees might devour most of the damages. The first attacks on this system were made by the states. Georgia in 1856 and Iowa in 1862 abolished the fellow-servant rule for railroad accidents; Colorado was the first to eliminate the defense altogether; and by 1910 twenty-three states and the national government had laws covering employers' liability. Finally, in 1912, in the *Second Employers' Liability Cases,* the Supreme Court upheld a Federal statute making railroads engaged in interstate commerce liable for accidents to employees.[10] It seemed highly unjust to ask a single employee to bear the costs, economic as well as physical, for an injury he may well have been unable to prevent. Legislatures and courts deemed it far better to assess the employer and let him pass it on to the customer as one of the costs of the industry. This was called the "doctrine of liability without fault." Other employers eventually had to accept these and other costs and restrictions.

Changing Attitudes of the Courts. Some indication has been given already of the hesitancy of the courts to accept social welfare legislation. It is of course the judges' interpretation that makes the law what it is. In general, the judges, and especially the judges in higher courts, were men who had been successful lawyers. That meant that they had probably devoted much time to advising corporations and to protecting the business interests of their clients. Their acquaintances, their experience in court, their sympathies (if only as a result of habit), their knowledge of the law, all tended to make their interpretations of the law and of the Constitution favor the employers' viewpoint.

Legal counsel for employers relied heavily upon the first clause of the Fourteenth Amendment in opposing social welfare legislation. This stated, "Nor shall any state deprive any person of life, liberty, or property, without due process of law." The original intention of the clause was to prevent Southern states from depriving newly freed Negro slaves of the civil rights accorded to them following the Civil War. But corporation lawyers early gave this clause an additional interpretation. According to law, a corporation was a legal or artificial "person." "Liberty" meant an individual's liberty to make his own contract even though he could do so only under disadvantageous conditions. "Property" meant also the enjoyment of income from property, for without income, property would have little value. "Without due process of law" meant in a legal and reasonable manner. "Reasonable" in turn usually meant not contrary to established custom. Thus the clause meant to the corporation lawyer and to the sympathetic judge listening to him, "No state legislature shall deprive any

[10] 223 U.S. 1 (1912).

individual of the liberty to make the best contract that he can, even if it be under disadvantageous conditions, nor deprive any corporation of the customary enjoyment of income from its property by enacting a law that is unreasonable because it oversteps the bounds of custom."

Shrewd lawyers made use of the due process clause of the Fourteenth Amendment to oppose hour and wage laws on the ground that they infringed the worker's freedom of contract. Their concern for the preservation of his civil rights sometimes caused wry smiles. Likewise, using the due process clause, they opposed efforts at rate regulation of grain elevator or railroad rates, installation of health measures and safety devices in factories, and all manner of prohibitions and regulations to promote the social welfare. Virtually every one of these interfered with someone's enjoyment of his income, if for no other reason than that they cost money and so reduced the profit margin. Until about the end of the century, the Federal Supreme Court followed these interpretations of the Fourteenth Amendment, except that the regulation of grain elevator and railroad rates was declared to be within a state's province after 1877.

Supporters of the workingman and advocates of social welfare legislation countered the due process clause with the argument that the police power of the state authorized it to protect the health and welfare of its citizens. Under this rather elastic power the state might invade a person's property rights or infringe on his freedom to make a contract with an employer if it were in the public interest to do so. The turning point was the already mentioned case of *Holden v. Hardy* in 1898, upholding Utah's law limiting miners' hours of work to ten. From this time on, the courts gave increasing weight in their decisions to the police power argument; they began to accept the due process clause argument with growing qualifications.

Wage and Hours Gains. Between the Civil War and World War I, the hours of labor were materially shortened. In 1860 the average working day was eleven hours; in 1890 it was ten hours; and by 1914 it was nine hours. Not all occupations gained equally in this regard. For example, workers in the building trades enjoyed a shorter than average workday; men in the steel industry worked longer than average hours—steel plants did not abandon the twelve-hour day until 1923.

His real wages should have interested the worker more than anything else. By real wages is meant what the worker can buy in goods or services for the money wages he gets. If part of his pay is, say, room and board, those too are part of his real wages. Only real wages really matter. Real wages cannot rise very much unless workers are producing more, for it is out of what they produce that the employer gets the money to pay his men. Since production was increasing in this period, it is not surprising to find real wages rising. According to Professor Alvin Hansen, who has made a study of real wages between 1860 and 1923, the chief gains were made between 1860 and 1890. Real wages rose 68 per cent, and this was despite a 33 per cent drop during the Civil War inflation. After 1873 money wages declined somewhat, but prices fell even more so that the workers' real wages increased. Between 1890 and 1913 money wages rose about one-third, but so did prices, with the result that real wages had not improved at the end of that twenty-three year period.[11] In general, rising prices often tend to rob laborers of the money wage gains that they have made because of increased productivity. Of course real wages of different occupations varied. For example, the unskilled suffered more in poor times than the skilled workers. Teachers made the greatest advances and were followed by farm laborers, salaried and clerical workers in manufacturing and transportation, and building trades workers in that order. The gains of teachers and farm laborers were long overdue, as both had been poorly paid in the previous generation. Wage earners in manufactures, public utilities and railroads, coal miners, postal employees, and unskilled laborers about held their own. Government employees, other than in post offices, and ministers were distinctly worse off, especially the former.[12] On the whole, the position of the wage earner was much better in 1914 than in 1860 whether he belonged to a union or not.

Relative Welfare of Organized versus Unorganized Workers. Union leaders and union members both believed that union membership benefited them materially. About 3 per cent of all workers belonged to unions in 1900 and about 7 per cent in 1914. Union men believed that their unions were largely responsible not only for the wage, hour, and welfare gains that they enjoyed, but also for those that their nonunion brothers enjoyed. This would be very difficult to demonstrate, although it is hard to believe that all their agitation and striking did not bring them some gains. In general, nonunion workers of the same occupation tended to receive lower rates of pay than union workers. On the other hand, there is strong reason to believe that worker productivity and worker scarcity were the prime factors in raising wage rates. It was pointed out above that in the post-Civil War period of rising real wages, teachers, farmer laborers, and salaried and clerical workers in manufacturing made the greatest gains. Unions were virtually nonexistent in these occupations. Next in order came persons in the building trades, wage earners in manufactures, public utilities and railroads, and coal miners, all of whom were to a considerable degree unionized. Trailing were unskilled workers, government employees, and ministers, all of whom again represent a relatively nonunionized group. In short, some nonunionized occupations

[11] Alvin Hansen, "Factors Affecting the Trend of Real Wages," *American Economic Review*, vol. 15 (March, 1925), p. 32.

[12] Millis and Montgomery, *Labor's Progress*, p. 102.

made greater progress than some unionized ones, and some made less. Advocates of unions would reply that all nonunionized groups would be better off if they unionized. Opponents would reply that any gains made by labor must be at someone else's expense, for the pie is only so big. If labor gets a bigger slice, others get a smaller one. Moreover, since labor got two-thirds of the pie anyway, there was really not a great deal more to be divided.

CHAPTER 22

The Overexpansion of Agriculture

Between the Civil War and World War I, agricultural production expanded enormously. Acreage in farm land more than doubled while farmers adopted equipment and techniques which raised productivity. This combination of new land and improved methods pushed output beyond the market demand for farm products. Thus, farmers suffered chronically from overproduction and declining prices. The underlying causes of the trouble in farming are not to be found in any one particular development; they appear, instead, in the several changes which took place within farming and in the national shift from a land of small farmers to a highly industrialized society.

EXPANSION

Extent of Growth. Growth of farming can be measured successfully in several ways. Population engaged in agriculture, number of farms, amount of land under cultivation, value of property used in farming, and income from agriculture are all useful in determining the magnitude of expansion. Table 22-1 indicates these quantitative changes. In respect to

Table 22-1
Expansion of Agriculture, 1860–1910

Year	Population on farms (millions)	Farm population, per cent of national total	Number of farms (millions)	Acres in farm land (millions)	Acres in crops (millions)	Value of land, buildings, implements, and livestock (millions)	Net farm income (millions)	Farm income, per cent of national total
1860	19	60	2.0	407	163	$ 8,000	$1,250	31
1910	32	35	6.4	879	347	42,000	5,600	22

SOURCE: U.S. Bureau of the Census, *Historical Statistics of the United States, 1789–1945* (Washington, 1949), pp. 95–100.

farm population, statistical data are largely inadequate for the years before 1900; however, the best sources estimate 19 million people on about 2 million farms in 1860. By 1910, 32 million persons lived on 6.4 million farms. Thus, the population on farms rose by 68 per cent and the number of farms more than tripled. Even so, the percentage of total population engaged in farming fell from 60 to 35.

Real and personal property and income from farming both increased substantially from 1860 to 1910. The value of land, buildings, implements, and livestock holdings rose from about \$8 to \$42 billion. Total acreage in farm land grew from 407 to 879 million; cropland increased similarly, moving upward from 163 to 347 million acres. Thus, farmers took up more land in 50 years than in the 250 years before 1860. Realized income from farming more than quadrupled; however, as a share of national income, it fell from 31 to 22 per cent. Hence, as in the case of population, the absolute increase did not keep pace with the national trends; agriculture fell behind other segments of the economy.

General Factors in Expansion. Much of the agricultural expansion was simply a continuation of the pre-1860 trends. National growth was so rapid after the Civil War that agriculture could hardly have failed to participate. Population tripled between 1860 and 1910 and farmers occupied a vast domain of virgin soil. The rise of the city and industrialization provided wider markets; better transportation facilities gave farmers access to distant markets both at home and abroad. Meanwhile, laborsaving equipment and scientific methods increased the productive power of the individual farmer.

TECHNOLOGICAL ADVANCEMENT

The Civil War stimulated the more widespread adoption of farm implements introduced before 1860. Wartime demands, plus the exodus of thousands of farm people to serve in the armies, forced farmers to utilize improved plows, reapers, threshers, mowers, and seeders and to substitute, where possible, animal and steam power for manpower. Greatest progress occurred in the production of small grains—a standardized product for which there was a mass market.

Grain Harvesting. The McCormick reaper had greatly increased the productivity of labor in grain harvesting by 1860. Subsequent inventions brought equally significant progress. A harvester, built and perfected by the Marsh brothers of De Kalb County, Illinois, in 1858 and 1859, had a platform large enough for two men to stand on and bind the cut grain. The Marsh harvester appeared commercially in 1864, and by 1870 farmers were buying about 1,000 annually. The Marsh machine enabled two men to do the work of four or five binders working on the ground;

furthermore, they accomplished it more easily. The next step in the harvesting of grain was the invention of a mechanical binder. Around 1873 or 1874, the Walter A. Wood Company sold twenty-five wire binders, attached to Marsh harvesters. Two mechanical "arms compress the bundle [of cut grain], while a third puts the wire around and twists or ties it, when it is thrown out by one of the arms and laid on the ground about 12 feet from the standing grain."[1] The wire binder dispensed with the services of two men and permitted the use of wider cutters, which further increased labor efficiency. Unfortunately, the wire binder's success in the field did not overcome other weaknesses. Farmers found the wire to be a nuisance, millers complained that pieces of broken wire ruined their machinery, and there were reports of cows having died from eating straw containing wire. Nevertheless, 20,000 of the machines were in use in 1878 when John Appleby patented his twine binder. Appleby's invention had gained almost universal acceptance by 1890.

A further evolutionary step was the combining of the cutting and threshing operations. California wheat growers were the first to adopt the process on a wide scale. Favorable climatic and topographical factors had encouraged the use of "headers" rather than harvesters in cutting California grain. The header removed just the heads of standing grain; an endless apron carried the heads back to a wagon. The grain was then stacked at a convenient location where it was threshed at the farmer's convenience. The big advantage of the header was that it eliminated the binding operation. But since grain had to be fully ripened before stacking, the header was not well suited to wheat harvesting in the more humid regions of the Mississippi Valley. Around 1880, a shortage of labor in California encouraged the adoption of the combined header-thresher. Its use spread slowly at first, but by 1900, combines accounted for about two-thirds of California's wheat crop. After 1889, a number of manufacturers adapted the combine to steam power. Large steam-traction engines, capable of delivering 110 horsepower, propelled combines cutting a 42-foot swath; such rigs threshed wheat for less than 25 cents per acre as compared to $1.75 for animal-operated combines.[2] (See Fig. 22-1.)

Mechanization greatly reduced the time required to harvest and thresh wheat. Before 1830, more than 60 man-hours were generally needed to produce 1 acre (20 bushels); in the 1890s, the time was cut to 15 hours in Illinois, 7 in the Dakotas, and to as little as 2.5 in California. This made possible wheat farming on a large-scale basis. Along the Northern Pacific Railroad in the Dakota Territory and in Minnesota, Oliver

[1] Leo Rogin, *The Introduction of Farm Machinery* (Berkeley, Calif.: University of California Press, 1931), p. 111.

[2] Reynold M. Wik, *Steam Power on the American Farm* (Philadelphia: University of Pennsylvania Press, 1953), p. 87.

Dalrymple managed wheat farms totaling 75,000 acres, with 30,000 acres usually in wheat. The farms employed 1,000 men, 800 draft animals, and 30 steam engines. The Dalrymple experience was duplicated in other parts of the country in the closing decades of the nineteenth century.

Steam Power. The use of steam in bonanza wheat farming suggested the wider substitution of steam for animal power. From 1870 to 1910, steam engines performed an increasing amount of farm work. By 1880, steam provided 1.2 million horsepower for agriculture, reaching a peak level of 3.6 million in 1910. The lighter gasoline tractor steadily replaced

FIG. 22-1. A combined header-thresher, powered by thirty-three mules and tended by five men, developed in the 1880s. (*Courtesy of Caterpillar Tractor Co.*)

steam power after 1910. For forty years, however, steam was the only successful substitute for animals. In comparison with draft animals, steam provided a single concentrated source of power which was economical when applied to large-scale operations. Furthermore, its speed was of great importance, especially in harvesting and threshing grain. Another advantage was that steam tractors did not require feed and care the year around. They consumed vast quantities of fuel and water during operations, but when the crop was in, the farmers had only to oil the engines and store them for the winter.

Steam power helped farmers build roads, saw lumber, and haul freight, but it achieved more success in threshing grain (see Fig. 22-2) and in plowing. By 1910, some 70,000 steam threshing outfits were in use. The giant rigs delivered 200 to 400 bushels of grain per hour, often totaling 4,000 bushels a day. Because of the scarcity and high cost of coal in the wheat regions, some of the engines burned a part of the threshed straw as fuel. In spite of the widespread use of steam engines for threshing purposes, few farmers could buy their own machines; a large thresher cost about $4,000. Consequently, wheat farmers hired custom threshermen, who in turn hired their crews from the thousands of migratory workers who appeared each year at harvest time. Migratory labor was necessary because the farmer could not afford to employ twenty-five to forty men, except for the brief harvesting season; a 5,000-acre farm required only two or three men for the rest of the year. The migratory workers started in the winter wheat regions in the early summer and

FIG. 22-2. Threshing with steam power. (*Courtesy of U.S. Department of Agriculture.*)

moved northward into the spring wheat belt, sleeping in hastily contrived shelters and hiring out to the highest bidder in each new area. The wheat growers became equally dependent upon the owners of the steam threshing machines and upon the migrants. At times, threshing costs rose to such high levels that some farmers formed cooperative "threshing rings" to buy their own threshers and furnish their own labor. Whatever the arrangement, the steam thresher became somewhat of an institution in the American West between 1885 and 1914. Wheat farmers viewed with mixed emotions its replacement by the internal-combustion engine.

Steam plows never reached the degree of popularity achieved by steam threshers. Early experiments, dating from the 1850s, generally failed because the first steam plows were impractical. Most of them were slow and cumbersome, breaking down or miring in the fields. By 1900, large farms in the West used improved steam tractors to pull breaking or gang plows. Yet in 1910, only one in 20,000 acres was plowed by tractors. Steam plows were too expensive for the average farmer to buy ($4,000 to $5,000) and their size and cost of operation further discouraged their use. Steam plows required from 1,500 to 5,000 pounds of coal and 12,000 to 25,000 pounds of water for a ten-hour day. Fuel loss was enormous—98 of each 100 pounds of coal was wasted. Even so, in terms of efficiency, steam plows compared favorably with horses, since farm animals were idle most of the year.

Other Improved Implements. Improvements in other farm implements continued after 1860 as farming spread over the Great Plains. There, farms were generally larger than in the Middle West and the East, and gang plows and sulky plows eased the physical exertion of farmers. The Northern plains required heavier, more efficient breaking plows to turn over the virgin buffalo sod. Also, the old brush and straight-toothed harrows proved inadequate on the plains; farmers adopted the disk-type, rotary harrow in the 1870s. This implement became of paramount importance in seedbed preparation on gigantic wheat farms. Another improvement, the spring-toothed harrow, gained wide acceptance in the East and the Middle West in the 1880s. Inventors perfected seed drills, which, when used in large-scale planting, effected a great saving of labor. Horse-drawn broadcast seeders also relieved farmers of the monotony of hand sowing, although grain still had to be covered with a harrow or cultivator. A combination cultivator-broadcast seeder, introduced in the 1860s, became popular in some regions.

Dry Farming and Irrigation. Improved farm technology extended into the nonmechanical realm. Farmers had to overcome the limitation imposed by insufficient moisture in the semiarid (10 to 20 inches of precipitation annually) zones to the west of the 98th meridian. Farmers invaded these dry regions during the Civil War and enjoyed a few years of good crop yields. After the destruction of the grass cover, the land quickly lost its accumulated water. Searing summer temperatures and high winds evaporated moisture with great rapidity. The farmers' frontier expanded and contracted in rhythm with nature's wet-dry cycle. By the early 1870s and again in the 1880s, dry spells forced a reversal in the Westward Movement. Frontier farmers painted slogans on their covered wagons like "In God We Trusted, in Kansas We Busted" as they retreated eastward before the harshness of the weather. Hardier souls remained to conquer nature.

Two methods of farming brought relief. The first to be used widely was dry farming. Dry-land tillage was not new in the 1880s, having been practiced in ancient times around the Mediterranean Sea and by the Mormons in Utah in the 1850s. It gained wider acceptance, however, with the perfection of more suitable tillage implements after 1880. A pioneer in dry-farming techniques was Hardy W. Campbell, a wheat farmer in the southern Dakota Territory. Campbell began experimenting in 1882; by 1894, when he moved to Nebraska, he had developed a "system." Campbell's system rested upon an elementary principle: where rainfall is slight, allow no loss of moisture from the soil. To achieve this objective, Campbell disk-harrowed his topsoil into a fine dust mulch to a depth of about 4 inches. This served two purposes: the mulch readily absorbed falling rain and it prevented subsoil evaporation. Campbell had observed that, without the mulch, moisture rose through tiny pores or capillaries and passed off into the air. Thus, after each rain, he harrowed his fields as soon as possible to retain the new moisture. After a year of intensive cultivation by such a method, the land could be planted to a crop. Campbell claimed that winter wheat yielded three to four times as many bushels per acre, when produced in this manner.

Campbell's system, while widely adopted in Nebraska, Colorado, and Wyoming and even to an extent in remote places like Germany, Hungary, Spain, and South Africa, did not escape harsh criticism. For one thing, dry farming exposed the topsoil to wind erosion. Also, the system required too much detailed attention for most farmers. Irrigation, either from wells pumped by windmills or from natural streams, was more reliable, albeit more expensive; after 1900, it became more commonplace.

The Mormons had experimented successfully with irrigation in Utah in the late 1840s, but there was little irrigated land elsewhere before 1890. In that year, the United States had some 3.7 million acres under irrigation, including the flooded rice fields in Arkansas and Louisiana. That was less than 1 per cent of the nation's farm land. Through the Desert Land Act (1877), the Carey Act (1894), and the Newlands Act (1902), the Federal government offered encouragement and financial aid to irrigation. Irrigated acreage rose to 7.7 million in 1900 and to 14.4 million by 1910. The scarcity of water and the expense of putting water on the land imposed serious limitations. Mountain streams provided a good source for the small areas which they served, but their use could not be greatly extended. Irrigation from rivers supplied only the bottom lands. Some areas pumped water from deep wells, but excessive use depleted the source after a time. Furthermore, ditches, reservoirs, wells, and pumps were costly; few farmers could afford to install their own equipment and facilities. This explains the more widespread use of irrigation after the Federal government began to finance the projects.

DISSEMINATION OF KNOWLEDGE

An important aspect of agricultural expansion was the increase in scientific farming. Many agencies, both public and private, disseminated scientific knowledge. Agricultural societies, journals, state and Federal departments of agriculture, public and private secondary schools and colleges, and interested business corporations are among the many institutions which helped spread the gospel of better farming. The Grange, established in 1867, was the outstanding agricultural society in the post-Civil War era. At regular meetings of thousands of local granges, members exchanged ideas, read papers, and heard lectures on scientific farming. The pre-1860 agricultural press continued to emphasize efficiency and progress in its journals. Older papers like the *Prairie Farmer* and the *Southern Cultivator* were joined by new ones such as *Colman's Rural World*, *Wallace's Farmer*, and *Campbell's Scientific Farmer*. Greater public education and social intercourse allowed the journals to reach more farmers. In the last half of the nineteenth century, many states created state boards of agriculture, some of which matured into departments of agriculture. Georgia created the first full-fledged department in 1874, with its commissioner elected directly by the people. Eleven other states created similar departments by 1907. These boards and departments publicized and encouraged improved practices.

The Federal government did very little to promote better farming until the Civil War. Then, in 1862, two important things happened. First, Congress passed the Morrill Act, by which it donated to each state 30,000 acres of land for each senator and representative; the state had to use the proceeds from the sale of the land to establish and maintain colleges of agriculture and mechanical arts. The act and subsequent amendments gave to the states nearly 11 million acres, an area about twice that of New Jersey. Secondly, Congress established a Department of Agriculture, largely at the urging of the United States Agricultural Society. The new department had a commissioner of agriculture rather than a secretary. In 1889 Congress elevated the head of the department to cabinet status. The department's primary duty was to acquire and disseminate new and useful information. The work included study of plant and animal diseases and experimentation in agricultural chemistry.

Another step forward came in 1887 when Congress passed the Hatch Act to establish experiment stations. The measure granted $15,000 annually to each state for the purpose of setting up stations. The Adams Act doubled the appropriation in 1906, permitting more elaborate testing. Then, in 1914, the Smith-Lever Act authorized Federal-state collaboration in establishing the county agent system. Starting with an annual appropriation of $10,000 per state, to be matched by the states, Congress increased the appropriations for seven years until the total for all states reached $4,580,000. The county agents, working closely with state institutions, offered free, practical instruction and demonstrations to farmers and their wives.

A seldom recognized influence in the dissemination of better farm knowledge is the role of corporations. Railroads, especially the land grant roads, encouraged better and more profitable agriculture in their territories. They pursued a policy of enlightened selfishness: prosperous farm communities meant prosperous railroads. By 1914, most of the major lines had agricultural development departments, each of which spent thousands of dollars annually to stimulate farm output. Many companies, such as the Great Northern and the Burlington, maintained model farms. They also operated special educational trains to publicize and encourage the adoption of superior methods. Concerns like the International Harvester Company engaged in much the same type of promotional activity.

REGIONAL DEVELOPMENT

12 The trend toward regional specialization which had developed before 1860 continued after the Civil War. Farmers in the Northeast (New England and the Middle Atlantic states) increasingly stressed dairying, truck farming, and fruit growing. The North Central region[3] produced grain and livestock. The South supplied cotton, tobacco, sugar cane, and rice as it had before 1860. West of the 98th meridian a new farming region specialized in wheat and beef cattle. Pacific coast farmers turned to fruit growing and truck farming after adequate transportation made it feasible to ship fresh produce out of the area.

The Northeast. The pre-1860 decline of Northeastern farming continued in the late nineteenth and early twentieth centuries. Improved farm acreage decreased only slightly for the region as a whole, but it fell by about a third in New England. There, farm abandonment reached sizable proportions as the former occupants moved to the cities or to Western lands. Many New England farms became summer homes for professional or business people in the cities. Farmers who chose to remain on their land had to adopt new methods and become more specialized if they were to succeed. Maine potatoes, Connecticut broad-leafed cigar-wrapper tobacco, and Vermont maple syrup became famous. Dairy products from New England and New York supplied metropolitan markets, as did vegetables and fruits from orchards and truck gardens.

The North Central States. The region drained by the Upper Mississippi and its chief tributaries, the Missouri and the Ohio, comprises the agricultural heart of North America. The eastern portion had already become a great cereal and livestock kingdom, specializing in wheat, corn, beef, and pork. The half century after 1860 witnessed further concentration. The chief developments were the westward movement of centers of

[3] This is virtually synonymous with "Middle West." It includes twelve states: Ohio, Indiana, Illinois, Michigan, Wisconsin, Minnesota, Iowa, Missouri, North Dakota, South Dakota, Nebraska, and Kansas.

wheat and corn production, further mechanization in grain farming, large-scale dairying, and pen feeding of cattle.

The North Central region, which produced 55 per cent of the nation's wheat in 1860, increased that percentage to 74 by 1910. The geographic center of production moved westward from Indiana to west-central Iowa. The leading states in 1860 were Illinois and Indiana, but by 1890 Minnesota had taken the lead. North Dakota assumed the leadership in 1910, while Kansas, producing hard-winter wheat, steadily gained prominence. By the end of the era, wheat production centered in the Mississippi-Missouri River Valleys.

The center of corn production also shifted westward between 1860 and 1910, although to a lesser degree. It moved from southern Indiana to west central Illinois, with Ohio, second-ranking state in 1860, surrendering its place to Iowa. Illinois, first in 1860, remained the leading state in 1910. Further evidence of the westward shift is the fact that the North Central states *west* of the Mississippi River produced only 15 per cent of the nation's corn crop in 1860; those same states produced 39 per cent of the total in 1910. By then, Ohio, Indiana, Illinois, Iowa, Missouri, Kansas, and Nebraska produced 63 per cent of the national output and clearly constituted a "corn belt."

Little of the corn entered commercial channels directly. As in the earlier era, it was either marketed on the hoof or in jugs. About 85 per cent of it went to fatten hogs and cattle. Open-range production of livestock in this region ended about the time of the Civil War as settlement pushed the cattle frontier onto the Great Plains. In the last third of the nineteenth century, the corn belt developed as a stock-fattening region; farmers bought Western cattle and fed them in pens until ready for market. By 1910, the North Central states had 45 per cent of the nation's cattle, compared to about 33 per cent for the entire Southwest and West. Hog raising was tied even closer to the corn belt; the North Central states produced over 60 per cent of United States' swine in 1910. Iowa, the leading state with more than 7.5 million hogs, had 3½ times as many as all the Northeastern states combined.

Dairying moved westward with grain and livestock. The growth of cities around the Great Lakes created a demand for milk, butter, and cheese. New York, the leading cheese-producing state in 1860, gave way to Wisconsin. By 1910, Wisconsin produced nearly half of the national total. The twelve states of the North Central region had about half of the country's dairy cows in 1910. Wisconsin, Iowa, Minnesota, and Illinois were the leading states in milk production, while Michigan ranked fourth in butter making behind Wisconsin, Iowa, and Minnesota.

13 **The South.** Southern agriculture suffered badly from the Civil War. The war bankrupted most Southern planters, destroyed the slave labor system,

and wrought destruction on livestock and crops. It left the people demoralized and destitute. The job of rebuilding Southern farming was long and painful. Land values fell to a tenth of the prewar level and buildings and farm implements were either demolished or in bad repair. An instable labor supply and an extreme capital shortage further handicapped reconstruction.

The free status of Negroes complicated the labor problem. At first, the ex-slaves maintained a futile hope of receiving "40 acres and a mule" from the Federal government. Facing starvation, many of them soon wandered back to their old plantation homes and became "wards" of their former owners. In some cases, they worked for wages, but the arrangement satisfied neither Negro nor landowner. After several years of experimentation, the share-cropping system appeared to be the best solution to the problem. It gave the "most constant supply of submissive labor at the lowest cost."[4] Under the system, the Negro (and poor whites) agreed to produce a crop for the landowner. The agreement generally provided for the division of the proceeds from the crop into three equal parts—one for labor, one for land, and one for operating expenses and supplies. The laborer, or share cropper, received two-thirds if he provided the operating expenses as well as the labor. In parts of the South, tenant farming, rather than share cropping, prevailed. Under tenancy, the farmer signed a lease calling for a fixed rent in cash or produce. Only occasionally did the fixed-rent system invade the cotton belt, however.

Control of the share croppers depended to a large degree on the credit system. Shortage of working capital in the South led to the development of the crop lien, which bound agricultural workers to the land. This method of granting credit became prominent after 1865, as local merchants began to supply the funds needed for farming. The storekeeper gave credit for groceries, seed, fertilizer, and other supplies to the farmers who in turn pledged their current or future crops as collateral. Because the risk to the merchant was high, interest rates ran as much as 40 to 110 per cent—usually concealed in the exorbitant prices of goods bought on credit. Merchants dictated to their debtors the amount and kind of crops. They always demanded more and more cotton because cotton was easily marketed and was difficult for the farmer to conceal from the merchant, especially in the many localities where the merchant owned the cotton gins. Abuses under the system were widespread, although the merchants rarely got rich from their somewhat shady dealings. They learned to juggle their account books so as to keep the farmers

[4] Fred A. Shannon, *The Farmer's Last Frontier* (New York: Farrar & Rinehart, Inc., 1945), p. 87. Most of the material in this section on the South comes from this source.

in debt and tied to the land; they did this by adjusting the prices of cotton or of goods sold to the farmer.

The share-cropping and crop-lien systems were inherently bad. They perpetuated the bondage of the Negro and drew the poor whites into a similar relationship. They accentuated the South's dependency upon the one-crop system of farming and contributed heavily to the oversupply of cotton. They further resulted in inefficiency and waste. Finally, they retarded the development of a landowning class of small farmers in the South. Contrary to much popular opinion, the Civil War did not bring a revolution in the size of Southern farms. The average size of farms did not decline; rather, a change in ownership took place in which absentee owners acquired land which they then put under share-cropping and tenancy arrangements.

Under the new labor and credit systems, the South steadily increased its cotton production from 1866 to 1914. It was not until 1877 that it equaled the 1859 record crop of 4.5 million bales, however. By 1914, output reached 16 million bales. Meanwhile, overproduction and poor quality forced prices to disastrously low levels. From about 30 cents per pound in 1865, cotton fell to 4.6 cents in 1894. Not until World War I did the price climb much above 14 cents.

Other Southern crops remained much the same as in the prewar years. Farmers curtailed tobacco production greatly during the war and by 1870 total output had reached only 270 million pounds—only two-thirds of the 1860 crop. But just before World War I, the United States produced 1,250 million pounds. Southern states grew 85 per cent of this, about half of which entered foreign trade. Rice growing moved from the Atlantic coast to the Mississippi Delta in Louisiana, which turned out about 75 per cent of the annual crop after 1900. Louisiana continued to grow sugar cane, although the 1861 record output was not matched until 1893. Cereal production increased except in the cotton belt, where corn growing had almost vanished by the 1880s and 1890s. New lands in Oklahoma and northern Texas, planted to wheat and corn, accounted for the over-all increase. Little change took place in livestock raising, except in Texas. The Southeastern seaboard states increased truck farming and fruit growing after better rail transportation and refrigerator cars gave access to Northern markets.

The Great Plains and the Far West. Beyond the 98th meridian, in the semiarid and arid zones, wheat growing and livestock raising predominated. On the Great Plains, the cattleman made the first agricultural use of the land, but the railroads brought in the pioneer farmer and the sheepherder. The plow and barbed-wire fences closed an epoch on the Plains around 1900. Before that time, however, ranchers built a Cattle Kingdom, never equaled before or since.

The Cattle Kingdom originated in the diamond-shaped area of Texas south of San Antonio and east of Laredo on the Rio Grande. There, wild Spanish cattle had roamed freely for centuries before the Civil War. Even before 1860, Texans drove herds of 2,000 or 3,000 head overland to markets in St. Louis and Chicago. The war interrupted these long drives, but soon afterward trail herds moved northward again. Profits tempted many to enter the business: Eastern cattle prices ranged from $30 to $40 a head, while Texan longhorns, in unlimited quantities, could be rounded up for a tenth as much. As settlement extended westward from Missouri, the long drives to St. Louis and Chicago gave way to shorter trips to the railhead at Sedalia, Missouri. Missouri and Kansas farmers effectively resisted the trespassing herders and forced the trails farther west. Joseph G. McCoy, a large livestock shipper in Illinois, suggested a solution to the marketing problem in 1867.

McCoy proposed to establish a site where Eastern buyers and Texan drovers would meet and from which rail transportation eastward would be available. He arranged with the Kansas Pacific Railroad and the Hannibal & St. Joseph Railroad to ship live cattle to Chicago over their lines. Then he laid out the first "cow town" of Abilene, Kansas. He built stockyards and loading chutes and by 1871, almost a million and a half head of Texas longhorns passed through the town. An oversupply of cattle at Abilene in the early 1870s caused some of the owners to winter their stock on the surrounding plains. Within a few years, the industry spread across the free grasslands. A great cattle boom followed, which lasted down to the mid-1880s. As buffalo vanished from the Plains, the Indians no longer blocked expansion. Cattle grazers usurped the open ranges from Texas to Montana, driving longhorns northward to stock the grasslands of the Plains. Speculation in cattle grew rampant, leading to the overstocking of the ranges early in the 1880s. By the summer of 1882, the boom reached a peak. Capital poured into the industry from the East and from Europe. Then, disaster struck. A Texas drought in 1883, falling prices in 1884, and the tragic winters of 1886–1887 ended the boom. Fortunes were lost and the industry changed sharply in nature. After 1887, fenced pastures, better-grade cattle, improved care and feeding, and more railway transportation revolutionized the Cattle Kingdom. The industry became a business rather than an adventure.

The day of the cattleman left a rich heritage. It saw the full development of the management of cattle on horseback, the growth of institutions like branding, roundups, and vigilante committees, and opened and publicized the Great Plains to permanent settlers. Even so, the Cattle Kingdom was never the chief cattle region of the country. The North Central and the Eastern states always had more of the national total. Even at the peak of the boom, in 1880, the Plains area had only 28 per cent. "The East did a large business on a small scale; the West did a small business magnificently."[5]

On the Pacific coast, fruits and vegetables came to rival wheat as important commercial crops. The west coast states produced a variety of fruits, with grapes (for wines, especially), peaches, prunes, apricots, pears, and cherries the most important. Citrus fruit became more important toward the close of the era. Potatoes, cabbages, cauliflowers, and tomatoes were among the vegetables shipped eastward in the 1890s. The region had important livestock and dairying industries as well.

FARM DISCONTENT

Despite the greater output, greatly improved technology, and higher income the farmers' *share* of the national income declined steadily. They reacted to this inequality by organizing social, economic, and political bodies to seek relief. They complained enough to bring about extensive government regulation of business before 1914. The causes of the agrarian movement, some of which were not apparent to the farmer himself, can now be traced clearly.

Causes of Farm Discontent. An underlying cause of farm discontent was the changing economic order. The Civil War ended the dominance of the country by farmers and brought forth an industrial society. Farmers were not prepared for the transition. Yet steadily their influence diminished. By 1870, for the first time, less than half of the population lived on farms. Agriculture's share of the national income diminished as manufacturing, transportation, trade, and finance took on greater importance. In terms of absolute income and wealth, farm families made substantial gains. Per capita farm income (in current dollars) rose from about $70 in 1859 to approximately $112 in 1900; wealth per capita similarly increased from $416 to $755. When these increases are considered alongside the deflation of the era, it is obvious that *real* farm income was much higher in 1900 than in 1860. But farmers did not view their changing economic status in this light. They saw instead that farm income declined from 31 to 21 per cent of the national total between 1859 and 1900, while farm wealth fell from 40 per cent of the national total in 1860 to 16 per cent in 1900.[6] Much of the farm discontent resulted from this relative loss of income to nonfarm sectors of the economy. Meanwhile, large-scale mechanized farming transformed successful agriculture from a "way of life" to a business enterprise. Industrialism became a giant whirlpool which

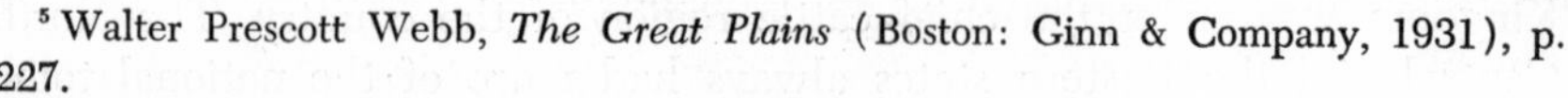

[5] Walter Prescott Webb, *The Great Plains* (Boston: Ginn & Company, 1931), p. 227.

[6] Shannon, *Farmer's Last Frontier*, pp. 353–354.

sucked everything into its vortex; only those farmers who could become efficient managers of their business could survive the ordeal.

Farmers tried to escape the whirlpool of industrialism. They demanded relief from monopolistic practices by railroads and manufacturers and from the deflation which followed the Civil War. They blamed middlemen for much of their trouble, singling out grain-elevator operators, railway companies, farm-implement manufacturers, and banks. Farmers in-

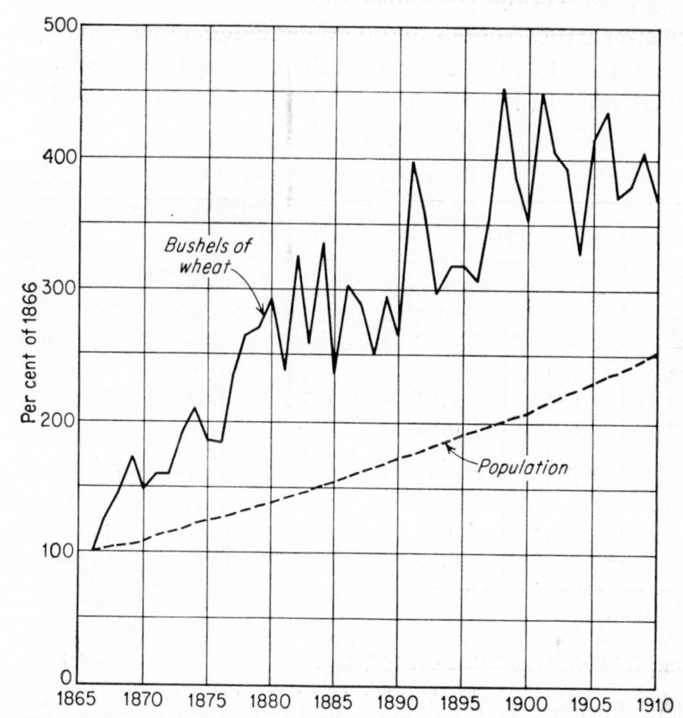

CHART 22-1. Indexes of population growth and wheat production, 1866–1910 (1866 = 100). (*Adapted from U.S. Bureau of the Census, Historical Statistics of the United States, 1789–1945, Washington, 1949, pp. 26, 106.*)

sisted that the Federal government stop the deflation, which especially burdened those who had gone into debt to expand production during the war. Farm prices fell by 1896 to about one-fourth of the 1865 level, while nonfarm prices dropped to about one-third. This meant that the purchasing power of a bushel of wheat or a bale of cotton declined, making it even more difficult for the farmer to get out of debt. Frequent droughts and other hazards of nature dealt additional damaging blows.

So much attention to external factors obscured the most basic trouble—overproduction of staple commodities (see Table 22-2 and Chart 22-1).

Agricultural expansion had caused production to outrun the aggregate demand for farm products. Accordingly, prices fell sharply and many farmers could not cover their costs of production. This is best illustrated in the case of wheat. In 1859, per capita wheat output amounted to 39.22 bushels; by 1879, the figure had risen to 53.79, and in 1889 it stood at 55.89.[7] When coupled with deflation, this increase reduced the price of wheat from $2.06 per bushel in 1866 to 49 cents in 1894. Other staples suffered a similar fate.

There are six possible solutions to the problem of overproduction. Two obvious ones are to (1) increase the demand, and (2) decrease the supply. Others are to (3) subsidize, (4) allow competition to eliminate the

Table 22-2
Crop Statistics, 1866–1914

Year	Wheat		Corn		Cotton	
	Million bushels	Price per bushel	Million bushels	Price per bushel	Thousand bales	Price per pound
1866	170	$2.06	731	$0.66	1,948	$0.16*
1870	254	1.04	1,125	0.52	4,025	0.12
1880	502	0.95	1,707	0.39	6,357	0.10
1890	449	0.84	1,650	0.50	8,562	0.09
1894	542	0.49	2,671†	0.21†	10,026	0.05
1900	599	0.62	2,662	0.35	10,124	0.09
1910	625	0.88	2,853	0.47	11,609	0.14
1914	897	0.99	2,524	0.64	16,112	0.07

* Estimated.
† 1896.
SOURCE: *Historical Statistics,* pp. 106, 108.

inefficient farmers, (5) cut costs of production, and (6) raise price through inflating the money supply.

Farmers were powerless to increase demand for or decrease the suppl of their products. Since the aggregate demand for farm products is rela tively fixed, little attention was given to expanding markets. On the sup ply side, if an individual farmer had reduced his output, it would no have affected the *total* supply of farm products. Each farmer's contribu tion to the national supply of wheat or corn was like one grain in a bushel basket: its addition or subtraction would pass without notice Hence, a single farmer would only suffer a loss of income if he cut hi output. One Kansas woman urged farmers to "raise less corn and mor hell," but beyond that recommendation, voluntary reduction in suppl

[7] Louis B. Schmidt, "The Internal Grain Trade of the United States, 1860–1890," *The Iowa Journal of History and Politics,* vol. 19 (April, 1921), pp. 196–245.

was basically out of the question. Only natural disasters or extreme governmental regimentation, which was contrary to the prevalent philosophy of the age, could have reduced output substantially.

The third alternative, subsidization, was equally unlikely. The political lip service paid to *laissez faire* precluded any financial aid to individuals in the late nineteenth and early twentieth centuries. The Populist leader, William Peffer, suggested that the Federal government make low interest loans to farmers, with commodities like wheat and cotton as collateral, which would have acted as a subsidy. No such aid was forthcoming, however. President Grover Cleveland demonstrated the general view when he vetoed a congressional appropriation of only $10,000 in 1887. The money would have allowed the United States Commissioner of Agriculture to purchase and distribute seed to farmers in drought-stricken Texas. Cleveland denied that the Constitution permitted the Federal government to relieve individual suffering through the use of public funds. He declared that "though the people support the Government, the Government should not support the people." Farm sympathizers justly accused the government of being inconsistent; it had given lavish subsidies to the land grant railroads and generous although less obvious aid to mining, lumbering, and manufacturing concerns through land laws and tariffs.

The fourth solution, that of letting competition eliminate the inefficient farmers and thereby eliminate excess production, was naturally unpalatable to farmers. Furthermore, it did not work in practice. Farmers managed to stay on the land, year after year, in spite of losses. They could nearly always raise enough food to avoid starvation. Consequently, the number of farms increased rather than decreased. The remaining two approaches proved to be the most practical at the time: much of the farmers' economic and political action was directed toward cutting costs and inflating the money supply.

The Granger Movement. The rising spirit of unrest among farmers crystallized in the late 1860s and early 1870s. It found a convenient vehicle for expression in the newly formed Patrons of Husbandry, or the Grange, as it was commonly known. A clerk in the Commissioner of Agriculture's office, Oliver Hudson Kelley, founded the Grange in 1867. Kelley got the idea while on an official tour to study conditions among Southern farmers. He observed their distressing economic and social plight and decided that a national organization of farmers would promote their social and intellectual advancement. Upon his return to Washington, he established the first chapter of the Patrons of Husbandry in that city. Together with six associates, Kelley drew up a ritual, following closely the organizational framework of the Masonic Lodge, of which he was a member. A major exception was the admission of women to full membership in the Grange. Kelley became the first national secretary of the Patrons. He was an energetic man—a friend described him as "an engine with too much steam on all the time"—and he worked endlessly toward the fulfillment of his dream of a strong national organization.

The first years were discouraging to Kelley. He resigned his government job and set out from Washington for home in Minnesota. He tried to establish subordinate granges en route, starting with Harrisburg, Columbus, Chicago, and rural Fredonia, New York. Only the last became an active chapter. He first achieved real success in Minnesota; there were thirty-seven active granges in that state by the close of 1869. Farmers in the Upper Mississippi Valley joined the Grange to promote their economic and political interests. After 1869, the organization experienced a mushroomlike growth, reaching a peak membership of 750,000 in 1874, made up of more than 20,000 granges. By then farmers had long since replaced Kelley's social and intellectual goals with economic and political objectives.

Economic Cooperation through the Grange. The Grangers sought to improve their economic conditions through cooperation. They tried to cut costs by taking over the middleman's function where possible. Local granges established cooperative stores, in which the members bought stock. The ventures rarely succeeded. Competition from regular merchants often squeezed out the Grange cooperatives; members did not remain loyal to their own organization when they could buy more cheaply elsewhere. Upon the failure of a Grange store, the merchants in the area generally raised their prices back to the old levels. Around 1876, the national Grange recommended the Rochdale plan of cooperative retail stores, based on an English system. The members of the Grange bought stock in the stores, which sold goods at regular prices rather than trying to undersell others. At the end of the year, after a small stock dividend, the store divided the remaining profits among the customers on the basis of purchases made during the year. The plan worked reasonably well in the East and South, but Middle Western Grangers basically ignored it. When the Grange turned toward marketing, they were more successful. Cooperative creameries and grain elevators in several states added to the farmers' profits directly through higher prices and indirectly through offering competition to existing businesses.

The least sensible and most tragic of all the Grangers' business ventures was the attempt to manufacture farm implements. Large manufacturers of plows and harvesting equipment consistently refused to sell to the Grange cooperatives at reduced prices. The Iowa Grange tried to overcome this problem by purchasing a harvester patent, and in 1874 it produced about 250 machines. The National Grange, blinded by this limited success, scoured the country for other patents and planned factories in several states. The scheme collapsed in 1875 with the failure of the Iowa harvester factory. The Iowa Grange, lacking business and manufacturing experience, turned out defective machines which broke down in the fields. Furthermore, much of their working capital went to defend patent infringement suits. When competitors began underselling the Grange, prices fell below the cost of producing the harvesters. The manufacturing project went under, bankrupting the Iowa State Grange in the process. The collapse injured the National Grange as well.

Political Actions. Politically, the Grange focused its primary attention on the questions of business monopoly, grain dealers, railway rates, and cheap money. Farmers believed that much of their trouble stemmed from unfair advantages held by private corporations—such as banks, meat packers, many manufacturers, and railroads. They attacked the monopoly power with a degree of success, helping to pass the Sherman Antitrust Act in 1890 (see Chapter 18). Through state legislatures, they brought railway and grain elevator charges under public control, resulting in the Interstate Commerce Act in 1887 (see Chapter 16). They campaigned vigorously for cheap money, first in behalf of Greenbackism and later in the cause of free silver (see Chapter 19). Actually, the Grange itself faded into insignificance after 1875, only 4,000 chapters remaining in 1880 out of the 20,000 in 1874. The failure of many business ventures and preoccupation with politics hastened the decline. The void thus created was filled by other organizations such as the Farmers' Alliance and the Agricultural Wheel; groups such as the Greenback and the Populist parties carried on the political fights. The farm protest was a major cause of the early twentieth century reform movement, Progressivism. It was the return of business prosperity in the late 1890s, however, that finally satisfied the farmers. From about 1896–1897 up to the business depression following World War I, the farmer's economic position was better than it had been at any time since the Civil War.

In spite of its business failures and its limited political success, the Grange succeeded admirably in certain respects. It taught the farmers the lesson of self-help and proved to businessmen that the farmer could lash out in protest. On the other hand, it gave the farmer more respect for the businessman. The many failures of cooperative enterprise showed the farmers that middlemen indeed filled a vital and useful function. Socially, the Grange helped to break down the dreadful isolation that had bred backwardness and superstition among rural people. It encouraged reading and public speaking on the part of many farmers, thus broadening them intellectually. In all, the Grange had an uplifting influence on the lives of hundreds of thousands of farmers.

SUMMARY OF PART THREE

The period following the Civil War and up to 1914 witnessed the settlement of territories acquired before the Civil War and a tremendous expansion in industry. Goods poured from the factories and fields in seemingly endless quantity. If business were to remain profitable, businessmen either had to find new ways of marketing these goods or else limit production. They did both. At first consumers could buy a greater variety of articles at lower prices. Later on they also found themselves faced with regional or national monopolies so powerful that they were quite unable to cope with them. They asked the government to step in. The various segments of the economy defended themselves in different ways.

Population tripled from 31 to 92 million in the half century between 1860 and 1910. The rate of growth was slowing down and a large proportion of the new population was immigrants. After 1882 the immigrants came from southern and eastern Europe instead of northern and western Europe. As always, they represented a cheap form of labor and were primarily useful in heavy, unskilled work in factories and railroad building. Other changes in the population were the marked tendency for people to live in the cities, the continued migration of people toward the West, and the tendency of the population to age. The median age rose from nineteen to twenty-five between 1860 and 1910.

Following the Civil War, which devastated parts of the South and freed the slaves, the seceded states had to rejoin the Union and to rebuild themselves economically. It was 1877 before the Union army withdrew entirely, and it was even longer before the South completed its economic reconstruction. Meanwhile, Congress admitted fourteen new states between 1863 and 1912. Most of them were in the West, each as large as Great Britain but sparsely populated. Nonetheless, population in the West grew more rapidly than in the East. Congress sought to encourage this by offering any citizen who had not fought against his country a 160-acre homestead virtually free if he would live on it for five years. Settlements under the law were disappointing, however, for the government simultaneously made it easy for large operators to acquire land cheaply in the best locations. Thus many settlers bought from speculators; those who bought from railroads probably fared the best. Pioneers on part of this frontier lived in sod houses instead of log cabins. Now that the United States had acquired all the territory between the 49th parallel and the Rio Grande, any new acquisitions had to be found elsewhere. It acquired Alaska from Russia in 1867, Hawaii in 1898, the Philippines, Puerto Rico, and Guam in 1898, and the Canal Zone in 1904. All this increased the nation's territorial extent by nearly a quarter.

Improved transportation was essential to reach and to develop much of the new territory. Between 1860 and 1910 railroad mileage grew from 31,000 to 240,000 miles and six transcontinentals were laid across the nation. Railroads made many improvements, too, such as steel rails for iron ones, a uniform gauge, improved car couplers and four standard time zones. Freight rates fell two-thirds between 1865 and 1900, which helped make the United States one national market for many products. Because of their heavy investment and hence high overhead costs, railroads were "natural monopolies." It was inevitable that they would exploit this opportunity and equally inevitable that governments would have to regulate them. At first the states did so with their Granger laws, and in 1887 Congress began doing so with the Interstate Commerce Act. An unsympathetic Supreme Court deprived the regulating commission of most of its powers, but starting in 1903 and 1906 Congress restored them, the Hepburn Act being the most important of the restorative acts. About the time that Congress imposed effective regulations on the railroads because they were transportation monopolies, they began to experience growing competition from lake boats, coastwise shipping, and pipelines. And even greater rivals of the future, automobiles and airplanes, were being born. Equally important improvements appeared in communication, such as the telephone and advances in the telegraph, postal service, and newspapers. All these knit the country closer together, made Americans more alike, and reduced the possibility of another civil war.

In manufacturing, the tendency was for more and more articles to be made in factories instead of by hand, and for the companies in almost every line to become larger and fewer. The cotton textile industry was losing its position of industrial leader, except in the South where it inaugurated a new industrial revolution as it had earlier in New England. Meat packing enjoyed national markets, thanks to refrigeration, and was a pioneer in the "disassembly" line and in the use of by-products. More and more industries, however, were depending for their raw materials on metals rather than on agricultural products. Steel became a veritable giant following the introduction of the bessemer process for making cheap steel, providing the nation with rails, building girders, and all manner of machinery. After 1908 an even better process, the open-hearth, supplanted the bessemer method. Meanwhile, furnaces became bigger, hotter, more efficient, and more costly. Henry Ford with his low-cost automobile, manufactured with assembly-line methods, perfected a new method of production already foreshadowed by the inventions of Oliver Evans and Eli Whitney and by the meat packing industry. Steam engines provided most of the power to run the railroads and the factories. Backward factories still used water power, but the most advanced ones were turning to electric power. Both steam and electric power were generally obtained from coal.

All these railroads and factories were expensive to build. Some of the funds to produce all this equipment came from private savings put away in savings banks, trust companies, insurance companies, and other such institutions. Most of it, however, was profits plowed back by the companies themselves. They generally used half the profits for expansion. Large companies were usually incorporated, for this permitted the mobilization of capital from many stockholders and yet placed decision making in the hands of a few energetic individuals. The corporations turned to investment bankers, such as J. P. Morgan, to market their bonds and stocks. Morgan and his colleagues, desiring to offer only reliable securities, watched the progress of their corporations with parental eyes, quieting disputes that might damage dividend or interest payments. Morgan encouraged higher business ethics and also monopolies.

Monopolies, or "trusts" as the industrial ones were called when they were nationwide in character, became very prevalent at this time. Ever-cheaper transportation helped make them possible, as well as tariffs, which kept out foreign competition, and the large investment in many of the companies. Some of them were "natural monopolies" almost as much as were railroads; the chief difference was that they touched the public less directly. They abused their opportunities; first the states and then Congress passed antitrust laws. But the Sherman Antitrust Act was of little use in the 1890s because of unfavorable Supreme Court decisions. Then in 1904 Theodore Roosevelt began to "bust" the trusts. The leading owners of trusts made huge fortunes in those days before there was an income tax. It was the age of *laissez faire*, which came to an end only after the turn of the century when its abuses became all too apparent. In this era the government regulated business very little, imposed few taxes, and let depressions run their unhappy course.

Monetary problems beset the nation in this era. The Federal government was not prepared for a long war when the Southern states seceded. and thus had to issue $431 million of greenbacks until it could set up satisfactory taxation and borrowing programs. The price levels nearly doubled during the war and in doing so benefited farmers and some debtors and businessmen but hurt creditors and laboring people. Then for some thirty-one years after the war the price level drifted downward, falling about two-thirds by 1896. That hurt farmers and debtors but helped creditors and laboring people. The farmer-debtor group sought to defend themselves, first by demanding further issues of greenbacks and later by demanding free coinage of silver at 16 to 1. Either program would have tended to stop the deflation and set inflationary forces in motion. The remedy was dangerous, but the farmer-debtor group had a real grievance. After 1896 the price level again turned upward.

Congress seized the occasion of the Civil War to enact the National Banking Act, which provided the nation with federally chartered commercial banks, with high standards of banking and with bank notes acceptable at par everywhere. From this time on, people did the great bulk of their business through checking accounts. The National Banking System was a great improvement, but it had some serious faults, nonetheless. It lacked a central bank, the notes were inelastic, and the banks' reserves were too scattered, which made the banks vulnerable to runs in time of panic. In 1913 Congress superimposed the Federal Reserve System on the National Banking System to remedy these defects.

It was of prime importance to sell all the goods coming from the factories and mills and workshops. Never before in American history had the marketing function been of such importance. Merchants responded to the challenge and came forth with a variety of new selling institutions and methods. Among the new institutions were department stores, chain stores, variety stores, and mail-order houses. Among the new selling methods were installment selling, the one-price system, prompter payment of bills, growing emphasis on salesmanship, and much more imaginative advertising. The efforts of the merchant, together with the steady decline in transportation costs, in this era made it possible for many products to have national markets. There was increased regional specialization, and goods crisscrossed the nation in every direction going to market. Foreign trade grew also, but not as rapidly: the United States stood third in the world by 1914. As America became more industrialized, it exported more manufactured goods and imported a growing proportion of raw materials. Europe remained the best market and also the chief source of imports, but Canada, Mexico, the Caribbean area, and South America grew in importance. One probable reason for the relative decline in manufactured imports was the policy of high tariffs. Congress raised them to help finance the Civil War and never substantially reduced them until 1913. On the other hand, Congress granted but meager subsidies to the merchant marine, which declined steadily in importance. Although that was dangerous from a military viewpoint, it at least meant that foreign nations could pay for American products with the proceeds of shipping services which they sold to Americans.

The organization of industry into larger units, even to the point of trusts, caused at least two segments of the economy to organize in self-defense, namely, labor and the farmers. By the postwar period unions were becoming national in scope; they conducted more strikes and they were strong enough to survive depressions. Although they made repeated efforts to enlist the unskilled and had occasional success, unions along craft lines such as Samuel Gompers' American Federation of Labor and the four Railroad Brotherhoods were the most successful. Whereas the National Labor Union, the Knights of Labor, and the Industrial Workers of the World wanted to abolish the wage system and somehow to remake the economy, the AFL and the Brotherhoods accepted the world as they found it and endeavored to obtain the best bargains possible. In general, also, unions did better by resorting to collective bargaining than by trying to put across legislative reforms. Nevertheless, the state legislatures, the Congress, and the Supreme Court gradually adopted a more enlightened attitude toward the problems of labor. They began by limiting the hours of work of children and of women, and then of men in dangerous occupations. Then they made employers more liable for accidents to employees. The healthy able-bodied laborer, however, was deemed quite able to care for himself. In general, the status of the laboring man had improved materially by the end of the period. The average working day had fallen from about eleven hours to about nine, and real wages had risen very substantially. How much of all this gain the unions had brought about it would be difficult to say, for some of the greatest gains were in occupations which were not unionized, and some of the smallest were in unionized occupations. Yet in general, the union worker in any trade got higher pay than his nonunion colleague.

Although farmers made fewer advances toward mechanizing farming than industrialists were making, agricultural progress was substantial. The bulk of the progress was in the production of small grains, especially wheat. Harvesters with wire binders appeared and were in turn supplanted by twine binders and headers and combines, the last appearing principally in the Far West. Steam threshers and, to a lesser extent, steam plows operated on large Western farms. There was a strong tendency toward crop specialization in various regions of the nation. For example, the Northeast went in for truck gardening, the Middle West for corn, beef, and hogs, the Missouri Valley for spring wheat in the north and winter wheat around Kansas. The South returned to cotton production, achieving its prewar peak output by 1877 and then quadrupling the figure by about 1914. The far West specialized in vegetables, wheat, and later in fruits. To farm in the Plains region it became necessary to adopt dry farming. Farmers in general, because they were advancing more slowly than industry, were unhappy in this period. The Middle West was the center of discontent. Basically, the trouble was overproduction, brought about by putting too much land under cultivation, by machine methods, and by low-cost transportation, which made one national market out of many local ones. There are six remedies, of varying effectiveness, to the overproduction problem—namely, increase the demand, decrease the supply (by organizing a monopoly), subsidize the industry, do nothing (and force the marginal farmers out), reduce costs, and raise the price level (farm prices go up first). For various reasons, chiefly because this was a laissez-faire economy, the first four were out of the question. Accordingly, the farmers, through their Granges, tried to reduce railroad rates and middleman costs; through the Greenback movement and the Free Silver movement, they tried to raise the price level.

[illegible] the supply [illegible] substituting the [illegible] and thus the [illegible] costs, [illegible] the price level [illegible] For various reasons [illegible] [illegible] Silver [illegible] the price level.

PART FOUR

Problems of Plenty—Governmental Solutions

INTRODUCTION

An American born in 1914 would be in his middle forties today and during his life he would have witnessed two world wars (1914–1918 and 1939–1945) and one regional war in Korea (1950–1953) and two long periods of responsibility and worry on the part of his people and his government. One of these was over the Great Depression of the 1930s and what it did to the lives of millions of people, and the other was over the "cold war" against the Communist menace, which has been going on almost continually since 1945. In that half-century span there was only one period of "normalcy" and relaxation, and that was the short but joyous one from 1922 to 1929. These eras of wars and of worries left the American people with two fear psychoses, both of which have at times had a deep influence on public attitudes and hence on governmental policies. They are fear of depression and fear of communism. The wars and threats of war also caused the nation to build up its industrial strength faster than it might otherwise have done, although even without this stimulus America would have been an industrial giant.

The United States has productive capacity to the point that the average individual has 100 energy slaves available to do his bidding each day. Compared to the average family in the rest of the world, the average American family is wealthy. As behooves citizens of greater wealth in the world community, Americans have shouldered some important social responsibilities. That has been the mature course of action. They have showed their responsibility for the welfare of their fellow man in America by enacting much social legislation, such as the Social Security Act of 1935 to protect workers against unemployment and old age. They have shown their responsibility for the welfare of the western world as well by participating in three wars, by helping to found the League of Nations and the United Nations, and by carrying much of the heavy burden of stemming the spread of communism. Only an extremely productive nation could afford to carry such heavy responsibilities.

As a result of economic growth during the one era of normalcy in the 1920s, too much capacity was developed in certain lines, and the resultant overproduction in some industries helped to bring on the Great Depression. But this depression was unlike any that had gone before. It was bigger and in the end the government's attitude toward it was different. For the first time, the government tried to bring relief to the unemployed and to help business to recover. Paradoxically, the method used by government to aid business was the same one that Rockefeller and Morgan had used to help business back in the days of trusts. It was to encourage monopoly and restriction of output. This was the basis of the National Industrial Recovery Administration, set up in 1933 to help business. That act suspended operation of the antitrust laws. It was the basis of the Agricultural Adjustment Administration, likewise inaugurated in 1933 and sometimes called an "agricultural trust." And it was the basis of labor unions which the government encouraged so much between 1933 and 1947. There was one big difference: this time it was the government which offered monopoly as a solution, made the ground rules, and to some extent determined the profits.

CHAPTER 23

Growth and Responsibility

The nearly half century since 1914 has seen great changes both in the size of the American population and in its attitude toward the rest of the world. The population nearly doubled, although the nation added no new large territory and not until 1959 did Alaska and Hawaii become states. The real advance lay in the development of a more mature outlook on the part of Americans. They became aware that the country's resources were not inexhaustible and must be husbanded. Also they learned that they could not live apart from the rest of the world, joining in its affairs only when it seemed attractive to do so. Three great wars made Americans realize that. By the end of the second one, the United States was the world's leading military power, and peace in the civilized world depended upon how intelligently it exercised that power. The nineteenth century had been known for Pax Britannica; the twentieth century is not yet known for Pax Americana.[1] Internally, the people through their governments have undertaken to protect and help the weak and oppressed elements of their own nation. The Great Depression did much to develop a feeling of responsibility in this respect.

POPULATION TRENDS

Population Growth. Between 1910 and 1958 the population nearly doubled (see Table 23-1). The country is today adding almost three million new persons every year. Within that half century, the rate of growth slowed down substantially between 1910 and 1940; it reached its low point during the depression decade of the 1930s but then rose sharply again during the 1940s and 1950s. This declining rate of growth between 1910 and 1940 is attributable to the disappearance of cheap land, increased urbanization, immigration restrictions, and a rising standard of living, which up to a point often means smaller families. The births per 1,000 persons fell from 25 in 1915 to 18 in 1940 and recovered

[1] By holding the balance of power, Britain allegedly kept the number of significant wars to a minimum. That was Pax Britannica—British peace.

again to 25 by 1957. Paradoxically, the chief reason for the increase in the birth rate and the more rapidly growing population was probably a rising standard of living after 1940. Just as some people spent their larger incomes on finer cars or better houses, others used it to raise more children. The decline in the death rate per 1,000 from 14.7 in 1910 to 9.4 in 1956 was also a contributing factor to the rising population. It is remarkable that the death rate declined in view of the aging of the population and that the birth rate has risen since 1940 despite the fact that immigrants are much less important in the make-up of the American population.

Table 23-1
Population Statistics, 1914–1957
(Thousands omitted)

Date	Total	Pacific coast	Negro	Immigrants, decade ending	Birth rate per thousand	Urban, per cent	Median age	Aged 65 and over, per cent
1910	92,406	4,192	9,828	8,796	.....	45.7	24.5	4.3
1914	99,118	......	....	......	25.0*	....	....	4.4
1920	106,466	5,567	10,890	5,706	23.7	51.2	25.6	4.6
1930	123,077	8,194	11,891	4,107	18.2	56.2	26.9	5.5
1940	131,970	9,733	12,866	528	17.9	56.5	29.5	6.8
1950	151,683	14,487	15,042	1,035	23.6	64.0	30.2	8.3
1957	175,000§	18,412	17,100†	2,074‡	25.0	63.0	29.8	8.6

* 1915.
† Estimated.
‡ 1951–1957.
§ 1958.

SOURCES: U.S. Bureau of the Census, *Historical Statistics of the United States, 1789–1945* (Washington, 1949), pp. 26, 29; U.S. Bureau of the Census, *Statistical Abstract of the United States, 1957* (Washington, 1957), pp. 5, 11, 25.

Immigration. Almost a million immigrants entered the country each year between 1900 and the outbreak of World War I, but between 1916 and 1920 only 1.3 million came in. A fear that there would be a tidal wave of immigration out of war-torn Europe to America led to stricter immigration laws. Consequently, during the 1920s only 4.1 million immigrants reached American shores. During the depressed 1930s America ceased to look like the land of opportunity and only 0.5 million came over. In the 1940s 1 million entered, chiefly after the war, and between 1951 and 1957 another 2 million arrived. Thus between 1916 and 1957, 9 million immigrants entered, but 2.5 million departed, leaving a net gain of 6.5 million. By the standards of former times, the flow of immigration to America has slowed to a trickle.

The restrictive measures that Congress took, starting just before World War I, accounted largely for the decline. In 1917 it put an $8 head tax on all immigrants and required that they know how to read and write either English or their native language. In 1921 Congress passed the first quota law, which limited immigration from any country to 3 per cent of the persons of that nationality living in the United States in 1910. In 1924 Congress reduced the quota to 2 per cent and put the base year back to 1890. One purpose of this was to favor the so-called "old immigration" that consisted of persons from northern and western Europe. There was much criticism of this assumption that "Nordic" people were more desirable immigrants, and in 1927 Congress moved the base up to 1920. However, it fixed the total quota at 150,000 a year, where it has remained, with minor changes, to 1959. Immigrants from Canada, Mexico, Cuba, and Latin-American nations are not included within the quota; there is no numerical limitation on their entry. Following World War II Congress passed laws to screen out Communist sympathizers among incoming immigrants. In 1952 it passed the McCarran-Walter Immigration and Nationality Act, which codified all previous laws and added a few new features. Immigrants must now have immigrant visas; to obtain them, they must undergo a close screening process before leaving Europe. The new law removed the head tax and gave special preference to aliens whose skills were in particular demand in America. After the war, two special laws permitted the entry of 415,000 "displaced persons." These were persons who, chiefly for political reasons, had had to flee from their former homes in Communist-controlled countries in central Europe.

This change in immigration policy and immigration flow has had several significant consequences. With fewer new immigrants entering, the "melting pot" has functioned better: the little Italies, little Hungaries and many other indigestible lumps in the big cities have almost disappeared. There are fewer immigrants available to industry as strikebreakers: this is a gain from the unions' viewpoint. But most important, the buyers of cheap labor have had to look elsewhere than to European immigrants for it. Immigration from other parts of the Americas has remained open. Chiefly, however, the change has helped to stimulate more internal migration.

Internal Migration. Between 1850 and 1900 the percentage of persons residing in the state of their birth declined, but since 1900 it has risen again.[2] In 1910 nine out of ten Negroes lived in the South, with the remaining tenth about equally divided between the Northeast and the

[2] The figure was 24.0 in 1850, 20.6 in 1900, and 25.2 in 1950. The Westerners are the chief movers, the New Englanders the chief stay-at-homes. U.S. Bureau of the Census, *Statistical Abstract of the United States, 1956* (Washington, 1956), pp. 39–41.

North Central regions. The West had very few. By 1950, however, less than seven out of ten Negroes lived in the South. About an eighth were in the Northeast and another eighth in the North Central regions, and 4 per cent lived in the West, chiefly in California. It was opportunities first in domestic services and then in industry that caused them to leave the South. The majority ended up in cities such as New York, where they congregated in Harlem, or Chicago, Detroit, and Philadelphia. Like the immigrants, they settled together and were difficult to assimilate, resulting in social problems. One of the most troublesome of these was whether to provide them with separate schools or to integrate the children in one school system. Integration became the answer in the North, but when in May, 1954, the United States Supreme Court ruled that Southern states must cease to discriminate against Negroes, the South keenly resented it and several states would not bow to the ruling. The most important consequence of this internal migration of Negroes, however, was to provide Northern industries with a new source of somewhat cheaper labor and thus to level out wage rates in different parts of the nation. A second example of this kind of migration is that of Puerto Ricans to New York.

Another important internal migration consisted of a general movement into less-developed parts of the West and South that were rich in resources or that had especially pleasant climates. Between 1910 and 1957 the population of California, Arizona, and Florida approximately quadrupled, whereas it about doubled for the nation as a whole.

Urbanization. The trend from country to city which had been so marked before World War I continued almost unabated. Whereas 46 per cent of the population in 1910 was urban, by 1950 64 per cent was urban. The number of towns of 2,500 or more about doubled and now numbered about 5,000. Those of 100,000 or more had also doubled and now totaled about 100. There were five cities of over a million, namely, New York with nearly 8 million, Chicago, Philadelphia, Los Angeles, and Detroit. The next five had nearly a million and, counting their suburbs, were already over the mark. They were Baltimore, Cleveland, St. Louis, Washington, and Boston. Indeed, the most important trend was not to the cities themselves but to their suburbs. Although the slum problem in large cities was still serious, it was less acute than before 1910, partly because immigrants had been absorbed and partly because the suburbs had grown so much.

Aging of Population. The population continued to age and was now more comparable in average age to the populations of European nations. The average age rose from 24.5 in 1910 to 30.2 in 1950. The percentage over 65 doubled from 4.3 to 8.6 between 1910 and 1957; the percentage under 20 declined but the percentage between 20 and 64 remained about the same. It was the group in this age bracket that had to support the others. Before World War II these shifts in age groups were already

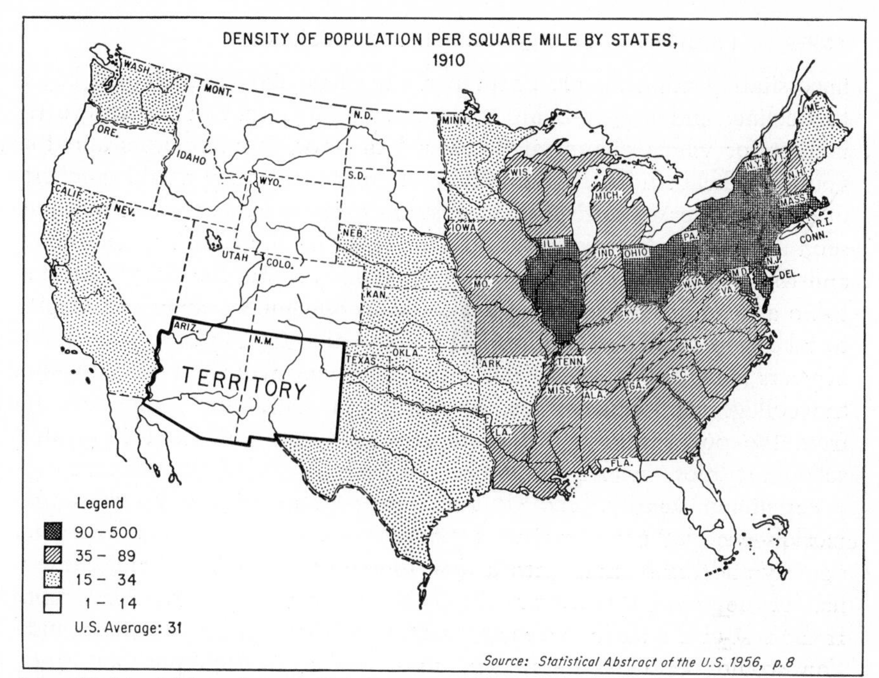

MAP 23-1A. (*Adapted from U.S. Bureau of the Census, Statistical Abstract of the United States, 1956, Washington, 1956.*)

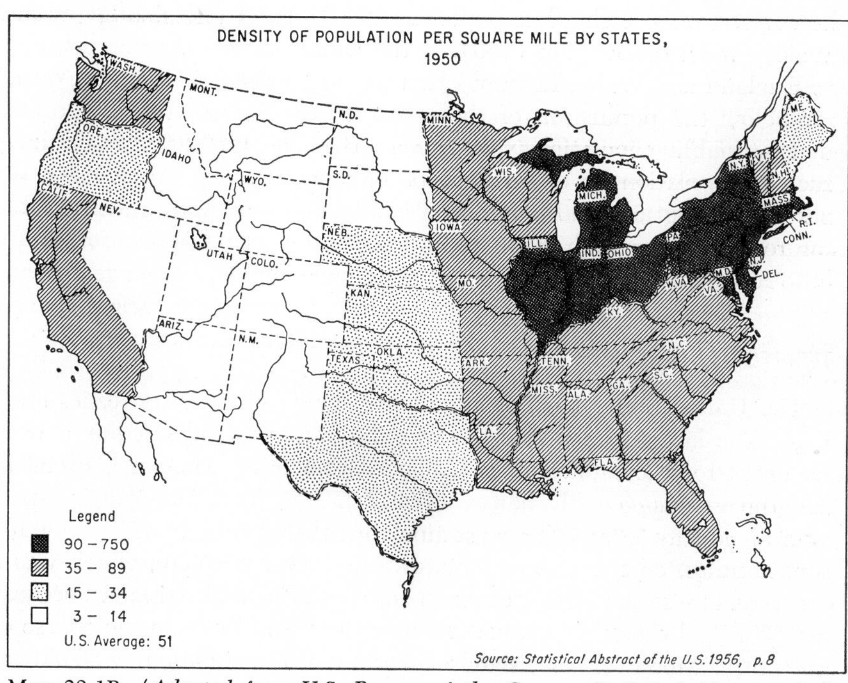

MAP 23-1B. (*Adapted from U.S. Bureau of the Census, Statistical Abstract of the United States, 1956, Washington, 1956.*)

necessitating adjustments. Enrollments in elementary schools had begun to decline, and it was being jokingly suggested that in the future the market for wheel chairs might exceed that for perambulators and that young medical students would find more business if they would specialize in cardiac diseases instead of in obstetrics. These ideas seemed outdated soon after the outbreak of World War II, when the birth rate picked up and the obstetricians were again busy. While serving the aged continued to be a good business, the nation could hardly build schools fast enough to take care of all the children. The population bulge of the World War II years is in 1959 storming the high schools and will shortly be invading the colleges and universities. Meanwhile, a continuing bulge resulting from the postwar high birth rate is demanding additional elementary school facilities.

Population Density. The United States has about 7 per cent of the world's land area and about 7 per cent of its population. There are densely and thinly settled areas, just as in the rest of the world. Close to half of the population lives north of the Ohio and east of the Mississippi. If the rest of the nation were as populous as this region, the total population would be 800 million. The most densely settled portions of the United States are the three lower New England states (Massachusetts, Connecticut, and Rhode Island) with 539 persons per square mile. These, however, are somewhat less populous than Holland (764), England and Wales (753), or Belgium (750). If the United States were as populous as England and Wales, its population would be about 2.70 billion, or not far below the population of the world. If the present rate of growth, that is, doubling every fifty years, should continue, the nation would have such a population by about 2160. Very obviously, the problems of the past—peopling an almost unsettled continent—and the problems of the future—finding enough elbow room for a still growing population—have little in common.

TERRITORIAL GROWTH

The United States has not added any significant new territories since 1914. The last actual possession was the Virgin Islands, acquired from Denmark for $25 million in 1917. The harbor of St. Thomas is excellent and the islands, roughly halfway between New York and Panama, provide an ideally located naval station. But the islands, totaling only 138 square miles, cost the United States about $283 per acre, which was a great deal more than the 3 cents an acre paid for the Louisiana Purchase in 1803. Real estate values had risen in the New World in the course of a century! Moreover, the islands already had a population of 26,051, or 188.4 per square mile, and their standard of living was low. Since then, to better their economic well-being, the government has spent on them more than the original purchase price.

Following World War I, the victorious allies divided up the colonial empire of defeated Germany, but the United States refused to share in the spoils.

Shortly after World War II, Japan's former colonies or mandates either went to the victorious powers outright or were assigned to the guardianship of one of them. Manchuria and Formosa went to China, for example; the United States assumed trusteeship of the Caroline, the Mariana, and the Marshall Islands. All these are in the Pacific and had been German colonies which Japan had later held as mandates. Again, the United States acquired no territories outright as a result of this war.

In short, the United States has throughout this period adopted a nearly model attitude in the matter of political imperialism. The American government sent troops to preserve order in the Dominican Republic in 1916 but withdrew them in 1924; and the Americans also withdrew their marines from Nicaragua in 1933 and their police from Haiti in 1933. Congress repealed the Platt amendment in 1934; it had permitted American intervention in Cuba to preserve order if need be. Congress had given the Philippines a considerable measure of self-government between 1916 and 1921 with only fair results. In 1934, by the terms of the Tydings-McDuffie Act, America promised the Philippines their complete independence on July 4, 1946. True, the fact that the leading beet sugar producing states enthusiastically supported the law somewhat sullied the generosity of the gesture. The sugar states did not want to face the competition of imported Philippine sugar. The Philippines gained their independence on the appointed day, but not before the Japanese had conquered them and held them in bondage for four years. The Filipinos fought gallantly to throw out their oppressors and having won their independence the hard way, they no doubt cherished it the more.

CONSERVATION

It took generations before Americans fully appreciated the natural resources which they inherited with their country. Most frontiersmen and farmers paid something for their land, and trappers, miners, and lumbermen likewise paid a little for the resources which they took. Yet for several centuries the price that they paid for these riches seemed amazingly low by standards prevailing in most parts of the world. Small wonder then that since these people obtained land and resources fairly easily, they often exploited them thoughtlessly. It was a case of "easy come, easy go." As people today look back on the way in which soil was misused, animals slaughtered, timber girdled, slashed, and even burned, and natural gas thrown away, they are aghast at what they regard as sheer waste. But it may well be asked whether one can waste a "free good." Is it possible today to waste the air that we breathe or the water in the ocean? Some of the resources in that bygone time seemed almost that plentiful. Thomas Jefferson remarked in 1803 that it would be 1,000 years before all the land *east* of the Mississippi would be settled. In 1827 the Secretary of the Treasury estimated that it would still take 500 years to settle the public domain which the United States possessed. Land and resources were so plentiful that it is difficult today to visualize it.

On the other hand, the other two economic factors of production were less plentiful than they are today. Labor was still scarce; that is a basic reason why slavery persisted. Capital was also scarce. Accordingly, Americans economized on these expensive factors at the expense of the cheap factor, land and its resources. Why waste the time of valuable laborers teaching them how to conserve cheap land? That made little sense to a businessman or to a farmer. True, land and resources became expensive in the East while they were still quite plentiful in the Middle West, and later they became more scarce in the Middle West while they were still plentiful in the Far West. There is some evidence that some Easterners were becoming conservation-minded long before "conservation" struck the public consciousness in 1908.

Conservation is the economical use of natural resources. It is not hoarding or stock-piling, although to some extent it does include rationing what this generation may use so that the next may have some. There is not too much evidence of the conservation idea before the Civil War except in state game laws in the East. Hunters reduced the herds of 100 million bison existing in 1866 on the Great Plains to perhaps 1,000 fifteen years later. Yet it was not until the late 1880s that William Hornaday aroused public interest in preserving this nearly extinct form of American wildlife. The Timber Culture Act, encouraging tree planting on the plains, and the Desert Land Act, encouraging irrigation of certain arid regions, paid lip service to the growing need for conservation. Under the Carey Act of 1894 the Federal government offered lands to states and corporate enterprises, provided they would irrigate them and cause them to be settled. The Newlands Act of 1902 provided for the establishment of irrigation projects from the proceeds of public land sales.

Throughout the last third of the nineteenth century men of science were especially active in sensing the need for greater conservation of natural resources, in gathering and publishing statistics to demonstrate the need, and in urging conscientious government officials to take long-overdue action. Thanks to the American Association for the Advancement of Science, the Federal government set up a Bureau of Forestry in 1890 in the Department of Agriculture. The first national forests were created the following year. Some years later, Gifford Pinchot and others pointed out that where man had removed the forests, floods and droughts were more frequent.

The stage was set by the start of the twentieth century for the conservation movement. All that was needed was the man and the occasion to launch it. President Theodore Roosevelt, a lover of the outdoors, was the man. When just out of Harvard, he had lived a while on a ranch in the Dakota Bad Lands. He became enamored of the West and wanted to prevent the spoliation of its resources. In March of 1907 Roosevelt appointed an Inland Waterways Commission to report on the effect of forests on inland navigation. The commission stressed the interrelationship of all kinds of natural resources. It urged Roosevelt to call a conference of governors the following year, since the problem obviously touched on the administrative practices of many states.

The conference met at the White House on May 13, 1908. Present were representatives from every state, thirty-four of them governors, congressmen, senators, members of the Supreme Court, and many other dignitaries. Such a gathering highlighted the topic of conservation and started the newspapers and general public talking about it. The conservationists particularly emphasized the "extravagant and reckless waste of the past." The governors pointed out that the prosperity of the future depended upon the conservation of natural resources. Congress shortly appointed a National Conservation Commission of forty-nine politicians, industrialists, and scientists, with Gifford Pinchot as chairman, to take an inventory of the nation's natural resources under the headings of minerals, waters, forests, and soils. The Commission made its report in December, 1908, and later published it in three volumes. In February of 1909, Roosevelt held a North American Conservation Conference to which he invited representatives of Canada, Newfoundland, and Mexico. Soon he was talking of a world conference. As a result of all this, the United States added 148 million acres of forests on the public domain to the national forest reserve, withdrew 80 million acres of coal lands in the West from private entry, set aside 1.5 million acres of water-power sites on twenty-nine streams, and reserved nearly 5 million acres of phosphate lands in three Western states. The total was 234 million acres of land, or an area the size of Texas and New Mexico. Congress evinced less enthusiasm for the Conservation Commission, refusing to appropriate even a meager $25,000 for its expenses for one year. Nevertheless, since that day Americans have remained aware of the conservation problem, not only because of the publicity but also because of the basic truth that land and resources are no longer a plentiful factor of production. Labor and capital have become relatively more plentiful than before. All this was another way in which the passing of the frontier made itself felt.

In the 1930s President Franklin Roosevelt, like his fourth cousin, took a considerable interest in conservation. Congress enacted the Civilian Conservation Corps Act in 1933 to provide work for young men, mostly just out of high school but without a job. Their families had to be on relief for them to qualify. They were to clean out trash in the forests and remove other fire hazards. When the Supreme Court found the Agricultural Adjustment Act unconstitutional in 1936,[3] Congress threw the Soil Conservation Act into the breach. It reasoned that if land might not be set aside to raise farmers' incomes, certainly it could be rested to improve its fertility and benefit the national well-being. Likewise Congress put an end to the Homestead Act of 1862—after 1935 a citizen could no longer declare his intention to acquire 160 acres of land by living on it for five years. Actually, of the 160 million acres left, very little was worth having. Most important, in 1933 Congress enacted the Tennessee Valley Authority to erect a series of dams in the Tennessee Valley which would provide a chain of artificial lakes, supply the region with cheap electric power, effect adequate flood control, and help reforest the region. The heavy rains were yearly carrying away millions of tons of fine soil and making a desert of that once beautiful country. Thanks to the TVA it regained its fertility and became a prosperous industrial area as well as an ideal vacation land. The New Deal administration also appropriated funds to build dams along the Colorado and Columbia Rivers to provide water for irrigation in these arid but fertile areas (see Fig. 23-1). They were likewise to provide the local inhabitants with low-cost power. The New Deal administration was not especially bothered by the fact that its giant dam program was adding lands while its AAA program was paying farmers not to use other lands.

The government showed its interest in conservation in other ways, such as protecting the salmon in the rivers of the Northwest, the seals in Alaskan waters, and many other forms of wildlife. For half a century it has maintained some 200 million acres of national forests. Private lumber companies may arrange to cut timber on government lands, but only if they follow prescribed practices. The government does not permit companies to cut more than one thirty-fifth of its mature timber in any year, the companies must not leave high stumps, and they must plant replacement trees for those they have taken.

Conservation has probably been most noticeable in forestry. The northeastern quadrant of the nation is the most densely settled and most people live in homes built of wood. Before the Civil War many Americans got the timber to build their homes from nearby forests in New York or Pennsylvania; later they found it in Michigan or Wisconsin, and since 1929 they have had to haul most of it all the way from the far

[3] *United States v. Butler*, or Hoosac Mills Case, 297 U.S. 1.

Northwest. This has showed up in the cost of lumber and in the cost of housing. How can the lumber shortage be remedied? Paper mills, which use much wood pulp to produce newsprint, have adopted the practice of raising trees as a farmer does a crop. This is possible when it takes only fifteen to twenty years to raise the kind of tree needed, but where it takes fifty years or more to grow hardwoods, the government has to step in and do some long-range planning. Businessmen cannot wait that long to reap their profits.

FIG. 23-1. Water stored in and distributed from the Hoover Dam irrigates millions of acres of land that would otherwise have little use. (*Courtesy of U.S. Bureau of Reclamation.*)

One of the difficulties faced by the conservationists is that they appear to be "crying 'wolf'" when there is no wolf. In 1909 it was pointed out that at the current rate of use, known oil reserves would last only about twenty years. Twenty years later, although output had quadrupled, known reserves, it was alleged, would last only about thirteen years. Twenty years after that, output had more than doubled again, but alarmists were saying that known reserves would last only about thirteen years at the current rate of use.[4] Something was obviously wrong; in fact, there were several things wrong. On the one hand, companies minimized

[4] American Petroleum Institute, *Petroleum Facts and Figures* (New York, 1950), p. 182.

their reserves to keep their taxes down. Companies were constantly exploring, making new discoveries, and adding to the known reserves. On the other hand, companies have had to seek oil at deeper levels, and in more remote places, as under the sea. That increases the costs; and obviously there is, in this finite world, a limit somewhere to the oil supply. To that extent the alarmists are right. But, say the optimists, by the time that oil gives out, man will have developed other sources of energy, such as liquefied coal or atomic power or solar energy. Man's ingenuity will save the day. It frequently has: when whale oil became too expensive, man discovered petroleum. But can man replace every kind of natural resource? What can replace forests as flood control devices or as manufacturers of rich soil? What can replace an adequate underground water supply? Perhaps man's ingenuity can solve these problems, too, but even if it can, is the solution cheaper than conservation?

GROWING RESPONSIBILITIES AT HOME

As the United States grew in size, population, and economic strength and complexity, it had to shoulder additional responsibilities, both in its domestic and foreign affairs. These necessitated changes in attitude of far-reaching importance on the part of the American people.

The Great Depression of the 1930s. The Great Depression changed the economic and social outlook of many Americans. The power of the Federal government to regulate the lives of millions of citizens increased appreciably. And just as the conservation movement reflected a higher regard for land and other natural resources, so the New Deal reflected a higher regard for labor and a lesser respect for capital.

Americans sowed the seeds of speculation and overexpansion in the years before President Herbert Hoover took office in March of 1929. Eight months later he began to "reap the whirlwind" of panic and long-drawn-out depression. Some 9,000 banks failed in five years. Prices fell 25 per cent. Businesses by the thousands went into bankruptcy. By late 1932 there were close to 12 million unemployed, about one workingman out of every four.

President Hoover was an able and conscientious administrator who had made a tremendous reputation in World War I relieving millions of starving people in Europe. He believed strongly that worthwhile Americans could find or make jobs if they wanted to, even in a depression, for he had done that himself back in the 1893–1895 depression. He thought that the country would just have to live through the depression: the government had never done anything significant to help the unemployed in the past. But he was having difficulties handling this greatest depression of all time in that customary manner. Private charities could not take care of the millions of unemployed. People were increasingly impatient. It helped little for Hoover to say that America was "fundamentally sound" or that "prosperity was just around the corner." Hoover finally concluded that if government were to help to alleviate the depression it should chiefly make emergency loans to big businesses like railroads and banks which employed thousands and whose failure would bring distress to many homes. His administration set up the Reconstruction Finance Corporation in 1932 to do this. There was much logic in the idea, but it offended many because it seemed to favor the rich and ignore the poor.

A Democratically controlled Congress lost faith in Hoover and would not appropriate much for his use when he finally requested funds. His administration had gone $4 billion "into the red" by the time he left office in March of 1933; he was a failure in the eyes of many Americans. Too many people were tired of standing too many years (or so it seemed) in too many bread lines. They wanted someone who would do something; they wanted a leader. Agreeable, cheerful Franklin D. Roosevelt, the newly elected President, was the man of the hour.

To the extent that Roosevelt had a program, he soon scrapped it. That can be seen from his criticisms of Hoover during the 1932 presidential campaign. For example, he denounced Hoover for piling up the greatest deficit in American peacetime history and promised that when he took office, he would cut expenses 25 per cent and balance the budget. He said he was in favor of "sound money." He criticized government spending for the farmers and called the Agricultural Marketing Act of Hoover's Secretary of Agriculture a "cruel joke." He was against government ownership of public utilities. He denounced "the tendency to concentrate power at the top of a government structure." Finally he said, "I am opposed to any form of 'dole.' I do not believe that the state has any right merely to hand out money." He may well have believed all this at the time. But the program that he subsequently provided reproduced in an exaggerated form many of the very policies he had criticized.

The New Deal. Roosevelt had little understanding of economic principles. His political principles were to help people in distress and to maintain his popularity. Those principles carried him to what came to be called the "New Deal." It was a collection of palliatives and a hodgepodge of the wishes of the liberals and the conservatives who influenced President Roosevelt. There were some of both in his cabinet and among his close advisers, who were called the "brain trust." The important thing, however, is that the whole turned out to be a plausible program, although conservative economists thought it an unsound one.

There were five main features of the New Deal as it worked out.

1. From the outset there was much talk of "a planned economy." It was said that capitalism had the nation in ruins because it was a system with-

out a plan except that it ran on the profit motive or human selfishness. A planned economy presupposes an over-all plan. That can come only from government and it makes that government more powerful. The desire of the people and of the Congress for a leader, after four years of drifting, made it possible for Roosevelt to assume great power. But he was not the dictator type; he liked too much to be agreeable. Nor could he draw up and personally carry out all the plans. He had to delegate these to bureaus, committees, commissions, and the like. A giant bureaucracy arose which ruled by administrative decree. Thus the New Deal developed a strong central government. How this came about can be seen from the execution of some of the first plans.

2. A way had to be found to restore prosperity as soon as possible. Much of the early New Deal thinking was devoted to this very proper aim. The extremists in agriculture, the liberals in labor, and the conservatives in industry all had one basic idea of the best way to restore prosperity in their afflicted segments of the economy. Stripped of details, it was this: *we need the support of the government to get a monopoly.* Roosevelt was agreeable. (*a*) Agriculture got its Agricultural Adjustment Act, which set up a government-sponsored monopoly of farmers to restrict production of certain crops and thus raise the prices received for them to get more income for the farmers. (*b*) To satisfy labor, Congress said in clause 7(a) of the National Industrial Recovery Act, and later in the Wagner Act, that employers must bargain collectively with unions. That enabled unions to organize more laborers and to increase their bargaining power. More unions achieved a closed shop and this increased the number of labor monopolies. (*c*) As for industry, Congress suspended the antitrust laws in enacting the National Industrial Recovery Act and invited the various industries to draw up their codes of business practices. The leaders in nearly 700 industries did most of the talking and rule making. They set prices, or forbade selling below cost, or restricted production, or made it hard for new businesses to enter. These are the warp and woof of monopoly.

3. The New Deal gradually devised a new economic philosophy. The English economist, John Maynard Keynes, supplied part of it, and some American economists contributed to it, too. It rested on a number of beliefs such as the following: The American economy has reached maturity and any further growth will be slow. As people's incomes rise they save more, and the average American income has risen in the last generation. A major cause of the depression is oversaving and not enough spending. The best way to end the depression is to put more purchasing power in the hands of consumers. The Federal government itself should do this directly and promptly by work relief and public works projects. Low interest rates will encourage business and others to borrow and spend;

therefore the government should keep interest rates low. Operating the government at a deficit, "deficit spending," will help bring the country out of the depression. Fear of inflation is exaggerated, especially in a depression; unemployment is the menace to be dealt with and removed.

4. Financing the New Deal required overhauling the money and banking system. The administration tried to raise prices in the hope of restoring prosperity. That was the purpose of the 1933–1934 devaluation of the dollar. The New Deal also abandoned domestic redemption of money in gold, lest a panicky demand for gold restrict the government's spending operations and hamper all the planning. Congress also rewrote some Federal Reserve legislation so that both business and government could borrow more easily than before. The government had to sell its bonds and other I.O.U.'s to get money to cover its annual deficits and the banks had to absorb most of them, with help, when needed, from the Federal Reserve banks.

5. Since about 1933 the vast majority of the American people have more or less consciously resolved that, come what might, they would not have another depression like the one of the 1930s if the government could possibly prevent it. They would elect only an administration that would promise to take prompt action the moment a depression threatened.

It may be asked how successful the New Deal program was. The Supreme Court declared the AAA and the NIRA unconstitutional and threw them out. It did not seriously challenge labor's laws, however. The farmers got their AAA restored as a conservation measure. Industries had to go back to living under antitrust laws and even to being prosecuted under them. The New Deal became increasingly partisan to farmers and laborers, and during the years 1935 to 1937 especially, had a strong antibusiness bias. The revenue law of August, 1935, put a heavy tax on corporation surpluses, lest such oversaving provoke a new depression. Congress enacted a number of social welfare measures, such as the Social Security Act of 1935 (once opposed by Roosevelt), interstate child labor laws, and maximum hour and minimum wage laws. There was much reform but little recovery. The New Deal was not able to pull the nation out of the depression. By 1940 the Federal government had incurred deficits averaging almost $4 billion a year for seven years and there were still 10 million unemployed. It took World War II with its mobilization of millions into the armed forces, its additional years of scarcities of civilian goods, and its colossal spending to bring the Great Depression to an end.

The chief legacies of the New Deal were changed economic and social attitudes and a stronger Federal government. Americans became increasingly concerned with the welfare of their fellow man. Fear of unemployment grew and respect for saving and capital declined. Americans willingly surrendered a part of their cherished freedom in return for greater economic security. People depended more on the Federal government and less on themselves. A new brand of economics came into fashion. A wave of humanitarianism and social reform swept the nation. Federal and state government legislation and policies reflected all these.

GROWING RESPONSIBILITY ABROAD

World War I. For over a century the United States had largely left Europe alone and Europe had for the most part left this country alone. But the world was becoming "smaller," thanks to improved means of transportation, and the United States was becoming larger. World War I ended America's career of peaceful isolation. Henceforth, try as it might to withdraw, it would have to take an ever-greater part in world affairs.

Although the United States was in the war only nineteen months, they were among the most momentous in this country's twentieth century history. By the war's end, America's little army of 50,000 had grown to 4,000,000, and half of them were in Europe. Germany asked for an armistice and received it on November 11, 1918. The Germans overthrew their own monarchy and set up a republic in its place. Germany then signed a treaty of peace at Versailles in June of 1919. Four men were the chief architects of this treaty, namely, Woodrow Wilson, the American President, and three prime ministers, Georges Clemenceau of France, David Lloyd George of Britain, and Vittorio Orlando of Italy. The victorious Allies dismembered Austria-Hungary, reduced Germany in size and took its colonies from it, and set up a flock of small nations on Wilson's principle of national self-determination.

Wilson had one other goal which he devoutly hoped to achieve. That was to establish a League of Nations, the beginnings of a world government in which the nations of the world would be equally represented, much as the individual states are represented in the United States Senate. He hoped that nations could avoid wars by debating controversial matters. The Allied powers accepted Wilson's proposed league and set it up in Geneva, Switzerland, but Wilson was unable to persuade his own Congress to approve the United States' joining it. During the next twenty years this country generally had an observer at its sessions and participated in the activities of most of its subordinate organizations, although it never joined the League. The League prevented some minor wars from breaking out and may have delayed World War II.

World War I cost the participants some 8.6 million dead and 21.2 million wounded. The estimated direct cost was $186 billion. The United

States lost 126,000 dead and 234,000 wounded, and paid out $22 billion.[5] This nation made loans to its allies to the amount of $7 billion during the war. After the armistice it loaned them several more billions. It eventually collected only a part of all this. Whereas the total cost of the Federal government had been about $0.7 billion in 1913, it averaged $4.5 billion during the 1920s, two-thirds of which was attributable to national defense and the recent war. The public debt had shot up from $1.2 to $26.3 billion. People soon began to ask themselves what they had bought with all this expenditure. Very clearly, modern war was extremely costly. The United States had entered World War I with the hope of "making the world safe for democracy" and spreading this gospel to many other countries. And many Americans had even thought that this war would put an end to war as a way of settling disputes.

Attempted Return to Isolationism. Most of the peoples of Europe did not have the background of experience and traditions in democratic government to make democracy work as it did in Anglo-Saxon countries. Strong men took over the reins of power in one European country after another. In 1933 Adolf Hitler became the "Führer" or leader of Germany. All these dictators had strong armies and were in a position to exercise power arbitrarily. If this was "making the world safe for democracy," many Americans now became sadly disillusioned. From an economic point of view, they were disillusioned also, as their prosperity bubble of the 1920s burst in their faces with the stock market crash of October, 1929. As for avoiding future wars, increasingly it seemed only a matter of time before World War II would break out. England, France, and the United States, working through the League of Nations, were unable to muster enough courage to prevent Japan from invading Manchuria in 1931. Italy's dictator, Benito Mussolini, deciding in 1935 that backward but independent Ethiopia in North Africa would be a suitable colony to have, conquered it with cynical disregard for world opinion. Despite the feeble protests of England, France, and others, Germany's Hitler sent troops into the Rhineland, which was supposed to remain demilitarized. When a civil war broke out in Spain, Germany aided the royalists and Russia assisted the rebels. These two totalitarian powers had a warm-up war, with bombed cities and all, at Spain's expense. The American people were by this time thoroughly disgusted.

In the early 1930s groups of college students across the nation signed statements that in the event that the United States was drawn into another European war, they would not fight. Scholarly works appeared showing that the case for Germany in World War I had been better than

[5] Leonard Ayres, *The War with Germany* (Washington: U.S. Government Printing Office, 1919), p. 138.

many had supposed. Munitions manufacturers, "merchants of death," had encouraged war. Investment banking houses such as J. P. Morgan allegedly had done their utmost to get the United States into the conflict on the Allied side. All these were exaggerations, but they show that the pendulum had swung the other way; many believed these revelations as they had once believed the war propaganda. By the time that Hitler came to power in 1933, some Americans had a higher opinion of Germany, the recent enemy, than of France, the recent friend. France was trying to extract the last dollar of reparations from Germany but complained bitterly about paying a greatly scaled-down war debt to the United States. Many a war veteran remarked bitterly that the United States should never have got into Europe's mess in the first place. The swing was back to the life of peace and the spirit of isolationism of the pre-World War I days. All this drawing away from Europe was bound to manifest itself in legislation.

Congress in 1934 passed the Johnson Debt Default Act, which forbade loans to foreign governments that had defaulted on their debts to the United States. This was to prevent a repetition of the Morgan firm's alleged involvement of the United States in World War I. When Italy launched its unprovoked war on Ethiopia in 1935, Congress, fearing a general outbreak of war in Europe, forbade Americans to travel on belligerent ships except at their own risk. It also required that the State Department license exporters of arms and temporarily forbade exports of arms to nations at war. Yet it did not forbid the export of basic materials such as copper, steel, and oil, which could easily be converted to military use. Another law in 1936 forbade loans to any belligerents. By this time civil war had broken out in Spain, and a new law was needed to take care of this war *within* a nation. A 1937 law made unlawful travel by Americans on belligerent vessels and required that belligerents pay cash and themselves carry away any arms that they bought from America.

However, from about 1938, Americans became increasingly concerned over the mounting power of Hitler's rearmed Germany and of the war lords of Japan. England and France gave in to Hitler's threats and, despite a treaty of alliance with Czechoslovakia, let him dismember that model democracy before their eyes. Germany finished devouring Czechoslovakia in the spring of 1939 and Italy occupied Albania. A Gallup poll in 1939 showed that 57 per cent of all Americans wanted a change in the neutrality law to permit England and France to buy war materials from this country. The second era of isolationism was about over.

World War II, 1939–1945. Emboldened by its repeated successes, Germany virtually demanded that Poland agree to let Germany have the free port of Danzig, on the Baltic Sea. Poland refused, and the Germans invaded Poland. This was one too many aggressions for France and England: they declared war on Germany in September of 1939. Poland was no match for Hitler's armies. Russia also pounced on its hapless neighbor, and the two dictatorships divided the carcass between them. To the dismay of the West, Germany and Russia now seemed to be allies. At first, little happened in the West, where the conflict was called a "phony war." In the spring of 1940, however, Germany launched a "blitzkrieg," or lightning war, against Holland, Belgium, France, Denmark, and Norway, overrunning all of them. Britain for a time was the sole combatant left. In September, 1940, it narrowly staved off invasion by defeating the German Air Force. Meanwhile, matters were not going well between Germany and Russia: Josef Stalin was fearful of Germany's success. In June of 1941 Germany attacked Russia. The United States was increasingly sympathetic to Britain and did "everything short of war," and much that overstepped the mark, to help. Congress had already repealed the neutrality legislation. America gave Britain 50 over-aged destroyers and sent war supplies; in March, 1941, Congress passed the Lend-Lease Act authorizing the government to grant, lend, or lease up to $7 billion to any nation whose defense the President deemed vital to that of the United States.

Meanwhile, in another part of the world another military-crazed nation, Japan, was threatening not only its weaker neighbors but even the colonies of defeated or harassed nations such as France and the Netherlands. The United States sought to restrain the Japanese, but in the end Premier Tojo of Japan announced that England and the United States must be driven out of Asia. On Sunday, December 7, 1941, Japan launched its surprise attack on part of the American navy anchored at Pearl Harbor in Hawaii. Germany declared war on the United States the next day, and Japan also attacked the Philippines. The United States found itself in a major war, against two great military powers; it was unprepared; and it had suffered a crushing naval defeat at the outset.

The war lasted until May 8, 1945, in Europe but continued three more months in Asia. The cost to the world of this war was 25 million killed and at least 25 million more wounded, and about half a trillion dollars. Of this staggering total, the American share was 408,000 lives and $221 billion.[6] In World War II the United States' financial aid to its allies took a different form. America contributed money as well as men, without stint, wherever needed. There was no distinction between giving the men and lending the money: this was the basic concept of Lend-Lease. By the end of the war the government had spent $50.2 billion under the Lend-Lease Acts.

[6] "Cost of War to the United States since 1917 Computed," *The New York Times*, Sept. 13, 1954.

In 1945 the victors did much as they had in 1919: they redrew boundary lines, imposed reparations, occupied defeated nations, assigned guardianships over colonies, and set up a new supergovernment. The United Nations, with headquarters in New York, replaced the League of Nations located in Geneva, Switzerland. But there were also important differences in the handling of the 1945 peace. Russia was a victor and kept not only the Baltic nations (Lithuania, Latvia, Estonia) which it had swallowed up during the war but gained control over nearby nations in eastern Europe, such as Hungary, Poland, and Yugoslavia. In 1948 it added Czechoslovakia to this "satellite" group but in that same year Yugoslavia squirmed loose. The victorious powers divided Germany and Austria into four zones, one each to be occupied by Russia, the United States, Britain, and France, and jointly occupied their capitals. Russia soon made its German zone virtually another satellite power. In 1949 the three western powers granted independence to their three zones, henceforth known as Western Germany. In 1955 all four powers pulled out of Austria. American forces have remained in Germany, however, first as an occupying army, and since 1949 as a guaranty against aggression by Russia. A somewhat similar situation has prevailed in Japan, with America the sole occupying power.

When the war ended, many persons believed that greater friendship than previously would prevail between the United States and England on the one hand and Russia on the other, largely because they had been comrades in arms. The Russians quickly dispelled this illusion. They endeavored to spread the gospel of communism across the world. They tightened their grip on Eastern Germany and they threatened to take over Greece. They seemed to wield considerable influence in the councils of the disturbingly large Communist parties in several western European nations, especially Italy. Their most alarming success in these early years was the subjugation of Czechoslovakia.

In June of 1947 the American Secretary of State, George Marshall, announced that the United States would grant financial aid to various European nations to speed up their economic recovery from war. Most nations of western Europe accepted the offer. It was primarily calculated to make the peoples of these countries less susceptible to Communist propaganda, which was most effective in nations whose standard of living had sunk, or was low to begin with. In April, 1949, twelve western powers set up the North Atlantic Treaty Organization, a military alliance, to protect western Europe against Russian aggression.

Meanwhile, in China in 1947–1949 the Russians had won an even greater victory than in Czechoslovakia by helping the Communist Chinese forces defeat those of Nationalist China.

At the end of the war Korea had been divided between Russian and

American guardianship. In 1950 it appeared that the Communist forces in northern Korea intended to take over the entire nation. The United States, having induced the United Nations to oppose this invasion, put up most of the troops and supplies for a war lasting three years. The war ended in a stalemate in 1953, having cost the United States 54,000 lives, 103,000 wounded, and $91 billion.[7]

Since 1953 limited wars instigated by the Communists have threatened to break out in various parts of the world, such as in Indo-China, Suez, Indonesia, and Guatemala. Again and again the United States has had to shore up the defenses of faltering governments. Britain and France, weakened by two world wars, have preferred to pass the financial and political responsibility over to the United States. Germany, twice defeated and badly mauled as well the second time, has lost its stomach for a large military establishment. Today any nation that resists Communist Russian aggressions, and many who are just lukewarm about doing so, receive generous American economic aid. Between 1945 and the end of 1958 the United States spent approximately $55 billion on economic and military aid to foreign countries. These were not loans, but outright payments. There were $11 billion in loans in addition. The philosophy of the American government has been that it is far cheaper to prevent wars and to defend our nation by helping others to defend themselves than it is to fight a war with most of the hostilities probably taking place in America.

The constant drain on the American taxpayer is enormous to keep this country ahead of Russia in atomic weapons, giant bombers, speedy fighters, and guided missiles. President Eisenhower has announced a $77 billion budget for 1959–1960. Of this, 60 per cent is to be spent for purposes of national security and another 20 per cent goes for interest, veterans' services, and international affairs. In other words, 80 per cent goes to pay for past wars or to avoid future ones. The United States has taken on the responsibility for protecting as much as possible of the world from Communist slavery and to keep peace as well, if it can be done. It is hard to see how American boundaries could extend very much farther. Indeed, many Americans have begun to feel that they have already been extended too far. There are two viewpoints on this. One is that Americans are entering a new era of postwar isolationism, as in the 1920s and 1930s, and trying to lay aside their world responsibilities. Another is that no nation can save the whole world, not even wealthy America. To save itself, the United States must limit its world-wide efforts and remain strong internally.

[7] *Ibid.*

CHAPTER 24

Modernization of Transportation and Communications

Transportation and communication facilities continuously improved after 1914. At the time of World War I, railroads dominated the transportation scene, accounting for nearly all intercity freight and passenger traffic. Inland waterways, especially the Great Lakes, and oil pipelines offered the only effective competition. Highways were largely local in nature, not permitting much utilization of motor trucks, and aviation was in its early experimental stage.

The four decades after 1914 witnessed a second "transportation revolution." Full-scale development of highway transportation elevated trucking to first place among the railroads' freight competitors; oil pipelines expanded greatly and the rehabilitation of rivers and canals arrested the decline of waterways. Mass-produced automobiles in the 1920s and commercial air transportation in the 1940s deprived railroads of most of their passenger traffic. In spite of steady progress in operating efficiency, railroads surrendered a mounting share of the nation's transportation business (see Chart 24-1).

These changes required a new approach in government regulation. Whereas railroads had a virtual monopoly on transportation in the late nineteenth century when regulation was first imposed, now keen interagency competition made some of the regulatory structure obsolete. Railroads requested less rate regulation and greater reliance upon competitive forces, but the Federal government responded by imposing its authority upon the newer forms of transportation as well.

In communications, progress in electronics produced first the radio and then television. Even so, the nation continued to rely heavily on the established telegraph and telephone and the postal service for business and personal contacts and on newspapers for mass communications.

MODERN RAILROADS

The railroad network reached its maximum physical size in 1916. In that year, 254,000 miles of first track were in operation. The figure has declined to about 219,000. Although the railroads abandoned 35,000 miles of first track, they increased their capacity to handle freight and passengers. Thus, they hauled more than twice as many ton-miles of freight in 1958 as in 1914, with only 86 per cent as much mileage. This was possible because of improvements in facilities and equipment.

Railroads in World War I. World War I found the railroads poorly prepared for the emergency. Most of the war traffic moved through the badly congested Northeastern ports, overtaxing facilities. The run-down

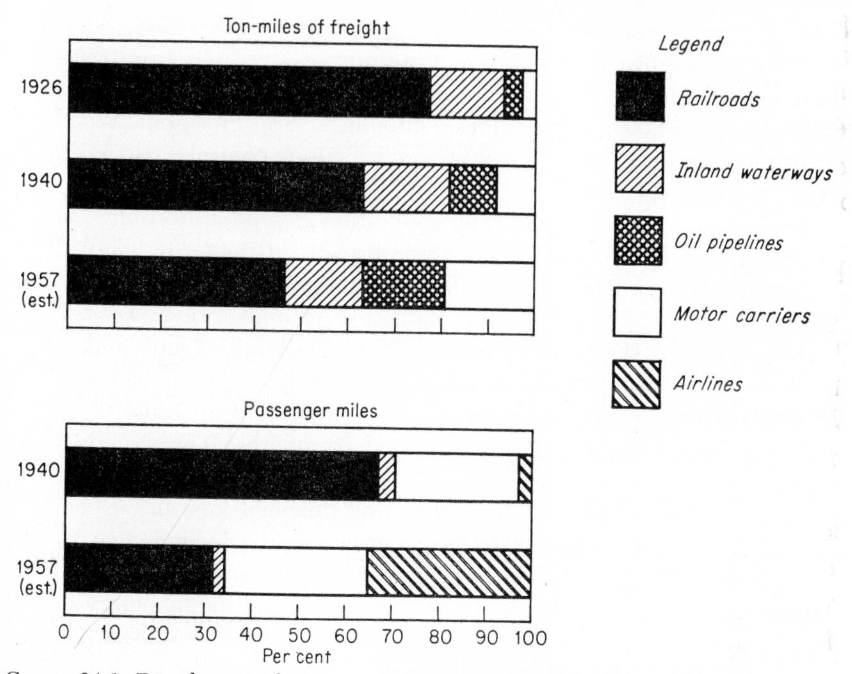

CHART 24-1. Distribution of intercity freight and commercial passenger traffic, 1926–1957. (*Adapted from Association of Western Railroads, Railroad Facts, 1958 ed., Chicago, 1958, p.* 5.)

condition of many of the Eastern lines compounded this problem. Federal regulation since the Hepburn Act (1906) had not taken into consideration the need of railroads to attract new capital. The Interstate Commerce Commission had based its rate decisions on the original investments of the companies, with low rates of return sometimes resulting. Many Eastern lines had not kept their tracks and rolling stock up to date or in good repair.

The burden of heavy traffic threatened to break down the Eastern network. Freight shipments piled up awaiting delivery. The railroads voluntarily formed the Railroad War Board in April, 1917, to promote greater coordination of rail facilities, but the Board proved inadequate for the task at hand. Its work was handicapped by government purchasing agents, who, armed with priority permits, indiscriminately loaded freight cars with supplies. Congestion near Eastern ports grew worse instead of better. Near the end of 1917, the Pennsylvania Railroad claimed that 85 per cent of its freight from Pittsburgh to Philadelphia moved under government priority orders. At Philadelphia, thousands of freight cars, loaded with shipbuilding materials, stretched for miles back into the country, awaiting unloading. Many had been dispatched to the Philadelphia shipyards weeks before unloading facilities were ready. Such unwise use of freight cars for warehousing purposes created an extreme car shortage. Eastern roads reported 180,000 stationary loaded cars and a shortage of 158,000. Under these circumstances, President Woodrow Wilson, acting under emergency war powers, took control of the railroads on December 28, 1917.

Within a short time, the railway congestion cleared noticeably. During the remaining months of the war, the railroads satisfactorily handled the freight and troops. The railway officials retained their positions but took orders from the United States Railroad Administration, headed by Director General William G. McAdoo. The USRA raised rates and wages to railway employees. The government, meanwhile, guaranteed a return to stockholders equal to the average from June, 1914, to June, 1917.

The period of Federal operation lasted 26 months. It was a costly experience in that the USRA lost about $1.2 billion—an average of $1.5 million per day. In spite of the staggering financial loss, the experience did not necessarily prove that the government was incompetent to run the railroads. It is doubtful that the competing companies could have cooperated enough to achieve the wartime task; and the monetary loss to the taxpayers was simply another cost of war. President Wilson had not considered profitability when he decided to take over the roads in 1917. On March 1, 1920, the government returned the railroads to the stockholders. This was accomplished through the Transportation (Esch-Cummins) Act of 1920, an important amendment to the Interstate Commerce Act of 1887.

Transportation Act of 1920. The bill was the most complex of any regulatory measure up to that time, and it reflected the multiplicity of problems created by the war. The carriers had suffered declining earnings even before the war, and their securities had lost their attractiveness for potential investors. Furthermore, some lines were in worse condition than others, a situation which posed a serious rate-fixing problem for the Interstate Commerce Commission. These circumstances called for a shift in the basic philosophy of railroad regulation. In the Act of 1920, Congress recognized railroads as "natural monopolies" and admitted that enforced competition had often been a mistake, resulting in evils which nullified any advantages.

The Act of 1920 overhauled the rate-making powers of the ICC. The earlier laws had been largely restrictive, designed to protect the public from unreasonably high and discriminatory charges. They gave no consideration to the adequacy of rates to protect the railroads. In a sense, the laws worked at cross purposes, since a line which could not earn enough to keep its plant in good working order rendered poor service to the public. The Esch-Cummins Act embodied a positive approach. It provided that the Commission should establish rates high enough to enable the roads "as a whole" to earn a fair return on a fair value of their property, "under honest, efficient and economical management." This clause did not apply to individual commodity rates nor to individual carriers; rather, the new policy called for a reasonable return to all railroads within a given section of the country.

Obviously, rates which allowed some lines a fair return would permit other companies to earn more or less than the average. Congress took care of that through a "recapture clause." Companies had to turn over to the government one-half of all earnings in excess of 6 per cent. The remaining half had to remain in a company reserve fund which the company could use only for certain purposes. The government put its share of excess earnings into a fund out of which the ICC could make loans to qualified carriers or could purchase equipment to rent to firms in trouble. The recapture clause brought howls of protest from the railroads, especially the stronger lines. They challenged its legality before the courts, but to no avail.[1] Even so, the recapture clause did not benefit the weaker lines. The terms of loans were too strict (6 per cent with good collateral): the same companies could borrow from private sources on as good or better terms. In 1933 Congress repealed the recapture clause and refunded all payments made since 1920.

The Transportation Act of 1920 also gave the ICC the power to fix *minimum* rates. This extension of authority was a recognition that rates could be too low for the public interest. Unreasonably low rates burdened other commodity rates as well as freight charges at noncompetitive points. The new power enabled the Commission to eliminate cutthroat competition, which had frequently proved harmful to rival firms.

In keeping with the recognition that competition was not always desirable, the law wrought decided changes in the legal relationship among carriers. Most revealing was the requirement that the ICC draw up a plan of consolidation, combining the nation's railroads into a few competitive systems. No carrier was required to consolidate, however. This provision proved difficult to administer because participation by indi-

[1] *Dayton-Goose Creek Railway Co. v. United States,* 263 U.S. 456 (1924).

vidual railroads was voluntary. A master scheme, worked out by the Commission in 1929, never went into effect. Another indication of the shift in regulatory philosophy was the provision which allowed pooling, with ICC consent, whenever such action was in the public interest. The Commission could also permit stock control of one company by another and sanction interlocking directorates under certain circumstances.

The Esch-Cummins Act contained other miscellaneous points. Carriers had to obtain the consent of the ICC to issue securities. The Commission had to approve all new rail construction and rail abandonment. Congress increased the number of commissioners from nine to eleven. And finally, it created the Railway Labor Board to handle disputes between the carriers and employees.

Performance of Railways, 1920–1941. The changed attitude of the government, plus the costly wartime experience, heralded a new era in railroading. Management became more progressive and went about the job of renovating and modernizing facilities. Between 1921 and 1940, the railroads spent nearly $11 billion for equipment, roadway, and structures; net investment increased by some $5 billion. Most of this capital expenditure came from corporate earnings. Technological improvements were myriad. Some of the most important were the introduction of diesel-electric locomotives (1925), centralized traffic control (1927), mechanical air conditioning of passenger cars (1927), adoption of lightweight streamlined passenger trains (1934), two-way train telephone communications (1937), and improved automatic couplers (1938). Diesel engines and centralized traffic control merit special consideration.

A diesel-electric locomotive operates on electric current generated by an oil-burning engine. It is about four times as efficient, in terms of fuel utilization, as a coal-burning steam locomotive. More important, a diesel requires less time for routine maintenance and is therefore available more hours per day and more days per year than a steam engine. Diesels were first used in switching yards in 1925 but not adapted for use with streamlined passenger trains until 1934. After 1941 they entered long-distance freight service, but they did not surpass steam engines in numbers until 1952.

Centralized traffic control is a refinement of automatic signaling. Its use permits an operator to direct train movements over many miles of line by remote control. An electronic panel shows the position of each train at all times. Knobs and levers control all signal devices and switches. The operator, with such precise visual information, can speed up passing and switching of trains and thereby greatly increase the traffic capacity of a given amount of track.

World War II and After. These and other improvements equipped the railroads to meet the challenge of World War II. In addition, coordination of aims among the railroads, government agencies, and shippers avoided much of the congestion of the first war. Joseph B. Eastman, Chairman of the Interstate Commerce Commission, became director of the Office of Defense Transportation, established in 1941. The railroads gave an outstanding performance by handling 98 per cent of military personnel and 91 per cent of military freight within the country. They did so with one-fourth to one-third less rolling stock than they had in World War I. Freight volume increased 2½ times and passenger traffic 4 times from 1938 to 1944. A number of factors made this possible. Freight-car capacity had increased by 13 per cent since World War I, locomotives were 33 per cent more powerful, and the length of the average freight run rose by 50 per cent. An important factor was the efficiency of management; it maintained its plant and equipment at high standards during the war in spite of many problems. The rail traffic in petroleum affords a good example of the railways' outstanding record. Delivery of ocean tankers to England and the action of enemy submarines forced railroads to handle the great bulk of petroleum, which normally moved by sea. In July, 1943, railroads hauled over 1 million barrels of oil per day, as compared with 11,250 barrels daily before the war. The railroads played a major role in America's winning war effort.

The technological progress of the prewar years continued after 1945. The railroads poured another $11 billion into improvements in the next ten years. They built new yards, terminals, sidings, and roadways and installed up-to-date signaling and communications equipment. They added over 20,000 diesel-electric units as well as 585,000 new freight cars. The application of roller bearings to freight cars speeded up service. Glass-domed observation cars on some of the streamlined passenger trains made rail travel more attractive. In 1948 experimentation with a powerful gas-turbine-electric locomotive began, and in the 1950s railway engineers considered the prospects of an atomic-powered locomotive. Railway progress has generally led to more efficient operation. Table 24-1 indicates the results of dieselization, better freight cars, and improved operating techniques. Revenue per ton-mile has remained virtually constant through thirty-five years although unit costs of labor, fuel, and materials have about doubled.

Financial Record since 1920. Since 1920, the financial well-being of railways has fluctuated with the business cycle. During the prosperous 1920s their net income rose from $351 million in 1921 to $977 million in 1929. This surplus turned into a $122 million deficit in 1932, however, as the carriers had to serve the public even at a loss. The financial crisis prompted Congress to authorize loans to railroads through the Reconstruction Finance Corporation and to amend the Bankruptcy Act of 1898 to facilitate financial reorganization of railroad companies. Low returns prevailed through the depression and the roads ran at a deficit again in 1938. During World War II, net income rose to $993 million in 1942 but then receded to $335 million by 1946. Since 1945, net income has varied from around $500 to $960 million in 1955. Net income in 1957 fell to $734 million. These income figures mean more when viewed in terms of return on investment. Although the Transportation Act of 1920 established 6 per cent as a fair return, Class I railways attained this rate but twice in thirty-seven years; in other years, they earned considerably less. For example, the 1957 rate of return was only 3.35 per cent. This reflects competition from other transportation agencies and suggests that government regulation may have remained too strict even after 1920.

Table 24-1
Railway Freight Operating Averages, 1921–1957

Year	Revenue per ton-mile, cents	Distance per locomotive per day, miles	Net load hauled per train, tons	Net load per freight car, tons	Number of cars per train	Average train speed between terminals, mph
1921	1.275	78.2	651	27.6	37.4	11.5
1930	1.063	89.6	784	26.7	47.9	13.8
1940	0.945	107.5	849	27.6	49.7	16.7
1950	1.329	119.3	1224	31.7	58.7	16.8
1957	1.445	146.2	1439	33.4	69.3	18.8

SOURCE: Bureau of Railway Economics, *Railroad Transportation: A Statistical Record, 1921–1957* (Washington: Association of American Railroads, 1958), p. 24.

Regulation since 1920. Two major acts to regulate railroads have gone on the books since 1920. These were the Emergency Railroad Transportation Act of 1933 and the Transportation Act of 1940. A third law, the Motor Carrier Act of 1935, affected railroads in that it placed highway transport under the jurisdiction of the amended Interstate Commerce Act.

The Emergency Railroad Transportation Act of 1933 stemmed from the depression. Many carriers, burdened with bonded indebtedness, were in danger of bankruptcy. The Reconstruction Finance Corporation helped some, but the railroads needed something more to check the steady decline in earnings. In June, 1931, they had sought a 15 per cent freight rate increase and had been denied it. The ICC correctly pointed out that rate increases would result in further losses of traffic at a time when low volume of business already plagued the roads. The Commission recommended congressional action instead, and Congress responded with the Emergency Act in June, 1933. This law created a post of Federal Coordinator of Transportation to encourage and promote cooperation among carriers in the use of facilities and to reduce operating expenses wherever possible. Joseph B. Eastman, an Interstate Commerce Commissioner, served as coordinator for three years, after which the emergency provisions of the 1933 law terminated. The railroads got very little immediate help from this work. The 1933 act contained some lasting provisions, however. It repealed the 1920 recapture clause and directed the Commission, in setting rates, to consider the needs of carriers for revenues sufficient to provide good service.

Railroad earnings stayed dangerously low throughout the 1930s. After the recession of 1938, nearly a third of all railway mileage in the country belonged to companies in bankruptcy or receivership. In its annual report for 1938, the Commission argued that the dismal economic conditions of the railroads were not the result of the depression alone. The rise of competition from highway, water, and air carriers accounted for no small part of the railways' troubles, it said. Accordingly, Congress adopted a new transportation policy—one which recognized that railroads were no longer the only major means of public transportation. The Transportation Act of 1940 declared that the national transport policy thenceforth would be to "provide for fair and impartial regulation of all modes of transportation subject to the provisions of this Act, so administered as to recognize and preserve the inherent advantages of each . . . all to the end of developing, co-ordinating, and preserving a national transportation system by water, highway, and rail . . . adequate to meet the needs of . . . the United States . . . ." The law placed inland water carriers under the ICC. It also applied to motor carriers as well as to railroads, pipelines, and express companies.

The 1940 law proved difficult to administer. Railroads in particular have questioned whether or not the ICC has been fair and impartial in upholding the inherent advantages of long-distance railway transportation. Accordingly, in 1954, President Eisenhower established a Cabinet Committee on Transport Policy and Organization to recommend changes in the laws. The Cabinet Committee Report, released in 1955, attracted much attention because of its basic proposal that greater reliance should be placed on competitive forces in rate setting. The railroads, in general, applauded the report, while motor carriers and water transportation companies opposed it vigorously. Congress, acting on the Cabinet Committee's Report, passed the Transportation Act of 1958. Among other things, the new law directed the ICC to follow more consistently the 1940 policy of recognizing the inherent advantages of each form of transportation; it gave the Commission new jurisdiction over the discontinuance of trains and railroad ferries; it authorized the Commission to guarantee loans to railroads under limited circumstances; and it provided for further Senate inquiry into national transportation problems. Meanwhile railroads continued to lose business to competing agencies.

The loss of traffic has placed the railroads in a precarious position. Net working capital declined from $1.6 billion in 1945 to $397 million in January, 1958. Railway employment fell in that same period from 1,420,000 to 862,000. The Senate Subcommittee on Surface Transportation summarized the causes of the railroads' troubles as (1) competition from highway, air, and water carriers, (2) government subsidies to the railroads' competitors, (3) overregulation by Federal and state authorities, and (4) lack of foresight and aggressiveness by railroad management.[2] Spokesmen for the railway industry generally agree with these statements, but they argue that railway labor unions have also contributed to the loss of business. For example, locomotive engineers receive nine days' pay for a Chicago to New York passenger run; an airline company pays a pilot one day's wages for the trip. Union work rules simply have not kept pace with technology.

HIGHWAY TRANSPORTATION

Motor carriers, traveling the nation's 3 million miles of intercity and rural roads, cut deeply into the railroads' dominant position. In 1914, automobile transportation was still in its early stage; but in the 1920s improved roads and pneumatic tires pushed highway transportation into the limelight. Motor trucks, operating as common carriers or as private or contract carriers, took over an increasing amount of railroad intercity freight, while cars and buses began to take passenger business away from the railroads. The major causes of these trends were the building of a highway system and the development of the automobile industry.

Highway Improvement. America had neglected highway transportation during the railway age. A better-roads movement began late in the nineteenth century, derived for the most part from bicycle enthusiasts and from the demands of rural areas for closer links with towns. Rural free delivery of mail, inaugurated in 1896, was a part of this trend. The building of automobiles for mass markets gave the highway movement its greatest impetus. The Federal government, inactive in highway construction since the national road project a century earlier, started an extensive aid program in 1916 by appropriating $75 million, to be matched by participating states, to assist in improving post roads. It left construction, maintenance, and supervision to the states. As the nation's highways became increasingly inadequate, Congress revised the Federal-aid program beginning in 1944. The biggest change came in the Federal-aid Highway

[2] *Report of the Subcommittee on Surface Transportation of the Committee on Interstate and Foreign Commerce*, 85th Cong., 2d Sess., April 30, 1958, p. 4.

Act of 1956—a plan to complete a 41,000-mile National System of Interstate and Defense Highways by 1969. To implement the $25 billion project, Congress raised the Federal government's share of building costs and granted wider authority over construction standards, highway access, and vehicle weight limits. The law also changed the formula for apportioning Federal funds among the states in order to reflect more accurately the relative highway needs of the various states. As of 1957, the United States had about 3.5 million miles of rural and municipal roads, of which approximately two-thirds were surfaced. An elaborate system of numbered routes facilitates highway travel.

Fig. 24-1. A modern highway grade separation in Los Angeles, Calif. (*Courtesy of Portland Cement Association.*)

Highway Freight. Motor trucks, which had proved dependable for hauling goods in World War I, came into prominence after 1920. Only 10,000 trucks had been registered up to 1910, but over 1 million were officially recorded in 1920. The number reached 4.6 million in 1940 and over 9 million in 1955. Several factors contributed to the rise of intercity trucking. In addition to highway improvements and better trucks were the low capital requirements and consequent ease of entering the trucking business. Furthermore, motor carriers possessed great flexibility in service. Freight in less-than-carload lots moved very slowly by rail, but truckers could give fast and frequent service on small shipments, usually on a door-to-door basis.

Railroads were slow to recognize the importance of motor trucks and tended to ignore the possibility of coordinating rail and highway systems. But after trucking proved itself, many railroad companies began to operate their own motor carriers to supplement rail facilities. The inherent advantage of trucks—their flexibility—enabled them to take over much traffic between nearby places. Also, they captured business where speed was important, especially perishables. Railways were best equipped, however, for the movement of volume shipments over long distances. This caused railroads to adopt "piggy-back" service, especially after 1945. Specially constructed flat cars carry highway trailers between cities like New York and Chicago, where they are attached to a tractor and hauled to their destination. "Trailer-on-flat-car" freight offers some hope of relief from the highway congestion which threatens to make the nation's road network highly inadequate.

Passenger Travel. In 1914, most Americans traveled by rail when moving from one city to another. Forty years later, 88 per cent of their travel was by automobiles and another 4 per cent by motor bus. The highways turned railroad passenger service from a profitable operation into a losing endeavor; the nation's railroads have run a deficit in their passenger service in all but four years (1942–1945) since 1936. The railways have had to keep expensive trains in operation, even though the public has largely abandoned rail travel. Railroad companies have introduced special features into their passenger service in an effort to recover lost ground. They have offered air-conditioned, streamlined coaches with reclining seats, reasonably roomy bedroom compartments, vista-dome coaches, reduced rates for family travel, and "ride-now-and-pay-later" credit arrangements. Yet even these have not checked the steady decline in rail passenger travel.

The major problem in highway travel is the high number of accidents and deaths. About 100 persons a day die in traffic mishaps. Superhighways, an increasing number of which are toll roads, have not yet reduced the accident rate on the roads. At best improved divided highways have increased the comfort of car travel and decreased the driving time between major cities.

Government Regulation. The Motor Carrier Act of 1935 placed interstate highway transportation under the jurisdiction of the Interstate Commerce Commission. States had already regulated trucks and buses, but they were unable to cope with traffic from other states. The 1935 legislation grew out of this problem. The railways and some shippers were demanding that the Federal government regulate highway transportation. Generally, the Motor Carrier Act safeguarded the rights of states to tax highway users and left the states with power to regulate trucks hauling interstate traffic wholly within state lines. The act gave the Commission exclusive power to issue interstate trucking certificates or permits, depending on the "public convenience and necessity" of the service. This clause has acted as a barrier to free entry into the industry, and according to some critics it has harmfully restricted competition. The Commission also received the power to control the rates, fares, and charges of common motor carriers, much as with railroads. An important exception was that the law did not require trucks to establish through routes and joint rates, largely because of difficulties involved in arranging them.

Controversy has centered on whether or not trucking concerns should enjoy subsidies in the form of highway right-of-ways. Unsympathetic critics claim that heavy trucks destroy road surfaces and make highway travel more dangerous; they would require trucking concerns to pay a greater share of highway costs. They point out that railways must build and maintain their own roadbeds and then pay property taxes on their rails and roadbeds as well. Supposedly, this gives truckers an unfair competitive advantage. Proponents of the trucking industry reply that trucks pay license fees—often very high—and fuel taxes which more than pay for the use of the roads. Their companies also pay property and income taxes just as the railroads do. And they always remind the railway men that the government gave land and other subsidies to the railroads in the nineteenth century. National transportation policy, in spite of the declaration set forth in the Act of 1940, seems dedicated to subsidizing and supporting, without regard to economic costs, any agency of transportation which the public demands. A well coordinated regulatory system does not appear on the horizon, notwithstanding the Cabinet Committee Report of 1955.

AIR TRANSPORTATION

World War I marked the beginning of the aviation industry. War provided the incentive for building large numbers of planes and for training pilots. During the 1920s and 1930s, stunt flyers at county fairs and daring adventurers like Charles A. Lindbergh popularized aviation. Meanwhile, improvements in planes and pilot training paved the way for the growth of commercial air transportation. The air age did not arrive until World War II, however, even though the long-distance movement of mail and passengers by air was already well established.

The history of commercial air transportation is closely linked with the movement of mail by air. As early as 1911, the Post Office Department experimented with air mail and in 1918 it established regular service between New York and Washington. The Kelly Air Mail Act of 1925 allowed the Postmaster General to award air-mail contracts on the basis of private bidding. These contracts proved important in the success of the early lines. As with earlier subsidies to railways and ocean shipping, fraud tainted the air-mail contracts, causing Postmaster General James A. Farley to cancel them in 1934. The Air Mail Act of that year charged the Interstate Commerce Commission with the responsibility for setting air-mail rates, ending private bidding. Since 1938 the Civil Aeronautics Board has fixed mail payments at a level sufficient, when added to other revenues, to enable the airlines to operate profitably.

FIG. 24-2. A trimotored aircraft of an early commercial airline, a predecessor of American Airlines. (*Courtesy of American Airlines.*)

Air-mail subsidies, averaging over $20 million a year from 1939 to 1956, were meager compared to other forms of governmental aid. From the start, local, state and Federal authorities provided most airport facilities, the Federal government built and maintained a civil airways system of navigation aids, and the military furnished most of the research in aircraft construction. The value of these different aids cannot be measured precisely in dollars and cents, but they exceeded $100 million annually in 1955. The public has regarded this expenditure as necessary to develop a new, promising form of transportation, just as the people earlier favored aid to railroads. But there are critics who say that the commercial airlines have existed long enough to prove their worth and should now stand on their own. They also argue that public policy does not take clearly enough into account the effects on other forms of transportation, such as railroad passenger traffic.

Growth of commercial aviation has been phenomenal, especially in terms of passenger-miles flown. In 1939, airline companies flew 683 million passenger-miles; in 1957, they flew 28,900 million. The 1939 figure represented only 2 per cent of commercial intercity travel. In 1957, all air carriers[3] accounted for 35 per cent of such traffic. The number of passengers carried increased twenty-three times in that same period, and the number of cities served rose from 286 to about 700. The speed of fast airliners grew from 220 to 360 mph. Jet cruisers of the future will greatly exceed these figures. Since 1939, rates for first-class air travel have remained fairly constant. For example, a ticket from New York to Chicago cost $44.95 in 1939. In 1959, the same ticket sold for $47.95. Meanwhile, comfort and safety of passengers have greatly improved. Fear of death in airplane crashes has not been eliminated, but since 1950 the fatalities per 100 million revenue passenger miles has been less than *one.* This compares with from three to four fatalities for an equivalent number of passenger miles in automobiles and taxicabs. Commercial air freight, except for mail cargoes, has not proved feasible for most commodities. Although aircraft carried 600 million ton-miles of cargo in 1957, air freight was only about ½ of 1 per cent of all intercity freight.

The nineteenth century experience with unregulated railroads caused the Federal government to bring air carriers under control. The Kelly Act of 1925 and the Air Commerce Act of 1926 placed aviation under some control by the Post Office Department and the Department of Commerce. The Air Mail Act of 1934 divided authority over air-mail rates between the Post Office and the ICC. The Civil Aeronautics Act of 1938 and a reorganization in 1940 created a Civil Aeronautics Administration and a Civil Aeronautics Board. The CAA has jurisdiction over the airways system and enforces safety regulations and supervises airline traffic. The CAB administers the federal *economic* controls, much as the ICC supervises land traffic. It issues certificates of convenience and necessity to domestic airlines and can fix rates and govern intercorporate relationships. The CAB looks after the financial health of the certified lines, adjusting mail payments to help the weak lines maintain profitable operations.

PIPELINES

In 1957, oil pipelines carried approximately 17.2 per cent of all intercity freight in the United States. This was only 2 per cent less than highway freight and amounted to more than one-third of rail freight. The 139,000 miles of petroleum pipelines moved over 200 billion ton-miles of oil products in 1957. Moreover, oil pipelines are only a portion

[3] 1957 statistics include private operations while 1939 figures do not.

of the total pipeline mileage in the country. In 1957, trunk and gathering lines extended more than 635,000 miles—enough to reach around the equator twenty-five times. In addition to crude oil, the major products which move by pipeline are gasoline and natural gas. Early in 1957, a revolutionary event was the opening of the world's first coal pipeline from an eastern Ohio strip mine to Lake Erie. The 108-mile line carried "slurry"—a mixture of small particles of coal and water—for use in generating electricity. It can deliver more than 3,400 tons of coal each day, or the equivalent of two 100-car freight trainloads. Other commodities such as limestone, wood pulp, and iron ore may also move by pipe in a similar manner.

INLAND WATER TRANSPORTATION

There was a revival of interest in river and canal transportation around 1900, after fifty years of decline. Some of the reasons for that revival were the interest in conservation, the belief that water transportation was inherently cheaper than railroad transportation, the hostility toward railroad monopolies, and the feeling that railroads could not handle the growing volume of freight traffic. Another influence, while not economically warranted, was the desire of localities to benefit financially from Federal funds for river projects. Thus, much of the river and harbor legislation of the twentieth century was of the "pork barrel" type. In spite of the renewed interest and some Federal aid, river and canal traffic developed slowly before 1920. Inability of the railroads to cope with the increased burden of wartime traffic convinced Congress that more adequate inland waterways were essential to national security. In the 1920s, the Federal government increased its financial outlay for improving rivers. Then during the Great Depression the New Deal gave the matter even greater attention. Traffic on the Ohio, Mississippi, Missouri, and Illinois Rivers increased substantially after 1930. By 1918, New York had rehabilitated the Erie Canal and enlarged it into the New York State Barge Canals at great cost. The efforts were disappointing, however; traffic on the system responded only modestly to the improved and enlarged facilities. For the inland waterways as a whole, excluding the Great Lakes, freight movements increased from 8.4 billion ton-miles in 1925 to 115 billion ton-miles in 1957. This raised the share of national freight movements by river and canal from less than 2 to 8.5 per cent in the same period. River and canal freight consists of heavy, bulky commodities such as coal, sand, gravel, lumber, some iron and steel products, and petroleum.

The primary advantage which river and canal transportation allegedly has over land agencies is cheapness. The advantage is often more imaginary than real. The costs of building and maintaining waterways should be added to the operating costs of water carriers, although this rarely happens. One scholarly study[4] of comparative costs of water and rail transportation concluded that railroads were generally cheaper to construct and maintain than canals or river channels. Even though rivers are "natural" waterways, they are expensive to maintain. The difference between the rates charged by water carriers and the true economic costs of the facilities clearly amounts to a subsidy for the users of this "cheap" transportation. Advocates of this type of policy claim that water transportation furnishes vital competition for railroads and trucks and that savings to shippers fully offset the costs to the taxpayers.

For most of the twentieth century, shipping on the Great Lakes was far more important than that on rivers and canals. Iron ore, coal, grain, and lumber are the chief commodities in this traffic. Costs for canals and channels have been relatively small on the Great Lakes; public aids amount to a fraction of a cent per ton-mile of freight. This places lake steamers in a class by themselves in moving bulky commodities. Of course, harbor facilities, built with public aid, have been expensive, but even so lake transportation is cheap. In 1957, lake vessels transported 117 billion ton-miles of freight—or 8.7 per cent of the nation's intercity freight.

Also, coastwise ocean traffic remained important. The coastwise merchant marine had over 9 million gross tons registered in 1957—about 50 per cent as much as the tonnage engaged in foreign commerce. The opening of the Panama Canal in 1914 stimulated intercoastal trade. It diverted much transcontinental freight away from the railroads and gave encouragement to industrialization on the Pacific coast. The canal also gave American merchants an advantage over European competitors along the west coast of South America.

Inland water transportation received a boost in May of 1954 when President Eisenhower signed the Wiley-Dondero Act, authorizing United States participation in the St. Lawrence Seaway project. Canada and the United States began serious study of the development of a deep-water channel from the Great Lakes to the St. Lawrence River just after World War I, but Congress steadfastly refused to ratify agreements worked out by the two nations. Finally, after Canada asserted willingness to proceed without United States help, Congress passed the Wiley-Dondero Act. The St. Lawrence Seaway, as it is currently planned, will have a 27-foot channel from the Gulf of St. Lawrence to the Detroit River. This will supposedly enable ocean-going vessels to carry iron ore or grain into and out of the Great Lakes region without reloading onto

[4] Harold G. Moulton et al., *The American Transportation Problem* (Washington: Brookings Institution, 1933), chap. 22.

canal barges. The argument in favor of the Seaway rested on three main points: (1) the need to open the landlocked mid-continent to cheap ocean shipping, (2) the severe power shortage in southern Ontario, and (3) the importance of the Seaway in continental defense. Opponents contend that a much more costly 35-foot channel is needed to accommodate most of the deep-draft vessels engaged in foreign trade. They also argue that the Seaway will provide cheap water transportation at taxpayers' expense and that it will be closed by ice during four or five months out of each year. Railroads will have to carry the Seaway's traffic during those winter months—a situation which poses a serious problem for the railway companies. Can they survive on five months' seasonal traffic?

OCEAN SHIPPING

The United States had to build a merchant marine during World War I. When the war began, the gross tonnage engaged in foreign trade was slightly more than 1 million—wholly inadequate to meet the demands of the national emergency. Immediately Congress eased the formerly exclusive registration policies and brought about a twofold increase in tonnage in two years. Greater reliance upon American shipping by the Allies and the activities of German submarines left the merchant marine still inadequate. Congress created the United States Shipping Board in 1916 to assume complete authority over the merchant marine and organized the Emergency Fleet Corporation in 1917 to construct new vessels. Delays kept the project from getting under way early enough to do much good. The Corporation did not stop building ships when the war ended (November, 1918), however; it kept ordering ships until it acquired some 1,500. By 1921 the size of the foreign trade fleet reached a respectable total of 11.1 million gross tons. Unfortunately, many of the ships built for the war were of inferior construction—some of wood and some even with concrete hulls. They were worthless almost as soon as they were finished.

The government revamped its shipping policy after 1920. The Jones Merchant Marine Act of that year ordered the Shipping Board to sell or lease its ships to private companies. The inferior ships went to the scrap heap, while soundly built steel vessels passed into the hands of shipping concerns at about 10 per cent of the original cost to the United States. This was but one facet of a subsidy policy designed to prevent another decline of the merchant marine. Mail subsidies and low-interest loans to shipping concerns were tried in vain. Registered tonnage fell off steadily through the 1920s and 1930s. Under the Merchant Marine Act of 1936, the government offered operational and construction subsidies but failed to stop the decline. By 1941, gross tonnage stood at just over 3 million; World War II again caught America unprepared.

Congress created a War Shipping Board just after the United States declared war on Japan in December, 1941. The Board took charge of enlarging and operating the merchant fleet; the Maritime Commission, established by the Merchant Marine Act of 1936, supervised new construction. Liberty and Victory ships slipped into the water at a rate of

FIG. 24-3. The coordination of rail and water facilities in New York Harbor is typical of large ports. The *Queen Mary* is in the background. (*Courtesy of the Port of New York Authority.*)

one a day, once the program began to function smoothly. By the war's end, the merchant fleet engaged in foreign shipping had grown to nearly 30 million gross tons—almost a tenfold increase since 1941. The nation did not need such a large merchant marine for peacetime purposes. The Merchant Ship Sales Act of 1946 permitted the sale of surplus cargo vessels at a fraction of the construction costs. Some Liberty ships were not fit for further sea service after 1945, and the government sold them as scrap metal—in some cases to razor-blade manufacturers. These sales reduced the United States foreign trade fleet to about 19 million gross tons in 1951; the tonnage has fluctuated near that level since then. The Federal government, in its postwar merchant marine policy, has endeavored to prevent a recurrence of the post-World War I decline. The Federal Maritime Board, successor to the Maritime Commission, pays subsidies equal to construction and operating cost differentials between America and foreign nations. The government agreed in 1957 to pay out $120 million in the fiscal year 1958. This huge outlay is considered essential to national security; it has little economic justification.

COMMUNICATIONS

In 1914, Americans used the post office, telegraph, and telephone for personal communications and had newspapers and magazines for mass communications. These agencies all grew in importance after that time, although radio in the 1920s and television in the 1940s became important mass media.

The postal service grew with the nation. In 1910, the system handled about 15 billion pieces of mail compared with over 61 billion pieces in 1958. Parcel post, inaugurated in 1912, greatly stimulated the mail-order business and offered stern competition to the express companies. The post office also offered its patrons savings certificates and money order service. The costs of these varied services to individuals and businesses have rarely been matched by post office receipts. Since 1914, the Post Office Department has run a deficit in every year except 1945.

The telegraph and telephone serve those persons who wish speedier contact than postal service can provide. The telegraph industry actually had fewer miles of wire in operation in 1958 than in 1914. The increased use of the telephone accounted in part for the relatively small growth of the telegraph industry. The number of telegrams sent in 1956 was 152 million, only 45 million more than in 1912. Meanwhile, the number of telephones mushroomed from 10.5 million in 1915 to 63.6 million in 1957. Long-distance service between New York and San Francisco began in 1915, and in 1923 the first wirephoto passed over telephone wires. The teletype, perfected in 1930, greatly facilitated business operations. In 1959, the nation awaits the installation of a direct-dialing long-distance service which will give instantaneous contact between the most distant parts of the nation.

Commercial radio broadcasting in 1920 had widespread social and economic effects. The popularity of radio listening grew rapidly in the 1920s, with the number of sets increasing from about 400,000 in 1922 to 5,700,000 in 1926. The industry became so big that Congress placed it under Federal control in the Radio Act of 1927. Then, in 1934, the Federal Communications Commission assumed control of radio along with telegraph, cable, and telephone (and later television) service. It regulated the issuance of licenses for broadcasting stations and rates and services of telegraph, cable, and telephone companies. The number of radio networks and stations expanded rapidly after the 1920s; by 1957 there were seven networks and about 3,500 stations. More than 97 per cent of American families owned radio sets in 1958. In addition to breaking the isolation of rural areas, the radio proved useful to the business world. Radio advertising enabled producers and retailers to reach millions of households daily.

The popularity of radio lessened with the success of television. The first television transmission occurred in 1927, but the first commercial telecasts did not begin until 1941. During World War II there were only six transmitting stations, as the emergency of war curtailed the production of television sets. But between 1948 and 1957, the number of stations increased thirty times. These stations joined, for the most part, three national networks, which in 1958 sent entertainment into four-fifths of all American homes. The economic significance of the television industry is twofold: it is a major advertising medium, and it is an important manufacturing industry. The retail sales value of television sets in 1957 exceeded that of any other household appliance.

Newspapers remained the primary agency for keeping the public informed. In 1957, 1,755 daily papers averaged 58 million paid circulation. These were supplemented by 540 Sunday papers and perhaps 8,000 weekly and other papers. The 5- or 10-cent daily paper, which carries local, national, and world news to its readers, is made possible by the payments of advertisers. In 1954 these provided more than two-thirds of the newspapers' total receipts of $2.9 billion.

CHAPTER 25

Expansion in Manufacturing

Manufacturing has expanded rapidly since the outbreak of World War I. Primarily, this has been the continuation of a trend that began early in the previous century. But today the United States is the world leader in manufacturing, and manufacturing has far outdistanced its one-time rival, farming. Whereas in 1914 the value added in manufacturing was only about 50 per cent greater than cash farm income, today it is four times as great. And whereas in 1914 there were about 50 per cent more persons engaged in farming than in manufacturing, today there are almost twice as many in manufacturing as in farming.

Two world wars and the Korean War particularly stimulated the growth of manufacturing calling, as they did, for the speedy output of large amounts of standardized products, with price a secondary consideration. Enterprisers bought costly capital equipment that made possible greater output in a shorter time at lower per unit costs and thus enhanced profits in the long run. This same period also brought on one major depression and one sizable secondary one (1920–1922). These set manufacturing back for a time—the Great Depression did so for several years—but they had the virtue of weeding out inefficient producers and of obliging the survivors to improve their methods. Manufacturing prospered and suffered in accordance with the phases of the business cycle. The number of persons engaged in manufacturing fluctuated much more sharply than those engaged in farming.

World War I and Manufacturing. At the time World War I began in 1914, there was a moderate depression going on in America, but it ended soon. The English blockade prevented the United States from selling to the Central Powers, but the Entente Allies sent American manufacturers ever larger orders. The Allies needed foodstuffs, steel, copper, cotton, and all kinds of machinery. Within a year American exports had doubled; within two years, five major Allied nations had tripled their imports from this country to $3 billion. The industries which made munitions and other kinds of war matérial prospered tremendously. Steel companies especially thrived; the Bethlehem Steel Company's net manufacturing profits shot up from $9.4 million in 1914 to $60.1 million in 1916. But the prosperity was not evenly distributed, for the war's demands raised the costs of raw materials in many civilian goods industries and obliged them to slacken operations and lay off workers. The construction industry, in particular, suffered in 1915.

In April, 1917, the United States declared war on Germany and her allies, and gave wartime prosperity another boost. Not only did the United States continue to supply its Allies with war matériel but it now had to equip and supply its own army of 4 million men, half of whom went overseas. Industries trying to fill government orders for war supplies had to obtain essential raw materials such as steel, copper, cotton, and the like as quickly, cheaply, and easily as possible. Obviously, nonessential industries should get only a minimum of them. During 1917 matters were not working that way at all. Accordingly, early in 1918, to straighten things out and to do this vital job, the President put Bernard Baruch at the head of the War Industries Board. This board controlled all resources and essential manufacturing plants and had the power to allocate raw materials and fix prices. Baruch's dictatorial but able direction brought order out of industrial chaos, and American industry greatly increased its output of munitions and other war matériel. The rule often used in government contracts with private individuals was that the producer would receive cost plus 10 per cent—an arrangement which greatly stimulated production. Admittedly, it gave rise to some shameless profiteering, but also it brought forth the goods to win the war.

Postwar Adjustments. The coming of peace necessarily brought adjustments to industries which had expanded during the war to produce munitions, airplane parts, cannon, ships, and other military necessities. Such industries had to reconvert themselves to fill peacetime demands. For some it was not too difficult to shift from making airplane parts and tanks to making automobiles. The government kept the shipyards producing for three years after the armistice. But other war industries simply had to shift from a feast to a famine existence. Meanwhile, industries like construction, which had been starved for several years, had their turn at the banquet table, at least when times were good. A short-lived but serious depression began in mid-1920 and lasted for about two years but was followed by seven prosperous years. It was the automobile industry as much as any single industry which helped to lift the country from the 1920–1922 depression. The faster development of a number of important industries characterized the period of the 1920's. In addition to automobiles, there were the radio, refrigerator, road-building equipment, cigarette, and the chemical and dye industries. Aviation and television did not develop as rapidly as many expected them to. On the other hand, silks and cotton textiles, pianos, coal mining, cigars, breweries (because of Prohibition), and the manufacture of ice declined in this period.

There was also considerable talk of technological unemployment during the decade of the 1920s. It was taking fewer workers less hours to turn out more goods. For example, in 1923 about 8.2 million wage earners added $24.6 billion dollars of value to manufactured goods. Six years later, 8.4 million wage earners added $30.6 billion of value to manufactured goods. In other words, 2½ per cent more workers added almost 20 per cent more value. Furthermore, the 1929 employment force contained a larger proportion of unskilled and semiskilled workers than the 1923 force. But the 1929 employees worked in somewhat better organized plants and had the use of better equipment. What, it may be asked, had happened to the more skilled workers? Some had grown old and retired; some had been down-graded; and some had been laid off. There was a consoling economic theory which said that when a machine and a semiskilled attendant supplanted a skilled worker, he would be able to find a job in some other type of work. Events in the United States, and especially in this period, demonstrated that considerable time was needed for such an adjustment, and that in all probability the worker whose skill the machine had displaced would never be as well off again. Some persons even blamed the unemployment of the depressed 1930s on technological changes. However, this exaggerated grossly the impact of technological advance. Moreover, those who criticized technological changes forgot that every invention that had contributed to the American high standard of living had done so by increasing the buying power of many in a small way, although injuring the livelihood of a few in a large way. The rising standard of living attested to the fact that the small gains of the many outweighed the heavy losses of the few. The causes of the depression were deeper than technological change.

Another industrial change in the 1920s probably contributed more to the depression. That was the increase for a time in the number of rather expensive articles demanded by the public. As income rose, the proportion of it which people spent on the essentials of life—food, clothing, and shelter—tended to decline. People saved some of the remainder, but much of it they spent on automobiles, radios, washing machines, and refrigerators, to name only a few. The factories producing these experienced for a while a tremendous demand for their products and they hastened to meet it by expanding their plant capacity. But once they had enlarged their plants, the companies were under pressure to sell a larger level of output every year. Meanwhile, the proportion of the population owning these autos, refrigerators, radios, and washing machines was nearing the saturation point. True, some machines were always wearing out and had to be replaced, new families were forming, the more well-to-do customers wanted the most up-to-date models, and manufacturers could reach new customers by clever advertising. Yet the machines lasted too long—from the manufacturers' viewpoint—and the cost of reaching new customers rose. Just as the nation had overinvested in railroads in 1857 and 1873, so, there is some reason to believe, it overinvested this time in factories to turn out certain consumer durable goods, and most especially automobiles.

Manufacturing in the Depression. The Great Depression began in the autumn of 1929. It was not unduly severe in 1930 but reached its low point in 1932–1933. Thereafter, the economy made a slow recovery, almost emerging in 1937, but then a recession set in which lasted until the outbreak of World War II. Between 1929 and 1933 the number of manufacturing establishments declined by one-third. So did the number of persons engaged in manufacturing; and the value added by manufacturing was halved. Total wages paid were also cut in half. The industries that suffered especially were the capital equipment industries—those making machines, steel, and the like—together with the consumer durable goods industries—those making automobiles, refrigerators, and washing machines. For example, between 1929 and 1932 the output of automobiles declined 76 per cent. Although one heard repeatedly that "recovery is just around the corner," the corner, like a mirage, never seemed to come any nearer. To achieve recovery and to eliminate some of the worst aspects of cutthroat competition, Congress created the National Industrial Recovery Administration, under which each industry set up its own rules to police itself. The Supreme Court found it unconstitutional in 1935. Congress put nothing in its place, for by then, some recovery was being felt. By 1937 industry was temporarily back on its feet. Then rising labor costs, brought on in part by successful strikes of the new Committee for Industrial Organization, helped set industry back once more. This recession continued until some months after the outbreak of war in Europe.

Manufacturing in World War II. When World War II broke out, manufacturing had been marking time for a full decade. The Federal Reserve Board's index of industrial production (1935–1939 = 100) had reached 110 in 1929, fallen sharply in the Great Depression, then climbed above that point in 1937, slipped again, and was back to 109 in 1939. In previous decades, industry had shown an average growth of about one-third every decade; now, for an entire ten-year period, American industry had shown no growth. There were economists who said the United States had a mature economy and that further growth would henceforth be slow. There were still 10 million unemployed early in 1940, and many industries were operating far below capacity. But the war tremendously stimulated manufacturing. First the orders came from Europe, then from the American government preparing for the possibility of war, and finally because this nation was at war after December, 1941. Chart 25-1 shows how manufacturing came to life and grew, especially the manufacture of durable goods such as transportation equipment. Production of durable goods rose 2½ times between 1939 and the peak year of 1943.

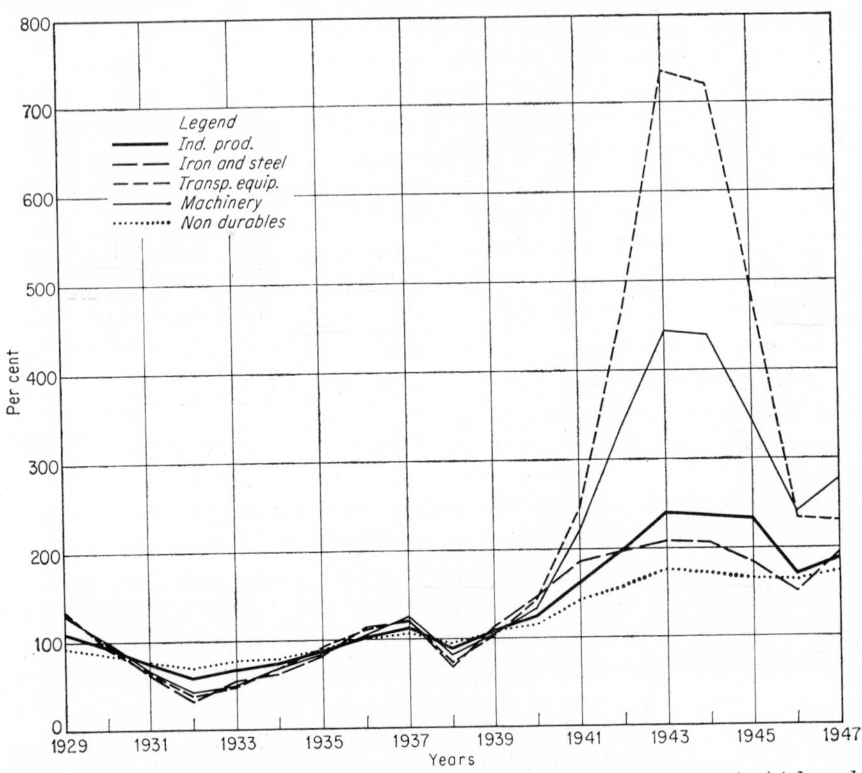

CHART 25-1. Indexes of industrial growth, 1929–1947 (1935–1939 = 100). (*Adapted from U.S. Bureau of the Census, Statistical Abstract of the United States, 1946, Washington, 1946, p. 811.*)

Within that category, iron and steel production nearly doubled, machinery production went up almost fivefold, and transportation equipment rose over sevenfold. The over-all index of industrial production about doubled. Miraculously the United States undertook the physical cost of fighting a two-front war and yet maintained its standard of living on an "as usual" basis. When President Franklin Roosevelt early in the war spoke of producing 50,000 airplanes within a year's time, the German High Command scoffed at his braggadocio. And few Americans really believed that the nation could do it. Building a plane still required much skilled hand labor. But just as other wars had caused manufacturers to put the making of other articles on an assembly-line basis, so did this one. The United States built airplanes as it did automobiles. It built ships on an assembly-line basis, too. The government built its own aluminum plants, airplane factories, and atomic bomb factory, the last costing about $2 billion to put into production.

Late in 1944, with the Germans retreating fast, it looked as though the war could not last much longer, and some economists voiced the fear

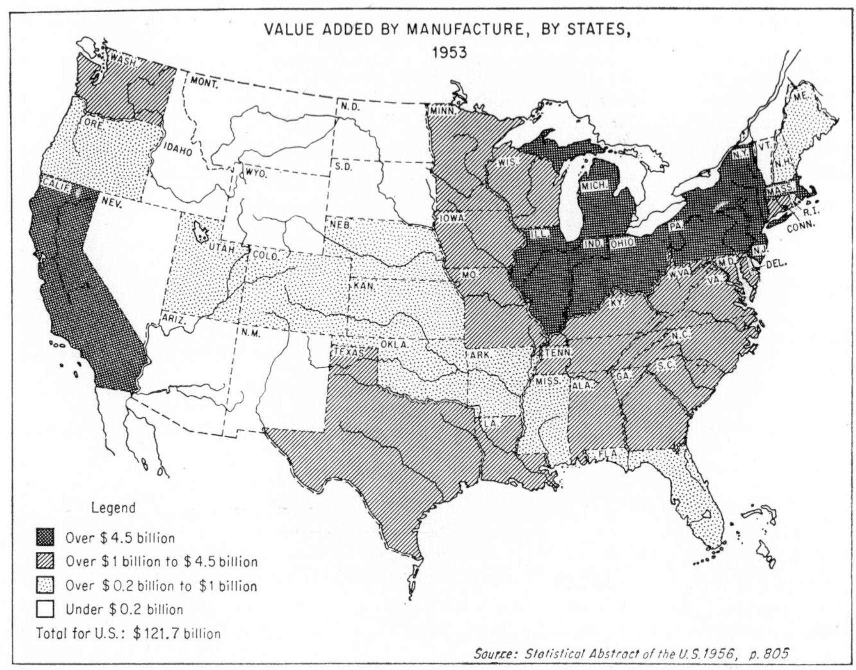

MAP 25-1. (*Adapted from U.S. Bureau of the Census, Statistical Abstract of the United States, 1956, Washington, 1956.*) See similar maps on page 316.

that the nation would slip back into a depression and that there would be some 8 or 10 million unemployed soon after the war ended. There would no longer be demand for the products of many war installations. Reconverting them to peacetime uses would take time. The pattern after the Civil War and World War I certainly suggested a depression shortly after this war, too.

Manufacturing since World War II. As Chart 25-1 shows, there was a drop-off in the manufacture of durable goods at the end of the war. A few months before it ended, the government cut back its orders to many plants. This hardly caused more than a mild recession, however, and the postwar depression which economists and businessmen alike anticipated did not materialize. There was an enormous backlog of replacements to provide, not only for the period during the war itself, but for the depressed decade before. People had cars to replace, homes to repair or build, equipment to replace, and factories had plants to renovate and expand. Instead of a depression being the chief problem, the United States was producing enough to satisfy the demands of a boom market. Whereas the average automobile in 1940 was five years old, by 1946 it was nine years old. Table 25-1 indicates the extent of growth in various

Table 25-1
Growth of Industry, 1930–1958
Production indexes: (1947–1949 = 100)

Year	Total industrial	Nondurable goods	Durable goods	Automobiles	Television sets
1930	49	51	45	56*	
1940	67	69	63	74*	
1944	125	99	159		
1945	107	96	123	2*	
1947	100	99	101	....	70
1948	104	102	104	93	
1949	97	99	95	122	217
1950	112	111	116	159	561
1953	134	118	153	146	541
1954	125	116	137	131	522
1958	134	130	142	99	365

* Estimated.

SOURCES: U.S. Bureau of the Census, *Statistical Abstract of the United States, 1957* (Washington, 1957), pp. 784, 785; Charles B. Fowler et al., *Economic Handbook* (New York: Thomas Y. Crowell Company, 1955), p. 32; *Federal Reserve Bulletin*, February, 1959, pp. 194, 198.

kinds of manufacturing since the end of the war. Durable goods such as steel, autos, tractors, and lumber have grown more rapidly than nondurables such as textiles, rubber, leather, printing, food, and tobacco. Automobile production has been uneven, but on the average it has doubled since 1940. The television business was in the prime of its life but, like radio in the late 1920s, it finally passed the period of easy expansion and had to face severe competition. The amazing aspect of manufacturing after 1945 is that it expanded fairly steadily, enjoying some fourteen years of prosperity. True, there were minor recessions in 1945, 1949, 1953–1954, and 1957–1958, and industries have not prospered equally. But there was no major depression, whereas there had been one, if not two, within ten years after the close of each previous war. One explanation has been that new industries are constantly appearing and that the old ones have managed not to have their individual depressions simultaneously.

PROGRESS IN INDIVIDUAL INDUSTRIES

Iron and Steel. Although the iron and steel industry was less important relatively in 1954 than in 1914, it was still one of the basic industries in highly industrialized America. One industrial worker out of three worked on a product made wholly or partly of iron or steel. The industry grew rapidly in this forty-year period. The two world wars especially stimulated steel's growth, as Table 25-2 shows. The iron and steel industry

Table 25-2
Production of Steel Ingots and Castings, 1914–1958

Year (Jan. 1)	Production, million long tons	Capacity worked, per cent	Business cycle stage
1914	23.5	57	Depression
1916	42.8	86	Prosperity
1918	44.5	82	Prosperity
1921	19.8	34	Depression
1929	56.4	87	Prosperity
1932	13.7	20	Depression
1939	47.1	64.5	Depression
1944	80.0	95.5	Prosperity
1949	69.6	81.1	Recession
1951	93.9	100.9	Prosperity
1958	125.6	73	Recovery

SOURCE: American Iron and Steel Institute, *Annual Statistical Report*, various years (New York: American Iron and Steel Institute).

is a "prince or pauper" or "feast or famine" industry. Its business is either prospering or doing poorly. That is because it supplies the raw materials for durable consumer goods and for equipment for industrial expansion. When times are good, people buy expensive items like refrigerators and automobiles, and industries enlarge their plants; when times are bad, consumers restrict their expenditures to necessities like food and clothing, and industrial plants see no need to enlarge their capacity. Consequently, the factory customers of iron and steel mills give them few orders.

Within this period of nearly half a century, there were a number of significant developments in the iron and steel industry, both on the technical side and on the business side. There has been a strong tendency for the steel industry to become less concentrated in the Pittsburgh area. In 1904 plants in that area made half of the steel, but by 1955 they made about one-third. The East and South likewise declined in importance, whereas the Great Lakes area grew until it was producing nearly a third of the steel by 1955. Another important business trend was the persistent tendency for iron and steel plants to become consolidated into a few big companies. Bethlehem Steel has since 1922 bought or built new plants at Buffalo, Johnstown, Sparrows Point, Maryland, and on the Pacific

FIG. 25-1. Modern blast furnace at U.S. Steel works at Morrisville, Pa. (*Courtesy of United States Steel Corporation.*)

coast. Bethlehem and Youngstown Sheet and Tube for several years sought to consolidate but the Justice Department and a lower Federal court decision prevented the marriage. In 1930 Republic Steel bought three large rival companies. Steel, like automobiles, is an industry in which a few giants do the bulk of the business. The largest of all the steel companies is still United States Steel, with its major plants in Pittsburgh and Gary. The Second World War gave the steel industry an opportunity not only to enlarge its plants but also to discard much obsolete equipment. The doubling of capacity that took place represented improved efficiency as well as additional furnaces. Some of this drive toward improvement arose from the fact that the steel industry, despite its consolidations and its trend toward oligopoly (production and sale by only a few large companies), had become more competitive than it was about 1910. Increased competition and the necessity of having to deal with stronger labor unions since 1937 have been major causes of concern to the steel industry. On the other hand, the industry has gained in stability in recent years from government armament orders, from the

FIG. 25-2. Modern rolling mill at U.S. Steel works at Morrisville, Pa. (*Courtesy of United States Steel Corporation.*)

nation's rising standard of living, and from the fact that since 1940 there has not been a major business depression.

There have been important technical improvements in iron and steel in at least five major respects. (1) Since 1908 an increasing proportion of steel has been produced by the open-hearth method rather than by the bessemer process. By 1915 the ratio was 4 to 1 in favor of the open-hearth method; by 1935, 8 to 1; and by 1957, 41 to 1. The open-hearth process yields a purer, more reliable steel. (2) Since 1948 electric steel has also outdistanced bessemer and now holds about a 3 to 1 ratio over it. Electric has replaced crucible steel as the method of making high-grade steels. (3) Since 1914 the steel industry has greatly mechanized its operations, especially in rolling mills where it has developed to a high degree the "continuous rolling" process. By this method, white-hot ingots are passed along on rolls and run through a series of grooves which narrow and form them into the structural shape desired. The machinery to do this is ingenious, elaborate, and requires almost no human assistance (see Fig. 25-2). (4) Still another important development, especially since the 1930s, has been the growing importance of "light steels," such as go into modern streamlined railroad trains. Steel has thus found ways to meet the competition of aluminum. (5) Finally, steel has gone chemical, so to speak. The use of alloy steels had begun before 1914, but in the last generation it has developed to a high degree. Depending on the use to which it will be put, steel will contain varying amounts of such alloying elements as titanium, manganese, tungsten, molybdenum, nickel, chrome, and vanadium. One will make the steel springy; another enables it to resist great heat; still another gives it the ability to withstand high pressures or continuous pounding. Making steel has become complicated again, as it was before Bessemer discovered his process a century ago.

The Automobile Industry. Once a rich man's toy, the automobile has become virtually a necessity of life in the United States. Some 68 per cent of the world's passenger automobiles are in America, and three families out of four owned one in 1958. Motor vehicles traveled 628 billion miles in 1956. The average car scrapped in 1956 was eleven years old; there were some 4.2 million scrapped in 1957. Thus replacement of worn-out cars alone means much to the automobile industry. As Chart 25-2 shows the number of cars has been growing steadily for over half a century. The success of the automobile industry is vital to a host of other industries, such as gasoline, rubber, steel, glass, upholstery, plastics, and cement, to name some of the major ones. Like iron and steel, the auto industry is also somewhat of a "prince or pauper."

World War I gave the automobile industry quite a stimulus. There were at times more Ford cars being made than all other cars combined, but Henry Ford lost ground after 1921. Ford lost the lead to General Motors about 1927: he had stayed with the "tin Lizzie" too long without making substantial improvements. Secondhand cars took over the low-priced field. Twice Ford closed down his plant to retool, coming out with the new Model A in 1928 and then with the V-8 in 1932, but he never regained the lead again. Henceforth General Motors held it, although another large company, Chrysler Motors, became a strong competitor from 1928 on.

William Crapo Durant was the head of General Motors. He was a financial wizard rather than a mechanical genius like Ford. Beginning with carriages, he entered the automobile business in 1904 to assist the Buick Motor Company. In 1908 he formed General Motors, worth $3.5 million, and temporarily outproduced Ford. In the next two years he bought up eleven companies, including the Cadillac and Oldsmobile;

twice he offered to buy out Ford. But Durant tried to do too much at once; he went too deeply in debt. If something went wrong, he stood a good chance of failing. When Buick sales fell off, banker interests took over and forced Durant out. He then formed a new company, the Chevrolet Motor Company, and gained the assistance of the Du Ponts. In 1916, by a Napoleonic maneuver, Durant and his friends regained control of General Motors. Once again he overborrowed and overexpanded; this time it was the Panic of 1920 that forced him out. The Du

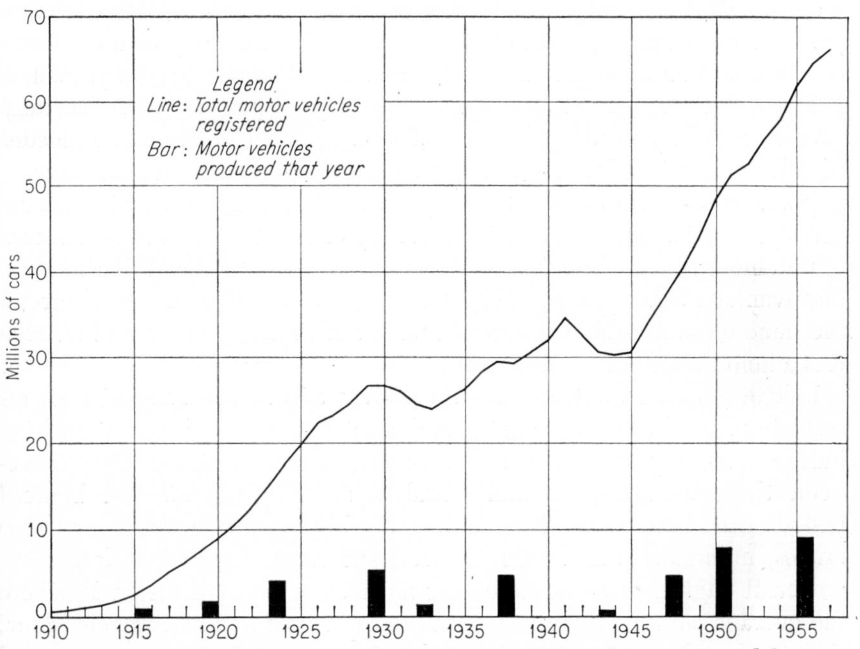

CHART 25-2. Growth of the motor vehicle industry. (*Adapted from Automobile Manufacturers Association; Automobile Facts and Figures, 1957.*)

Ponts bought out his interests and in 1922 Alfred Sloan, Jr., became president of General Motors. General Motors sales boomed from $464 million in 1922 to $1,504 million in 1929 to $10,990 million in 1957. By then it produced nearly as many cars as all other automobile companies combined. General Motors and its two nearest rivals, Ford and Chrysler, make about 97 per cent of the cars in the United States. The other two companies left in the passenger-car business, American Motors and Studebaker-Packard, are relatively small. From the 1890s to the present some 1,500 companies have made motor vehicles, but in 1921 only forty-four were left in the passenger-car business, only eleven in 1940, and but five today.

There are numerous reasons why the small companies simply have not been able to compete with the larger ones. First, the Big Three, especially Ford, are quite extensively "integrated." Ford has its own coal and iron mines, lake boats, steel plants, glass factories, and tire factories. Admittedly, when times are bad, the cost of idle plant is sizable. To avoid this difficulty, the companies have integrated themselves only to the point that they can supply a major part of their own needs; the rest they buy from independents. Secondly, the large companies change styles and make improvements almost yearly. The smaller companies must do likewise, but for them the retooling involved is extremely expensive. For example, a set of dies to stamp out the body of a car costs nearly a million dollars. If Ford or General Motors or Chrysler produces half a million cars with the dies, that is only $2 per car, whereas for a smaller company producing only 50,000 cars, it is $20 per car. The cost of advertising is relatively heavier for small companies, too, and it is impossible for them to have as many dealers to sell and repair their cars. Finally, they cannot offer as wide a variety of cars to potential customers. Maintaining several brands and styles might at first glance seem to be a disadvantage for, say, General Motors, but it is not. Car parts made from the same dies are usable in several makes and models so that, on balance, it is a help rather than a hindrance.

Improvements in automobiles themselves and in the conveniences of motoring have been a constant stimulus to the growth of the automobile business. Among the many major improvements since the 1920s have been the self-starter, hydraulic brakes, safety glass, all-steel bodies, balloon tires, better rear vision, automatic shifting, power steering, power brakes, numerous push-button devices, and more economical and more powerful engines that move the car more smoothly and faster. By 1956 the average car had twice as long a life as in 1925 and had traveled four times as far. On the highway itself, the motorist now has the convenience of concrete highways, which the states first built in great number in the 1920s, a numbering system to guide him, and adequate gasoline stations, repair shops, and motels. It became possible in 1956 to travel from New York to Chicago by turnpike, without encountering a traffic signal. A rugged driver could make the 800-mile trip in a day. All this is a far cry from one author's memories of his first long automobile trip from New Jersey to Maine, 600 miles, in the summer of 1919. Since virtually all the roads were dirt, the passengers wore "dusters." There was no highway numbering system and a scarcity of signs, and the journey took six days to accomplish. No wonder that with today's conveniences the automobile business is a giant.

The Chemical Industries. The chemical industries represent a new type of industry and one quite typical of the twentieth century. Edward Slosson, former popularizer of chemistry, once pointed out that man, in his struggle to make a living, has passed through three stages in his use of nature's resources. Early man simply appropriated food from the forest. A later civilization was more imaginative and cultivated plants, kept animals, and made nature cater to his needs. There followed a third stage, a "creative" one, in which man broke down what nature offered into its basic chemical elements and then rebuilt them into what he wanted. Now the world is entering a fourth stage, in which scientific man has probed even back of the elements into the secrets of the atom

Table 25-3
Growth of the Chemical Products Industries

Year	Index of production in chemical industries (1929 = 100)	Sulfuric acid (million tons)	Rayon yarns (million pounds)
1899	19	0.3	
1914	42	1.9	2
1919	52	2.2	8
1921	42	2.0	15
1929	100	4.1	121
1933	84	2.6	213
1937	124	3.9	322
1939	133	3.8	329
1945	329	9.5*	
1949	286	10.9*	
1956	501	16.0*	

* Not closely comparable with previous figures.
SOURCES: U.S. Bureau of the Census, *Historical Statistics of the United States, 1789–1945*, p. 186; *Continuation to 1952*, p. 26; *Statistical Abstract, 1956*, pp. 792, 823; *1957*, pp. 784, 817.

itself. This may in time make the dreams of the alchemists come true—making gold out of lead—and should unleash formidable power resources at low cost for man's use.

The so-called chemical industries, according to the National Bureau of Economic Research and the Federal Reserve Board, have shown astounding growth in the last two generations, as Table 25-3 clearly shows.

The chemical industry includes such diverse products as sulfuric acid, soda ash, explosives, dyes, nylons, and numerous drugs. The first sulfuric acid plant was set up in 1793, but the product was not important until the twentieth century. Output has increased nearly tenfold since 1914 (see Table 25-3). About a quarter of it is the by-product of other industries, especially copper refining. Sulfuric acid is of prime importance to the fertilizer industry and it is essential in petroleum refining. A very large number of other industries use it at one stage or another. Thus it is a good indicator of business conditions. Soda ash is made of salt, limestone, coke, and ammonia by the Solvay process (named for its Belgian inventor) and is essential to the processing of glass, soap, paper, and petroleum.

There are many large and important chemical companies, but the largest and probably best known is Du Pont de Nemours of Wilmington, Delaware, founded in 1802. During the nineteenth century it specialized in gunpowder and dynamite, and later added paints. Because World War I prevented the United States from obtaining its synthetic dyestuffs from Germany, the customary source, Du Pont went into the business. According to the company, Du Pont invested $40 million and five years of research before it began to earn a profit. About the turn of the twentieth century, chemists had perfected several ways of making artificial silk out of cellulose. By the 1920s the so-called rayon industry was thriving. About 1938 Du Pont came out with a better product, nylon, which it made chemically from coal, air, and water. More recently, Du Pont has perfected dacron and other fibers.

There are certain characteristics that are common to most of the chemical industries. First of all, they maintain close connections with universities and they have large research staffs of their own. They allocate sizable budgets each year to perfect existing products and to develop new ones. Du Pont announced in 1948 that 20,000 of its employees were making products that twelve years before either were unknown or at least not in commercial production. A few years later the company estimated that over half of the products it would be producing in 1970 had not yet been discovered. An industry that invents and discovers so many new products and methods must deal with a rapid rate of obsolescence in its equipment. Also, to support their costly research programs, the companies have to be large. To stand the risk of failure in the case of some projects, they have to be diversified. Finally, the cost of developing artificial dyes or nylons or, more recently, dacrons is so great that the companies must strive to operate on the basis of large output and low cost.[1]

Electronics.[2] The newest of the major industries is electronics and it is most representative of modern industry: it relies on science. Electronics deals with "devices in which a controlled and variable flow of electrons results in a signal containing information." To be electronic, a device generally has to use a vacuum tube or transistor. Electronics began with

[1] E. B. Alderfer and H. E. Michl, *The Economics of American Industry* (New York: McGraw-Hill Book Company, Inc., 1957), chap. 15.

[2] Material for this discussion came from William B. Harris, "The Electronic Business," *Fortune* (April, 1957), pp. 137ff.

wireless telegraphy invented by Marconi about 1896 or perhaps with the telephone invented by Alexander Bell in 1876. It took on the proportions of an important industry with the coming of home radios from 1922 onward, and since then it has added several new major products to its list. Radar developed quite rapidly during World War II as a military device, and since then commercial airlines have adopted it. From 1947 on, television developed rapidly, just as radio had done a quarter of a century before, and since 1950 electronics has done an ever-increasing business in producing guided missiles for the government. The electronics industry produces computing machines which will do in minutes problems that it would take humans years to solve. It is the basis of automation. This industry rose from forty-ninth in 1939 to fifth in 1956. In 1939 it employed 150,000 persons and its total sales were under $1 billion; by 1956 its 500 manufacturers employed 1.5 million persons and its sales amounted to $11.5 billion. As already indicated, it is a collection of industries with common characteristics. These characteristics are very much the same as those of the chemical industries: the electronics industry must devote much attention to research, expect rapid obsolescence, and diversify its activities to a considerable degree.

There is a distinct pattern of development in new industries, whether the automobile, chemical, or electronics. At the outset, a few individuals with a modicum of capital and technical ability can start the industry. Competition is keen and casualties many—especially in times of depression. The average life of a passenger automobile company between 1903 and 1926 was five years. As soon as the public had bought its fill of automobiles, radios, or television sets and the profit honeymoon was over, the smaller and weaker companies dropped out or the larger ones absorbed them. Eventually a few large companies emerged, as in the automobile business, and dominated the field. This pattern has shown itself again and again in the history of American industry.

DEVELOPMENTS IN FUEL AND POWER

Fuel, and the power derived from it, are the muscles of the American industrial giant. The sources and character of the fuels used have changed materially in the last half century, as can be seen from Chart 25-3.

Half a century ago, coal was king among the fuels. Coal production reached its zenith with an output of 678 million tons in 1918. It slipped to 360 million tons in the depth of the Great Depression, but prospered again during World War II. Since then, total production has once more declined, reaching 421 million tons in 1958. All but five per cent is bituminous coal and the rest anthracite. Over three-quarters of all coal comes from five states: West Virginia, Pennsylvania, Kentucky, Illinois, and Ohio (important in that order). The coal mining industry has generally been very competitive. In recent decades, because of the competition of other fuels, it has often been a sick industry. The monopoly grip that the United Mine Workers have held on the industry since about 1933 has kept its costs up and accelerated the decline of coal as the major fuel.

To effect economies, the larger coal mines have installed expensive and elaborate machinery to dig, load, and carry away coal, all in one operation. In large mines it is fairly common to find $100,000 of equipment in

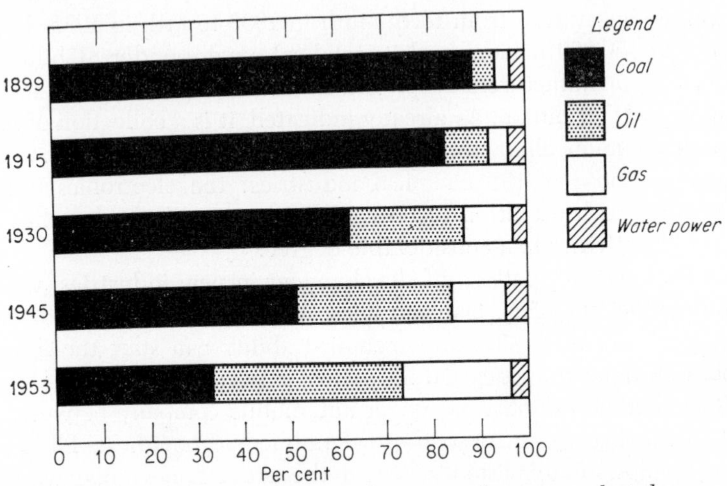

CHART 25-3. Relative importance of sources of energy, selected years, 1899–1953. (*Adapted from U.S. Bureau of Mines, Minerals Yearbook, 1950, p. 333; and 1953, p. 1.*)

use at each coal face. Only in the older or smaller mines are mules, picks, and dynamite still to be found. Thanks to mechanical improvements, the American miner in 1956 averaged 10.3 tons of coal per day, compared to 3.5 in 1910 and 5.2 as recently as 1940. Another reason for this increased productivity is that nearly a quarter of all coal mined (1956) comes from strip mines. Huge excavators remove the overburden from a vein of coal, digging down perhaps as much as 60 feet. Then somewhat smaller shovels dig out the whole vein of coal. This method requires fewer men, causes fewer accidents, and leaves virtually none of the coal behind (for pillars). However, it necessitates very expensive equipment and largely destroys the land for any further use for centuries.

For many years the consumption of coal was fairly evenly divided between the railroads, steel mills, other industries, homeowners, and the public utilities. Since about 1948 homeowners have been shifting to oil and natural gas and railroads have been changing from coal locomotives to diesel-powered ones. The coal mines' chief customers now are the utilities, the steel mills, and other industries. Even though coal has been slipping, it is still a large producer of energy.

In the days when Rockefeller made his millions, oil was used chiefly in kerosene lamps, but about 1914 gasoline passed kerosene as the chief product derived from petroleum. By 1920 petroleum supplied 15 per cent of all fuel energy; in 1957 it provided 41 per cent, surpassing coal. It supplied it in the form of crude oil, diesel fuel, and kerosene as well as gasoline. Between 1910 and 1957 the production of petroleum increased twelvefold. Moreover, through cracking and other improvements, the industry extracts twice as much gasoline from a barrel of oil as it did in 1910. About half of this enormous output went to propel 66 million motor vehicles over 628 billion miles in 1956. The other half, in the form of crude oil, diesel oil, and kerosene, ran tractors, railroads, factories, ocean vessels; it also heated homes and offices and provided some lighting. Nearly seven-eighths of the 33,000 railroad locomotives in 1956 were diesels, but the diesel engine is very economical in its use of oil. The United States produced two-thirds of the world's petroleum in 1914 and today produces almost half of it. Five states, Texas, California, Louisiana, Oklahoma, and Kansas, supply three-quarters of the American output. The nation imports a substantial amount of oil from abroad as well.

Natural gas is the cleanest and easiest of all the fuels to use. It can be piped to the furnace or cooking stove just as it comes from the ground. For many years oil producers had to throw it away because they had no storage tanks near the wells and no pipelines to carry it to the large cities. Gas is produced chiefly in Texas, Louisiana, Oklahoma, California, and New Mexico, but its market is in the more populous New York and Great Lakes areas. The government constructed two huge pipelines—Big Inch (24 inches in diameter) and Little Inch (20 inches)—from Texas to near New York in 1943 and 1944 to carry oil and gasoline. After the war these were converted to carry natural gas. Between 1930 and 1957 the consumption of natural gas more than sextupled, and gas provided over a quarter of the energy in 1957. Industry consumed nearly three-quarters of it, and homes used the remainder for heating and cooking.

The type of power most characteristic of the recent period is electricity, which may be turned on or off with the flick of a switch. There are enormous dynamos to furnish it and tiny fractional horsepower engines to use it. Coal produces most of the energy that becomes electric power, although water power and oil and gas contribute also to making electricity. Let the power go off in a city and people realize quickly how much they depend on it. It provides light, operates the refrigerator and deep freeze, the television set and radio, many a cook stove and air conditioning unit, the vacuum cleaner and washing machine, the toaster and electric shaver, and many other useful devices. On farms it milks cows, separates cream, and does numerous other chores. It provides the power for telephones, serves industry, and runs railways in parts of the East.

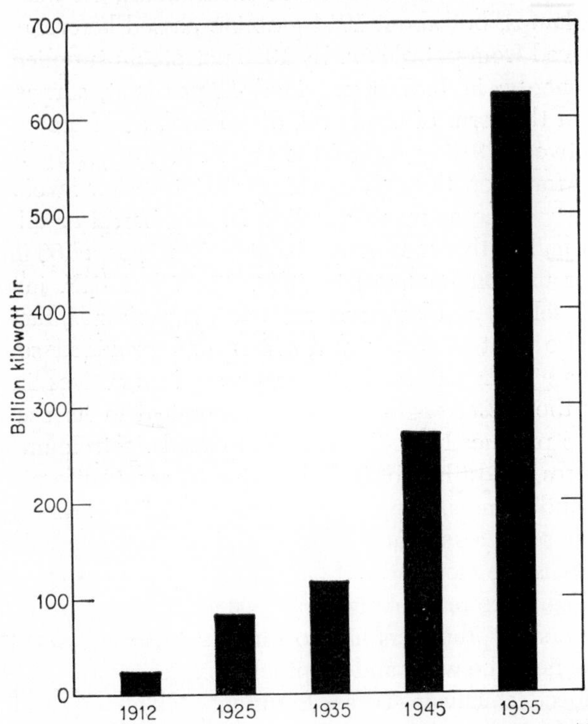

CHART 25-4. Growth in use of electric power, 1912–1955. (*Adapted from U.S. Bureau of the Census, Historical Statistics of the United States, 1789–1945, Washington, 1949, p. 156, and U.S. Bureau of the Census, Statistical Abstract of the United States, 1956, Washington, 1956, p. 529.*)

Chart 25-4 shows the phenomenal increase in the use of electric power in the period since before World War I. Electricity provides the invisible slaves of a modern age that make the fable of Aladdin's lamp come true.

In 1945 the United States dropped two atomic bombs on Japanese cities and demonstrated the immense power of atomic energy for destruction. Atomic energy obviously has power for construction once science has mastered its mysteries (see Fig. 25-3). Already man has learned to run submarines with it, and railroad engineers have promised to operate trains with it. When cheap power comes, man will be able to

FIG. 25-3. Nuclear core of world's first full-scale atomic electric generating station devoted exclusively to civilian needs, at Shippingport, Pa., 1957. (*Courtesy of Duquesne Light Company.*)

perform many tasks which he now considers too costly. At the same time it is well to remember, in dealing with power, that a very large part must be used to transmit itself from the source of energy to the place of use.

CHAPTER 26

Capital Expansion and Trusts

The standard of living of the average American was twice as high in 1956 as in 1914. Greater production of goods and services made this possible. Since the average worker put in a shorter workday, his output per hour of work had to be more than twice as great. This advance de-

Table 26-1
Factors Contributing to the Rising Standard of Living, 1914–1958
(Dollars in billions, except per capita GNP)

Year	Gross national product (current $)	Personal income (current $)	Gross private savings (current $)	Gross private domestic investment (current $)	Per capita gross national product (1947 $)	Phase of business cycle
1914	39.1	31.2*	....	....	925	Depression
1919	84.6	62.9*	....	....	1,024	Prosperity
1921	70.0	56.7*	....	....	857	Depression
1929	104.4	85.8	15.7	16.2	1,225	Prosperity
1933	56.0	47.2	1.9	1.4	825	Depression
1941	125.8	96.3	22.6	18.1	1,486	Prosperity
1944	211.4	165.7	54.2	7.1	1,938	War prosperity
1949	257.3	206.8	36.2	32.5	1,621	Mild recession
1954	360.5	287.6	55.0	47.2	1,855	Prosperity
1958	437.7	334.4	60.9†	54.4	1,939	Recovery

* Not closely comparable with figures for 1929 on.

† 1957.

SOURCE: National Industrial Conference Board, *Economic Almanac, 1956* (New York), pp. 423, 434, 444, 445; *1958*, p. 407; *Economic Indicators*, February, 1959 (Washington, 1959), pp. 2, 4, 9.

pended on several factors, such as better organization of the job and greater skill on the worker's part, but most of all upon better equipment. The equipment was capital, which in turn came from the investment of savings. Table 26-1 illustrates how these developments have raised the standard of living. Note that the per capita gross national product, in terms of 1947 dollars, doubled in this forty-year period and that domestic investment more than tripled from 1929 to 1958. As people received higher incomes, they saved more. Except in depression times, they invested more in plant and equipment, increasing the productivity of the nation. In the twelve years 1946 to 1957, net private capital formation averaged close to $20 billion a year. The savings in banks, insurance companies, and pension funds grew from $18 billion in 1914 to $259 billion in 1954. According to the National Bureau of Economic Research, by the early 1950s Americans had 5 billion energy slaves working for them. A recent study by the Twentieth Century Fund estimated that men and work animals supplied 14 per cent of the horsepower-hours in production in 1910 and fuel and machinery the remaining 86 per cent. By 1950 fuel and machinery were providing 98.5 per cent.[1] The horsepower per employed worker changed from 2 in 1890 to 4½ in 1920 and to 5½ in 1950. Meanwhile the efficiency of machines improved greatly. All this made it possible to increase the output per worker. But it also took efficient organization of capital on the part of business to achieve this.

Basic Importance of the Corporation. The corporation is still the most important form of business organization in industry, just as it was in 1914. In 1914, 28 per cent of all industrial establishments were incorporated; by 1947, 49 per cent were incorporated. In 1914 these corporations produced 83 per cent of all manufactured goods, whereas by 1947 they were responsible for 92 per cent of all the value added in manufacturing. They also had nine out of ten manufacturing employees. Corporations had grown in importance in mining, transportation, and finance, and to a lesser extent in merchandising. The corporation had several outstanding virtues. It was easy to organize; the enterpriser could limit the amount he wanted to invest in it and thus enjoy some degree of safety; and, for its size, it was easy to direct. Because corporations were generally ruled by a few persons who were interested in seeing them grow, they often plowed back a large portion of their earnings. In the nineteenth century the proportion had been half, but by the 1920s it had slipped to a quarter. During the depressed 1930s, corporations in most years paid out more in dividends than they earned; with the return of prosperity in the 1940s they tended once again to pay about half out in dividends and to plow back the other half to expand the business. Over the past 150 years the chief cause of capital growth in the United States has been converting a respectable fraction of profits into better equipment and larger plants.

Institutions Encouraging People to Save. Before the Civil War a number of new financial institutions appeared that encouraged people to save by

[1] J. Frederic Dewhurst and Associates, *America's Needs and Resources* (New York: The Twentieth Century Fund, Inc., 1955), p. 1116.

providing a place of safekeeping for their funds and promising them a reasonable rate of return. After the Civil War these institutions grew considerably in size and importance, and since 1914 they have grown enormously. They include mutual savings banks, savings and loan associations, trust companies, life insurance companies, since 1924 investment trusts, and especially since the 1930s pension funds. Table 26-2 shows the growth in assets of some of these institutions. Their investable funds roughly doubled every decade. By the mid-1950s they had approximately $2 billion a month to invest, either from new savings left with

Table 26-2
Growth of Institutions to Encourage Savings and Investment
(Dollars in billions)

Date	Mutual savings banks (deposits)	Savings and loan associations	Trust companies	Life insurance companies	Investment trusts	Pension funds	Other savings accounts in banks	Total
1914	3.9	0.9	4.5	3.4	....	....	4.9	17.6
1929	8.8	6.2	.....	12.8	....	1.7	19.4	48.1
1939	10.5	4.1	.....	23.0	1.1	6.0	16.5	61.2
1949	19.3	12.5	36.2*	50.2	2.8	38.7	39.3	162.8
1954	26.3	27.3	.....	69.3	7.3	54.2	49.0	233.4
1956	30.0	37.3	.....	78.1	10.3	61.2	52.2	269.1
1957	31.7	41.9	.....	.....	9.9	....	56.4	

* 1947.

SOURCES: *Economic Almanac, 1956,* p. 409; *1958,* pp. 77, 384; U.S. Bureau of the Census, *Historical Statistics of the United States, 1789–1945* (Washington, 1949), p. 271; Arthur Wiesenburger, *Investment Companies, 1958* (New York: A. Wiesenburger Co., 1959), p. 19.

them or from returns on earlier investments. There were, of course, limitations on what some of them could purchase as investments. Banks and life insurance companies might not invest in common stocks; savings banks and savings and loan associations invested almost exclusively in mortgages; investment trusts preferred corporate stocks and bonds; and trust companies could invest in only a limited amount of stocks. The important point is that here were savings looking for a place in which to be safely and profitably invested. They constituted the supply. Where was the corresponding demand for them?

Institutions Seeking Savings. Some of these same institutions were in the business of lending money as well. Persons seeking to borrow against property on a mortgage came to savings banks, building and loan associations, commercial banks, and even to insurance companies. But trust companies, life insurance companies, investment trusts, and pension funds had savings to lend to Federal, state, and local governments. They also invested their money through the stock market or bond market, or they bought new issues of securities through investment banks.

Investment Banking. Investment banking declined in importance after the death in 1913 of J. P. Morgan, the elder, for a number of reasons. The primary one was that investment bankers are basically middlemen in the marketing of securities and, just as in other areas of marketing, large buyers and large sellers began to deal more directly with one another. A survey of the main developments in investment banking since 1914 will reveal some of the other reasons. The decline was uneven

Table 26-3
Liberty Bond Campaigns
(Dollars in billions)

Name	Date	Interest rate, per cent	Goal	Accepted by Treasury
First Liberty Loan	May, 1917	3½	2.0	2.0
Second Liberty Loan	October, 1917	4	3.0	3.8
Third Liberty Loan	April, 1918	4¼	3.0	4.2
Fourth Liberty Loan	September, 1918	4¼	6.0	7.0
Victory Liberty Loan	May, 1919	4¾	4.5	4.5
Total	....	...	18.5	21.5

rather than steady, and after World War II investment bankers regained some of their former importance.

When the elder J. P. Morgan died, his son, also J. P. Morgan, succeeded him; the younger man, however, lacked his father's prestige and powerful personality. The Morgan firm, comparatively speaking, lost its dominance over other investment bankers. While its prestige was still high, in 1915, it led a syndicate of sixty-one New York houses in floating a $500 million loan to France and England. This was the first of a number of such loans which were essential if the Allies were to continue buying war supplies from America. They had used up their cash and the United States was not yet in the war.

With the entry of America into World War I in April of 1917, the government floated the first of its five gigantic Liberty Bond issues. Over two years, millions of citizens bought Liberty Bonds totaling $21.5 billion (Table 26-3). Many bought bonds through their banks, not infrequently borrowing some of the money to buy them, which amounted to buying them "on a margin." Not since the Civil War had the American public received such a practical education in the purchase and ownership of securities. Yet investment bankers had virtually nothing to do with this tremendous marketing operation.

During the 1920s the two outstanding developments were the rise of commercial bank affiliates and the tremendous interest evinced by the public in common stocks. For example, in 1925 Edgar L. Smith published *Common Stocks as Long-term Investments,* in which he showed that "in buying a well-diversified group of representative common stocks in essential industries, our chances of coming out even, or of making a profit in principal values are: within 1 year, 78 in 100; 2 years, 87 in 100; 4 years, 94 in 100."[2] Experience subsequently showed that the public did not diversify their purchases, or buy in essential industries, or hold the stocks long enough, or show very good judgment in what they bought. For the moment, however, Smith's arguments were appealing. Growth of such industries as the Ford Motor Company, General Motors, General Electric, and Standard Oil of New Jersey, and the outlook for radio and cigarette companies, had made many people believe that common stocks in such concerns were the investments to buy. Heretofore, the public had considered common stocks as risky, except those of leading railroads. There was no lack of new institutions to offer new issues to people with money to invest. Thus the older investment banks acquired a new type of competitor.

Investment affiliates—investment companies associated with large commercial banks—could serve the small investor as neither the investment bank nor the commercial bank could. Investment banks sold securities wholesale; commercial banks did not sell corporate securities at all, although many an investor came to his banker for advice. To fill this need, or to capture this market, large commercial banks founded investment companies that were essentially parts of their organizations. For example, the National City Bank of New York founded the National City Company as early as 1911 by declaring a 40 per cent dividend to be taken in the form of the stock of that investment company. To ensure that the two institutions remained affiliated, the stock certificates of the bank and of the company were printed on opposite sides of the same piece of paper.

Many other banks formed affiliates in the 1920s when this business really began to grow. These engaged in the investment banking business and sold stocks and bonds both retail and wholesale. It was easy for a banker to direct a customer to go to the affiliate's offices. Likewise, it was easy for the affiliate to circularize the bank's depositors. If the bank had bonds which did not meet the bank's own investment standards, it could dispose of them to customers through its affiliate. The heads of several of

[2] E. L. Smith, *Common Stocks as Long-term Investments* (New York: The Macmillan Company, 1925), p. 82.

these large banks sometimes forgot their sense of responsibility in the desire to sell more and more securities to an enthusiastic public and to establish new sales records each year. The rewards for new sales records, in the way of commissions and bonuses, were generous, which gave a strong incentive to sell stocks and bonds as if they were so many pulp magazines or brushes. Charles Mitchell, head of the National City Bank, and Albert Wiggin, head of the Chase National Bank, New York City's two largest banks, later paid heavily with their reputations for forgetting the serious responsibility that a banker owes to his customers.[3] Their ethics did not measure up to the investment banking standards established earlier by the elder J. P. Morgan. Between 1924 and 1929, offerings of new issues of stocks and bonds grew from $6.4 to $10.2 billion. Then came the Panic of 1929 and new offerings dropped to $0.7 billion by 1933. Congressional investigations followed; these ruined the reputations of leading bankers and Congress enacted reforms.

There were three outstanding events in investment banking in the decade of the 1930s. They were the divorce of investment affiliates from their commercial banks, the passage of acts regulating securities and exchanges, and the fact that government agencies rather than investment banks supplied much of the nation's long-term capital funds. The Banking Act of 1933 simply gave investment affiliates the choice of remaining in the investment banking business or of returning to commercial banking; they could not do both. Then Congress enacted The Federal Securities Act in 1933 to regulate the sale of new securities by investment houses, and the Securities Exchange Act of 1934 to regulate the activities of stock exchanges. The 1934 law set up a five-man Securities and Exchange Commission to oversee the securities marketing business. The new law required the registration of all proposed issues of stocks and bonds. A prospectus had to contain full information about the company. If the securities later proved bad, a buyer could sue the investment house and probably collect his losses, if he could show that the investment house had withheld vital information which might have discouraged him from buying. It was said that the law altered the old rule of the market place, "Let the buyer beware," and made it read, "Let the seller beware." It added risks to investment banking that were not there before. This law, coming on top of a devastating depression, made investment bankers very cautious. Whereas in the five years from 1926 to 1930 investment banking houses had put out $39.4 billion of new issues, in the five years from 1936 to 1940 they offered only $11.8 billion.

Meanwhile, one government agency, the Reconstruction Finance Corporation, established in 1932, had made loans by 1938 amounting to a

[3] Ferdinand Pecora, *Wall Street under Oath* (New York: Simon and Schuster, Inc., 1939), chaps. 4–8, especially p. 93.

total of $4.8 billion. At the close of 1938 some seventeen other government agencies had loans and preferred stock holdings of $7.3 billion. By the end of World War II the Reconstruction Finance Corporation had loaned some $50 billion. The agency's head, Jesse Jones, was the government-appointed equivalent of the elder J. P. Morgan of a generation earlier. The RFC had helped to finance the building of steel mills, aluminum plants, shipyards, chemical plants, and airplane factories.

World War II brought with it a new series of war loans, like the Liberty Loans of World War I in some respects. Altogether the Federal government sold $157 billion of war bonds to the public in eight campaigns during and just after the war. This time the experience of owning securities was somewhat less novel to the public than before. The end of the war did not bring a renewal of the depression, and so times improved somewhat for investment bankers.

Between 1946 and 1950, new issues of securities came to $38.1 billion, and during the following five years they exceeded $60 billion. The government was by now less of a competitor, but the investment bankers had to compete with commercial banks again, in another way, and with insurance companies too. For example, commercial banks were willing to make loans to companies payable in five to ten years, thus sparing them the necessity of floating a bond issue. These "term" loans grew in popularity with banks after the war. Sometimes a large bank made a tie-in arrangement with a large insurance company to lend a company money for as long as fifteen years. The bank would advance the money for the first five years, and the insurance company would then pay off the bank and assume the loan for the final ten years. In 1952, close to one-fourth of the loans of the big New York and Chicago banks were in the form of term loans.

Investment banks also met stiff competition from insurance companies in another way, especially from 1945 on. Large insurance companies simply bought entire issues directly from a corporation, thus eliminating the investment banker middlemen. By resorting to such "private placements," the corporation got a better price for its bonds and the insurance company paid less than if it had bought from an investment bank. In 1951 Equitable Life Assurance Company bought 84 per cent of its investments directly. The most that investment bankers could hope to earn from such arrangements was a small fee for bringing interested buyers and sellers together to complete their own arrangements. That was a far cry from the power and profits once enjoyed by J. P. Morgan and his colleagues. Despite these inroads on their business, investment bankers still carried on a large business in marketing securities. They were, however, no longer as closely associated with the monopoly or trust problem as they were in the days of the elder Morgan.

TRENDS IN TRUSTS, 1914–1956

The trust problem never again became as acute in the mind of the general public as it did in the opening years of the twentieth century. True, it is still common to hear the monopolistic practices of big business condemned. The government occasionally prosecutes some big business for breaking the antitrust laws and once in a while wins a conviction. Only once has the Justice Department prosecuted firms in droves as it did before World War I, and the owners of trusts have been very careful about flaunting their power. The public's attitude toward trusts has undergone repeated changes since 1914.

Indifference to Trusts, 1914–1935. No sooner had President Woodrow Wilson got two new antitrust laws on the federal statute books in 1914 than the nation lost interest in this one-time bugbear. The public's attention centered on a greater menace—an arrogant and powerful Germany, perhaps about to subjugate all Europe. As soon as America entered the war in 1917, the government suspended the antitrust laws. Indeed, it encouraged industries to pool their knowledge and resources in order to produce goods more efficiently and thus win the war. The tendency shifted definitely toward combination. For example, the Federal government took over all the railroads and operated them as a unified whole under an all-powerful Director General. Congress set up a War Industries Board to regulate production and to prevent competition among agencies purchasing war supplies. The government encouraged private manufacturers to standardize the shapes and sizes of their products, and the government also exercised price-fixing powers. Congress passed the Webb-Pomerene Act in 1918 to exempt organizations of American exporters from prosecution under the antitrust laws.

After the war, it was impossible to revive the old crusading spirit against the trusts. The spirit of the postwar age was one of almost cynical disillusionment. America had entered the war with high ideals—to make the world safe for democracy, to end all wars—but it was not long before Americans realized how unreal such hopes had been. The war taught them also that inflation as well as profits caused high prices. The government itself had encouraged combinations during the war. In 1920 Congress finally agreed to look upon railroads as "natural monopolies" and largely removed them from prosecution under the antitrust laws. In 1922 it passed the Capper-Volstead Cooperative Marketing Act to exempt farmers' cooperatives from the antitrust laws.[4] What showed the govern-

[4] In 1932 the Norris-LaGuardia Act freed organized labor from injunctions when the courts issued them to prevent a conspiracy in restraint of trade under the antitrust laws.

ment's attitude most clearly was the Supreme Court decision in 1920 in the case against the United States Steel Corporation.[5] The Court said the company was not guilty of monopoly and added, "The law does not make mere size an offense or the existence of unexerted power an offense."

Actually, United States Steel by itself was not a monopoly; rather, virtually all the companies in the steel industry were working in collusion. The device by which they held themselves together was known as "Pittsburgh Plus." A South Chicago steel company delivering rails costing, say, $65 a ton to a Chicago elevated railway line would charge the elevated railway company $65 a ton plus, for the sake of example, $4 freight from Pittsburgh to Chicago. Since the rails never came from Pittsburgh, the $4 charge for "phantom freight" simply went into the coffers of the Chicago steel company as additional profit. The Chicago company did not have to be a branch of the United States Steel Company to enjoy this. The system was even contrived to work to the advantage of the United States Steel Company's main plant, located at Pittsburgh. That plant did not have as modern equipment as some of the so-called "independents." Under competitive conditions, these might well have invaded its market. Under the Pittsburgh Plus system, however, any independent company shipping steel to Pittsburgh not only received no phantom freight bonus but had to pay the freight costs out of its own pocket. The Chicago company would have received $65 less $4 transportation for its rails. The system thus assured the United States Steel Company of a protected market in its own Pittsburgh area. The Justice Department's lawyers believed that the different prices, say for rails quoted by different companies, meant that they were competing, whereas the difference was merely one of varying phantom freight costs. The Supreme Court, in handing down its decision exonerating United States Steel, failed to realize that the whole steel industry was a trust. All this was encouraging to those thinking of promoting trusts. The Pittsburgh Plus device, however, was more than the steel trust could hope to keep much longer, and in 1923 the steel companies abandoned it, adopting in its place the more subtle but equally monopolistic *multiple* basing point system.

During the 1920s the tendency toward combinations and mergers was strong again. This time, however, it did not take place in heavy industry, as had been the case between 1898 and 1903. That would have flouted the antitrust laws too obviously. Nor did most industries dare employ the security holding company device, for the Clayton Act forbade its use where the effect would be to lessen competition. Nevertheless, between 1925 and 1930 there were 1,238 consolidations and 7,000 companies disappeared via the merger route. Public utilities, which were admittedly monopolies to start with, were able to make free use of the security hold-

[5] *United States v. United States Steel Corporation,* 251 U.S. 417 (1920).

ing company device. Between 1919 and 1928, 4,500 of these combined. Banking mergers, retail store chains, and moving picture company mergers were also popular. The era of 1927–1929 was one of consolidations second only to that of 1898–1903. Some of these were trusts. Both were eras of lush prosperity culminating in panic.

The Great Depression was characterized by many business failures. Whereas between 1927 and 1929 there had been 23,000 a year, the average rose to 29,000 in the next three years and the losses were greater. In some large businesses, it was possible to restrict production and yet hold up prices. A few examples of this appear in Table 26-4. Industries whose prices were "sticky," that is, did not fall, were widely suspected of

Table 26-4
"Sticky Prices," 1929–1933

Industry	Drop in prices, per cent	Drop in production, per cent
Agricultural implements	6	80
Motor vehicles	16	80
Cement	18	65
Iron and steel	20	83
Textile products	45	30
Food products	49	14
Petroleum	56	20
Farm commodities	63	6

SOURCE: Gardner C. Means, *Industrial Prices and Their Relative Inflexibility*, Senate Doc. no. 13, 74th Cong., 1st Sess. (Washington, 1935), p. 8.

enjoying a monopoly position. This suspicion was sometimes unjustified. But in the business world of this era, monopoly was not the unforgivable sin. Rather it was drastic price cutting, sometimes called "chiseling." Many firms were guilty of it, for the simple reason that they were on the verge of bankruptcy. If they did not sell more goods, they could not pay their bills. The best way to attract customers seemed to be to offer them better bargains. Each decline in prices brought more concerns into the danger zone of bankruptcy. When President Roosevelt asked business leaders what reforms were needed to bring about recovery, they asked for an end to "chiseling" so that they could make a profit and survive.

In June of 1933 President Roosevelt signed the National Industrial Recovery Act (NIRA). It set up the National Recovery Administration (NRA) headed by General Hugh S. Johnson. One of the ten purposes of this act was "to eliminate unfair competitive practices." The law instructed each industry to draw up its own code of fair practices. Since that obviously involved collusion by competing companies, NIRA specifically suspended the antitrust laws. The codes were not supposed to encourage monopoly or to operate unfairly against the small businessman. Once accepted by the President, they were to become the standards of the industry, and any violation of them was to be unfair competition within the meaning of the Federal Trade Commission Act. Companies operating under such codes displayed a "Blue Eagle" sticker in their window or on their premises. Within the first month, over 400 industries had filed their codes, and the total eventually reached 677. These included activities ranging from producing steel to pressing pants; many of the codes were rather hastily drawn. The program extended farther than Congress had originally contemplated and included some businesses of rather secondary importance.

In most industries the big companies took the lead in drawing up the codes. Some industries drew up codes that gave them monopolistic powers. For example, the copper and petroleum codes provided for the limitation of output by means of plant quotas; the textile industry and nearly sixty others controlled production by limiting the number of hours that companies might operate machines. Other codes had provisions forbidding sales below cost. The soft-coal industry set for itself such a generous minimum price for coal that it stimulated mine operators to produce more coal than they could dispose of at that price. The operators then broke their own agreements and had to abandon their code.

The NRA was short-lived; in May, 1935, the Supreme Court unanimously declared it unconstitutional in the case of *Schechter v. United States*, a suit involving violations of the Live Poultry Code.[6] This ended the experiment in self-government by business, and its close restored antitrust legislation. The NRA had helped to improve business ethics, but it also represented the extreme in legislation favorable to monopoly. Henceforth, except during World War II, the trend was to be the other way.

Renewed Prosecution of Trusts after 1936. It was to be expected that an administration as cool to businessmen as Roosevelt's would regulate them in the matter of monopoly profits as it did in many other regards. Congress enacted two new laws affecting trusts in 1936 and 1937; one limited their activities and one rather favored them. The Robinson-Patman Act of 1936 was an amendment to the Clayton Act of 1914. Its goal was to reduce the advantage that chain stores had over independent stores because of the quantity discounts that the chains received. This hampered somewhat the growth of the chain-store business. The Miller-Tydings Act of 1937 permitted manufacturers to set retail prices, which was a

[6] 295 U.S. 495 (1935). The Supreme Court ruled that the NIRA unconstitutionally delegated legislative authority to the President and that it illegally regulated *intrastate* commerce.

help to big business. Both of these acts are treated more fully in Chapter 28 on commerce. The significant point about both of these so-called anti-trust laws is that they were aimed at price reductions. That is the opposite of the usual complaint against monopolies. It was not the consumers who wanted these laws; rather, it was the independent stores, the distributors, and, for a time, the manufacturers. Both laws were belated efforts to reduce price cutting, which had been the major crime in the eyes of business in the early 1930s.

The Antitrust Division of the Justice Department became quite active in the late 1930s, during the period when Thurman Arnold was in charge. It initiated proceedings against the country's then outstanding trust, the Aluminum Company of America, which controlled an estimated 99 per cent of the nation's aluminum ingot production. It investigated and publicized agreements between European cartels and American companies, such as patent exchanges between America's Du Pont and Germany's I. G. Farbenindustrie. President Roosevelt stressed the need for revising the antitrust laws. In June, 1938, Congress set up the Temporary National Economic Committee (TNEC) to find a way to reconcile existing anti-trust legislation and the growing concentration of economic power, and to recommend appropriate legislation. The Committee heard volumes of testimony and concluded that concentration was growing at an alarming rate and further legislation was needed. Meanwhile, it had not been difficult to convince the courts that companies were conspiring in restraint of trade. By 1940 Arnold had more cases under way than the government had tried during the first twenty years of the Sherman Act. He seemed especially interested in conspiracies in the building trades. After the nation went to war in 1941, Congress never got around to enacting the antitrust legislation which the TNEC had called for.

Just as during World War I, the government suspended antitrust prosecutions for the duration of hostilities. Again, it was more important for industries to pool their resources and ideas, to cooperate rather than compete, and to produce as much as possible in order to win the war. The War Production Board and other agencies encouraged cooperation. Economics professors who served the Office of Price Administration later reported to their university colleagues that, in instance after instance, all that they needed to do to obtain cooperation from an industry was to call the presidents of the half-dozen leading companies. These generally controlled three-quarters or more of the output. Although Congress set up the Office of Defense Transportation to coordinate the activities of all forms of commercial transportation, the government did not take over the railroads as it had in World War I. The government did erect several aluminum plants to supplement those of the Aluminum Company of America.

In 1946 the Antitrust Division of the Justice Department reported, "The monopoly problem in American industry is today more serious and widespread than at any time since the passage of the Sherman Act." It commenced antitrust investigations of the activities of 122 large companies. Although the Aluminum Company of America had been a well-behaved trust, the government felt that the company's complete domination of the industry was unhealthy. After the war the government disposed of its own war-built aluminum plants to independent companies such as Reynolds and Kaiser to ensure that the Aluminum Company of America would have competition. The Justice Department ordered the company to sever relations with Aluminium Limited of Canada and to make certain of its patents available to Kaiser and Reynolds. Other government successes included dissolving an important patent pool which dominated the glass container industry, ordering the Pullman Company to dispose of either its operating or its manufacturing business, and breaking up the Crescent theater combine (a collection of theater chains). In 1957 it at last won its case to make Du Pont dispose of its large holding of General Motors stock. The Antitrust Division was unsuccessful in its prosecution of the leading meat packers as a monopoly. Its widely heralded suit against the Atlantic and Pacific Tea Company grocery chain for controlling 5 per cent of the grocery business achieved very little. Sometimes the courts got themselves into strange predicaments on antitrust matters; for example, they held professional football subject to antitrust laws, but not professional baseball.

The Justice Department's greatest postwar success came in 1948, when the Supreme Court ordered the Cement Institute (a monopolistic association of cement manufacturers) to abandon its multiple basing point system (a subtler version of "Pittsburgh Plus").[7] By implication, this affected about twenty-five other industries employing the device, among them the steel industry. Since the 1930s the steel industry has become more competitive than it was before that time.

In summary, the Antitrust Division has had a larger staff and more funds with which to prosecute trusts in recent years than ever before. It has become easier to persuade the courts that a conspiracy in restraint of trade exists. Mere largeness is today almost tantamount to being considered a trust. Industries take special care to avoid being suspected of infringing the antitrust laws. The public, however, no longer becomes as excited about the evils of industrial monopoly; it is more worried about

[7] *Federal Trade Commission v. Cement Institute,* 333 U.S. 683, (1948). Under the multiple system the arrangement was similar to Pittsburgh Plus. A Chicago customer getting cement from Pittsburgh would pay freight only from the nearest of the basing points, Chicago. The effect was nonetheless to encourage monopoly. Every company was assured an advantage in its local market: it cost a competitor heavily to invade it.

the evils of big labor unions.[8] Actually, there are few if any trusts left of the sort that existed about 1900. Informal working agreements through trade associations or "follow the leader" agreements very likely exist but are not easy to detect. Rather, it is oligopoly that is commonplace in today's economic world. This is control of an industry by a few large companies, for example, the control of about 97 per cent of the passenger automobile industry by General Motors, Ford, and Chrysler. The question is to what degree such companies work in collusion and to what degree they compete vigorously. If it could, would General Motors really want to kill off its competitors? It would then surely be declared a trust and ordered to dissolve. Yet if it does not compete to the best of its ability and beat prices down, is not that reluctance to some degree a conspiracy to keep prices up? Whatever it does, a huge company like General Motors is open to criticism simply because it is large.

TAXATION

The finances of the United States were in excellent condition in 1914. The public debt was $1.2 billion, which was no burden at all, and the Federal budget amounted to only $0.7 billion. The country had just adopted the Sixteenth Amendment authorizing an income tax and Congress had enacted an income tax law. The nation was on a gold coin standard which was working well, and Congress had just established the Federal Reserve System. If it were possible to be prepared for the costs of a major war, this country was ready.

In contrast, by 1958 the Federal debt had risen to about $283 billion, which was approximately equal to the disposable personal income for one year. The proposed budget for 1960 amounted to $77 billion; Federal income taxes took a fifth of personal income, with rates varying from 20 per cent for low incomes to 87 per cent for incomes over $400,000. The nation no longer had a gold coin standard, although it was one of the few countries left in the world with a semblance of a gold standard. The purchasing power of the dollar had declined two-thirds since 1913. The Federal Reserve System operated smoothly, but it had only recently regained its freedom, in 1951, to set interest rates at what it considered a financially healthy level. Considering that the country had been through two world wars and a major one in Korea, it was still in good financial shape, although it clearly showed the financial effects of these experiences. It is the Federal taxation developments of some forty years that are of most concern here.

[8] G. Cowles, "What the Public Thinks about Big Business," *Look Magazine*, vol. 19 (Feb. 8, 1955), pp. 19ff.

In 1913, customs duties and excise taxes supported the Federal government, and a 1 per cent income tax on incomes over $3,000 contributed a trifle to the Treasury. By the end of World War I, as Table 26-5 and Chart 26-1 show, income taxes provided the Treasury with 58 per cent of

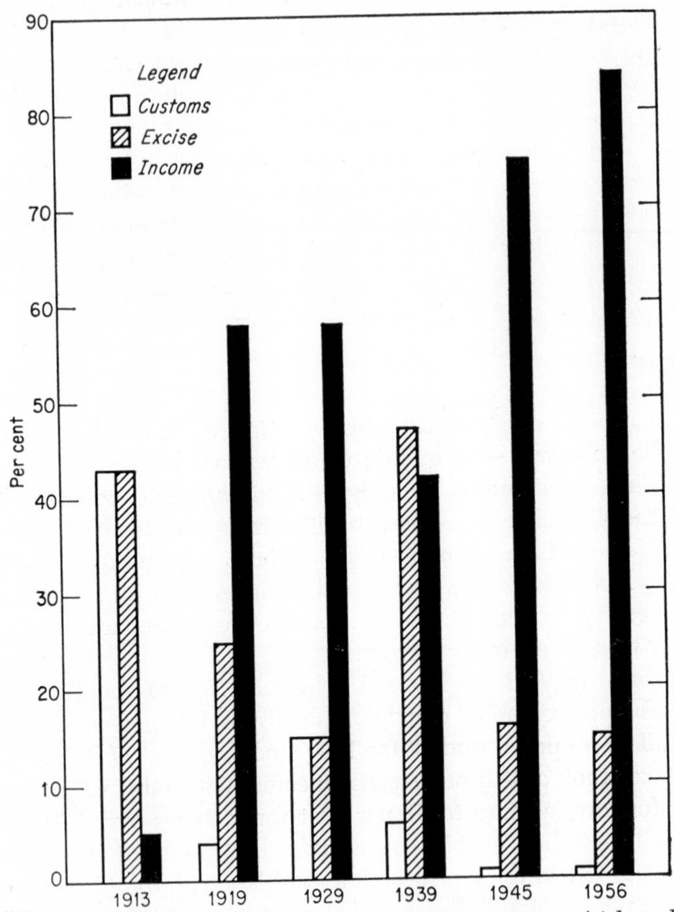

CHART 26-1. Major sources of Federal tax moneys. (*Adapted from U.S. Bureau of the Census, Historical Statistics of the United States, 1789–1945, Washington, 1949, and U.S. Bureau of the Census, Statistical Abstract of the United States, 1956, Washington, 1956.*)

its income. Rates were 6 per cent on incomes over $2,000 up to a maximum of 77 per cent. The great contributions of Secretary of the Treasury Andrew Mellon during the 1920s were lowering the income tax rates and at the same time accumulating enough surplus revenue to reduce the national debt by nearly $1 billion each year. Nevertheless, Federal, state, and local taxes absorbed between two and three times as much of the citizen's income as they had in 1913. Starting in 1931, the budget went unbalanced nearly every year. During the depressed 1930s taxes rose and deficits were chronic. The deficits were about equal to each year's tax collections. The public debt rose steadily, and national income averaged about 15 per cent less than in the prosperous late 1920s. The Federal government was footing the bill for relieving unemployment, subsidizing

Table 26-5
Government Finance Statistics
(Dollars in billions)

Year	Total Federal receipts	Federal receipts, as percentage of national income	Deficit (−) or surplus (+)	State and local taxes	All taxes, as percentage of national income	National debt
1913	0.7	2	......	1.6	7	1.2
1919	5.2	8	−13.4	......	...	25.5
1921	5.6	10	+	1.2*†	...	24.0
1929	4.0	5	+ 0.7	2.1†	...	16.9
1932	2.0	4	− 2.5	7.4	20	19.5
1939	5.2	8	− 3.5	......	...	40.4
1945	46.5	31	−53.9	9.2	37	258.7
1949	42.8	23	− 1.8	14.8	30	252.8
1951	53.4	25	+ 3.5	17.6	31	255.2
1954	64.7	23	− 2.7	22.1	34	271.3
1957	71.6	20	+ 1.6	29.0	28	270.5

* 1922.
† State only.
SOURCES: *Historical Statistics, 1789–1945*, pp. 295–296, 305, 315; *Continuation to 1952*, pp. 38, 39; *Statistical Abstract, 1956*, pp. 357–358, 399; *1958*, pp. 366, 390; *Economic Almanac, 1956*, pp. 423, 442; *1958*, p. 428.

the farmers, setting up a Social Security program, and paying for other social benefits that it had never before undertaken. People complained that the tax burden was heavy and that the mounting public debt ($40 billion in 1939) would ruin the economy. Nevertheless, as late as the years 1937–1940 individual income taxes averaged only about $1 billion and only about 3 million persons paid such taxes. World War II made all this seem quite mild by comparison.

During the height of World War II the Federal government was spending money at the rate of $1 billion every four days. During 1944 and 1945 it collected $45 billion each year. This was nine times what it collected in 1939, and yet it had a deficit of about $50 billion in each of those years. Individual income taxes amounted to almost $20 billion a year. The rates varied from 3 per cent on taxable incomes between $500 and $1,000 to 91 per cent on taxable income of $1 million in 1944, when some 45 million people were paying taxes.

The end of the war brought hopes that the government would lower taxes as it had in the 1920s and cut back the national debt, which was $259 billion in December, 1945. The public was largely disappointed. Although the huge deficits disappeared and there were even occasional surpluses (1947, 1948, 1951, 1956, and 1957), Congress did little to cut income taxes. The Federal government's annual income continued on the $45 billion level. In 1948 a Republican Congress sought a mild across-the-board reduction of taxes at all income levels, but President Harry Truman vetoed the bill because it did not provide greater tax relief to the low-income groups. Soon after the war ended, it became apparent that Russia was thinking of absorbing western Europe and that only a strongly armed and alert United States could deter it from doing so. Continued expenditures for armaments kept taxes up. Then between 1950 and 1953 the Korean War necessitated higher taxes once more. Individual income taxes reached $32 billion in 1954 and total Federal government expenditures were about $67 billion. To that, state and local governments were adding their levies of some $22 billion. The average taxpayer was handing over to his various governments a third of his annual income. Even after the Korean War ended, the costly "cold war" with Russia went on.

BUSINESS CYCLES

In the period since 1914, the country has suffered several secondary depressions and one of the worst major depressions in all its history. The great one left the public with the determination that whatever might be the cost, they would prevent such a depression from happening again. Political party leaders were especially depression-conscious from that time forward. Economists, turning to the study of the cause and cure of depressions, produced a new brand of economics whose basic aim was to prevent unemployment at the expense of capital, instead of protecting capital at the cost of unemployment. This gave the Federal government, more than ever before, the responsibility for tending to the security of its citizens.

The Great Depression was the most severe of a long series of depressions which had been happening periodically for more than a century. In the recent period, one took place in 1914, caused in part by the outbreak of war in Europe. When World War I ended in November, 1918, a year and a half of lush prosperity ensued, during which merchants speculated heavily in commodities and prices continued to rise. But wages did not keep up with prices, and a buyers' strike in April, 1920, set off a short but severe postwar depression. The wholesale price level fell from 247 in May, 1920, to 146 in May, 1921—the sharpest price drop the nation had ever experienced.[9] The depression lasted only about two years. A boom

FIG. 26-1. Floor of the New York Stock Exchange.

in the automobile industry helped to pull the country out of it. There followed seven years of prosperity punctuated in 1924 and 1927 by two short recessions.

A growing mania of speculation characterized the closing years of the 1920s. There were numerous reasons for the optimism that led to this speculation. The country was prosperous, and several fast-growing indus-

[9] Bureau of Labor Statistics index, using a 1913 base.

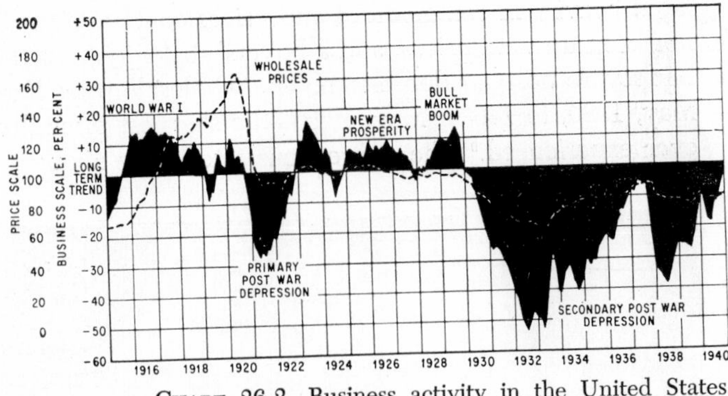

CHART 26-2. Business activity in the United States,

tries—automobiles, refrigerators, radios, cigarettes—seemed to augur ever-growing prosperity. Business had labor unions fairly well under control. Every year Secretary of the Treasury Andrew Mellon was cutting taxes and reducing the national debt. Real incomes were rising and the rate of interest was falling. It seemed to be a good time to bet on America's future. As has already been pointed out, common stocks in industries and utilities seemed to be the answers. Some persons invested their savings in them; others sought to speed up their profit taking a bit. Just as some people were learning how to buy a car on the installment plan, so others learned how to buy stocks on a margin. A speculator in stocks paid, say, $1,000 down, ordered $10,000 of Radio Corporation of America stock, left the stock with his broker as collateral for the other $9,000 which the broker had borrowed for him and waited for the price to rise. It usually did; between 1924 and 1929 the average value of all stocks more than doubled, and some stocks rose ten and twenty times. At least 1½ million people and perhaps many more invested or speculated in stocks in this period. The fact that many were buying on margin meant that the market might topple like a house of cards if the buyers' rosy optimism should turn to black pessimism. In October, 1929, that happened. During the next few years, the estimated value of securities slipped from $90 billion at the peak to $16 billion at the bottom. Many persons gave up plans to buy cars, build homes, or spend their money in countless other ways. Business fell off sharply. The disaster on the stock market plunged the nation into a deep depression which lasted throughout the 1930s.

Herbert Hoover was President when the crash came. By present-day standards he did little to relieve the unemployed and help the bankrupt, but by previous standards he did quite a lot. He instituted a farm program and established the Reconstruction Finance Corporation. However, no president could have hoped to weather a major depression; Franklin

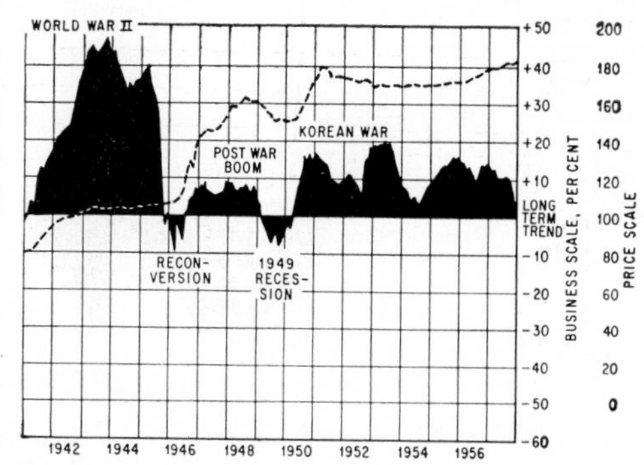

1915–1957. (*Courtesy of the Cleveland Trust Company.*)

Roosevelt defeated him in 1932. Roosevelt instituted the New Deal program to relieve unemployment, to aid the farmers, and to help business recover. He accepted the advice of economists who said the nation could spend its way out of the depression.

By late 1936 the depression seemed to be about over. A new period of prosperity arrived and stock prices began to climb again. Then a series of major strikes and a tightening of bank reserves made the future seem black again to businessmen. The nation plunged back into depression, or "recession" as it was called this time. As late as January, 1940, there were still 10 million unemployed. Prosperity finally returned after the outbreak of World War II.

Some government economists prophesied that when the war ended there would be some 8 million unemployed and another depression. Within ten years of the end of the two previous major American wars there had been two depressions—a minor one and then a major one—which was accepted as the pattern. Nevertheless, in thirteen years there were only four dips—1945–1946, 1949, 1953–1954, and 1957–1958. (See Chart 26-2.) For several years, people awaited the inevitable depression. The government enacted a Full Employment Act in 1946, and the Federal Reserve System prepared to use its arsenal of financial weapons the moment that a depression reared its ugly head. Stock market investors refrained for several years from committing themselves heavily. Then came another war—this time in Korea in 1950–1953—and the Republicans finally elected a president again, Dwight Eisenhower. After that, the business public forgot its inhibitions and decided to enjoy a new era of plenty and prosperity. Business boomed and the stock market rose again, although this time speculators could not buy stocks on a thin margin. By 1959 there had been nineteen years of only briefly interrupted prosperity, the longest in the nation's entire history.

CHAPTER 27

Money and Banking

In studying eighteenth-century finance, it was necessary to study money alone, for banking did not appear in the United States until 1781. In studying nineteenth-century finance, the two subjects were treated separately despite the fact that (the chief money before the Civil War was bank notes and the chief money afterward was checking accounts.) In the present century, it is very difficult to study the two topics separately. That is especially so after the mid-1930s when America abandoned the gold coin standard and gradually substituted in its place for some fifteen years what some economists have called a "low interest rate" standard, which was carried on through the banks. This will be explained later. Thus it is barely possible to study monetary history up to about 1934 without much reference to banking; after that it becomes impossible.

MONETARY HISTORY, 1914–1934

The United States had an excellent monetary system between 1914 and 1934. Considering the strains under which it had to operate, it worked well. In 1914, along with most other major nations of the world, the United States had a gold coin standard. Over a sixth of the money in circulation was gold coins. Another third was gold certificates: these were Treasury notes backed 100 per cent by gold held in a special fund (see Table 27-1). The rest of the circulating money consisted of greenbacks (10 per cent), national bank notes (20 per cent), silver certificates and silver dollars (16 per cent), and silver, nickel, and copper change.

The Gold Coin Standard. In 1914 the gold coin standard was looked upon as the soundest in the world. This country, before 1879, and many others, from 1890 on, had gone to much trouble to achieve such a standard. Its outstanding advantage was that it obliged the Treasury to limit its issues of money and thus prevented serious currency depreciation. Any time that citizens became fearful that the government was embarking on unsound monetary policies, they had the privilege of demanding gold for their silver or paper money. That made money "tight" or scarce because each gold dollar in a bank was legal reserve for several checking account dollars. Thus when citizens demanded gold, it forced banks to make fewer loans to customers. This served warning on Congress or the Treasury or the banks that the public was worried about current financial policies. That in turn tended to stop a speculative boom or inflation before it proceeded too far. The gold coin standard, like the right to vote, protected the public against its government by making possible a

Table 27-1
Money in Circulation in the United States, 1914–1958
(Dollars in millions)

Year	Total circulation*	Gold	Gold certificates	Silver and silver certificates	Greenbacks	National bank notes	Federal Reserve notes	Demand deposits adjusted
1914	3,459	612	1,026	549	338	715	......	10,082
1919	5,697	475	328	242	274	639	2,450	17,624
1921	6,173	447	201	225	259	721	2,600	17,113
1929	6,603	368	935	431	262	653	1,693	22,540
1933	7,992	321	265	389	269	920	3,061	14,411
1939	10,483	...	.....	1,496	266	Fed. Res. bank notes	4,484	27,355
1945	30,492	...	.....	1,776	323	527	22,867	69,053
1949	31,368	...	.....	2,225	319	309	21,209	81,877
1953	35,395	...	.....	2,612	345	192	27,680	104,452
1958†	36,524	...	.....	2,352	317	59	27,173	110,300

* Total circulation includes money in Federal Reserve banks. Totals also include Federal Reserve bank notes before 1939, subsidiary coin, minor coin, unaccounted-for moneys no longer in circulation, such as Treasury notes of 1890, gold certificates after 1933, national bank notes after 1937, etc.

† November.

SOURCES: U.S. Bureau of the Census, *Historical Statistics of the United States, 1789–1945* (Washington, 1949), pp. 274–275; *Continuation to 1952*, p. 35; *Federal Reserve Bulletin*, February, 1954, p. 159; *ibid.*, January, 1959, pp. 31–32.

periodic check. The gold standard was not foolproof, but it worked well in the nineteenth and early twentieth centuries. Countries with a gold coin standard or its near equivalent such as England, Germany, France, the United States, and the Scandinavian nations had very reliable currencies.

Effect of World War I on Money Systems. World War I ruined many of the world's best currencies and did some damage to all of them. Germany's mark went from 4 to the dollar to 4 trillion to the dollar; France's franc fell from 5 to the dollar to 25 to the dollar, and England's pound sterling lost two-thirds of its purchasing power. All these nations inflated their currency to some extent to help meet the terrific costs of World War I. Their financial manipulations were more subtle than they had been in the nineteenth century: they avoided crude resort to the printing press. Instead, they sold their bonds to banks, either central banks or commercial banks, or both. In return, they took the central banks' notes or had the banks credit their checking accounts. The end result, however, was the same as if they had used the printing press. In Europe the central banks instead of the Treasury used printing presses. In America government-induced inflation took the form chiefly of a sharp increase in demand deposits. Persons who were not fooled by all this financial sleight-of-hand sometimes called the government's enormous demand deposits in banks "invisible greenbacks." The name was appropriate.

As noted before, there are three basic ways of financing a war, namely, by taxation, by borrowing, and by creating money. They are both difficult and desirable in the order cited. The United States paid about 20 per cent of the cost of World War I by taxation, about 50 per cent by borrowing, and the remaining 30 per cent by creating money. The government had paid for only 12 per cent of the Civil War by creating money. The government did not finance World War I as well as it had financed the Civil War, and the government had not handled that especially well. Table 27-1 shows that both the money supply and the total of demand deposits increased by about two-thirds between 1914 and 1919. Most of the currency increase was the addition of $2,450 million in Federal Reserve notes. These were the bank notes of the new central banking system. Between 1914 and 1919 the country added some $10 billion dollars, visible and invisible, to its total money supply.

This sharp increase in the money supply was likely to cause some people to doubt the soundness of the dollar and thus to demand gold in order to "play it safe." The government accordingly imposed an embargo on gold exports in September, 1917. Government restrictions also made it virtually impossible for a citizen to obtain gold from his bank. That situation lasted until June, 1919. Within this interval the United States had suspended specie payments and therefore had temporarily abandoned the gold coin standard. Nearly every other nation in the world had done the same. After the war the United States was the first country to return to the gold standard. In 1922 at a conference in Genoa the other major nations resolved to return to gold as soon as practical. By 1930 over thirty had done so, and the United States had assisted several in this endeavor.

The Trend of Prices. The near doubling of the money supply caused price levels to rise. Prices about doubled between 1914 and 1920. That was because in this period the nation did not noticeably increase its total supply of goods and services. The last column of Table 27-2 shows that between 1914 and 1919 national income rose a little less than the wholesale price level. Thus real national income did not rise at all. The behavior of prices in this period illustrates again most of the generalities already cited about price trends during periods of inflation and deflation (see Chapter 19). Wholesale prices rose more rapidly during the war than the cost of living. Then they fell more sharply in the 1920–1922 depression after the war. Farm prices were more sensitive than wholesale prices during both the inflation and the subsequent deflation.

Table 27-2
Price Level, Money, and National Income Indexes, 1914–1923
(1913 = 100)

Year	Wholesale prices	Farm prices	Cost of living	All labor, real wages	Money and demand deposits*	National income*
1914	98.1	102.6	103	99	105	99
1917	177.2	189.6	142	89	143	147
1919	206.4	230.8	188	98	193	200
1920	226.2	217.9	209	112	216	172
1921	146.9	123.7	177	123	189	183
1923	153.7	141.2	171	127	206	208

* Indexes calculated by D. L. Kemmerer.

SOURCES: *Historical Statistics, 1789–1945,* p. 68; National Industrial Conference Board, *Economic Almanac, 1956* (Washington, 1956), p. 423; U.S. Bureau of the Census, *Statistical Abstract of the United States, 1926* (Washington, 1926), p. 347; Board of Governors of the Federal Reserve System, *Banking and Monetary Statistics* (Washington, 1943), p. 34.

Farmers prospered during the war period but had a hard time meeting payments on mortgages after the war and had to lower their standard of living again. Thanks probably to unions, wage earners fared better in World War I than in the Civil War. As in the Civil War and afterward, the inflation brought undeserved pains to creditors during the inflation—they got back less valuable dollars than they had loaned. And it brought some unmerited gains during the deflation afterward—they got back more valuable dollars than they had loaned.

The period between 1923 and 1929 was one of very level prices, both wholesale and retail. Almost no one gained unfairly at the expense of someone else because of shifting price levels. Economists and others began to entertain high hopes that they had learned how to keep the price level stable. Then disillusionment came swiftly and cruelly.

Monetary and Price Trends, 1929–1933. The stock market break of October, 1929, led many people to curtail purchases and that, in turn, led to canceled orders and layoffs at factories. The result was a sharp decline in prices of all kinds, as Table 27-3 shows. Businessmen borrowed less at banks, and banks, for their part, were more careful in making loans. Since it is these loans that give rise to many of the demand deposits that serve as checking account money, the total money supply diminished noticeably. Actually, the circulating money increased, but the checking accounts declined so sharply that the total of the two resulted in a 20 per cent over-all decline (Table 27-3). As in previous depressions,

Table 27-3
Price Level, Money, and National Income Indexes, 1929–1939
(1926 = 100)

Year	Wholesale prices	Farm prices	Cost of living*	Real wages*	Money and demand deposits†	National income†
1929	95	105	96	102	102	108
1932	65	48	77	87	80	64
1937	86	86	82	112	120	94
1939	77	65	79	118	130	93

* Converted from 1923 to 1926 base by D. L. Kemmerer.
† Calculated by D. L. Kemmerer.
SOURCES: *Economic Almanac, 1956*, p. 423; *Banking and Monetary Statistics*, p. 34; *Statistical Abstract, 1939*, p. 331; *ibid., 1941*, p. 371.

the prices of farm goods fell most sharply. Even real wages fell somewhat, reaching their low point at 87 in 1932.

As in past periods of falling prices, many self-appointed money experts came forward with remedies. These blamed the troubles of the nation on insufficient money or on a growing shortage of gold or on an antiquated monetary system. "It was as though the patient had chills and various well meaning people were explaining how to repair the thermometer." After all, it was the economy, not the money system, that had suffered a breakdown. Yet Britain had made the gold standard the scapegoat for its troubles and abandoned it in 1931, dragging some fifteen other nations with her. Only a small bloc of nations such as France, Italy, Belgium, Holland, and Switzerland, most of whom had unhappy memories of inflation in World War I, clung to the protection of gold. During the 1932 presidential campaign, it was known that the Democratic candidate, Franklin D. Roosevelt, was listening to persons who believed that the United States, too, should abandon the gold coin standard.

Suspension of Specie Payments. Up until the winter of 1932–1933 the public had shown no lack of confidence in the dollar itself. At the same time the public had ample reason to distrust banks, for many had failed. But it is significant that people were hoarding paper dollars, not gold ones. About a month before Hoover left office and Roosevelt came in, the public's distrust of the dollar itself began to appear. During February, 1933, anxious citizens withdrew over a quarter of a billion gold dollars from banks. On March 6 the accumulation of bank failures forced the incoming President to declare a "bank holiday" which lasted a week, during which he closed all banks. On March 9 he forbade further exportation of gold except with Treasury permission. That amounted to suspension of specie payments and of the gold standard. Unless the movement of gold is free, the gold standard is not truly in operation. On April 5, 1933, the President "nationalized" gold, that is, he forbade the hoarding of gold coin, bars, or certificates, and required persons and banks to deliver all that they had over $100 to the nearest Federal Reserve bank or branch. On April 18 the Treasury let it be known that it was refusing to grant licenses to export gold. That suggested strongly that the government might be going to debase the dollar. Its value declined in terms of other nations' moneys. Things were happening rather fast to the dollar, but more startling events were still in store.

Congress attached a significant amendment to the Agricultural Adjustment Act in passing it on May 12, 1933. This so-called Thomas amendment gave the President authority, on a moment's notice, to take one or all of four major steps. (1) He might devalue the dollar by as much as 50 per cent. (2) He might order the Treasury to issue $3 billion in greenbacks. (3) He might order the Federal Reserve to buy $3 billion in government bonds; that would tend, in time, to increase demand deposits by a much greater amount. (4) He might put the nation on a bimetallic standard, as Bryan had once wanted to do. The President took none of these steps right away, but the fact that he had these powers made many fearful for the future of the dollar. The dollar's value continued to decline on the foreign exchange markets.

The possibility of bimetallism in 1933, as in 1896, came following a period of falling prices which unfairly hurt the well-being of several economic classes, especially farmers and debtors. As had happened before, there were many people who remembered a recent wartime inflation and wanted to avoid a repetition of that experience. Many feared that the proposed cures for deflation would shortly produce inflation and might prove more harmful in the long run than the disease.

On June 5, 1933, the President prohibited further use of the "gold clause" and declared that past use of it was void and unenforceable. Since Civil War days lawyers had regularly put a clause in debt contracts stating that the debtor must pay the creditor in gold dollars of the same weight and fineness as the ones that he had borrowed. The Supreme Court judges later had some sharp things to say about this rescinding of the gold clause, but they upheld it. This step also pointed to the government's probable intention to debase the dollar.

Meanwhile, the prime ministers of England, France, and Holland had talked with President Roosevelt about holding a monetary and economic conference late in June (1933) in London. Roosevelt explained to the nation in a fireside talk that a major objective of the conference would be "the setting up of a stabilization of currencies in order that trade and commerce can make contracts ahead. . . . The great international conference that lies before us must succeed . . . ; we have each of us pledged ourselves to the best joint efforts to that end." In the years just before, it had seemed that nations were racing to see which one would devalue its currency the most. Each time that a nation devalued its currency, that step stimulated its export trade and gave it a temporary advantage. The conference was to stop any such debasement race. It was also intended to lower tariff barriers. Before the London Conference got under way, however, Roosevelt changed his mind about the importance of the dollar's relationship with other currencies. Someone had persuaded him that it was more important to raise the price level inside the country than to maintain it at an even level with other currencies outside the country. Therefore, he wired our delegates that they should not concern themselves with foreign exchange stabilization. "The United States seeks the kind of a dollar which a generation hence will have the same purchasing and debt-paying power as the dollar we hope to attain in the near future." That left the London conference nothing of importance to do.

In August of 1933 President Roosevelt ordered gold miners to sell newly mined gold to the Treasury. Then in October he announced the Gold Purchase Plan and on October 25 set the price which the Treasury would pay for newly mined gold at $31.36 an ounce. He explained that it was the definite policy of the government "to restore commodity price levels." Once restored, presumably at levels familiar in the prosperous 1920s, he intended "to maintain a dollar which will not change its purchasing power and debt-paying power during the succeeding generation." He said flatly that he was making a move "toward a managed currency" and assured the public that "a sound currency will accompany a rise in the American price level." The President and his Secretary of the Treasury, Henry Morgenthau, were taking the advice of a Cornell University agricultural economist, George Warren, who believed that the government could alter the general price level within a short time by changing the gold content of the dollar. During the autumn of 1933, the

Treasury periodically raised the price that it would pay for newly mined gold. On January 30, 1934, Congress passed the Gold Reserve Act which was, in a sense, the ultimate goal of these months of preparations.

That law debased or devalued the dollar by 41 per cent. This the President had power to do under the Thomas amendment. The new gold dollar thus contained 41 per cent less gold than the old one. Instead of containing 23.22 grains of pure gold, it contained 13.71 grains. Out of every old gold dollar, the Treasury could make up 1.69 new ones (23.22 divided by 13.71 equals 1.69). The price which the Treasury was paying for gold was also 69 per cent higher than it had been before: it was $35 an ounce instead of $20.67. Professor Warren and the Treasury apparently were figuring that if they had 69 per cent more gold dollars, and they paid 69 per cent more for gold, this would push the price level up 69 per cent. The price level prevailing back in "normal," prosperous 1926 was about 69 per cent higher than that prevailing at the bottom of the depression. It all fitted together very neatly. So also did the preparations of the previous year. The Treasury's $4 billion of 1932 gold dollars were worth $6.8 billion in 1934 gold dollars. The government would not have had that "profit" if it had not prevented the export of gold, suspended specie payments, forbade hoarding, insisted that everyone turn in his gold to the government, and ordered mines to sell new gold only to the government. The profit would have gone, instead, to countless persons trying to protect themselves against inflation or speculating on the dollar. This might have protected these people against government manipulation of the money, as the gold coin standard was intended to do. The gold coin standard interfered with the government's planned solution of the money and price problems; it had to go, or at least it had to suffer considerable modification. The old gold coin standard's purpose was to protect the people's money against government manipulations; the new monetary standard was to prevent the people from interfering when the government saw fit to manipulate the money.

The Gold Reserve Act of January, 1934, placed the nation part way back on the gold standard, but gold coins no longer circulated. The Treasury stood ready to buy gold at $35 an ounce in unlimited amounts. Since this was 69 per cent higher than the old price of gold, it proved a tremendous stimulus to the gold mining business. Gold poured into the country during the next few years from South African and Canadian mines and from hoards all over the world. American holdings of gold rose from $7 billion in 1934 to $22 billion in 1940. The Treasury would, however, sell gold at $35 an ounce to any foreign central bank or treasury if such a sale were needed to settle international debts. Thus, although the new gold standard did not give the citizen the chance to protect himself, as the old one had, it nevertheless provided a measure of protection and stability. It was far better than the paper currencies of many other nations.

The Warren scheme for raising the price level, which the administration had adopted and followed, did not succeed. Prices rose, but they rose slowly, and they did not rise by 69 per cent for many years. Moreover, some of the rise was clearly owing to the end of the depression and the coming of World War II. Between 1933 and 1937 wholesale prices rose 13 per cent, and the cost of living rose 12 per cent. Then both drifted slightly downward again until World War II. It was 1946 before

Table 27-4
Commercial Banking Statistics, 1914–1933
(Dollars in billions)

Year	Total banks	National banks	State banks	National bank loans	State bank loans	National bank total deposits	State bank total deposits	State bank failures as per cent all failures
1914	25,517	7,525	17,992	6.4	6.7	8.6	8.8	88
1919	26,822	7,785	19,037	11.0	10.5	15.9	16.8	97
1921	28,197	8,154	20,043	12.0	14.1	15.1	17.8	89
1925	26,392	8,072	18,320	12.7	17.9	19.9	25.7	80
1929	23,332	7,536	15,797	14.8	20.8	21.6	28.2	90
1931	20,332	6,805	13,527	13.2	13.4	22.2	20.3	82
1933	13,245	4,902	8,343	8.1	7.7	16.7	15.3	92

SOURCES: *Banking and Monetary Statistics*, pp. 20–23, 283; *Historical Statistics*, pp. 263–264.

wholesale prices had risen 69 per cent and 1947 before the cost of living had done so. Doubtless the war was the immediate cause in both instances.

Further developments in money and prices are so inextricably involved with those in banking that it is necessary to treat them in terms of banking history.

BANKING

Commercial Banking, 1914–1929. There were 25,517 commercial banks in the United States in 1914. Somewhat under a third of them, 7,525, were national banks; the rest were state-chartered. Table 27-4 shows, however, that in 1914 the national banks made 49 per cent of all commercial bank loans and had 49 per cent of the deposits. Many of the state commercial banks were small and served relatively rural areas. Their charters let them loan to farmers against real estate collateral, but they also had the distinction of having more failures. Consistently, the state banks accounted for 80 to 90 per cent of all bank failures. If the chief crop in a region failed or its leading industry fell on hard times, the local bank was likely to fail, for it could not collect on a large part of its loans.

During World War I and after, the national banks made much more rapid progress than the state banks, especially in the matter of deposits. They also became substantial holders of investments about half of which were government bonds. Banks could not hold stocks, however. One reason that the national banks ran ahead of the state banks was that they all belonged to the new Federal Reserve System, whereas only a relatively small number of state banks were "member" banks. Federal bank examination standards were higher than those of many states, and member banks gained a measure of protection from the Federal Reserve System.

The Federal Reserve System. As was pointed out in Chapter 19, the Federal Reserve System which went into operation in November, 1914, was a system of bankers' banks superimposed on the National Bank System. Bankers' banks do for banks what banks do for their customers. (1) Federal Reserve banks lent to any member bank which needed a loan and had adequate collateral to protect it. (2) Federal Reserve banks held deposits for member banks. These deposits were the member banks' legal reserves. (3) The Federal Reserve banks could create their own credit, either in the form of Federal Reserve notes or of created deposits. The Federal Reserve bank added such deposits to the account (legal reserve account) of the borrowing member bank. The Federal Reserve banks dealt with banks, almost never with individuals.

Member banks used the Federal Reserve System as a clearing house, since all had accounts in it. That worked fairly simply. Suppose that Smith, who banked with the First National of Savannah, drew a $100 check on his bank and sent it to Jones, who banked with the Citizens and Southern National Bank of Atlanta. Jones of Atlanta promptly deposited the check to his account. The Atlanta bank would send the check to the Federal Reserve bank of Atlanta to clear. The Federal Reserve would deduct $100 from the Savannah bank's account and add it to the Atlanta bank's account. It is important to keep in mind that these accounts were the legal reserve accounts of these banks held in the Atlanta Federal Reserve bank. If a legal reserve account kept falling, the member bank either had to replenish it or refrain from lending as much. One way to replenish the legal reserve account was to borrow from the Federal Reserve bank.

The borrowing bank had to pay interest on such a loan, which meant it was not too profitable. Banks like to loan the money of their demand depositors which they get free; they like much less to lend borrowed money.

The Federal Reserve in World War I. During World War I the Federal Reserve System acted more like a manufacturer of money than like a central bank whose duty it was to keep people from going too deeply into debt. The government needed funds to pay for the war, and it wanted to encourage the public and even banks to buy bonds. Consequently, the Federal Reserve System enouraged credit expansion, which is another way of saying that it encouraged debt expansion. The government was the big debtor. The main aim at this point was to win the war, and the Federal Reserve System was doing its part to achieve that goal.

When the war ended, it fell to the Federal Reserve to discourage this credit expansion. The only tool the Federal Reserve had with which to accomplish this was its discount rate, that is, the interest which it charged member banks when they came to borrow. The Federal Reserve should have raised its discount rate to banks, which would have caused them to raise their interest rates to customers. That would have discouraged customers from borrowing to buy and hold, say, cotton, wheat, or copper for a price rise. Quite a number of firms and people speculated in such commodities after World War I. The Federal Reserve was slow to raise its discount rate because the Treasury Department urged it not to do so. The Treasury wanted to borrow some more also and wished to keep down the cost of such loans. Now that the war was over, the Federal Reserve should have ignored the Treasury. The Federal Reserve Board still had its offices in the Treasury building, however, and the Federal Reserve and Treasury people had worked closely together during the war, so that it was difficult to make this change in attitude. Speculation got out of hand and wholesale prices climbed higher and higher. Finally, the Federal Reserve acted, late in 1919 and again early in 1920. The bubble burst in May, 1920, a panic was on, and a depression followed. The Federal Reserve System had not performed well in its first test as a credit control authority. It did poorly in the depression which followed. In a depression a central bank should give generous help to sound banks which are temporarily short of funds, but the Federal Reserve banks kept interest rates up and reduced loans.

Discovery of Open Market Operations. About 1922 the Federal Reserve authorities became aware of another credit control device that was more effective than raising the discount rate. That was open market operations. It was not exactly a new discovery. Other central banks, and even the Federal Reserve, had known of it before; they now became more aware of its usefulness. Open market operations were effective because so many banks used the Federal Reserve banks as a clearing house. The new device worked in this fashion: if the Federal Reserve wanted to discourage credit expansion, it offered some of its own government bonds for sale. Whoever bought them paid for them with a check on his bank. Very likely, many of these checks were on national banks. When the Federal Reserve collected on those checks it automatically reduced the legal reserves of those national banks. That discouraged the national banks from making as many loans. Or else they had to borrow from the Federal Reserve, which probably raised its discount rate at this point.

Contrariwise, if the Federal Reserve authorities felt that times were too dull, they might offer to buy government bonds. The sellers usually deposited the checks which they got from the Federal Reserve in their own banks. That automatically increased these banks' legal reserves. The banks had more funds to lend and so became less strict in their lending policy.

When the Federal Reserve authorities first tried open market operations, the device worked very well. They thought that they had discovered a control device which would enable them to prevent future panics and depressions and to keep the price level quite stable. They were very optimistic.

When there was a little recession in 1924, the Federal Reserve made credit more plentiful and the country seemed to respond, as a car does when the driver steps on the accelerator. Somewhat later they discouraged a boom with apparently equal success. However well the Federal Reserve passed these little tests of keeping the price level even and avoiding boomlets and recessions, it failed the really big test.

The 1929 Collapse. From about 1925 on, speculative purchases in real estate and in securities increased sharply. The real estate boom, which was largely in Florida, collapsed about 1926, but the boom in securities continued. When the Federal Reserve authorities discouraged credit expansion early in 1928, it was high time for action. That summer, however, they relaxed the controls again and security prices resumed their upward climb. There have been various explanations for this reversal. One is the illness in February, 1928, and then death in October of Benjamin Strong. He was the head of the New York Federal Reserve Bank and New York's most influential banker in the 1920s. His bank was the largest of the twelve Federal Reserve banks. Strong actually had more power than the Federal Reserve Board in Washington. Some admirers later said that if he had lived, he would have brought the boom under control. For months no one assumed leadership, and the boom grew in size. Then in February, 1929, the Board finally applied pressure to limit further credit expansion. It even wanted to deny loans to banks that were known to be lending to speculators. But some big New York banks and the New York Federal Reserve Bank itself would not cooperate. Furthermore, corporations with cash surpluses, and wealthy individuals, sent funds directly to brokers to lend to speculators. The banks had no control over these "loans from others." By 1929 anyone who had tried to stop the prosperity party would have received no thanks for his pains: he would only have been blamed. The collapse came in October of 1929. As in 1920–1921, the rescue operations of the Federal Reserve System were more effective than its ability to prevent the calamity. But by this time many banks were beyond rescue.

Bank Failures, 1921–1933. Between 1921 and 1933, the number of commercial banks in the United States declined from 28,197 to 13,245, that

Table 27-5
Bank Failures, 1921–1933*

Year	Number of banks failing	Total deposits of failed banks ($ in millions)
1921–1928	4,763	1,548
1929	628	223
1930	1,292	822
1931	2,213	1,669
1932	1,416	698
1933	3,891	3,583
Total.	14,203	8,543
1934	44	35

* Includes only national and state banks.
SOURCE: *Federal Reserve Bulletin* (Washington, 1937), pp. 1209, 1213.

is, by more than half. Nearly all the decline resulted from bank failures. Table 27-5 shows the appalling magnitude of this loss. It went on not merely in the depression, but even during the preceding prosperity; about 450 failed in only one year (1922). Actually, 1929 was an average year in the matter of bank failures. 1930 was twice as bad as the year before, with nearly a billion dollars of deposits tied up. Then 1931 was twice as bad as 1930, and finally 1933 was nearly twice as bad as 1931.

With banks failing in such numbers, cautious persons began to withdraw their money and hoard it. That created a need for a greater supply of money, since hoarded funds were idle; it tended to lower the price level, and it endangered the remaining banks. To help the banks out of this predicament, Congress in 1932 passed the Glass-Steagall Act. It permitted Federal Reserve banks to back up Federal Reserve notes with government obligations, something not previously permitted. It was a step back toward the Civil War days when national bank notes were backed by government bonds. The law would later make it easier to inflate the currency, too. Nevertheless, the hoarding continued and so did bank failures.

By the fall and winter of 1932–1933, the country was extremely jittery. Starting on October 31 in Nevada, state after state declared a bank moratorium, temporarily excusing banks from having to pay out deposits on demand. Louisiana had a bank holiday on February 4, Michigan on February 14, and Maryland a few days after that. Each one put greater pressure on the banks in the remaining states. Between March 1 and 3, seventeen states declared bank holidays. Many states made Inauguration Day, March 4, 1933, also a bank holiday. President Roosevelt was no sooner in office than he declared a four-day nationwide moratorium, March 6 to 9. In the interim, Congress passed the Emergency Banking Act, which provided among other things for the orderly reopening of the solvent banks. This authorized the Comptroller of the Currency to appoint conservators for weak or insolvent banks. Some 2,000 banks never reopened. It also authorized the Reconstruction Finance Corporation to help other banks by buying newly created preferred stock from them. And it permitted the Federal Reserve banks to issue a new type of Federal Reserve bank notes, backed by assets not normally considered suitable. The law also let nonmember banks borrow temporarily from Federal Reserve banks.

Reform Legislation of 1933–1935. The banking laws which Congress had enacted in 1931, 1932, and 1933 were largely emergency measures. Later in 1933, in 1934, and in 1935 Congress passed two major banking acts and two acts dealing with the securities and exchange businesses but touching on banking as well. Taken together, these four acts constituted a basic revision of the banking system almost as important as that which occurred in 1913–1914. Viewed in their entirety, these laws sought to accomplish four things: namely, (1) to restore confidence in banks in general; (2) to strengthen the banks; (3) to remove some of the temptations to speculate; and (4) to increase the powers of the Federal Reserve System.

The failure of over ten thousand banks was bound to shake the confidence of the public. The cross-examination by a Senate committee of Charles Mitchell and Albert Wiggin, the presidents of New York's two largest banks, confirmed the worst suspicions of people who had suspected the ethics of big business. These two men had shown an appalling lack of responsibility.

Since 1929 many individuals had been withdrawing their deposits from banks. Yet it would have proved a great handicap to the nation's economic recovery and growth if Americans had turned into a nation of hoarders. Therefore, it was essential to restore the public's confidence in banks. The Banking Act of 1933 set up a Federal Deposit Insurance

Corporation (FDIC) to insure every depositor in a member bank against losses up to $10,000. The Treasury and the Federal Reserve System provided it with the capital to start. All members of the Federal Reserve System had to belong: other banks might if they met its requirements. By 1958, 97 per cent of all commercial banks belonged to the FDIC. In 1935 the insurable maximum was cut to $5,000, but then in 1950 it was set up to $10,000 again. All members of the system must pay a premium of 1/12 of 1 per cent of their deposits each year. Since the founding of the FDIC, bank failures have virtually ceased. The FDIC examines banks carefully: if one is shaky, it arranges a merger or liquidates the bank before it fails.

In order to strengthen the banks, the new laws sought to encourage more small banks to join the Federal Reserve System. To do this, Congress had to make some concessions. It was willing to lower its standards in some respects in the hope of getting more banks under the Federal Reserve's direct control, which it felt would be a net gain. The new laws eased the old prohibitions against banks' having branches and permitted them some freedom in making real estate loans. The effort to draw more banks into the Federal Reserve was not especially successful, or at least it took a long time to produce moderate results. In 1936, 42 per cent of all commercial banks were members; and by 1956 this had only risen to 47 per cent. There are still more banks outside of the Federal Reserve System than in it.

To remove some of the temptations to speculate, Congress obliged banks to get rid of their investment affiliates, that is, their investment banking companies (see "Investment Banking" in Chapter 26). And the Federal Reserve banks might refuse to loan to any bank which was lending "undue" amounts of its credit to speculators.

Meanwhile, Congress saw to it that the over-all direction of the Federal Reserve System rested with the Board of Governors[1] in Washington, and not with the head of the New York Federal Reserve Bank. Moreover, the Board could remove just about anyone from the organization that it wanted to. The Board determined whether to expand or contract credit. In this connection, it acquired two new credit control devices. It could raise margin requirements and thus lessen speculation on the stock exchanges. It could also raise reserve requirements of member banks up to double the old rate. Thus the Board now had four weapons with which to bring a boom under control.

The New Economic Philosophy. The Great Depression left the American people determined to avoid any further depressions and mass unemployment. In order to achieve a stable economy, the nation's leaders had to

[1] Congress changed the name of the Federal Reserve Board to Board of Governors in 1935.

have some theory as to what was likely to undermine economic stability. The theories of an English economist, John Maynard Keynes, gained a wide acceptance in America at this time, especially with the Roosevelt administration. Accordingly, Keynes had a profound effect on governmental policies.

Keynes' theory in a simplified form was as follows: The United States had become a mature economy. Population growth and business expansion were leveling off and the country should no longer expect the mushroom growth it had experienced in the past. At the same time, the American standard of living was high and people with a high living standard save more; in fact, they may save too much. It would be all right if they invested these savings in productive enterprises, but all too often they hoarded the money or speculated on the stock markets or in real estate as they had in the 1920s. That withdrew funds from productive activities and led to unemployment and depression. It was therefore essential to discourage oversaving, hoarding, and speculation and to encourage genuine investment.

Low interest rates would encourage investors to borrow. Insuring bank deposits discouraged hoarding and high margin requirements discouraged speculation. The government even imposed high taxes on corporate savings in 1936 to make corporations spend them in dividends or plant expansion. If private business would not invest enough, it meant that the government itself must step in and spend money, stimulate buying, and encourage business expansion. The ultimate goal was to put an end to unemployment and prevent its recurrence. Yet in a mature economy, private investment might easily become discouraged; therefore, the government always had to stand ready to spend more to bolster it. And interest rates should remain low to encourage investors. The government kept them artificially low (see Table 27-6, page 546). A "low interest rate standard" had replaced the gold coin standard. Because the administration felt obliged to spend generously, the Federal budget was regularly unbalanced. Such a theory had political merits as well. Harry Hopkins, one of President Roosevelt's close advisors, remarked on one occasion that the administration's policy was "to tax and tax, spend and spend, and elect and elect."

If the administration were to run deficits each year, it needed a Federal Reserve System and a banking system that would be willing to absorb some of the growing public debt. It needed a Federal Reserve System that would employ its credit controls to keep interest rates low most of the time. With that thought in mind, President Roosevelt in 1934 put Marriner Eccles at the head of the Federal Reserve System. Eccles was sympathetic in his thinking to Keynesian or New Deal economics and to deficit financing. Government bonds had made up 11 per cent of the earning assets of commercial banks in June, 1929, but by June, 1939, they were 39 per cent and by the end of 1945 they were 72 per cent. At this point, commercial banks were serving the Federal government far more than they were private enterprise. Yet this new economics did not put an end to the Great Depression. In January of 1940 there were still 10 million unemployed. It took the war to put an end to the Great Depression.

Banks and War Financing. The government handled the financing of World War II somewhat better than it had handled that of World War I. It collected more in taxes at the time and it inflated the currency less. It paid for approximately 40 per cent of the war by taxes and approximately 50 per cent by borrowing. Created money and credit paid for only about 10 per cent. Part of this damage took place early in the war when the government permitted banks to buy bonds directly from the Treasury, thus creating "invisible greenbacks." Later in the war the Treasury permitted banks to buy only 90-day treasury bills (I.O.U.'s) or treasury certificates (one year, usually), or to purchase on the open market long-term bonds which had less than ten years' maturity remaining. This arrangement also created invisible greenbacks, as will be explained shortly. Just as Civil War financing was less crude than that of the Revolution, and World War I financing was more subtle than that of the Civil War, so that of World War II was even more difficult to follow. It also had inflation built into it: the problem was to detect it.

The Treasury tried to profit from the mistakes made in financing World War I, but in doing so it made some mistakes of its own. People who had patriotically bought Liberty Bonds in World War I, especially of the Fourth Loan, had had to sell their bonds at a considerable loss after the war if they wanted cash. This time the Treasury was determined that all government securities should stay at par or better. It decided that everyone who bought directly from the government would know exactly what interest he would get and that this would not vary from one bond drive to the next. The Treasury also determined that these interest rates should be low. That would have two advantages: it would keep down the cost of borrowing money to finance the war, and it was in keeping with Keynesian economics. Once the war was over, the country would again face problems of a mature economy, underinvestment, and unemployment, and it seemed advisable to pursue a consistent interest rate policy.

The low interest rate policy, however, was definitely inflationary. Whenever banks had a chance to buy bonds with less than ten years remaining to maturity, they did so and sold some of their treasury bills. That tended to depress the price of treasury bills. To prevent this happening, the Treasury asked the Federal Reserve System to buy those bills at no loss to the banks. By the war's end (August, 1945) the Federal Reserve banks held $19.5 billion of bills and certificates which they had had to buy. Purchasing them amounted to an open market buying operation. It made credit easy. It added to the reserves of member banks, which could, as a result, loan freely to customers. It amounted to creating invisible greenbacks.

This support of the government securities market should have ended soon after peace came, but it did not.[2] The Treasury did not want to see interest rates rise, for that would make it more costly to float new bond issues. There were also many government policymakers who feared a renewal of the depression. They wanted to continue the low interest rate standard. Accordingly, the Federal Reserve went right on buying bonds any time that their price threatened to go below par.

No real depression took place after the war. Business boomed and factories turned out goods to fill long-felt needs. Businessmen could borrow at banks, and even if the Federal Reserve authorities feared an inflation or an unhealthy boom, they could do almost nothing to stop it. The cost of living rose one-third between 1945 and 1950. The Federal Reserve authorities were powerless to use their credit control devices, such as open market selling operations, higher discount rates, and higher reserve requirements for banks. The commercial banks would simply put some of their vast supply of bonds on the market and the Federal Reserve would have to absorb them or else bond prices would fall below par. The Federal Reserve had promised the Treasury not to let that happen. When the Federal Reserve bought the bonds, it created more credit, made it possible for banks to lend more, and caused further inflation. As long as the Federal Reserve obeyed the wishes of the Treasury, there was no way to break out of this "vicious circle."

Matters were getting out of hand in the late fall of 1950; wholesale prices were rising 1 per cent a month; and something had to be done. The Treasury and the Federal Reserve finally reached an "accord" in February, 1951, under which the Federal Reserve no longer had to "support" the government bond market. Within another year, the inflation came to a halt. Government bond prices dropped below par and interest rates, for the first time in some twenty-five years, began to climb back to levels that had been considered normal back in the 1920s. That was the last time that economic and political conditions had been reasonably normal. The Federal Reserve System had regained its "independence"; it was again in a position to discourage lending when that seemed desirable. Nevertheless, the return to a normal level of interest rates, after many years of artificially low ones, made many people believe

[2] After 1947 the Federal Reserve banks refused to support the bill or certificate market any longer, but they continued to support the government bond market.

that the Federal Reserve System was being unduly severe and that it was making the money supply unreasonably "tight."

After World War II, banks resumed their earlier function of lending primarily to business people rather than to the government. Table 27-6 shows that loans have risen and bank holdings of government securities

Table 27-6

Commercial Banking and Price Level Statistics, 1939–1958

Year	Loans ($ in billions)	Government securities held ($ in billions)	90-day treasury bills—yields, per cent	Demand deposits ($ in billions)	Cost of living index*	Wholesale price index*
1939	17.2	16.3	0.023	32.5	59.4	50.1
1945	26.1	90.6	0.375	105.9	76.9	68.8
1947	38.1	69.2	0.604	95.7	100.0	96.4
1950	52.2	62.0	1.218	104.7	102.8	103.1
1952	64.2	63.3	2.09	116.6	113.5	111.6
1955	82.6	61.6	1.73	126.9	114.5	110.7
1958†	96.0	67.3	2.77	128.8	123.9	119.2

* 1947–1949 base.

† November.

SOURCES: *Federal Reserve Bulletin,* December, 1953, pp. 1345, 1357; January, 1959, pp. 33, 41, 72; *Statistical Abstract, 1956,* pp. 320, 324.

have declined. Nevertheless, demand deposits have grown, and both cost of living and wholesale prices have risen. It is noteworthy that most of the inflation took place not *during* the war, but after it. Between 1939 and 1952 the dollar lost each year about 5 per cent of its remaining value. Then followed four years of relatively stable prices. The price level began to rise again early in 1956.

CHAPTER 28

Domestic and Foreign Commerce

The American people normally spend half of their incomes each year in retail stores. It is true in merchandising, as it is in manufacturing, that a minority of the merchants do a majority of the business. For example, in 1948, 3.8 per cent of all the 1,770,000 retail stores in the United States made 42 per cent of the sales. Domestic commerce, and that included all kinds of wholesaling operations as well as retailing ones, continued to grow more rapidly than foreign commerce. The ratio was 9 to 1 in 1908; it doubled to 18 to 1 in 1939 and then fell back in 1948 and 1954 (see Table 28-1). This was despite the fact that foreign commerce itself had

Table 28-1
Relative Expansion of Domestic and Foreign Trade
(Dollars in billions)

Year	Wholesale trade	Retail trade	Total domestic trade	Foreign trade	Ratio
1908	.....	.....	28.0	3.2	9–1
1929	66.7	48.3	115.0	9.6	12–1
1939	54.9	42.0	96.9	5.5	18–1
1948	188.7	130.5	319.2	19.8	16–1
1954	235.0	170.0	405.0	25.3	16–1

SOURCE: National Industrial Conference Board, *Economic Almanac, 1956* (Washington, 1956), pp. 144, 149, 481.

greatly increased. In fact, early in World War I American foreign commerce became the largest in the world, instead of ranking third as it had in 1913. American domestic commerce grew enormously in this period, partly because of the capability of the American manufacturer to produce goods in quantity cheaply and partly because the standard of living of the consuming public had increased so sharply. Obviously growing production, rising buying power, and mounting sales are all interrelated. The point was made in Chapter 20 that merchants had to devise new retail institutions and new selling techniques in order to dispose of all the goods that the new factories were capable of turning out. That continued to be the situation after 1914. In addition to further progress in already established institutions such as specialty stores, department stores, chain stores, variety stores, and mail-order houses, a new crop of retail institutions appeared. These were economy stores, combination stores, supermarkets, gasoline stations, shopping centers, drive-ins, and discount houses. There were also advances made in selling methods, advertising, branded products, and marketing research. As transportation and communication improved and stores grew in size, various wholesalers declined in importance. Retailers and manufacturers took back some of the functions which they had conceded early in the industrial revolution to jobbers, brokers, commission merchants, and other wholesalers.

RETAIL TRADE INSTITUTIONS

Progress or Decline in Old Forms. General stores faded rapidly in the twentieth century. In 1958 they were found only in rural areas, notably in upper New England, the South, and the Plains and Mountain states. Their number declined from 104,000 in 1929 to 17,000 in 1954, making them only 1 per cent of all retail establishments; they made only about ½ of 1 per cent of all sales. Specialty stores had almost supplanted them. To some extent, the modern drugstore and the variety store had taken over the general store's function of offering a little bit of everything.

The specialty stores continued to be by far the most important type of store in existence. The chief ones were grocery stores, meat markets, automobile agencies, gas stations, restaurants, liquor stores, drugstores, lumber yards, hardware stores, shoe stores, clothing stores, furniture stores, and appliance firms. Stores could be more specialized in large cities than in small towns. New York City has clothing stores for tall girls, but in Middlebury, Vermont (population 3,600), in the 1950s the same merchant combined the specialties of furniture selling, radio repairing, and undertaking in one establishment. Certain types of specialty stores rose and others declined after 1914. Dry goods stores, saloons, stationery stores, bicycle shops, and saddle and leather shops all slipped, whereas soda fountains, liquor package houses, automotive supply firms, and gasoline stations grew in importance.

Department stores exist in most towns of about 55,000 or more persons; in fact, it seems to be a rule of thumb that if one appears, there may soon be three. Department store statistics now include mail-order houses. When the automobile invaded rural America, many farmers preferred to shop in town rather than to order from catalogues. Accordingly, mail-order houses set up local stores, which became department stores of a kind. There was this important difference, however: mail-order stores carried many heavy items such as farm equipment, household appliances, hardware, and the like. They were often more of a man's store than was the normal department store. Mail-order houses also continued to do a mail-order business, but that constituted only about a third of their total sales. The catalogue business was still growing but not as fast as the store sales.

In 1929 department stores made over 9 per cent of the sales of all retail stores, but by 1954 their share had declined to 6 per cent. In terms of total sales, department stores grew nearly fivefold between 1919 and 1958. This growth was especially noteworthy in Texas and in the Southeast, where improvement in the standard of living was marked. Department stores added many special services to attract and keep their customers, such as escalators, restaurants, beauty parlors, delivery services, parking grounds, and even playrooms where the weary housewife could deposit her young while she shopped in some degree of peace. Because of modern driving and parking problems, the shopper is more than ever desirous of doing most of her shopping in one or a few places. Since department stores fill that need, they continue to prosper.

Chain stores have had a phenomenal growth since 1914. In 1956 they sold about a fifth of all goods sold by retail. The types of stores which found that the chain organization met their needs were the following, given in order of importance in 1955: grocery stores, department stores, variety stores, building materials, women's apparel stores, drugstores, shoe stores, and service stations. Grocery stores and department stores make more than half of all chain store sales.

Among the variety stores, Woolworth's, Kresge's, Kress', and Grant's head the list. For example, in 1957 Woolworth's had 2,121 stores in operation and made $824 million of sales. Since Frank Woolworth's death in 1919, this store and its competitors have given up being strictly "5 and 10 cent" stores. The World War I inflation by itself made that an impossibility. Today some of their merchandise sells for several dollars. In fact, they sometimes maintain two stores in a shopping district, one that sells articles of less than $1 and one that sells the more expensive items. Many of the basic principles of Woolworth are still in operation, however. The merchant places the goods on display in such a way that no personal "selling" is needed. The great majority are low-priced items. The clerks do little more than put the customer's purchase in a bag and accept his money. Variety stores are continually adding new goods to their large offerings and they are careful to choose locations where traffic is heavy. Like the department stores, they offer the shopper an opportunity to do a considerable part of his purchasing in one place.

New Types of Retail Institutions. Most of the new types of retail stores are improved variations of the old ones. "'Throughout the history of retailing, new types of merchandising outlets have emerged as a result of innovations in the fields of transportation and communication.' Each of these merchandising methods, whether it be the fair, the market, the shop, the trading post, the general store, the specialty store, the department store, the chain store or the supermarket, has been based on lower cost of distribution resulting in better consumer service . . . ; the increased concentration of population was largely responsible for the department store while the railroads and the Parcel Post System gave impetus to the mail order house."[1]

About 1908 an early "cash and carry" store appeared. Some imaginative independent merchant was trying out an idea that he had. In 1913 the Atlantic & Pacific grocery chain inaugurated its version of "cash and carry," called "economy" stores. Since housewives did not want to carry their groceries any great distance, A & P had to set up many small neighborhood stores. The A & P chain had 3,100 stores in 1917 and 15,500 in 1930. By then their sales totaled over $1 billion. Meanwhile, other merchants were making experiments. Clarence Saunders opened his first Piggly-Wiggly store in Memphis, Tennessee, in 1916. Its distinguishing feature was that the customer waited on himself. This method had already been tried with success in cafeterias. The saving in clerks' wages meant, of course, lower prices to the customer. Still another innovation that appeared was the combination food store. Instead of having to go to three or four specialty stores, the housewife could now buy canned goods, meat, and green vegetables all in one store.

During the 1920s the shopper acquired two new aids which greatly changed his shopping habits. Between 1919 and 1929 the number of automobile registrations rose from 7.7 to 26.5 million, and many families acquired electric refrigerators. These two changes meant that the housewife could travel farther to market, make a larger purchase, and have a cool place to store the more perishable items. It was not that refrigerators were so much roomier than the old-fashioned icebox; rather, many persons bought refrigerators who had not owned iceboxes. When all these ideas and changes were put together about 1930, they resulted in the birth of a new retail trade institution—the supermarket. The early ones appeared in garages and warehouses, some distance removed from the center of business, the shelves were of wood, the walls were bare, and the whole atmosphere was austere. But the prices were abnormally low, which had appeal, especially in the depressed 1930s. For several years the large grocery chains resisted this idea, but in 1937 A & P began erect-

[1] William Clem, *An Analysis of the Impact of Shopping Centers on Retailing*, unpublished master's thesis (Urbana, Ill.: University of Illinois, 1955), p. 24.

ing supermarkets. For every one that A & P put up, it abandoned about three neighborhood "economy" stores: its stores decreased from 14,700 in 1937 to 4,500 in 1951. Other grocery chains did likewise, but most of the change-over occurred in the 1940s. The supermarket combined a number of advantages. It was a cash and carry and also a self-service store; it was a combination food store; it was located in a low-rent district; and its coming meant that the company had one store to administer and supply instead of three or four. For the customer all these factors meant lower-cost groceries, greater convenience in shopping, and usually less difficulty in finding a parking place.

In an ever-changing world, even the supermarket did not remain the ideal solution. Traffic congestion became heavier every year on American city streets and the problem of finding a parking place became a major one. Either the supermarket had to pay high real estate prices for a parking area in the center of town, which ran up its expenses, or it went without a parking area and lost potential customers, or it moved to the edge of town, which meant that the housewife had to make another stop in town to complete her shopping. Supermarkets tended for a time to select the edge of town; frequently other stores, such as gas stations, laundries, perhaps a furniture mart, joined them. A small local market sprang up, spontaneously and unplanned. Some withered early because they had not allowed themselves adequate parking space.

The planned shopping center has come into vogue in recent years. J. C. Nichols founded one in Kansas City as far back as 1908, but the shopping center did not become significant until after World War II. The essential features of a shopping center are that it have ample parking places, for as many as 1,000 cars, that it have a branch of a reasonably well-known department store or mail-order house, and that there be several other types of specialty stores represented, such as a grocery store (which should be a supermarket), women's apparel shops, a branch of a bank, and a drugstore. The shopping center's customers are chiefly women. In 1953 there were 948 shopping centers either planned or under construction in the United States, with the greatest activity in the East and the Middle West. (See Fig. 28-1.)

The tendency has been for chain operations of all kinds, except the variety stores, to reduce the number of their stores and yet to increase their volume of business. This has been true even of gasoline stations, which prosper when carefully located at busy intersections but often fail when set along an open highway.

From their very nature, gasoline stations were the first drive-in type of store. Drive-ins for gas or for food and soft drinks have grown in importance ever since the surge in automobile registration in the 1920s. Stands dispensing ice cream, root beer, hot dogs, or quick lunches dot American highways to serve the millions who have just a few minutes for a gulp and a bite. Americans spend more on food and drink than on anything else, and they spend next most on cars and their care. Truly we are a nation of people who eat and run (on wheels). Merchants who expected to sell to Americans had to take into account the great importance of the automobile in their customers' thinking, behavior, and motivations. In recent years the drive-in idea has invaded such lines as package liquor

Fig. 28-1. A modern shopping center at Yonkers, N.Y. (*Photo by Fairchild Aerial Surveys, Courtesy of John Wanamaker.*)

stores, laundries, dry cleaning, banking, and of course motion picture entertainment.

Somewhat akin to the drive-in but on a more modest scale is the vending machine. Candy and chewing gum machines were in use before World War I, and later cigarette machines were added. In recent years the manufacturers of these machines have become very ingenious. Vending machines sell hot coffee, pour out cold drinks in a paper cup, serve food, and offer fresh milk in cartons. There are often nearby auxiliary machines that will make change. Likewise, coin machines will now do a man's laundry or shine his shoes. The common denominator running through many of these devices is the substitution of cheap capital for dear labor. Eliminate the labor cost, or reduce it, and the merchant can sell his commodity or service at a lower price and make a bigger profit. Moreover, machines work twenty-four hours a day, are rarely discourteous, and pose no human relations problems to the manager. This makes them increasingly popular.

The discount house is a new way, and an old one, of winning customers. For at least a century, the offer to sell "at wholesale prices" has drawn customers as honey does bees. New York auctions, mail-order houses, factory outlets, supermarkets, and wholesale agents all more or less played on this theme. It has been most prevalent in time of depression when a buyer's market existed. Its latest form is the "discount house" which has appeared in considerable numbers since the Korean War. Discount houses sell the most popular items of a great many brands, especially appliances. Although they may have a few items in stock, they order most of them for the customer from a catalogue. If the product is faulty, the customer sometimes finds that he has less recourse than if he had bought from a regular dealer.

The pattern of new retail institutions has been that they started very simply. They were usually the invention of an ingenious merchant who was seeking to attract customers by offering them a real bargain if they would forego some of the usual services that ran up costs. Economy stores, early self-service stores, supermarkets, and others have had this characteristic. Owners of more established types of stores, faced with this keen competition, have often rationalized that it was unfair and have sought to secure legislation to limit it.

FEDERAL LEGISLATION AFFECTING NEW RETAIL INSTITUTIONS

By the early 1920s independent stores were contending that "There ought to be a law" against chain stores. In 1929 chains were 11 per cent of all stores and did 22 per cent of the business. Maryland in 1927 passed a law to limit the number of chain stores in each county, but the circuit court ruled it unconstitutional. Pennsylvania also tried to limit chains, but the Federal Supreme Court declared that unconstitutional. Finally Indiana succeeded in imposing a tax on mercantile companies for having more than one store; the Supreme Court upheld this 5 to 4 in 1931. Other states followed this lead. In 1935 Congress investigated the alleged existence of a superlobby of chain stores and produced evidence that chain stores sometimes received generous discounts for large orders or for local advertising which they conducted on behalf of the manufacturer. Out of this came the Robinson-Patman Act in 1936, an amendment to the Clayton Antitrust Act of 1914. The act forbade price discrimination between buyers in interstate commerce if the effect was to limit competition substantially and tend toward monopoly. Congressman Wright Patman sought principally to lessen the buying advantages of chain stores over smaller rivals who could not enjoy the economies of volume buying. It has been a difficult law to enforce.

The Miller-Tydings Act of 1937, a so-called "fair trade law," was aimed at merchants who cut prices on nationally advertised brands in order to attract customers. The act legalized price fixing from manufacturer to consumer: it upheld resale price maintenance contracts. After all, the choice of any brand as a "loss leader" to attract customers might hurt the reputation of the brand, hence of the manufacturer, as well as disturbing local business conditions.

There was much to be said on both sides of this question. On the one hand, both the manufacturer and his local representative had an investment in a nationally known product. The manufacturer had spent much to advertise it and to associate a certain value with it; the local store sometimes offered repair service if the item had moving parts and also served the manufacturer's customers in other ways. On the other hand, supporters of price fixing, price stabilization, or resale price maintenance often overlooked an important truth. Cutting prices is an integral part of the competitive process. It is one of the chief ways by which the more efficient merchant or producer enlarges his market at the expense of his less efficient rival. It has been one of the secrets of the improving American standard of living. To say that a merchant may cut prices in one manner but not in another is to set up a rule extremely difficult to enforce and perhaps not desirable.

The Miller-Tydings Act had only limited success in its early years but seemed to work fairly well during the 1940s. This era, however, was one of wartime scarcities; it was a sellers' market. By the early 1950s consumers had satisfied their pent-up demand and manufacturers began again to have surpluses of which to dispose. Some disposed of these surpluses to "discount houses," which offered the goods to the public at a bargain. At that point, the courts took the attitude that if a manufacturer was going to undercut his own local representative, the court was not going to oblige the local representative to maintain the brand price. The courts contended that the fair trade laws did not apply to retailers who had not signed resale price maintenance contracts.[2] This rendered the Miller-Tydings Act useless, since a manufacturer could not obtain the thousands of individual signatures necessary for effective price maintenance. The fair trade advocates then exerted enough pressure on Congress to obtain a new law—the McGuire Act of 1952—which permitted the use of nonsigner clauses in resale contracts. State supreme courts in Georgia, Florida, and Michigan immediately ruled against the nonsigner clause,

[2] *Schwegemann Brothers v. Calvert Distillers Corporation,* 341 U.S. 384 (1951).

but the supreme courts of some seventeen other states upheld the principle.

NEW METHODS IN SELLING, CHANGES IN OLD METHODS

Since 1914 there has been a definite decline in door-to-door selling. The consumer now has a car and prefers to buy in town where the selection is greater and where he is surer of recourse in case something goes awry. The one-price system is even more firmly established than it was in 1914. More companies guarantee their products and the guarantees are more meaningful. More emphasis is placed nowadays on salesmanship. The salesman receives training in the virtues of his product and in how to persuade the customer to buy it.

One way of persuading the customer to buy is to show him how easy it is to have the product now and pay for it later, "in easy payments" over a period of time. To sell expensive appliances in quantity, such plans are virtually essential. The amount of consumer credit has grown rapidly; that was especially true during the 1920s and 1930s and after World War II. Table 28-2 shows that consumer credit has hovered around 10 per cent of personal disposable income. That means that the average person was in debt for autos, appliances, personal loans, and merchandise bought for an amount equal to 10 per cent of the income he had left after paying all his taxes. The chief component parts of consumer credit have been noninstallment credit and installment credit. The noninstallment credit is a third to a quarter of all consumer credit. Only half is charge accounts. Installment credit consisted for years of two major items: loans to finance automobile purchases and loans to finance the purchase of appliances, such as washing machines, television sets, and air conditioners. Recently, personal loans by finance companies and banks have become a third important item.

Automobile financing enabled millions of families to buy cars in the 1920s. Allegedly, it was also a major factor in pulling the nation out of the 1920–1921 depression, and it played a part in lifting the nation, for a time, out of the depression of the 1930s. There were misgivings later, however, that excessive installment selling had been a factor in bringing on the 1929 panic and ensuing depression. During World War II there were restrictions on most kinds of consumer credit. When the war ended, the government lifted the restrictions, and banks and finance companies again expanded their credit to consumers. By the mid-1950s the percentage of consumer credit had reached its all-time high of 15 per cent of personal disposable income. That seemed to many to be a dangerously high level.

During World War II the Federal Reserve System's restrictions on consumer credit were collectively known as Regulation W and first went into operation in 1941. In general, Regulation W required the consumer to pay about one-third of the purchase price down and to pay off the remainder within one year's time. He had to pay all charge accounts within two months' time. The purpose of Regulation W was to prevent prices from rising. It kept those who had little cash from competing with

Table 28-2
Consumer Credit, 1923–1958
(Dollars in billions)

Year	Total	Automobile	Other goods	Charge accounts	Consumer credit as per cent of disposable income	Phase of business cycle
1923	3.8*	....	2.3	...	6	Prosperity
1929	6.4	1.4	1.8	1.6	8	Prosperity
1933	3.5	0.5	1.1	1.0	8	Depression
1937	6.7	1.5	2.5	1.3	10	Recovery
1939	7.2	1.5	3.0	1.4	11	Recession
1943	4.9	0.4	0.8	1.4	5	Prosperity, but
1945	5.7	0.5	0.8	1.6	4	wartime restrictions
1949	17.3	4.6	3.7	2.8	9	Recession
1950	21.4	6.1	4.8	3.3	9	Prosperity
1954	32.3	9.8	6.8	4.3	13	Recession
1958†	43.5	14.1	8.5	4.3	14	Prosperity

* Not closely comparable with 1929 figures and after.

† November.

SOURCES: *Economic Almanac, 1956* (New York, 1956), pp. 101–102; *Federal Reserve Bulletin*, January, 1959, pp. 56, 74; U.S. Bureau of the Census, *Historical Statistics of the United States, 1789–1945* (Washington, 1949), p. 13; *Continuation to 1952*, p. 1.

those who could pay cash on the spot or within a relatively short time. It held many consumers out of the market: this was understandable as a device to prevent inflation during a war. After the war automobile and appliance firms and finance companies complained that Regulation W was singling out their businesses unfairly. Regulation W expired in 1947; Congress revived it temporarily in 1948 and again during the Korean War, but it finally lapsed in 1952.

The credit card is one of the more recent selling innovations. Just as tourists traveling abroad have long carried letters of credit from their bank, so travelers within the United States carry credit cards permitting them to charge purchases of goods or services at any branch of the granting company's far-flung chain. Service stations, hotels, and airlines have done this for several years. Recently Diners' Club, American Express Company, and others have made it possible for subscribing independent restaurants and other merchants to attract the patronage of persons who like the freedom of a charge account away from home, and yet are good credit risks. Another advantage to the card holder is that he has evidence of his expenditures for expense account and tax purposes. The advantages from the sellers' viewpoint is that they retain or gain his patronage. Also the card holder's right to "charge it" may tempt him to spend more freely than he otherwise would. Credit cards have enlarged substantially the range of consumer credit.

WHOLESALE TRADE INSTITUTIONS

The term "wholesale," it will be recalled, has a broad and a narrow meaning. In the broad sense it includes not only wholesale houses but manufacturers' sales branches and offices, petroleum bulk stations, brokers, agents, and assemblers of farm products. The total sales made by these is considerably greater than that by full-service wholesale houses. That explains why wholesale sales involve more dollars than retail sales—some sales are actually counted twice in the wholesale statistics (see Table 28-1).

Among the more important wholesalers in 1954, in the narrow sense of the word, were houses handling groceries (22 per cent), machinery, furniture, dry goods, apparel, lumber, electrical appliances, liquor, hardware, automobiles, metals, and drugs. They were important in about that order. Such wholesale houses made $101 billion of sales. In addition, manufacturers' branches sold $70 billion more, and merchandising agents and assemblers each $39 billion more.

The most significant point about wholesalers in general since 1914 is that they have become less important. Their heyday was between 1880 and 1910. There are several basic reasons for their decline. Trucks, fast freight trains, or even airplanes make more rapid deliveries than were formerly possible. Communication by telephone is now fast and cheap (transcontinental phone service began in 1915). Business between retailers and manufacturers is simply better organized than formerly. Accordingly, the retailers keep smaller inventories. Also it is no longer essential in many lines for the wholesale merchant to buy, store, assemble, and risk commodities for his retail house customers. Many retailers order directly from the factory, on relatively short notice, and get quick delivery. Brokers, jobbers, and commission merchants have also declined in importance. The manufacturer has increasingly taken back the functions that he once was happy to let the wholesalers handle. The large retailers likewise have reached out and taken over some of the functions of wholesalers.

One important way in which manufacturers took over the middleman's selling function was in advertising. Advertising merchandise by brand name, trade-marks, or slogans increased after the Civil War, but it grew especially rapidly after 1914. Some manufacturers spent millions of dollars to make their product well known so that many consumers would probably ask for it. Once a product is well-known and highly regarded by the public, such as Camel cigarettes, which formerly the customer would walk a mile to buy, the manufacturer can ask a higher price for it or allow the retailer a narrower margin of profit. Since 1914, manufacturers of nationally distributed items have spent many billions of dollars advertising on highway billboards, in newspapers and magazines, over the radio (since 1922), and by television (since about 1947). It is these advertisements which enable the public to buy their newspapers for 10 cents (in the 1920s it was 2 cents), their *Saturday Evening Post* for 15 cents (in the 1920s and 1930s it was 5 cents), and to hear their radio and television programs free. The amount spent on advertising was $1.7 billion in 1935; it was $10 billion in 1956. Before World War II the annual total was about equally divided between national and local advertising; since the war, the national advertisers have paid for two-thirds of all advertising. Advertising absorbs about 2 to 3 per cent of national income; but the cost of advertising some branded products, especially ones such as cigarettes, soaps, cosmetics, and deodorants, is considerably more than 3 per cent of their manufacturing cost.

In general, the marketing of goods is about half of their cost. On the average, a product which costs 50 cents to manufacture will sell for $1. Out of the second half dollar many costs must be paid, such as for shipping, assembling, insuring, advertising, selling, losses from bad debts, overstocking, faulty merchandise, etc. To reduce these costs a new economic science—marketing research—has developed. If a company is to spend hundreds of thousands on advertising, it wants to know in what magazines it will reach the greatest number of buyers with the least cost, or what sort of television programs appeal to its customers and at what hours. Soap companies, accordingly, have sponsored continued melodramas in the morning when the housewife listens to her radio while doing housework. These "soap operas" have proved a highly successful advertising medium. Marketing research organizations stand ready to study any manufacturer's problem and advise him on the best way to advertise and sell his product.

FOREIGN TRADE

Soon after the outbreak of World War I, the United States assumed leadership in the world's foreign trade and has held it since that time.

Between 1914 and 1957 merchandise imports and exports of the United States increased just eightfold, from $4.2 to $33.4 billion. This was about the same increase that occurred between 1860 and 1914. Foreign trade tripled during World War I, then fell back during the 1920s and more in the early 1930s. By 1932 it equaled the 1914 figure again but improved again during the later 1930s. By 1940 war was going on in Europe and America was assisting her former allies. In 1944 foreign trade reached five times the 1914 figure, largely because of the sharp upsurge in exports as well as the price rise. Exports declined somewhat after the war but still remained high, for America was now helping to rebuild Europe. The steady rise in imports from $4 billion in 1945 to over $13 billion in 1957 accounts for the final increases in foreign trade since World War II.

Major Trends in Foreign Trade. Many of the trends in foreign trade, which had begun before the Civil War and had become unmistakable in the next period, became very pronounced after 1914. Exports consisted, to an ever-greater degree, of manufactured products, whereas imports were made up primarily of semimanufactured goods, food, and crude materials. Europe remained of major importance both as a market and as a source of imports, although Canada and Asia now challenged Europe's supremacy. The United States relied less than previously on foreign shipping but American tourists swarmed in ever greater numbers to Europe every summer. The United States became a creditor nation about 1916: it loaned heavily in the 1920s, and it saw many of these debts become bad in the 1930s. America both gave and loaned heavily once again in the 1940s and 1950s.

In 1914 raw materials, crude stuffs, food, and semimanufactures were 57 per cent of exports, whereas manufactured articles and manufactured foods were 43 per cent of the total. The manufactured items achieved equality with the others in 1925, and they were two-thirds of the total by 1956. All this reflected America's progress as an industrial nation. By 1956 the leading American exports were automobiles, industrial machinery, grains and their preparations, chemical products, iron and steel, and electrical apparatus. Only one of the six was agricultural in origin. Raw cotton, which in 1860 had outranked all other exports combined, had sunk to ninth place despite the fact that the nation was exporting more cotton in 1956 than a century before.

As for developments in imports, in 1914 raw materials, crude stuffs, food, and semimanufactures had constituted 65 per cent of imports; by 1956 they had risen to 70 per cent. Outwardly there appeared to have been little change. Closer inspection revealed marked changes in the nature of the raw materials and semimanufactured goods. Whereas in 1914 the leading five imports had been hides, coffee, sugar, raw silk, and crude rubber, all agricultural in origin, by 1956 the leading five imports were nonferrous metals and ferroalloys, petroleum and products, coffee, paper and paper materials, and sugar. Only coffee and sugar were clearly agricultural. Only two were left from the 1914 list.

Europe had been the market for almost 60 per cent of American exports in 1914, but by 1955 Europe took under 30 per cent; its share had been cut in half. Canada was this country's best customer, in terms of single countries: it received a fifth of all American exports. The rest of the world, made up of Asia, Africa, Australia, and Oceania, had taken only about 5 per cent of American exports in 1914. In 1956 they bought almost as much as Canada. Japan and the Philippines (now independent)

Table 28-3
Percentage Changes in Origin of Imports and Destination of Exports of the United States, 1910–1914 to 1956
(to nearest 5 per cent)

Type of trade	Year	Europe	Canada	Southern North America	South America	Asia, Africa, Australia
Imports..........	1910–1914	50	15	15	10	20
Imports..........	1956	25	25	10	20	20
Exports..........	1910–1914	60	10	20	5	5
Exports..........	1956	30	20	15	15	20

SOURCES: *Historical Statistics*, pp. 250–251; *Statistical Abstract, 1957*, pp. 888–909. Also Louis Hacker and others, *The United States: A Graphic History* (New York: Modern Age, Inc., 1937), pp. 143–145.

were the leading customers in Asia. The Union of South Africa got nearly half of all that America sent to Africa. South America had also improved as a customer; there Venezuela and Colombia were the leaders.

Whereas Europe had provided America with half of its imports in 1914, it supplied less than a quarter of them in 1956. Canada alone did somewhat better than all of Europe, South America about as well, and Asia almost as well (see Table 28-3). No nation supplied a quarter as much as Canada. The next major suppliers were Brazil, Britain, Venezuela—all three about equal—and then another trio of Japan, Western Germany, and Cuba. Canada sent in wood pulp and iron; Brazil provided coffee and Cuba the sugar to go with it. Venezuela sent oil, and Britain, Germany, and Japan provided a good part of the manufactured articles that America still imported.

Throughout nearly all this period, the United States was a creditor nation. When World War I began, Americans owed people in other countries, especially in Europe, more than others owed them. The net indebtedness was between $2 and $4 billion. The war was terrifically costly to France and England, and their governments bought up American securities owned by their citizens and sold them in America to buy war supplies. In addition, Americans became heavy purchasers of Anglo-French war loans. By 1916 America was, on balance, a creditor nation. During the 1920s Americans made long-term investments overseas averaging $1.1 billion every year. The bulk of them were in mining and railroads, in Canada, the Caribbean area, and South America. Europe got

Table 28-4
Balance of International Payments of the United States, 1920–1956
(Dollars in billions)

Items	1925		1935		1956	
	Exports	Imports	Exports	Imports	Exports	Imports
Merchandise	5.0	4.3	2.4	2.5	17.3	12.8
Investments of capital (i.e., securities imported)	0.2	0.9	1.5	...	3.4	1.8
Tourists' expenditures	0.1	0.3	0.1	0.2	0.7	1.3
Payments on investments	0.9	0.2	0.5	0.2	2.5	0.6
Specie	0.1	...	...	1.8	...	0.3
Shipping freight	0.3	0.4	0.1	0.2	1.6	1.4
Immigrant payments	...	0.4	...	...	...	0.5
Miscellaneous, chiefly government	...	0.1	0.1	0.1	0.5	7.3
Omissions	...	0.1	0.4			
Total	6.6	6.7	5.1	5.0	26.0	26.0

SOURCE: *Statistical Abstract, 1957*, p. 876.

less than one-quarter of the total. When the Great Depression struck, many of these investments proved bad; losses were especially heavy in so-called portfolio investments, for example, in foreign government bonds. American companies which had made direct investments fared better. An example of a direct investment is an American copper company developing a copper mine in Chile. During the 1930s Americans invested only $0.1 billion a year of capital overseas, less than a tenth of what they had invested in the 1920s. With the outbreak of World War II American investments abroad increased once more to the level of the 1920s. Nevertheless, during much of World War II the United States was again a debtor nation, by a small amount. Most of what it sent abroad, it gave, and most of what it took in, it borrowed. Following the war America's annual investments reached new highs, achieving a peak of \$8.6 billion in the one year of 1947 and then averaging about \$2.5 billion during the next seven years. Between 1939 and 1956, the total of American investments abroad grew from \$12.5 to \$49 billion. Total foreign investments in this country rose from \$12.8 billion in 1939 to \$31.6 billion in 1956.

As Table 28-4 shows, most of American business with other countries consisted of merchandise imports and exports, security imports and exports, and government grants to friendly foreign nations. All else was

FIG. 28-2. The busy port of New York, with the *Queen Elizabeth* docking. (*Courtesy of the Port of New York Authority.*)

usually of secondary importance only. By 1956, American tourists were buying annually over \$1 billion of travel and sightseeing services. This is a so-called "invisible import." Americans today render about as much in shipping services as they receive. Back in the middle 1930s, right after the United States devalued the dollar, there was a substantial inflow of specie for several years. Devaluation raised the price of gold from \$20.67 to \$35 an ounce and made America an attractive place to which to sell gold.

Ports. New York has remained the nation's leading port, handling a quarter of the nation's general cargo volume. New Orleans and Philadelphia come next, far behind New York. New York still preserves the distinction of being chiefly an import port, although during a few years, just after World War II, its exports exceeded imports by substantial amounts. Tonnage-wise, its imports were four times as great as its exports in 1955 because they included so many raw materials. Considerable trade also came over the Canadian border to Lake ports such as Detroit, Superior, and Huron. Houston was in 1955 the leading port in the Southwest.

TARIFFS

Reformers contend, with considerable logic, that tariffs are a cause of war. The opposite, wars cause tariffs, is also true. Several American wars have been followed by a hike in tariff rates, namely, the War of 1812, the Civil War, and World War I. World War I demonstrated to the American people their insufficiency in the matter of producing chemical dyes, optical instruments, and other items which they needed badly during the war. This experience plus the return of the Republican party to power between 1921 and 1933 meant a return to the high tariff policy so familiar in the 1861–1913 period. The imposition of higher duties was different in one respect this time. Congress did not impose them during the war to get revenue but after the war to provide protection.

The Emergency Tariff of 1921 was the first of three Republican high tariffs. It was a temporary law, intended primarily to help farmers without delay. The European nations were able to restore their agricultural production to a normal level soon after the war and thus could dispense largely with American farm goods. In the drop of wholesale prices in 1920–1922, farm prices especially fell sharply. Farmers believed that a tariff on wheat, corn, meat, sugar, cotton, and wool would help them. There was little economic logic behind this thinking: competition from foreign suppliers in American markets was not a major cause of the farmers' distress. It was the loss by American farmers of their European market, which an American tariff could not remedy. Nevertheless, the farm lobby thought it would help, and the newly elected Republican majority, with equal blindness, acceded to their wishes.

Congress enacted a permanently higher tariff act the following year. This was the Fordney-McCumber Act of 1922, which imposed rates about as high as those in force under the Payne-Aldrich Act of 1909 (see Table 28-5). It made the high rates on agricultural commodities permanent and even raised a few. It protected the dyestuff industry. In fact, it allegedly gave some protection to just about every industry in the country. The law gave the President power to increase tariffs by executive order on any commodity needing more protection. The basic theory was that the tariff should "equalize production costs" between American industries and foreign industries. Some senators said they would vote for rates of 500 per cent if that much were needed to equalize protection. This also was nonsense economics, for the simple reason that cost of production varies from one firm to another. Whose cost of production should be equalized? The least efficient firm's? If so, an even less efficient one would soon appear and ask for protection, too. Nevertheless, equalizing cost of production was the slogan that characterized this tariff. Quite another excuse for higher tariffs made much more sense. That was that the still-depreciating currencies of several European countries made it unusually easy for them to sell their goods in American markets. American manufacturers needed protection against this abnormal situation. The 1922 tariff was also the first one in which Congress had the assistance of a permanent Tariff Commission. Created in 1916, it helped to establish orderly procedures in the administration of the law.

The third Republican tariff was the Smoot-Hawley Act of 1930. This pushed rates even higher than the Fordney-McCumber Act of 1922 had done, and even higher than the Dingley tariff of 1897. Again it was the discontented farmers who demanded another upward revision of the tariff. A few manufacturing interests also obtained increased protection for their products in an early version of the bill, but the agricultural bloc in the Senate eliminated most of these in the final act. There were vigorous protests against the law, and 1,000 economists signed a petition urging President Hoover to veto it. The economists pointed out that limiting imports would also limit America's ability to export. It would likewise invite retaliation from other countries. However, President Hoover signed the bill. Whether in retaliation or in self-defense, other nations soon raised their tariffs, including even Great Britain in 1932. The 1930 law was the last of America's high tariffs.

High tariffs were particularly out of place in the United States in the 1920s. This country was by then a creditor nation. It occupied the position that Great Britain had held during most of the previous century. The people of a creditor nation obviously wanted to receive dividends and interest on the money that they had loaned abroad. They wanted to get the principal back when a loan finally matured. As a creditor nation, the United States should have had an excess of imports. It should not have expected to collect in gold or silver year after year: there was not enough of those metals available, for one thing. Great Britain's record shows an excess of imports during most of the nineteenth century as it collected on its investments abroad. Britain wisely pursued a low tariff policy to enable the imports to come in so that it could profit from its investments. That was all quite logical. The United States in the 1920s, however, imposed high tariffs which discouraged imports. That made it difficult to collect on overseas investments or to collect on the war debts which England, France, Italy, and others owed America. The American attitude was that the Europeans had "hired" the money; now they should pay for it. Yet by erecting high tariffs, America made it difficult, sometimes almost impossible, for its debtors to pay. There was logic in the situation at only two points. American industry wanted protection from foreign competition: the high tariff provided it. And when Europeans and others wanted more American goods or capital, this country made them additional loans. This was what made possible a continued excess of exports. The most likely end of such a policy, as long as the tariff remained high, was eventual default by many foreign borrowers. Exactly that happened in the early 1930s. In 1931, President Hoover publicly urged a moratorium on reparations and war debt payments. Payments ceased on both and were not resumed. They also ceased during the depression on many private loans. The absurdity of the high tariff policy then became more apparent.

The Democrats, with their low tariff traditions, took over the Presidency and Congress as well in 1933. In 1934 Congress enacted a basically new tariff law, the Reciprocal Trade Agreements Act, which is still in operation (1959). This law gave the President the power to lower or raise a duty by up to 50 per cent of the original rate. The Tariff Commission makes the studies and the recommendations, and the State Department negotiates the treaties.

The United States shortly made reciprocal agreements with several dozen nations to reduce tariffs. Each agreement contained a "most favored nation" clause which assured that nation that it would receive treatment as good as the most favored nation on any deal which it made with the United States. When the United States offered to cut duties on imported French wines if France would cut duties on American typewriters and other machines, it also made France a further promise. If at a future date this country made a further cut in wine duties to please, say, Chile, French wine exporters would automatically receive the benefit of the same cut. Lest this appear to be overgenerous on America's part, it should be emphasized that the Tariff Commission has been careful to make the first reduction on any commodity with the chief supplier of it to the United States.

In 1945 Congress granted the President authority to cut or raise any then-existing duty by 50 per cent. Thus if a duty on wine had been reduced from an original level of 80 per cent a gallon to 40 per cent, it could be reduced again to 20 per cent. And in 1955 Congress authorized the President to cut duties an additional 15 per cent; thus he could reduce the duty on French wine from 20 per cent to 17 per cent. Altogether, the Reciprocal Trade Agreements have worked well. Albeit with some grumblings, Congress has renewed the law repeatedly for one, two, or three years. The average of rates has come down especially fast since World War II. In 1947 the United States ceased relying purely on the bilateral approach and began making what it called a General Agreement on Tariff and Trade (GATT). The first of these took place in Geneva in 1947 with twenty-two nations participating and another occurred in

Table 28-5
Tariff Levels, 1909–1957

Act	Years	Duties collected as percentage of value of all dutiable imports
Payne-Aldrich Act of 1909	1910–1913	40.8
Underwood-Simmons Act of 1913	1913–1922	27.0
Emergency Tariff Act of 1921	1921	
Fordney-McCumber Act of 1922	1922–1930	38.5
Smoot-Hawley Act of 1930	1930–1933	52.8
Reciprocal Trade Agreements Act of 1934	1939	37.3
General Agreement on Tariff and Trade	1947	15.3
General Agreement on Tariff and Trade	1957	11.0

SOURCES: Lawrence W. Towle, *International Trade and Commercial Policy* (New York: Harper & Brothers, 1956), p. 595; *Statistical Abstract of the United States*, 1955 (Washington, 1955), p. 899; *1958*, p. 904.

1952. By 1957 duties were 11 per cent of the value of dutiable goods imported. Thus rates are lower than they have been in almost 150 years. Meanwhile, a growing proportion of the American public has come to the conclusion that this country, because it is a creditor nation, should have lower tariffs than formerly.

CHAPTER 29

The Labor Movement

Organized labor, in 1914, stood on the threshold of its most fruitful era. Workers enjoyed an ever-increasing standard of living and their right to form labor unions, although not safeguarded, was widely recognized. The Clayton Antitrust Act (1914) declared "that the labor of a human being is *not* a commodity or article of commerce" and that unions should *not* be considered conspiracies in restraint of trade. Still, the mass of laborers remained unorganized. Out of a nonagricultural working force of 28.4 million, only 2.6 million were in unions. Of these, more than three-fourths belonged to the American Federation of Labor. Thus, unskilled workers were almost entirely without union representation. Their greatest union growth came after 1933 under the protection and encouragement of the New Deal.

THE IMPACT OF WORLD WAR I

The prosperity engendered by World War I enabled labor unions to expand their membership. The AFL doubled its numbers from 2 to 4 million by 1920 and total union membership rose to slightly over 5 million. The growth conformed to the traditional patterns of union activity during periods of prosperity and depression.

Labor's Record. Labor's war record was generally good, in spite of the lack of support from radical elements. A March, 1917, conference of labor leaders, made up primarily of AFL and Railway Brotherhood officials, adopted a resolution to support the national war effort. The unions insisted, however, that the government safeguard the workers' status. Labor remained free to organize and bargain for wage and hour benefits and it refused to surrender the right to strike. The Wilson administration accepted these conditions and generally tried to avoid strife. Samuel Gompers, AFL leader, served on the Advisory Commission of the National Council of Defense; other representatives of labor served on the War Labor Conference Board and its successor, the National War Labor Board, in 1918. Still, under the pressure of wartime inflation, industrial peace broke down. More than 4,400 strikes occurred in 1917, involving more than a million workers. The National War Labor Board, established to settle labor disputes, eliminated most harmful work stoppages after April, 1918. Labor gave a "no strike" pledge, and in return, the government backed labor's demands for an eight-hour day, collective bargaining rights, and similar objectives. Labor emerged from the war in a favorable position, especially from the standpoint of numerical strength.

The 1919 Strikes. The end of the war brought renewed hostility between labor and management. The government removed most economic controls soon after November, 1918, and prices climbed steadily to May, 1920. Without government support, unions resorted to strikes to gain wage increases. A number of serious labor disturbances followed, causing general public alarm. An anti-Bolshevik hysteria, occasioned by the Russian Revolution of 1917, had seized the nation; the fear of communism caused employers and the public to identify labor agitators as "reds." The 1919 strikes played decisive roles in molding the future of labor. The Seattle general strike, the Boston police strike, the bituminous coal strike, and the steel strike were among the most important outbreaks.

The steel strike was probably the most important of all. Low wages and a seventy-two hour week prevailed in the steel industry. The mass of workers had no union affiliation. In 1918, William Foster, former radical leader of the IWW, led a drive to organize the entire industry. Within a year, some 100,000 workers joined the movement. They asked that the steel producers negotiate new wage contracts but were turned down. U.S. Steel's board chairman, Judge Elbert H. Gary, made clear his company's position. He said, "Our corporation and subsidiaries, although they do not combat labor unions as such, decline to discuss business with them." In reply, 350,000 workers left their jobs in September, 1919. The strike was bitter and prolonged. The steel companies hired strikebreakers and bombarded the public with newspaper propaganda. They branded the strike a Bolshevist plot to overthrow American capitalism. The public withdrew its prolabor sympathy, and hungry, ragged workers began drifting back to work. The strike failed in January, 1920. The steel corporations were too big to defeat. Their surplus funds, built up during the lush war years, equipped them to break any such strike. A national union of steel workers was a lost cause for another two decades. The effects of the 1919 strikes were far-reaching. The failure of the steel strike meant that other mass-production industries remained unorganized. The Communist influence, either real or imagined, brought public disfavor, and labor suffered a loss of prestige similar to that in the 1880s and 1890s following the Haymarket Square Riot. With public sentiment strongly against organized labor, it was an easy matter for employers and government to consolidate and further weaken labor's position. The opportunity came shortly. The depression of 1920–1922, with nearly 5 million unemployed, broke the rise in union membership which had gone on since 1914. The prosperous era which followed that depression was one of retreat for unions.

STAGNATION FOR LABOR UNIONS

The decade of the 1920s offered the unions little promise for recovering the losses of 1920–1922. Union membership declined until 1924 and

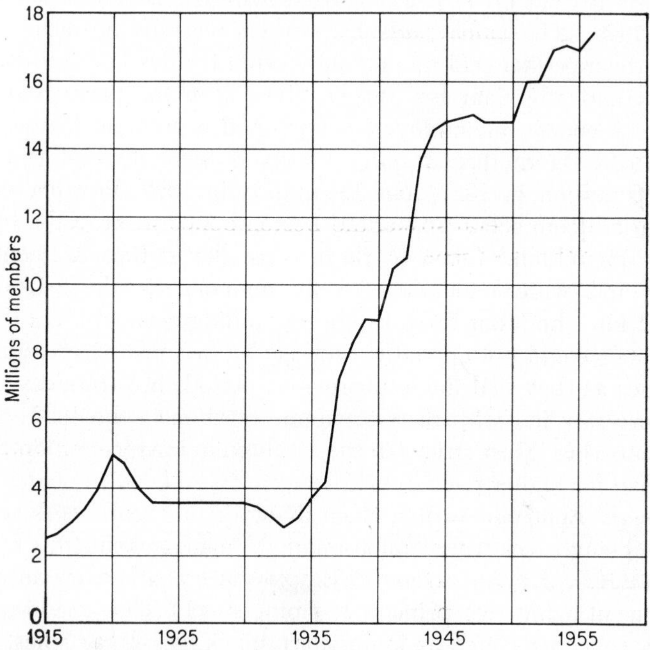

CHART 29-1. Estimated labor union membership in the United States, 1915–1956. (*Adapted from U.S. Bureau of the Census, Historical Statistics of the United States, 1789–1945, Washington, 1949, p. 72; estimates since 1945, Bureau of Labor Statistics, Bulletin 1222, Washington, 1958, p. 10.*)

then leveled off at about 3.5 million until 1930. The gains of World War I had been largely lost through the 1919 strikes and the ensuing depression. Ordinarily, labor had regained its strength as soon as prosperity returned. The 1920s marked the first major prosperity period when union activity did not pick up appreciably (see Chart 29-1). The reversal in the normal trends was caused by general economic conditions, by employers' tactics, and by governmental attitudes.

Economic Conditions. Much of the economic expansion of the 1920s was in the new mass-production industries where unions had not yet gained a foothold. Also, farm people supplied much of the new labor force after 1920; by their standards, existing wages were high. Like many immigrants in the nineteenth century, they accepted low wages and were not good union material. Meanwhile, real wages rose anyway, which hampered union activity even more.

The biggest gain in real wages came during the postwar depression. Between 1919 and 1923, real weekly earnings increased by 9 per cent; the gain from 1923 to 1929 amounted to 5 per cent. Real hourly pay rose even more; it went up 11 per cent from 1919 to 1923 and 8 per cent from 1923 to 1929.[1] The gains made by workers were by no means uniform. "Sick" industries like coal mining and cotton textiles had frequent unemployment and attendant low wages. Even after the postwar depression had run its course, unemployment remained a problem in several years in the 1920s. More than 2 million workers were unemployed in 1924, about 1.6 million in 1927, and 1.9 million in 1928. In other years, the figure varied from 430,000 to 820,000, or 1 to 2 per cent of the total labor force of 45 million.[2] Some of these were the victims of technological progress and were unemployed only temporarily—they were usually absorbed into the labor force by the expanding economy. On the whole, labor unions could not appeal to workers by promising to remedy falling real wages as they had done in previous periods of prosperity. Laborers were more satisfied with their economic position in the 1920s than they had been earlier. Most strikes in the 1920s were for recognition of unions, rather than for higher pay.

Employers' Antiunion Tactics. Even though rising real wages kept workers from being excessively "union-minded," management took no chances on the revival of union strength. Employers embarked on an antiunion campaign, utilizing two primary techniques. (1) They made use of the traditional weapons such as injunctions, black lists, labor spies, lockouts, yellow-dog contracts, and the refusal to recognize unions as bargaining agents. (2) They employed the theory of welfare capitalism. This was the idea that unionism could be discouraged by making working conditions so favorable that unions would be of little value to the workers. Recreation facilities, intramural athletic competition, clean and comfortable washrooms, cafeterias, company magazines—these were among the attractions offered by enlightened management to build morale and loyalty among employees. Some companies sold stock to their workers and thus shared the profits from the business. Many firms promoted the

[1] Carroll R. Daugherty and John B. Parrish, *The Labor Problems of American Society* (Boston: Houghton Mifflin Company, 1952), p. 154.

[2] U.S. Bureau of the Census, *Historical Statistics of the United States, 1789–1945* (Washington, 1949), p. 65.

company-type union, over which the employer could exercise strong influence. The company union, however, meant little to the workers, especially since such unions rarely had strike funds. Furthermore, the employer did not have to deal with leaders from outside, as in the case of the established trade unions. Actions of this type undoubtedly retarded union growth.

Government Attitude. Management found that some unions threatened to grow strong in spite of concessions to independent workers. In such cases, it turned to the government for assistance. Since the Republican administrations under Harding, Coolidge, and Hoover generally looked with favor on business, it is not surprising that they contributed to the antiunion pressures. The public feeling that labor was unduly influenced by radical elements, especially pro-Russian groups, gave the Federal government an excuse for its strong bias. Still, the threat of subversion hardly justified the extreme position taken by successive administrations. The government contributed to labor's troubles in two general ways: (1) the courts freely issued injunctions to prevent labor's use of strikes, secondary boycotts, and similar weapons, and (2) legislatures took no positive action to protect workers from certain abusive practices by management. The Clayton Act, hailed by Samuel Gompers as labor's "Magna Carta," had limited the use of injunctions in labor disputes, but a loophole, designed to protect property rights, negated the benefit to unions. In 1928, the AFL published a list of 389 injunctions issued since 1919 by either Federal or state courts. When Arizona outlawed all injunctions in labor disputes, the United States Supreme Court invalidated the law. It claimed that the state law violated the property rights of citizens, guaranteed by the Fourteenth Amendment.[3] Equally crippling to unions was the government's sanction of yellow-dog contracts, by which employees agreed not to join a union and were subject to dismissal if they did. The Supreme Court had earlier nullified both Federal and state laws banning such contracts. It claimed that those laws violated the freedom of contract granted to individuals by the Fifth and Fourteenth Amendments.[4] This view prevailed throughout the 1920s; it was not until 1932 that Congress finally outlawed the use of yellow-dog contracts (see "The Norris-LaGuardia Act," p. 572).

LABOR IN THE GREAT DEPRESSION

Labor's inability to strengthen its position during the prosperous 1920s contributed to its vulnerability during the Great Depression. Union membership declined from 3.6 million in 1929 to 2.9 million in 1933,

[3] *Truax v. Corrigan,* 257 U.S. 312 (1921).

[4] *Adair v. United States,* 208 U.S. 161 (1908); *Coppage v. Kansas,* 236 U.S. 1 (1915).

chiefly because of the widespread unemployment. The army of unemployed grew steadily to 2.9 million in 1930 and 11.8 million in 1933, representing about one-fourth of the total labor force.[5] For these millions, earnings dwindled to nothingness. Even for wage earners in manufacturing who held their jobs, real weekly earnings fell 14 per cent between 1929 and 1932 because of a decline in the number of hours worked. Loyalty to unions, which required payment of dues and refusal to work for less than union wage scales, faded. Hopefully, the nation endorsed the New Deal program, advanced by the Democratic candidate, Franklin D. Roosevelt, in 1932. During the campaign, Roosevelt expressed sympathy for the workingman's cause. He promised direct relief and employment for the "forgotten man at the bottom of the economic pyramid." After his election, a business upturn and Federal work relief caused unemployment to diminish until a recession in 1938 reversed the trend. Meanwhile, union membership had tripled by 1939. The Federal government's reversal of its earlier hostility toward unions was the primary cause of labor's gain in power.

The Norris-LaGuardia Act. The first labor reform bill of the 1930s preceded the New Deal. The Norris-LaGuardia Act, passed in March, 1932, imposed strict limitations on the power of Federal courts to issue antilabor injunctions. It asserted the rights of a worker to "full freedom of association, self-organization, and designation of representatives of his own choosing, to negotiate the terms and conditions of his employment. . . . " It held that workers should be "free from the interference, restraint, or coercion of employers . . . for the purpose of collective bargaining or other mutual aid or protection. . . . " In keeping with this philosophy, the Norris-LaGuardia Act restricted the use of injunctions in labor disputes to clearly defined circumstances where "unlawful acts have been threatened and will be committed unless restrained . . . " and where "substantial and irreparable injury to complainant's property will follow. . . . " The law further outlawed yellow-dog contracts and sanctioned labor's use of strikes, picket lines, and secondary boycotts. The antiinjunction bill represented a turning point in Federal attitude toward unions. In the past, the central government had used its power to restrict union activity; now, it gave encouragement to unions.

Section 7(a) of the National Industrial Recovery Act. The Norris-LaGuardia Act established the *general* view that labor should have the right to organize without interference from management. The National Industrial Recovery Act, signed by Roosevelt in June, 1933, *specifically* guaranteed that right to certain workers. In Section 7(a) of the NIRA, Congress provided that the industrial codes, formed under the law, had to include a guaranty that employees would have the right to form

[5] *Historical Statistics,* pp. 65, 72.

unions for purposes of collective bargaining. The codes also had to specify that no worker could be forced to join a company union and had to contain provisions for maximum hours and minimum wages. Under the law, unions recruited a net of about 400,000 members in 1934 and another 500,000 in 1935. But many employers, especially in the mass-production industries like steel and automobiles, refused to abide by the labor provisions of the codes. Early in 1935, the failure of the NIRA to bring harmony between labor and management or to promote industrial recovery became obvious. When the Supreme Court declared the act unconstitutional in the Schechter Poultry case (May, 1935),[6] the public felt little remorse. Furthermore, the New Deal administration was prepared for the ruling. Eleven days before the Court's announcement, the Senate adopted a far stronger labor law—the National Labor Relations Act, popularly called the Wagner Act.

The Wagner Act. Except for the wage and hour provisions, Congress reenacted the principles of Section 7(a) of the NIRA. In addition to the protection of workers' rights to organize and bargain collectively, the Wagner Act denied to management the use of certain practices. It declared illegal the following employers' actions: (1) any interference with the exercise of employees' rights to form unions; (2) the promotion of company unions; (3) discrimination against union members in hiring or firing; (4) refusal to bargain collectively with unions. The act created the National Labor Relations Board to administer and enforce these provisions. The Board, made up of three members chosen by the President, received the sole authority to determine the bargaining agent or union to represent the workers. For this purpose, the NLRB conducted elections, either at the request of workers or on its own initiative. The results of such elections were binding upon both management and *all* workers in a firm. A second major function of the Board was to hear and investigate complaints of unfair labor practices. The Board had the authority to issue "cease and desist" orders to employers and to petition the Federal courts for enforcement.

From the beginning, many employers refused to recognize the law, contending that it was unconstitutional. Many criticized the NLRB for its extreme prolabor bias. For a while, it appeared that employers might succeed in their resistance. But in April, 1937, the Supreme Court upheld the constitutionality of the Wagner Act. In *NLRB v. Jones & Laughlin Steel Corporation,*[7] Chief Justice Charles Evans Hughes showed how far the nation had moved toward endorsing labor unions. He said that "Employees have as clear a right to organize and select their representa-

[6] See page 518. The Supreme Court ruled against the wages and hours provisions of the NRA codes but *not* against the collective bargaining rights.

[7] 301 U.S. 1.

tives for lawful purposes as . . . [a corporation has] to organize its business and select its own officers and agents. . . . " He argued that a single worker was helpless to deal with an employer and that labor unions were essential to give employees ample opportunity to deal with management. With its authority thus strengthened, the Board went about the business of enforcing the law.

Employers harshly criticized the administration of the Wagner Act in several respects. They claimed that the NLRB should have protected employers from harmful jurisdictional disputes between rival unions. They felt that the Board was unduly biased in many of its actions. The NLRB undoubtedly assisted unions in their progress after 1937. Prolabor observers as well as some neutrals pointed out that the past conduct of businessmen made this bias necessary; otherwise, labor could never have gained equal status at the bargaining table. These persons favored the creation, by government action, of a countervailing power to offset an earlier concentration of economic power in the hands of employers. Under the trying circumstances of the Great Depression, when unemployment and low incomes conditioned the thinking of most Americans, such sentiments were understandable. After economic conditions improved, however, the public began to put pressure on the government to neutralize labor's newly won strength. Even though changes in personnel made the NLRB more impartial after 1940, employers firmly insisted that Congress amend the Wagner Act. Labor successfully resisted these demands until after World War II.

Social Security. Labor's greater bargaining strength would have been meaningless as long as millions were out of work. During the Great Depression, the New Deal sought to put people back to work through the Public Works Administration, Civil Works Administration, Works Progress Administration, and other such projects. But these were emergency measures. A growing feeling developed that society as a whole should assume the risks of future unemployment. Because the separate states were reluctant to adopt unemployment insurance, the Federal government took the lead. The Social Security Act of 1935 encouraged the states to set up their own programs within the framework of Federal law and by July, 1937, all states had such laws. The Federal government levied a 3 per cent payroll tax on employers for unemployment compensation. The states received 90 per cent of these funds to pay unemployment benefits. Although the "insurance" varied in details from state to state, the state programs were generally similar. Illinois, in 1959, provided $10 to $40 per week for a maximum of twenty-six weeks for employees of firms hiring four or more persons.

The Social Security Act and its amendments also committed the Federal government to an enormous old-age pension program. Employers and employees each contributed equal amounts, a percentage of the first $4,200 earned each year, to a federally administered fund. In 1958, eligible retired workers or their eligible survivors received from $30 to $162.80 per month after reaching age sixty-five (age sixty-two for women). Congress had brought an ever-increasing number of persons under Social Security and augmented the size of benefit payments. The Amendments of 1954 left only certain professional groups without participation.

The Fair Labor Standards Act. Another New Deal measure reflected the full shift of the government's attitude toward labor. The Fair Labor Standards Act of 1938 established minimum wage and maximum hour requirements and outlawed child labor in shops whose output entered interstate commerce. The act instituted an ascending scale of minimum wages, beginning at 25 cents per hour in 1938 and reaching 40 cents by 1945. The minimum was raised to 75 cents in 1949 and to $1 in 1956. Hours per week could not exceed forty-four in 1938 or forty after 1940, unless the worker received 1½ times his regular hourly rate. The chief effect of the law was that it tended to equalize wage rates for union and nonunion shops and it definitely lessened the use of child labor. More important was the government's resolution to protect workers' wage scales.[8]

Changing Industrial Organization. In soil so thoroughly cultivated by the New Deal, a new type of labor organization took root. The craft union of the past century did not fit the needs of the new industrial order. The constant widening of markets stimulated the rise of mass-production industries in which labor became increasingly specialized. The meaning of "skilled labor" changed when the assembly line replaced the handicraftsman's shop. It was inevitable that this would affect the craft unions. Some of them merged or amalgamated rather than wither away. Others admitted to membership thousands of laborers who had little special skill.

The changes in industry and unions posed at least two major problems. First, jurisdictional disputes promoted ill feeling among unions. For example, in railroad repair shops where there were several AFL unions, the boilermakers, sheet metal workers, blacksmiths, machinists, and

[8] For the most part, the courts had held unconstitutional any state or Federal legislation fixing wages or hours, claiming that such laws violated the freedom of contract guaranteed by the Fifth and Fourteenth Amendments. *Lochner v. New York,* 198 U.S. 45 (1905), and *Adkins v. Children's Hospital,* 261 U.S. 525 (1923), reflect this view. But in 1937, the Supreme Court upheld a Washington state minimum wage law in *West Coast Hotel Co. v. Parrish,* 300 U.S. 379, opening the door to Congress to pass the Fair Labor Standards Act. The Court substantiated the action in *United States v. Darby Lumber Co.,* 312 U.S. 100 (1941), by a unanimous decision. The pendulum had completed the full swing from right to left.

electricians came into frequent conflict. Who should attach the headlight on the locomotive? Second, there was rivalry between skilled and unskilled workers. The Knights of Labor had disintegrated over this point. In the twentieth century, the skilled workers in some unions feared that they would lose control. Leaders of strong craft unions grew jealous of the rising power of the industrial unions. In turn the leaders of industrial unions like the United Mine Workers became impatient with the old-fashioned tactics of the craft organizations.

The Committee for Industrial Organization. In 1935, the AFL decided not to promote industrial unions in certain mass-production industries. Consequently, eight affiliated unions left the AFL and formed the Committee for Industrial Organization on November 10, 1935. The new organization had 1 million members. John L. Lewis, head of the United Mine Workers, the largest constituent union, became president. The withdrawal was at first temporary in nature, but it became permanent when the AFL formally expelled the dissenting unions in 1937. The CIO adopted the same federal framework as the AFL. The chief structural difference was the organization of local unions by industry rather than by craft. In two years the CIO formed twenty-four additional national unions, partially organizing the automobile, steel, oil, and rubber industries. Its membership mounted to 3,700,000. In 1938 it adopted the new name, Congress of Industrial Organizations.

The new unions sometimes showed more spirit and ingenuity than respect for the law. Rejoicing in their new-found strength, they were anxious to make up for lost time. The CIO had difficulty controlling the leaders of the national unions, who in turn were unable to restrain the enthusiasm of their membership. Public opinion, somewhat sympathetic toward workers, was repeatedly shocked by the new unions' excesses. The General Motors strike of 1937 illustrated this vividly.

General Motors Sit-down Strike. Most of the workers in the automobile industry possessed little skill, since four jobs out of five could be learned in a brief period of time. But life on the assembly line was dull, tedious, and very wearing; some workers were unable to endure the pace, which they claimed increased steadily. Although the pay was at times high on a daily basis, work fluctuated so that annual wages were not good after 1929. Furthermore, numerous labor spies made union membership hazardous, and company policy based on the strategy of "divide and rule" encouraged dissension among any unions which managed to form. After 1933, the United Automobile Workers, at first an AFL industrial-type union, gained power. It deserted to the CIO and in December, 1936, endeavored to negotiate with General Motors officials. When the company refused to recognize the union as a bargaining agent, a strike broke out at the Fisher Body plant and spread to other factories. The workers, instead of staying home as most strikers in the past had done, sat down in the factories and refused to move. The corporation stressed that the men were trespassing, often destroying property, and preventing the operation of valuable equipment whose idleness was costly. General Motors obtained a court order requiring the men to vacate, but Governor Frank Murphy of Michigan, fearing bloodshed, failed to enforce it. Instead, he brought about a peaceful settlement in which the union achieved recognition. The company also agreed to survey speed-up abuses, to pay time and a half for overtime, and to stop discrimination against unionists.

The sit-down strike was novel and highly effective at a time when the unions needed victories to give their membership self-confidence. It was declared illegal in the Fansteel case of 1938, but CIO tactics continued to make headlines.

RAILWAY LABOR: A SPECIAL CASE

The four Railway Brotherhoods—engineers, firemen, conductors, and trainmen—developed independently of the AFL and the CIO. Their traditional conservatism and the high caliber of their members, plus the fact that railways are in the nature of a public utility, require their consideration as a special case.

Early Railway Labor Legislation. Even though the Federal government waited until the 1930s to enact far-reaching labor legislation, it had passed certain laws affecting railway labor at a much earlier date. In 1898, the Erdman Act forbade railroads to use yellow-dog contracts and prohibited discrimination against employees because of union membership. The Supreme Court declared the law unconstitutional in *Adair v. the United States* (1908).[9] A federal Employers' Liability Act (1906), which made interstate common carriers liable for death or injuries to their employees, also fell victim to the Court's hostility in 1908.[10] In that year, Congress passed a revised statute which met the constitutional objections of the earlier act. Then, in 1916 the Adamson Act established an eight-hour workday for railroads at wages then in effect for the ten-hour day. The Supreme Court upheld the law in *Wilson v. New* (1917), citing the public nature of transportation.[11] The Transportation Act of 1920 established the Railway Labor Board to mediate railway labor disputes.

The Railway Labor Act of 1926. With these early efforts to serve as precedents, Congress passed the Railway Labor Act in 1926. It guaran-

[9] 208 U.S. 161.
[10] *First Employers' Liability Cases*, 207 U.S. 463.
[11] 243 U.S. 332.

teed to railway employees the right to organize and bargain collectively without employer interference and it set up procedures for dealing with different kinds of labor disputes. Both railway management and labor leaders participated in drafting the bill. They designed it especially to curtail strikes and government interference. A 1934 amendment to the act created the National Railway Adjustment Board and endowed it with power to interpret labor contracts. The railway labor laws have held serious railway labor disputes to a minimum.

LABOR DURING WORLD WAR II AND AFTER

Labor in World War II. Unemployment during the late 1930s limited labor's progress. In spite of New Deal efforts to promote recovery, 10 million persons were unemployed as late as January, 1940. But World War II soon solved the unemployment problem and allowed unions to make further gains. Membership grew from 9 million in 1939 to 15 million in 1946, with the CIO claiming 6 million and the AFL 7.2 million. The majority of manufacturing workers belonged to unions by that time, but two-thirds to three-fourths of the labor force remained unorganized. Unions employed various devices to force workers into membership and to keep them there. The closed shop or union shop principle, sanctioned by the Wagner Act, obliged workers to join a union to obtain or to hold a job. Checkoffs of union dues by employers kept members from defaulting financially. Union treasuries swelled and the power of union leaders expanded. Organized labor received representation on many of the major war councils, as it had in World War I. The War Production Board and the War Manpower Commission both had labor representatives, as did regional and Federal War Labor boards.

Despite the loss of much personal freedom, few union members objected because of the numerous benefits they received. From January, 1937, to April, 1945, average weekly earnings of all manufacturing workers almost doubled. Part of this increase came from overtime wages paid for work in excess of forty hours per week; but average hourly earnings rose by some 60 per cent. While labor officials took a no-strike pledge in 1941 and Congress froze wages for the duration of the war in October, 1942, the war period witnessed both strikes and rising wages. Disputes in coal mines, steel mills, aircraft factories, and elsewhere brought pay adjustments from sympathetic War Labor boards. The rising cost of living caused the National War Labor Board to grant a 15 per cent cost of living raise to workers by the Little Steel formula of July, 1942. A coal strike in May, 1943, led to a Federal order to seize the mines and prompted Congress to pass the Smith-Connally War Labor Disputes Act that same year. This gave the President the power to take over any establishment in which a strike threatened the war effort. Although

Congress passed the measure over his veto, President Roosevelt used the seizure power some forty times.

Aside from some unsavory strikes, the war record of labor was generally one in which the vast majority could take pride. Output of war materials for the Allies, plus almost as much civilian goods as in peacetime, attested to their productivity. Many laborers purchased war bonds regularly and served as civil defense workers.

Reconversion and Labor Strife. The return to peacetime witnessed an outbreak of serious strikes. As overtime work became less necessary, the size of workers' pay checks diminished. Labor reasoned that business had grown fat during the war and could afford to restore wartime take-home pay from excessive profits. President Harry S. Truman supported labor in this by publicly stating that wage increases were possible without price increases owing to technological improvements and the economies of large-scale production. Management resisted union demands because it saw profits squeezed between rising wages and continued price ceilings imposed by the Office of Price Administration. Numerous and prolonged strikes brought great losses to both labor and management, as well as to other industries and to the public. More man-days were lost through strikes in the first half of 1946 than in any year in history—indeed, more than in the five previous years combined.

The wave of strikes commenced in the fall of 1945 with the walkout of the United Automobile Workers in General Motors plants. The UAW had demanded a flat 30 per cent pay increase; when General Motors rejected the demand, 150,000 production workers left their jobs. The strike ended in March when Federal mediators helped work out a satisfactory agreement. The UAW gained 18 cents an hour plus other benefits, although loss of overtime left take-home pay below the wartime levels. Meanwhile, the United Steel Workers called out 750,000 members in January, 1946, cutting steel production to about 6 per cent of capacity. Again the union gained a sizable wage increase. The automobile and steel strikes were but opening actions by the unions. Major work stoppages followed in General Electric and Westinghouse, in the meat packing industry, and in both the bituminous and anthracite coal mines. All told, there were thirty-one strikes, each involving 10,000 or more workers. About 3 million laborers took part. These strikes, plus the obvious power of organized labor in gaining concessions, caused the American public to withdraw its sympathy from labor. Just as the "robber barons" of the late nineteenth century had abused their power under *laissez faire*, so likewise had the later czars of labor—men like Caesar Petrillo of the musicians' union and John L. Lewis of the United Mine Workers—abused the new power. The nation learned painfully that when the rules of making a living are relaxed, the men who come out on top are those who exploit their advantage to the utmost. Laws adequate to protect the public should be impartially enforced on both management and labor. Lewis's outright defiance of the Federal government during the coal strike late in 1946 made a new labor law inevitable. The Republican party's victory in the congressional elections of that year added to the certainty.

The Taft-Hartley Law. The lawmakers set to work immediately to revise the National Labor Relations Act. On June 23, 1947, a thoroughly aroused Congress overrode Truman's veto of the Taft-Hartley Labor-Management Relations Act. It was the answer to more than a decade of demands for changes in the New Deal's prolabor laws. Union leaders fought the measure every step of the way, and after passage, they condemned it as "a slave labor law." President Truman, in his veto message, had called its provisions "shocking—bad for labor, bad for management, bad for the country." In spite of these protests, the Taft-Hartley law proved to be a practical measure which, in 1958, had withstood all attempts by labor to bring about a repeal. Every Congress since 1947 has convened with the avowed purpose of amending it or even repealing it outright. Yet, no Congress has made a single major revision.

The primary purpose of the Taft-Hartley law was to restore a semblance of equality between the powers of labor and management at the bargaining table. The law retained all the protections of workers' rights guaranteed by the Wagner Act, but it granted certain comparable rights to employers. It outlawed the closed shop and put the union shop in its place; it required unions to bargain in good faith with management and outlawed as unfair labor practices such weapons as featherbedding (pay for work not performed), jurisdictional strikes, secondary boycotts, and coercion of employers to violate the law. It protected workers from abusive union conduct by upholding their right to reject union membership, except under union-shop contracts. The act prohibited involuntary dues checkoffs and subjected union financial affairs to closer scrutiny. The general public benefited from the procedure for handling labor disputes of a national emergency nature; the act provided for a Federal board of inquiry into such disputes, an eighty-day "cooling off" period before strikes, a secret ballot of employees to determine the willingness of workers to participate in strikes, and a report to Congress. These benefits to employers, workers, and the public, the continued strength of organized labor, and the failure of Congress to revise the law offer rather positive proof that it is anything but a "slave labor law." Yet, it has certain basic weaknesses which one of its framers, the late Senator Robert Taft of Ohio, favored correcting. The national emergency provisions have not always proved effective; certain restrictions on labor leaders are clearly discriminatory in favor of management; and the law has appeared vague and inconsistent in some respects.

The reaction to the Taft-Hartley Act demonstrated the power of labor leaders. When they denounced the law for its "slave labor" provisions, *Look Magazine*[12] conducted a public opinion poll among both union and nonunion workers, asking whether they favored or opposed the Taft-Hartley Act; 54 per cent opposed, 31 per cent favored, and 15 per cent had no opinion. Of union members, two out of three were opposed. Then the pollsters asked for opinions on ten of the major provisions of the law. The average of the ten surveys showed that 73 per cent of those interviewed were in favor of the separate provisions. On no single issue did a majority of union members oppose the major issues. Workers had accepted union leaders' opinions that the law was bad without pausing to consider its contents.

Since Taft-Hartley. After 1947, labor continued to display great strength. There were major strikes, such as the crippling steel strike of early 1952. President Truman refused to use the national emergency clause of the Taft-Hartley Act but instead seized the industry to prevent a shutdown. The Supreme Court ruled that Truman had exceeded his constitutional powers and ordered the mills returned to their private owners. The delayed strike followed and lasted about eight weeks. The final settlement granted major concessions to the steelworkers. Of far greater significance were two later developments: labor's desire for a guaranteed annual wage and the merger of the AFL and the CIO.

The CIO especially pushed the demand for a guaranteed annual wage. In certain industries, as in automobiles, production is not regularized over the full year. Unions have long sought protection against seasonal unemployment, and they have pressed for contracts which would pay workers during idle months. A Bureau of Labor Statistics study in 1952 reported that of some 2,600 contracts surveyed, less than 200 carried any kind of a guarantee. Only twenty gave substantial assurance of wages or employment. About 1952, the United Steel Workers and the United Automobile Workers stepped up their campaign for a guarantee of full pay for a full year, except for certain short-service workers. The cost of such plans would be paid by employers through state unemployment compensation taxes and through additional direct payments into a guaranteed annual wage fund. The automobile workers signed such a contract with the major producers late in 1955. The steelworkers and other major unions such as electrical workers, rubber workers, teamsters, and railway shop workers continue to seek the same success.

The consummation of the long-awaited merger of the AFL and the CIO came about in December, 1956. The deaths of William Green and Philip Murray, presidents of the two organizations, allowed George Meany and Walter Reuther to take over. The new leadership eliminated

[12] Sept. 30, 1947.

most of the personality conflicts and permitted the merger. One cause of the merger was the fact that no significant prolabor legislation has been enacted since the New Deal. Inability to bring about a repeal of the Taft-Hartley law prompted labor to consolidate to achieve greater effectiveness in national elections. A serious doubt exists, however, as to whether or not the AFL-CIO can control the votes of its 15 million members and their families. If it can, there is a good chance that labor can stop the loss of political power which has been evident since 1946. An economic reason for the merger was the fact that growth in union

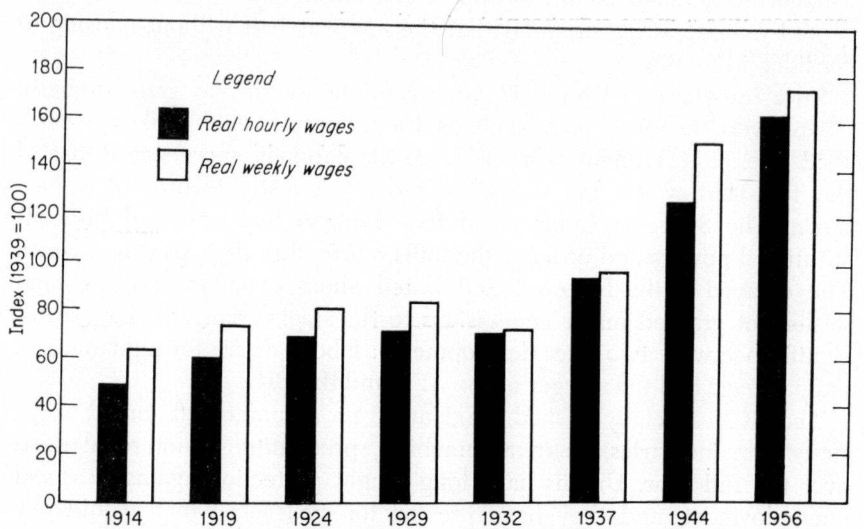

CHART 29-2. Rise of real wages for manufacturing workers, 1914–1956. (*Adapted from Carroll R. Daugherty and John B. Parrish, The Labor Problems of American Society, Houghton Mifflin Company, Boston, 1952.*)

membership slowed down after World War II. The unions realized that jurisdictional disputes complicated the problem of organizing the remaining masses of workers, especially in the South. The 1956 merger should enable unions to increase their numerical strength.

LABOR'S PROGRESS

The workingman has made great gains since 1914. Increased real wages, shorter working hours, greater bargaining strength through favorable Federal and state laws, and greatly increased union membership are aspects of this progress.

Wages. The higher real wages since 1914 (see Chart 29-2) have come through sporadic increases; they have by no means been equally distributed among all groups of workers. During World War I, the real earnings of men engaged in transportation and manufacturing rose noticeably despite the inflation; coal miners, unskilled laborers, and farm workers also registered gains. White-collar workers, teachers and ministers, and workers in the building trades lost ground. After the price collapse of 1920, labor made its greatest gains in real wages; all but the coal miners, unskilled workers, and farm hands gained. By 1924, the real weekly earnings of manufacturing workers were 28 per cent above the 1914 level. They increased slightly up to 1929 and then declined 14 per cent in three years. Of course, the mass unemployment of the Great Depression was a more significant factor than the level of wages. With some economic recovery in 1933, real wages started a steady climb. Except for

Table 29-1
Average Gross Weekly Earnings of Workers in Selected Industries, 1950–1957

Year	All manufacturing	Primary metal industries	Automobiles	Textiles	Bituminous coal mining	Consumers' price index (1947–1949 = 100)
1950	$59.33	$67.24	$73.25	$48.95	$70.35	102.8
1957	82.39	98.75	99.85	58.35	110.53	120.2
Increase, per cent......	39	47	36	19	57	17

SOURCES: U.S. Bureau of Labor Statistics, *Monthly Labor Review*, vol. 82 (January, 1959), pp. 93–112; U.S. Bureau of the Census, *Statistical Abstract of the United States, 1955* (Washington, 1955), pp. 213–215.

1938, the rise continued through 1944. Inflation and loss of overtime pay led to a three-year fall, but by 1950 workers had recovered most of the postwar loss.

Since 1950, real wages of workers in manufacturing and mining have moved upward. Table 29-1 reflects this gain, and it also shows that wages in the most strongly unionized industries such as coal mining, metalworking, and automobiles have advanced far more than those in industries like textiles, where unions are not nearly so powerful. Many persons such as white-collar workers, teachers, persons living on retirement income, and fixed-income groups have suffered a loss in real income since 1939.

An obvious conclusion is that labor unions have benefited their members through higher wages. There can be little doubt that this is true, but higher *real* wages are possible only through greater productivity. Wages have risen faster in those industries where technological advancement has been most rapid. Investment in new technology has increased worker productivity and has permitted higher wages. If the total flow of goods and services to the public does not increase, a rise in real wages for one group must come at the expense of another. Thus, higher wages for union workers sometimes result in losses for nonunion labor. In at least one instance, unorganized workers equaled union wage gains: the earnings of farm laborers nearly tripled between 1940 and 1945, chiefly because of labor scarcity.

Hours. The historical trend toward shorter working hours continued after 1914. In a century and a half, the hours in the average work week declined from eighty to forty. In 1914, the average for all workers was nine per day and fifty-four per week. This dropped steadily during the 1920s, fell off further during the unemployment of the 1930s, picked up because of the overtime hours of World War II, and has stabilized at around forty hours per week and eight hours per day since 1945. This gain has come from greater productivity of the labor force. Per capita national income doubled between 1919 and 1950, owing primarily to the accumulation of capital and to technological improvements. Greater leisure time was one of the fruits of this progress.

State and Federal legislation followed, rather than led, in this trend toward shorter hours. States passed laws fixing the maximum hours of labor in the middle of the nineteenth century, but it was not until after 1900 that the courts looked with favor upon that type of legislation. Since then, states have intervened more and more, primarily to safeguard the health of female workers. By the 1950s nearly all states limited women to eight hours per day or forty-eight hours per week or both. All states restricted child labor and required school attendance to age fifteen or sixteen. There was little regulation of male workers' hours by states.[13] The Federal government's most decided action came in 1938. The Fair Labor Standards Act eliminated child labor in interstate industries and fixed the average work week at forty hours with a standard eight-hour day. Constant improvements in technology and pressure from labor unions point to further reductions; a goal of unions in the 1950s is a four-day, thirty-hour week.

good or bad?

Closely associated with the gains in wages and hours are fringe benefits for members of the labor force. Accident and health insurance, unemployment compensation, pensions for disabled and retired workers, and guaranteed annual wages were some of the established principles in operation in 1958.

Union Strength. Labor unions achieved great economic power after 1914. The greatest strength came with the New Deal legislation, which placed the Federal government in the position of "sponsor" for organized labor. The National Labor Relations Act (1935) and the favorable deci-

[13] See pages 414 and 416 for the exception to this general view.

sions of the courts provided the nourishment necessary for spontaneous growth. In the decade after 1935, total union membership skyrocketed from 3.7 to 14.8 million. The CIO accounted for more than half of the 11-million increase. The numerical strength of unions stabilized after World War II at around 15 million; by 1958, total membership had moved upward again to about 17.5 million. The unions still had about 75 per cent of the total labor force left to organize.

CHAPTER 30

Agriculture in an Industrial Economy

Instability has plagued farming in the twentieth century. During periods of wartime prosperity, farmers have prospered. But in peacetime "normalcy" they have failed to share proportionately in the national well-being. They have also suffered more than other groups in times of depression. Agriculture underwent profound changes in the first half of the twentieth century, but many farmers were unable to make the transition successfully. The alternate periods of prosperity and depression for millions of farm families were painful. A growing social conscience, which

Table 30-1
Agricultural Change, 1910–1957

Year	Number of farms (millions)	Cropland acreage harvested (millions)	Average acres per farm	Value of farm land, buildings, equipment, and other items (billions)	Population on farms, per cent of national total
1910	6.4	322	138.1	$ 42.0	35
1920	6.5	362	148.2	78.7	30
1930	6.5	359	157	57.8	25
1940	6.4	321	174	41.9	23
1950	5.6	345	215.3	102.4	17
1957	4.9	333*	242.2*	119.7*	12

* 1954.

SOURCES: U.S. Bureau of the Census, *Statistical Abstract of the United States, 1958* (Washington, 1958), pp. 611–612; U.S. Bureau of the Census, *Historical Statistics of the United States, 1789–1945* (Washington, 1949), pp. 65, 99.

became most pronounced during the Great Depression, dictated that the Federal government should undertake to "solve the farm problem." The complexities of the problem, plus the fact that agriculture is a declining industry, has defied governmental solutions. Tables 30-1 and 30-2 and Chart 30-1 portray certain fundamental changes which have occurred in farming and help to explain some of the problems.

Table 30-1 and Chart 30-1 set forth some of the quantitative changes between 1910 and 1957. The number of farms declined while the cropland harvested remained roughly constant, causing an increase in the average acreage per farm. At the same time, the population on farms diminished steadily, as did the number of workers employed in agricul-

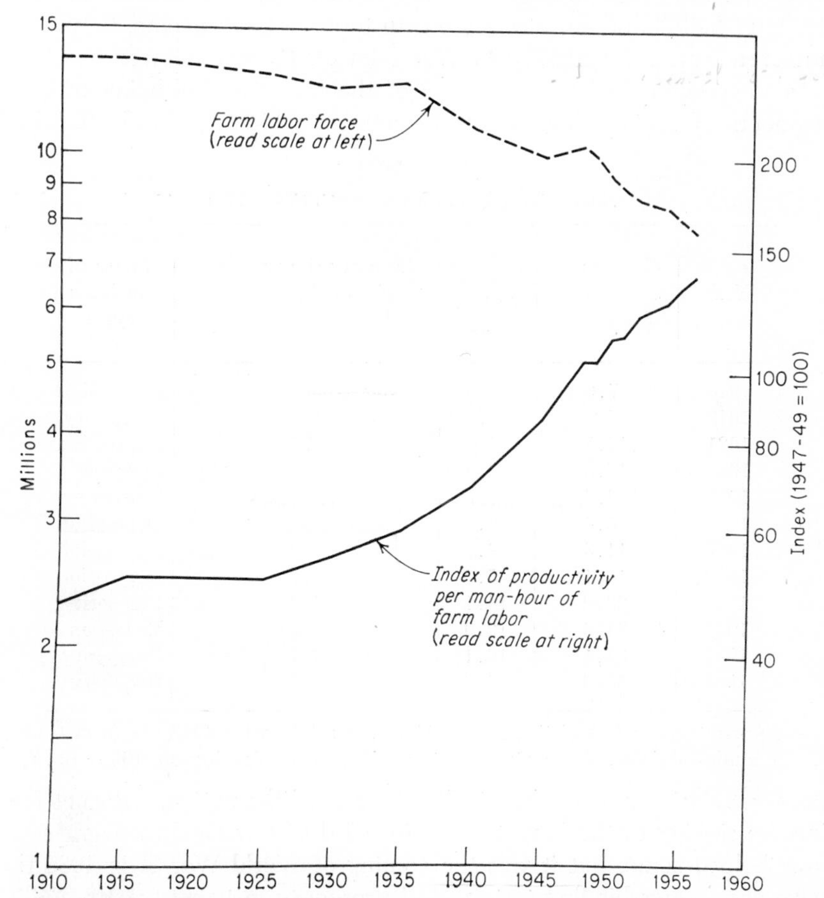

CHART 30-1. Comparison of change in size of the farm labor force and in farm labor productivity, 1910–1956. (*Adapted from U.S. Bureau of the Census, Statistical Abstract of the United States, 1955, Washington, 1955, p. 659; 1957, pp. 210, 649.*)

ture. Yet the nation's population rose from 92 to 170 million. The productivity of farm labor and the value of farm land, buildings, machinery, and other selected items almost tripled.

While these changes occurred, farm income fluctuated wildly, as revealed in Table 30-2. During World War I, income more than doubled for farmers, and a large part of that increase came in the form of real earnings, since farm prices rose faster than nonfarm prices. Then the postwar depression left farmers in a weak position; 1921 net income was less than in 1914 and the purchasing power of the farmer's dollar was even lower. During the prosperity which followed 1922, agriculture recovered some of the lost ground, but farmers were never able to reach the lofty heights of the war period. In terms of real income, they could not even match the pre-World War I levels. Farmers viewed the 1920s as a depression decade, regardless of the material well-being of other segments of society. The Great Depression which followed 1929 hurt

Table 30-2
Fluctuations in Farm Income, 1914–1958

Year	Gross farm income ($ billions)	Net income ($ billions)	Ratio of prices received to prices paid by farmers (1910–1914 = 100)	Phase of business cycle
1914	7.6	4.5	99	Depression
1918	16.2	9.7	118	Prosperity
1921	10.5	3.8	75	Depression
1925	13.6	6.9	92	Prosperity
1929	13.8	6.7	89	Prosperity
1932	6.4	2.3	55	Depression
1937	11.3	6.1	92	Depression
1938	10.1	5.0	77	Depression
1943	23.0	14.1	119	Prosperity
1949	31.6	12.9	100	Recession
1951	37.1	16.1	107	Prosperity
1958	38.0	14.2	85	Recovery

SOURCES: *Historical Statistics, 1789–1945*, p. 99; data after 1943 are from Council of Economic Advisers, *Economic Indicators*, Feb., 1959 (Washington, 1959), pp. 7, 25.

farmers relatively more than it did the rest of the nation, with net farm income sinking to the lowest level since 1910. New Deal recovery measures helped some, but it was the coming of World War II in 1939 that gave the farmer his first taste of full prosperity in twenty years. Falling farm prices in 1948–1949 threatened another serious crisis, but the Korean War, 1950–1953, brought renewed hope. Since 1951, however, farm income and farm purchasing power have declined constantly in spite of heavy government subsidies. Price and income instability and uncertainty are normal conditions for modern agriculture.

THE EFFECTS OF WORLD WAR I

The outbreak of war in Europe in 1914 caused American agriculture to expand immediately. Demand was especially heavy for grain and livestock products, and farmers extended their land holdings and bought additional equipment to take advantage of rising prices. Land and capital investments exceeded the bounds of "prudential restraint," as many mortgaged their farms to buy extra land and machinery. Farmers unwisely plowed up grazing lands west of the 98th meridian to raise more wheat. Some wheat farmers, who had diversified their risks with dairy farming and poultry raising, took a backward step by returning to grain production. Wheat acreage expanded 33 per cent between 1914 and 1919. Production rose by only 6 per cent, however, attesting to the low productivity of the extra lands planted. Meanwhile, wheat brought higher prices, averaging $2.16 per bushel in 1919, as compared to $0.97 in 1914. Hog slaughtering increased by 20 per cent, while pork prices climbed to more than double the 1914 level. These prices pushed net income to farmers from $4.5 billion in 1914 to $9.9 billion in 1919.

The war-inspired prosperity lasted only temporarily. The dizzy upward spiral of prices leveled off in 1919 and moved downward in mid-1920. Livestock prices broke first late in 1919 and crop prices began falling in 1920, dropping to 52 per cent of the wartime peak. Since costs of farming declined less sharply, net farm income slumped from $9.9 billion in 1919 to $3.8 billion in 1921. In the short depression which followed, businessmen took losses on stockpiled inventories and manufacturers cut back output. The nation quickly bounced back from the depression, making a successful adjustment by the end of 1922. Between 1923 and 1929, only certain "sick" segments of the economy failed to enjoy unprecedented prosperity. Agriculture, along with a few other industries, never fully recovered from the postwar depression.

CAUSES OF AGRICULTURAL INSTABILITY

Loss of Markets. Farmers planted their 1920 crops in anticipation of high prices. Even those who could foresee a price decline were unable to reduce production to prewar levels. They had to maintain output or lose their heavy investments. Farm mortgage debt had more than doubled between 1914 and 1921; annual interest payments represented high fixed costs which farmers had to cover. But the markets for farm products, especially for cereals and livestock, began to shrink after the war. Foreign markets declined as European farmers returned to production after some five years of curtailed activity. Also, cheap fertile lands in more recently developed countries poured forth wheat and meat products at lower prices than American farmers cared to meet. The Russian Ukraine, Argentina, Canada, and Australia had begun to compete with United States wheat and livestock growers as early as the 1870s and 1880s. They released an ever-increasing flow of products. The United States gave ground, much as New England had done a century earlier in the face of Western competition. United States exports of crude foodstuffs fell from $918 million in 1920 to $257 million by 1923. Lower prices caused some of the decrease, but volume also diminished. Wheat exports dropped from 369 million bushels in 1920 to 160 million in 1923. The decline in wheat exports had the same effect as a 45 per cent *increase* in domestic output; it added 209 million bushels to the 470 million bushels consumed in 1920.

Not only did farmers lose foreign markets, but their domestic markets diminished as well. The expansion of demand for foodstuffs slowed as the rate of population growth decreased. A declining birth rate and restrictions on immigration meant that there were fewer new "mouths to feed." Urbanization made the populace more sedentary, reducing the need for high-energy foods. Changes in dietary habits resulted in greater consumption of fresh fruits, green vegetables, and choicer cuts of lean meat, with less demand for fat pork and starches. Also, the need for hay and feed grains was less as gasoline tractors and automobiles replaced horses and mules on most farms. This eventually released about 60 million acres of land for other uses.

Increased Productivity. While demand fell off, the American farmer's ability to produce mounted rapidly. Mechanization and better methods caused the productivity of farm workers to rise by 25 per cent in the decade after 1910 and by another 9 per cent by 1931. Progress in farm technology after World War I was astounding.[1] It permitted a steady decline in the number of persons engaged in farming, but it also produced new "problems of plenty."

Foremost among the innovations in modern farming was the internal-combustion engine, which became commonplace after World War I. Tractors gave greater flexibility and speed to farming than the use of animal or steam power, especially after the perfection of pneumatic tires. In 1920, farmers owned about 250,000 tractors; in the mid-1950s, there was slightly less than one for each of the 4.8 million farms. Many improvements in farm equipment followed the adoption of the all-purpose tractor. Mechanical corn and cotton pickers, tractor-drawn combines, windrow hay balers, and manure loaders lightened the farmer's chores. In 1920 combines cut only 5 per cent of the nation's wheat crop; in 1938 they handled 50 per cent of the total. The use of automobiles and motor trucks also added to the mechanization of farm life. Electrification, especially after the Rural Electrification Administration came into being in 1935, further contributed to mechanical progress. In addition to the blessings of home lighting, farmers installed electric motors for many farm

[1] William L. Calvert, "The Technological Revolution in Agriculture, 1910–1955," *Agricultural History*, vol. 30 (January, 1956), pp. 18–27.

Fig. 30-1. A diesel tractor pulling three 9-foot disk plows on a 10,000-acre Minnesota farm. (*Courtesy of Caterpillar Tractor Co.*)

Fig. 30-2. A modern cotton picker. Note the thoroughness with which the machine picks a row. (*Courtesy of International Harvester Co. Photo from National Cotton Council.*)

jobs. Dairy farming changed markedly with the introduction of electric milking machines and cream separators.

Crop technology advanced with similar rapidity. For example, the corn belt experienced two particularly revolutionary developments: the perfection of hybrid corn and the commercial production of soybeans. Hybrid corn, introduced about 1926 after years of experimentation, increased the yield per acre about 20 per cent on the average. Between 1936 and 1946, acreage planted to hybrid corn in the North Central states increased from 2 to 91 per cent. Soybeans, unlisted in the census of 1910, became the fifth leading crop in the 1950s in terms of cash sales and sixth in terms of acreage. The technological development of soybean utilization made possible this great increase. A variety of human and animal food products are derived from soybeans converted to meal or oil, while industrial uses, especially plastics manufacture, consume vast quantities of soybeans. Increased crop yields also came from better seed selection, greater reliance upon scientific soil testing, application of varied fertilizers, and chemical weed control. Irrigation in regions of moderate to light rainfall offered hope that the drought hazard could be partially eliminated. Aerial spraying was used successfully to eradicate plant diseases and insect pests.

Agricultural scientists also made giant strides in livestock husbandry. They devoted greater attention to the protein, vitamin, and mineral requirements in meat, dairy, and poultry feeding; more recently, they adapted antibiotics and hormones to animal nutrition. Selective breeding, partly through artificial insemination, raised productivity in all lines. The swine and poultry industries benefited from disease control; major aspects of this were the development of a hog cholera serum and encouragement of sanitary methods.

These modern advancements made farming much more complex than it was in 1914. Farmers had to become better managers with knowledge of business administration, mechanics, fertilizers, and nutrition. Farms became larger, and the investment in machinery and other equipment required great capital outlay.

Technological progress tripled the productivity of farm labor in forty-five years. One farm worker in 1910 produced enough to support 6.8 other persons; each farm hand in 1955 supported almost 20 others. In that period, total agricultural output almost exactly kept pace with the growth of the population although the farm labor force declined by 40 per cent.

GOVERNMENT SOLUTIONS IN THE 1920s

Farmers in the 1920s felt that they were victims of circumstances not of their own making. The Federal government had encouraged greater production during the war and the overproduction of staple commodities was beyond the control of the individual farmer. His high fixed costs made reductions in his output unrealistic. Farmers of the late nineteenth century had tried to solve a similar problem privately by cutting costs; those of the 1920s turned to the Federal government for assistance. The government made a number of gestures toward solving the farm problem in the 1920s, but none of them gave any significant measure of relief. It tried to help by erecting tariff barriers against foreign competition, by granting more liberal credit to the debt-burdened farmers, by imposing stricter regulations on the middlemen who handle farm products, by exempting agricultural marketing cooperatives from the antitrust laws, and by a number of surplus disposal schemes.

The Effect of Tariff Policy. Farmers believed that competition from foreign producers had caused the price collapse and that high duties on commodities like wheat, corn, cotton, and meat would restore prices to their 1919 level (see "Tariffs," page 563). Congress agreed and passed the Emergency Tariff Act of 1921 and the Fordney-McCumber Act of 1922. These bills boomeranged. Other nations retaliated with higher tariffs of their own, adding to the restrictions on American agricultural exports. As a remedy for overproduction, the general effect of tariffs was the reverse of that intended. In spite of the failure of the 1921 and 1922 laws, however, farm-state politicians pushed through the Smoot-Hawley Tariff of 1930 and raised the level of duties even higher.

Farm Credit. Farm leaders had long protested the inadequacy of agricultural credit. Partly as a result of this pressure, Congress had passed the Federal Farm Loan Act in 1916 to provide five- to forty-year mortgages on first-class farm real estate at reasonable rates of interest. But this did not meet all the critical financial needs of rural areas. Farmers still found it difficult to finance their operations from early spring to late fall. Accordingly, in 1923 the Federal government set up the Intermediate Credit System for making medium-length loans, ranging from six months to three years in maturity. These easier credit provisions filled a long-time need, but they did not solve the problem of overproduction; in fact, they did not remedy the farm debt problem. Total farm mortgage debt remained at about $10 billion throughout the decade of the 1920s, and the annual number of bankruptcy cases filed by farmers more than tripled between 1920 and 1922 and more than doubled again by 1924. The rate varied from 4,500 to 7,900 annually from 1923 down through 1930.

Regulating the Middleman. Just as the Patrons of Husbandry had sought to reduce the profits of the middleman as a solution to their problems, so did the farm leaders of the 1920s. Agricultural interests pushed three laws through Congress, all designed to raise profits to farmers. The Packers and Stockyards Act of 1921 forbade unfair and discriminatory practices, the manipulation of livestock prices and supplies, and other devices which might give meat packing firms an advantage over farmers. The Grain Futures Act of 1922 regulated speculative transactions on the grain exchanges in an attempt to eliminate market control by dealers. The Capper-Volstead Cooperative Marketing Act, also passed in 1922, exempted agricultural cooperatives and associations from the antitrust laws and allowed cooperative buying and selling by farmers in interstate commerce. But these measures did not cope with the basic problem of overproduction.

Surplus Disposal Schemes. The Federal government toyed with a number of surplus removal schemes in the twenties. Most observers recognized oversupply as the major cause of the farmers' troubles, and some of them advocated plans designed to take a part of agricultural production out of the American market. Most elaborate of these schemes was the McNary-Haugen proposal, introduced into Congress for the first time in 1924.

The purpose of the plan was "to improve the marketing of farm products, to insure a fair return from farm operations, to stabilize farm securities, to facilitate farm finance, and to secure equality for agriculture in the benefits of the protective tariff." The measure called for a Federal agency to purchase the annual surplus of "basic commodities"—cotton, wheat, corn, rice, tobacco, and hogs—at prices high enough to give farmers "a fair exchange value at home." The government intended to hold the surplus off the market until prices should rise, or else "dump" it overseas for whatever price it would bring. To maintain domestic prices above world market levels, the law called for a protective tariff on all the basic commodities. Any losses suffered by the government were to be borne by the farmers themselves; an ingenious "equalization fee" took care of this. For example, if the government bought, under the plan, 200 million bushels of wheat at $1.40 per bushel and sold it for $1 per bushel on world markets, it would lose $80 million. Assuming that wheat growers produced 1,000 million bushels of wheat, each grower paid the government 8 cents per bushel grown, thus spreading the loss over the entire wheat crop. Supposedly, farmers would receive the world price of $1 per bushel without the McNary-Haugen plan; under the scheme they would get $1.40, less the 8-cent equalization fee, or a net of $1.32. An import duty of about 40 cents per bushel would keep out foreign wheat. The McNary-Haugen plan never became law; it failed in Congress in 1924 and President Coolidge vetoed it in 1927 and again in 1928. He thought that the plan would encourage additional overproduction and that the dumping of surpluses would invite retaliation from foreign countries. Congress considered a similar plan—the export debenture scheme—after 1928, but President Hoover declared his intention to veto any such measure. The farm bloc agreed to compromise and helped to pass the Agricultural Marketing Act of 1929.

Congress designed the Agricultural Marketing Act to raise farm prices without dumping surpluses on foreign markets. The act created the Federal Farm Board and appropriated $500 million for promoting producer cooperatives and establishing government-owned commodity stabilization corporations. The Board set up the Cotton Stabilization Corporation, the Wheat Stabilization Corporation, and similar agencies to which it made low-interest loans to purchase and store excess staples. The program succeeded in holding up farm prices only briefly; the stabilization corporations accumulated vast stocks of cotton and wheat while commodity prices fell after the early months of 1930. In some respects, the program simply encouraged farmers to produce more of the price-supported commodities. When the Federal Farm Board ceased operations in 1933, it had lost between $300 and $350 million, largely to no avail.

AGRICULTURE IN THE GREAT DEPRESSION

The farmers' poor position in the 1920s became much worse after the stock market crash of October, 1929. As the economy crumbled, net farm income fell from $6.7 billion in 1929 to $2.3 billion in 1932. Farm income lost purchasing power at the same time; the ratio of prices received by farmers to prices paid declined by 38 per cent from 1929 to 1932. The principal reason for this was that farmers reduced production very little, if indeed at all, in the basic commodities, while most manufacturing concerns cut their production. For example, agricultural production fell only 6 per cent from 1929 to 1933 while prices dropped 63 per cent; manufacturers of farm implements cut output 85 per cent and reduced prices a mere 6 per cent. Control of output and prices was necessary to give farmers equality in the market place. Since farmers were powerless to develop such control on their own initiative, the Federal government took charge through the Agricultural Adjustment Administration.

The Agricultural Adjustment Act of 1933. The Democratic party had promised prompt action to help farmers during the campaign of 1932. After Franklin D. Roosevelt's election, a Democratic Congress proceeded to carry out the platform pledge to enact "every constitutional measure that will aid the farmer to receive for basic farm commodities prices in excess of the cost of production." It passed the Agricultural Adjustment Act on May 12, 1933, setting up the Agricultural Adjustment Administration (the AAA) to administer the law. The basic purpose of the bill was to raise the purchasing power of farmers for industrial products in order "to relieve the existing national economic emergency. . . . " It planned to balance the production and consumption of farm products in order to raise farm prices. The goal was farm prices which would have a purchasing power, with respect to nonfarm articles, equal to that from August, 1909, to July, 1914. In other words, Congress hoped to raise farm prices to "parity" or equality with nonfarm prices, accepting as ideal the price relationships of the pre-World War I era. For example, if wheat averaged 90 cents a bushel in the base period and a pair of work shoes averaged $4.50 in the same years, a pair of shoes cost 5 bushels of wheat. If a similar pair of shoes sold for $3 in 1933, wheat should bring 60 cents a bushel.

The AAA employed three primary methods to raise farm prices. First, Congress classified seven products as "basic" commodities—wheat, corn, cotton, rice, tobacco, hogs, and dairy products. For each of these, the AAA asked producers to sign voluntarily agreements to limit production. At the same time, it authorized a Commodity Credit Corporation to make stabilization loans to farmers, so that producers could keep their crops off the market until prices rose. The Corporation, using Federal funds, stood ready to lend a specific amount per pound of cotton or bushel of corn. If the market price were below the announced loan figure, the farmer could get a government loan, using the cotton or corn as collateral. Later, if the market price climbed above the loan price, the farmer could sell the crop, repay the loan, and pocket the difference. If the market price stayed below the loan price, the farmer surrendered the crop to the government agency.

Second, the government supplemented farmers' incomes by subsidy payments to those farmers who signed restrictive agreements. The payments were based on the difference between market and parity prices. A tax levied on the first processor of the basic commodity provided the funds for the payments. For example, millers paid a small tax on each bushel of wheat which they processed; they added the tax to the price of a bag of flour.

Third, the AAA encouraged the organization of processors, distributors, and agricultural cooperatives to exercise central control over marketing. It exempted these from the antitrust laws. The Secretary of Agriculture could then enter into agreements with these groups for more orderly marketing. For cotton and tobacco, Congress imposed strict marketing quotas in separate laws in 1934; these laws levied a penalty tax on the sale of commodities in excess of an allotted quota.

The AAA went into operation too late in the year to affect cotton and pork production in 1933. Accordingly, Secretary of Agriculture Henry A. Wallace paid farmers to plow under 10 million acres of cotton and to slaughter 6 million brood sows and pigs. The irony of destroying pork while millions of people lacked adequate food aroused public indignation. Few persons cared that many of the old sows and baby pigs were scarcely fit for human consumption or that some of the edible meat was used in the free-lunch program of the public schools. They failed to see the logic of converting meat animals into fertilizers—this was the destiny of much of the pork—which the AAA then gave to farmers to raise more corn to raise more hogs. It seemed that the New Deal was ready to exchange "two birds in the hand for one in the bush." The public protest caused Wallace to abandon the destruction program after 1933.

Any appraisal of the AAA is difficult. Farm prices and incomes rose decidedly between 1932 and 1935. Cotton moved from 6 to 11 cents per pound and wheat from 38 to 83 cents per bushel. Average farm prices were 60 per cent higher and net farm income increased from $2.3 to $5.1 billion. Farm purchasing power rose some 53 per cent. The success of the program was by no means uniform, however. Many farmers continued to suffer from low incomes, as did millions of city people. As for the actual influence of the AAA, one can only surmise. Severe drought conditions in the summer of 1934 damaged the crops and limited output effectively. Without this influence, it is doubtful that the AAA could have reduced surpluses appreciably. Many farmers refused to sign agreements, and those who did often produced as much as before on the restricted acreage by applying extra fertilizer and farming their land more intensively.

GOOD WORK FARMERS!

The AAA of 1933 lasted but three seasons. In January, 1936, the Supreme Court demolished it in the case of *United States v. Butler*.[2] The Court ruled that the processing tax was unconstitutional because it taxed one group (consumers) to benefit another (farmers). Furthermore, the Constitution did not give Congress the power to regulate agricultural production; the Tenth Amendment reserved this right to the states. The New Deal had to find a new justification for its farm policy.

IMPORTANT

Later New Deal Measures. The government changed its approach in the Soil Conservation and Domestic Allotment Act of 1936. The purpose remained the same as in the AAA of 1933: to raise farm purchasing power. Congress circumvented the Supreme Court's objections to the processing tax by paying farmers to plant soil-conserving crops (like alfalfa and clover) instead of staple commodities. Benefits to cooperating farmers came from general tax funds rather than from a special processing tax. But the 1936 measure did not control overproduction. Wheat and cotton crops, under the stimulus of higher prices, increased; the 1937 cotton crop was the largest in the nation's history. Some gains were made in conservation, but as a remedy for surplus output the act failed. A third law, the Agricultural Adjustment Act of 1938, replaced the Soil Conservation and Domestic Allotment Act.

The AAA of 1938 retained the farm income parity objective and the soil conservation methods of the earlier laws. But the droughts of 1934 and 1936 had produced embarrassing shortages of feed grains and caused Secretary of Agriculture Wallace to advance the "ever-normal granary"

[2] 297 U.S. 1.

idea. Under this plan, the government purchased and stored surpluses to prevent future shortages. Subsidies, ranging from 52 to 75 per cent of parity, went to farmers who restricted acreages of five basic crops—wheat, corn, cotton, tobacco, and rice. The Commodity Credit Corporation made crop loans to stabilize prices. The law empowered the AAA to impose marketing quotas upon approval of two-thirds of the producers of a basic commodity. All producers of the commodity, whether they approved or not, received a quota or allotment; if they sold more than their quota, they had to pay a penalty tax on the excess sold. As a part of the program, the Department of Agriculture removed surpluses from the market. It supported a free school-lunch program, subsidized the export of cotton and wheat, and experimented with new uses of farm products. The Act of 1938 also introduced another idea. It established the Federal Crop Insurance Corporation to protect wheat farmers against loss from unavoidable risks (such as drought, flood, hail, and plant disease).

The government's experience with the AAA of 1938 was too brief to permit adequate evaluation. With the start of World War II in the fall of 1939, the need to restrict output and support farm income dissolved in the stream of new demands for farm products, both at home and abroad. By the time America entered the war late in 1941, government policy had shifted to one of expanding farm production. Meanwhile, the Supreme Court upheld the act as a legitimate regulation of interstate commerce: it ruled that the government was now using marketing controls, not production controls.[3]

Farm Credit and Rural Resettlement. The New Deal had likewise turned its attention to that serious problem of farm indebtedness. The Farm Credit Administration, established in 1933, took control of all Federal farm credit facilities. It coordinated the functions of existing agencies and provided easier credit at low interest, refinancing many long-term mortgages on more favorable terms for farmers. It made available emergency short-term credit to farmers who could not get loans elsewhere. Federal farm mortgage legislation in 1933 and 1934 also provided emergency loans to help farmers hold their property. The Frazier-Lemke Farm Bankruptcy Act in June, 1934, also had this aim. It gave additional credit to farmers faced with mortgage foreclosures and allowed the repurchase of farm property at reappraised values and reduced interest. In the event that creditors should oppose the new terms, the law suspended bankruptcy proceedings for five years. The Supreme Court declared the law unconstitutional in 1935 on the grounds that it deprived creditors of their property rights without just compensation.[4] Congress promptly enacted

[3] *Mulford v. Smith,* 307 U.S. 38 (1939).

[4] *Louisville Bank v. Radford,* 295 U.S. 555 (1935).

a second Frazier-Lemke bill providing for a three-year moratorium on foreclosures and required farmers to pay a reasonable and fair rental to mortgage holders during the stay period.

In spite of the liberal credit arrangements, many farmers lost their land. The New Deal set up an agricultural Resettlement Administration to rehabilitate and relocate dispossessed and impoverished farm families. The Farm Security Administration replaced the Resettlement Administration in 1937 and continued the same general work. The FSA also made loans to tenant farmers who wished to purchase their own farms.

Rural Electrification. Many isolated rural areas had living conditions as primitive as those met with in backward countries. It was to improve these conditions by increasing the use of electricity on farms that Congress created the Rural Electrification Administration in May of 1935. The REA made low interest loans to cover the entire cost of erecting power lines. In 1934, less than 11 per cent of the nation's farms had electricity; the figure rose to over 30 per cent in 1940 and to more than 90 per cent in the 1950s. Much of the credit for this progress belongs to the REA.

Appraisal of the New Deal's Farm Program. The administrations of Franklin Roosevelt sought to raise farm income by curbing the output of staple commodities. Net farm income rose from $2.3 billion in 1932 to $5.3 billion in 1939. It would be erroneous to assume that the entire rise resulted from New Deal policies, although about a billion dollars of 1939 income came from government benefit payments. Normal economic recovery accounted for some of the increase in farm income, and the weather played a major role in restricting farm output from 1934 through 1936. Furthermore, it was World War II which finally eliminated crop surpluses and made American farmers prosperous again.

The New Deal tried all but two of the six possible solutions to the problem of overproduction. It (1) restricted output; (2) sought new uses and better markets for farm products with limited success; (3) devalued the gold dollar to inflate the currency and raise prices (see pp. 533–536); and (4) subsidized farm income out of tax funds. It rejected the alternative possibilities of (5) cutting costs and (6) doing nothing and letting economic hardship drive inefficient farmers out of farming. In fact, the New Deal fostered a "back to the land" movement during the depression, encouraging people to retain their farms and aiding impoverished people to take up agriculture.

WORLD WAR II AND POSTWAR READJUSTMENT

World War II. The American economy responded to the stimulus of World War II and the resulting prosperity spilled over into agriculture.

The government took off the restrictions on production and appealed to the farmers to increase their output "to win the war." The volume of production rose by about one-third over the depression years. The farmers' net income soared to record levels, exceeding $14 billion in 1943; real income rose even faster as the ratio of farm to nonfarm prices jumped from 77 in 1939 to 119 in 1943. Price supports and subsidies were unnecessary during the war years. Farmers still remembered the post-World War I collapse, however, and they insisted that the government protect

Fig. 30-3. A row of "Butler huts," used for storing Commodity Credit Corporation grain, at Forsythe, Iowa. (*Courtesy of U.S. Department of Agriculture.*)

them from the inevitable fall in farm prices after the war. In 1942 Congress established price supports for wheat, cotton, corn, tobacco, rice, and peanuts at 90 per cent of parity; these supports were to remain in force for two years after the end of the war.

Farmers emerged from the war in exceptionally good financial condition. Real estate values were high, mortgage debt was reduced to $5 billion—the lowest figure since 1920—and farm prices showed no sign of collapsing as they had in 1920. In fact, they continued upward until 1948, largely because of relief shipments abroad, financed by American aid programs.

Postwar Federal Farm Policy. Farm surpluses reappeared in 1948, causing Congress to extend for two additional years the high price supports which were to have expired in January, 1948. The farm bloc in Congress succeeded in gaining further extensions until 1955, at which time the Farm Bill of 1954 became operative. The 1954 measure instituted a sliding scale of price supports, ranging from 82.5 to 90 per cent of parity for most protected commodities. The purpose of the sliding or flexible supports is to permit the Secretary of Agriculture to raise or lower the level of guaranteed prices in order to encourage or discourage production of certain products. For example, if surpluses of corn continue to pile up under a 90 per cent of parity support, the Secretary can reduce the guaranteed price in the expectation that farmers will shift to some other cash grain.

The primary result of postwar farm policy has been the accumulation of vast stocks of farm products. Since 1948, storage bins have bulged with government-owned wheat, corn, and cotton; lesser amounts of dairy products, eggs, rice, peanuts, and other items have run the total government holdings in excess of $8 billion in 1956–1959. Except for the years of the Korean War (1950–1953), the surpluses have mounted and farm income has declined from 1948 through 1956. Neither rigid 90 per cent price supports nor sliding scales of guarantees appear capable of preventing wide fluctuations in farm income, even though net farm income turned slightly upward in 1957 and 1958. Nor does the "soil bank" idea, adopted in 1956, offer a certain solution to the problem of overproduction. Under this plan, the Secretary of Agriculture pays farmers to retire a part of their farm land; but, as in the past, farmers frequently retire the poorest land and then apply extra fertilizers and effort to the remaining acres. This often results in higher, not lower, farm output. It is ironic that war alone has been able to cope satisfactorily with the farm problem in the twentieth century. Meanwhile, the Federal government continues to grope for an alternative solution.

Agribusiness. A recent trend in agriculture has been the closer integration of business and farming. In some respects, a new agricultural revolution is taking place. The change is remaking the family farm in the image of a small business. The individual farmer is becoming a link in the chain of suppliers and processors for the big corporations which deal with farm products. Some of the independence of the farm family disappears, but with it go many of the extreme risks. The essence of "agribusiness" is that farmers become contractors, turning out products at known costs and prices, instead of producing for a free market, with a free price system. Agriculture is one of the few segments of the economy which produce for a free market and then accept whatever price the purchaser is willing to pay. Corporations, like General Motors, enter into contracts with other producers to obtain parts for assembling automobiles. The contracts call for a specified quantity of a certain product at a set price. General Motors has an assured flow of parts to its factories, it knows the costs of these parts, and it can regulate the output of finished cars in accordance with demand. Using production contracts lessens the risks of unanticipated market fluctuations. Firms with high fixed costs must of necessity keep their plant in constant use.

Some agricultural producers have already profited from these established concepts. In the past twenty years, the poultry industry, and to a lesser extent the beef and pork industries, have undergone a remarkable change. Earlier, the production of frying chickens was a seasonal thing. Farmers kept chickens as a part of their regular farming operation and sold broilers only during the summer. Frying chickens were rarely cheap enough for the average household. Processors of broilers could not afford to establish large packing plants for just a few months' use each year. In the 1950s, chickens became the "common man's food" throughout the year as the monthly output of broilers remained reasonably steady. What caused the change?

Big concerns like Swift and Company, with large plants and plenty of working capital, regularized poultry production. They developed a system whereby farmers signed contracts to raise broilers on a year-around basis. The company supplied baby chicks, feed, and a guaranteed return to the farmer. The farmer put up a building and furnished the labor. The farmer's risk declined greatly in that he no longer had to supply his own working capital and run the chance of selling his output on a weak market. For example, his contract might call for delivery of 20,000 frying chickens every ten weeks to Swift and Company. The farmer would receive a flat rate of 5 cents per bird. His gross receipts would average $100 per week under such a contract. By adding a helper, he could increase his output to 60,000 per ten-week period. The farmer thus became a contractor, much like the supplier of wheel bearings for Chevrolet automobiles. True, he lost much of the independence long associated with farming; on the other hand, he gained a large measure of security.

The Mid-century Position of Agriculture. The dominant characteristics of agriculture at the halfway mark in the twentieth century point to the conclusion that farming is a declining industry. The miraculous growth of the American economy has meant that an increasingly smaller percentage of the population is needed to produce the foods and fibers necessary to feed and clothe the people. As national income has grown, the percentage of that income spent for farm products has grown smaller. Meanwhile, the productive capacity of agriculture has outrun the ability of the people to consume the output. This is actually a healthy sign for the economy as a whole. Progress in living standards requires fewer productive resources to turn out necessities like food and clothing so that more resources can be devoted to luxury and nonessential items. The decline in farm population should not be viewed with alarm. Of the five million farms in the United States, the top two million yield approximately 85 per cent of all commercial farm products—and they could undoubtedly increase their output enough to account for the other 15 per cent. This means that about three million farms (60 per cent of the total) are not needed for wheat, cotton, corn, livestock, and similar commodities. The real problem is one of effectively utilizing the labor potential of

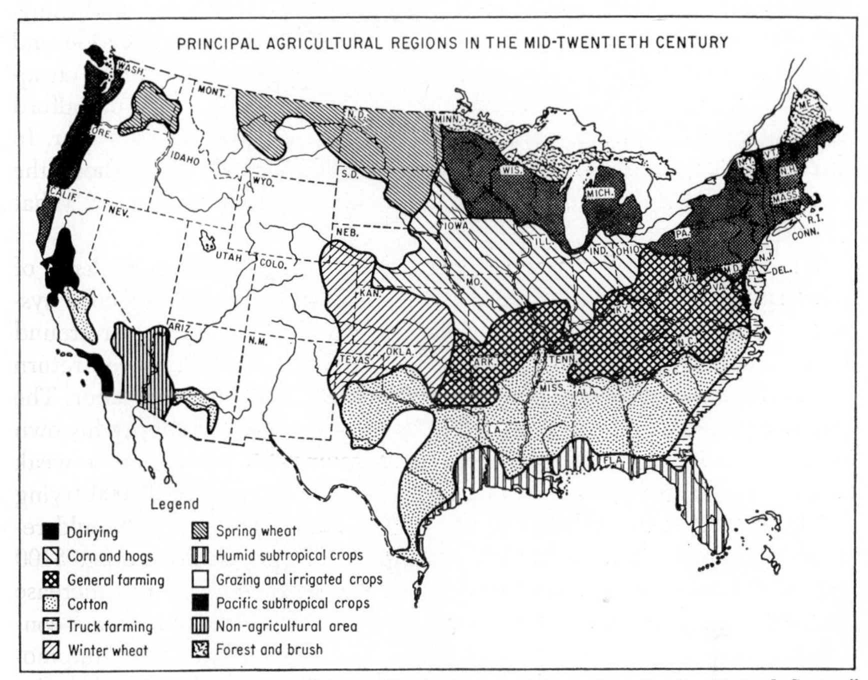

MAP 30-1. (*Adapted from "Generalized Types of Farming in the United States," Agricultural Information Bulletin no. 3, U.S. Bureau of Agricultural Economics, Washington, 1950.*)

some three million farm families to produce things that the general population wants and needs to advance the standard of living. The greatest obstacles to shifting these people out of farming is the lack of educational opportunities, the low standard of living, and the lack of mobility in backward rural areas.

Recent trends in the thinking of farm policymakers include greater emphasis on increasing the mobility of rural people. Some experts advocate a "reversed homestead law" to provide homes and jobs in industrial regions for the excess farm population. This idea finds great opposition from those individuals who believe that the social values of the family farm are vital to the maintenance of a democratic society and that America will deteriorate if the family farm is not preserved. There is little historical evidence to substantiate this fear. The course of United States history since the Civil War has been toward industrialization and the relative decline of farming. But any solution to the farm problem runs squarely into the fact that political, social, and other noneconomic factors are inextricably interwoven into the farm scene.

CHAPTER 31

The Ultimate Achievement

A higher standard of living for the consumer has at all times been an ultimate purpose of work on the part of most Americans. A basic reason for making the economy increasingly specialized has been to produce more goods and services with less effort. The year 1957 is exactly 350 years after the founding of Jamestown and about 175 years after the close of the Revolutionary War. Americans have achieved most of their material progress since the Revolution, indeed since 1900. They have done much more than open a continent 3,000 miles wide, settle it with 175 million people, and provide a strong government. They have made their country the richest and most powerful nation in the world. They have raised their standard of living about fivefold, as Chart 31-1 clearly shows. Americans are today at least three times better off than they were at the time of the Civil War and twice as well off as they were about 1900. In addition, there have been qualitative improvements in living standards which do not show up in per capita income even when it is reduced to comparable dollars. The automobile that cost $1,200 in 1914 was hardly comparable with the car that can be bought for $3,600 today (allowing for a depreciated dollar). Better-quality medical service, canned foods, silk stockings, plumbing, and countless other items are available at the same, indeed, even at lower prices, than in 1914. Thus Americans today live in more comfortable homes, eat better food, and have more mechanical conveniences than ever before. Three-fourths of all families have automobiles; about as many have television sets; even more have radios. True, not all regions of the country enjoy this high standard of living to an equal degree as Map 31-1 shows. The average person in Northern states like Delaware ($2,858) or some Western ones like California ($2,419) did better in 1956 than the national average ($1,940), whereas the average person in some Southern states like Mississippi ($964) or one Western one, South Dakota ($1,330), was not nearly as well off as the average American.

There are other ways of measuring the progress that Americans have made than in counting material goods. They have more leisure than they

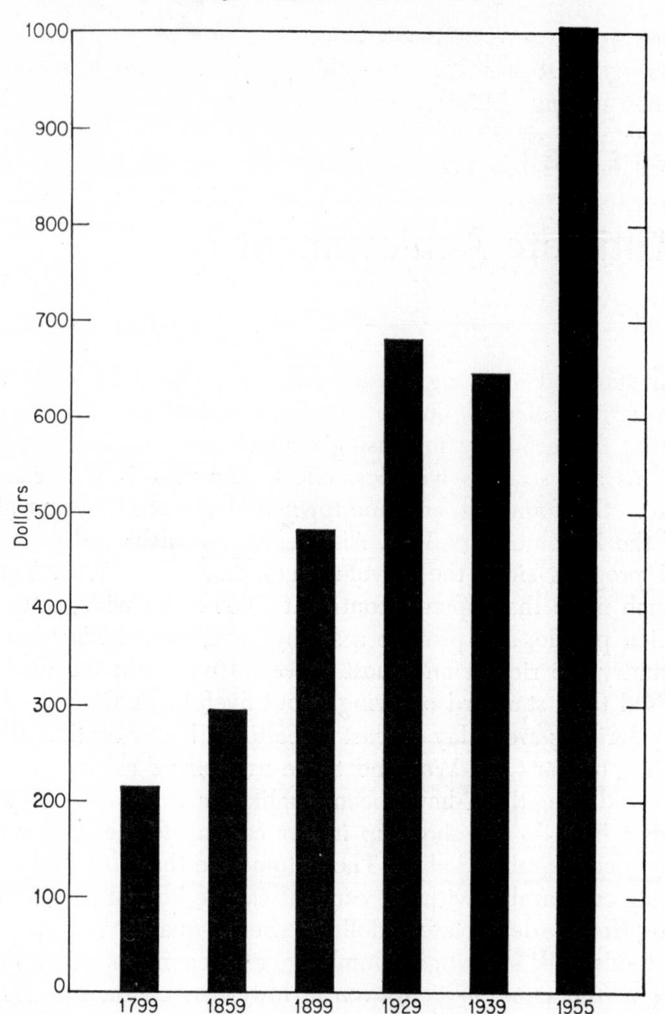

CHART 31-1. Per capita income in 1926 dollars. (*Adapted from National Industrial Conference Board, Economic Almanac 1956, New York, 1956, pp. 423, 442.*)

used to have. A century and a half ago, the average workday was about thirteen hours; by the Civil War it had fallen to eleven hours; it fell to ten in 1890, to nine in 1914, and today it is about eight with a five-day week. This allows Americans more time to become educated.

Education is said to enable people to govern themselves better, to understand their fellow humans here and abroad better, and to observe more sharply what is happening all around them. If that is true, then Americans have made progress in this area, too, for five-sixths of the population five to seventeen years of age is in school, whereas seventy-five years ago, just over half were. Moreover, they attend school nearly three times as long. And the schools spend over twenty times as many dollars to educate students as they did in 1870 (see Table 31-1).

Perhaps the most complete and important test of progress appears in the figures for life expectancy at birth (see Table 31-2). For example, in Massachusetts in 1789, life expectancy at birth for boys was 34.5 years; for girls it was 36.5 years. It is very likely that the life expectancy figure

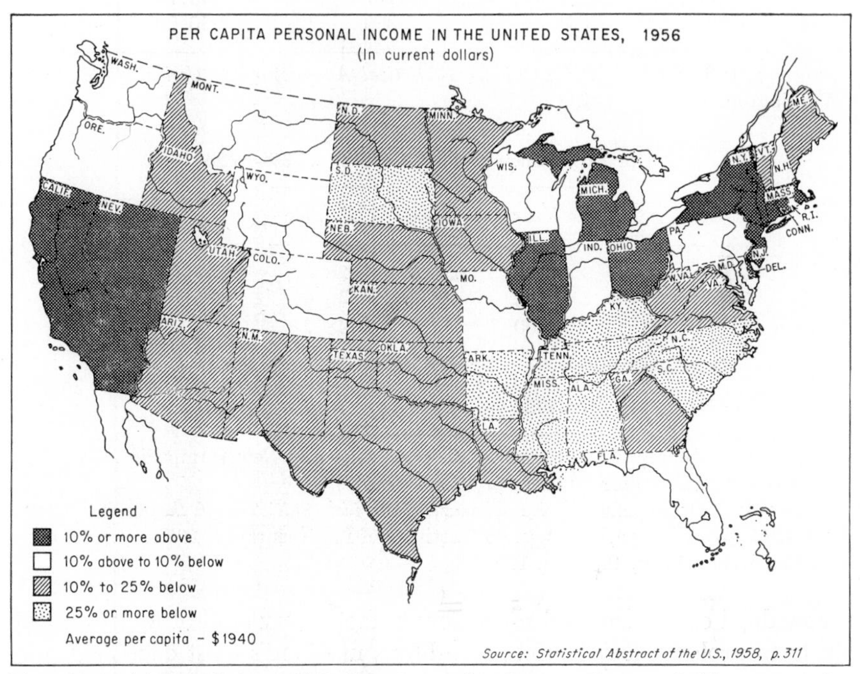

MAP 31-1. (*Adapted from U.S. Bureau of the Census, Statistical Abstract of the United States, 1958, Washington, 1958, p. 311.*)

was even lower in other states, for they were less advanced than Massachusetts. A major reason for the short life lay in the fact that so many babies died in infancy. Once a man or woman reached 20, his life expectancy was still about 34 years. By 1855 life expectancy at birth was around 40 in Massachusetts, and by the start of the present century it was nearing 50 in the United States. Today it is about 70. Women outlive the men by nearly six years, on the average. This rise in life expectancy represents not merely great medical progress in the care of infants of under one year; it also embraces all manner of advancements. It includes better food, more comfortable homes, more leisure time, bet-

Table 31-1
Education Statistics, 1870–1954

Year	Population aged 5 to 17 in schools, per cent	Number of days attended per pupil per year	Expenditure per student in average attendance
1870	57	78.4	$15.55
1900	72.4	99.0	20.21
1930	81.3	143.0	108.49
1940	85.5	151.7	105.74
1954	83.5	158.9	350.90

SOURCE: U.S. Bureau of the Census, *Statistical Abstract of the United States, 1958* (Washington, 1958), p. 114.

Table 31-2
Life Expectancy at Birth (White), 1789–1956

Year	Male	Female
1789	34.5*	36.5*
1855	38.7†	40.9†
1900	46.6	48.7
1930	59.7	63.5
1940	62.1	66.6
1956	67.3	73.7

* Data for 1789 are for 62 towns in Massachusetts and New Hampshire.
† Data for 1855 are for all races in Massachusetts.
SOURCES: U.S. Bureau of the Census, *Historical Statistics of the United States, 1789–1945* (Washington, 1949), p. 45; Institute of Life Insurance, *1958 Life Insurance Fact Book* (New York, 1958), p. 109.

ter medical care, increased sanitation, in fact, every kind of improvement likely to prolong human life. Since life is mankind's most cherished possession, an economy that provides a standard of living that prolongs it is accomplishing the ultimate.

SUMMARY OF PART FOUR

Americans have taken an ever-increasing interest in their fellow men since 1914. That is true with regard to those who are economically less fortunate in America and also with regard to people living in regions that are politically dangerous or economically "backward." It is said that an optimist looking at a half-filled glass of water reports it is half full, whereas a pessimist describes it as half empty. So the optimist may say that Americans are taking a more responsible attitude toward their own social problems and their duties to the world at large. The pessimist, on the other hand, may feel that millions of Americans are becoming increasingly dependent upon their government for economic protection and support, that Europeans receiving aid from this country are becoming dependent on us, too, and that America is interfering too much in the political affairs of other nations. Whoever is right, and both may well be to some extent, the American government has undertaken tremendous new responsibilities in the last half century.

This broadened interest in the world and greater participation in its affairs took the place of the Westward Movement after 1914. The United States tipped the balance of power which enabled the Allies to win World War I. President Wilson then helped remake the map of Europe and set up the League of Nations. The effort of the United States in the 1920s and especially in the 1930s to draw back into its prewar shell of isolationism did not succeed. When World War II broke out, America quickly became involved. Since that war, this country has spent some $55 billion trying to rebuild the war-torn world and save it from the Communist menace. America even fought a war in Korea with that aim in mind, with rather little help from its recent allies.

Within its borders the United States has made great material progress since 1914. This is true in every segment of the economy. The railroad no longer dominates transportation as it did fifty years ago. Trucks, pipelines, barges, passenger cars, buses, and airplanes are among its competitors. The government regulates transportation more closely now than it did half a century ago. This also is true of other segments of the economy. Once given power, a government commission or bureau has rarely relinquished it. The number of these agencies is constantly multiplying, and the power of government over business has grown and grown.

The relative importance of industries has changed since 1914. More of the major ones today depend for their raw materials on metal rather than agricultural products, and they rely increasingly on the assistance of scientists and engineers. Steel is still the basic industry, but the chemical and electronics industries characterize the modern age in contrast to textiles and meat packing in the previous era. Many of these new industries are tremendously productive and sometimes turn out more goods than the public can readily absorb. That is one reason why the economy got seriously out of order during the 1930s.

Back in the late nineteenth century whenever overproduction or overcapacity was the problem, some business leader usually came to the fore and set up a monopoly to limit supply and hold the price at a profitable level. Sometimes it was a far too profitable level. Accordingly, the government enacted antitrust laws. When this same situation appeared in the early 1930s, the government encouraged industries to set up monopolies; it even encouraged agriculture and labor to do the same. Thus the government suspended the antitrust laws to make the NIRA practical. The AAA program for farmers was basically a government-sponsored farm monopoly. And Section 7(a) of the NIRA encouraged labor to form stronger unions for better protection in dealing with management. Thus the New Deal in its early years encouraged monopoly. This solution was apparently acceptable as long as the government proposed it and watched over it. After 1935 the government attitude toward manufacturing changed, and except during World War II, it prosecuted trusts much as it had done before World War I. Indeed, any industry that is merely very big today is in real danger of being judged guilty of breaking the antitrust laws.

Capital no longer enjoys the respect that it did in the nineteenth century. Americans then used their resources generously, even wastefully, but economized on labor and capital. By 1900 they were setting greater value on resources, as is shown by the conservation movement, and they were increasingly critical of capitalists, as is shown by the antitrust movement. Labor had become so plentiful, thanks partly to immigration, that it often received rather shabby treatment. By the 1940s another change had come about. Labor was now the scarce factor of production, and thanks to the help given it by the New Deal, it was in a stronger position to influence public policy. Owing to bitter experiences during the depression, labor leaders knew what they wanted to be protected against. They wanted protection against unemployment, poverty-stricken old age, and helplessness in dealing with employers. They became powerful in the councils of government and influential with political parties. Both major parties wanted to avoid serious unemployment. In 1946 Congress passed the Full Employment law which said, in effect, that the government would do its utmost to prevent unemployment. Labor and capital, however, could not be protected simultaneously. Henceforth the government manipulated the money system with the chief aim in mind of preventing a depression. That was the goal of the "low interest rate standard" which replaced the gold coin standard. The new economics gave much more thought to the workingman's job, and less to his and to his employer's savings. If necessary, it would sacrifice the value of savings to preserve jobs.

As in the previous era, merchants had the responsibility of finding markets for all that the manufacturers were turning out. They came forward with several new retailing institutions such as economy stores, combination stores, supermarkets, shopping centers, and discount houses. They went a long way toward eliminating the wholesaler and other middlemen. Thanks to improved transportation and communication, factory managers and retailers were in much closer touch with one another than ever before. The retailer did not have to carry such a large inventory and the factory manager had a better sense of how well his goods were selling. This reduced losses to both merchant and manufacturer and made depressions somewhat less likely.

In the 1914–1959 era, government took a much more active hand in the lives of citizens. It imposed more regulations and spent a far larger portion of their money for them. Each year citizens observed national tax day, sometime in May, after which, allegedly, the average citizen might keep for himself what he earned. Up to that time, he had been working for his governments. This dramatized that governments took about a third of national income in taxes. The Federal government had to spend $81 billion in 1958–1959. This was needed to help pay for three costly wars, prevent others from happening, provide millions of citizens with social security benefits, and preserve the farmers' way of life. State and local governments, for their part, had to educate many millions of children and provide services of all kinds, from penal institutions and parks to sanitary water supplies and superhighways. As the nation has become older and more populous and people have had to live closer together, the various governments have had to do more and more to protect people from one another. The new way of giving people the maximum of liberty is by protecting them from the selfish acts of others. Letting everyone do pretty much as he pleased was the old way, but that will no longer work in a country as crowded and in an economy as complex as ours.

Selective Bibliography

GENERAL

The student in American economic history should know something of the general histories, bibliographies, encyclopedias, atlases, statistical sources, learned journals, and pictorial histories which the scholars of the profession find most useful.

Bibliographies. Henry P. Beers, *Bibliographies in American History: Guide to Materials for Research* (New York: H. W. Wilson, 1942) is a bibliography of bibliographies. Chapter 5 deals with American economic history. Oscar Handlin and others, *Harvard Guide to American History* (Cambridge: Harvard University Press, 1954) is the modern revised edition of Channing, Hart, and Turner's classic *Guide* first published in 1912. The American Historical Association has long published a list of all books and articles on American history that have appeared during the year, *Writings on American History* (Washington, annually). The series is several years in arrears. David M. Matteson, *Index to the Writings on American History, 1902–1940* (Washington, 1956) is the collected series from its beginning in 1902 to 1940. All the better American economic history texts also carry fairly extensive bibliographies. Attention is particularly called to the fifty-page one in E. L. Bogart and D. L. Kemmerer, *Economic History of the American People* (New York: Longmans, 1947). See also the Carnegie Institution series volumes. Anne M. Boyd, *United States Government Publications* (New York: H. W. Wilson, 1952) is an excellent reference on the uses of government publications.

General Histories. There are many good political histories of the United States. One is H. U. Faulkner, *American Political and Social History* (New York, Appleton-Century, 1957). Charles and Mary Beard, *The Rise of American Civilization, 1492–1927* (2 vols., New York: Macmillan, 1927) and Charles Beard, *America in Mid-passage* (2 vols., New York: Macmillan, 1939) are classics, famous for their sweeping yet penetrating generalizations and for their emphasis on the economic motivations of many American political leaders. John B. McMaster, *History of the People of the United States, 1784–1860* (8 vols., New York: Appleton, 1885–1913) was written extensively from original documents and newspapers. For a work of its time it contains much economic and social as well as political history. Curtis Nettels, *The Roots of American Civilization* (New York: Crofts, 1938) is the best one-volume history of colonial America for the economic historian. Joseph Dorfman, *The Economic Mind in American Civilization, 1606–1948* (3 vols., New York: Viking, 1946–1949) is a standard source on the history of American economic ideas. There have been two major efforts to write a series of books on American economic history. One was begun half a century ago under the auspices of the Carnegie Institution of Washington, D.C. Most of the authors were economists, but they drew their material largely from original sources. Each volume has an extensive bibliography and the quality of the scholarship is high but the series was never completed. Among the chief works in the series are Victor Clark, *History of Manufactures in the United States, 1607–1929* (3 vols., New York: McGraw-Hill, 1929); L. C. Gray, *History of Agriculture in the Southern United States to 1860* (2 vols., New York: Peter Smith, 1941); P. Bidwell and J. Falconer, *History of Agriculture in the Northern United States to 1860* (New York: Peter Smith, 1941); Caroline MacGill, *History of Transportation in the United States to 1860* (Washington: Carnegie, 1917); Emory Johnson and others, *History of Domestic and Foreign Commerce of the United States* (Washington: Carnegie, 1915); and John R. Commons and others, *History of Labour in the United States* (to 1896) (2 vols., New York: Macmillan, 1918). More recently Farrar & Rinehart has been publishing a nine-volume series, chronological in approach, from colonial times to the present, written largely by historians. Fred Shannon, *The Farmers' Last Frontier, 1860–1897* (New York, 1945) and George Taylor, *The Transportation Revolution, 1815–1860* (New York, 1951) stands out in this series, which is not yet complete.

Published Source Materials. Henry Steele Commager, *Documents of American History* (New York: Appleton-Century-Crofts, 1958) is the standard one-volume collection. Three source collections in American economic history are: Ernest L. Bogart and C. M. Thompson, *Readings in the Economic History of the United States* (New York: Longmans, 1916); Felix Flugel and H. U. Faulkner, *Readings in the Economic and Social History of the United States* (New York: Harper, 1929), and Guy C. Callender, *Selections from the Economic History of the United States, 1785–1860* (Boston: Ginn, 1909). Louis M. Hacker, *The Shaping of the American Tradition* (2 vols., New York: Columbia University Press, 1947) is a well-chosen selection of sources with helpful comments by the editor. N. S. B. Gras and H. Larson, *Casebook in American Business History* (New York: Crofts, 1939) has business history sources. Joseph T. Lambie and Richard V. Clemence, *Economic Change in America: Readings in the Economic History of the United States* (Harrisburg, Pa.: Stackpole, 1954) is a collection of significant articles since about 1940 from various economic history journals. The leading magazines taken by business leaders a century ago contain a wealth of material. These were *Niles Weekly Register* (Baltimore, 1811–1849); *Hunt's Merchant and Commercial Review* (New York, 1839–1870); and *DeBow's Review* (New Orleans, 1847–1869).

Encyclopedias. *The Encyclopedia of Social Sciences* (15 vols., New York: Macmillan, 1930–1935) contains many articles on American economic history topics, each with a short bibliography. James T. Adams, *Dictionary of American History* (5 vols. and index vol., New York: Scribner, 1940) carries brief explanations of major laws, events, catch phrases, etc., in American history. Each article has a bibliographical note. Two handy one-volume references are: Gordon Carruth and associates, *The Encyclopedia of American Facts and*

Dates (New York: Crowell, 1956) and Richard B. Morris, *Encyclopedia of American History* (New York: Harper, 1953).

Biographical Dictionaries. Allen Johnson, *Dictionary of American Biography* (21 vols., New York: Scribner, 1928–1944) is the standard reference on outstanding Americans. No living person may be listed. *Who's Who in America* (Chicago: A. Marquis, biannually since 1899) contains biographical facts on tens of thousands of living Americans. *Who Was Who in America*, vol. I, 1897–1942 (Chicago: Marquis, 1943) and vol. II, 1943–1950 (1950) give biographical data on persons now deceased and formerly listed in *Who's Who in America*. It has many names not distinguished enough or not deceased early enough to be listed in the *Dictionary of American Biography*.

Statistical Sources. The most important single source for the American economic historian is the Federal census, which has been taken every ten years since 1790. At first the census takers did little more than count heads but as time passed they gathered all kinds of other information. In recent decades the census has run to dozens of volumes and has covered a wide range of topics such as manufacturing, agriculture, housing, internal commerce, etc. W. Stull Holt, *The Bureau of the Census: Its History, Activities and Organization* (Washington: Brookings, 1929) tells what each new census added. Up to 1930 there was an abstract or compendium for each census, but the *Statistical Abstract of the United States* (Washington, annually since 1878) has now replaced these and is the most important single volume statistical source. Bureau of the Census, *Historical Statistics of the United States, 1789–1945* (Washington, 1949) and *Continuation to 1952 of Historical Statistics* (Washington, 1954) contain series of value to historians but no longer carried in the *Statistical Abstract*. Many of the statistical tables in the monthly *Survey of Current Business* (Washington) continue those in the *Statistical Abstract* down to three months back. Two early forerunners of the *Statistical Abstract*, in use over a century ago, are Adam Seybert, *Statistical Annals of the United States* (1818) and Timothy Pitkin, *Statistical View of American Commerce* (several editions, 1817–1835). For population estimates before 1790, see Evarts B. Greene and V. Harrington, *American Population before the Federal Census of 1790* (New York: Columbia University Press, 1932). Arthur H. Cole, *Wholesale Commodity Prices in the United States, 1700–1861* (Cambridge: Harvard University Press, 1938) is the authority on early price statistics. National Industrial Conference Board, *The Economic Almanac* (New York, annually since 1940) is next in importance only to the Bureau of the Census publications. W. N. Peach and Walter Krause, *Basic Data of the American Economy* (Homewood, Ill.: Irwin, 1955) is a graphic as well as tabular presentation of some outstanding statistical series. J. Frederic Dewhurst and associates, *America's Needs and Resources: A New Survey* (New York: Twentieth Century Fund, 1955) is the second attempt to use past statistical trends to estimate future needs. Willard Thorp and Wesley Mitchell, *Business Annals, 1790–1925* (New York: National Bureau of Economic Research, 1926) gives the business conditions for each year in many nations for more than a century.

Edwin T. Coman, *Sources of Business Information* (New York: Prentice-Hall, 1949) tells where statistics on a wide variety of subjects may be found.

Most large trade associations, such as the automobile manufacturers, insurance companies, etc., publish fact books annually full of pertinent data on their industry. The Board of Governors of the Federal Reserve System, *Banking and Monetary Statistics* (Washington, 1943) is a summary of statistics that appeared monthly in the *Federal Reserve Bulletin* (Washington, 1914 to 1941). Other specialized statistical publications are Department of Agriculture, *Agricultural Statistics* (Washington, annually); U.S. Department of Labor, *Handbook of Labor Statistics, 1950* (Washington, 1951) and *The Monthly Labor Review* (Washington) for current figures; U.S. Department of Commerce, *Foreign Commerce Yearbook* (Washington, irregularly); Bureau of Mines, *Minerals Yearbook* (Washington, irregularly), and the Tax Foundation, *Facts and Figures on Government Finance* (New York: Tax Foundation, annually). For key current figures, see Council of Economic Advisers, *Economic Indicators* (Washington, monthly).

Learned Journals. The chief learned journal for American economic historians is the *Journal of Economic History,* quarterly since 1941. Of almost equal importance is the *Bulletin of the Business Historical Society,* published since 1927, now renamed the *Business History Review.* An older journal, the *Journal of Economic and Business History,* lasted four years, from 1928 to 1932, but has many good articles. When economic historians have not had their own journals, they have relied on more general publications such as the following: *The American Historical Review,* since 1895; *The Mississippi Valley Historical Review,* since 1914; some of the better historical society publications in the individual states; journals of regional historical associations in the South or on the Pacific coast; *Agricultural History,* since 1927; *The American Economic Review,* since 1908; *The Quarterly Journal of Economics,* since 1886; *The Southern Economic Journal,* since 1933; *The Journal of Finance,* since 1946; *The Industrial and Labor Relations Review,* since 1947; and *The Journal of Political Economy,* since 1892. It is in these journals that scholars often first publish the results of their research. Such journals also generally carry reviews of major books in economic history soon after they appear.

Recent Events. Person's Index, *Facts on File* (New York, annually since 1941) is a weekly condensation of current events, handy for tracking down recent happenings. The student can also use the *New York Times Index* (since 1913), which will lead him to that newspaper's account at the time of the event.

Atlases. Charles O. Paullin, *Atlas of the Historical Geography of the United States* (Washington: Carnegie, 1932) is the best American economic history atlas. The index is in the center; black numbers refer to map plates. Clifford L. Lord and Elizabeth H. Lord, *Historical Atlas of the United States* (New York: Holt, 1944) is an excellent, inexpensive atlas. Clinton Lewis and J. D. Campbell, *The American Oxford Atlas* (New York: Oxford, 1951) has fine physical maps.

Pictorial Histories. Ralph Gabriel, *The Pageant of America* (15 vols., New Haven: Yale University Press, 1926–1929) has five volumes on economic history topics such as agriculture, transportation, commerce, manufacturing, and the Westward Movement. Although somewhat elementary and now dated, it is still the best pictorial American economic history. James T. Adams, *Album of*

American History (5 vols., New York: Scribner, 1944–1949) is more recent but has less economic history than the *Pageant*. There are many good specialized pictorial histories and more are constantly appearing. A few examples are: Oliver LaFarge, *A Pictorial History of the American Indian* (New York: Crown, 1956); Bernard DeVoto, *Across the Wide Missouri* (Boston: Houghton Mifflin, 1947) on life on the Great Plains in the mid-nineteenth century; Joseph H. Jackson, *Gold Rush Album* (New York: Scribner, 1949); John Durant and Alice Durant, *Pictorial History of American Ships* (New York: Barnes, 1953); Lucius Beebe, *Hear the Train Blow* (New York: Dutton, 1952) on railroads; Paul H. Giddens, *Early Days of Oil* (Princeton: Princeton University Press, 1948); Mitchell Wilson, *American Science and Invention* (New York: Simon and Schuster, 1954); and John Kouwenhoven, *The Columbia Historical Portrait of New York* (New York: Doubleday, 1953). The student can also find pictures in *Harpers Weekly* and *Leslie's Illustrated Weekly* of the latter nineteenth century and in *Life* magazine for the past generation.

Historical Novels. Ernest L. Bogart's list of historical novels having a bearing on economic history was published in *History Teachers' Magazine*, vol. 8 (September, 1917), pp. 226–231. A. T. Dickinson, Jr., *American Historical Fiction* (New York: Scarecrow Press, 1958) carries an annotated list of 1,224 novels since 1917. See, too, the list in Handlin's *Harvard Guide*, pp. 238f.

THE WESTWARD MOVEMENT

Westward Movement. The spirit and significance of the Westward Movement are best interpreted by Frederick J. Turner, *The Frontier in American History* (New York: Holt, 1921). Chapter 1 is a classic. Frederick L. Paxson, a student of Turner's, gives a detailed account of many aspects of the Westward Movement in his *History of the American Frontier, 1763–1893* (Boston: Houghton Mifflin, 1924). A more recent treatment, also in the Turner tradition, is Ray Billington, *Westward Expansion* (New York: Macmillan, 1949). His Chapter 1 explains the significance of Turner. Charles A. Beard and Mary Beard in their classic, *Rise of American Civilization* (New York: Macmillan, 1927), especially Chapters 9, 11, 13, 19, and 24, paint the picture of westward expansion in broad strokes.

Geographical Influences. Ellen C. Semple and C. Jones in *American History and Its Geographic Conditions* (Boston: Houghton Mifflin, 1933) show how geography shaped the course of the Westward Movement.

Contemporary Accounts of the West. Contemporaries too wrote colorfully of the Westward Movement. One of the most valuable is Timothy Flint's *Recollections of Ten Years' Residence in the Valley of the Mississippi* (Boston: Cummings Hilliard, 1826) and *History and Geography of the Mississippi Valley* (2 vols., Cincinnati: Flint and Lincoln, 1828; 2d ed., 1832). Turner drew generously from J. M. Peck, *A Guide for Emigrants* (Boston: 1831, 1837). Morris Birkbeck in his *Notes on a Journey in America* (Philadelphia: 1817) and *Letters from Illinois* (London: 1818) has given some of the most readable accounts of pioneer living. Reuben G. Thwaites (ed.), in his *Early*

Western Travels (32 vols., Cleveland: 1904–1907), has collected many colorful contemporary accounts of Western travel and exploration. Also notable is his *Journals of Lewis and Clark* (7 vols., Cleveland: 1904–1907).

Middle West. R. Carlyle Buley has written a very full and detailed account of pioneering days in the Middle West in *The Old Northwest* (2 vols., Bloomington: Indiana University Press, 1951). Governor Thomas Ford of Illinois wrote a detailed *History of Illinois* (New York: 1854) that gives a clear picture of life in his day. Much research has been devoted to the early life of Abraham Lincoln. He lived the life of a pioneer in the Middle West of the 1830s and 1840s. Carl Sandburg, although more a poet than a historian, has caught the spirit of that life in his *Abraham Lincoln: The Prairie Years* (New York: Blue Ribbon, 1926). Lincoln lived for seven years in the frontier shopping community of New Salem, which lasted only a decade but has since been reconstructed. Benjamin Thomas accurately describes life there in a little book entitled *Lincoln's New Salem* (Springfield, Ill.: Abraham Lincoln Association, 1934). J. W. Pratt, *Expansionists of 1812* (New York: 1925) shows the Westward Movement into the Middle West to be a chief cause of the War of 1812.

Great Plains and Far West. Katherine Coman has written one of the best accounts of the settlement of the Plains and Mountain regions in her *Economic Beginnings of the Far West* (2 vols., New York: Macmillan, 1930). Another comprehensive study of the settlement of the West is Cardinal Goodwin, *The Trans-Mississippi West, 1803–1853* (New York: Appleton, 1922). Constance L. Skinner, in *Adventurers of Oregon* (New Haven: Yale University Press, 1920), gives a brief account of the early settlement of that region. For the post-Civil War period the story of the settlement of the plains is well told by Walter P. Webb in *The Great Plains* (Boston: Ginn, 1931). A detailed account of life on the treeless northern plains is found in Everett Dick, *The Sod-house Frontier, 1854–1890* (New York: Appleton-Century, 1937).

California. Crossing the Plains to California is described in Joseph E. Ware, *The Emigrant's Guide to California* (St. Louis: 1849, and reprinted, Princeton: Princeton University Press, 1932). This was the guidebook used by tens of thousands. Stewart E. White, *The Forty-niners* (New Haven: Yale University Press, 1918) has a readable account of the times. In more recent years Irene Paden has retraced the steps of the forty-niners and presented much of the lore of those days with great charm in *Wake of the Prairie Schooner* (New York: Macmillan, 1945). Walker D. Wyman has compiled a representative collection of *California Emigrant Letters* (New York: Bookman Associates, 1925). Pioneering days in California, including the gold rush, are described in R. G. Cleland, *A History of California* (New York: Macmillan, 1923).

Indians. No account of the Westward Movement would be complete without some mention of the Indians who barred the way, defending their own less advanced civilization. Clark Wissler, *The American Indian* (New York: Oxford, 1938) is a good one-volume account of Indian culture. A reference on all aspects of Indian life and customs is Frederick W. Hodge, *Handbook of American Indians North of Mexico* (2 vols., Washington, 1907). Francis Parkman, *The Oregon Trail* (New York: Scribner, 1924) is a classic account of early contacts between whites and Indians in the Northwest. David Lavender,

Bent's Fort (New York: Doubleday, 1954) depicts the conflict of pioneers and Indians in the far Southwest. Another colorful account of the Indians, with many pictures, is Bernard De Voto, *Across the Wide Missouri* (Boston: Houghton Mifflin, 1947).

Public Lands. The standard work on the public lands is Thomas Donaldson, *The Public Domain, Its History with Statistics* (Washington: Government Printing Office, 1884). All authorities quote this tome. A later classic is Benjamin H. Hibbard, *A History of Public Land Policies* (New York: Macmillan, 1924). A more recent comprehensive study is R. M. Robbins, *Our Landed Heritage: The Public Domain, 1776–1936* (Princeton: Princeton University Press, 1942). Paul Gates, in his article, "The Homestead Act in an Incongruous Land System," *American Historical Review* (July, 1936), and also in *Frontier Landlords and Pioneer Tenants* (Ithaca: Cornell University Press, 1945), deals with the large operations of land speculators. George Sakolski in *The Great American Land Bubble* (New York: Harper, 1932) catches the spirit of frontier speculation. The story of how one railroad disposed of its lands is told in Richard C. Overton, *Burlington West* (Cambridge: Harvard University Press, 1941). A convincing defense of the railroads by R. S. Henry, "The Railroad Land Grant Legend in American History Texts," appeared in the *Mississippi Valley Historical Review* in September, 1945. It stirred considerable controversy, which will be found in the March and June, 1946, issues. One of the best short accounts of railroad land grants is W. S. Greever, "A Comparison of Railroad Land-grant Policies," *Agricultural History* (April, 1951).

Safety-valve Theory. Turner's writings and those of his disciples led some to think that free or cheap land raised wages in this country and also that it served as a safety valve in time of depression. The best attack on this second theory is by Fred A. Shannon, "A Post Mortem on the Labor Safety-valve Theory," *Agricultural History* (January, 1945). The best defense, by an economist, is Norman J. Simler, "The Safety-valve Doctrine Re-evaluated," which appeared also in *Agricultural History* (October, 1958).

Frontier Industries. Intimately connected with the Westward Movement were such pioneer industries as fur trapping, cattle raising, and mining. On the fur trade, H. M. Chittenden, *The American Fur Trade of the Far West* (3 vols., New York: 1903) is outstanding. A short comprehensive study is Arthur H. Clark, *The Fur Trade and Early Western Exploration* (Cleveland: Arthur Clark, 1929). Dale Morgan has written a fine biography of one of the famous early fur trappers and mountain men in his *Jedidiah Smith and the Opening of the West* (Indianapolis: Bobbs-Merrill, 1953). The classical contemporary account of the post-Civil War cattle business is Joseph McCoy, *Historic Sketches of the Cattle Trade* (Washington: The Rare Book Shop, 1932). On mining see George D. Lyman, *The Saga of the Comstock Lode* (New York: Scribner, 1934).

Conservation. An epilogue to the Westward Movement was the realization that the land and natural resources were more limited than supposed. Charles R. Van Hise and Loomis Havemeyer in their *Conservation of Our Natural Resources* (New York: Macmillan, 1937) trace the history of the conservation movement. A later treatment is A. E. Parkins and J. R. Whitaker, *Our Natural Resources and Their Conservation* (New York: Wiley, 1939). Gifford Pinchot wrote an autobiography, *Breaking New Ground* (New York: Harcourt, Brace, 1947). A conservationist's view of the lumber shortage problem is Arthur H. Carhart, *Timber in Your Life* (Philadelphia: Lippincott, 1955). William J. Trimble wrote a provocative article on "The Influence of the Passing of the Public Lands" in *The Atlantic Monthly* (June, 1914); he explains some of the economic aspects of conservation in an understandable way.

TRANSPORTATION AND COMMUNICATIONS

General. No recent, comprehensive general history of transportation exists. Some older works which are still good are Balthasar H. Meyer (ed.), *History of Transportation in the United States before 1860* (Washington: Carnegie Institute, 1917), written by Caroline MacGill; Seymour Dunbar, *History of Travel in America* (4 vols., Indianapolis: Bobbs-Merrill, 1915); Archer B. Hulbert, *Historic Highways of America* (16 vols., Cleveland: A. H. Clark, 1902–1905) and *Paths of Inland Commerce* (New Haven: Yale University Press, 1920); and Malcolm Kier, *The March of Commerce* (New Haven: Yale University Press, 1927). George Rogers Taylor, *The Transportation Revolution, 1815–1860* (New York: Rinehart, 1951) is a general economic history with excellent chapters on transportation before 1860.

Early Roads. The general works all discuss early roads. Two famous roads are the subjects of Robert L. Kincaid, *The Wilderness Road* (Indianapolis: Bobbs-Merrill, 1947) and Philip D. Jordan, *The National Road* (Indianapolis: Bobbs-Merrill, 1948). W. Turrentine Jackson describes early Western roads in *Wagon Roads West: A Study of Federal Road Surveys and Construction in the Trans-Mississippi West, 1846–1869* (Berkeley: University of California Press, 1952).

Inland Waterways. Before the age of steam, river currents supplied motive power for flatboats and keelboats. Leland D. Baldwin shows the importance of this in *The Keelboat Age on Western Waters* (Pittsburgh: University of Pittsburgh Press, 1941). Excellent accounts of steamboats are found in Louis Hunter, *Steamboats on the Western Rivers* (Cambridge: Harvard University Press, 1949) and Charles H. Ambler, *A History of Transportation in the Ohio Valley* (Glendale, Calif.: A. H. Clark, 1932). The canal era is portrayed by Alvin F. Harlow in *Old Towpaths* (New York: Appleton, 1926). Archer B. Hulbert devotes two entire volumes of his *Historic Highways of America* to canals; volumes XIII and XIV are entitled *The Great American Canals* (Cleveland: A. H. Clark, 1904). The rise of the Great Lakes in inland transportation is set forth in James C. Mills, *Our Inland Seas: Their Shipping and Commerce for Three Centuries* (Chicago: A. C. McClurg, 1910).

Ocean Shipping. Samuel Eliot Morison depicts the golden era of sailing vessels in a literary masterpiece, *The Maritime History of Massachusetts, 1783–1860* (Boston: Houghton Mifflin, 1921). Robert G. Albion, *Square-Riggers on Schedule* (Princeton: Princeton University Press, 1938) and Carl C. Cutler, *Greyhounds of the Sea* (New York: Putnam, 1930) are both classics. The general history from the Revolutionary War to World War I is best told by John G. B. Hutchins in *The American Maritime Industries and Public Policy, 1789–1914* (Cambridge: Harvard University Press, 1941).

Railroads. The greatest body of historical literature on transportation deals with railroads, yet there is no recent single work on the subject. The first sixty years of railroads are covered in Lewis Henry Haney, *A Congressional History of Railways in the United States to 1850* (Madison: University of Wisconsin Press, 1908) and *A Congressional History of Railways in the United States, 1850–1887* (Madison: University of Wisconsin Press, 1910). Another older history is Slason Thompson, *A Short History of American Railroads* (New York: Appleton, 1925). A brief but meritorious book is George Rogers Taylor and Irene Neu, *The American Railroad Network, 1861–1890* (Cambridge: Harvard University Press, 1956); the authors analyze the problems of developing an integrated rail system from many diverse segments.

Some regional railway studies which help clarify the national picture are George W. Baker, *The Formation of the New England Railroad System* (Cambridge: Harvard University Press, 1937); Edward C. Kirkland, *Men, Cities, and Transportation: A Study in New England History* (2 vols., Cambridge: Harvard University Press, 1948); Robert C. Black, *Railroads of the Confederacy* (Chapel Hill: University of North Carolina Press, 1952); John F. Stover, *The Railroads of the South, 1865–1900* (Chapel Hill: University of North Carolina Press, 1955); and Robert E. Riegel, *The Story of Western Railroads* (New York: Macmillan, 1926).

Strong and colorful personalities stand out in the railway industry. Many of these people appear in the pages of John Moody, *The Railroad Builders* (New Haven: Yale University Press, 1919) and in Matthew P. Josephson's derogatory story, *The Robber Barons: The Great American Capitalists, 1861–1901* (New York: Harcourt, Brace, 1934). A more objective treatment of railway executives is Thomas C. Cochran, *Railroad Leaders, 1845–1890: The Business Mind in Action* (Cambridge: Harvard University Press, 1953), in which the author analyzes correspondence and notes of sixty railway men in an effort to determine why they made certain decisions. The biographies of some of the great railroad financiers and builders contain much railway history. Some good ones are Wheaton J. Lane, *Commodore Vanderbilt: An Epic of the Steam Age* (New York: Knopf, 1942); Julius Grodinsky, *Jay Gould, His Business Career, 1867–1892* (Philadelphia: University of Pennsylvania Press, 1957); James Blaine Hedges, *Henry Villard and the Railways of the Northwest* (New Haven: Yale University Press, 1930); Henrietta Larson, *Jay Cooke, Private Banker* (Cambridge: Harvard University Press, 1936); and Joseph G. Pyle, *The Life of James J. Hill* (New York: Doubleday Page, 1916). Much of the history of railway finance can be gleaned from the pages of Alfred D. Chandler, *Henry Varnham Poor, Business Editor, Analyst, and Reformer* (Cambridge: Harvard University Press, 1956).

There are numerous company histories which can be read with profit. Among these are Edward Hungerford, *The Story of the Baltimore & Ohio Railroad, 1827–1927* (2 vols., New York: Putnam, 1928); Alvin F. Harlow, *The Road of the Century* (New York: Creative Age, 1947), which is the account of the New York Central; and Nelson Trottman, *History of the Union Pacific* (New York: Ronald, 1923).

On the question of public aid to railroads, the reader should consult the Federal Coordinator of Transportation, *Public Aids to Railroads* (4 vols., Washington: Government Printing Office, 1938–1940). A special study of public aid is Harry H. Pierce, *Railroads of New York: A Study of Government Aid, 1826–1875* (Cambridge: Harvard University Press, 1953). The pioneer work in how a railroad disposed of its Federal land grant is Paul Wallace Gates, *The Illinois Central and Its Colonization Work* (Cambridge: Harvard University Press, 1934). Another outstanding study of this type is Richard C. Overton, *Burlington West: A Colonization History of the Burlington Railroad* (Cambridge: Harvard University Press, 1941).

Early abusive practices in railroad operations are seen in Charles Francis Adams, *Chapters of Erie, and Other Essays* (Boston: J. R. Osgood and Co., 1871) and in Oscar Lewis, *The Big Four: The Story of Huntington, Stanford, Hopkins, and Crocker, and of the Building of the Central Pacific* (New York: Knopf, 1938). A specific type of abuse is described and analyzed in Julius Grodinsky, *The Iowa Pool: A Study in Railroad Competition, 1870–1884* (Chicago: University of Chicago Press, 1950). The government regulation which followed these abuses has been set forth by Emory R. Johnson in *Government Regulation of Transportation Agencies* (New York: Appleton-Century, 1938). The operations of the Interstate Commerce Act of 1887 and its amendments, plus the law cases involving the Interstate Commerce Commission, are best covered in I. L. Sharfman, *The Interstate Commerce Commission* (4 vols., New York: Commonwealth Fund, 1931–1937). More recent aspects of regulation can be found in D. Phillip Locklin, *Economics of Transportation* (4th ed., Homewood, Ill.: Irwin, 1954) and in Stuart Daggett, *Principles of Inland Transportation* (4th ed., New York: Harper, 1955).

The Railroads' Competitors. An excellent analysis of the competitive situation in American transportation is found in the books by Locklin and Daggett listed above. Also helpful is Harold G. Moulton, *The American Transportation Problem* (Washington: Brookings, 1933). For a history of pipelines, the best book is Arthur Menzies Johnson, *The Development of American Petroleum Pipelines: A Study in Private Enterprise and Public Policy, 1862–1906* (Ithaca: Cornell University Press, 1956). A recent book on highway transportation is Merrill Denison, *The Power to Go: The Story of the Automotive Industry* (Garden City: Doubleday, 1956). Also the official history of the Ford Motor Company traces the development of the industry through one of the leading automobile producers. This history is by Allan Nevins and Frank Ernest Hill, and the first two volumes are *Ford: The Times, the Man, the Company* (New York: Scribner, 1954) and *Ford: Expansion and Challenge, 1915–1933* (New York: Scribner, 1957). Henry Ladd Smith traces the growth of air transportation in *Airways: The History of Commercial Aviation in the United States* (New York: Knopf, 1942), as does John H. Frederick in *Commercial Air Transportation* (Homewood, Ill.: Irwin, 1955).

Communications. Older books on communications are Alvin F. Harlow, *Old Wires and New Waves: The History of the Telegraph, Telephone and Wireless*

(New York: Appleton-Century, 1936) and Malcolm Keir, *The March of Commerce* (New Haven: Yale University Press, 1927). The early history of the telegraph industry is found in Robert L. Thompson, *Wiring a Continent: The History of the Telegraph Industry in the United States, 1832–1866* (Princeton: Princeton University Press, 1947).

AGRICULTURE

General. The best general survey, although brief, is Everett E. Edwards, "American Agriculture—the First 300 Years," *Yearbook of Agriculture, 1940* (Washington, 1940). An older account is Albert H. Sanford, *The Story of Agriculture in the United States* (Boston: Heath, 1916). Louis Bernard Schmidt and Earle Dudley Ross (eds.), *Readings in the Economic History of American Agriculture* (New York: Macmillan, 1925) is arranged to give insights into most aspects of agricultural history. O. E. Baker (compiler), *Atlas of American Agriculture* (Washington: Government Printing Office, 1936) is a highly useful geographic guide to accompany these general works.

Period histories up to 1900 are outstanding. The colonial and pre-Civil War eras have been covered in an exhaustive manner in two outstanding works: Percy Wells Bidwell and John I. Falconer, *History of Agriculture in the Northern United States, 1620–1860* (New York: Peter Smith, 1941) and Lewis C. Gray, *History of Agriculture in the Southern United States to 1860* (2 vols., New York: Peter Smith, 1941). Equally adequate is Fred A. Shannon, *The Farmer's Last Frontier: Agriculture, 1860–1897* (New York: Farrar & Rinehart, 1945). The same author is preparing a history of farming since 1897, but at present no general history of that period exists. Ronald L. Mighell presents a statistical view of farming since 1900 in *American Agriculture: Its Structure and Place in the Economy* (New York: Wiley, 1955). Also, a recent popularly written book, useful for showing some of the changes since 1920, is John H. Davis and Kenneth Henshaw, *Farmer in a Business Suit* (New York: Simon and Schuster, 1957).

Regional Studies. In addition to Gray's *History of Agriculture in the Southern United States to 1860* (mentioned above), Avery O. Craven, *Soil Exhaustion as a Factor in the Agricultural History of Virginia and Maryland* (Urbana: University of Illinois Press, 1926) throws much light on practices of progressive farmers of the upper South. Ulrich B. Phillips, *Life and Labor in the Old South* (Boston: Little, Brown, 1929) describes plantation agriculture in the Deep South before the Civil War. A recent extensive and highly readable study of cotton farming is David L. Cohn, *The Life and Times of King Cotton* (New York: Oxford University Press, 1956). Readers interested in the technical aspects of cotton should consult Harry Bates Brown and Jacob Osborn Ware, *Cotton* (3d ed., New York: McGraw-Hill, 1958); this book also contains a brief history of cotton. Sugar cane and tobacco production are best covered in J. Carlyle Sitterson, *Sugar Country: The Cane Sugar Iudustry in the South, 1753–1950* (Lexington: University of Kentucky Press, 1953); Joseph C. Robert, *The Story of Tobacco in America* (New York: Knopf, 1949); and the same author's *The Tobacco Kingdom* (Durham: Duke University Press, 1938).

The early history of the Middle West is the subject of R. Carlyle Buley, *The Old Northwest: Pioneer Period, 1815–1840* (2 vols., Bloomington: Indiana University Press, 1951). Much agricultural history is included in Everett Dick, *The Sod-house Frontier, 1854–1890* (New York: Appleton-Century, 1937) and in Walter Prescott Webb, *The Great Plains* (Boston: Ginn, 1931). Further treatment of the Great Plains' farm problems appears in a more recent book, Mary W. Hargreaves, *Dry Farming in the Northern Great Plains, 1900–1925* (Cambridge: Harvard University Press, 1957). Excellent specialized studies of wheat farming are James C. Malin, *Winter Wheat in the Golden Belt of Kansas* (Lawrence: University of Kansas Press, 1944) and Harold E. Briggs, "Early Bonanza Farming in the Red River Valley of the North," *Agricultural History*, vol. 6 (1932).

Livestock Industry. The standard work on the livestock industry is Rudolf Alexander Clemen, *The American Livestock and Meat Industry* (New York: Ronald, 1923). Two of the best books on the range-cattle industry are Ernest S. Osgood, *The Day of the Cattlemen* (Minneapolis: University of Minnesota Press, 1929) and Edward Everett Dale, *The Range Cattle Industry* (Norman: University of Oklahoma Press, 1930). A recent book, unexcelled for its literary quality, is Mari Sandoz, *The Cattlemen* (New York: Hastings House, 1958). The sheep industry receives its best treatment in Charles Wayland Towne and Edward Norris Wentworth, *Shepherd's Empire* (Norman: University of Oklahoma Press, 1945).

Land Tenure and Capital. Most of the general histories contain material on land tenure, and Shannon's *Farmer's Last Frontier* is especially good. Charles L. Stewart gives the subject full treatment in *Land Tenure in the United States, with Special Reference to Illinois* (Urbana: University of Illinois Press, 1916). Carey McWilliams, *Ill Fares the Land* (Boston: Little, Brown, 1942) discusses farm tenancy in the Southwest. The writings of Paul Wallace Gates on Federal land policy and its effects on land tenure are best on the growth of farm tenancy; among Gates's numerous contributions are *Frontier Landlords and Pioneer Tenants* (Ithaca: Cornell University Press, 1945) and "The Homestead Act in an Incongruous Land System," *American Historical Review*, vol. 41 (1936). Another outstanding book which deals with a different aspect of land tenure is Allan C. Bogue, *Money at Interest: The Farm Mortgage on the Middle Border* (Ithaca: Cornell University Press, 1955). A recent technical study examines the role of capital in farming: Alvin S. Tostlebe, *Capital in Agriculture: Its Formation and Financing since 1870* (Princeton: Princeton University Press, 1957).

Farm Technology. The broad sweep of farm technology is presented in Earle D. Ross, "Retardation in Farm Technology before the Power Age" and William L. Cavert, "The Technological Revolution in Agriculture, 1910–1955," both in *Agricultural History*, vol. 30 (1956). Leo Rogin, *The Introduction of Farm Machinery in Its Relation to the Productivity of Labor* (Berkeley: University of California Press, 1931) contains a history of most of the important farm machines and is a meticulous study of the impact of implements on the output of human labor. The best treatment of steam power in agriculture is Reynold M. Wik, *Steam Power on the American Farm* (Philadelphia: University of Pennsylvania Press, 1953). For the development of the reaper, William T. Hutchison, *Cyrus Hall McCormick* (2 vols., New York: Appleton-Century, 1935) is excellent. Cotton-harvesting machinery is the principal subject of James H. Street, *The New Revolution in the Cotton Economy: Mechanization and Its Consequences* (Chapel Hill: University of North Carolina Press, 1957).

Agricultural Education. A. C. True, *A History of Agricultural Education in the United States, 1785–1925* (Washington: Government Printing Office, 1929) and the same author's *A History of Agricultural Experimentation and Research in the United States, 1607–1925, Including a History of the United States Department of Agriculture* (Washington: Government Printing Office, 1937) are the basic works on the subject. A monumental study is Henry C. and Anne Dewees Taylor, *The Story of Agricultural Economics in the United States, 1840–1932* (Ames: Iowa State College Press, 1952). Edward Danforth Eddy, Jr., looks at agricultural colleges in *Colleges for Our Land and Our Time: The Land-grant Idea in American Education* (New York: Harper, 1957). Two scholarly studies which show the dissemination of agricultural knowledge by the press are Albert Lowther Demaree, *The American Agricultural Press, 1819–1860* (New York: Columbia University Press, 1941), and John T. Schlebecker and Andrew W. Hopkins, *A History of Dairy Journalism in the United States, 1810 to 1950* (Madison: University of Wisconsin Press, 1957).

Agricultural Organizations and Farmers' Movements. General histories of agricultural organizations and farm protest movements are Edward Wiest, *Agricultural Organization in the United States* (Lexington: University of Kentucky Press, 1923) and Carl C. Taylor, *The Farmers' Movement, 1620–1920* (New York: American Book, 1953). The standard history of the Grange is Solon Justice Buck, *The Granger Movement: A Study of Agricultural Organization and Its Political, Economic and Social Manifestations, 1870–1880* (Cambridge: Harvard University Press, 1913) while John D. Hicks, *The Populist Revolt: A History of the Farmer's Alliance and the People's Party* (Minneapolis: University of Minnesota Press, 1931) is outstanding for the 1880 to 1900 era. Hicks joined Theodore Saloutos in continuing the study through the Great Depression in *Agricultural Discontent in the Middle-West, 1900–1939* (Madison: University of Wisconsin Press, 1951). James H. Shideler makes a penetrating analysis of the post-World War I scene in his excellent book, *Farm Crisis, 1919–1923* (Berkeley: University of California Press, 1957) and Gilbert C. Fite examines the role of one of the leaders for agricultural legislation in the 1920s in *George N. Peek and the Fight for Farm Parity* (Norman: University of Oklahoma Press, 1954).

Agricultural Policy. The highly controversial nature of Federal farm policy has aroused the interest of countless writers. Readers must approach most books on the subject with extreme caution. A generally objective work is Murray Reed Benedict, *Farm Policies of the United States, 1790–1950* (New York: Twentieth Century Fund, 1953). A sequel to this study is Benedict's *Can We Solve the Farm Problem? An Analysis of Federal Aid to Agriculture* (New

York: Twentieth Century Fund, 1955). Harold G. Halcrow employs more economic analysis than history in *Agricultural Policy of the United States* (Englewood Cliffs, N.J.: Prentice-Hall, 1953), as does Theodore W. Schultz in *Agriculture in an Unstable Economy* (New York: McGraw-Hill Book Co., 1945). Lauren Soth, *Farm Trouble in an Age of Plenty* (Princeton: Princeton University Press, 1957) is probably the clearest nontechnical explanation of the causes of the mid-twentieth century farm problem and possible solutions. Willard W. Cochrane in *Farm Prices: Myth and Reality* (Minneapolis: University of Minnesota Press, 1958) argues through historical presentation that unstable farm prices and incomes are normal, not abnormal, conditions for agriculture; he advocates a government policy which recognizes this situation.

MANUFACTURING

General Sources. There is a tremendous amount of material on manufacturing in the census, early state papers, and other government publications. Alexander Hamilton's *Report on Manufactures* (1791) is one of the first and most famous studies of this topic. Hamilton's capable assistant, Tench Coxe, made a study on the 1810 census of manufactures, which is printed in *American Finance State Papers*, vol. II (Washington, 1814), pp. 666–812. Albert Gallatin wrote a *Report on Manufactures* in this same volume. Another mine of information is Louis McLane, *Report on Manufactures* (House doc. no. 308, 22nd Cong., 1st Sess., 2 vols., Washington, 1833). The introductions to the census volumes on manufacturing of the 1860, 1880, and 1900 censuses are all helpful. E. D. Durand, director of the 1910 census, wrote a book, *American Industry and Commerce* (New York, 1930), that is based largely on census material. In 1904 and 1914 there was a census of manufacturing taken in the middle of the decade, and from 1921 to 1937 a census of manufacturing was taken every two years. That ceased with World War II, resumed in 1947, and ceased again. For the World War I period Bernard Baruch, *American Industry in the War* (New York: Prentice-Hall, 1941) is the authority. For World War II consult the War Production Board's *Wartime Production Achievements* (Washington, 1945).

General. The most complete work on the history of American manufacturing is Victor D. Clark's *History of Manufactures in the United States, 1607–1929* (3 vols., New York: McGraw-Hill, 1929). It is one of the series published by the Carnegie Institution on the economic history of the United States. Older than Clark, and not as well-organized but rich in material, is J. Leander Bishop's *A History of American Manufactures from 1608 to 1860* (3 vols., Philadelphia, 1866). Malcolm Keir, *Industries of America: Manufacturing* (New York: Ronald, 1928) is a dated but good one-volume history of manufacturing. Another one is James B. Walker, *The Epic of American Industry* (New York: Harper, 1949). A fine treatment of modern industry is E. B. Alderfer and H. E. Michl, *Economics of American Industry* (New York: McGraw-Hill, 1957). Likewise good on modern industry is J. G. Glover and W. B. Cornell, *The Development of American Industries: Their Economic Significance* (New York: Prentice-Hall, 1951).

Home Industry. Colonists and other pioneers did much of their manufacturing at home with simple materials. Marion N. Rawson, *Of the Earth Earthy: How Our Fathers Dwelt upon and Wooed the Earth* (New York: Dutton, 1937) tells of their methods. Her *Little Old Mills* (New York: Dutton, 1935) is likewise very readable. Jared van Wagenen, Jr., *The Golden Age of Homespun* (Ithaca: Cornell University Press, 1953) is in a similar vein.

Textiles. The industrial revolution in one nation after another has begun with cotton textiles. Rolla M. Tryon, *Household Manufactures in the United States, 1640–1860* (Chicago: University of Chicago, 1917) tells of the beginnings of clothmaking in America. George S. White, *Memoir of Samuel Slater, the Father of American Manufacturers Connected with a History of the Rise and Progress of the Cotton Manufacture in England and America* (Philadelphia, 1836) is an early account of the first successful cotton factory in America. Caroline Ware, *The Early New England Cotton Manufacture* (Boston: Houghton Mifflin, 1931) discusses the rapid progress in cotton textiles made before the Civil War. Melvin T. Copeland, *The Cotton Manufacturing Industry of the United States* (Cambridge: Harvard University Press, 1923) is the definitive study on cotton textiles. Constance M. Green, *Holyoke, Massachusetts. A Case History of the Industrial Revolution in America* (New Haven: Yale University Press, 1939) shows the effect of industrialization on one town. Arthur H. Cole, *The American Wool Manufacture* (2 vols., Cambridge: Harvard University Press, 1926) is the leading study on woolen textiles. Arthur H. Cole and Harold F. Williamson, *The American Carpet Manufacture* (Cambridge: Harvard University Press, 1941) is the authority on that industry. John S. Ewing and Nancy Norton, *Broadlooms and Businessmen* (Cambridge: Harvard University Press, 1955) is a good business history.

Iron and Steel. Victor Clark's chapters on iron and steel in his first volume of *History of Manufactures* are especially good. An often-quoted classic on iron is James M. Swank, *History of the Manufacture of Iron in All Ages* (Philadelphia: J. M. Swank, 1884). Joseph G. Butler, Jr., *Fifty Years of Iron and Steel* (Cleveland: Penton, 1922) describes steelmaking methods in an important growth period of the industry. Andrew Carnegie's *Autobiography* is the life and ideals of a great steel manufacturer. Ida M. Tarbell, *The Life of Elbert H. Gary* (New York: Appleton, 1925) is the biography of the head of the United States Steel Corporation in its early years.

Miscellaneous Industries. Blanche Hazard, *The Organization of the Boot and Shoe Industry in Massachusetts before 1875* (Cambridge: Harvard University Press, 1921) shows very clearly the evolution of the factory system from home to factory building. There is a condensed version of this article in the *Quarterly Journal of Economics* (February, 1913). Charles B. Kuhlmann, *The Development of the Flour Milling Industry in the United States* (Boston: Houghton Mifflin, 1929) was long the authority on this important industry. A more recent, broader account is John Storck and Walter D. Teague, *Flour for Man's Bread: A History of Milling* (Minneapolis: University of Minnesota Press, 1952). J. E. Defebaugh, *History of the Lumber Industry of America* (2 vols., Chicago: The American Lumberman, 1905–1907), although old, is the chief work on the lumber industry. Whaling long provided the oil to light homes.

Two authorities on this are W. S. Tower, *A History of the American Whale Fishery* (Philadelphia: University of Pennsylvania Press, 1907) and Elmo P. Hohman, *The American Whaleman* (New York: Longmans, 1928). On fisheries, see R. McFarland, *A History of the New England Fisheries* (Philadelphia: University of Pennsylvania Press, 1911). Rudolf A. Clemen, *The American Livestock and Meat Industry* (New York: Ronald, 1923) is the authority on meat packing history. Louis F. Swift, *The Yankee of the Yards* (New York: A. W. Shaw, 1927) is a biography of Gustavus Swift, one of the great meat packers, by his son. John K. Winkler, *Tobacco Tycoon: The Story of James Buchanan Duke* (New York, Random House, 1942) is a popular biography of the founder of the American Tobacco Company. Pearce Davis, *The Development of the American Glass Industry* (Cambridge: Harvard University Press, 1949) is the most definitive study on glass. William B. Harris, "The Electronic Business" in *Fortune* magazine, April, 1957, is a good account of a new industry. *Fortune* carries many fine articles on new developments in industry.

Oil Industry. Paul H. Giddens, *The Birth of the Oil Industry* (New York: Macmillan, 1938) is the best introductory account of this industry. It should be supplemented by his pictorial *Early Days of Oil* (Princeton: Princeton University Press, 1948). Samuel T. Tait, Jr., *The Wildcatters* (Princeton: Princeton University Press, 1946) tells of prospecting for oil, chiefly in the twentieth century. Allan Nevins, *John D. Rockefeller: The Heroic Age of American Enterprise* (2 vols., New York: Scribner, 1940) is a history of the oil industry as well as a fine biography of its leading figure. John T. Flynn, *God's Gold: The Story of Rockefeller and His Times* (New York: Harcourt, Brace, 1932) is a good earlier account of oil and Rockefeller. Neither Nevins nor Flynn is especially critical of Rockefeller. Ralph and Muriel Hidy, *Pioneering in Oil* (New York: Harper, 1955) on the early history of the Standard Oil of New Jersey is the latest and most definitive study of Rockefeller's development of oil refining.

Automobiles. Allan Nevins, *Ford: The Times, the Man, the Company* (New York: Scribner, 1954) and *Ford: Expansion and Challenge, 1915–1933* (New York: Scribner, 1957) are the final works on Ford and his automobile. It is also a good history of a large part of the auto industry. Keith Sward, *The Legend of Henry Ford* (New York: Rinehart, 1948) is a good but somewhat less friendly account. Charles Sorenson, *My Forty Years with Ford* (New York: Norton, 1956) are the memoirs of one of Ford's chief engineers and production men. Harry Bennett, *We Never Called Him Henry* (New York: Fawcett Publications, 1951) is a racy account by Ford's personal bodyguard who nearly took over the business. Automobile Manufacturers Association, *Automobile Facts and Figures* (Detroit, annually since 1919) is full of statistics on the growth and present status of the auto industry.

Mining. As the industrial revolution advanced, metals rather than agricultural products became the chief raw materials of industry. Victor Clark, *History of Manufactures*, mentioned earlier, is one authority on metals. Another is T. A. Rickard, *A History of American Mining* (New York: McGraw-Hill, 1932). William B. Gates, Jr., *Michigan Copper and Boston Dollars: An Economic History of the Michigan Copper Mining Industry* (Cambridge: Harvard University Press, 1951) is an excellent history of one company, the once-famous

Calumet-Hecla. On sulfur, see William Haynes, *The Stone That Burns: The Story of the American Sulphur Industry* (New York: Van Nostrand, 1942).

Inventions. Waldo Kaempffert's *A Popular History of American Invention* (2 vols., New York: A. L. Burt, 1924) is very suitable for the reader who is not technically inclined. Albert P. Usher's *A History of Mechanical Inventions* (New York: McGraw-Hill, 1929) deals with basic principles. John W. Oliver has recently written *A History of American Technology* (New York: Ronald, 1956). Roger Burlingame has done a trilogy, *March of Iron Men* (New York: Scribner, 1938), *Engines of Democracy* (New York: Scribner, 1940), and *Backgrounds of Power* (New York: Scribner, 1949). Four of America's great inventors were Eli Whitney, Oliver Evans, Cyrus McCormick, and Thomas Edison. Constance McLaughlin Greene has written a very readable yet penetrating biography of Whitney, *Eli Whitney and the Birth of American Technology* (Boston: Little, Brown, 1956). Greville Bathe and Dorothy Bathe have compiled a scholarly volume on *Oliver Evans* (Philadelphia: Historical Society, 1935). Two good ones on McCormick are William T. Hutchinson, *Cyrus Hall McCormick: Seed-time, 1809–1856* (New York: Century, 1930) and *Cyrus Hall McCormick: Harvest, 1856–1884* (New York: Appleton-Century, 1935). There are many biographies of Edison. One readable one is George S. Bryan, *Edison: The Man and His Work* (Garden City: Garden City Publishing Co., 1926).

Mechanization. Siegfried Giedion, *Mechanization Takes Command* (New York, Oxford, 1948) is broad in its coverage. A more statistical analysis is Harry Jerome, *Mechanization in Industry* (New York: National Bureau of Economic Research, 1934). Machines of course greatly increased production and productive capacity and created new economic problems. Two standard works are Arthur Burns, *Production Trends in the United States since 1870* (New York: National Bureau of Economic Research, 1934) and Edwin G. Nourse, *America's Capacity to Produce* (Washington: Brookings, 1934). William T. Hogan, *The Development of American Heavy Industry in the Twentieth Century* (New York: Fordham University Press, 1954) is a recent authority on this topic, although Victor Clark, *History of Manufactures,* should be consulted for the pre-1930 era.

Industrial Power. Once industry derived most of its power from water. A much-read book then was Oliver Evans, *The Young Millwright and Miller's Guide* (9th ed., Philadelphia, 1836). Bathe and Bathe's *Oliver Evans,* mentioned above, discusses the significance of his various steam engines and mills. When steam replaced water power, coal grew rapidly in importance. A leading study on the highly important coal industry is Howard N. Eavenson, *The First Century and a Quarter of American Coal Industry* (Pittsburgh: Koppers Building, 1942). In making steel only coking coal could be used. A biography of the coke king is George Harvey, *Henry Clay Frick: The Man* (New York: Scribner, 1928). Steam in turn gave way to electricity. On this the authority is Malcolm McLaren, *The Rise of the Electrical Industry during the Nineteenth Century* (Princeton: Princeton University Press, 1943).

The South. The industrial revolution began later in the South. A good history of this region is Emory Q. Hawk, *Economic History of the South* (New York:

Prentice-Hall, 1934). J. T. D. De Bow, *The Industrial Resources of the Southern and Western States* (3 vols., New Orleans: De Bow's, 1852) is a selection from *De Bow's Preview,* the leading commercial magazine of the South a century ago. Broadus Mitchell and George S. Mitchell, *The Industrial Revolution in the South* (Baltimore: Johns Hopkins Press, 1930) discusses the rise of the textile industry after the 1880s.

CAPITAL, CORPORATIONS, TRUSTS, TAXATION, AND BUSINESS CYCLES

National Income. Robert F. Martin, *National Income in the United States, 1799–1938* (New York: National Industrial Conference Board, 1939) is the longest series available, but Simon Kuznets, the leading authority on national income, has questioned the validity of the much-used Martin estimates in "National Income Estimates for the United States prior to 1870," *Journal of Economic History* (vol. 12), Winter, 1952, pp. 115ff. Simon Kuznets, *National Product since 1869* (New York: National Bureau of Economic Research, 1946) is reliable. Simon Kuznets, *National Income and Its Composition* (2 vols., New York: National Bureau of Economic Research, 1941) is a standard work for the years after 1919. Recent national income figures appear in various Federal government publications, but attention is called to the analyses in the February and July issues of the *Survey of Current Business* and in the National Industrial Conference Board's annual *Economic Almanac.* Richard Ruggles, *An Introduction to National Income and Income Analysis* (New York: McGraw-Hill, 1949) explains the uses of national income statistics. New capital is, of course, a part of national income.

Capital Formation. Carl Snyder, *Capitalism the Creator: The Economic Foundations of Modern Industrial Society* (New York: Macmillan, 1940) vigorously emphasizes the importance of capital in man's material progress. Chapters in Victor Clark, *History of Manufactures in the United States,* show historically how capital has been formed. Harold G. Moulton, *The Formation of Capital* (Washington: Brookings, 1935) is analytical. Harold Williamson and O. Smalley, *Northwestern Mutual Life* (Evanston: Northwestern University Press, 1957) discusses one of the sources of capital—savings for insurance. Debts, reflecting savings by the lender, are another. Two books dealing with American public and private debts are Evans Clark, *The Internal Debts of the United States* (New York: Macmillan, 1933) and Leonard Kluvin, *Private Long-term Debt and Interest in the United States* (New York: National Industrial Conference Board, 1936). See the National Industrial Conference Board's *Economic Almanac* for more recent figures.

Government Assistance to Industry. Government aid to early industry was essential sometimes if industry was to start at all, for liquid capital was scarce. Victor Clark, *History of Manufactures,* shows this. So also does Oscar Handlin, *Commonwealth of Massachusetts, 1774–1861* (New York: New York University Press, 1947), who contends that there was much more government activity in business in the so-called laissez-faire period than is usually recognized. Jesse H. Jones and Edward Angly, *Fifty Billion Dollars* (New York: Macmillan,

1951) shows government aid to business during the Great Depression and after.

Corporations. A good beginning is C. C. Abbott, *The Rise of the Business Corporation* (Ann Arbor: University of Michigan Press, 1936). The leading study of early business corporations is Joseph S. Davis, *Essays in the Earlier History of American Corporations* (2 vols., Cambridge: Harvard University Press, 1917). Three good specialized studies to supplement these are J. G. Blandi, *Maryland Business Corporations, 1783–1852* (Baltimore: Johns Hopkins, 1934); R. C. Larcom, *The Delaware Corporation* (Baltimore: Johns Hopkins, 1937); and John W. Cadman, Jr., *The Corporation in New Jersey Businesss and Politics, 1791–1875* (Cambridge: Harvard University Press 1949). Shaw Livermore, "Corporations and Unlimited Liability," *Journal of Political Economy*, vol. 43, pp. 674ff., throws light on this mystery. Livermore contends in his book, *Early American Land Companies* (New York: Commonwealth Fund, 1939) that these were the origin of early American corporations. Lincoln Steffens, "New Jersey: A Traitor State" in *McClure's Magazine*, vol. 25, pp. 41ff. (May, 1905) is a "muckraker" article and should be used with care but shows the abuses of which later corporations and some states could be guilty. G. Heberton Evans, *Business Incorporations in the United States, 1800–1943* (New York: National Bureau of Economic Research, 1948) provides a partial census of incorporating and draws conclusions on the trends. The Twentieth Century Fund, *Big Business: Its Growth and Its Place* (New York, 1937) contains statistical information on the growth of corporations and their relative importance in various industries. For the legal aspects of corporations in more recent times, see Adolph Berle and G. Means, *The Modern Corporation and Private Property* (New York: Macmillan, 1948).

Foreign Investors and Investments. In the early years Americans borrowed heavily abroad. Four books on this are: Cleona Lewis, *America's Stake in International Investment* (Washington: Brookings, 1938); Leland H. Jenks, *The Migration of British Capital to 1875* (New York: Knopf, 1927); Ralph H. Hidy, *The House of Baring in American Trade and Finance: English Merchant Bankers at Work, 1763–1861* (Cambridge, Harvard University Press, 1949); and Reginald C. McGrane, *Foreign Bondholders and American State Debts* (New York, Macmillan, 1935) which deals chiefly with the 1830s. For America in the role of lender, see Cleona Lewis again and Max Winkler, *Foreign Bonds: An Autopsy* (Philadelphia: Swain, 1933); and Herbert Marshall, F. Southard, and K. Taylor, *Canadian-American Industry: A Study in International Investment* (New Haven: Yale University Press, 1936). The *Statistical Abstract* and the *Economic Almanac* have recent figures on foreign loans.

Investment Banking. A good introduction to the history of investment banking is H. Parker Willis and J. I. Bogen, *Investment Banking* (New York: Harper, 1936). John Moody, *Masters of Capital* (New Haven: Yale University Press, 1919) is an old and brief account containing colorful episodes. The most scholarly historical analysis is Chapter 21 of Fritz Redlich, *The Molding of American Banking* (2 vols., New York: Hafner, 1951). In it he traces the development of several investment banking firms. Henrietta Larson, *Jay Cooke*

(Cambridge: Harvard University Press, 1936) is standard on the financier of the Civil War. There are several biographies of J. P. Morgan. A good fairly recent one is Frederick L. Allen, *The Great Pierpont Morgan* (New York: Harper, 1949).

The Stock Exchanges. A history of the stock market and of the adjoining New York money market appears in Margaret G. Myers, *The New York Money Market* (4 vols., New York: Columbia University Press, 1930). Older and briefer treatments are found in J. E. Meeker, *The Work of the Stock Exchange* (New York: Ronald, 1930) and Sereno S. Pratt, *The Work of Wall Street* (New York: Appleton, 1926). Alexander D. Noyes, *The Market Place* (Boston: Little, Brown, 1938) is an anecdotal account. Henry Clews, *Twenty-eight Years in Wall Street* (New York: Irving Publishing Co., 1887) is similar for an earlier period. H. P. Willis and J. I. Bogen, *Investment Banking*, mentioned above, cover stock selling and stock exchange reforms. The atmosphere of rivalry between tycoons of big business and the speculative fever of the 1920s may be recaptured in Arthur Pound and S. T. Moore, *They Told Barron* (New York: Harper, 1930). Barron, editor of the *Wall Street Journal*, kept a diary of what leading financiers told him. Kenneth Galbraith, *The Great Crash—1929* (Boston: Houghton Mifflin, 1955) likewise retells the stock market story before 1929. William Z. Ripley, *Main Street and Wall Street* (Boston: Little, Brown, 1927) discusses security selling practices of the 1920s. Ferdinand Pecora, *Wall Street under Oath* (New York: Knopf, 1939) is a synopsis of the 1932–1934 Senate investigations of stock market abuses of the 1920s. Pecora was the Senate's attorney. The *Yearbook of the New York Stock Exchange* gives statistics on its activities over a long period of time. Lewis H. Kimmel in 1952 made the first scholarly attempt to estimate how many Americans hold stock and wrote *Share Ownership in the United States* (Washington: Brookings, 1952).

Trusts. The trust question never ceases to fascinate economists and the flow of literature is continuous. Eliot Jones, *The Trust Problem* (New York: Macmillan, 1924) is old but is one of the clearest exposés of the problem ever written and is historical in much of its treatment. John Moody, *Masters of Capital* (New Haven: Yale University Press, 1919) gives highlights of the days of giant trust formations. Andrew Carnegie, who was partly responsible for the giant United States Steel Corporation trust, gave his version of why monopoly appears in *Empire of Business* (New York: Doubleday, 1902). The *Report of the Industrial Commission* (19 vols., Washington, Government Printing Office, 1900–1902), especially vols. I and XIX, shows the situation at the start of the century.

Some of the outstanding analyses of the trust problem, selected from those appearing over more than a half century are: Richard T. Ely, *Monopolies and Trusts* (New York: Macmillan, 1900); W. Z. Ripley, *Trusts, Pools and Corporations* (Boston: Ginn, 1905); Arthur Burns, *The Decline of Competition* (New York: McGraw-Hill, 1936); Thurman W. Arnold, *The Folklore of Capitalism* (New Haven: Yale University Press, 1937); and George W. Stocking and M. Watkins, *Monopoly and Free Enterprise* (New York, 1951) and S. N. Whitney, *Anti-trust Policies* (New York, 1958), both Twentieth Century Fund books.

Sometimes trusts can be understood better by studying individual examples. Much has been written about the Standard Oil Company, and each time the treatment is less hostile. Investigation began with such indignant exposés as Henry D. Lloyd, *Wealth against Commonwealth* (New York: Harper, 1902) and Ida Tarbell, *History of the Standard Oil Company* (2 vols., New York: Macmillan, 1904). John Flynn, *God's Gold* (New York: Harcourt, Brace, 1932) is a popular and sympathetic account by a former liberal, and Allan Nevins, *John D. Rockefeller* (2 vols., New York: Scribner, 1940) is in a similar vein. Ralph and Muriel Hidy, *Pioneering in Big Business* (New York: Harper, 1955) and its successor volume by George Gibb and Evelyn Knowlton, *The Resurgent Years* (New York: Harper, 1956) are based on thorough investigations of the records and papers of the company. Frank A. Fetter, *Masquerade of Monopoly* (New York: Harcourt, Brace, 1931) is a critical study of the oil and steel monopolies.

Consequences of Trusts. Some of the informal literature reflecting the consequences of trusts would include Thorstein Veblen, *Theory of the Leisure Class* (New York: Modern Library, 1934); the *Autobiography of Lincoln Steffens* (New York: Harcourt, Brace, 1931), which represents "muckraking" literature at its best; and Theodore Roosevelt, *An Autobiography* (New York: Scribner, 1929), especially Chapter 12 on trusts. Frederick L. Allen, *The Big Change* (New York: Harper, 1952) contrasts social values in 1900 and 1950. Ward McAllister, *Society as I Have Found It* (New York: Cassell, 1890), by its "social lion," shows how wealthy families squandered their millions.

Regulating Trusts. Regulation of trusts is discussed in nearly all the books on trusts. Eliot Jones, *Trust Problem*, mentioned above, is clear on this subject down to 1924. A compilation of the early cases is found in James A. Finch, *Federal Anti-trust Decisions, 1890–1912* (4 vols., Washington, 1912). Hugh S. Johnson, *The Blue Eagle from Egg to Earth* (Garden City: Doubleday, 1935) describes an interlude in trust busting from 1933 to 1935. Johnson headed the government's effort to encourage self-regulation by business. Leverett S. Lyon and others, *The National Recovery Administration: An Analysis and Appraisal* (Washington: Brookings, 1935) also describes the NRA Temporary National Economic Committee. Investigation of Concentration of Economic Power, *Final Report and Recommendations* (Purs. Pub. Res. no. 113, 77th Cong., 1st Sess., Doc. 35, Washington: Government Printing Office, 1941) sums up the sweeping 1938 investigation of trusts. Monograph no. 16 of the same report by Walton Hamilton, *Anti-trust in Action* (Senate, 76th Cong., 3d Sess., Washington, 1941) discusses problems of "trust busting" from the government's viewpoint. Corwin D. Edwards, *Maintaining Competition: Requisites of a Governmental Policy* (New York: McGraw-Hill, 1949) is by a member of the Federal Trade Commission.

Taxation. Material on the history of taxation in the United States may be found in Paul Studenski and H. Krooss, *Financial History of the United States* (New York: McGraw-Hill, 1952) and also in W. Shultz and M. R. Caine, *Financial Development of the United States* (New York: Prentice-Hall, 1937).

Business Cycles. The subject of business cycles is complicated. Leonard Ayres, *Turning Points in Business Cycles* (New York: Macmillan, 1939) is a good book to start with. A very complete treatment, historical and otherwise, is Norman J. Silberling, *Dynamics of Business* (New York: McGraw-Hill, 1943). The book that was long the classic, although largely theoretical in its treatment, is Wesley C. Mitchell, *Business Cycles* (New York: National Bureau of Economic Research, 1927). Another classic is Joseph Schumpeter, *Business Cycles* (2 vols., New York: McGraw-Hill, 1939). The business cycle in terms of Keynesian analysis may be found in Dudley Dillard, *The Economics of John Maynard Keynes: The Theory of a Monetary Economy* (London: Lockwood, 1948).

Separate histories have been written on a number of the major depressions. For example, Reginald McGrane is the authority on *The Panic of 1837* (Chicago: Chicago University Press, 1927); George Van Vleck covered *The Panic of 1857* (New York: Columbia University Press, 1943); and Lawrence Sullivan did a polemic, *The Prelude to Panic* (Washington: Statesman's Press, 1936) on the bank holiday of March, 1933. Kenneth Galbraith, *The Great Crash—1929* (Boston: Houghton Mifflin, 1955) is a lively account of the events leading up to October, 1929.

MONEY AND BANKING

General Financial History. There are seven financial histories of the United States. The oldest is Albert S. Bolles, *Financial History of the United States, 1774–1885* (3 vols., New York: Appleton, 1879–1886), which deals largely with the Treasury's activities. The classic for many years, famed for accuracy rather than light reading, was Davis R. Dewey, *Financial History of the United States* (12th ed., New York: Longmans, 1939). Alonzo B. Hepburn, *A History of Currency in the United States* (New York: Macmillan, 1915) deals with the subject of nineteenth century money and banking. Alexander D. Noyes, long the financial editor of *The New York Times*, wrote a trilogy: *Forty Years of American Finance* (New York: Putnam, 1909); *The War Period of American Finance*, 1908–1925 (New York: Putnam, 1926); and *The Market Place* (Boston: Little, Brown, 1938). W. J. Shultz and M. R. Caine, *Financial Development of the United States* (New York: Prentice-Hall, 1937) is a clear one-volume treatment. Benjamin M. Anderson, for years the economist of the Chase National Bank, wrote *Economics and the Public Welfare* (Princeton, N.J.: Van Nostrand, 1949). It covers the recent period and is conservative in its views. The most recently published financial history is Paul Studenski and Herman Krooss, *Financial History of the United States* (New York: McGraw-Hill, 1952). John C. Schwab, *The Confederate States of America* (New York: Scribner, 1901) is the authority on Confederate finances.

Colonial Money. There are numerous special studies and some general ones on the moneys of colonial times. Scattered through Curtis H. Nettels, *The Roots of American Civilization* (New York: Crofts, 1938) are helpful sections on money. He also wrote *The Money Supply of the American Colonies before 1720* (Madison: 1934). W. B. Weeden covers Indian wampum in his *Indian Money as a Factor in New England Civilization* (Baltimore: Johns Hopkins, 1884). "A History of Paper Money in Colonial New Jersey, 1668–1775," by

Donald L. Kemmerer, appears in *The Proceedings of the New Jersey Historical Society*, vol. 74 (April, 1956). A good early account of colonial money is Henry Phillips, Jr., *Historical Sketches of the Paper Currency of the American Colonies* (2 vols., Roxbury, Mass., 1865). W. Z. Ripley wrote about *The Financial History of Virginia, 1609–1776* (New York: Columbia University Press, 1893). Finally, there is the very scholarly study by W. M. Davis, "Currency and Banking in the Province of Massachusetts Bay," in the *Publications of the American Economic Association*, 3d series, vols. 1 and 2 (New York, 1900–1901). Charles Bullock's *Monetary History of the United States* (New York: Macmillan, 1900), although old, is still worth consulting.

Coinage. The first authority to consult on American money in the nineteenth century is Neil Carothers, *Fractional Money* (New York: Wiley, 1930). Next is Alonzo Barton Hepburn, *A History of Currency in the United States*, mentioned above. D. K. Watson's *A History of American Coinage* is an earlier authority on coinage. Any annual *Report of the Director of the Mint* (Washington: Government Printing Office) will give needed statistical information on the amount of coins minted each year since the 1790s.

Greenbacks and Resumption in 1879. The leading authority on greenbacks is Wesley C. Mitchell, *A History of the Greenbacks* (Chicago: University of Chicago Press, 1903). Also excellent is Don C. Barrett, *The Greenbacks and Resumption of Specie Payments, 1862–1879* (Cambridge: Harvard University Press, 1931). An earlier authority is John Jay Knox, *United States Notes* (New York: Scribner, 1884). No study of the return to the gold standard in 1879 would be complete without examining John Sherman, *Recollections of Forty Years in the House, Senate and Cabinet: An Autobiography* (2 vols., Chicago: Werner Company, 1895).

Bimetallism. The bimetallic or silver question in the latter nineteenth century produced a vast amount of literature. All financial history texts deal with it. J. L. Laughlin, *History of Bimetallism in the United States* (New York: Appleton, 1900) is the standard work. Noyes has a good account in his *Forty Years of American Finance*, mentioned above. Recommended from a political viewpoint are James Barnes, *John G. Carlisle, Financial Statesman* (New York: Dodd, Mead, 1931) on Cleveland's Secretary of the Treasury; Frederick L. Allen, *The Great Pierpont Morgan* (New York: Harper, 1949); Paxton Hibben, *The Peerless Leader: William Jennings Bryan* (New York: Farrar & Rinehart, 1929); and William J. Bryan, *The First Battle* (Chicago: Conkey, 1896), which is a story of the 1896 campaign containing his speeches on silver. W. H. Harvey, *Coin's Financial School* (Chicago: Coin Publishing Co., 1894) was widely read propaganda in favor of bimetallism.

The 1933–1934 Devaluation. The monetary disturbances leading to the abandonment and partial readoption of the gold standard in 1933–1934 are described in several books; Leo Pasvolsky, *Current Monetary Issues* (Washington: Brookings, 1933) is a good introduction. Another account is James D. Paris, *Monetary Policies of the United States, 1932–1938* (New York: Columbia University Press, 1938). There are some pertinent chapters in E. W. Kemmerer, *Kemmerer on Money* (Philadelphia: Winston, 1934), in Frederick A. Bradford, *Money and Banking*, mentioned below, and also in Benjamin M.

Anderson, *Economics and the Public Welfare,* cited above. The views of devaluationists are found in George Warren and F. A. Pearson, *Prices* (New York: Wiley, 1933), in Irving Fisher, *Stabilizing the Dollar* (New York: Macmillan, 1925), and in Lauchlin Currie, *The Supply and Control of Money in the United States* (Cambridge: Harvard University Press, 1934). George Brown, *The International Gold Standard Reinterpreted* (2 vols., New York: National Bureau of Economic Research, 1940) takes the viewpoint that the gold standard has proved a failure. Walter E. Spahr, Edwin W. Kemmerer, and Benjamin M. Anderson in their many writings defend the gold standard. The gold clause cases are available in 294 U.S. Reports.

First and Second Banks of the United States. J. T. Holdsworth and Davis R. Dewey wrote *The First and Second Banks of the United States* (Washington: Government Printing Office, 1911) for the National Monetary Commission. These are strictly factual. The classic account on the second Bank is R. C. Catterall, *The Second Bank of the United States* (Chicago: University of Chicago Press, 1903). A more recent book, by an economist, is Walter B. Smith, *Economic Aspects of the Second Bank of the United States* (Cambridge: Harvard University Press, 1953). These may be supplemented by good political biographies of Alexander Hamilton, Thomas Jefferson, and Albert Gallatin, for the first Bank and of Andrew Jackson, Henry Clay, and Thomas H. Benton for the second Bank. Arthur M. Schlesinger, Jr., in his *The Age of Jackson* (New York: Little, Brown, 1945) is hostile to the second Bank. Bray Hammond defends Biddle ably in "Jackson, Biddle and the Bank of the United States" in the *Journal of Economic History,* vol. 7 (May, 1947). Reginald McGrane, *The Correspondence of Nicholas Biddle* (Boston: Houghton Mifflin, 1919) gives insight into Biddle's character and motives. David Kinley is the authority on the Independent Treasury System. See his *The History, Organization and Influence of the Independent Treasury of the United States* (New York: Crowell, 1893).

Pre-Civil War Banking. Much has been written and much remains to be written about state banking before the Civil War. Horace White provides a clear introduction in his *Money and Banking* (New York: Ginn, 1936) and so does Louis A. Rufener in *Money and Banking in the United States* (Boston: Houghton Mifflin, 1936). Davis R. Dewey wrote *State Banking before the Civil War* and Robert E. Chaddock wrote *The Safety Fund Banking System in New York, 1829–1866,* both of them for the National Monetary Commission (Washington: Government Printing Office, 1910). Bray Hammond in an article, "Banking in the Early West: Monopoly, Prohibition and Laissez-Faire," in the *Journal of Economic History,* vol. 8 (May, 1948), shows the varied character of frontier banking philosophy. He elaborated on this in *Banks and Politics in America* (Princeton: Princeton University Press, 1957). The authority on early Illinois banking is George W. Dowrie, *The Development of Banking in Illinois, 1817–1863* (Urbana: University of Illinois, 1913). Many historians have drawn on William Gouge's *A Short History of Paper Money and Banking in the United States* (Philadelphia: 1833) for examples of bad banking practices. Hugh McCulloch, later Secretary of the Treasury, helped make the state bank of Indiana successful. His *Men and Measures of Half a*

Century (New York: Scribner, 1888) has some helpful chapters. Finally, William H. Dillistin, *Bank Note Reporters and Counterfeit Detectors, 1826–1866* (New York: American Numismatic Society, 1949) exposes the unhealthy condition of some of the banking of the period.

National Banking System. The National Monetary Commission made several studies of the National Banking System. These include Andrew M. Davis, *The Origin of the National Banking System* (Washington: Government Printing Office, 1910) and Oliver M. W. Sprague, *History of Crises under the National Banking System* (Washington: Government Printing Office, 1910). Alexander D. Noyes's short study, *History of the National Bank Currency* (Washington: Government Printing Office, 1910), shows why that currency was inelastic, sometimes perversely so. James G. Cannon is the authority on *Clearing Houses* (Washington: Government Printing Office, 1910). The text of the law and its amendments may be found in *Laws of the United States: Concerning Money, Banking and Loans, 1778–1909* (Washington: Government Printing Office, 1910). The use of checks was greatly stimulated by the National Banking System. On that the authority is David Kinley, *The Use of Credit Instruments in Payments in the United States* (Washington: Government Printing Office, 1910). Biographies of Salmon P. Chase, the father of the National Banking System, and of J. P. Morgan, who helped save it in 1907, are also helpful. The head of the National Banking System, in so far as it had one, was the Comptroller of Currency, and his office has published an *Annual Report* from 1864 on.

Federal Reserve System. The literature on the Federal Reserve System is vast. E. W. Kemmerer and D. L. Kemmerer in their *ABC of the Federal Reserve System* (12th ed., New York: Harper, 1950) provide a brief history and an explanation of the system. Nathaniel Stephenson's *Nelson Aldrich* (New York: Scribner, 1930) gives the political background of the man who contributed so much to it at the outset. Paul M. Warburg, *The Federal Reserve System* (2 vols., New York: Macmillan, 1930) shows this also. Among those who later reshaped the law and put it through Congress were Carter Glass and his advisor, H. Parker Willis, later secretary of the Federal Reserve. Glass wrote *An Adventure in Constructive Finance* (Garden City: Doubleday, 1927) and H. Parker Willis wrote several books on the Federal Reserve System and its functions. Rixey Smith and Norman Beasley wrote a popular biography of *Carter Glass* (New York: Longmans, 1939). The second chairman of the Board, W. P. G. Harding, wrote *The Formative Period of the Federal Reserve System* (London: Constable, 1925). Benjamin M. Anderson in his *Economics and the Public Welfare* has much to say, a good deal of it critical, about the Federal Reserve in the 1920s. Other able discussants of it are W. Randolph Burgess, *The Reserve Banks and the Money Market* (rev. ed., New York: Harper, 1936); E. A. Goldenweiser, *The Federal Reserve System in Operation* (New York: 1925); and S. E. Harris, *Twenty Years of Federal Reserve Policy: Including an Extended Discussion of the Monetary Crisis, 1927–1933* (2 vols., Cambridge: Harvard University Press, 1933). Ray W. Westerfield in his encyclopedic *Money, Credit and Banking* (New York: Ronald, 1947) is particularly good. So also is Frederick A. Bradford, *Money and Banking* (New

York: Longmans, 1949). In more recent years, George L. Bach has written a penetrating analysis of the everyday operations of the Federal Reserve in his *Federal Reserve Policy Making* (New York: Knopf, 1950). Marriner S. Eccles, head of the System from 1934 to 1948, gives his version of events in his autobiography, *Beckoning Frontiers* (New York: Knopf, 1951). Statistical information on the Federal Reserve is available in the monthly *Federal Reserve Bulletin* and in the *Annual Report of the Board of Governors.* Both are available at the Federal Reserve headquarters in Washington. The monthly bulletin figures, to 1941, are collected in *Banking and Monetary Statistics* (Washington: Federal Reserve, 1943).

Price Level Trends. The best source for price level trends in colonial times is Arthur H. Cole, *Wholesale Commodity Prices in the United States, 1700–1861* (Cambridge: Harvard University Press, 1938). Anne Bezanson has made an exhaustive study in *Prices and Inflation during the American Revolution* (Philadelphia: University of Pennsylvania Press, 1951). On the pre-Civil War period there is Cole's study and also that of Thomas S. Berry, *Western Prices before 1861: A Study of the Cincinnati Market* (Cambridge: Harvard University Press, 1943). Norman Silberling in his *Dynamics of Business* (New York: McGraw-Hill, 1943) uses some price series that are difficult to find elsewhere. The price level section of *Historical Statistics* is also recommended for the nineteenth century. A still used but now somewhat discredited series is the *Aldrich Report on Wholesale Prices, Wages and Transportation, 1840–1890* (Senate doc. no. 1394, 52nd Cong., 2d Sess., 4 vols., Washington: 1893). George Warren and F. A. Pearson in *Prices* (New York: Wiley, 1933) provide extensive price statistics. There are recent series in the *Statistical Abstract of the United States,* in the *Economic Almanac* of the National Industrial Conference Board, and in the *Federal Reserve Bulletin.*

DOMESTIC AND FOREIGN COMMERCE

Foreign Trade. The most authoritative account of the history of American foreign trade is Emory R. Johnson and others, *History of Domestic and Foreign Commerce of the United States* (2 vols., Washington: Carnegie Institution, 1917), a portion of the Carnegie Institution series on American economic history. A very popular treatment of American foreign commerce, with many illustrations, is Malcolm Keir, *March of Commerce* (New Haven: Yale University Press, 1927). The authority on the Embargo of 1807 is W. W. Jennings, *The American Embargo, 1807–1809* (Iowa City: University of Iowa Press, 1921). Samuel E. Morison in his *Maritime History of Massachusetts, 1783–1860* (Boston: Houghton Mifflin, 1921) gives a charming account of New England commerce, with only one dull phrase in the book, the title. The function of factors in the handling of cotton, at one time 60 per cent of American exports, is well covered by N. S. Buck, *The Development of the Organization of Anglo-American Trade, 1800–1850* (New Haven: Yale University Press, 1925). Sections on the early and recent history of American commerce are to be found in some of the textbooks on foreign trade. Especially recommended are J. P. Young, *The International Economy* (New York: Ronald,

1951) and Asher Isaacs, *International Trade: Tariff and Commercial Policies* (Homewood, Ill.: Irwin, 1948).

Foreign Commerce Statistics. Statistics on foreign commerce are available in Timothy Pitkin's *Statistical View of the Commerce of the United States of America* (Hartford: Hosmer, 1816) and in Adam Seybert's *Statistical Annals* (Philadelphia: 1818) and during the twentieth century in the Department of Commerce's *Foreign Commerce Yearbook* (Washington: Government Printing Office). Some of this is also printed in the annual *Statistical Abstract of the United States. Historical Statistics, 1789–1945* should also be consulted.

Merchant Biographies. One of the best ways of studying foreign commerce in the nineteenth century is through the biographies of various well-known merchants. Freeman Hunt, of *Hunt's Merchant Magazine,* ran a series of biographies of prominent merchants of the mid-nineteenth century and then collected them in *Lives of American Merchants* (2 vols., New York, 1858). As might be expected, the quality of these articles varies. Harry E. Wildes has done a good life of Stephen Girard, *The Lonely Midas* (New York: Farrar & Rinehart, 1943). Stuart Bruchey, *Robert Oliver, Merchant of Baltimore, 1783–1819* (Baltimore: Johns Hopkins, 1956) is a careful study. So also are Elva Tooker, *Nathan Trotter, Philadelphia Merchant, 1787–1853* (Cambridge: Harvard University Press, 1955) and William Hurd Hillyer, *James Talcott, Merchant and His Times* (New York: Scribner, 1937). An interesting source is Vincent Nolte's *Fifty Years in Both Hemispheres or Reminiscences of the Life of a Former Merchant* (New York: 1854). See Colonial Commerce section below too.

Ports. The nation's outstanding port has been New York. Robert G. Albion has written its commercial history in *The Port of New York* (New York: Scribner, 1939). Thomas J. Wertenbaker has covered *Norfolk: Historic Southern Port* (Durham: Duke University Press, 1931). Wyatt W. Belcher describes the rivalry between interior cities in *The Economic Rivalry between St. Louis and Chicago, 1850–1880* (New York: Columbia University Press, 1947).

The Tariff. The outstanding treatment of the tariff is Frank W. Taussig's *Tariff History of the United States* (New York: Putnam, 1931). He also has a study of the effect of the tariff on each of several industries, *Some Aspects of the Tariff Question* (Cambridge: Harvard University Press, 1924). A more protectionist approach to the tariff question is found in Edward Stanwood, *Tariff Controversies in the 19th Century* (2 vols., Boston: Houghton Mifflin, 1903). Ugo Rabbeno, *American Commercial Policy* (New York: Macmillan, 1895) is a critical appraisal of American protectionist policy during the nineteenth century. The late nineteenth century economic thinking that favored lower tariffs is found in David Wells, *Recent Economic Changes* (New York: Appleton, 1897). W. S. Culbertson, *Reciprocity: A National Policy for Foreign Trade* (New York: McGraw-Hill, 1937) supports a reciprocal trade policy. A more recent treatment of the tariff is available in Lawrence W. Towle, *International Trade and Commercial Policy* (New York: Harper, 1956).

Colonial Commerce. Curtis Nettels, *Roots of American Civilization* (New York: Crofts, 1938) is a good introduction to commerce in the colonial period.

Arthur M. Schlesinger, *The Colonial Merchants and the American Revolution, 1763–1770* (New York: Facsimile, 1939) provides some specific illustrations. A superb account of the problems faced by colonial merchants in making ends meet is James B. Hedges, *The Browns of Providence Plantations: Colonial Years* (Cambridge: Harvard University Press, 1952). William T. Baxter has written a readable story of *The House of Hancock* (Cambridge: Harvard University Press, 1945), whose chief was active in the American Revolution. Robert A. East describes business during the American Revolution in *Business Enterprise in the American Revolutionary Era* (New York: Columbia University Press, 1938).

Mercantilism. Mercantilism is most clearly treated by George Louis Beer in *The Origins of British Colonial Policy, 1578–1660* (New York: Macmillan, 1907) and *The Old Colonial System* (2 vols., New York: Macmillan, 1912). England's attitude toward its former colonies after the Revolution is set forth in Lord J. B. H. Sheffield's bitter but calculated *Observations on the Commerce of the United States* (2d ed., London: 1784).

Piracy and Privateering. Piracy, privateering, and smuggling were forms of trade that flourished in colonial times. J. F. Jameson (ed.) has compiled a source book on *Privateering and Piracy in the Colonial Period* (New York: Macmillan, 1923). C. H. Haring has written authoritatively on *The Buccaneers in the West Indies in the XVII Century* (London: Methuen, 1910) and John Esquemeling, a Dutch pirate of the seventeenth century, has written the racy classic, *The Buccaneers of America* (London: Routledge, 1931). A popular account is Edward R. Snow, *Pirates and Buccaneers of the Atlantic Coast* (Boston: Yankee Publishing Co., 1944).

Internal Commerce. Internal commerce is well treated in Emory Johnson, *Domestic and Foreign Commerce.* A rich but unexpected source of information on domestic commerce is the report of Israel D. Andrews entitled *Andrew's Report on Colonial and Lake Trade, 1852* (Executive doc. no. 112, 32d Cong., 1st Sess., Washington: 1853). A different classic of the mid-century is Josiah Gregg's *Commerce of the Prairies,* edited by Milo Quaife (Chicago: Donnelly, 1926), which deals with the Santa Fe trade.

Early Retailing. Probably the best account of early peddling is Richardson Wright, *Hawkers and Walkers in Early America* (Philadelphia: Lippincott, 1927). The general store was the next stage in retailing. The outstanding authority on this is Lewis Atherton, *The Pioneer Merchants in Mid-America* (Columbia: Missouri University Press, 1939). More popular accounts are Gerald Carson, *The Old Country Store* (New York: Oxford, 1954) and R. E. Gould, *Yankee Storekeeper* (London: Whittlesy, 1946). Also good is T. D. Clark, *Pills, Petticoats and Plows: the Southern Country Store* (Indianapolis: Bobbs-Merrill, 1944).

Middlemen. The nineteenth century was the heyday of the middleman. Fred Jones's fine monograph treats *Middlemen in the Domestic Trade of the United States, 1800–1860* (Urbana: University of Illinois Press, 1937). Ray B. Westerfield is the authority on the *Early History of American Auctions* (New Haven: Yale University Press, 1920). Asa Greene, *Perils of Pearl Street* (New York: Betts and Anstice, 1834) discusses wholesaling in the 1830s in New York.

Much of the material on wholesalers, jobbers, and commission merchants is still rather fragmentary and must be taken, in the form of half generalities, from standard texts. A good one of these is Paul D. Converse, H. Huegy, and R. V. Mitchell, *The Elements of Marketing* (Englewood Cliffs, N.J.: Prentice-Hall, 1958). Samuel Crowther, *John H. Patterson* (Garden City: Doubleday Page, 1923) is the life of the head of the National Cash Register Company, who did much to advance the art and science of salesmanship. Richard M. Clewett, *Marketing Channels* (Homewood, Ill.: Irwin, 1954) is another good general treatment by a number of experts.

Department Stores. There are several histories of department stores. Ralph Hower, *History of Macy's, 1858–1919* (Cambridge: Harvard University Press, 1943) is one of the most scholarly. Herbert Adams Gibbons, *John Wanamaker* (2 vols., New York: Harper, 1926) is a popular account. So also is Joseph Appel, *The Business Biography of John Wanamaker* (2 vols., New York: Macmillan, 1930). The best available on Woolworth is John Winkler's *Five and Ten* (New York: McBride, 1940), which is very readable but not a definitive study. Robert W. Twyman has written a scholarly *History of Marshall Field & Co., 1852–1916* (Philadelphia: University of Pennsylvania Press, 1954). On mail-order houses, B. Emmet and John E. Jeuck, *Catalogues and Counters* (Chicago: University of Chicago Press, 1950), treating Sears, Roebuck, is outstanding.

Advertising. Material on advertising history is widely scattered, and marketing texts should be consulted. Charles H. Sandage, *Advertising: Theory and Practice* (Homewood, Ill.: Irwin, 1953) gives some historical background and an understanding of advertising principles. Ralph H. Hower has written *The History of an Advertising Agency, 1869–1939* (Cambridge: Harvard University Press, 1939), the story of N. W. Ayer and Son of Philadelphia, one of the oldest and best-known companies in the field. A century ago patent medicine manufacturers were the pioneers in modern advertising. Jean Burton in *Lydia Pinkham Is Her Name* (New York: Farrar, Strauss, 1949) has done a popular short biography of one of the most famous patent medicine personalities.

LABOR

General and Histories. The history of the labor movement is complex. Somewhat dated but still a good introduction is Selig Perlman, *History of Trade Unionism in the United States* (New York: Macmillan, 1922). This is to a considerable degree an abridged version of John R. Commons and associates, *History of Labour in the United States* (2 vols., New York: Macmillan, 1918). Commons' is an institutional approach (that is, he stresses customs, methods, and facts and makes few generalities). These two volumes, which carry the history to 1896, were later supplemented by Don D. Lescohier and Elizabeth Brandeis, *History of Labor in the United States, 1896–1932* (vol. III, New York: Macmillan, 1935) and Selig Perlman and Philip Taft (vol. IV, same title and publisher). Some of the basic source material for the first two volumes appears in John R. Commons and associates, *A Documentary History of American Industrial Society* (10 vols., Cleveland: 1910). An excellent and detailed study of the field of labor is Carroll Daugherty and John Parrish, *The Labor Problems of American Society* (Boston: Houghton Mifflin, 1952). Another modern authority is Harry A. Millis and Royal E. Montgomery, *Labor's Progress and Problems* (New York: McGraw-Hill, 1938). Three other general histories are Richard T. Ely, *Labor Movement in America* (New York: Crowell, 1886), which was a pioneer work; A. Bimba, *The History of the American Working Class* (New York: International, 1936), whose approach is definitely radical; and Foster R. Dulles, *Labor in America* (New York: Crowell, 1949). A more down-to-earth approach is found in Florence Peterson, *American Labor Unions: What They Are and How They Work* (New York: Harper, 1952) and Robert R. Brooks, *When Labor Organizes* (New Haven: Yale University Press, 1938), which explains why and how unions are organized and what their early problems are.

Why Labor Organizes. There have been numerous attempts to analyze the labor movement, but again Selig Perlman offers the best beginning in his *A Theory of the Labor Movement* (New York: Macmillan, 1928). A. M. Simons, *Social Forces in American History* (New York: Macmillan, 1912) presents a radical interpretation. A. M. Ross's two articles in the *American Economic Review*, "Trade Unions as Wage Fixing Institutions" in the September, 1947, issue, and "Wage Determination under Collective Bargaining" in the December, 1947, issue (vol. 37), point out that union behavior is more logical if unions are viewed as political bodies rather than as primarily profitmaking organizations. John A. Fitch also sought the answer in *The Causes of Industrial Unrest* (New York: Harper, 1924).

Labor in Colonial Times. On labor in the colonial period Richard B. Morris, *Government and Labor in Early America* (New York: Columbia University Press, 1945) and Morris W. Jernegan, *Laboring and Dependent Classes in Colonial America, 1607–1783* (Chicago: University of Chicago Press, 1931) are the chief authorities. Indentured servants and slaves performed much of the labor then. Slavery is treated in a separate section of this bibliography. The best modern study on indentured servants is Abbot E. Smith, *Colonists in Bondage: White Servitude and Convict Labor in America, 1607–1776* (Chapel Hill: University of North Carolina Press, 1947). An older but very good account is Cheesman A. Herrick, *White Servitude in Pennsylvania* (Philadelphia: McVey, 1926). Back in the 1890s scholars at The Johns Hopkins University made a series of studies of indentured servitude in various colonies. Two of these are James C. Ballagh, *White Servitude in the Colony of Virginia* (Baltimore: Johns Hopkins Press, 1895) and Eugene I. McCormac, *White Servitude in Maryland* (Baltimore: Johns Hopkins Press, 1904). Foster Dulles, *Labor in America* (New York: Crowell, 1949) is good on colonial labor. There are also sections on this subject in Curtis Nettels, *Roots of American Civilization* (New York: Crofts, 1938).

Before 1860. Material on the labor movement before 1860 is fragmentary outside of the John R. Commons and Perlman studies already mentioned. Norman J. Ware, *The Industrial Workers, 1840–1860* (Boston: Houghton Mifflin, 1924) is quite pessimistic in its viewpoint. Helene Zahler, *Eastern Workingmen and National Land Policy, 1829–1862* (New York: Columbia

University Press, 1941) is limited in its approach. Louis Arky's article, "The Mechanics Union of Trade Associations and the Formation of the Philadelphia Workingmen's Movement" in *Pennsylvania Magazine of History and Biography,* vol. 76 (April, 1952), pp. 1412ff., indicates what needs to be done on a much greater scale for us to understand this period. Not one labor leader stands out in that era. Hannah Josephson describes the Lowell system in *The Golden Threads: New England's Mill Girls and Magnates* (New York: Duell, Sloan & Pearce, 1949). John Bach McMaster, historian, delivered a series of lectures on *The Acquisition of Political, Social and Industrial Rights of Man in America* (Cleveland: Imperial Press, 1903). In this era reformers rather than laboring people themselves sometimes looked upon utopianlike communities as the best solution of the labor problem. Albert Brisbane, *The Social Destiny of Man, or Association and Reorganization of Industry* (Boston: 1840) is representative. Charles Nordhoff has written *The Communistic Societies of the United States from Personal Visit and Observation* (New York: 1875). More recent is Arthur Bestor, *Backwoods Utopias* (Philadelphia: University of Pennsylvania Press, 1950). Norman Ware in his *Industrial Worker* has an excellent summary of these movements. A good biography of one of the leading reformers, who was active in America as well as England, is Richard Leopold, *Robert Dale Owen* (Cambridge: Harvard University Press, 1940).

Knights of Labor. The literature on the Knights of Labor is fairly generous. Perlman's account of them is excellent. Norman J. Ware, *The Labor Movement in the United States, 1860–1895,* is more detailed but less clear. George E. McNeill, an early state labor official, wrote *The Labor Movement: The Problem of Today* (Boston: 1887). Terence Powderly, for years the Grand Master of the Knights of Labor, related his experiences in two books, *Thirty Years of Labor* (Columbus: 1889) and *The Path I Trod* (New York: Columbia University Press, 1940). Henry J. Browne, *The Catholic Church and the Knights of Labor* (Washington: The Catholic University of America Press, 1949) shows how events in the Catholic Church's history at this time affected the Knights. Joseph R. Buchanan, a labor editor and organizer of this period, tells of his life in *The Story of a Labor Agitator* (New York: Outlook, 1903).

The AFL. There are several histories of the American Federation of Labor. The most recent and probably the best is Philip Taft, *The A. F. of L. in the Time of Gompers* (New York: Harper, 1957). Others include L. L. Lorwin, *The American Federation of Labor* (Washington: Brookings, 1933) and Leo Wolman, *Growth of American Trade Unions, 1880–1923* (New York: Bureau of Economic Research, 1924) but any of these need to be supplemented by Samuel Gompers's own autobiography, *Seventy Years of Life and Labor* (2 vols., New York: Dutton, 1925). Others prominent in the AFL have been *John Mitchell,* whose biography Elsie Gluck has written (New York: John Day, 1929), and *John L. Lewis,* whom Saul Alinsky portrayed (New York: Putnam, 1949). Cecil Carnes also wrote on Lewis (New York: Speller, 1936). A good recent collection of labor leader biographies is Charles Madison, *American Labor Leaders* (New York: Harper, 1950).

The IWW. The very radical Industrial Workers of the World has been described by Paul F. Brissenden, *The I. W. W., A Study of American Syndicalism*

(New York: Columbia University Press, 1919); J. S. Gambs, *The Decline of the I. W. W.* (New York: Columbia University Press, 1932); and John G. Brooks, *American Syndicalism: The I. W. W.* (New York: Macmillan, 1913). In addition, the student should consult the biographies of Eugene Debs, Daniel DeLeon, and William D. Haywood.

The CIO. The most scholarly account of the rise of the CIO is found in Harry A. Millis and Royal Montgomery, *Organized Labor* (New York: McGraw-Hill, 1945). More colorful accounts are Benjamin Stolberg, *The Story of the C. I. O.* (New York: Viking, 1938); Herbert Harris, *Labor's Civil War* (New York: Knopf, 1940); and the biographies of John L. Lewis. The relatively recent merger of the AFL and CIO is well covered in "The Proposed A. F. L.-C. I. O. Merger" by E. B. McNatt in *Current Economic Comment,* vol. 17 (May, 1955).

Labor Violence. Because laborers have at times felt that their cause, though just, was not being given a proper hearing, they have resorted to violence. This spirit is portrayed in Louis Adamic, *Dynamite* (New York: Viking, 1934). Anthony Bimba tells of the activities of *The Molly Maguires* (New York: International, 1932) in the Pennsylvania anthracite coal fields in the 1870s. Henry David has written *The History of the Haymarket Affair* (New York, Farrar & Rinehart, 1936). An excellent account of a major strike is Donald McMurray, *The Great Burlington Strike of 1888* (Cambridge: Harvard University Press, 1956). The Chicago Railway Strike of 1894 was the most famous in the 1890s. Almont Lindsey describes it in *The Pullman Strike* (Chicago: University of Chicago Press, 1942). See also Grover Cleveland, *Presidential Problems* (New York: 1904) and the U.S. Strike Commission, *Report on the Chicago Strike of June–July, 1894* (Sen. doc. no. 7, 53d Cong., 2d Sess., Washington, 1894). Vernon Jensen has described violence in mining in *Heritage of Conflict: Labor Relations in the Non-ferrous Metals Industry to 1930* (Ithaca: Cornell University Press, 1950). Another violent flare-up took place in 1919. The Commission of Inquiry of the Interchurch World Movement put out its *Report on the Steel Strike of 1919* (New York: Harcourt, Brace, 1920). A more recent chapter in labor violence, which took place in southern Illinois in the 1920s, is described by Paul M. Angle in *Bloody Williamson* (New York: Knopf, 1952).

Labor Reforms. The most successful period of labor reform has been the last thirty years. Harry A. Millis and R. E. Montgomery discuss those in *Labor's Progress and Problems,* and also in *Labor's Risks and Social Insurance* (New York: McGraw-Hill, 1938).

Labor Law. Labor law has become an intricate subject, which is constantly changing. Charles O. Gregory, *Labor and the Law* (New York: Norton, 1949) is probably one of the best accounts. Volumes III and IV of Commons, *Documentary History,* are devoted to labor conspiracy cases of the 1806–1842 era. Felix Frankfurter wrote *The Labor Injunction* (New York: Macmillan, 1930) on the most effective weapon management used against labor. New cases are always described in *The Monthly Labor Review,* 1915 on, and in *The Labor Relations Reporters,* 1937 on.

Statistics. The student should first consult *Historical Statistics, 1789–1945,* for wage statistics. Millis and Montgomery in *Labor's Progress and Problems* have many tables on real wages in various occupations. Alvin Hansen prepared a table and supporting article entitled "Factors Affecting the Trend of Real Wages" in the *American Economic Review*, vol. 15 (March, 1925), covering the years 1820 to 1923. Paul Douglas made a most elaborate study of *Real Wages in the United States, 1890–1926* (Boston: Houghton Mifflin, 1930). Paul Brissenden prepared a series on *Earnings of Factory Workers, 1899–1927* (Census Monograph no. 10, Washington, 1929). The oldest series on wages is the so-called Aldrich Report which, although still used, is now looked upon with suspicion. It is entitled *Wholesale Prices, Wages and Transportation, 1840–1890* (Sen. doc. no. 1394, 52d Cong., 2d Sess.; 4 vols., Washington, 1893). For more recent information the best authority is the United States Department of Labor's *Handbook of Labor Statistics* (Washington: 1950) and of course the *Monthly Labor Review*. The *Statistical Abstract of the United States* carries helpful series, too.

SLAVERY AND THE CIVIL WAR

General. Ulrich B. Phillips, an outstanding authority on slavery in the South, sympathetically traces the history of slavery in *American Negro Slavery* (New York: Appleton-Century, 1940). Kenneth M. Stampp challenges many of Phillips's conclusions about the necessity of slavery in *The Peculiar Institution: Slavery in the Ante-bellum South* (New York: Knopf, 1956). Much of the general history of slavery is also found in Lewis C. Gray, *History of Agriculture in the Southern United States to 1860* (2 vols., New York: Peter Smith, 1941). A contemporary critic of slavery was the British economist, John E. Cairnes, who denounced slavery as inefficient in *The Slave Power, Its Character, Career, and Probable Designs* (London: Parker, Son, and Bourn, 1862); however, Cairnes did not personally observe American slavery. He relied heavily on the writings of a New Englander, Frederick Law Olmstead, who traveled widely through the South and recorded with impartiality and accuracy what he saw. Part of Olmstead's observations appear in *The Cotton Kingdom* (New York: Knopf, 1953), edited by Arthur M. Schlesinger.

State Studies. Special state studies of slavery are useful for seeing the differing conditions under which Negro slaves worked. Among the best are Ralph B. Flanders, *Plantation Slavery in Georgia* (Chapel Hill: University of North Carolina Press, 1933) and Weymouth T. Jordan, *Hugh Davis and His Alabama Plantation* (University, Ala.: University of Alabama Press, 1948).

Economic Aspects of Slavery. L. C. Gray, *History of Agriculture in the Southern United States to 1860,* and Ulrich B. Phillips, *Life and Labor in the Old South* (Boston: Little, Brown, 1929), examine the economic aspects of slavery. More precise studies are Robert Worthington Smith, "Was Slavery Unprofitable in the Ante-bellum South?" *Agricultural History,* vol. 20 (1946) and Chester McArthur Destler, "David Dickson's 'System of Farming' and the Agricultural Revolution in the Deep South, 1850–1885," *Agricultural History,* vol. 31 (1957).

Slave Trade. A standard work on the African slave trade is W. E. Burghardt DuBois, *The Suppression of the African Slave-trade to the United States of*

America, 1638–1870 (Cambridge: Harvard University Press, 1896). The domestic slave trade is discussed in Frederic Bancroft, *Slave-trading in the Old South* (Baltimore: J. H. Furst Co., 1931).

Economic Causes of the Civil War. Countless volumes have been written on the causes of the Civil War. An excellent short statement of various views is Howard K. Beale, "What Historians Have Said about the Causes of the Civil War," *Theory and Practice in Historical Study: A Report of the Committee on Historiography* (New York: Social Science Research Council, 1946). James F. Rhodes, *History of the United States from the Compromise of 1850* (7 vols., New York: Macmillan, 1893–1906), exclusively blamed slavery for the war. Among the first to challenge the single-cause theory was Charles A. Beard, who explained the war as a conflict between two divergent economic systems in Charles and Mary Beard, *Rise of American Civilization* (New York: Macmillan, 1933). Fred Albert Shannon, *America's Economic Growth* (3d ed., New York: Macmillan, 1951) has an excellent chapter on economic sectionalism as the primary cause of the war. Among many outstanding books on the causes of the war are Avery O. Craven, *The Coming of the Civil War* (2d ed., Chicago: University of Chicago Press, 1957) and Roy F. Nichols, *The Disruption of American Democracy* (New York: Macmillan, 1948).

The crusade to abolish slavery was one of the most dramatic causes of the sectional conflict. The abolitionists' attack, led by William Lloyd Garrison and Theodore Dwight Weld, intensified the South's determination to defend her labor system. Gilbert Hobbs Barnes, *The Anti-slavery Impulse, 1830–1844* (New York: Appleton-Century, 1933) considers abolitionism generally. Theodore Dwight Weld presented his own case for abolition in *American Slavery As It Is: Testimony of a Thousand Witnesses* (New York: American Anti-slavery Society, 1839). The most dramatic of the abolitionist literature was Harriet Beecher Stowe, *Uncle Tom's Cabin* (2 vols., Boston: John P. Jewett, 1852); the book, a best seller, pictured slavery in an unfavorable light. A newly freed slave, Frederic Douglas, made a strong case against slavery in *My Bondage and My Freedom* (New York: Miller, Orton and Mulligan, 1855). Hinton R. Helper, a small North Carolina farmer, supported abolitionists in *The Impending Crisis of the South* (New York: Burdick Brothers, 1857). George Fitzhugh ably defended slavery in *Sociology for the South or the Failure of Free Society* (Richmond: A. Morris, 1854). Other proslavery arguments appear in William Sumner Jenkins, *Pro-Slavery Thought in the Old South* (Chapel Hill: University of North Carolina Press, 1935). Throughout the 1850s *De Bow's Review* printed many articles both in defense of Negro slavery and to show how the North exploited the South.

Index

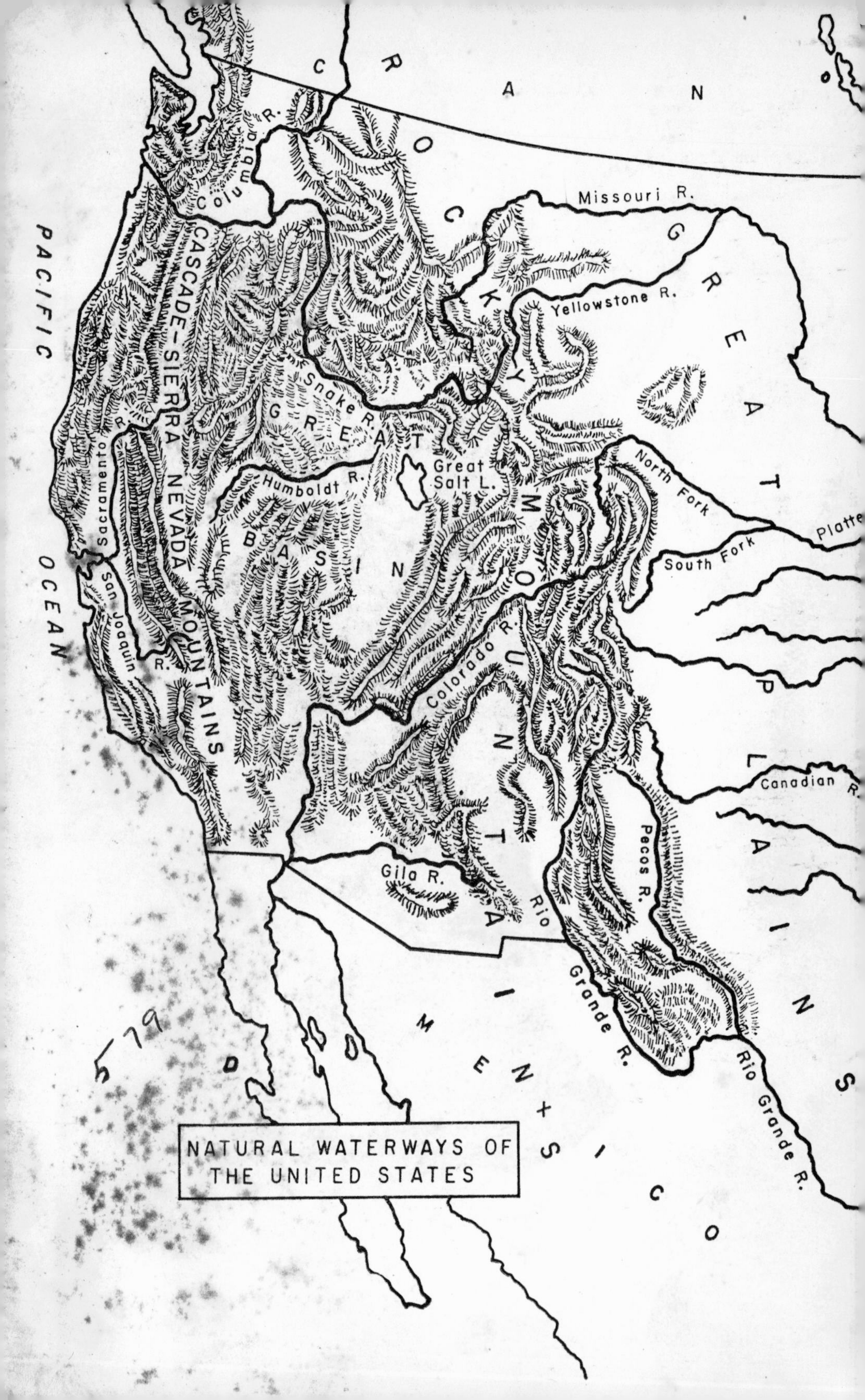

NATURAL WATERWAYS OF THE UNITED STATES